The Battle of Moscow, 1941–1942: The Red Army's Defensive Operations and Counteroffensive Along the Moscow Strategic Direction is a detailed examination of one of the major turning points of World War II, as seen from the Soviet side. The Battle of Moscow marked the climax of Hitler's "Operation Barbarossa," which sought to destroy the Soviet Union in a single campaign and ensure German hegemony in Europe. The failure to do so condemned Germany to a prolonged war it could not win.

This work originally appeared in 1943, under the title "Razgrom Nemetskikh Voisk pod Moskvoi" (The Rout of the German Forces Around Moscow). The work was produced by the Red Army General Staff's military-historical section, which was charged with collecting and analyzing the war's experience and disseminating it to the army's higher echelons. This was a collective effort, featuring many different contributors, with Marshal Boris Mikhailovich Shaposhnikov, former chief of the Red Army General Staff and then head of the General Staff Academy, serving as general editor.

The book is divided into three parts, each dealing with a specific phase of the battle. The first traces the Western Front's defensive operations along the Moscow direction during Army Group Center's final push toward the capital in November–December, 1941. The study pays particular attention to the Red Army's resistance to the Germans' attempts to outflank Moscow from the north. Equally important were the defensive operations to the south of Moscow, where the Germans sought to push forward their other encircling flank.

The second part deals with the first phase of the Red Army's counteroffensive, which was aimed at pushing back the German pincers and removing the immediate threat to Moscow. Here the Soviets were able to throw the Germans back and flatten both salients, particularly in the south, where they were able to make deep inroads into the enemy front to the west and northwest.

The final section examines the further development of the counteroffensive until the end of January 1942. This section highlights the Soviet advance all along the front and their determined but unsuccessful attempts to cut off the Germans' Rzhev–Vyaz'ma salient. It is from this point that the front essentially stabilized, after which events shifted to the south.

This new translation into English makes available to a wider readership this valuable study.

Richard W. Harrison earned his undergraduate and master's degrees from Georgetown University, where he specialized in Russian area studies. In 1994 he earned his doctorate in War Studies from King's College London. He also was an exchange student in the former Soviet Union and spent several years living and working in post-communist Russia.

Dr. Harrison has worked for the US Department of Defense as an investigator in Russia, dealing with cases involving POWs and MIAs. He has also taught Russian history and military history at college and university level, most recently at the US Military Academy at West Point.

Harrison is the author of two books dealing with the Red Army's theoretical development during the interwar period: *The Russian Way of War: Operational Art, 1904–1940* (2001), and *Architect of Soviet Victory in World War II: The Life and Theories of G.S. Isserson* (2010). He has also authored a number of articles on topics in Soviet military history. He is currently working on a history of the Red Army's high commands during World War II and afterwards.

Dr. Harrison currently lives with his family near Carlisle, Pennsylvania.

THE BATTLE OF MOSCOW 1941–1942

THE BATTLE OF MOSCOW 1941–1942

The Red Army's Defensive Operations and Counter-offensive along the Moscow Strategic Direction

Soviet General Staff

Edited and translated by Richard W. Harrison

AUSA
ASSOCIATION OF THE UNITED STATES ARMY

Helion & Company

Published in cooperation with the Association of the United States Army

Helion & Company Limited
Unit 8 Amherst Business Centre
Budbrooke Road
Warwick
CV34 5WE
England
Tel. 01926 499619
Email: info@helion.co.uk
Website: www.helion.co.uk
X (formerly Twitter): @Helionbooks
Facebook: @HelionBooks
Visit our blog at https://helionbooks.wordpress.com/

Published by Helion & Company 2015, in cooperation with the Association of the United States Army. This new edition 2025
Designed and typeset by Mach 3 Solutions (www.mach3solutions.co.uk)
Cover designed by Paul Hewitt, Battlefield Design (www.battlefield-design.co.uk)

ISBN 978-1-806720-62-0

British Library Cataloguing-in-Publication Data.
A catalogue record for this book is available from the British Library.

Contents

List of Maps

List of Tables

Preface to the English-language edition

The Battle of Moscow 1941–1942: The Red Army's Defensive Operations and Counter-Offensive Along the Moscow Strategic Direction is a direct translation and slight reworking of the original Russian-language publication *Razgrom Nemetskikh Voisk pod Moskvoi*, which appeared in 1943 under the auspices of the Red Army General Staff's military-historical section. This work was edited by Marshal B.M. Shaposhnikov (1881-1945), who served a number of times as chief of the Red Army General Staff, before poor health forced his retirement in mid-1942. Shaposhnikov was then appointed to head the General Staff Academy and was also instrumental in helping the army command systematize the experience of the ongoing war, of which this book is the first major product.

The actual work of compiling and writing was carried out by a commission under the leadership of Lt. Gen. Ye.A. Shilovskii, who was at the time a professor at the General Staff Academy and a prominent military historian. He was assisted by a group of officers, including Lt. Gen. A.N. Bakhtin, Col. A.V. Vasil'ev, Col. K.N. Vakhterov, Col. A.F. Korablev, Col. I.S. Korotkov, Col. N.I. Frenkel', Lt. Col. G.P. Meshcheriakov, Maj. G.V. Kuz'min, and others.

This work was later declassified and published in Russia in 2006, under the same title. This work was further augmented by the addition of a section examining the defense of Tula during the Moscow operation. The present work excludes this addition and adheres strictly to the original General Staff study.

The study consists of three parts. The first part chronicles the second general offensive by the German forces on Moscow and the defensive fighting around Moscow (November 16—December 5 1941); the second part details the Red Army's counteroffensive along the Western Front and the defeat of the German forces around Moscow (December 6—24 1941). The third part describes the Soviet offensive from the line of the Lama, Ruza, Nara and Oka rivers (December 25 1941—January 31 1942), with concluding remarks regarding the overall conduct of the operation. The work is liberally supported by various tables.

The book contains a number of terms that may not be readily understandable to the casual reader in military history. Therefore, I have adopted a number of conventions designed to ease this task. For example, a *front* is a Soviet wartime military organization roughly corresponding to an American army group. Throughout the narrative the reader will encounter such names as the Western Front, the Kalinin Front, the Southwestern Front, etc. To avoid confusion with the more commonly understood meaning of the term front (i.e., the front line); italics will be used to denote an unnamed *front*. Similar German formations (i.e., Army Group Center) are spelled out in full.

Due to their large number and frequent appearance, I have chosen to designate Soviet armies using the shortened form (i.e., 20th Army, 1st Shock Army, etc.). German armies, on the other hand, are spelled out in full (i.e., Second Panzer Army). In the same vein, the few Soviet corps are designated by Arabic numerals (1st Guards Cavalry Corps), while German units are denoted by Roman numerals (e.g., XXIV Panzer Corps). Smaller units (divisions, brigades, etc.) on both sides are denoted by Arabic numerals only (8th Guards Rifle Division, 106th Infantry Division, etc.).

Given the large number of units involved in the operation, I have adopted certain other conventions in order to better distinguish the two sides' units. For example, Soviet armored units are called tank divisions and brigades, etc., while the corresponding German units are denoted by the popular term *panzer*. Likewise, Soviet motorized units are referred to as motorized rifle, while the German units are listed as motorized. Likewise, Soviet infantry units are designated by the term rifle, (e.g., 8th Guards Rifle Division), while the corresponding German units are simply referred to as infantry (e.g., 106th Infantry Division).

The work subscribes to no particular transliteration scheme, because no fault-free one exists. I have adopted a mixed system that uses the Latin letters ya and yu to denote their Cyrillic counterparts, as opposed to the ia and iu employed by the Library of Congress, which tends to distort proper pronunciation. Conversely, I have retained the Library of Congress's ii ending (i.e., Rokossovskii), as opposed to the commonly-used y ending. I have also retained the apostrophe to denote the Cyrillic soft sign.

The original work contains a number of footnotes inserted by the authors, in order to explain this or that technical question. These have been retained in the present text as endnotes and have been supplemented by a number of appropriately identified editorial notes, which have been inserted, where necessary, to highlight factual errors in the text, or as an explanatory guide to a number of people and terms that might not be readily recognizable to the average reader.

Elsewhere, I have taken some liberties as regards the book's overall organization. This primarily involves leaving out some maps and copies of orders, the inclusion of which would have made the final product too long. On the other hand, I do not take issue with some of the claims made in the text, although I have attempted to highlight and note obvious factual mistakes. Neither have I attempted to make the language more "literary," and have striven throughout to preserve the military-bureaucratic flavor of the original.

Richard W. Harrison
Translator and editor

Introduction

Having perfidiously attacked the Soviet Union, the German-Fascist leadership intended to quickly end the war. The USSR's defeat, according to this plan, should be completed in one to one and a half months.

Fascist Germany's striving for a "lightning war" was determined by its strategic situation, its central location in Europe and its limited potential resources in comparison with its enemies. The rapid end of military activities on this or that theater of the war was conditioned for Fascist Germany by the opportunity of operating along internal strategic lines for the purpose of defeating its enemies in detail.

The prolongation of the war was clearly unprofitable for Germany.

> … it lacked both the forces and equipment; a prolonged war might exhaust it to such a degree that further fighting might prove useless and impossible;
> … it was both difficult and dangerous for Germany to wage war on two fronts; a prolonged war with the USSR would enable England and America to organize their forces and employ them in the fight against Germany.

In the event of the Soviet Union's quick defeat, the Hitlerite command counted on receiving its enormous matériel resources (grain, oil, coal, iron, and others) and use them in a war against England and the USA in order to achieve world domination.

The realization of the plan for a lightning war against the Soviet Union seemed possible to the German supreme command for the following considerations:

1 At the time the war began (June 22 1941) Germany's mobilized forces were superior to the Red Army's opposing forces.
2 The German-Fascist armed forces already had two years of wartime experience; some of their armies had gained versatile combat experience on various fronts and under diverse conditions.
3 The Fascist army possessed powerful military equipment and enjoyed superiority in motor-mechanized forces and air power.
4 Fascist Germany began the war with us with a perfidious attack, without a declaration of war, and by covering its preparations with assurances of friendship and non-aggression.
5 The Fascist German troops had been raised in the spirit of "invincibility" and disdain for the enemy; they were drunk from their previous victories; this was supposed to facilitate the maintenance among them of an offensive spirit and guarantee speedy and decisive activities.

Through a series of powerful blows along several directions, the German-Fascist armed forces were supposed to pierce the Red Army's front and, thrusting deep into the USSR, to split up our forces into a number of uncoordinated groups, and to encircle and destroy them before the country's main forces could be mobilized for the war with Germany. The fascist command's strategic plan included: the seizure of Moscow as the country's main organizational center; the seizure of Leningrad as a large industrial center and the gate to our northern regions, and; the seizure of Ukraine, the breadbasket of the USSR, as well as the Donets Basin and Rostov, the latter an important point on the road from the Donbas to the riches of the Caucasus and the Baku oilfields.

The following forces were deployed for these purposes:

Army Group North under von Leeb in the general direction of Leningrad;
Army Group Center under von Bock towards Moscow;
Army Group South under von Rundstedt in the direction of Kiev, Khar'kov, and Rostov.

Russia's great expanses, for the conquest of which Napoleon expended a significant part of his troops, did not frighten the Fascist command. Hitler was convinced that the motor should eat up this space.

The Red Army's valorous resistance and the Soviet people's struggle under comrade Stalin's leadership, overthrew these calculations.

In two months of war Fascist Germany suffered enormous losses in men and matériel: more than 2,000,000 men killed, wounded and taken prisoner; around 8,000 tanks, 10,000 guns, and more than 7,200 aircraft were put out of commission.

At the end of August the German armies continued to attack, but the speed of their advance fell sharply.

The enormous losses suffered by the German-Fascist troops in the fighting against the Red Army forced them to go over from an offensive along the entire front to blows along the most important operational-strategic directions. In September 1941 these directions were:

1 Leningrad-Tikhvin, with a further blow against Cherepovets and Vologda. Objective: to complete the encirclement of Leningrad and force it to surrender; to seize the Soviet Baltic Fleet; to link up with units of the Finnish army around Lake Onega; to cut off the USSR's central region with the north and thus cut the USSR off from its communications with England and America.
2 Moscow direction, with a possible further advance toward Gor'kii, and south of Moscow, to Yelets, Michurinsk, Penza, and Kuibyshev. Objective: to seize the capital of the USSR, Moscow, and occupy its important industrial area; reach the Volga and separate the country's central region from the south.
3 Rostov, with a further advance on Stalingrad, the Northern Caucasus, and toward Baku. Main objective: seizing Soviet oil resources.

Of the three enumerated directions, the Hitlerite command considered the Moscow one the most important. The capture of Moscow, according to this thinking, would greatly facilitate the remaining operational-strategic tasks, as well as the chief objective—the defeat of the Soviet Union.

Thus the Germans' main efforts in the autumn of 1941 were directed at the capture of Moscow.

A new grouping of German-Fascist forces, created during the second half of September, envisaged the concentration of fascist forces along the Moscow strategic direction. Gen. von Bock's Army Group Center in this area was significantly reinforced.

These troops were assigned decisive objectives—to capture Moscow as quickly as possible, so as to force the USSR to capitulate and end the eastern campaign before the onset of winter.

The seizure of Moscow (as the Fascist command saw it) would remove the USSR from the war. In any case, it would create an enormous impression throughout the world, it would create the illusion of the war's end, or at least enable the Germans to speak of the end of the war in the East. Finally, in the event of this plan being realized, it would place an enormous city with its great resources in the hands of the German plunderers.

Thus the military activities along the Moscow strategic direction in the fall of 1941 acquired a great scope and played out as a series of very large operations, the outcome of which exercised a decisive influence on the further course of the 1941-42 fall-winter campaign on the Soviet-German theater of war.

Part I

A short description of the theater of military activities

The Moscow operation played out across an enormous expanse, the boundaries of which are the following:

north—the Volga River from Kalyazin to Rzhev;
west—the lateral railroad Rzhev-Vyaz'ma- Bryansk (as far as Dyat'kovo);
south—the line Ryazhsk-Gorbachevo station-Dyat'kovo;
east—Kalyazin-Ryazan'-Ryazhsk.

The straight-line distance from Kalinin to Moscow is 160 km; from Moscow to Tula, 170 km; from Vyaz'ma to Ryazan', 350 km.

The surface of the theater represents a broad plain, covered by a series of small, flat heights and ridges of small hills. The northern part of the Central-Russian Uplands intrudes into the theater. The uplands have a low relief and do not impede large troop movements; only in the area of Tula and Kaluga does one encounter significant gullies with steep banks, and rivers flowing through deep valleys, which can make troop movements difficult.

The Smolensk-Moscow ridge stretches through the northwestern part of the theater in the general direction from Smolensk through Vyaz'ma and Gzhatsk toward Klin. The average height of this ridge is 200-250 m.; the highest point—height 286—is located near Volokolamsk. The Klin-Dmitrov ridge is a continuation of the Smolensk-Moscow ridge, and runs from Klin through Dmitrov to Yur'ev-Pol'skii as far as Vladimir.

Lowlands are encountered along the entire expanse of the theater and usually stretch along the rivers. More significant lowlands, of a forest-marsh type, are in the north in the area of Taldom and the Moscow Sea, and to the southeast of Moscow (the Meshchorsk depression) in a band between the Klyaz'ma, Moscow and Oka rivers, and along the northern bank of the Oka River in the area of Serpukhov and Kolomna. During the operation the lowlands to the west of Moscow along the course of small rivers (Lama, Ruza, Nara and others) had a material effect.

Forests cover about 25% of the surface and are located predominantly in the northeastern and central parts of the theater. The largest forest tracts are located mainly in the lowlands, along river valleys, as well as lake and swampy areas, which make entry into these sectors more difficult. There are fewer forests in the southern part of the theater and the terrain is more open.

Of the large rivers one must note: in the northern part of the theater—the Volga River (its width at Rzhev is 100 m. and at Kalinin 150-200 m., although there are fords; further to the east the river widens) in the southern part—the Oka River (the width as far as Belev is 70-90 m., at Kaluga 150 m., and at Serpukhov 300 m.). The Volga, which flows in a generally northeastern direction, divides along with the water system of the Moscow Sea and the Volga Reservoir, forces operating from the west to the east. It also covers the Moscow area from the north. The Oka River flows from south to north as far as Kaluga, forming a defensive line in a north-south direction. Farther along it turns to the northeast and thus divides forces in a latitudinal direction. It also covers the Moscow area from the south.

Between these two large water lines (the Volga and Oka) there lies a broad zone of terrain (220 km. along the line Rzhev-Kaluga), representing the shortest and most convenient route to Moscow, along which, running from the "Smolensk Gates," enemies have more than once have invaded the Russian state from the west at various times in history. Here, in the central part of the zone, west of the city of Mozhaisk, lies the famous Borodino battlefield, where in 1812 Napoleon's glory was first dimmed.

The Moscow River to the west of Moscow is narrow (about 50 m. in width); from the Moscow-Volga Canal its width increases and reaches 100-300 m. The Moscow-Volga Canal, at 80-90 m. in width (and wider in some places), with a depth of 5-6 m., along with its steep banks, presents a serious operational obstacle. It was along this line that the Germans' offensive misfired to the north of Moscow.

In accordance with the operational situation, the small rivers west of Moscow (Lama, Ruza, Nara), which flow approximately in a north-south direction, played an important role as defensive lines. Information on these rivers is presented in the description of the corresponding operations.

Lakes and artificial reservoirs are located predominantly in the northern part of the theater. Heavy fighting took place in the area of the Moscow Sea and the Istra Resevoir.

The average temperature for the Moscow area is as follows: November—minus 3 degrees celsius, December—minus 8 degrees, and January—minus 11 degrees. However, the winter of 1941-42 was very severe, with a deep snow cover. The average temperature for the winter of 1941-42 was as follows: November—minus 5 degrees celsius, in December—minus 12 degrees, and in January—minus 19 degrees. At certain times in January the frosts reached minus 35-40 degrees. The thickness of the snow cover reached 50-65 cm.

Communications routes were highly developed. The thickest network of railroad, paved and dirt roads, as well as a large amount of waterways, is located in the central part of the theater, in the Moscow area. Moscow is the central junction of the railroad network not only for the Western Front, but of the entire European part of the USSR, and is fed from various directions by 11 railroad lines, having an overall peacetime capacity of 500 pairs of trains per day. The paved-road network is primarily radial (much like the railroad network) with its center in Moscow. From Moscow radiate the most important highways to Leningrad, Warsaw, Khar'kov, Voronezh, Gor'kii, and other cities. The most important road is the Moscow-Smolensk highway; its peacetime carrying capacity is estimated at 10-15 pairs of trains. However, the radial direction of the railroads and paved roads and the absence of lateral roads, forced us to carry out troop and freight transfers mainly through the Moscow junction. This caused difficulties in carrying out shipments from east to west and back.

In the Western Front's immediate rear lay Moscow—the capital of the Soviet Union—the political, economic and cultural center of a great country. Moscow is one of the great cities of the world, with a patriotically-inclined population and a numerous and heroic working class, with the latest powerful modern technology. Moscow is a very important junction for railroads, paved and dirt roads, waterways, and air routes for the USSR. Moscow's great political and military significance to a significant degree determined the type of operations conducted by the Western Front.

In the operational-strategic sense, the retention of the Moscow area afforded a number of advantages to the Red Army over the enemy's opposing forces. Moscow actively aided the front with people, equipment, and its entire mighty organization. Moscow increased our defensive and offensive capabilities and strengthened our situation at the front and in the rear. The retention of the Moscow area created favorable conditions for carrying out rapid maneuver by the Red Army in almost any direction. A series of defensive lines and fortified areas were constructed for the defense of the Moscow area during the course of the war.

Thus the location of Moscow in the immediate rear of the Western Front had a salutary effect on the activities of its forces, aiding their resolve, and guaranteeing an uninterrupted flow of forces, as well as their maneuver. The abandonment of Moscow (even temporarily) would have been not only a fact of great political significance, but would have sharply worsened the operational and strategic position of the Western Front, would have been reflected on other fronts, and would have complicated their communication and coordination. It was necessary at any cost to halt and defeat the enemy before Moscow.

The theater of military activities under consideration embraced a single vital strategic direction—the Moscow direction. This strategic direction included three main operational directions (running north to south).

1 Kalinin—connecting the western with the northwestern theater and with Leningrad. During the operation the Kalinin direction became an independent operational-strategic direction, embracing a large number of forces and its own *front* command.
2 Moscow—the central and most important one, covering the immediate approaches to the capital. It will be examined more thoroughly in describing Moscow and its environs.
3 Tula—covering the important Tula industrial and communications junction and connecting the Western Front with the Southwestern Front. The Tula direction acquired an important significance in November in connection with the unfavorable situation along the junction with the Southwestern Front as the result of the withdrawal of the *front's* right-flank army and the resulting 40-60 km gap between the *fronts*. The armies of the Western Front's left wing later successfully attacked along the Tula operational direction.

Within the confines of the Moscow area (during the fighting of November-December 1941), the following local operational axes were noted (from north to south).

1 Klin—located near the junction of two *fronts* and flanking Moscow from the north toward Dmitrov and Zagorsk and leading into the rear of the Western Front. The presence of two paved roads to the southwest toward Moscow also eased the advanced of mobile formations immediately against the capital from the area of Klin and Rogachevo.
2 Volokolamsk—including the Volokolamsk-Moscow road, enabling the enemy to turn the capital's flank from the northwest. A well-developed communications network to the north and northwest of Moscow, within the confines of these two operational axes, and their favorable flanking position in relation to the capital, contributed to the fact that in the beginning the German-Fascists' northern flanking group, followed by the counteroffensive by our armies along the Western Front's right wing unfolded primarily along these axes. Here the decisive events transpired.
3 Zvenigorod—allowing movement from the town of Ruza to Zvenigorod to the north of the Moscow River. The Germans took advantage of this axis in November in order to outflank the Mozhaisk axis, which was securely sealed along the front.
4 Mozhaisk—including the shortest route to Moscow from the west and from Moscow to the west, had a well-developed road network (a highway, the Mozhaisk road). However, its central position between the other possible axes meant that the two sides' actions here were essentially head-on offensives, frontal collisions and breakthroughs of the enemy defense.
5 Maloyaroslavets—leading to Moscow from the southwest through Naro-Fominsk and Podol'sk. It includes the important Moscow-Brest-Warsaw highway. Within the confines of these two axes, cut by a series of defensive lines (for example, the Nara and Protva rivers), stubborn frontal battles by both sides transpired and events developed here more slowly than along both wings. Here the central German-Fascist group unsuccessfully attempted to break through to Moscow and split our front, encountering the stubborn resistance of the Western Front's center armies. Later offensive operations were carried out here by our center armies.
6 Serpukhov—including the shortest approaches to Moscow from the south and outflanking Moscow from the southeast through Kolomna and Bronnitsy. Two paved roads lead from the area of Serpukhov and Kashira to the capital.

After overcoming the crisis caused by the offensive of the German-Fascist troops in the Tula area, in December and January successful maneuver operations by the armies of the Western Front's left wing unfolded along the Serpukhov and Tula-Ryazan' axes.

The Red Army air force's network of airfields included 85 airfields by the middle of November; about half of these were free; part of the frontline area's airfield net was created while preparing for the operation. The airfield network fully met the basing needs of the available forces and had a significant reserve of unoccupied airfields. The network was inferior to that of the enemy as to the quality of equipment, which restricted the maneuver of our planes in poor weather.

The Germans' airfield network consisted of airfields located on our territory temporarily under enemy occupation. For the most part, these airfields were operational and suitable for flying. The main airfields had landing strips, which enabled planes to land and take off regardless of the wetness of the soil on the airfields. The main basing airfields were located in the area of Vitebsk, Orsha, Roslavl', and Smolensk. Airfields in the forward zone were located within 30-50 km from the front line.

Thus according to the topography and development of the communications routes, the theater of military activities allowed for large-scale maneuver operations by both sides, using all kinds of modern military equipment. The men and matériel of the Moscow area, located in the immediate rear of the Western Front, improved its situation and mitigated the conduct of defensive and offensive operations by the troops of that *front*. Here, on the approaches to Moscow, unfolded the vivid and important events of this period of the Patriotic War.

Part II

The failure of the first offensive of the German-Fascist troops on Moscow. The general situation on the Western Front at the beginning of November 1941

In the first half of October broad maneuver operations unfolded along the Moscow strategic direction. They were the result of a new and large offensive, begun by the Germans on October 2 on the Soviet-German front. The German-Fascist leadership placed great hopes on the forthcoming operations. On October 2, at the beginning of the new offensive, Hitler declared in an order for the Eastern front:

> In a few weeks the three main industrial areas will be completely in our hands. At last the prerequisites have been created for delivering the final huge blow, which must bring about the destruction of the enemy before the onset of winter. All the preparations, insofar as is humanly possible, have been completed. This time the preparations were carried out systematically, step by step, in order to place the enemy in such a position in which we can now inflict a fatal blow to him. Today begins the final great and decisive battle of this year.

The three main industrial areas mentioned in the order were evidently: 1) Leningrad, 2) Moscow and, 3) the Donbas and Rostov-on-Don. Thus the Germans' October offensive pursued decisive political and strategic goals: the defeat of the Red Army, the seizure of the main industrial areas, and the rapid completion of the campaign and the war.

Army Group Center under von Bock, including the Ninth and Fourth armies, the Third and Fourth panzer groups, and the Second Panzer Army, was to attack along the Moscow strategic direction. The chief objective was the defeat of the opposing forces of the Red Army and the seizure of Moscow.

The shortest and most convenient routes to Moscow lie in the topographical zone between the Moscow Sea and the Oka River at Serpukhov. However, the experience of the preceding battles evidently had an influence on the German command. It took into account the presence of fortified lines and areas on the approaches to Moscow from the west as well as the possibility of flank attacks by the Red Army from the north and south against German troops during the fighting for Moscow. To attempt to take Moscow through a frontal blow, particularly while attacking along a narrow front that could be enveloped was an expedient that evidently did not guarantee success, according to the opinion of the German command. Therefore the Germans strove to secure their flanks by an advance in the center toward the capital, while at the same time to occupy a favorable flanking operational position *vis a vis* the Red Army's forces covering Moscow. By directing their blows at Kalinin and Tula, the wanted to split Moscow from the north and south and isolate it.

At present we still do not have complete information regarding the plans of the German command. But the enumerated considerations allow us to explain the circumstance by which along with the movement of part of the German forces in the direction of Moscow, toward our Mozhaisk defensive line, powerful groupings of German mobile formations, supported by aircraft and infantry divisions, unleashed offensive operations along both flanks, to the north and south of Moscow. This led in the north to the Kalinin operation and in the south to the Tula operation. The blow in the direction of Kalinin, covered by the northwestern line of the Volga River, would enable the Germans to penetrate into the operational depth of our entire position, to disrupt the work of the rear organs, to cut the shortest communications links between Moscow and Leningrad, and to complicate the *fronts'* coordination. The blow against Tula would put the Germans into an important industrial region and would be carried out at the junction of our two *fronts*—the Western and Bryansk. During the course of further operations, it was planned to cut Moscow off from Yaroslavl' and Gor'kii and to surround it.

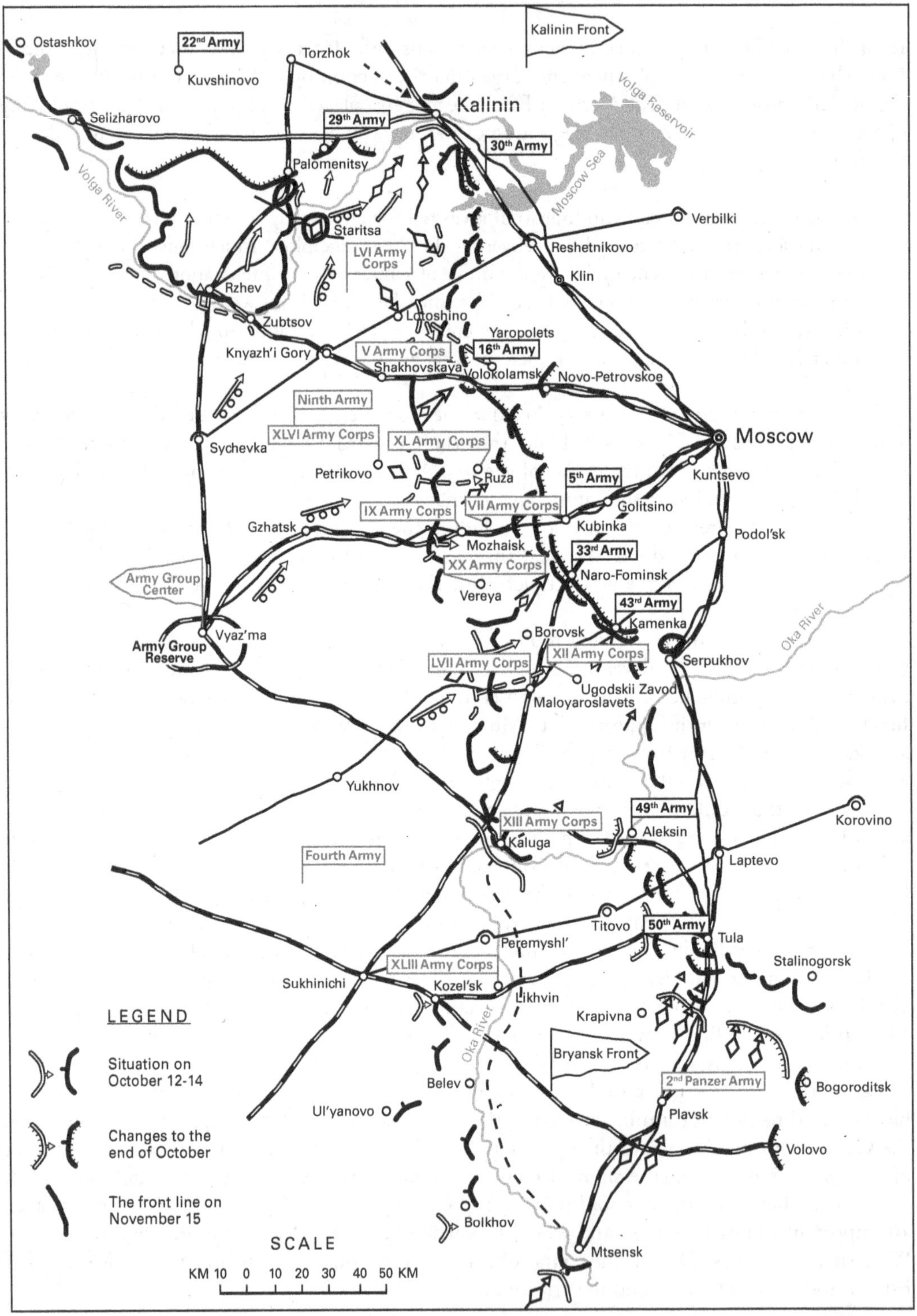

Map 1 The Situation Along the Moscow Strategic Direction, October 12-November 15

The battles which unfolded in October along the Kalinin and Tula axes were connected in the strategic sense with the Germans' Moscow operation, but they operationally transpired independently of each other.

The Kalinin axis, which formed part of the Western Front's area of responsibility, later on acquired independent significance due to developments and on October 17 was removed from the Western Front. A separate Kalinin Front was formed, subordinated directly to the *Stavka*. The boundary with the Western Front ran as follows: Berendeevo station-Verbilki-Reshetnikovo station-Knyazh'i Gory- Sychevka.

The Tula axis at first formed part of the Bryansk Front, but due to further developments at the end of October and beginning of November, became more closely tied to the Moscow direction. Thus on November 10 it was included with the Western Front, with the *front's* southern boundary running along the line Spassk-Ryazanskii-Mikhailov-Uzlovaya station-Krapivna-Belev-Dyat'kovo (all points within the Western Front).

During the course of the October 12-14 fighting the troops of the Red Army occupied the following position. On the right flank our units were holding the Ostashkov area; then the front of the 22nd and 29th armies followed the course of the Volga from Selizharovo to Rzhev, Zubtsov, and Staritsa. There were no significant forces further to the east as far as the Moscow Sea; here there was a gap, in which a group of German forces had formed a wedge all the way to Kalinin. All our available forces were hurriedly thrown to the Kalinin area in order to hold it and stabilize the situation. From the western extremity of the Moscow Sea the front line went through Yaropolets-to the west of Volokolamsk-west of Mozhaisk-west of Borovsk-toward Maloyaroslavets-Kaluga, and to southward.

On October 14 the enemy, with a force of about a motorized division, reinforced with tanks and supported by 50-60 aircraft, threw back our weak units near Kalinin and seized the town. During the following days the German strength in the area grew to 1-2 panzer and 1-2 motorized divisions.

The nearest fortified region in the path of the German forces advancing toward Moscow was the Mozhaisk defensive line. The Mozhaisk defensive line included four main fortified areas: Volokolamsk, Mozhaisk, Maloyaroslavets, and Kaluga. They had the following operational tasks: a) the Volokolamsk fortified area—to cover the axis Rzhev-Volokolamsk-Moscow; b) Mozhaisk fortified area—to cover the axis Gzhatsk-Mozhaisk-Moscow; c) Maloyaroslavets fortified area—to cover two axes: Medyn'-Maloyaroslavets-Moscow, and Kaluga-Maloyaroslavets-Moscow; d) the Kaluga fortified area—to cover the following axes: Yukhnov-Kaluga; Sukhinichi-Kaluga-Serpukhov; Kozel'sk-Kaluga. By the time the German troops reached the Mozhaisk defensive line the readiness of the structures in the main defensive zone stood at 40-80%. This will be covered more fully in the section on the Moscow Defense Zone. The Western Front commander, in view of the developing offensive by the German-Fascist troops, ordered on October 13 the commander of the 16th Army to take over the troops of the Mozhaisk fortified area, with the mission to stubbornly defend it. Similar orders followed concerning the other fortified areas, which were located in the operating areas of the corresponding field armies.

On October 17 the Western Front's right wing, which was occupying the former line, was concentrating its forces in order to retake Kalinin. In the center and on the left wing there was fighting with the enemy's tanks and infantry, which in some areas have driven a wedge into the depth of our defense. The enemy was concentrating his main forces along the Kalinin, Mozhaisk, Naro-Fominsk and Serpukhov axes.

The Bryansk Front's troops were conducting a fighting retreat to the east.

On October 19 a decree by the State Defense Committee declared Moscow to be under a state of siege. In the decree, signed by comrade Stalin, it was stated that the defense of the capital along the lines 100-120 km. distant from Moscow was entrusted to the commander of the Western

Front, Gen. Zhukov, and that the defense of the approaches to Moscow to the commander of the Moscow garrison, Lt. Gen. Artem'ev. The capital's workers were called upon to take part in the heroic struggle and to deal ruthlessly with provocateurs, spies and other enemy agents. The State Defense Committee called upon all the workers of Moscow to maintain order and calm and to render the Red Army forces defending the capital all possible assistance.

On October 19 the stubborn struggle continued against the enemy's groups of tanks and motorized infantry that had broken through along the Volokolamsk, Mozhaisk, and Maloyaroslavets axes. In the morning the enemy renewed his attack, with the objective of moving from the Ostashevo area into the rear of the Volokolamsk fortified area, and on the Mozhaisk and Podol'sk axes—to break through into the depth of the fortified lines. Our aviation actively aided the ground troops, carried out reconnaissance, strafed and bombed the enemy's infantry and motor-mechanized units in the areas of Lotoshino, Luk'yanovo, Ostashevo, Mozhaisk, Maloyaroslavets, Vorob'i, and Tarutino. On October 21 169 air sorties were carried out, destroying up to 50 tanks and 70 vehicles and inflicting significant losses on enemy personnel. On October 22 364 air sorties were carried out, during which 80 tanks and about 200 other vehicles and other equipment were destroyed. The aviation's combat service continued in the days ahead.

On the Bryansk Front's right wing units of the 50th Army were approaching Belev.

During October 22-23 the forces of the Kalinin Front held off in the center an attack by up to two enemy divisions in the direction of Lukovnikovo and were attacking the enemy's Kalinin group of forces.

On October 23 our forces on the Western Front's right wing held their positions. In the center, along the Dorokhovo, Naro-Fominsk and Podol'sk axes, they were engaged in heavy fighting with the enemy's tanks and infantry, which were attempting to develop the offensive to the east and northeast. Artillery and mortar fire was conducted along the remaining sectors of the Western Front. During this period the most significant and stubborn fighting took place in the area of Volokolamsk, the area of Mozhaisk and Dorokhovo, and near Naro-Fominsk along the Maloyaroslavets axis. Here our forces resisted the enemy, wore him down and destroyed him and then counterattacked, launching some small counterblows. In connection with the overall situation, the Western Front's military council demanded that the troops exert themselves to the utmost and stubbornly fight to the point of self-sacrifice. "There can no longer be a question of taking a step back," the orders read, and this demand was reinforced by corresponding measures along all lines.

During the course of October 25 and the following days the Kalinin Front's forces continued to wage holding actions against the Germans' Rzhev and Staritsa groups of forces, and on the left wing attacked the enemy's Kalinin group of forces. The Western Front also fought stubbornly, holding back the enemy's attack along the Volokolamsk, Naro-Fominsk, and Serpukhov axes, while carrying out attacks along the Mozhaisk and Maloyaroslavets axes. On the Bryansk Front's right wing the troops of the 50th Army fell back; they fought along the Likhvin and Belev axes, and in the area of Krapivna and Plavsk, holding off the pressure by the enemy's motorized infantry and tanks. This created a threat to the Tula area, to where units of the 50th Army retreated in the following days.

On November 1 the Western Front included five armies (16th, 5th, 33rd, 43rd, and 49th), operating along a front of 275 km. (minus small twists and turns). The troops consolidated their positions, organized a defense, improved their position and fought the Germans' reconnaissance parties. The Bryansk Front's right wing (50th Army) fought stubbornly against units of the Second Panzer Army in the Tula area, repelling multiple attempts by the enemy's tanks and motorized infantry to take the city.

As a result of their October offensive, the German-Fascist armies managed to advance 230-250 km. in the center in the direction of Moscow (along the line Yartsevo-Dorokhovo) and develop the operation on the flanks on either side of Moscow towards Kalinin and Tula. The enemy's great superiority in equipment enabled him to carry out maneuver operations, advancing at an average speed of 10 km per day, inflicting serious losses on the troops of the Western Front.

But they failed to achieve their main goal: they did not take Moscow, nor did they destroy the Red Army. As a result of the fighting along the Kalinin Front the front line moved to the north to the line Selizharovo-Kalinin. However, a significant part of the German forces were pinned down in stubborn fighting around Kalinin and were thus unable to take part in the offensive on Moscow. Nor was the fighting around Tula crowned with success for the Germans. They were unable to take Tula from the march and frontal attacks were becoming prolonged and bore little result. Attempts were made to take Tula by means of a turning movement.

Thus the operations on both flanks failed to yield the Germans a decisive success. The fighting took on a prolonged character. The German troops were pinned down around Kalinin and Tula and could not be immediately used for a concentric offensive on Moscow.

In the center, along the Mozhaisk axis, the enemy, having encountered growing resistance by the troops of the Western Front, and deprived of support from the flanks, advanced only slightly in the latter half of October and the beginning of November.

Following the fighting along the line Volokolamsk-Mozhaisk-Maloyaroslavets-Kaluga our troops consolidated along their defensive positions to the east of these towns, reequipped, rearmed and prepared for local counterattacks against enemy forces which had appeared in the area. The heavy casualties suffered by the Germans, the necessity of bringing their units up to strength, as well as the ongoing regroupings, forced the enemy to leave facing the Western Front at the end of October only eleven infantry divisions, three panzer divisions, and up to five motorized divisions in the front line. By this time we had managed, using the breathing space, to bring up forces and equipment, organize and perfect our defense, which had earlier been carried out using insufficient forces. The Western Front's operational situation on the approaches to Moscow became significantly stronger.

The country, in the throes of a patriotic upswing, and answering the call of the government, the party and comrade Stalin, contributed more and more new forces for the struggle with the German-Fascist invaders. In these critical days many new units and formations appeared on the approaches to Moscow. They, together with the old, veteran troops of the Western Front, barred the enemy's way, took the blow on themselves and repulsed the enemy attack, and brought forth thousands of new hero-patriots. The enemy suffered heavy losses in men and matériel. His offensive gradually slowed down. Our stubborn and active struggle wore out and exhausted his troops and destroyed his forces. By the end of October his pressure weakened and his offensive faltered and from the beginning of November the fighting along the Mozhaisk axis became local in character. On a number of sectors the enemy went over to the defensive, evidently in order to accumulate forces for further operations.

The Germans' first offensive against Moscow failed. The enemy was halted on the far approaches to Moscow. Neither on October 16 or 25 (the deadlines mentioned by Hitler) did the German forces enter Moscow. The planned capture of Moscow by German troops on November 7 also came a cropper. On that day the great leader of the Soviet people and Supreme Commander-in-Chief, comrade Stalin, took the Red Army's parade on Red Square in Moscow. The foreign press interpreted this as a brilliant Soviet victory. Speaking at a solemn meeting on November 6, comrade Stalin said:

> The German invaders were counting on the weakness of the Red Army and Red Navy, supposing that the German army and navy would be able from the first blow to overwhelm and scatter our army and navy, thus opening the way for an unfettered advance into the depth of our country. But here the Germans cruelly miscalculated, having overestimated their forces

and underestimated our army and navy. Of course, our army and navy are still young, having fought only four months and have not yet had time to become fully cadre forces, while facing at the same time the Germans cadre navy and army, which have been waging war for two years. But, first of all, the morale condition of our army is higher than that of the German army, because they are defending their motherland against foreign invaders and believe in the rightness of their cause, while the German army is waging an aggressive war and robbing another country, without the possibility of believing for one minute in the rightness of their repulsive cause. There can be no doubt that the idea of defending one's fatherland, in the name of which our people are fighting, must give rise to, and is really giving rise in our army to heroes who are strengthening the Red Army, while the idea of invading and pillaging another country, in the name of which the Germans are waging war, must give rise to and really gives rise in the German army to professional brigands, deprived of any sort of moral foundations, which break down the German army. Secondly, the German army, by advancing into the depth of our country, is moving further from its German rear and is forced to subsist in a hostile environment, is forced to create a new rear in another country, which is already being razed by our partisans, which seriously disorganizes the German army's supply and forces it to fear its own rear and destroys within it faith in the strength of its situation, while our army is acting in its home environment, enjoys the unending support of its own rear, has a guaranteed supply of men, armaments, food and strongly believes in its rear. This is why our army proved stronger than the Germans believed and the German army weaker than one could have assumed given the boastful statements of the German invaders. The defense of Leningrad and Moscow, where our divisions recently destroyed tens of German cadre divisions, shows that in the fire of the patriotic war are being forged, and have already been forged, new Soviet soldiers and commanders, pilots, artillerymen, mortar troops, tank troops, infantrymen, and sailors, who tomorrow will become a threat to the German army.

These calm and assured words of the leader poured new strength into the ranks of the defenders of Moscow and inspired them to new feats.

Part III

The second general offensive on Moscow by the German-Fascist troops and the defensive battle on the Western Front (November 16-December 1941)

1

The initial situation and the opposing plans. The outline of the German offensive on Moscow

In the first half of November all types of intelligence began to show that the enemy was bringing up and building up forces in front of the Western Front, and that the German-Fascist troops were preparing shock groups and trying to occupy a favorable jumping off point for the resumption of a full-scale offensive. During the period November 1-11, according to our intelligence, the enemy forces facing the Western Front increased by nine divisions. It was becoming clear that in the near future we must expect the Germans' second attempt to capture Moscow.

By the beginning of the German-Fascist troops' second offensive the Western Front staff and the Red Army staff had, on the whole, correct information regarding the enemy's forces and possible intentions.

As early as November 5 the chief of the Western Front staff's operational section, in a document compiled by him, defined the likely German plan in the following manner: the enemy is evidently preparing a blow along both flanks of the Western Front:[1] 1) to the north—toward Klin and Istra; 2) in the south—toward Podol'sk and Lopasnya. But the enemy will require a certain amount of time to bring up reserves and put his forces and rear services in order, for rest and arranging his matériel-technical support. The enemy forces are now concentrated into several groups: a) the Volokolamsk group (5-6 divisions, of which two are panzer and one motorized), slated for likely operations from Volokolamsk toward Klin and Dmitrov, in order to outflank Moscow from the north; part of these forces may be directed through Istra directly against Moscow; b) the Dorokhovo (Mozhaisk) group (4-5 divisions), located along the shortest route to Moscow, with the axis of its advance along the Moscow-Mozhaisk road; c) the Maloyaroslavets group (4-5 divisions, of which one is armored), which is evidently aimed at Podol'sk and then at Moscow from the south. To the west of Serpukhov another concentration of forces was noted (the Tarusa-Serpukhov group), consisting of 4-5 divisions (one of them armored) for possible operations toward Serpukhov.

In the center, in the Naro-Fominsk area, it was supposed that the enemy had concentrated weaker forces (about three infantry and one panzer divisions), slated to maintain contact between the two active wings. Operational reserves were calculated at 3-4 divisions, located near Mozhaisk, Maloyaroslavets, east of Gzhatsk, and near Kaluga. In all, according to the available information, there were concentrated 25-30 divisions and up to 350-400 aircraft based at forward airfields.

1 One should bear in mind that at this time the Tula axis was not part of the Western Front. The 50th Army was subordinated to the Western Front on November 10. The boundary line between the Western and Bryansk fronts was as follows: Spassk-Ryazanskii-Mikhailov-Uzlovaya station-Krapivna-Belev-Dyat'kovo (all within the Western Front).

Further data refined and complemented this earlier information. A prisoner, captured on November 12 along the 33rd Army's front, stated that preparations for the offensive had been completed and that the offensive could begin that night or in the morning of November 13; according to him, his regiment would pin down the Red Army's defending forces, while the others would outflank them.

On November 14 the Western Front's military council reported to comrade Stalin on the situation along its left flank: "Left-flank units of the Southwestern Front's 3rd Army are continuing their uninterrupted withdrawal to the southwest toward Yefremov. With each day the gap between the right flank of the Southwestern Front's 3rd Army and the left flank of the Western Front's 50th Army is increasing and by the end of November 13 had reached 60 km.

> The enemy, having failed to take Tula from the south and suffering a reverse in trying to break through to Tula from the northwest, and having suffered heavy losses in the attempt, has taken advantage of the retreat by units of the Southwestern Front's 3rd Army and during the course of November 12-13 began to concentrate tank and infantry formations to the left flank of the 50th Army. The enemy continues with impunity to create a powerful grouping south of Dedilovo and Uzlovaya for a blow to the north and northeast to outflank Tula from the east against the flank and rear of the 50th Army.

In mid-November our intelligence organs in the capital came to the conclusion that the most powerful German groups were located in the following areas: a) in the Volokolamsk-Dorokhovo area; b) at the junction of the Western and Southwestern fronts in the Tula area (XXIV and LXVII Panzer corps). The German command's measures should be viewed as the preparation for an offensive against the Western Front's wings to bypass Moscow (along the right flank in the direction of Klin and Dmitrov, and on the left in the direction of Tula and Kolomna), in conjunction with a frontal blow from the Naro-Fominsk area.

The number of infantry divisions concentrated for the attack approximated that available to the Germans when they went over to the offensive against the Western Front on October 2 1941 (26 infantry divisions in the first line, two infantry divisions formed the army reserve, about seven infantry divisions in the army group's reserve; in total, 35 divisions). The number of panzer formations (up to ten panzer divisions, in all 800-900 tanks) enables the enemy to begin the offensive with blows by large mobile groups along the most important axes. The following speaks to the likelihood of such an enemy attack:

a) the German command's desire (already a cliché) to employ its beloved method in operations: employing two flank shock groups ("wedges"), to encircle the intended target (running the gamut from ordinary "Cannaes," having as their objective completely encircling the enemy's main forces, to the "pincers," lopping off, encircling and destroying one of the separate groups or one of the parts of the enemy's operational formation). In this regard, the encirclement was usually carried out by motor-mechanized forces (the so-called "tank encirclement"), and then the enemy sought to consolidate this with the follow-on infantry divisions ("infantry encirclement"). In the present case such an approach would have enabled the enemy to achieve the flanks of our Moscow group and subsequently encircle the capital and the Western Front's main forces.
b) the difficulties of a frontal offensive for the Germans in the current situation and their attempts to take Moscow head-on.
c) local conditions; particularly the possibility of covering the German northern shock group's left flank and the southern group with water barriers (the Moscow Sea and the Volga Reservoir in the north and the Oka River in the south);
d) the observed transfer of enemy troops at the end of October and beginning of November: from

Kalinin to the Volokolamsk area from October 30 through November 2; to the Orel, Mtsensk and Tula areas from October 25 through November 8.

In the first half of November the Western Front's armies continued to wage predominantly local battles for the purpose of improving their positions, while repulsing attempts by the enemy to break into our position. In the main, the more significant fighting unfolded on both of the Western Front's flanks: along the Volokolamsk axis, and also in the area southeast of Aleksin, from which area the enemy tried to get into the rear of Tula from the north.

Our troops strengthened their defensive positions, carried out small regroupings, and also received reinforcements of men and matériel. New formations arrived—rifle, tank and cavalry, the result being that our strength was augmented. For example, on November 12 the 16th Army, which was covering an extremely important axis towards Moscow, was reinforced with five cavalry divisions.

On November 10 Gen. Belov's 2nd Cavalry Corps arrived along the Serpukhov axis and after unloading concentrated in the area to the northeast of Lopasnya. On the following day the 112th Tank Division arrived in the Lopasnya area.

The concentration of tanks and cavalry along the Klin-Volokolamsk and Serpukhov axes was undertaken so as to break through on both wings into the enemy rear in order to wreck his offensive preparations. Such a measure by the *Stavka* speaks of an active defense on the Western Front, the results of which told in the following period.

On November 15 the front line of our troops followed the general line from the western shore of the Moscow Sea to the south, east of Volokolamsk, east of Dorokhovo (on the Mozhaisk axis), then to Naro-Fominsk, west of Serpukhov, further along the Oka River to Aleksin, west of Tula and west of Uzlovaya station. The forces of the Western Front (16th, 5th, 33rd, 43rd, 49th, and 50th armies) beat off attacks by the enemy's infantry and tanks along the 16th Army's center and continued fighting along the 49th Army's front and on the right flank of the 50th Army, eliminating the Germans' attempts to encircle Tula from the northwest.

On the Western Front's right flank, at the junction with the Kalinin Front south of the Moscow Sea, was the 16th Army, which had grouped its main forces along the Volokolamsk axis. The 5th Army operated along the Mozhaisk axis, and the 33rd Army covered the Naro-Fominsk axis. Further to the south were the 43rd and 49th armies. The 50th Army, recently subordinated to the Western Front, defended the Tula area.

The boundary with the Kalinin Front to the north was as follows: Verbilki-Reshetnikovo station-Knyazh'i Gory-Sychevka (all within the Western Front);[2] in the south the boundary with the Southwestern Front lay along the line Spassk-Ryazanskii-Mikhailov-Uzlovaya station-Krapivna-Belev-Dyat'kovo (all within the Western Front). The overall length of the front (minus small turns) as of November 15 was about 330 km.

In all, the Western Front numbered (including the 30th Army): 31 rifle divisions, three motorized rifle divisions, nine cavalry divisions, 14 tank brigades, two tank divisions, and six aviation divisions.[3]

The combat and numerical strength of some formations was quite small. In all, as of November 15 the Western Front numbered (see the table showing the correlation of forces) around 240,000

2 From 2300 on November 17 the 30th Army was subordinated to the Western Front. The boundary with the Kalinin Front was then as follows (excluding): Kashin-Negotino (10 km south of Kalinin)-Staritsa-Rzhev.

3 In all, 49 divisions, with three tank brigades counting as one division.

troops, 1,200 field pieces, 500 tanks, 180-200 combat aircraft[4] (80 fighters, 80 bombers, and 20 assault aircraft).

The opposing enemy forces counted around 24-26 infantry divisions, four motorized divisions, and 11-13 panzer divisions; in all, around 40 divisions, deployed in front of the Western Front.

Combat troops numbered approximately 230,000 men, about 1,800 field pieces, 1,300 tanks, and 600-800 aircraft. In comparing the correlation of forces within the confines of the entire front we arrive at almost equal numbers of infantry, a German superiority in artillery, mortars and somewhat in aviation, and more than a two to one superiority in tanks. Thus quantitative superiority in equipment at the beginning of the second offensive favored the Germans.

Alongside the overall correlation of forces along the entire front, the correlation of forces along those axes where the decisive events unfolded also had great significance. As we will see further, the Germans were able to concentrate their main mobile forces on both wings in accordance with their operational plan (insofar as they held the initiative in the first half of November) and in the first period achieved an even more significant superiority in men and matériel along the shock sectors. This question will be thoroughly illuminated in describing the course of the operation.

Table III/1.1 The correlation of forces on the Western Front as of November 16 1941 – German forces

Unit	Divisions	Men	Field guns	Anti-tank guns	Mortars	Tanks	Aircraft
XXVII and LVI army corps, XLI Panzer Corps	3 infantry, 1 motorized 3 panzer	39,000	300	250	360	300	–
V Army Corps, XLVI and XL panzer corps	3 infantry 1 motorized 4 panzer	44,000	350	280	400	400	–
IX and VII army corps	5 infantry	30,000	300	230	350	–	–
XX Army Corps	3 infantry 1 motorized 1 panzer	29,000	210	160	300	100	–
XII Army Corps and LVII Panzer Corps	4 infantry 1 panzer	29,000	250	200	320	100	–
XIII and XLIII army corps	4 infantry	24,000	210	160	280	–	–
XLIII Army Corps, XXIV and XLVII panzer corps	2 infantry 1 motorized 4 panzer	38,000	260	220	330	400	–
TOTAL	41 divisions	223,000	1,880	1,500	2,340	1,300	600-800

*Note. Figures for the sides' strength and correlation of forces were compiled from various sources.

The enemy's operational-strategic situation in the theater of military activities and his quantitative superiority in tanks gave the Germans the opportunity to launch blows against Moscow with large mobile groups along the following axes:

4 This figure excludes aircraft subordinated to the High Command and the Moscow PVO (National Air Defense) Zone, i.e., around 600 active aircraft.

Table III/1.2 The correlation of forces on the Western Front as of November 16 1941 – Red Army

Unit	Men	Field Guns	Anti-tank guns	Mortars	Tanks	Aircraft
30th Army	23,000	110	25	75	20	–
16th Army	50,000	287	180	300	150	–
5th Army	31,000	217	85	160	65	–
33rd Army	30,000	114	45	95	37	–
43rd Army	34,000	146	115	150	85	–
49th Army	44,000	280	100	320	100	–
50th Army	28,000	100	45	175	45	–
TOTAL	240,000	1,254	595	1,275	502	600-800

a) Turginovo-Klin-Dmitrov (about 100 km.) and then outflanking Moscow from the northeast;
b) Teryaeva, Sloboda, and then to Klin (or directly on Solnechnogorsk) and then to Moscow, directing the main blow along the Leningrad road (about 120 km.);
c) Volokolamsk-Novo-Petrovskoe-Istra and then to Moscow (about 110 km.);
d) Dorokhovo-Kubinka and then to Moscow, employing the highway and the Mozhaisk road (70 km.);
e) the Naro-Fominsk axis, using as an axis the Naro-Fominsk-Moscow road (70 km.);
f) the Maloyaroslavets axis, afterwards branching either to Podol'sk or Krasnaya Pakhra and then on to Moscow;
g) the Serpukhov axis for an advance on Moscow from the south (90 km.), or in order to outflank Moscow from the southeast;
h) the Tula axis, with smaller branches to Mikhailov, Zaraisk, Venev, Kashira, or Serpukhov, moreover as the enemy's desire to outflank Tula from the southeast and encircle it had already been noted.

All of these axes were important and each of them had its own significance in the Western Front's defensive system, as the result of which it was necessary to reliably cover them in a situation of the enemy's impending attack. The shortest axes to the capital ran through our center, but the Germans' mobile groups, according the available information, were concentrated against our wings.

The Red Army Supreme High Command adopted measures for repelling the gathering enemy offensive.

The Supreme High Command's plan called for:

1 the creation in the country's rear of powerful strategic reserves (a large number of reserve formations, and the formation of reserve armies and other matters);
2 the construction of a series of fortified lines and areas along the far and near approaches to Moscow, which were supposed to form a multi-layered system of defense for the capital;
3 waging a stubborn and active defense on the approaches to Moscow from the west and the apportionment of forces necessary for this task, and relying on fortified positions;
4 the concentration of operational-strategic reserves near Moscow and their deployment behind the flanks, beyond the ring of the enemy's possible tank encirclement;
5 wearing down the enemy by launching counterblows and inflicting local defeats on the approaches to Moscow, so as to exhaust and halt him;
6 going over to a decisive counteroffensive at the proper moment, in order to defeat the enemy.

The main objective of the Western Front's forces in this situation was, by reliably securing the approaches to the capital, exhaust and wear out the enemy through an active defense along the most important axes, inflict local defeats upon him, halt his advance, and to delay him until favorable conditions arose for passing over to a decisive counteroffensive.

In such a situation the Western Front, under the command of Gen. Zhukov, took upon itself a blow by an enormous mass of men and matériel, delivered by the German command on November 15-16 during the second general offensive against Moscow.

As it later became known (after the beginning of the second German offensive), the German command had concentrated and thrown into the offensive against the Western Front by the beginning of December 30-33 infantry, 13 panzer and 4-5 motorized infantry divisions, in all 47-51 divisions. These forces were deployed in the following manner:[5]

a) against our right flank along the Klin-Solnechnogorsk axis—the Third and Fourth Panzer groups under generals Hoth and Hoeppner, including the 1st, 2nd, 5th, 6th, 7th, 10th, and 11th panzer divisions, the 36th and 14th motorized infantry divisions, and the 23rd, 106th, and 35th infantry divisions.
b) against the left flank along the Tula-Kashira-Ryazan' axis—Gen. Guderian's Second Panzer Army, including the 3rd, 4th, 17th and 18th panzer divisions, the 10th and 29th motorized infantry divisions, and the 167th Infantry Division.
c) against our center were the IX, VII, XX, XII, XIII, and XLIII army corps, and the 19th and 20th panzer divisions.

These forces were part of the Ninth and Fourth armies, the Second Panzer Army, and the Third and Fourth panzer groups, which formed Army Group Center (Gen. von Bock commanding, with headquarters in Vyaz'ma), operating along the Moscow strategic direction.

An order was issued by Hitler calling for the rapid capture of Moscow at any cost. The German-Fascist leadership's objective was to break through and deeply envelop our Western Front's flanks and get in our rear, to defeat the Red Army forces opposing them, and to encircle and capture Moscow. To this purpose, the enemy strove to: a) to capture Klin, Solnechnogorsk, Rogachevo, Dmitrov, and Yakhroma in the north; b) to capture Tula, Kashira, Ryazan' and Kolomna in the south; c) then to strike at Moscow from three sides: the north, west and south and to capture it. The German information bureau reported at the beginning of December:

> The German command will view Moscow as its main objective, even if Stalin tries to shift the center of military operations to another sector.

Thus the German command's operational plan came down to a concentric offensive against Moscow by means of launching the main blows with its mobile forces along the enveloping wings ("wedges"); the infantry formations located in the center were to carry out a supporting offensive. The northern German wing was to, after capturing the area of Klin, Solnechnogorsk and Dmitrov, and attacking with part of its forces towards Moscow, develop the blow and outflank the capital from the northeast and link up with the southern wing to the east of Moscow. The German southern wing's main objective (the core of which was the Second Panzer Army) was to quickly break through our front along the Tula axis and then through the line of the Oka River between Ryazan' and Serpukhov, to seize the important industrial cities of Tula, Stalinogorsk and

5 From the report by the Western Front's military council to comrade Stalin on December 12 1941, and an announcement by the Soviet Informburo on December 13 1941.

Kashira and then to encircle the capital from the southeast, closing the ring together with the northern group to the east of Moscow. According to the plan's first draft, the XXIV Panzer Corps was to break through at Tula to the crossings over the Oka River at Kashira and Serpukhov. The XLVII Panzer Corps, augmenting the blow by the XXIV Panzer Corps, was to capture the Kolomna area and create bridgeheads to secure the passage of troops across the Moscow River. The Second Panzer Army was reinforced for this operation with two army corps (XLIII and LIII). The German center was to first tie town with its army corps the Red Army forces on the near approaches to Moscow from the west, and then with the development of the operation on the wings, by launching blows through Zvenigorod and Naro-Fominsk, break through to the capital, so as to split our front into isolated segments and render impossible further resistance by the Red Army around Moscow.

This operational plan was no better or worse than the German command's other similar plans, the realization of which in other cases had brought about success. At first glance, the plan's idea seemed to correspond to the level of development of both military art and modern technology. Large forces had been gathered for the offensive, which occupied a favorable jumping-off position, and which were concentrically aimed at the capital of the Soviet state. By moving directly forward they must break into the flank and rear of the Western Front's forces and encircle Moscow. It seemed to the German-Fascist leadership that all the prerequisites were at hand for launching a final blow of enormous force, which should decide the fate of Moscow, the campaign, and even the war before the onset of winter. This was the plan of an experienced and skillful predator, eager for quick conquests.

However, the conditions in which the great Battle of Moscow took place were already different and more favorable to the Red Army than at the beginning of the war. The results of the preceding five-month struggle by the Red Army and the entire Soviet people, under the wise leadership of comrade Stalin against the Fascist invaders were beginning to tell. Under the new combat conditions, which had arisen along the western front in November-December 1941, in a political and strategic situation favorable to the Red Army, the German command's operational plan no longer corresponded to the situation. The plan proved to be impracticable and adventuristic and led the German-Fascist troops to defeat at Moscow.

The beginning of the German offensive. The description of the Moscow Operation

On November 16 the second general offensive by the German-Fascist forces on Moscow began along the western front.[6] The combat activities, which unfolded from the second half of November along a broad swath of territory from the Moscow Sea to Tula, were united by a single operational idea and the overall *front* command and represented a single large and complex operation. Aside from this, the combat activities along the northern wing, the center, and the southern wing, given the unity and mutual connection of operational events within the confines of a *front* operation, also contained their own order and a certain independence of development. They are also rich in instructive factual material and valuable for those operational-tactical conclusions that can be made within the confines of an army or several armies carrying out a common mission (an army operation, an operation by a group of armies).

In order to correctly understand the characteristic features and the specifics of the fighting along different operational axes at different periods of the battle (while at the same time not missing the mutual dependency of events), it is worthwhile viewing this grandiose epic according to the operation's major consecutive stages (the defensive battle around Moscow; the Red Army's

6 The German offensive began on November 15 along the Kalinin Front's left wing (30th Army).

counteroffensive on the Western Front; the further development of the offensive from the line of the Lama, Ruza, Nara, and Oka rivers). Inside each stage we must examine first of all the activities on the wings and in the center, after which he can connect them in accordance with each state of the *front* operation and draw the necessary conclusions. The further description of events will be conducted in this order. A number of the Supreme High Command's major problems and measures, which cannot be fitted into these confines (for example, the participation by High Command aviation, and others), will be removed and examined separately. The defensive battle around Moscow embraces the period from November 15-16 through December 5 1941.

2

The concentration of the 1st, 20th and 10th Reserve armies and other reserves

In order to defeat the German-Fascist troops advancing on Moscow, the Supreme Commander-in-Chief carried out a number of timely measures to strengthen the Western Front with fresh operational reserves. Beside those forces being send by order of the Supreme Commander-in-Chief as reinforcements or *front* reserves, within the depths of the country large operational reserves were being formed, designated for active combat along the decisive axes.

The advance of the enemy's panzer groups north and south of Moscow made it absolutely necessary to quickly concentrate large forces along these axes and in those areas lying outside of the possible tank encirclement of the capital. These areas were: the eastern bank of the Moscow-Volga Canal in the north and the Ryazan' area in the south. In accordance with this there were concentrated and deployed the 1st Shock Army and the 20th and 10th armies (see the register for the concentration of the 1st, 20th and 10th armies on pp. 31-33). Two reserve armies (1st and 20th) were to be concentrated behind the *front's* right wing by the beginning of December, assigned to defeat the German Klin-Solnechnogorsk Group; behind the left wing—one reserve army (10th) for launching a flank attack against the enemy's southern group.

These armies' concentration was carried out in the following manner:

The concentration of the 1st Shock Army

On November 20 1941 a directive by the Supreme Commander-in-Chief ordered the formation of the 1st Shock Army (initially called the 19th Army), to be directly subordinated to the Supreme Commander-in-Chief. This directive called for the army to include the following formations and units: the 55th, 47th, 50th, and 29th rifle brigades in the Dmitrov area; the 43rd and 60th rifle brigades in Zagorsk; the 71st Rifle Brigade in Yakhroma; the 44th Rifle Brigade in Khot'kovo; the 2nd, 3rd, 4th, 16th, 18th 19th, and 20th ski battalions in Zagorsk; the 1st, 5th, and 7th ski battalions in Dmitrov; the 6th Ski Battalion in Yakhroma; the 8th Ski Battalion in Khot'kovo, and; the 517th Artillery Regiment in Zagorsk.

It was planned to complete the concentration of the army's formations and units in these areas by November 27.

From November 25 the troops of the 1st Shock Army began to concentrate in their designated areas.

The concentration of the formations and units was somewhat delayed and made more difficult as the result of air attacks on the railroads. However, these attacks had no real influence and by December 1 the main formations were concentrated in their staging areas along the eastern bank of the Moscow-Volga Canal in the Dmitrov-Yakhroma area. The army's strength as of December 1 was as follows: 2,998 officers, 6,427 NCOs, and 27,525 enlisted men. In all, the army numbered 36,950 men.

A number of the army's formations were under strength at the time of concentration, not only among senior and junior officers, but among the NCOs as well, which naturally made the organization of troop control more difficult.

The army was completely outfitted with enlisted men.

The 1st Shock Army was also short of weaponry. For example, there were only 25,050 rifles, 245 heavy machine guns, 705 light machine guns, 684 Degtyarev machine guns, five heavy-caliber machine guns, 103 field pieces, and 335 mortars. The army also lacked howitzers and anti-aircraft weapons.

Besides this, the units were poorly outfitted with horses and auto transport. For example, the 50th Rifle Brigade had only 42 horses, with the 44th Rifle Brigade had 169. The 29th and 55th Rifle brigades were each 84 trucks short of authorized strength, while the 50th Rifle Brigade was 120 short, and the 56th Rifle Brigade 101 short.

While the army was concentrating it was further reinforced by the addition of the 126th and 133rd rifle divisions, and the 123rd Tank Brigade.

Upon completing its concentration, the army (29th, 44th, 47th, 71st, 84th, 50th, 55th, and 56th Rifle brigades, the 133rd and 126th rifle divisions, and 11 ski battalions) was subordinated to the Western Front and as early as December 2 the *front* commander had ordered it to carry out the following mission: from the morning of December 2 1941 the army was to decisively attack with all its forces in the general direction of Dedenevo and Fedorovka and the southern outskirts of Klin, with the immediate objective of freeing Gen. Zakharov's forces from encirclement in the area of Kamenka and Fedorovka.

As a subsequent goal, the army was to, in coordination with the 30th and 20th armies; defeat the enemy's Klin-Solnechnogorsk group.

The concentration of the 20th Army

The 20th Army, just like the 1st Army, was formed on the basis of the Supreme Commander-in-Chief's directive of November 20 1941 and was subordinated directly to the Supreme Commander-in-Chief.

The 20th Army at first consisted of the following formations and units: the 11th, 12th, 13th, and 16th Rifle brigades in Ranenburg, the 78th Rifle Brigade in Proskurov, the 35th Rifle Brigade (arrived from Tashkent) in Skopino, the 23rd and 24th Ski battalions in Ranenburg, the 21st and 22nd Ski battalions in Ryazhsk, and the 18th Artillery Regiment in Ranenburg. Besides this, the army also contained the 331st Rifle Division, and the 36th, 37th, 40th, 53rd, 54th, 49th, 28th, 64th, 43rd, 24th, and 31st rifle brigades.

It was planned to complete the concentration of the 20th Army's units by November 27 1941 in the area of Lobnya, Skhodnya, and Khimki.

The army's composition later changed and as of December 1 1941 it contained the 331st and 352nd rifle divisions, the 134th and 135th tank brigades, the 28th, 35th, and 64th rifle brigades, the 517th Artillery Regiment, and the 7th and 13th Guards Mortar battalions. These units contained 3,255 officers, 6,351 NCOs, and 28, 633 enlisted men, in all 38, 239 men. The army contained 27,826 rifles, 296 heavy machine guns, 639 light machine guns, 672 Degtyarev machine guns, four anti-aircraft machine guns, eight heavy-caliber machine guns, 158 field pieces, 34 howitzers, and 402 mortars.

On the basis of an order by the *Stavka* of the Supreme High Command of December 3 1941, the 20th Army (331st and 352nd rifle divisions, 43rd, 28th, 35th, and 64th rifle brigades, the 134th and 135th tank brigades was subordinated to the Western Front, where it received orders to attack in the general direction of Krasnaya Polyana.

In connection with the operational situation around Moscow, the 20th Army's units and formations were committed into the fighting upon the completion of their concentration, which took place on December 4.

The concentration of the 10th Reserve Army

The concentration of the 10th Reserve Army took place in the following fashion:

As early as October 20 the *Stavka* of the Supreme High Command issued a directive ordering the formation of the 10th Reserve Army by December 2 1941, to be subordinated directly to the *Stavka*.

The army consisted of the 326th Rifle Division in Penza; the 324th Rifle Division in Inza; the 322nd Rifle Division in Kuznetsk; the 330th Rifle Division in Syzran', and; the 323rd Rifle Division in Petrovsk. Aside from this, two rifle brigades were to arrive from the Ural Military District.

The army headquarters was deploying in the city of Kuznetsk.

On November 29 1941 the army's units were transferred to the following areas: the 328th Rifle Division to Turlatovo and Vygorodok; the 322nd Rifle Division to Rybnoe; the 330th Rifle Division to Ryazan'; the 323rd Rifle Division to Spassk-Ryazanskii; the 326th Rifle Division to Shilovo; the 57th Cavalry Division to Kanino (northeast of Ryazhsk), and; the 75th Cavalry Division to Ryazan'.

The army staff and communications units were located in Shilovo.

Just as with the 1st Army, the army's concentration was somewhat delayed: of 152 trains en route by December 1 only 64 had arrived in the designated areas; another 44 were en route, with another 44 still loading. For this reason, it was planned to complete the army's concentration on December 5, instead of the date of December 2 1941, established by the *Stavka*.

The army was incompletely outfitted. For example, the 57th and 75th cavalry divisions remained without weapons and accoutrements for their horses. The 325th and 326th rifle divisions were short of weapons and also lacked communications and transport.

The 324th Rifle Division lacked its full complement of heavy machine guns, Shpagin machine guns, anti-aircraft weapons, mortars, howitzers, communications and engineering equipment. The 322nd, 330th, 328th, and 323rd rifle divisions were outfitted with their main types of weapons and could be committed into the fighting upon concentration. They needed only to be slightly reinforced with weaponry and auto transport.

The 325th and 326th rifle divisions lacked anti-tank artillery and were poorly supplied with mortars and machine guns. Besides this, the army's units were poorly supplied with communications and engineering equipment and auto transport.

The army's units and formations continued to receive weapons during the rail trip to their concentration areas.

The army's strength was as follows: 94,180 men, 62,187 rifles, 409 heavy machine guns, 3,141 light machine guns, 646 mortars, and 215 artillery pieces.

By December 5 the units of the 10th Reserve Army were located in the following areas: the 385th Rifle Division, the 83rd Cavalry and 207th Rifle regiments in Ukholovo; the 346th Rifle Division in Ryazhsk; the 325th Rifle Division in Spassk-Ryazanskii; the 323rd Rifle Division in Troitsa; the 328th Rifle Division in Redino; the 761st Artillery Regiment in Ryazan', and; the 322nd Rifle Division in Khodynevo.

The army's movement had the objective of concentrating it closer to the front, at the junction of the Southwestern and Western fronts. Before December 6 the army was subordinated to the *Stavka* of the Supreme High Command, and on December 6 1941 it was subordinated to the

Western Front, consisting of the 325th, 323rd, 324th, 328th, 322nd, 326th, 330rd, and 239th rifle divisions, and the 57th, 75th, and 41st cavalry divisions.

However, as early as December 5 the army received the following directive from the Western Front's military council:

> The 10th Reserve Army is to launch its main attack in the direction of Mikhailov and Stalinogorsk from its jumping-off point in the area of Zakharovo and Pronsk. A division-sized supporting attack from the Zaraisk and Kolomna area will move through Serebryanye Prudy in the direction of Venev and Kurakovo.
>
> The beginning of the offensive from the jumping-off point is slated for the morning of December 6.

In this manner, all three reserve armies had completed their concentration in their designated areas by the start of the December counteroffensive and moved to carry out their assignments.

Besides these reserve armies, the Western Front received eight rifle and seven cavalry divisions, four rifle brigades, an airborne corps, and a large number of special units in November and December.

November 20 is an important date in the Supreme Commander-in-Chief's decision. Deep reserves were deployed along the line Vologda-Penza. The decision to transfer the reserve armies their new concentration areas essentially marks the adoption of a new decision for launching a counterblow around Moscow, and not just the passive defense of the capital. The reserves were concentrated, as already noted, behind our forces' flanks and against the enemy's outflanking groups.

The Supreme High Command's reserves played a decisive role in the course of the Battle of Moscow.

The role of rail transport in the Moscow Operation

Rail transport was one of the most important elements in the problem of concentrating the reserve armies.

If in the beginning of November the *front* command had to mainly use the railroads for ensuring the uninterrupted supply of those units at the front, by the end of November and the beginning of December this means of transportation was called upon to play an important role as a factor enabling the concentration of large reserves along the operational axes designated by the *Stavka* of the Supreme Command.

The German offensive, which was developing according to their plan north and south of Moscow, made it necessary to carry out maneuver using the railroad resources available to the *Stavka*. This peculiarity of the railroads' work noticeably told in that period when not only lateral, but deep railroad lines were factually subject to air attack by the enemy, who attempted to foil the concentration of our reserves by attacking the railroads with not only bombers from the sky, but with artillery fire (The October and Dzerzhinskii railroads). The transfer of large reserves under these conditions naturally demanded the fullest work of all transport.

One must point out the great distances which these troop transfers had to cover. For example, during the November 20-December 1 time period the railroads carried out the following transfers: the 44th Rifle Brigade from Krasnoyarsk to Zagorsk; the 56th and 71st rifle brigades from Chkalov to Zagorsk and Dmitrov; the 352nd Rifle Division from Bugul'ma to Khimki, and the 35th Rifle Brigade from Tashkent to Khovrino.

The distance between Bugul'ma and Khimki is 1,250 km, and was covered in three days, for an average speed of 400 km. per day. Long-distance transfers, such as from Krasnoyarsk (3,943 km), were carried out at a speed of around 500 km. per day. Such speeds of railroad transfer should be considered quite high, particularly under conditions of enemy air attack.

If one takes into account the fact that the railroads moved the troops of the 1st Shock and 20th armies, numbering 75,000 men and 300 guns during the preparation for the counteroffensive (not counting the remaining equipment park and horses), to the right wing and the 90,000 men and 200 guns of the 10th Reserve Army to the left wing, then it become clear that under intense combat conditions at the front the railroads were able to carry out their difficult work, which may rank among the highest achievements in the history of rail transport.

This great aid to the front enabled the *Stavka* of the Supreme Command to concentrate reserves along the most important axes and made it possible to create a decisive superiority in forces for going over to a counteroffensive.

Table III/2.1 Register of the concentration of the 1st Shock, 20th and 10th armies during the period November-December 6 1941

Unit	Beginning of embarkation transport	End of transport	Disembarkation area	Kilometers covered
1st Shock Army				
29th Rifle Bde	20.11.41 Balakhna	25.11.41	Dmitrov	476
50th Rifle Bde (Urals MD)	19.11.41 Lebyazh'ya	27.11.41	Dmitrov	2,102
44th Rifle Bde	19.11.41 Krasnoyarsk	27.11.41	Zagorsk	3,943
56th Rifle Bde	19.11.41 Chkalov	27.11.41	Zagorsk	1,533
71st Rifle Bde	19.11.41 Chkalov	30.11.41	Dmitrov	1,533
55th Rifle Bde	19.11.41 Chkalov	28.11.41	Dmitrov	1,533
47th Rifle Bde	19.11.41 Ufalei	25.11.41	Dmitrov	1,767
84th Rifle Bde	1.12.41 Ryazhsk	5.12.41	Zagorsk	113
126th Rifle Div	1.12.41 Ryazhsk	5.12.41	Zagorsk	113
133rd Rifle Div	24.11.41 Kushalino	27.11.41	Dmitrov	200
17th Ski Bn	20.11.41 Gor'kii	25.11.41	Zagorsk	546
18th Ski Bn	20.11.41 Gor'kii	25.11.41	Zagorsk	546
19th Ski Bn	20.11.41 Gor'kii	25.11.41	Zagorsk	546
20th Ski Bn	20.11.41 Gor'kii	25.11.41	Zagorsk	546
3rd Ski Bn	19.11.41 Slobodskoi	25.11.41	Zagorsk	976
4th Ski Bn	19.11.41 Slobodskoi	25.11.41	Dmitrov	976
5th Ski Bn	19.11.41 Slobodskoi	25.11.41	Dmitrov	976
6th Ski Bn	19.11.41 Slobodskoi	25.11.41	Yakhroma	976
7th Ski Bn	19.11.41 Kotel'nich	25.11.41	Dmitrov	814
8th Ski Bn	19.11.41 Kotel'nich	25.11.41	Zagorsk	814
20th Army				
64th Rifle Bde	19.11.41	27.11.41	Zagorsk	1,607
	To the 1st Shock Army from Nizhne-Serginsk			
35th Rifle Bde	19.11.41 Tashkent	1.12.41	Khovrino	3,329
1st Rifle Bde	19.11.41 Tashkent	1.12.41	Khovrino	3,329
28th Rifle Bde	20.11.41	25.11.41	Cheremukho to Zagorsk	4,899
31st Rifle Bde	3.12.41	8.12.41	From Vetluzhskii to Odintsovo	574
	To the Moscow Zone			

Unit	Beginning of embarkation transport	End of transport	Disembarkation area	Kilometers covered
24th Rifle Bde	3.12.41	8.12.41	From Vetluzhskii to Odintsovo	574
	To the Moscow Zone			
134th Tank Bde	3.12.41	8.12.41	From Vetluzhskii to Odintsovo	574
	To the Moscow Zone			
135th Tank Bde	3.12.41	8.12.41	From Vetluzhskii to Odintsovo	574
	To the Moscow Zone			
331st Rifle Div	25.11.41 Michurinsk	4.12.41	Khimki	407
352nd Rifle Div	28.11.41 Bugul'ma	2.12.41	Khimki	1,257
10th Army				
322nd Rifle Div	24.11.41 Kuznetsk	1.12.41	Rybnoe	830
323rd Rifle Div	24.11.41 Petrovsk	1.12.41	Kenzino	825
324th Rifle Div	27.11.41 Inza	4.12.41	Shilovo	700
326th Rifle Div	26.11.41 Penza	4.12.41	Kenzino	709
328th Rifle Div	24.11.41 Penza	3.12.41	Turlatovo	705
330th Rifle Div	24.11.41 Syzran'	3.12.141	Ryazan'	920
239th Rifle Div	11.11.41 Kuibyshev	17.11.41	Ryazan'	1,061
41st Cav Div	2.10.41 From Kovrov	6.10.41	Mtsensk	331
57th Cav Div	26.11.41 Kamyshlei	3.12.41	Kenzino	780
75th Cav Div	30.11.41 Glotovka	6.12.41	Ryazan'	728

The role of automobile transportation in the Moscow Operation

Automobile transport, while carrying out its usual work of hauling troop supplies, as a result of the German offensive on Moscow, was used for the operational transfer of troops and for concentrating reserves. This was called for by the character of the fighting along the given direction. By the start of our counteroffensive the 133rd Rifle Division, the 49th, 43rd, 28th, 30th, and 34th Rifle brigades and two ski battalions (see the table on the auto transport of forces) had been moved by auto transport. The movement of these forces was carried under conditions of little time and under constant attack by the enemy's aviation.

Thus it should be noted that auto transport also aided the rapid concentration and deployment of reserves in the Moscow operation for the goal of defeating the Germans.

Table III/2.2 Table of troop movements by automobile

Unit	Beginning of transport	Number of vehicles	Embarkation area	Disembarkation area	Time of arrival
133rd Rifle Div	23.11.41	778	Kushalino	Dmitrov	25.11.41
49th Rifle Bde	30.11.41	130	Rastorguevo	Nakhabino	1.12.41
43rd Rifle Bde	2.12.41	290	Zagorsk	Cherkizovo	3.12.41
28th Rifle Bde	2.12.41	55	Zagorsk	Khlebnikovo	3.12.41
30th Rifle Bde	13.12.41	130	Likhobory	Tarusskaya	14.12.41
34th Rifle Bde	13.12.41	150	Kozhukhovo	Tarusskaya	14.12.41
Two ski battalions	16.12.41	150	Khlebnikovo	Naro-Fominsk	17.12.41

3

The defensive battle on the Western Front's right wing: the situation by November 16

The operational situation that had developed on the right wing of the Western Front by the beginning of the second German offensive on Moscow was characterized by the following data:

1 The forces of the 16th and 5th armies continued to strengthen and improve their positions, repelling enemy attempts to break into our position.
   a) Gen. Rokossovskii's 16th Army, with part of its forces (17th Cavalry Division, a cadet regiment, 316th Rifle Division, 50th and 53rd cavalry divisions, 18th and 78th rifle divisions, and the 58th Tank Division) occupied defensive positions along the line Matyushkino-Kharlanika-Chentsy 2-Danilkovo-Shchelkanovo-Sloboda, with part of its forces (126th Rifle Division, 27th and 28th Tank brigades, 1st Guards Tank Brigade) in the second echelon in the area of Teryaeva, Sloboda, Il'inskoe, Chismena, Pashkovo, and Ustinovo. The 302nd and 301st Machine Gun battalions occupied and were developing the fortified line along the eastern bank of the Istra River from Rakovo and the town of Istra as far as Kryukovo. The 24th, 44th and 20th cavalry divisions, subordinated to the 16th Army by Western Front order no. 045, were concentrating west and southeast of Klin. The demarcation line with the Kalinin Front (30th Army) on the right was the line Verbilki- Reshetnikovo-Knyazh'i Gory, and with the 5th Army on the left—Zagorsk-Iksha-Povarovo-Istra-Tarkhanovo-Bulychevo, all locations being within the 16th Army's zone. The length of the army's front was 70 km. The 30th Army's (Kalinin Front) left-flank 107th Motorized Rifle Division occupied the eastern bank of the Lama River from Glukhino to Markovo.
   b) Gen. Govorov's 5th Army was defending with part of its forces (144th and 50th rifle divisions, 20th, 18th and 22nd tank brigades, 82nd Motorized Rifle Division, 36th Motorcycle Regiment, 32nd Rifle Division) along the line Fomkino-Kryukovo-Tuchkovo-Trufanovka-Brykino-Bol'shie Semenychi, having in its second echelon a rifle division in the area of Zvenigorod. The demarcation line on the left (33rd Army) was Kuntsevo-Maurino (to the 5th Army), and Kulakovo. The length of the army's front was 50 km.

2. The enemy, in preparing a new offensive against Moscow for more than two weeks (November 1-15), was completing the concentration of the right-flank units of the Ninth Army, the Third and Fourth panzer groups, and the left-flank forces of the Fourth Army, including the XXVII, XLI, LVI, V, XLVI, XL, IX and VII corps along the right flank of the Western Front. At the same time the Germans were improving their positions along the eastern bank of the Lama River-Bludi-Novo-Pavlovskoe-Mikhailovskoe-Gorbovo-Maurino-Naro-Fominsk, and were continuing to bring up supplies and fuel

The main forces were disposed as follows:

a) Gen. Hoth's Third Panzer Group (1st, 6th and 7th panzer divisions, 14th and 36th motorized divisions, 23rd Infantry Division) along the Klin-Solnechnogorsk axis.
b) Gen. Hoeppner's Fourth Panzer Group (2nd, 5th, 10th, and 11th panzer divisions, 106th and 35th infantry divisions, an SS infantry division) along the Volokolamsk-Istra axis. The 2nd Panzer and 106th infantry divisions were evidently designated for action in the general direction of Solnechnogorsk by outflanking the Istra Reservoir from the north and were the link with Hoth's group attacking toward Klin; the 5th, 10th and 11th panzer divisions and the SS infantry division comprised the Hoeppner group's shock unit, deployed in the Volokolamsk area for launching a blow against Solnechnogorsk and Istra. The SS division was designated to operate with the panzer divisions in order to cover them from the south, and for maintaining contact with units of the IX Army Corps attacking our 5th Army.

3 The 30th Army (5th and 185th rifle divisions, 107th Motorized Rifle Division, 46th Cavalry Division, 21st and 8th tank brigades, 46th Motorcycle, 2nd Motorized, and the 20th Reserve Infantry regiments, 276th Artillery Battalion, anti-tank and other attached units) defended the line (excluding) Malye Peremerki (six km southeast of Kalinin)-Kotovo-Slygino-Kamenka-Tsvetkovo-Luk'yanovo-Dorino and farther along the eastern bank of the Lama River.

During November 15-17 the enemy attacked along the 30th Army's front, launching his main blow to the south of the Moscow Sea.

The *Stavka* of the Supreme High Command, taking into account the operational situation and the blow along the boundary between the two *fronts* (Kalinin and Western) and the Western Front's right wing, transferred the 30th Army at 2300 on November 17 1941 to the Western Front. In accordance with this, the new boundary between the Kalinin and Western fronts lay along the following line: Kashin-Negotino-Staritsa-Rzhev (all three locales within the Western Front).

The objectives of both sides

The armies of the Western Front's right wing were given the following tasks:

a) to prevent a German breakthrough into the depth of our defense;
b) by means of stubborn holding actions on the far approaches to Moscow, to prevent the development of the German offensive operation and their deep outflanking of the *front's* right wing at the junction of the Kalinin and Western fronts;
c) by means of a stubborn and active defense of the most important axes, to defeat the enemy and win time for the concentration of our operational reserves behind the *front's* right wing, so as to subsequently go over to a counteroffensive;
d) during the course of the defensive battle the armies were tasked with wearing out and exhausting the enemy forces and inflict maximum losses on his men and matériel.

The German command, having concentrated by the end of the first half of November (November 15-16) along the Klin-Solnechnogorsk and Istra axes the Third and Fourth panzer groups, intended to break through and outflank, followed by a deep turning movement of the *front's* right-wing armies, to get into their rear and create a threat to encircle Moscow.

In accordance with this, the German command ordered the following:

a) by means of a short and sharp blow north of the Moscow Sea, to throw back our forces beyond the Volga and secure the left flank of its Klin-Solnechnogorsk group;
b) by attacking with its main forces toward Klin-Solnechnogorsk and Istra, to defeat the Red Army's opposing forces, turn the Western Front's right flank and reach Moscow.

Map 2 The Withdrawal of the Western Front's Right Flank in November, 1941

The distribution and correlation of the opposing forces

The distribution of the sides' forces by November 16 1941 reveals that along the main shock axes the German command enjoyed a decisive superiority in tank formations (according to the number of tanks).

The correlation of the sides' forces along the different axes changed during the course of the fighting, because lesser or greater regroupings of forces were occurring not only at the army, but at the *front* level as well.

The table below indicates the correlation of forces at the beginning of the enemy's offensive operation, including the troops of the 30th Army:

Table III/3.1 The correlation of forces as of November 16 – German forces

Unit	Divisions	Men	Guns	Anti-tank guns	Mortars	Tanks
XXVII and LVI army corps, XLI Panzer Corps	3 infantry 1 motorized 3 panzer	39,000	300	250	360	300
V Army Corps, XLVI and XL panzer corps	3 infantry 1 motorized 4 panzer	44,000	350	280	400	400
IX and VII army corps	5 infantry	30,000	300	230	350	–
TOTAL	11 infantry 2 motorized 7 panzer	113,000	950	760	1,110	700

Table III/3.2 The Correlation of forces as of November 16 – Red Army

Army axis	Men	Guns	Anti-tank guns	Mortars	Tanks	Width of front (in km)
Turginovo-Klin						
30th Army	23,000	110	25	75	20	80
2 rifle divisions						
1 motorized rifle division						
1 cavalry division						
2 tank brigades						
Volokolamsk-Istra						
16th Army	50,000	287	180	300	150	70
4 rifle divisions						
6 cavalry divisions						
4 tank brigades						
1 tank division						
Mozhaisk-Zvenigorod						
5th Army	31,000	217	85	160	65	50
4 rifle divisions						
1 motorized rifle division						
3 tank brigades						
TOTAL	104,000	614	290	535	235	200

10 rifle divisions
2 motorized rifle divisions
7 cavalry divisions
9 tank brigades
1 tank division

Correlation of forces by combat arm:
Infantry—1:1
Field Artillery—1:1.5
Anti-Tank Artillery—1:2.6
Mortars—1:2
Tanks—1:3 in favor of the enemy.

From the table it is clear that the enemy enjoyed superiority in equipment (particularly in tanks). According to the German command's thinking, the concentration of large mobile groups should ensure the success of the operational plan.

The overwhelming number of formations in the armies of the Western Front's right wing was small in strength. The tank formations had a serious shortage of tanks.

The 30th Army's defensive battles in the area of the Moscow Sea, November 15-17

By the morning of November 15 the 30th Army occupied the following line: 5th Rifle Division—the bank of the Volga River (six km south of Kalinin)-Vishenki-Kotovo and further along the northeastern bank of the Krapivna River, with the 257th Rifle Regiment (107th Motorized Rifle Division) in reserve in the area northeast of Chupriyanovka station; 21st Tank Brigade, 2nd Motorized Regiment and 20th Reserve Regiment along the line Salygino-Kamenka-Tsvetkovo-Zholnino-Luk'yanovo, with a separate group from the 21st Tank Brigade in Poddubki (five km south of Tsvetkovo); the 107th Motorized Infantry Division, 46th Motorcycle Regiment, and the 8th Tank Brigade defended the line south of the Moscow Sea along the eastern bank of the Lama River from Dorino to Silanuch'e (inclusive), and covering the surfaced road Dorino-Kozlovo-Novo-Zavidov with its right flank; the 185th Rifle Division formed the Kalinin Front's reserve in the Zhornovka area (six km north of Kalinin). The 30th Army's task was to defend the indicated front and prevent the German troops breaking through to the Leningrad highway north and south of the Moscow Sea and to the crossings over the Volga River in the Kalinin sector and the Moscow Sea.

In accordance with the operation's development in the area of the Moscow Sea, one may assume that the enemy's main task here was to launch a blow against the 30th Army so as to break through the front and with his mobile units reach the Leningrad highway.

The enemy was to launch his main attack south of the Moscow Sea in the general direction of Kozlovo, Novo-Zavidovskii and Reshetnikovo, with a supporting attack north of the Moscow Sea in the general direction of Redino. For this he concentrated north of the Moscow Sea the 129th and 86th infantry divisions and parts of the 1st Panzer Division. These forces' immediate task was to throw back our opposing forces beyond the Volga River and seize the railroad and road bridges across the Moscow Sea, so as to be able in the future to aid the development of the success of those units operating south of the Moscow Sea.

The German southern group, which included the 6th and 7th panzer and 14th Motorized divisions, had the task of breaking through south of the Moscow Sea and creating favorable conditions for the further development of the success of the entire Third Panzer Group along the Klin-Solnechnogorsk axis.

On November 14 the 107th Motorized Infantry Division's weak covering forces were thrown back from the line Turginovo-Bol'shie Gorki, and by the morning of November 15 the Germans had reached the front Selino-Sentsovo-Koidinovo.

From the morning of November 15 the enemy attacked along the entire front of the 30th Army. His attacks against the 5th Rifle Division, employing an infantry regiment and 12 tanks, did not achieve any great success. Up to an infantry division, supported by 50 tanks, attacked the 21st Tank Brigade and its attached units. The enemy supported by air attacks on our troops, pushed back units of the 21st Tank Brigade during the fighting along the whole front and by 1500 had taken Shcherbinino and Staryi Pogost, developing his further efforts to the southeast in the direction of Gorodnya, Kozlovo, and Redino. As a result, Gen. Konev, the commander of the Kalinin Front, ordered the commander of the 30th Army to move his 5th Rifle Division during the night of November 15-16 to the northeastern bank of the Volga River and take up defensive positions on the sector Poddub'e-Sudimirka; the 21st Tank Brigade and attached units fell back in a holding action to the southeast towards Bezborodovo. The 185th Rifle Division from the *front* reserve was ordered to the Zavidovo area at the disposal of the commander of the 30th Army.

South of the Moscow Sea the enemy's mobile units (14th Motorized and 6th and 7th panzer divisions), following heavy fighting, forced the Lama River and reached the front Dorino-Kur'yanovo. Their attempts to throw a bridge over the Lama River in the Sentsovo area were liquidated by our aviation and artillery. The enemy developed his main effort toward Dorino in the direction of Glukhino.

By the close of November 15 and the morning of November 16 the forces of the 30th Army occupied the following line: north of the Moscow Sea the 5th Rifle Division occupied a defensive position behind the Volga River along the sector Poddub'e-Sudimirka, having fended off enemy attempts to cross in the Pasynkovo-Staroe Semenovskoe area. The 21st Tank Brigade, with attached units, was engaged in heavy fighting with superior enemy forces along the line Novo-Semenovskoe-Mezhinino, and pulling back its main forces to the line Staraya Vedernya-Mezhevo. The enemy captured Pasynkovo, Myatlevo, Staryi Pogost, and Kozlovo and was directing his efforts in an eastern and southeastern direction. South of the Moscow Sea the 107th Motorized Rifle Division, the 8th Tank Brigade, and the 46th Motorcycle Regiment were engaged in fierce fighting with superior German forces along the line Dorino-Zelentsyno-Silanuch'e; the enemy was making his main efforts toward Kur'yanovo and Dmitrovo. A cadet regiment of the 16th Army was taking up position along the front Kharlanika-Uteshevo 2-Bykovo, to the left of the 30th Army.

During the course of the fighting of November 15 and the early hours of November 16 a difficult situation had arisen along the 30th Army's front: its right-flank units were isolated north of the Moscow Sea and a significant gap (16-18 km.) had developed between the 30th Army's left flank and the 16th Army's right flank.

The commander of the Kalinin Front, taking into account the situation, dispatched the 46th Cavalry Division by forced march on the morning of November 16 from the Mednoe area (the *front* reserve) to the commander of the 30th Army in order to occupy a defensive position along the eastern bank of the Volga River along the front Sudimirka-Sverdlovo.

Cavalry units were also moved into the gap between the 30th and 16th armies.

From the morning of November 16 the enemy continued to develop the offensive along the entire front; the attack was particularly strong south of the Moscow Sea. North of the Moscow Sea the 21st Tank Brigade, 2nd Motorized Regiment, and the 20th Reserve Regiment were engaged in fierce fighting along the line Staraya Vedernya-Mezhevo and were gradually withdrawing to the southeast along the Leningrad highway toward Gorodnya. By the end of November 16 enemy units of the 86th Infantry Division, with tanks and armored cars, were attacking between the Volga River and the line Tsvetkovo-Staryi Pogost-Redino and attempting to cross over to the

Volga's northern bank. However, all his attempts to infiltrate into the depth of the defense and cross the Volga were beaten back. South of the Moscow Sea the 107th Motorized Rifle Division, with attached units, was fighting a holding action along the Lama River, stoutly repulsing the attack by superior Fascist forces and inflicting losses on them. Nevertheless by 1200 the enemy managed to capture Dorino.

By the end of November 16 the 30th Army occupied the line: north of the Moscow Sea—along the left bank of the Volga River along the line Poddub'e-Sudimirka-Sverdlovo; on the right bank—the line Gorodnya-Krasnaya Gora (southeast of Redino): south of the Moscow Sea our front ran along the line east of Dorino-east of Kur'yanovo, toward Dmitrovo and Silanuch'e. By the end of November 16 a machine gun battalion from the High Command Reserve had taken up defensive positions in the area of the bridges across the Moscow Sea at Bezborodovo and Demidovo.

In two days of fierce fighting the 21st Tank Brigade had lost all of its tanks and 35% of its personnel. Units of the 107th Motorized Rifle Division, the 8th Tank Brigade, and the 46th Motorcycle Regiment also suffered heavily, although they also inflicted significant losses on the Fascists. For example, in two days of fighting the enemy lost 35 tanks, 28 armored cars, 38 anti-tank guns, 18 artillery pieces, 80 machine guns, five mortar batteries, and up to 2,500 officers and men.

Our aviation supported the 30th Army's forces and attacked concentrations of enemy's motor-mechanized units, auto transport and supply columns in Staryi Pogost, Sentsovo, and Dorino.

On November 17 fighting took place south of the Moscow Sea. During the day the enemy continued attacking with the forces of the 14th Motorized Division, and the 6th and 7th tank divisions, with their main blow in the direction of the paved road Dorino-Novo-Zavidovskii. By 1630 he had managed to break the resistance of the 107th Motorized Rifle Division and reach the western outskirts of Novo-Zavidovskii. By the morning of November 17 the 21st Tank Brigade (minus its tanks), the 2nd Motorized and 20th Reserve Infantry regiments had concentrated in the Novo-Zavidovskii area, where by order of the army's military council they had blown up the railroad and paved road bridges over the Moscow Sea during their retreat and were subordinated to the commander of the 107th Motorized Rifle Division. This division's right-flank units, following a fierce battle with superior enemy forces, also fell back to the Novo-Zavidovskii area; the division's remaining units waged stubborn battles along the line Dmitrovo-Grishkino.

Thus by the end of November 17 (that is, to the moment when the 30th Army was subordinated to the Western Front) the army's forces were located in three isolated groups: a) beyond the Volga, defending from Poddub'e to Sudimirka and to the southeast; b) on the south bank of the Moscow Sea in the area of Novo-Zavidovskii and Zavidovo; c) east of the Lama River along the Dmitrovo-Grishkino sector. The gap between Novo-Zavidovskii and Dmitrovo was more than 20 km.

The 185th Rifle Division (two regiments) and the 46th Cavalry Division continued to concentrate in their designated areas.

The 16th and 5th armies' battles on the Volokolamsk and Istra axes, November 16-17

The commander of the Western Front, Gen. Zhukov, in order to break up the concentration of German-Fascist troops along the Volokolamsk axis, ordered the commander of the 16th Army to launch an attack along the flank and rear of the enemy's Volokolamsk group.

In the early hours of November 16 the 16th Army carried out a partial regrouping and at 1000 went over to the attack. In his turn, the enemy decided on the morning of November 16 to attack the left-flank forces of the 16th Army with more than two regiments of infantry, plus tanks (5th Panzer Division). The Fascists attacked along the boundary between the 316th Rifle Division and

Dovator's cavalry group and started to push back our units. Both sides' offensive developed simultaneously on opposite flanks.

In the fierce fighting on the approaches to Moscow there was no small number of amazing feats performed by our units, groups and commanders, soldiers and political workers. Particularly outstanding among these was the feat of the 28 Soviet heroes of the former 316th Rifle Division—now the 8th Guards Red Banner Division named after Gen. Panfilov Rifle Division, which displayed unparalleled valor in battle.

The combat-hardened and small 316th, now the 8th Guards Rifle Division, engaged with battalion-sized enemy forces, supported by tens of tanks and bombers along the line Bykovo-Chentsy-Goryuny, covering the Volokolamsk paved road and the road to Istra and Moscow with its left-flank units. One of the division's regiments occupied defensive positions along the line height 251—Petelino—Dubosekovo station (7 km southeast of Volokolamsk).

The regiment covered the most important route to Moscow south of the Volokolamsk paved road, securing the road from a breakthrough by tank units from the southwest. The breakthrough of large tank forces along this axis could have had deleterious consequences for the 16th Army's entire operation. It was extremely important to hold the line. Company political instructor Klochkov-Diev and Sgt. Dobrobabin and a group of soldiers were located on the regiment's left flank.

They had already learned from intelligence that the Germans were preparing for a new offensive and that they had concentrated a regiment of tanks (80 tanks), around two regiments of infantry, six mortar and four artillery batteries in the area of Muromtsevo, Zhdanovo, Krasikovo; groups of automatic riflemen and motorcyclists were here as well.

From the morning of November 16 the enemy attacked with large forces from the Zhdanovo area in the general direction of Petelino and Matrenino. A group of soldiers under the command of Sgt. Dobrobabin, taking advantage of the favorable terrain, occupied a covered position near Dubosekovo station. The Fascists sought to take advantage of the covered approaches on the left flank of the 316th Rifle Division's regiment's defensive position, and attacked with company-strength infantry, supported by 20 tanks. Not expecting to meet any serious resistance here, the German infantry attacked standing upright.

The enemy, met by the unexpected but accurate fire from the 28 fearless Guards troops, lost up to 70 men killed and he was forced to halt. In the frozen trench near the Dubosekovo station the Guards troops swore to each other to fight the enemy to their last drop of blood. Among them were Russians, Ukrainians, collective farm workers from Talgar in Kazakhstan, and Kazakhs from Alma-Ata. Their warrior's comradeship, made fast by blood, became the embodiment of the combat friendship of the peoples of our countries, who rose up against their mortal foe. There were 28 heroes. The twenty ninth, who turned out to be a despicable coward, was killed by the Guards troops on the spot. The battle with the tanks continued more than four hours and the tanks were unable to break through the valorous defenders' defense. Fourteen tanks out of 20 lay motionless on the battlefield. Of the 28 glorious soldiers, seven were killed and gravely wounded. Brave Sgt. Dobrobabin was killed. But not one of the soldiers wavered or lost his composure. At this time another 30 tanks moved into the attack. In this heavy and unequal battle another 11 enemy tanks were put out of action. By this time the glorious defenders had run out of ammunition. The anti-tank rifles, bottles with flammable liquid, and grenade clusters were all used up. Political Instructor Klochkov-Diev, already wounded, hung a grenade cluster around himself and threw himself under a tank and blew it up. Fighting fearlessly against the enemy's tanks to the very end, the Guards troops died a hero's death, but valorously carried out their combat duty to the Motherland and inflicted heavy losses on the enemy, putting out of action 50% of the tanks taking part in the attack. The heroes' glorious battle near Dubosekovo station was not only a feat of bravery; it had great tactical significance, because it delayed the Germans' advance for several hours and made it possible for our units to occupy more favorable positions and prevented the breakthrough by a mass of enemy tanks to the paved road and enabled us to organize an anti-tank defense in this area.

Simple Soviet people, they became heroes of a great people, which rose to the defense of its independence and freedom. Burning hatred for the enemy aroused in their hearts contempt for death and a fierce determination to conquer even at the cost of one's life.

> No, you cannot force heroes to their knees!
> They rose up to their full height,
> So that there would remain in the hearts of generations
> The dark station of Dubosekovo!

As a result of these battles the 316th Rifle Division and the right flank of Dovator's cavalry group had to fall back on a new line under the pressure of superior forces. The enemy, supported by bombers, captured by the end of the day Mykanino, Goryuny, and Matrenino.

The situation of the 16th Army's units by the end of November 16 was as follows:

> the 17th Cavalry Division was fighting for Matyushkino, where there was a battalion of German tanks with armored cars;
> units of the 24th Cavalry Division were fighting along the line Vlasovo-Kuzyaevo, faced by up to a regiment of enemy infantry, with 30 tanks and 25 armored cars;
> the cadet regiment, securing the 58th Tank Division's right flank, reached the line Kuzyaevo-Shishkovo, continuing to attack toward Parfenkovo;
> the 58th Tank Division by 1200 had occupied Bludi and Bortinki;
> the 44th Cavalry Division was concentrated in the second echelon behind the 58th Tank Division in the Kharlanika 2 and Uteshevo area;
> the 126th Rifle Division occupied Botovo;
> the 20th Cavalry Division had concentrated in the Steblevo state farm and Popovkino.

On the 18th Rifle Division's sector more than a regiment of enemy infantry, with 30 tanks, captured Shchelkanovo and Kozlovo by 1700; at the same time a concentration of infantry was observed in Nizhnee Slyadnevo and up to 45 tanks in the Pokrovskoe area.

The 78th Rifle Division's left-flank regiment had reached the northeastern outskirts of Mikhailovskoe and Barynino by 1700.

At the close of the day the 16th Army, having begun an attack along its right flank, was in a difficult position, having encountered a counterblow along its left flank, where the enemy had enjoyed a certain amount of success. Following energetic counterattacks by units of the 316th (8th Guard Rifle Division) and Dovator's cavalry group the German's further advance was halted along the line Mykanino-Matrenino-Morozovo.

Troop control on that day was disrupted more than once as the result of breaks in communications with the divisions, while by the end of the day communications with the 17th Cavalry Division had not been restored at all. This division, as a result of the day's fighting with the enemy's tank units in the area of Yegor'e, Brykovo, and Glazkovo, was scattered and by the morning of November 17 had concentrated along the line Izosim'e-Kuzminskoe (on the northern bank of the Malaya Sestra River). Only 200 swordsmen remained in each of the division's regiments, which faced up to 80 German tanks.

The reasons for the lack of success by units of the 16th Army on the first day of battle were conditioned by the following circumstances:

a) as a result of the lack of time and the ceaseless fighting, the plan for the attack on Volokolamsk was drawn up by the army staff in the course of a single night, while the questions of coordinating units and concentrating them in their jumping-off positions were not thought through; as a result of this the units reached their jumping-off points late (the attack was scheduled for 1000, while a number of units, for example the 24th and 17th cavalry divisions, reached their jumping-off positions only by 1230);
b) the movement of the cavalry (20th and 44th cavalry divisions) slated for commitment into the breakthrough along the Volokolamsk axis was not exactly calculated (in accordance with their capabilities); the calculations were based on the units being in good condition, while the cavalry regiments actually had up to 50% of their horses unshod, while the shod horses did not have studs), etc.;
c) the army staff's communications with its units was poorly organized; telephone communication with the 17th, 24th and 44th cavalry divisions had not been established, while radio communication worked intermittently; the location of a number of division staffs (20th and 44th cavalry divisions, 126th Rifle Division) were unknown to the army staff;
d) the cavalry divisions' rear services were still short of the jumping-off position at 0800 on November 17, while a number of them did not even know the exact location of their units (44th Cavalry Division); some of the transport vehicles lacked fuel.

During the course of November 17 the enemy continued to attack from the area of Gorki, Petelino, Shit'kovo, Novo-Pavlovskoe, Shchelkanovo, in coordination with his aviation, to the east, northeast and north, and by the end of the day captured Matrenino station, Yazvishche and Gorodishche.

Prisoners taken from the 11th Panzer Division in the Morozovo area stated that the division's objective was to reach the line Shit'kovo-Novo-Pavlovskoe and from the morning of November 18 to continue the attack between the junction of the 2nd and 5th tank divisions.

By the end of November 17 the enemy had concentrated a powerful tank group (10th Panzer Division) to the south of Shchelkanovo.

Thus during November 16-17 the army was involved in fierce fighting, checking the offensive by the enemy's Fourth Panzer Group on its left flank and repeatedly launching counterattacks and inflicting losses in men and equipment on him. The Germans made their main efforts along the northeastern axis, so at to, in conjunction with the Klin group break into the rear of the 16th Army to surround and destroy it.

During November 16-17 the neighboring 5th Army to the south continued to consolidate along its former positions. The enemy here carried out artillery and mortar fire and in some sectors attempted to attack.

The fierce battles that took place during November 15-17 along the front of the 30th and 16th armies confirmed the concentration of large groups of German forces. One of these (Third Panzer Group) was evidently attacking along the Klin-Solnechnogorsk axis south of the basin of the Moscow Sea; the second (Fourth Panzer Group) was operating in along the Novo-Petrovskoe-Istra axis from the area of Volokolamsk.

Both panzer groups, coordinating their activities to capture the line Klin-Solnechnogorsk-Istra, according to the Fascist command's plan, were to further combine their efforts to complete the defeat of the 16th Army and envelop Moscow from the northwest.

The end of the 30th Army's defensive battles in the Moscow Sea sector, November 18

In the Moscow Sea sector fierce battles continued throughout November 18 along the center and left flank of the 30th Army. Units of the German XXVII Army Corps (129th and 86th infantry divisions) carried out an active reconnaissance of the crossings against the army's right wing along the western bank of the Volga River in the Peremerki-Novo-Semenovskoe-Gorodnya sector. In the area of Novo-Semenovskoe and Gorki small groups of enemy infantry attempted to cross the Volga, but were not successful.

South of the Moscow Sea on November 18 two main enemy groups continued to attack: the 6th Panzer and 14th Motorized divisions along the road to Zavidovo and Klin; the 7th Panzer and 106th Infantry divisions along the Yauza River toward Ovsyannikovo.

Along the Zavidovo axis, the Germans' motor-mechanized formations, meeting very stubborn resistance from our forces, sought to break through along the road to Zavidovo and Klin, while part of their forces operated along the northeastern axis toward Konakovo. The Germans' movement along the road to Zavidovo was hindered because our sappers had mined a number of sectors; for example, a group of German scouts and an armored car were blown up along the mined sector (2,000 mines) of the road between Dorino and Novo-Zavidovskii. This forced the enemy to move more slowly and with greater caution, while in certain places (the result of our sappers damaging the road) it was not possible for the enemy to use the road to advance quickly.

On November 18 the German advance was supported by aviation. In comparison with the previous days, it significantly increased its combat activities, conducting reconnaissance, covering the advance of the mobile groups, and bombing various targets in our rear. If before the enemy conducted 70-120 sorties per day (depending on the weather conditions), on November 18 270 sorties were carried out, with the great majority of them directed against the Western Front's right wing.

Our aviation, in its turn, assisted the 30th Army's forces in carrying out their tasks.

The 47th Air Division in the course of the day attacked the enemy's motor-mechanized units, bombed concentrations and columns of tanks and automobiles on the roads between inhabited areas in the areas of Dorino, Zelentsyno, and Maksimovo. They also carried out reconnaissance along the axis Novo-Zavidovskii-Turginovo, Maksimovo-Volokolamsk.

As a result of fierce battles with superior enemy forces the troops of the 30th Army by the end of November 18 had consolidated along the line: along the left bank of the Volga River on the front Poddub'e-Sudimirka and to the south; then Bezborodovo-(excluding) Novo-Zavidovskii-Zavidovo. Separate groups of the 107th Motorized Rifle Division were defending in the areas: southeast of Rabochii Poselok (southeast of Kozlovo), (exclusive) Dmitrovo, Glukhino, Kitenevo; the 143rd Tank Regiment was in Gologuzovo. The 25th Tank Brigade was moving to the Zavidovo area.

By this time the German 6th Panzer and 14th Motorized divisions had captured Lyagushino, Novo-Zavidovskii, and Chistyi Mokh, with their main group moving along the Zavidovo axis.

Southwest of the Moscow Sea the enemy's large forces (up to an infantry division, with 80-90 tanks) overcame the 107th Motorized Division's and 8th Tank Brigade's resistance and had reached the front Dmitrovo-Grishkino and continued to attack toward Glukhino.

At 1230 Fascist aviation bombed the 30th Army's troops in Zavidovo and Spas-Zaulok.

The operational significance of the 30th Army's defensive battles in the area of the Moscow Sea consisted of the following: first, these battles delayed the enemy's advance to the east and inflicted significant losses on him in men and matériel; secondly, they gave us the opportunity to get a better idea of the enemy's forces and intentions.

Defensive battles along the Volokolamsk Axis, November 18

The 16th Army, in conjunction with its neighbor to the right (30th Army), on November 18 waged intense battles with the attacking enemy. Particularly stubborn collisions played out on the sector Popovkino (8 km northeast of Volokolamsk)-Goryuny-Yazvishche. The fighting once again confirmed that the 16th Army faced the Fourth Panzer Group, consisting of the 2nd, 5th, 10th and 11th panzer divisions, an SS division, and units of the 106th, 35th and 87th infantry divisions, supported by aviation from the Second Air Fleet.

The most powerful enemy group was operating along the Volokolamsk axis, where from the morning of November 18 the forces of the 2nd, 5th, 10th and 11th panzer divisions and the 35th Infantry Division, supported by bomber and fighter aviation, attacked in an eastern and north-eastern direction.

The efforts of our units halted the German offensive along the front: 35th Infantry Division—Botovo-Strokovo; 2nd Panzer Division—Golubtsovo-Sitnikovo-Nikita-Shishkino; units of the 11th Panzer Division (two battalions of the 110th and 111th motorized regiments), with tanks—Annino station-Kopytsevo; 5th Panzer Division—Yazvishche-Greben'ki, and; 10th Panzer Division—Gorki-Pozhdestveno.

By the end of November 18 our troops had occupied the intermittent and broken line Vasil'kovo-Zhestoki-Kuz'minskoe-Kharlanika 2-Popovkino-Medvedkovo-Pokrovskoe-Davydkovo, and to the south Rozhdestveno, east of Pokrovskoe and Barynino.

The enemy's mobile group of four panzer divisions (350-400 tanks) advanced along a 35-40 km. front, which yields an average density of up to 10-12 tanks per km, and in some areas along the Volokolamsk road 30 and more tanks per km.

During November 19-20 the Fourth Panzer Group was concentrating along the line Buigorod (11 km northeast of Volokolamsk)-Goryuny-Den'kovo-Skirmanovo. According to prisoners' statements, it was established that the 252nd Infantry Division had concentrated in the area of Vayukhino and Mikhailovskoe.

At the same time the enemy's Fourth Panzer Group was attacking along the Volokolamsk axis against the 16th Army's center and left flank, seeking in conjunction with the Third Panzer Group to encircle and defeat the troops of the 30th and 16th armies, there was no large-scale fighting along the 5th Army's front. Only on certain sectors did the enemy carry out combat reconnaissance with forces up to a battalion of infantry.

The 5th Army's forces continued to occupy and fortify their former line and carried out active reconnaissance, having as their task pinning down the enemy on this front.

The German-Fascist troops, meeting fierce resistance from the armies of the right wing, which also counterattacked, moved forward slowly. The enemy's offensive, in the main, was conducted on and along the roads, which given the fact that our sappers had made the roads unusable in a number of sectors (mining, blowing up and destroying some sectors, etc.), reduced the mobility of the enemy's motor-mechanized units. Our aviation's activities in support of the ground troops, despite the poor weather conditions, also helped to slow down the speed of the enemy offensive.

The artillery helped to achieve the army's objectives and destroyed his men and tanks, particularly in places where they congregated. The artillery was quite successful in suppressing the enemy's weapons and interfered with the arrival of reserves, scattering them and causing significant losses.

The tank brigades, despite the small number of tanks, inflicted serious losses in men and matériel on the Germans. The tank brigades, as a rule, cooperated with the infantry formations, although there were instances in which several tank brigades were united to carry out independent tasks (the November 21 battle involving the 1st, 23rd, 27th, and 28th tank brigades in the area to the east of Novo-Petrovskoe.

The defensive fighting in the Moscow Sea sector and on the western approaches to Klin and Istra, November 19-20

During November 19-20 the enemy continued to attack with his Zavidovo and Turginovo groups and encountering our troops' stubborn and active defense. As before, units of the 129th and 86th infantry divisions, the 14th Motorized Division, and the 6th and 7th panzer divisions continued to operate against the 30th Army.

On the army's right flank (5th Rifle and 46th cavalry divisions) the enemy's attempts (129th and 86th infantry divisions) to cross over to the left bank of the Volga River during November 19-20 were beaten back.

The enemy, waging fierce battles with the forces of the 30th (center and left flank) and 16th armies, sought to split the armies' front into separate isolated parts and destroy them. The 30th Army's center and left-flank forces engaged in heavy fighting on November 19-20 with the enemy's superior number of infantry and tanks.

By the end of November 20 the army's forces occupied the line along the northeastern bank of the Volga River Shchelkovo-Pervomaisk- the Vladykino area-then Kontsovo-Zhukovo-Reshetnikovo-Kopylovo. The German 6th Panzer Division sought to attack from the Spas-Zaulok and Reshetnikovo areas and break through in the Klin area.

During November 19-20 the forces of the 16th Army carried out stubborn holding actions against enemy infantry and tanks along the entire front, falling back fighting to a new defensive line.

The enemy, having eased up the pressure on Chismena, directed his main efforts toward Tarasovo (along the Teryaeva Sloboda-Pavel'tsevo road), as well as Rumyantsevo (5 km southeast of Novo-Petrovskoe), Onufrievo (south of Lake Trostenskoe), striving here to move on the town of Istra. There was fierce fighting near Den'kovo and Novo-Petrovskoe.

By the end of November 20 the 16th Army, in accordance with an order from the *front* commander, had fallen back to a new defensive position along the line Puptsevo (five km west of Pavel'tsovo)-Filatovo-Savino-Nadezhdino-Yadromino, and south toward Sorokino.

In five days of offensive fighting (November 16-20) the Germans' mobile units had advanced 15-25 km. to the east of Volokolamsk, that is, advancing at a daily rate of 3-5 km. One must recognize this speed as quite small, even for infantry formations, not to mention motor-mechanized forces.

The enemy, despite the presence of a powerful motor-mechanized group, supported by aviation, was not able to break through our front and get into the operational depth of our defense in order to encircle and destroy the Red Army troops.

At the present stage of the operation the enemy had not managed to carry out his plan of cutting deep into our defense with a powerful armored wedge and splitting it into several separate parts.

On the 5th Army's front during November 19-20, the enemy's 87th and 78th infantry divisions, supported by a small number of tanks, attacked, with the objective, on the one hand, of supporting units of the Fourth Panzer Group, and on the other, pinning down our reserves along the 5th Army's front. The Germans, overcoming our forces' resistance, by the end of November 20 occupied Andreevskoe, Khaustovo and Lokotnya (15 km northwest, west and southwest of Zvenigorod). The 5th Army's right-flank units fell back and consolidated along a new defensive line Iglovo (12 km northwest of Zvenigorod)-Andriyankovo and to the south.

The defensive battles of the 30th and 16th armies in the Klin-Solnechnogorsk areas, November 21-26

On November 21 the offensive by the Germans' northern group continued. It attacked from the line Berezino (ten km southeast of Zavidovo)-Reshetnikovo-Semchino-Komlevo-Borikhino-Tarkhovo (on the Teryaeva-Sloboda-Klin road)-Volosevo, in two groups: the Zavidovo group, consisting of the 6th Panzer and 14th Motorized divisions, and the Turginovo group, consisting of the 86th Infantry and 7th Panzer divisions, in the direction of Klin and Solnechnogorsk.

On the 30th Army's right flank the troops continued to defend along their former line, repulsing attacks by the enemy's small reconnaissance groups (129th Infantry Division and units of the 86th Infantry Division).

In order the strengthen the 30th Army, the Western Front staff as early as November 18 ordered the 16th Army's 58th Tank Division was ordered to the area of Golovkovo and Spas-Zaulok (15 km northwest of Klin). The division, numbering 78 tanks and transferred by the *Stavka* to the Western Front on November 3, disembarked at Klin station and was moving to the line east of Tikhomirovo-Petrovskoe (16 km southwest of Klin). The division had the objective of covering the axes leading from the west to Klin.

The 58th Tank Division, while subordinated to the commander of the 16th Army, from November 8th through 17th was engaged in fierce fighting with units of the Fourth Panzer Group in the area northeast and southwest of Teryaeva Sloboda. The division, in these battles, faced with the enemy's superior forces, suffered significant losses in men and matériel. During November 18-20 the 58th Tank Division was already subordinated to the 30th Army and was engaged in heavy fighting with the enemy's Third Panzer Group and was delaying its offensive.

The 58th Tank Division (15 tanks, five guns, and 350 infantrymen), the 280th Rifle Regiment, and the 107th Motorized Rifle Division was fighting in the area of Minino (three km east of Spas-Zaulok) and Selevino with the enemy's motorized units (infantry and up to 100 tanks).

To the south units of the 107th Motorized Rifle Division, as a result of heavy fighting with the enemy's infantry and tanks, were thrown back and retreated to the area to the north of Yamuga, where the organized a defense. Along the line Khlynikha-Zhestoki (20 km west of Klin), the 25th Tank Brigade and 17th Cavalry Division were fighting off fierce attacks by the enemy's infantry and automatic riflemen.

The 30th Army's left flank and the 16th Army's right flank were covering the Klin axis and the approaches to Klin from the north and west. Thus it was extremely important to maintain the close cooperation of the troops along the junction of the two armies and hold Klin.

Taking the situation into account, Western Front commander Gen. Zhukov ordered the formation of a group, mainly from units of the 16th Army, under the command of Gen. Zakharov (126th Rifle and 24th Cavalry divisions, a cadet regiment, 8th and 25th tank brigades), with the objective of defending Klin. This group was to be the connecting link on the Klin axis.

During November 21 the 16th Army's forces waged stubborn battles along the entire front, and in particular fierce ones along the left wing in the area of Novo-Petrovskoe and Yadromino. Here, as was mentioned above, a powerful motor-mechanized group was operating, which was attempting to break through to Istra and making its main effort along the Istra road.

The 16th Army's right flank—the 126th Rifle Division—under heavy pressure from enemy infantry and tanks, was falling back in a disorganized fashion on Klin; by the end of November 21 the division's regiments were holding a defensive line southwest and south of Klin: 550th Rifle Regiment—Teterino-Reshetkino; 539th Rifle Regiment (one battalion)—Marfino; 366th Rifle Regiment—Kononovo-Strel'kovo-Nadezhdino.

On November 22 the 30th Army and the right flank of the 16th Army continued to wage stubborn battles, holding the offensive by the enemy's motor-mechanized units and infantry. On the 30th Army's left flank the enemy took Berezino and by 1530 his infantry and 60 tanks attacked Yamuga and took it. The 31st Tank Brigade occupied the northern and western outskirts of Klin, with part of its forces set aside for tank ambushes. The 58th Tank Division and units of the 107th Motorized Rifle Division fell back from the Yamuga area to the line Maidanovo-Malanino, northwest of Klin. The 24th Cavalry Division was moved to the area of Bol'shoe Shchapovo-Klin to secure Klin from the northeast. The 8th Tank Brigade (the *front* reserve) was occupying Voronino by the end of November 22.

The enemy's efforts were now directed toward encircling Klin. Units of the 126th Rifle Division, under enemy pressure, fell back from their positions toward Akulovo, Sokhino, and Misirevo (to the south of Klin). At 1530 the enemy's tanks broke into Misirevo and Frolovskoe, where the headquarters of the 126th Rifle Division was located, as a result of which communications with the headquarters were lost. Thus by the end of November 22 the Germans had managed to halfway encircle Klin from the north, west and south.

On November 23 fierce fighting continued between our troops and the enemy's motor-mechanized units and infantry, which were concentrating their blows along the Klin and Solnechnogorsk axes. From the morning of November 23 the enemy's mobile forces (6th, 7th and 2nd panzer, and 35th Infantry divisions) were fighting for Klin. To the north of Klin the situation was as follows: on the 107th Motorized Rifle Division's front (200 men, 15 tanks) the enemy (14th Motorized and 6th Panzer divisions), having lost up to two battalions of infantry, 15 tanks and 70 automatic riflemen, captured Maloe Ivantsevo Birevo and Bol'shoe Birevo; along the line Selyukhino-Shchapovo (to the northeast of Klin) the 24th Cavalry Division was holding its positions, while to its left the 58th Tank Division was covering Klin from the north (south of Yamuga). The enemy's infantry and tanks attacked these forces, enveloping them from the north and south. The Fascists' mobile units sought to complete the encirclement of Klin and narrow the ring around it.

To the west of Klin the enemy, attacking with large forces (7th Panzer and 106th Infantry divisions) toward Vysokovsk, threw back the remains of the cadet regiment and the 25th Tank Brigade, which were fighting half-surrounded, and on the night of November 23 fell back by order of the army command to the southwestern outskirts of Klin, as its reserve; the remains of the 17th Cavalry Division also fell back there. Units of the Germans' 2nd Panzer and 35th Infantry divisions, operating southwest of Klin, captured Gorki (six km south of Klin) during the first half of the day and attacked toward Klin. Part of the 2nd Panzer Division's tanks turned in a southeastern direction toward Solnechnogorsk. In order to ease Klin's situation, the 126th Rifle Division, 31st Tank Brigade, and tank battalions from the 129th and 146th tank brigades counterattacked the enemy forces in the direction of Reshetkino at 1230, but the counterattack was unsuccessful; units engaged in stubborn fighting with the enemy along the line Akulovo-Frolovskoe (four km south of Klin). In order to secure the 126th Rifle Division's left flank, on the orders of the *front* commander, Dovator's cavalry group was supposed to depart at 1200 and take up defensive positions along the line Kononovo-Radovan'e-Nikol'skoe-Sosnino, but because of the threat to Solnechnogorsk, instead took up position with the 44th Cavalry Division, two battalions of the 8th Guards Rifle Division, and the 129th and 146th Tank brigades' tank battalions along the line Kresty-Skorodum'e-Obukhovo-Krivtsovo (2-4 km south of Solnechnogorsk).

Developing the offensive in the face of our small and isolated units: the 8th Tank Brigade, 24th and 17th cavalry divisions, 126th Rifle Division, the remains of the cadet regiment, and the 25th Tank Brigade (11 tanks), the enemy forces energetically advanced from the area of Bol'shoe Birevo, Yamuga,

Kolosovo, Troitskoe, Reshetkino, and Sitnikovo, completing the encirclement of Klin. Attacking were the following units: from the northwest—the 14th Motorized, 1st and 6th panzer divisions; from the west—the 7th Panzer and 106th Infantry divisions, and; from the southwest—the 35th and 23rd Infantry divisions, and the 2nd Panzer Division and units from a motorcycle brigade. Thus our weak and small forces in the Klin-Solnechnogorsk area were being assaulted by no less than eight enemy divisions (four panzer, three infantry, one motorized divisions). By the end of November 23 a group of tanks broke into Klin from the northeast, while fighting continued in the city itself.

Our aviation (46th Air Division), despite the poor weather conditions, bombed and strafed enemy troop concentrations in the areas of Yamuga, Vysokovsk and Klin. The village of Misirevo, where a concentration of enemy motor-mechanized troops had been observed, was burned down.

Attempts by groups of tanks and automatic riflemen, who had penetrated as far as Solnechnogorsk, to take the town were repulsed by our defensive fire. During November 24 the fighting along the 16th Army's front became especially fierce, particularly in the Klin area, as well as in the Istra area along the army's left flank.

After taking Klin the German command reinforced its northern mobile group up to four panzer divisions (6th, 7th, 2nd, and 11th), two motorized infantry divisions (14th and 36th), and an infantry division (106th).

During November 24-25 this powerful group continued to attack toward Rogachevo and Dmitrov and along the Leningrad road toward Solnechnogorsk and Chernaya Gryaz'. A part of these forces simultaneously was fighting to completely capture the Klin area, where the 30th Army's small forces (107th Motorized Rifle Division, 24th Cavalry Division, the remains of the 58th Tank Division, and the 8th and 21st tank brigades), which by 0600 on November 24 were fighting northeast of Klin (Maloe Ivantsevo Birevo and Bol'shoe Birevo, and Voronino, east of Shchapovo), as well as the 16th Army's scanty units (126th Rifle Division, the remains of the cadet regiment, 25th and 31st Tank brigades), located to the south and southeast of Klin (Lavrovo and Frolovskoe).

Communications officers, sent by airplanes on November 24 by the 16th Army commander, failed to find these units. The aircraft were fired upon by machine guns from the southern and southeastern outskirts of Klin.

Taking into account the difficult situation in the Klin area, the Western Front commander ordered the commander of the 30th Army to organize on November 25 an attack with the objective of relieving those units surrounded in the Klin area. However, the 30th Army's forces on November 24-25, despite the difficult situation and the threat of our units' complete encirclement after the German capture of Davydkovo (southeast of Klin) and the infiltration of small enemy groups to Spas-Korkodino, were nonetheless forced to fall back to the east and southeast after exceptionally heavy fighting. The enemy captured Spas-Korkodino and the area to the north and continued attacking toward Rogachevo, which was defended by a small combined detachment (two rifle companies, 24 anti-tank rifles, three anti-tank guns, a machine gun battalion, and two armored cars). Units of the 30th Army (the remains of the 107th Motorized Rifle, 24th Cavalry, and 58th Tank divisions, and the 8th and 21st tank brigades) were removed by order of the army commander to the area of Aleshino, to the south of Rogachevo.

The situation that had arisen on the 30th Army's left flank significantly worsened the situation on the 16th Army's right flank. The enemy wanted to split both armies with his panzer divisions. The Germans' Klin-Solnechnogorsk group sought to quickly break through to the east and southeast in order to reach Moscow.

On November 24 the 16th Army's right-flank units (126th Rifle Division, the remains of the cadet regiment, and the 25th and 31st Tank brigades), as was mentioned earlier, were putting up stout resistance to the south of Klin and under the pressure of the enemy's superior forces were able to break out of the encirclement. These units, waging fierce battles with the 106th Infantry and 2nd Panzer divisions on November 25-26, fell back to the line Boriso-Glebskoe-Tolstyakovo-Timonovo. By that time a regiment of the 33rd Rifle Division, with the 2nd Battalion of the 511th Howitzer Regiment, and an anti-tank group, had been brought forward from the Fedorovka area in order to take up position along the line Popovskoe-Alad'ino and cover the withdrawal of the 30th Army's left-flank units to the south from Rogachevo.

In the Solnechnogorsk area the situation was as follows: Dovator's cavalry group, reinforced with the 44th Cavalry Division, two battalions of the 8th Guards Rifle Division, and tank battalions from the 129th and 146th Tank brigades, during the second part of the day, carrying out an order by the *front* commander, attacked Sterlino and Golovkovo, with the objective of striking a blow in the rear of the enemy attacking Solnechnogorsk from the west. During the second half of the day, attacking from the line Krivtsovo-Berezhki, the cavalry group captured Sterlino and nearby points, and continued to develop the success to the northwest. A tank reconnaissance, with the objective of determining the situation in Solnechnogorsk, was hit with artillery and machine gun fire upon approaching the southwestern outskirts of the town.

The enemy tried to attack from the north and northwest, but upon encountering our units' stubborn and well-organized defense along this sector, called off his attacks. However, our subsequent counteroffensive in this area was also unsuccessful. Due to heavy enemy fire, the group's units were forced to occupy a new defensive line. On November 26 they were fighting along the line Parfenovo (seven km south of Solnechnogorsk)-Melechkino.

The situation on the *front's* right flank called forth a number of measures by the *Stavka* of the Supreme High Command, the Western Front command, and army commands:

1 By order of the *Stavka* the 133rd Rifle Division was being shifted to Dmitrov by auto transport on November 23 from the Kushalino area (30 km northeast of Kalinin). The division was subordinated to the Western Front commander, who then transferred it to the 16th Army for occupying and securing the Fedorovka area (16 km southwest of Yakhroma). The division's lead rifle regiment was arriving at the designated area by 1500 on November 25. The division's remaining units were approaching the concentration area.
2 On the orders of the *Stavka*, the 7th Guards Rifle Division was transferred to the 16th Army. The division was part of the 49th Army at the beginning of November. The 7th Guards Rifle Division was defending the line Gur'evo-Drakino with one rifle regiment, while with two other rifle regiments was concentrating in the area of Shatovo, Ivan'kovo, and Kalinovo (five km south of Serpukhov) and up to November 23 was engaged in stubborn fighting with the enemy as part of the 49th Army. From November 23 the division was boarding trains at the Podol'sk station and was moving by rail to Povarovo station as part of the 16th Army. The 7th Guards Rifle Division's lead regiment on November 25 occupied the defensive line: the woods east of Yesipovo and Zhukovo (eight km southeast of Solnechnogorsk). The division's remaining units were concentrating, as they disembarked, in the area of Loshki (12 km southeast of Solnechnogorsk), Bukharovo, Radomlya, Bersenevo; the division was given the objective of occupying the defensive line Shelepanovo (five km north of Radomlya)-Terekhovo-Zhukovo, astride the Leningrad road.
3 On orders of the Western Front commander, the 133rd Rifle Division's 681st Rifle Regiment and an artillery regiment from the Moscow Military District's anti-tank defense were united under the command of the commander of the 8th Tank Brigade in order to reinforce the Rogachevo axis in the area of Arevskoe, Alad'ino, Novoselki, and Ivanovskoe. The brigade was involved in fierce fighting on the approaches to Rogachevo; it suffered heavy losses in men and matériel and was extremely small in strength.
4 By order of the Western Front staff, a regiment from the 251st Rifle Division (Kalinin Front) and the 2nd Motoized Rifle Regiment were concentrating on November 26 in the area of Dmitrovka (20 km southeast of Solnechnogorsk).
5 By order of the Western Front staff, on November 26 the 11th Motorcycle Regiment was sent to secure the Yakhroma area.
6 The 46th Motorcycle Regiment, in the 30th Army's commander's reserve, was concentrated on his order in Filimonovo (seven km southeast of Solnechnogorsk) on November 26.
7 By order of the 16th Army commander a combined group from the 126th Tank Battalion, a motorcycle battalion from the 1st Guards Tank Brigade, and the 1077th Rifle Regiment, was created with the objective of straddling the highway south of Peshki (6-7 km southeast of Solnechnogorsk) and preventing a breakthrough by enemy tanks in a southeasterly direction.

The air force supported our forces, despite the unfavorable weather. The 46th Air Division bombed an enemy concentration in the area of Vysokovsk and Kuznechikovo during November

25-26 and carried out reconnaissance in the area of Solnechnogorsk, Nudol', Teryaeva, Sloboda, Vysokovsk, and Klin. Enemy tanks and automobiles were destroyed by our bombers and assault aircraft in the area of Vysokovsk, Solnechnogorsk and Klin. The 47th Air Division reconnoitered the area of Solnechnogorsk and Klin and destroyed the enemy's motor-mechanized units in the area of Skirmanovo, Gorodishche, Petrovo, and Yadromino. During November 26 86 air sorties were carried out, including 58 by assault aircraft and bombers, 11 reconnaissance, and 17 escort sorties.

As a result of ten days of fierce fighting along the Klin-Solnechnogorsk axis, the Germans managed to achieve significant successes. They had approached closer to Moscow and driven a wedge between the 30th and 16th armies, inflicting serious losses on them. But the enemy, despite all his efforts, had not managed to break through our defense to its entire depth and get into the rear of the 30th and 16th armies. The front had become bent and porous and in places faced north, east or south. The enemy was unable to fully use the advantages of the offensive and carry the fighting to a decisive conclusion. Our units resisted stubbornly and inflicted large losses on the enemy in men and matériel and withdrew from under his blows to new defensive lines. To the northwest and west of Moscow the Red Army's front, hard-pressed and weakened, held and was ready for further battle.

The 16th Army's defensive fighting for the Istra Reservoir and the town of Istra, November 21-28. Cooperation with the 5th Army

In the Klin area the enemy enjoyed success thanks to the concentration of a powerful panzer group, although the tank units' offensive along the Istra axis was seriously slowed down as a result of the 16th Army's stubborn defense.

As has been shown, by the end of November 20 Dovator's cavalry group had withdrawn to the line Pospelikha-Nadezhdino. After several days' fighting there remained 160 cavalrymen in the 50th Cavalry Division and 514 cavalrymen and riflemen in the 53rd Cavalry Division.

It was in this state that the cavalry group further retreated in the direction of the northern shore of the Istra Reservoir, as if forming the army's right wing. The reservoir was a convenient natural line of defense, although it simultaneously divided the army's troops during their retreat.

The army's center and left wing were in the following situation:

The 316th (8th Guards) Rifle Division, pressed by the 35th Infantry Division and units of the 2nd Panzer Division attacking eastward, following fighting along the line Popovkino-Chentsy-Goryuny, fell back to the northeast with heavy losses. It was in this area on November 18 that the commander of the 8th Guards Rifle Division, Hero of the Soviet Union, Maj. Gen. Panfilov, was killed. By the close of November 20 the division was retreating under fire to the line Ustinovo (one km north of Novo-Petrovskoe)-Rybushki. This retreat was carried out under pressure from the enemy infantry, supported by tanks, moving directly behind the division. The division was covering the approaches to the reservoir from the west.

The 18th Rifle Division, with the 33rd Tank Brigade, following the fierce combat near Novo-Petrovskoe and Rubtsov, was forced to fall back to a new defensive line: Rybushki-Rumyantsevo-Yadromino. Individual inhabited areas (Andreikovo, Koren'ki, and Golovino) changed hands twice, but the enemy's significant superiority enabled him to take Novo-Petrovskoe. The seizure of this important road junction enabled the enemy to further attack to the northeast and southeast.

By the end of November 20 the 78th Rifle Division was engaged in heavy fighting with large enemy forces along the line Veretenki-Troitsa-Mansurovo, covering the Istra axis from the southwest.

The Western Front command during these critical days of fighting the German offensive, issued the 16th Army commander the following orders:

> ... we categorically confirm to you the order to consolidate on the present line and to not take a single step back without our authorization—if need be, up to and including the sacrifice of the unit and formation.
>
> ... Focus all your attention on organizing the enemy's repulse along your flanks... Zhukov, Bulganin.

The stubbornness of the defense by units of the 16th Army continually increased, despite the fierce fighting with the enemy, who took advantage of his tank units' maneuverability and superiority in equipment. The fighting on the 16th Army's left flank was conducted in close coordination with the 5th Army's forces, while the enemy sought to break through along the boundary between the 16th and 5th armies.

The 5th Army's forces were engaged in extremely heavy fighting in the area of Dyaden'kovo (ten km northwest of Zvenigorod), Sergievo, and Lokotnya. The enemy directed his main efforts against the army's right flank and center and by the end of the day had pushed back units of the 129th, 144th, and 50th rifle divisions and had reached the line Toropenki-Dyaden'kovo-Sergievo-Mikhailovskaya.

The Western Front command, taking into account the situation along the boundary of the 16th and 5th armies and the threat to Istra, moved up the 108th Rifle Division and the 145th Tank Brigade to the line Kotovo-Boriskovo-Nasonovo. Besides this, before the arrival of the arrival of the field troops to the line of the Istra River, the Western Front commander ordered the organization of a defensive line by the 301st and 302nd machine gun battalions.

The level of water in the Istra River was raised by 1-2 meters. The high bank of the Istra River and the woods immediately behind it influenced the defensive system in the sense of a certain linear placement of the guns; at the same time the woods secured the rear.

The anti-tank defense of the Istra area was organized by the forces of the 694th and 871st anti-tank regiments according to the instructions of the 16th Army's chief of artillery.

By November 21 the 16th Army's units were seriously under strength: the cavalry and rifle regiments numbered from 150 to 200 men each; the 1st Guards, 23rd, 27th, and 28th tank brigades had between them only 15 serviceable tanks; the 78th Rifle Division had on the average a 60% casualty rate in men. The same was true of the 126th Rifle Division, as in the other units. The 20th, 24th, and 44th cavalry divisions were short of men, because they had been so long involved in heavy fighting.

The enemy, as the result of our troops' actions on the approaches to the Istra Reservoir, had also suffered significant losses from our artillery, aircraft and infantry as the result of the stubborn resistance by the units of the 16th Army.

The character of the fighting during these days was determined by the necessity of halting the holding the German advance on Moscow at all costs, thus all units, recognizing the responsibility laid upon them by the party and government, fought with the enemy, not sparing their lives.

However, despite all the measures of the command of the *front* and armies, separate units and formations did not always display the proper resistance and sometime abandoned their positions without a fight, or following a collision with the enemy's forward units (the 126th Rifle Division in the area to the west of Klin and in the Klin area, and the 17th and 24th cavalry divisions in the Klin area).

On November 21 the *front's* military council issued directive no. 057, in evaluating the especially serious situation, characterized it as follows:

> The fight for the approaches to Moscow has taken on a decisive character in the last ten days.
>
> For six days the enemy has been straining his final efforts, and having collected his reserves, is attacking along the front of the 30th, 16th, 5th, and 50th armies.

> The combat experience of these six days shows that the troops understand the significance of the ongoing fierce battles. This is shown by the heroic resistance, at times going over to counterattacks, of the valorous 50th and 53rd cavalry divisions, the 8th Guards and 413th rifle divisions, the 1st Guards, 27th, and 28th tank brigades, and other units and formations. However, there have been instances of violations by individual commanders of the well-known order categorically forbidding any voluntary withdrawals from one's position, which is punishable by immediate execution. Such a shameful act was committed by the commanders and commissars of the 17th and 24th cavalry divisions.
>
> Now, at a time when the battle for Moscow has entered its decisive phase, the unauthorized abandonment of one's position is tantamount to treason and betrayal of the Motherland...

The combat actions of Dovator's cavalry group, the 8th Guards (316th) Rifle Division, and the tank brigades, was rated highly by the *front's* military council.

Only in those instances of extreme necessity in order to preserve the Red Army's men and matériel did the military council allow a retreat to new defensive positions.

As has been noted, right-flank units of the 16th Army were falling back to the north of the Istra Reservoir. Later the right flank along the Solnechnogorsk axis divided into two groups: a northern group, composed of the 17th and 24th cavalry divisions, a cadet regiment, and the 126th Rifle Division, was operating along the Klin axis (see the description of the fighting in the Klin area); a southern group, composed of Dovator's cavalry group, the 20th and 44th cavalry divisions, and the 8th Guards Rifle Division, were waging defensive battles in the area of the Istra Reservoir.

On the army's left flank the 18th and 78th rifle divisions had the task of holding the line of the Istra River and the town of Istra.

On November 22 the army's forces were involved in stubborn fighting along the entire front; particularly heavy fighting occurred on the left wing.

Two groups of German mobile troops tried to turn both flanks of the 16th Army from north and south. Up to two infantry regiments, reinforced by tanks, attacked from the line Petrovskoe (17 km southwest of Klin)-Zakharovo-Nagovo in the general direction of Solnechnogorsk, striving to get around the army's right flank. Simultaneously, up to three infantry regiments and two panzer divisions were attacking along the front Novo-Petrovskoe-Lake Trostenskoe to the northeast and in the direction of the town of Istra.

The 44th Cavalry Division, covering the army's right flank, was battling the enemy, which had taken Maleevka and Troitskoe (15 km south of Klin).

The 20th Cavalry Division had repulsed an attack by an infantry battalion, reinforced by 40 tanks, in the Nagovo area. However, the enemy's appearance in the Troitskoe area forced the division to fall back to the east.

Dovator's cavalry group had no contact with the enemy throughout November 22.

The 8th Guards Rifle Division was engaged in heavy fighting with two infantry regiments, reinforced with tanks, and holding their attack from Novo-Petrovskoe to the east.

The 18th Rifle Division and the 33rd Tank Brigade, as a result of stubborn fighting with an enemy infantry division, supported by a group of up to 100 tanks, fell back by the end of the day to the Rumyantsevo area.

The 78th Rifle Division on November 21 fought along the line of the Molodil'nya River south of Yadromino, covering the approaches to Istra. Due to the Germans' continuing pressure, the division was forced to fall back in the direction of Istra.

The overall operational-tactical situation along the 16th Army's front by this time demanded the withdrawal of its main forces to the main defensive line along the Istra Reservoir and the Istra River, so that, relying on it, to render more effective resistance to the enemy. Thus according to the army commander's order, the army slowly, stubbornly defending each inhabited point fell back to this line.

The blows by the enemy's Volokolamsk group were mainly directed against Solnechnogorsk and Istra. Besides this, the Germans' 87th Infantry Division was attacking along the boundary of the 16th and 5th armies toward Zvenigorod and Pavlovskaya Sloboda.

The fighting on the 5th Army's flank by this time had become quite intense. The 108th Rifle Division, in cooperation with the 145th Tank Brigade, by the end of the day were forced under the pressure of superior enemy forces to abandon Kotovo, Gorshkovo, Ivashkovo, and Nasonovo. However, as a result of a counterattack we were once again able to occupy the eastern part of Nasonovo. The 129th Rifle Division organized its defense in the Skokovo area. Along the remainder of the front the 5th Army's units had consolidated their line and were repelling the enemy's attacks.

The *front's* military council, considering further withdrawals inexcusable, issued a command to the division commanders of the 16th Army and the army's military council:

> ... there is nowhere left to fall back, and no one will allow you to do so...
>
> By using any and the most extreme methods, you must immediately bring about a turning point, to cease withdrawing and not only not surrender for any reason Istra, Klin and Solnechnogorsk, but drive the Fascists from these occupied areas...
>
> ... any further step backward on your part means disrupting the defense of Moscow and a shame for you and those units which you command...
>
> The entire command and political element, from top to bottom, is to be with their units, on the battlefield...

On November 24 the 16th Army, the central divisions of which were falling back to the line of the Istra River, continued to be involved in fierce battles on the right and left flanks

Dovator's cavalry group, moved to the eastern bank of the reservoir, was preparing to attack from the area of Krivtsovo and Berezhki toward Golovkovo, against the flank of that part of the Gemans' group that was trying to break through to Solnechnogorsk.

The 20th Cavalry Division, which had been covering the route to the reservoir's northern bank, was retreating from the Nagovo area so as to link up with Dovator's cavalry group.

The 8th Guards Rifle Division, while destroying the attacking German units in stubborn fighting, was falling back to the reservoir's western bank along the line Rozhdestveno-Martyushino.

The 18th Rifle Division was involved in fierce fighting, attacked by up to a division of enemy infantry and tanks. Following bloody collisions in the Glebovo area, the division continued to fall back to the Istra River.

The 78th Rifle Division was falling back to Istra under Fascist pressure and was fighting ten km west of the town.

During November 23-24 the Germans attacked the 16th Army's units along several axes. The entire eastern bank of the Istra River was shelled by artillery and mortar fire, and in many places subjected to bomber attacks. The counteroffensive by Dovator's cavalry group on the northern bank of the reservoir was not successful.

The 8th Guards Rifle Division, following the fighting along the line Rozhdestveno-Martyushino, was forced by enemy infantry and 50-60 tanks, to fall back to the eastern bank, crossing the Istra River in the area of the southern bank of the reservoir. Enemy tanks and machine gunners followed immediately behind the division's retreating units and by the end of November 24 had taken Buzharovo.

The 18th Rifle Division, following attempts to delay the German attack in the Bukarevo area, was falling back under the blows of two infantry regiments with tanks on the east bank of the Istra River on the sector of the reservoir and the town of Istra.

The 78th Rifle Division was holding the western approaches to Istra in the Yabedino area, from which the Germans would be able to shell the town with artillery.

On November 24 the Germans arrived in force at the line of the Istra Reservoir and the Istra River.

With the approach of the Germans to this line the reservoir's floodgates were blown up (after our troops had crossed), and as a result an area up to 50 km south of the reservoir was flooded to a depth of 2 ½ meters. The Germans' attempts to close the floodgates were not successful.

The enemy was forced to halt along the water boundary and organize a forcing of this barrier. Aside from this, the Fascists put no small effort into overcoming the intermediate defensive line that ran through here (Solnechnogorsk-Istra Reservoir-Istra-Pavlovskaya Sloboda), and which had earlier been prepared by our engineering units.

However, the shortage of time for organizing a stout defense along this line kept the 16th Army from halting the German offensive here. The German blows north of the Istra Reservoir in the direction of Klin and Solnechnogorsk (which their units had reached on November 23), and in the direction of Zvenigorod and Pavlovskaya Sloboda, threatened the army's forces on the eastern bank of the reservoir and the Istra River with encirclement.

On the 5th Army's right flank our units (108th Rifle Division) fought off enemy attacks (IX Army Corps) during November 24, but by the end of the day were pushed back on Lukino and Surmino, where the fighting continued. In repelling numerous attacks from the area of Petrovskoe (eight km south of Istra) and Natashino, the 108th Rifle Division stubbornly held its positions, but under pressure by superior enemy forces retreated at 2000 on November 25 to the line Ivanovskoe-east of Petrovskoe-east of Fun'kovo, where it fought during the course of November 26.

By November 25 the 16th Army's front followed the line of the eastern bank of the reservoir to the Istra River. Only the 78th Rifle Division, which was defending the town, remained on the western bank, straddling the Volokolamsk road.

The presence of the Istra line undoubtedly played a role in delaying the German offensive along this axis and in raising the steadiness of the army's units.

Only after three days of fighting (November 26-28) were the Germans able to throw our units back from this defensive position and continue the offensive to the southeast. However, the Germans' further offensive was soon halted along the line Kryukovo-Lenino.

By the end of November 26 the Germans were able to cross over to the river's eastern bank in some areas. From the morning of November 27 the 16th Army's forces (18th and 9th Guards rifle divisions and the 146th Tank Brigade) were engaged in stubborn fighting to hold Istra, along with right-flank units of the 5th Army's 108th Rifle Division.

The 18th Rifle Division, consisting of 800 riflemen, and the 146th Tank Brigade, during the daylight hours of November 27 repelled attacks by two enemy infantry regiments and 60 tanks in the area to the northeast of Istra (Kurtasovo, Yermolino, and Aduevo). The 9th Guards Rifle Division fought for Istra during the night of November 26-27. There was fighting in the town itself and along the eastern bank of the river south of town. The division's units occupied a line up to 15 km in length. The enemy attacked in large numbers along the road and simultaneously attempted to break through to the town's southwestern outskirts.

The Fascists' superior forces and the withdrawal of its neighbors forced the 9th Guards Rifle Division by 0400 on November 27 to withdraw to the eastern outskirts of Istra. The 18th Rifle Division, under the pressure of superior tank forces, by the close of November 28 was fighting along the line Novo-Sergovo-Dukhanino-Nebogatkovo. The enemy captured Adreevskoe and Nikulino (north of Istra) and advanced to the northeast along the road to Rychkovo. With part of his forces he launched an attack in the direction of the northern outskirts of Istra. The situation forced the 9th Guards Rifle Division to abandon the town with a fight and fall back to the east. In the fighting for Istra and to the east the enemy's aviation, in groups of 6-8 aircraft, ceaselessly bombed the 9th Guards Rifle Division's positions. By the end of the day the division had fallen back to the line Aleksino-Zhevnevo (six km west of Dedovsk), where it consolidated.

The 5th Army's right-flank units (108th Rifle Division) were subjected to attacks by large enemy forces from the Petrovskoe area (252nd Infantry Division) during November 27, and continued fighting along the line Ivanovskoe-Petrovskoe-Koz'mino. By the close of November 28 the situation along the division's front had not changed and its units consolidated on their positions.

In summing up the results of the Istra defensive battle, it's important to note the following:

1 The preparation by the 16th Army for its November 16 offensive in order to destroy the enemy's Volokolamsk group was conducted in haste and was not completed. The army had no success in carrying out a simultaneous offensive on mutually opposing flanks and was forced to go on the defensive and then retreat. The unfavorable operational situation in which it found itself on November 17 could have led to serious consequences (in the case of the Germans' breakthrough and rapid advance in the direction of Novo-Petrovskoe and Istra). However, organized control and the good combat work of the troops on the army's left wing (particularly Dovator's cavalry group) enabled the army's forces to subsequently wage more or less systematic holding actions.
2 During the course of the subsequent fighting on the approaches to the Istra Reservoir, the army's control problems became much more difficult: the maneuver battles required flexible and precise control. The army's fighting retreat along a broad front, given the enemy's great superiority in tanks (one of the most difficult operations) was successfully conducted by the 16th Army command (in conditions under which the Fascists were attacking along the entire right wing). Despite the difficulties of the situation along the army's front, by November 23 (the day the Germans took Klin), the 16th Army command had carried out a comparatively systematic withdrawal of its forces, while waging fierce battles and delaying and counterattacking the enemy. The 16th Army's combat activities unfolded under the immediate command and control of the *front's* military council, which during the most critical days (the Germans' arrival at Krasnaya Polyana) was with the troops (Gen. Zhukov and military council member Bulganin) and personally controlled them. One should note that the 16th Army's actions during this period deserve praise. Despite the Germans' superiority in equipment (tanks, aviation), its resistance and persistence in battle were high.
3 Large water lines and reservoirs, such as the Istra Reservoir, demand the operation's timely planning as to the disposition of forces and command organization. The division of the 16th Army's front into two almost isolated sectors under conditions of mobile defense was a factor that demanded especially precise and strict combat control for achieving the necessary unity of action.
4 During the first days the 16th Army operated along a 60-70 km front. The front later shrank to 35-40 km. In such a situation, despite significant losses, the army was able to hold off the extremely powerful pressure of the enemy's mighty motor-mechanized group and prevent it from breaking into the operational depth. The German-Fascist troops, while moving forward, were forced to constantly overcome the organized resistance of Red Army units.

The 30th and 16th armies' defensive battles east of Klin and Solnechnogorsk, November 27-29

The main forces of the Third Panzer Group, having taken Klin, moved on Rogachevo and Dmitrov, in order to split the Red Army's front, to develop the operational breakthrough between the 30th and 16th armies and then to encircle Moscow from the north and northeast.

Taking into account the threat to Rogachevo, the commander of the 30th Army Gen. Lelyushenko united all the units defending that area under the command of the 30th Army's chief of staff, Col. (later Gen.) Khetagurov. A detachment of infantry and tanks, a single 85mm gun, three Guards mortar batteries, and two companies from a reserve regiment were shifted to cover Rogachevo itself. An artillery battalion of 12 76mm guns was also concentrated there. The deputy chief of the army's engineering section was sent to strengthen Rogachevo's engineering defense.

In the Rogachevo area the remains of the 8th Tank Brigade, the 107th Motorized Rifle Division, and the 58th Tank and 24th Cavalry divisions continued to wage fierce battles with the attacking enemy during the first half of November 27. In these battles our units inflicted significant casualties on the enemy, destroying 70 heavy, medium and light tanks, 60 machine guns, and 25 guns; 2,000 enemy officers and men were killed. However, in the fighting of November 26-27 we suffered losses in the battles with superior enemy forces. For example, all the tanks in the 8th Tank Brigade were out of action. Only a few batteries and guns remained among the artillery.

By the close of November 26 the troops of the Third Panzer Group (6th and 7th panzer and 14th Motorized divisions), developing the offensive with their forward units, burst into Rogachevo and on November 27 advanced on Sin'kovo, Dmitrov and Yakhroma through Ivan'kovskoe.

In the Solnechnogorsk area the enemy's mobile group (2nd Panzer and 106th Infantry divisions) attacked from November 27 Kochergino and Khoroshilovo from the area of Redino and Obukhovo (to the south and southeast of Solnechnogorsk) and from the line Kochergino-Yesipovo to the south and southeast in the direction of Chernaya Gryaz' (two km north of Skhodnya).

The enemy's mobile units of his Klin group by the end of November 27 had reached the line Zver'kovo (northwest of Dmitrov)-Vysokovo-Malygino-Semenovskoe-Borodino (16 km east of Klin)-Vorob'evo-Timonovo (five km northeast of Solnechnogorsk) against the 30th Army's center and left flank.

On the right flank, the 30th Army's forces (5th Rifle, 46th Cavalry, 185th Rifle, and 18th Cavalry divisions) by the morning of November 28 were continuing to hold their defensive positions along the line Poddub'e-Sverdlovo-Pervomaisk-Borshchovka-Ust'-Pristan'-Kanalstroi. The enemy' attempts to infiltrate our position were repulsed.

Our forces' Rogachevo group (58th Tank and 107th Motorized Rifle divisions, the 8th Tank Brigade, 24th Cavalry Division, the 133rd Rifle Division's 681st Rifle Regiment, and the 251st Rifle Division's 923rd Rifle Regiment), following difficult defensive fighting, was falling back under the pressure of superior enemy forces s to the east and southeast. On the Dmitrov axis the remains of the 8th Tank Brigade, 58th Tank division, the 107th Motorized Rifle Division, and a special battalion (behind this group, on the eastern bank of the Moscow-Volga Canal, lay the 1st Shock Army's 55th Rifle Brigade along the line Udarnaya pier-Tatishchevo) were engaged in heavy fighting with the enemy and would counterattack, and by the end of November 28 held Savelovo, Marinino, Voldynskoe (west and southwest of Dmitrov). The 24th Cavalry Division was consolidating on the eastern bank of the canal (along the Tempy-Sorevnovanie sector). A rifle battalion from the 29th Rifle Brigade was moved to the Yakhroma area in order to cover the concentration of the 1st Shock Army on the eastern bank of the Moscow-Volga Canal. The battalion's mission was to occupy the defensive sector west of Yakhroma and prevent the enemy from taking the town and the bridge over the canal.

During the night of November 27-28 an enemy forward detachment of 12-15 tanks and a company of machine gunners, attacking from Fedorovka through Ol'govo on Yakhroma, and not meeting stubborn resistance from our units, pushed back the covering battalion's left flank in a brisk attack and broke into Yakhroma. By 0700 the enemy detachment (10-12 tanks and up to two platoons of automatic riflemen) captured the bridge and crossed over to the canal's eastern bank, where it halted. One may assume on the basis of materials that the enemy manifested a lack of decisiveness because he was unsure of the situation and scared of the predawn darkness. The

Germans fired from their machine guns in a disorderly manner and carried out reconnaissance with small groups of automatic riflemen before the break of day.

At dawn the enemy, reinforced by newly-arrived forces, continued to advance to the east. By 1000 they had taken Peremilovo, Il'inskoe, and Bol'shie Semeshki, to where he began to bring up new reserves. Fighting in the Yakhroma area continued with varying success all during the day of November 28. By means of a flank blow by the 58th Tank Division's 21st Tank Brigade (30th Army) from the north on Yakhroma we managed to somewhat halt the advance by the enemy's mobile units (7th Panzer Division).

At 1200 the 1st Shock Army's 29th and 50th rifle brigades, which were moving on Yakhroma, were ordered to delay the enemy's further advance on the canal's eastern bank, to cut off his retreat an destroy him. The enemy nevertheless managed to bring up more than a battalion of infantry (14th Motorized Division) with a large number of mortars and tanks (7th Panzer Division) to the area of Peremilovo and Bol'shie Semeshki. Our units' attempts on November 28 to take this area were not successful. During November 29, as the result of an organized counterattack by our 29th and 50th rifle brigades, supporting by artillery and aviation, the enemy was thrown back to the canal's western bank. The Germans lost up to 20 tanks, five aircraft, and many officers and men.

In this fashion the situation on the canal's eastern bank was restored. However, Yakhroma remained in enemy hands.

Our units made attempts to blow up the Yakhroma bridge so as to prevent the enemy's withdrawal to the western bank, but these efforts were not successful.

It was only after the enemy had been thrown back into Yakhroma that the bridge was blown up. However, two days later, the 1st Shock Army's forces, which had gone over to the offensive, spent a good deal of time and equipment in forcing the canal.

At the same time the enemy's Klin-Rogachevo group was attempting with part of its forces to overcome the resistance of the 30th Army's left flank and force the Moscow-Volga Canal, the Solnechnogorsk group (2nd Panzer and 106th Infantry divisions), continued to direct its main efforts against the 16th Army's right flank. The 16th Army's right flank (133rd Rifle and 17th Cavalry divisions, 25th Tank Brigade, the remains of the cadet regiment, and the 126th Rifle Division) was engaged in persistent fighting during November 27-28 along the entire front, while the enemy's main efforts were directed to the southeast along the road to Fedorovka.

By the close of November 28 the army's right-flank forces were consolidating along the line Kharlamovo (12 km west of Yakhroma)-Safonovo-Klusovo-Zakhar'ino-Timonovo and in immediate contact with the enemy. The Germans' repeated attacks (a motorized regiment and 40 tanks) in the Klusovo area in order to break through to the road were repulsed by counterattacks by the 133rd Rifle Division and the enemy was thrown beyond the Kamersha River.

The 16th Army's units in the center and left flank (31st Tank Brigade, 7th Guards Rifle Division, 2nd Guards Cavalry Corps, 20th Cavalry Division, 8th Guards, 18th, and 9th Guards rifle divisions) were involved in heavy fighting in the area to the south of Solnechnogorsk and to the east of the Istra Reservoir and Istra. The enemy's mobile groups sought to break out of Kochergino and Yesipovo to the southeast.

On November 27 the 24th Tank Brigade was moved to the Kamenka area and the 31st Tank Brigade to Kochergino, in order to secure the Kamenka-Iksha axis (12 km south of Yakhroma). During the latter half of November 27 separate groups of the enemy's motorized infantry and tanks from the area of Peshki and Yesipovo (on the Leningrad road southeast of Solnechnogorsk) managed to break through and reached the L'yalovo and Klushino area and attempted to advance further to the south; on November 28 these groups continued to remain in those areas occupied by them. By the morning of November 29 the 16th Army's forces were consolidating along the line Kharlamovo-Klusovo-Timonovo-Lake Senezhskoe, and to the south—Kochugino (six km south of Kochergino)-Zhukovo-Klochkovo-Novo-Sergievo-Aleksino-Zhevnevo (on the Istra River west of Dedovsk).

The enemy attacked along the following axes: the 23rd Infantry and 7th Panzer divisions attacked from the line Kharlamovo-Timonovo along the road toward Kamenka and Krasnaya Polyana; the 106th Infantry and 2nd Panzer divisions attacked along the Leningrad road toward Chernaya Gryaz' and Khimki; the 35th Infantry and the 5th, 10th and 11th panzer divisions attacked toward Kryukovo and from the Istra area toward Dedovsk and Krasnogorsk.

In order to destroy the enemy's tanks and motorized infantry, which had broken through to the area of L'yalovo, Kholmy and Klushino, the following units were concentrated in the area of Ozeretskoe, Chernaya Gryaz', and Bezverkhovo: 282nd Rifle Regiment, 24th and 145th tank brigades, a cavalry regiment, 31st Artillery Regiment, and the 509th Anti-Tank Artillery Regiment. At 1700 on November 28 these units attacked, although as a result of the enemy's stout resistance, they returned to their jumping-off positions by the end of the day.

During November 28 the Fascist aviation was particularly active; it carried out 180 single and 21 group sorties along the Western Front's front. The enemy aviation's increased activity was noted in the area south of Solnechnogorsk, Krasnaya Polyana, and Kryukovo, that is, where the Germans' main mobile groups were active. Our aviation (23rd, 43rd, and 47th air divisions), flying in support of the *front's* right-flank armies, bombed enemy tank and troop concentrations along the roads and in inhabited areas in the area of Klin, Solnechnogorsk and Istra.

The battles of this period show that the enemy, exerting his forces, sought to defeat as quickly as possible the opposing units of the Red Army and reach Moscow from the northwest. However, the stubborn and skillful resistance of our troops along a number of lines prevented him from quickly completing the operation on the Western Front's right wing and achieving decisive results. The enemy's troops, suffering significant losses in men and matériel, gradually became exhausted and worn out, which lowered their combat power.

Fighting on the near approaches to Moscow, November 29-December 3. The entrance of the reserve armies into the battle

During November 29-30 the battles along the Western Front's right wing continued with unabated energy.

From the morning of November 20 the enemy's mobile groups continued to attack from the line Yakhroma-Ol'govo-Timonovo-Yesipovo-Lopotovo-Polevshino-Vysokovo (five km east of Istra), seeking to force the Moscow-Volga Canal along its left flank, and in the center to break through from the Solnechnogorsk area to the southeast to Krasnaya Polyana and Kryukovo.

During November 29-30 the troops on the 30th Army's right flank continued to consolidate their positions; the enemy was not particularly active here.

There was local fighting in the army's center with small groups of the enemy's infantry; while on the left troops were regrouped. By the end of November 30 the army's units (5th Rifle, 46th Cavalry, and 185th Rifle divisions, 1319th Rifle Regiment) occupied their previous positions. Reinforcements arrived in the form of the 365th Rifle and 82nd Cavalry divisions. The following enemy units were located in front of the army's center and right flank: XXVII Army Corps (129th and 86th infantry divisions), the 36th Motorized Infantry Division, and part of the 1st Panzer Division.

The forces of the 16th Army, against which the enemy directed its main blow, during November 29-30, were involved in heavy fighting. The enemy's mobile units were attacking along the Kamenka-Ozeretskoe road, and along the Leningrad and Istra roads.

So as to more stoutly secure the line Ol'govo-Fedorovka-Vel'evo, units from the 133rd and 126th rifle and 17th Cavalry divisions, a cadet regiment, and the 24th and 21st tank brigades were unified into a group under the command of Gen. Zakharov. At 1200 on November 29 the group was engaged in stubborn defensive fighting along the line Ol'govo-Kharlamovo-Klusovo-Timonovo and further along the eastern shore of Lake Senezhskoe. Significant enemy forces (7th Panzer, 106th and 23rd infantry divisions) sought to outflank the group's units from the northeast in the Ol'govo area and from the northwest in the Timonovo area. After heavy fighting, the enemy, supported by tanks, captured Ol'govo. His attacks in the Klusovo area were beaten back.

On the group's left flank units of the enemy's 23rd Infantry Division captured Rigino and Vel'evo (four km northeast of Timonovo), and by the morning of November 30 his mobile units occupied Kamenka (ten km south of Ol'govo).

General Remizov's composite group (282nd Rifle Regiment, 145th Tank Brigade, and a cavalry regiment), created to oppose the enemy that had broken through in the Kholmy area, occupied the line Ozeretskoe-Lunevo, and along the southern bank of the Klyaz'ma River. The group battled the enemy along the entire front, maintaining its position.

Forces of the 16th Army (7th and 8th guards rifle divisions, 18th Rifle and 9th Guards Rifle divisions) were waging a fierce struggle by the end of November 30 along the line L'yalovo-Alabushevo-Kryukovo-Barantsevo-Nefed'evo-Lenino-Zhevnevo. Units of the 5th Army's 108th Rifle Division were defending west of Krasnovidovo. The 20th Cavalry Division was concentrated in the area of Krasnyi Oktyabr'; the 2nd Guards Cavalry Corps in the area of Bol'shaya Rzhavka, Nazar'evo and Savelki, and; the 1st Tank Brigade, the army reserve, in the area of Kamenka and Brekhovo.

During November 29, as a result of poor weather conditions, our and the enemy's aviation carried out limited combat activities.

On November 30 the Fascist aviation carried out 132 single and group sorties along the Western Front, primarily along the *front's* right flank.

Our aviation (43rd and 47th air divisions) carried out active reconnaissance of the area, bordered on the right by the line Kryukovo-Teryaeva Sloboda, and on the left by the line Zvenigorod-Ruza. Enemy motor-mechanized units were being destroyed in the area of Kochergino, Povarovo and Ovsyannikovo; enemy infantry and tanks were attacked in the areas of Mar'ino, Kurtasovo, and Kholmy.

In the last days of November north of Moscow along the Moscow-Volga Canal (in the Dmitrov-Yakhroma areas), and northwest of Moscow in the direction of Krasnaya Polyana and Kryukovo, a highly tense situation had developed. The Germans had driven deeply here and divided the main forces of the 30th and 16th armies; the fighting was now on the near approaches to Moscow. The situation for the Western Front's right wing was serious; an immediate danger hung over the capital. The Fascists were straining every fiber for the final blows, believing that final victory was near. But their calculations underestimated the Red Army's power of resistance and failed to take into account its powerful and deep reserves.

During the course of the prolonged and intense defensive battle along the Western Front's right flank, reserves (in the form of entire formations and separate units) were continually being dispatched from various directions to the threatened sectors. They, together with those forces fighting along the front line made it possible to achieve local successes, strengthened the front, and delayed and halted the enemy, but were still unable to bring about a turning point in the operation in our favor. The crisis of the fierce battle was approaching on the right wing. Large reserves of the Supreme High Command were committed into the battle in order to launch a decisive counter-blow and defeat the German group attacking toward Moscow.

For this purpose, during the period November 26-December 1, the forces of Gen. V.I. Kuznetsov's newly-formed 1st Shock Army (29th, 47th, 55th, 50th, 71st, 56th, 44th rifle brigades), which was concentrating in the Zagorsk-Dmitrov area, were moving to the eastern bank of the

Moscow-Volga Canal along the front Nikol'skoe (15 km north of Dmitrov)-Bol'shoe Ivanovskoe (22 km south of Dmitrov) (a more detailed description of the reserve armies' concentration is contained in Chapter 2).

Simultaneously, to the northwest of Moscow in the Lobnya-Skhodnya-Khimki area, units of the 20th Army (64th, 35th, 28th, 43rd rifle brigades, 331st and 353nd rifle divisions) were concentrating and moving to the line Chernaya (12 km north of Loynya)-Khlebnikovo-Mel'kisarovo (on the Klyaz'ma River)-Uskovo, occupying the front between the 1st Shock and 16th armies.

In connection with the 1st Shock Army's inclusion in the Western Front from December 1, the *front* commander's order no. 080 of November 30 established new boundary lines: a) between the 30th and 1st armies—Yeremino-Kanalstroi-Rogachevo-Klin (all within the 30th Army); b) between the 1st and 16th armies—Mitropol'e-Chernaya-Dmitrovka-Lake Senezhskoe (all within the 1st Army).

Gen. Zakharov's group was transferred from the 16th Army to the 1st Army and the latter's commander ordered to establish communications with it.

The Western Front commander also issued the following orders to the 1st Shock Army: 1) all forces are to go over to a decisive offensive from the morning of December 2 in the general direction of Dedenevo, Fedorovka, and the southern outskirts of Klin, and on that day relieve Gen. Zakharov's encircled group in the Kamenka-Fedorovka area; 2) in cooperation with the 30th and 20th armies, defeat the enemy's Klin-Solnechnogorsk group.

During December 1-3 the troops along the 30th Army's front continued to strengthen their position, carried out combat reconnaissance and a partial regrouping of their forces, with the mission of launching a counteroffensive. The enemy here had gone over to the defensive and was not particularly active, firing sporadically from artillery and mortars, and had begun to dig trenches and construction obstacles.

By the morning of December 3 the 30th Army's units were completing their partial regrouping along their former line, and were strengthening their defenses, having in front of them the 86th Infantry and 36th Motorized divisions, and an SS brigade; the 365th Rifle Division, included in the 30th Army, was concentrated in the area 20 km east of Konakovo (Nikol'skoe-Lipino-Tokarevo); the 21st Tank Brigade and the 24th and 18th cavalry divisions were defending along the line of the locks at Bol'shaya Volga-Sorevnovanie-Kanalstroi; the 82nd Cavalry Division was north of Kanakova (Skryl'evo-Fedorovskoe-Sazhino); the 107th Motorized Rifle Division in the Litvintsevo area; the 58th Tank Division in Kimry, and; the 8th Tank Brigade (the army commander's reserve) was in Aleksandrovka.

The *Stavka* sought to strengthen the 30th Army, and new formations were arriving from the High Command reserve—348th, 371st and 379th rifle divisions. The divisions arrived by rail and disembarked during the period December 2-5 exclusively: 348th Rifle Division—at the Zagorsk station; 371st Rifle Division—the Savelovo station; 379th Rifle Division—the Taldom station. As they disembarked, the divisions concentrated in their designated areas behind the army's front.

At the same time that the enemy before the 30th Army had assumed the defensive, covering the attack by the main forces on Moscow, on the front of the 1st and 16th armies he continued to make his final efforts, seeking to seize Moscow. Having by this time concentrated everything that was possible to pull from other sectors of the front, and employing special and rear units, the attacking enemy was losing blood, and sought to achieve success at any price.

As before, the enemy was particularly concentrating the efforts of his motor-mechanized groups along the Solnechnogorsk and Istra axes, seeking to tie down units of the 1st Army and defeat the 16th Army, so as to open the road to the capital. In order to render support to its northern wing, the enemy on the morning of December 1 attacked with the Fourth Army's left-flank units (IX and VII army corps) against the 5th Army.

The 16th Army was waging a fierce fight along the Solnechnogorsk and Istra axes, stubbornly holding the attack by the enemy's tanks and infantry. The Germans' Istra group (Fourth Panzer Group) was concentrating and committing into the fighting its last reserves.

On the 1st Army's front the Fascists on December 1 directed their main efforts from the line Doronino-Timonovo against Gen. Zakharov's group. As a result of the heavy fighting and the threat of its left flank being deeply turned, the group's units abandoned their position and by the end of December 2 had concentrated in the area Rtishchevo-Nikol'skoe-Belyi Rast. The enemy captured the Fedorovka area and was advancing quickly to the southeast.

The 1st Shock Army as early as the morning of December 1 had attacked with part of its forces (44th and 71st rifle brigades) and by the end of the day they were located 5-7 km west of the canal (Stepanovo, three km southwest of Yakhroma, and D'yakovo and Grigorkovo), having thrown a forward detachment as far as the area of Yazykovo and Sokol'nikovo. The Germans (23rd Infantry and 7th Panzer divisions) put up fierce resistance.

The army's units established through the fighting that the 1st Panzer Division, shifted from the Kalinin axis, was now in the Sokol'nikovo area.

The 1st Shock Army's remaining units occupied their former positions. Units of the 14th Motorized, the 23d Infantry, and the 1st, 6th and 7th panzer divisions were attacking along the army's front.

On December 2 the army's forces continued the battle; the attacking units (44th, 56th, 71st rifle brigades) were overcoming the enemy's stubborn resistance, which in some places involved launching counterattacks, with particularly heavy fighting occurring on the 44th Rifle Brigade's front, where more than two battalions of infantry, supported by 25 tanks, pressed our units back and again captured Stepanovo. The left flank of the 44th Rifle Brigade fell back to Medkovo. The 56th Rifle Brigade captured Strekovo (five km south of Dedenevo), faced by small enemy units. The 71st Rifle Brigade was fighting near Bornosovo and Sokol'nikovo against four battalions with tanks.

In carrying out the orders of the commander of the Western Front, the commander of the 1st Army decided on the morning of December 3 to continue the offensive in order to take Ol'govo and reach the front Yakhroma-Ol'govo-Svistukha (seven km southwest of Ol'govo).

The 44th, 50th, 56th, and 71st rifle brigades, the 701st Artillery Regiment, and the 3rd and 38th mortar battalions were designated for this purpose. The brigades received the following missions: a) the 50th and 44th brigades were to take the area of Yakhroma and Stepanovo and then attack toward Fedorovka; b) the 56th and 71st rifle brigades were to reach the line Ol'govo-Svistukha and then attack toward Fedorovka; c) the 29th Rifle Brigade was to defend the front Dmitrov-Peremilovo, while its left flank supported the 50th Rifle Brigade. The attached group (133rd and 126th rifle divisions, 17th Cavalry Division) was to secure the line Khoroshilovo (12 km southwest of Yakhroma)-Nikol'skoe. The 47th Rifle Brigade remained in the army commander's reserve.

On the morning of December 3 the 1st Army went over to the offensive. The enemy's infantry and tanks (23rd Infantry, 1st Panzer divisions) put up stubborn resistance and in places launched local counterattacks. During the latter half of December 3 the army's units were fighting along the line Voldynskoe-Mikishkino, outflanking Yakhroma from the north in the area of Leonovo and Stepanovo, south of Yakhroma; the front then moved toward Yazykovo, Sokol'nikovo and Staroe; the 55th Rifle Brigade was concentrating in the Neroshchino-Andreikovo area; the 123rd Tank Battalion was in Peremilovo, and the 133rd Tank Battalion in Kuzyaevo (both places in woods).

On December 2-3 the enemy pushed back Gen. Zakharov's group and occupied Belyi Rast (15 km north of Lobnya), but afterwards was not active.

A *Stavka* order of December 3 included the newly-formed 20th Army (64th, 35th, 28th, 43rd, rifle brigades, 331st and 353nd rifle divisions, and other units) in the Western Front. On December

1 the army's forces were occupying the line Chernaya (12 km north of Lobnya) – Lugovaya station-Khlebnikovo-Mel'kisarovo-Uskovo (three km south of Skhodnya). The 352nd Rifle Division continued concentrating in the Khimki area. In accordance with the operational situation, the *front* commander ordered the 20th Army to seize the area of Krasnaya Polyana, Vladychino, and Kholmy from the morning of December 2.

On the morning of December 2 the 20th Army's units (331st Rifle Division, 134th Tank Battalion, 7th Independent Guards Mortar Battalion, 28th Rifle Brigade, 135th Tank Battalion, and 15th Independent Guards Mortar Battalion) went over to the offensive with the mission of encircling and destroying the enemy in the indicated area. The 331st Rifle Division, with attached units, attacked toward Krasnaya Polyana and Ozeretskoe and by the end of December 3 had advanced 1-2 km toward Krasnaya Polyana, where up to a battalion of enemy infantry (106th Infantry Division) was located, with tanks. The division was reinforced with a 203mm battalion from the High Command Artillery Reserve for bombarding the Fascists' positions. The enemy put up stout resistance to our attack with mortar and artillery fire and employed anti-tank and anti-personnel barriers. There were no changes on the remainder of the 20th Army's front.

The 16th Army's forces on December 1-3 were involved in heavy fighting with the enemy's main group, which was attacking along the Solnechnogorsk axis along the Leningrad highway and on the Istra axis along the Volokolamsk road.

The Germans' shock groups were concentrating in the following areas: a) Krasnaya Polyana and Klushino (106th Infantry and 2nd Panzer divisions), from whence a blow was to be launched toward the northern outskirts of Moscow; b) L'yalovo, Alabushevo, Kryukovo, Bakeevo—5th and 11th panzer and 35th infantry divisions, attacking along the Leningrad highway; c) to the east of Istra—an SS infantry division and the 10th Panzer Division—operating toward Kozino and further to the southeast; d) southwest of Dedovsk—the 252nd and 87th infantry divisions along the Istra road toward Krasnogorsk. During this period the fighting along the 16th Army's front was particularly fierce. Several locations changed hands.

During December 2-3 the enemy, by means of straining to the utmost its men and matériel, managed to take Kryukovo, where there was fighting in the streets. However, the enemy's attempts to break through our lines on the remaining areas of the front ended in failure, causing heavy casualties.

The 354th Rifle Division, which had arrived in the Skhodnya area from the *Stavka* reserve, was included in the 16th Army and from the morning of December 3 went over to the attack and by 1600 had reached the southern outskirts of Matushkino (three km east of Alabushevo). Units of the 7th and 8th guards divisions were engaged in heavy fighting with the enemy's infantry and tanks for control of Kryukovo. Units of the 18th Rifle Division were also attacking from Brekhovo. The 9th Guards Rifle Division was engaged in heavy fighting with the enemy's infantry and tanks on the eastern outskirts of Nefed'evo; the 36th Rifle Brigade was also arriving here.

By the end of December 3 the army's units were located along the line Poyarkovo (seven km west of Krasnaya Polyana)-Bol'shie Rzhavki-(excluding) Alabushevo-the eastern part of Kryukovo-Brekhovo-Nefed'evo-Zelenkovo (on the Istra River five km southwest of Dedovsk).

During the first part of the day the 5th Army's forces fought the enemy's infantry and tanks along the entire front, while particularly heavy fighting went on between the Istra and Moscow rivers, where the enemy, having concentrated up to two infantry divisions with tanks (87th Infantry Division, part of the 78th Infantry and part of the 10th Panzer divisions), attacked along the following axes: a) Ivanovskoe-Pavlovskaya Sloboda; b) northeast of Zvenigorod. The enemy also launched a supporting attack with forces up to an infantry division in size to the south (along the front Ulitino-Mikhailovskoe).

Thus the enemy, with units from the IX Army Corps (87th and 78th infantry divisions) sought to coordinate with the Fourth Panzer Group attacking along the boundary between the 16th and 5th armies.

The 5th Army's right-flank units (108th, 144th rifle divisions), under pressure from superior enemy forces, were forced on December 1 to abandon several points in the wake of heavy fighting, while holding the remainder of their defensive front. The 108th Rifle Division was thrown back and torn to pieces. By the end of the day one rifle regiment was in Padikovo, a second east of Koz'mino (encircled), and the third in the area of Palitsy and Aksin'ino (seven km east of Zvenigorod). The enemy continued to attack and during the night of December 1-2 sought to drive a wedge in the 108th Rifle Division's position along its boundary with the 144th Rifle Division in the direction of Aksin'ino, attempting to outflank Zvenigorod from the northeast.

By 1200 on December 2 up to a regiment of infantry with tanks occupied Savkovo (nine km northeast of Zvenigorod) and, taking advantage of the situation, began to advance to the east.

Units of the 144th Rifle Division were holding the defensive line with their main forces and were destroying, along with a tank brigade, a group of Germans who had broken through. By the end of December 2 enemy activity in front of the 144th Rifle Division declined.

By the end of December 2 and during the night of December 3 the 5th Army's right-flank units continued to wage stubborn holding actions against the enemy, while preparing for a counteroffensive. The army's right flank (108th , 144th rifle divisions, 20th Tank Brigade), with the 252nd, 87th and 78th infantry divisions, supported by tanks in front of it, was holding the front Anosino (seven km southwest of Dedovsk)-Pokrovskoe-Aksin'ino-Kozino (five km east of Zvenigorod)-Dyut'kovo (three km northwest of Zvenigorod)-Yagunino.

From the morning of December 3 the 5th Army launched an attack in order to aid the 16th Army's left flank. The fighting was extremely heavy; Anosino changed hands four times. The fighting developed with mixed success and made no great change in the overall situation.

Our aviation and the enemy air force were not particularly active on December 1 as a result of the poor weather conditions. However, on December 2 the German air force carried out 310 sorties against the Western Front. A large number of these sorties were carried out to bomb and strafe the troops along the right wing and targets in our rear.

Our aviation (23rd, 47th, 43rd air divisions) on December 2-3 bombed concentrations of enemy infantry and motor-mechanized forces in the areas of Istra, Novo-Petrovskoe, Volokolamsk, and Yesipovo, as well as enemy automobile columns moving along the roads between Klin, Istra and Solnechnogorsk.

The Germans go on the defensive

On December 4 the armies on the *front's* right wing engaged in heavy fighting, holding off along several sectors the offensive of an enemy that was already fading, and with fire and counterattacks was destroying those groups which had infiltrated into the defensive depth. Our forces on the Solnechnogorsk and Zvenigorod axes were attacking so as to restore the positions lost and occupy more favorable lines for going over to a general offensive.

On December 4 the enemy was still striving, making his final efforts, to complete his offensive on Moscow along the blow's main axes and was putting up fierce resistance to our units by counterattacking with infantry and tanks.

By the close of December 4 the 30th Army was regrouping its forces in preparation for launching a counteroffensive with units from its center and left flank.

The enemy was passive along the army's front. The enemy was strengthening his lines and setting up barbed wire obstacles.

By a December 1 order of the Supreme Command, the 5th Rifle Division, with attached units, was removed from the 30th Army on December 4 and transferred to the Kalinin Front. A new boundary between the Kalinin and Western fronts was organized along the following line: Kalyazin-Sudimirka-Turginovo (all within 30th Army).

The 30th Army's new formations continued to arrive and concentrate: the 379th Rifle Division to the west of Taldom; the 348th Rifle Division in the area of Zaprudnaya, and; the 371st Rifle Division was unloading at Savelovo station.

During December 5 units of the 30th Army occupied their former defense lines and continued to concentrate in their jumping-off positions for the offensive, carrying out reconnaissance of the enemy's forward positions. The enemy was not particularly active and was consolidating in his positions.

The 1st Shock Army's forces continued to attack along the right flank and in the center on December 4 and the early hours of December 5, meanwhile repulsing attacks against its left flank, where the enemy had massed a large panzer group (1st Panzer Division).

The Fascists put up stubborn resistance to our attacking units and in some sectors launched counterattacks. The enemy concentrated his main efforts on the left flank in the direction of Belyi Rast, launching a blow along the boundary between the 1st Shock Army's left flank and the 20th Army's right flank.

The decision by the 1st Shock Army commander, taken on December 4, was as follows:

1 Launch a blow with the right flank to capture the area of Ol'govo (on the Yakhroma-Fedorovka road). To achieve this, it was planned to take the unnamed height to the west of Dmitrov and move up an active screen from a single brigade, with the mission of covering the army's right flank from the Rogachevo side.
2 Create a shock group of four rifle brigades (50th, 44th, 56th, 71st) along the line Novo-Kartsevo-Ol'govo-Yazykovo and attack in the direction of Fedorovka and Klin.
3 The 47th Rifle Brigade and the 133rd and 126th rifle divisions were to attack in the direction of Lake Senezhskoe and then toward Klin.
4 Hold the 55th Rifle Brigade as a reserve behind the army's center.

The army commander proposed to completely clean the enemy out of the area of Dmitrov, Yakhroma and Ol'govo by the evening of December 4 and the following day take the Fedorovka area.

Fearing a flank attack from the Rogachevo area, the army commander asked the 30th Army to render active support by attacking Rogachevo and also considered it necessary to hold yet another rifle brigade in reserve behind his right flank.

The army was faced by units of the 1st, 6th and 7th panzer divisions supported by two infantry divisions, which were occupying the area Rogachevo-the west bank of the Moscow-Volga Canal to the south of Kanalstroi (seven km north of Dmitrov) and further on to Kamenka, inclusively. The enemy was very stubbornly defending the Yakhroma-Ol'govo-Fedorovka road, putting up strong points and centers of resistance.

The fighting on December 4-5 was particularly fierce along the 1st Shock Army's front; a number of places changed hands.

The enemy was throwing in infantry on vehicles and tank units along the Fedorovka-Ol'govo-Yakhroma road, removing units from the 30th Army's left wing, and employing his assault aircraft to strafe our attacking forces. Our aviation had the mission of supporting our forces and fighting the German aviation.

With the appearance of the 1st Panzer Division along the boundary between the 1st Shock and 20th armies, and the threat of the enemy's tanks penetrating between them, the Western Front commander to organize on December 5 (using the anti-tank weapons from the composite group and the 1st Shock Army) a powerful anti-tank defense of the area Iksha-Belyi Rast-Chernaya. The commanders of the 1st and 20th armies were instructed to shift their tanks for cooperation with the left-flank group. The commander of the 20th Army was ordered to establish a dense and deep anti-tank defense in the area of Belyi Rast, Sukharevo, and Marfino, capable of repelling the enemy's massed tank attack. Also, the Western Front commander ordered to throw not less than 20 anti-tank guns, taken from the divisions' units, in order to strengthen the junction between the armies; to immediately refit the 24th and 31st tank brigades with repaired and new equipment.

By the end of December 5 the 1st Shock Army's forces, waging fierce battles, occupied the following position: the 29th Rifle Brigade was consolidating north of Yakhroma (along the line Voldynskoe-Mikishino-Pochinki); the 50th Rifle Brigade continued to fight for Yakhroma from the south and with its left flank defended the line Leonovo-Zhivitino; the 44th Rifle Brigade was consolidating south of Stepanovo; the 56th Rifle Brigade was fighting on the southeastern outskirts of Volgusha (one km south of Ol'govo) and Sokol'nikovo, but was unable to move forward; to the south the 55th Rifle Brigade and the 133rd and 126th rifle divisions were fighting along the line to the west of Khoroshilovo and Trutnev, while the 126th Rifle Division's left-flank units were fighting alongside the 20th Army's 64th Rifle Brigade east of Kuzyaevo; the 84th Rifle Brigade was concentrated in the area of Bashlaevo and Vasil'evskoe.

Although the 1st Army's forces had inflicted serious losses on the enemy during the two days of fighting, they were not able to completely carry out their instructions of December 4-5 because of the enemy's stubborn resistance and his creation of strong points.

During the fighting of December 4-5 680 German officers and men were killed, 26 captured, as were 400 rifles, 80 machine guns, and six 37mm guns, while 17 tanks, two airplanes, and two armored cars were knocked out.

The 20th Army, cooperating with the 1st Shock and 16th armies, continued the fight to take the area of Belyi Rast and Krasnaya Polyana on December 4-5.

The enemy put up stubborn resistance to our offensive by counterattacking and in some sectors organized a fixed defense.

The army was faced by units of the 1st Panzer and 106th Infantry divisions, and the 2nd Panzer Division. Fierce fighting took place in the area of Krasnaya Polyana. The 20th Army destroyed 11 tanks, five armored cars, six anti-tank guns, five motorcycles, seven tankers, and up to a company of infantry in the fighting for Krasnaya Polyana.

The fighting for Belyi Rast was also stubborn and the town changed hands twice.

By the end of December 5 the 20th Army's forces, repelling the enemy's savage counterattacks near Belyi Rast and Krasnaya Polyana continued fighting along the line lying east of Belyi Rast and south of Krasnaya Polyana (Kuzyaevo-Lugovaya station-Gorki-Shemyakino); the 31st Tank Brigade defended the area of Chernoe.

On December 4 the 16th Army's forces continued to wage persistent holding battles along their right flank against the enemy's attacking infantry and tanks. In the center and along the left flank (where the Fascist offensive was halted by our troops and where the enemy started to consolidate along a number of sectors) our units gradually developed the offensive, overcoming the enemy's fierce resistance.

The troops' main efforts were directed at taking Kryukovo and launching blows against the boundary of the enemy groups in the area along both sides of the Istra road (toward Shemetkovo and Rozhdestveno).

On December 4-5 the 8th Guards Rifle Division was fighting in Kryukovo itself. The enemy, having massed two battalions of infantry from the 35th Infantry Division and 60 tanks from the 5th Panzer Division, was resisting stubbornly, using tanks in ambushes from behind houses and barns. At 1300, following a number of counterattacks, the Germans managed to take a machine-tractor station (northeast of Kryukovo), but his further progress was halted. The fighting for Kryukovo continued until the night of December 5 with growing strength on both sides.

The 18th Rifle Division and the 145th Tank Brigade, which fought on December 4-5 to take Shemetkovo, by the evening of December 5 had broken the enemy's stubborn defense, had taken Shemetkovo and consolidated there. Up to a battalion of infantry from Turovo counterattacked against our units, but was dispersed by fire from the guards mortar men. While pursuing the Germans, our units took Nadovrazhino, where the captured four damaged tanks and one gun.

The 9th Rifle Division and the 17th Tank and 40th Rifle brigades attacked toward Petrovskoe and Nefed'evo (three km north of Dedovsk). Following heavy fighting, units from this group had taken Nefed'evo and Turovo by 1200 and were continuing the attack toward Petrovskoe. However, the attack on Rozhdestveno by left-flank units of the 40th Rifle and 17th Tank brigades was unsuccessful. There were no changes along the front of the 16th Army's other units.

The 5th Army's right-flank forces, in cooperation with the 16th Army's left flank, waged stubborn holding actions with units of the enemy's 252nd and 87th infantry divisions on December 4, and counterattacked along a number of sectors.

The right-flank 108th Rifle Division was involved in heavy fighting in the Anosino area (seven km southwest of Dedovsk) and Padikovo, where no less than two enemy regiments with tanks put up stubborn resistance and counterattacked.

The enemy managed to push back units of the 108th and 144th rifle divisions and take Pokrovskoe and Abushkovo.

From the morning of December 5 the 108th and 144th rifle divisions, supported by the 43rd Rifle and 20th Tank brigades, attacked and by the end of the day had taken Zakharovo, Abushkovo, Yur'evo, Palitsy, and Gryazi. Our aviation bombed the enemy positions.

The enemy began to fall back, covered by powerful artillery and mortar fire, from the area of Padikovo and Pokrovskoe.

Our aviation (46th, 47, 23rd air divisions) during the night of December 4-5 and the daylight hours of December 5 bombed enemy troop concentrations in the areas of Istra, Dorokhovo, Maurino, and other areas and carried out reconnaissance along the line: from the right—Kryukovo-Zavidovo; and from the left—Aksin'ino-Mikhailovskoe.

Despite enemy attempts to renew the offensive along parts of the broad front, the initiative had obviously passed to the Red Army.

Operational-tactical conclusions

1 In launching a new offensive, the enemy had the goal of breaking through and subsequently deeply outflanking the Western Front's right wing in order to get into the rear of our armies, encircle and seize Moscow. The realization of this mission was entrusted to the best German formations, and was supported from the air by the Second Air Force.

The German command scrupulously planned the forthcoming operation for more than a month and a half, and concentrated large forces for the task (particularly armored). Simultaneously, the regiments were brought up to strength, and ammunition and equipment was brought up in order to make up for the losses incurred during the time of the first offensive on Moscow.

The German command, while concentrating mobile tank groups (reinforced by a significant amount of automatic weaponry, mortars and other equipment) against the *front's* right-wing armies, planned to carry out a lightning blow: to break through the Red Army's front and break into Moscow from the northwest.

The operation, as conceived by the German-Fascist command along the Western Front's right wing, was conducted in the same way as other operations carried out by the Germans during the preceding period of the Great Patriotic War. This circumstance made it possible to foresee the necessary countermeasures by our side, and which facilitated the success of the defensive fighting on the approaches to Moscow.

2 The Fascists miscalculated by underestimating the Red Army's powers of resistance and failed to take into account the presence of our powerful and deep reserves. The 16th Army, holding off the main blow of the Germans' northern group, despite the initially broad front and the scattered location of its own units, was a model of persistence, skill and bravery in the fighting due to the command's firm leadership and valor of the rank and file.

At the battle's decisive moment, just as the Germans were driving a wedge between the 30th and 16th armies, fresh reserves in the form of the 1st and 20th armies entered the fighting. They, together with the front-line troops, halted the Germans and forced them on the defensive.

The Germans, having concentrated a large tank group (including the newly-arrived 1st Panzer Division in the Nikol'skoe-Belyi Rast area) during the fighting of December 4-5, and calculating on launching their latest blow along the boundary between the 1st and 20th armies by employing their favorite method of an armored wedge, not only were not able to carry out this blow, but as the result of timely measures by the Western Front command, were forced on to the defensive.

The successful actions of large tank groups (as large as a regiment) took place only on isolated sectors of the front, such as, for example, during the Germans' advance on Klin (November 21-23). However, they were unable to take advantage of the tactical result and transform it into a broad operational success.

During the German offensive against the 16th Army during the last part of the defensive battle, the army's units withstood (during December 1-5) unending and fierce attacks by four of the enemy's panzer divisions (2nd, 11th, 5th, and 10th), attacking with no less than 300 tanks along a 30-40 km front. However, despite the fact that the 16th Army could oppose this with only 86 tanks (according to the data of November 20), the Germans could not manage to achieve a decisive success and break through our positions.

This is explained by the fact that the entire defense of the Western Front's right wing was extremely stubborn, active, and elastic.

As a result of the defensive battle, the front line, which took on a fantastic and curved shape, was nowhere broken through in its entire depth.

3 The German command did not take into account the peculiarities of the theater of military activities along its own northern wing, where it was planned to carry out a lightning blow against Moscow from the northwest.

In the area where the Germans' mobile groups were operating there were a lot of forests. This caused certain difficulties for the massed employment of the panzer divisions. The Germans dispersed their tanks and only in certain cases in certain sectors did they employ tanks *en masse*, by concentrating their tank regiments.

If the wooded character of the terrain forced the tank formations to move primarily along the roads, the frosts gave the Germans the opportunity of carrying out movement b by their mobile units off the roads (in those places where there were no large woods).

It is also possible that the German command, aside from the enumerated circumstances, thought it expedient under the given conditions to carry out the offensive by means of a combined-arms battle, that is, by organizing the cooperation of tanks with infantry, which did not contradict their operational-tactical doctrine. The late autumn, short days, long and dark nights and the subsequent cold weather, restricted the conduct of operations, confined their forces' broad maneuver activities, and gradually tied the latter to inhabited areas. These conditions were also unfavorably reflected in the troops' matériel supply. The obstacles employed by our troops while retreating also played a vital role in slowing down the Fascists' advance.

4 The Germans, during the operation's decisive moments (given the presence of suitable weather conditions), sought to sharply increase their combat air activity. For example, on November 18 the enemy's air activity increased as it bombed various targets, carried out reconnaissance, and covered its forces.

During the conduct of operations around Klin the poor weather conditions significantly limited air activity; for example, on November 24, when the enemy carried out only 30 sorties along the entire Western Front. On November 27 the enemy air force once again sharply increased its activity in connection with the fierce fighting in the areas of Rogachevo and Istra.

On December 2 (during the critical period of the defensive fighting on the approaches to Moscow), the enemy air force once again increased its activity and rendered support to its ground troops.

Air activities were mostly directed against our troops on the battlefield. In this case, our troops and equipment in the immediate area of the front were subjected to air strikes. However, despite the overall well-organized cooperation with the ground forces, there were incidents of the Fascist aviation bombing its own units.

During the second half of November, with the worsening of the weather, the enemy bombed and strafed our forces from low altitudes, carrying out single-plane sorties. For example, on November 24 an enemy plane bombed a road near Dmitrov from a height of 15 meters.

5 The Germans sought such a disposition of forces and battle organization that would ensure a superiority in men and matériel along the most important sectors. During the battle the German command fully used its weapons and equipment and organized the cooperation between the combat arms. In a number of fights in the Klin area, that is, the decisive sector, the German command massed its most powerful group of mobile troops (three panzer and three infantry divisions).

During the offensive the German troops committed their forces into the first combat echelon, leaving no more or less large reserves. Only at the end of the offensive did a panzer division appear, having been transferred from the left to the right flank (1st Panzer Division). This happened because the Germans, during the preceding operations, suffered heavy losses in men and matériel. Also, the German command, evidently believed that it was very important to guarantee the force of the initial blow, which could break the resistance of our troops already weakened by the preceding operations. The possibility of our concentrating large reserves (the participation of which factually decided the outcome of the defensive battle on the *front's* right wing in our favor) was not foreseen by the Germans.

The rate of advance by the German mobile groups operating against the right wing of our front was small and reached 4-5 km per day (in 20 days the Germans advanced about 90 km).

During the offensive the Germans suffered greater and greater heavy losses in men and matériel and encountered growing difficulties along their way, as a result of which their offensive spirit gradually fell, while confidence in the battle's success among our troops grew.

6 The organization of the Red Army's defense on the *front's* right wing is worthy of attention for the following reasons: the defense was mainly built not as a continuous defensive position on the model of the First World War, but rather as a system of strong points and centers of resistance (created at the platoon-battalion level), employing concrete and wood and earth firing points, and using inhabited areas, where the buildings were adapted for defensive purposes. Examples of this are: a) the fortification of the 16th Army's defensive zone along the line Kharlanika-Chentsy (excluding)-Nelidovo-Skirmanovo-Lake Trostenskoe (the second defensive line was also fortified and occupied by units of the defense's second echelon along the line Teryaeva Sloboda-Den'kovo-Novo-Petrovskoe); b) the creation of a defensive line along the line of the Istra River. Also, the 16th

Army's defense on the line Kharlanika-Lake Trostenskoe was reinforced by the quite large reserves (a group of cavalry divisions stationed along the boundary with the 30th Army in the Klin area.

A positive factor during the defensive battle was the presence of reserves in the armies, which had a great significance during the fighting on the near approaches to Moscow along the 16th Army's front on December 2-5, when the 354th Rifle Division, and the 36th, 40th, and 49th rifle brigades were moved up from the *Stavka* reserve. This enabled the 16th Army's forces not only to actively defend their line, but from December 3 go over to a partial counteroffensive along their center (and the left flank from December 4).

7 During the defensive fighting the Germans encircled a number of our units several times. However, this did not lead to them laying down their arms. Our forces broke out of their encirclement and created a defense along new lines, and at the same time inflicted personnel and matériel losses on the enemy.

Examples of this are: a) the encirclement and breakout in the Klin area of the 107th Motorized Rifle Division, the 58th Tank and 24th Cavalry divisions, and the 21st Tank Brigade during the period 22-24 November; b) the encirclement of the 126th Rifle Division on November 22 southeast of Klin in the area of Akulovo, Misirevo, and Frolovskoe (the division managed to fight its way out in the area of Borozda, Karavaevo, and Kononovo by the end of November 22); c) the encirclement of the 17th Cavalry Division in the area of Khlynikha and Zhestoki on November 23 by enemy infantry and tanks (the division was able to fight its way out of the encirclement in the area of Olisovo and Polushkino).

The reasons are that, first of all, in a number of cases the Germans lacked the time, forces and equipment to fully complete the operational encirclement with a tactical encirclement and destruction; secondly, the terrain conditions (large woods) facilitated the waging of a defense while encircled for a more or less extended period; third, there was the important role of those measures undertaken by the high command of the Red Army, which involved rendering aid to the encircled troops through counterblows by other units; fourth, the activity, resoluteness, stubbornness, and flexibility of our units in an encirclement facilitated a favorable outcome, and; five, the high morale of the troops, who sought not only to escape from the encirclement, but to inflict as many losses as possible on the enemy.

8 The experience of the defensive fighting on the Western Front's right wing confirmed the enormous role of all types and calibers of artillery in the modern battle (particularly in fighting enemy tanks and automatic weapons). The artillery on the *front's* right wing (just as with mortars) supported the accomplishment of their mission by our infantry and tanks. The artillery interfered with the arrival of the enemy's reserves from the rear. One must emphasize the significance of the guards mortar battalions, the combat activity of which in destroying the enemy's men and matériel (both while massed in inhabited areas and while attacking our defenses) achieved good results.

9 The course of the fighting along the *front's* right wing confirms the significance of the proper organization of the battle and arranging the coordination of all units. Positive examples of the proper organization of the defensive battle are the actions of Dovator's cavalry group, which with comparatively small forces repulsed the efforts by the enemy's large infantry and tank forces to break through on the Volokolamsk road during November 15-21, as well as similar actions by other combat formations. Gen. Dovator's cavalry group (50th and 53rd cavalry divisions), as a result of a number of successful fights against the German invaders, was renamed the 2nd Guards Cavalry Corps.

10 In fighting the Germans' tank units, anti-tank defense, a description of which is contained above, had great significance.

In special cases, anti-tank areas and obstacles were created by order of the higher command in certain areas and along the boundaries between formations and armies. An example of this is the order by the commander of the Western Front on December 5 on the organization of an anti-tank defense area along the boundary between the 1st and 20th armies, in light of the appearance of a large enemy tank group in the Nikol'skoe-Belyi Rast area.

During the defensive fighting against large Fascist tank groups along the Klin and Istra axes, aside from field and anti-tank artillery, bomber aviation and anti-aircraft artillery from the Moscow city PVO (as anti-tank artillery) were employed. From November 23 through December 5 anti-aircraft artillery took part in combined combat actions with the troops of the right wing along those axes representing the greatest danger of tanks (in the area around the Klin fighting, Solnechnogorsk, and the Istra Reservoir).

Anti-tank anti-aircraft groups from the Moscow PVO were used in the 30th and particularly the 16th armies, where they delayed the German offensive with their fire, while at the same time protecting our troops from air attack. The 76mm and 85mm anti-aircraft guns showed themselves to be quite an effective weapon, from the tactical-technical point of view, for combating enemy tanks.

11 Control over the armies during the defensive battle was exercised by the issuing of episodic general orders, embracing all the combat activities of the *front's* right wing, as well as separate orders to the armies, depending on the situation on the given army's front; direct coded conversations by high-frequency means and by telephone; code; by radio; by the dispatch of communications officers on planes, automobiles, and a personal visit by the command.

These communications means had a positive result during the defensive battle.

4

Events in the center. The defense along the Nara River (November 16-December 5 1941)

The Nara River as a defensive line

The Nara River is one of the small rivers in the Moscow-area basin, not differing from other rivers in the area—the Istra, Ruza, and Protva. The river's width averages 20-25 meters, its depth ½ to two meters; the bottom is solid and sandy, and the banks are low along almost the entire course and marshy in some areas. The river flows from the northwest to the southeast; the current is slow and quiet.

The Nara River has long served as a serious water line, hindering the enemies of the Russian state from freely approaching Moscow. The Nara played such a role in the Patriotic War of 1812. Kutuzov's well-fortified Tarutino position was located on the Nara.

The defense of the Nara in 1941 unfolded in conditions of late autumn and the beginning of winter. Although ice had appeared by that time on the river, nevertheless the battle along the Nara acquired the character of a struggle for crossings. The Nara is crossed by a number of roads leading to Moscow; the enemy sought to seize these roads, as crossing the river off the roads kept him from widely using his motor-mechanized equipment. The defense organized along the line of the Nara River was a serious barrier on the path of the Germans and one which they could not overcome.

The situation on the Western Front's central sector before the second German offensive on Moscow

The enemy's disposition (determined on November 5) indicated the Germans' intention of launching blows with their motor-mechanized forces along the flanks and pinning down our forces in the center. However, there was a large concentration of enemy forces in the center (predominantly infantry formations). On a comparatively small front (about 100 km in a straight line) here were deployed parts of five corps (IX, VII, XII, XX army, and LVII Panzer), which indicated that the enemy on this sector would not limit himself to pinning down duties.

In light of the possibility that the enemy would launch a blow along the shortest route to Moscow, it was necessary to seriously and reliably strengthen the Nara River as the main line along which the enemy could be halted.

To this purpose, a directive (no. 0428 of October 30 1941) by the Western Front command to the troops of the central sector laid out the following tasks:

1 to create obstacles on their sectors and destroy the roads, bridges and some structures in front of them;

2 to construct anti-tank areas;
3 to create fire obstacles;
4 to prepare, where possible, for flooding the terrain;
5 to organize anti-tank, anti-artillery, anti-air, and anti-personnel defense;
6 to station tanks in the depth and in ambushes.

In furtherance of this directive, the following work was organized on site:
In combat units:
a) the construction of defensive positions;
b) the erection of anti-tank and anti-personnel obstacles;
c) the building of communications trenches;
d) the building of command and observation posts;
e) the building of shelters.

By division engineering units:
a) the building of mine obstacles on the forward edge;
b) the destruction of all crossings in front of the forward edge;
c) the building of barbed wire obstacles and erecting hard-to-see obstacles.

By army engineering units:
a) the preparation and construction of road obstacles;
b) the laying of minefields in the depth of the defensive zone;
c) the engineering preparation of anti-tank areas in the depth.

It was planned to cover the most important axes leading to Moscow with anti-tank artillery, and create anti-tank strong points in the depth.

On the *front's* central sector such strong points were planned in the following places: in the 5th Army's zone—Lokotnya, Mikhailovskaya, Zvenigorod, Dorokhovo, and Kubinka; in the 33rd Army's zone—Akulovo, Maurino, Tashirovo, Naro-Fominsk, and Petrovskoe; in the 43rd Army's zone—Kresty, Kamenka, Stremilovo, and Lopasnya.

In directive no. 0437 of November 1 1941 the troops were further instructed to:

1 practice the creation of a false forward zone, removing the real one back by 1-1½ km;
2 create false artillery positions and false tank positions using dummy tanks;
3 distribute the minefields in such a way that the enemy must either maneuver through them or, bypassing them, expose his flank to our artillery and mortar fire.

Finally, directive no. 0450 of November 3 1941 demanded that the troops begin erecting heavy defensive structures—wooden-earth firing points, which must be located not only along the forward edge, but in the depth as well.

It was necessary to complete this work quickly, because the enemy offensive was expected at the beginning of November and could be launched at any moment. A prisoner (captured along the 33rd Army's front on the night of November 12-13) testified to the following:

> The Germans' preparations for the offensive have been completed; the artillery and ammunition have been brought up and the motor-mechanized units whipped into shape; the offensive may begin today (the night of November 12-13) or tomorrow morning.

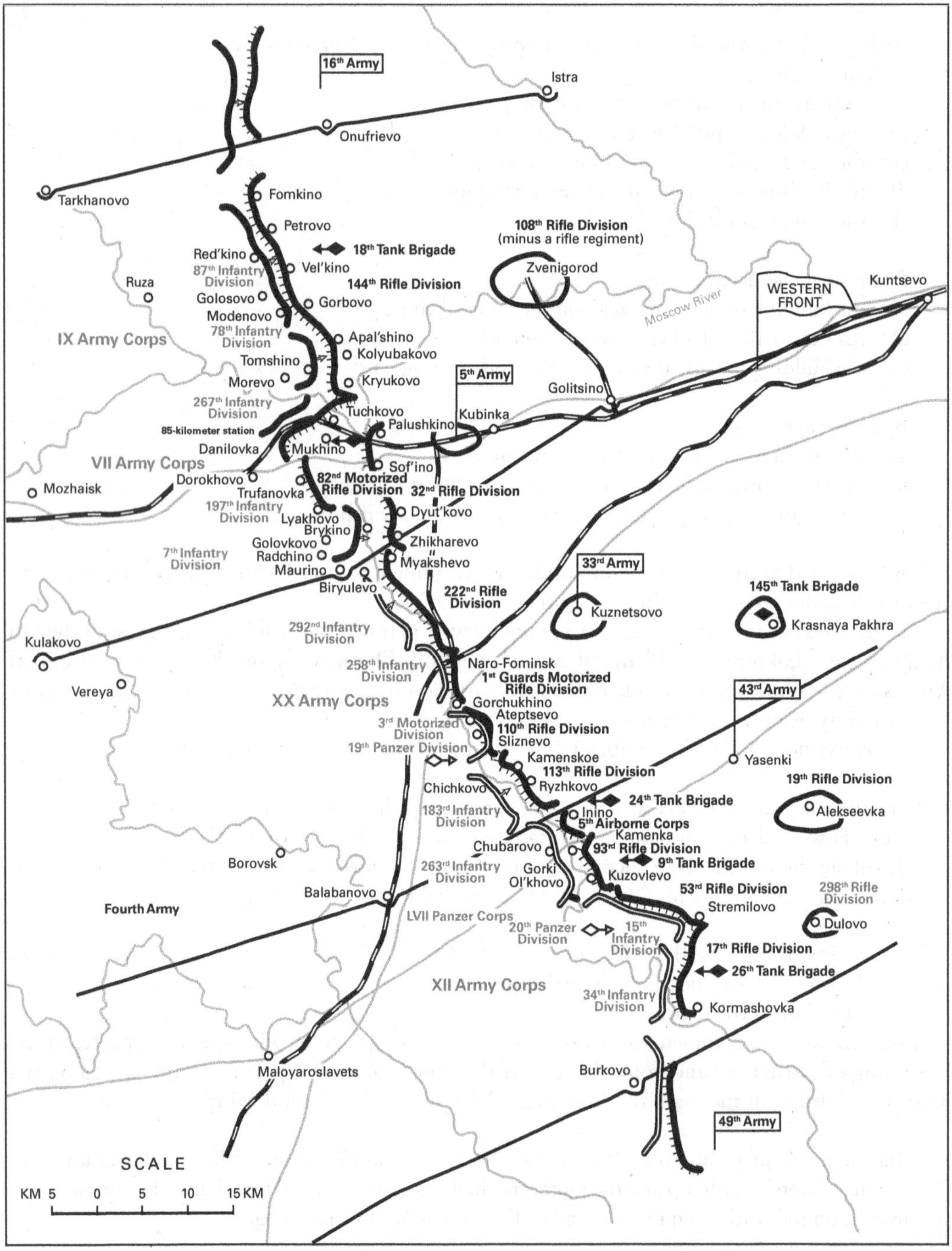

Map 3 The Armies' Defense of the Central Sector on November 16

Actually, it began on November 16. By this time the planned defensive works were not fully completed. In certain divisions they had been completed by 40-60%. In the main, trenches had been dug for the troops and weapons, and anti-fragmentation shelters, dugouts and communications trenches had been constructed. Work was being completed on the construction of anti-tank and anti-personnel minefields, while anti-personnel obstacles with barbed wire in 1-3 rows were being built; the edge of woods were ringed with barbed wire, hard-to-see obstacles were set up, and command and observation posts were being outfitted.

The quality of the fortifications work was not high. Many trenches and wooden-earth firing points lacked a sufficient field of view and fire. The haste in choosing sites for their construction told.

The combat correlation of forces at the beginning of the German offensive

By the start of the German offensive along the Western Front's central sector, the two sides' forces were deployed as follows:

Soviet		**German**	
Rifle divisions	11	Infantry divisions	12
Motorized Rifle divisions	2	Motorized divisions	1
Tank brigades	7	Panzer divisions	2
Motorcycle regiments	1		
Ind. Machine gun battalions	1		
Airborne corps	1		

The correlation of combat forces, according to our intelligence data, along the Western Front's central sector, is shown as follows:

Table III/4.1 Correlation of combat forces along the Western Front's central sector

Front	Total					Per Kilometer				
	Men	Field guns	Anti-tank guns	Mortars	Tanks	Men	Field guns	Anti-tank guns	Mortars	Tanks
5th Army (50 km)										
Soviet	31,000	217	85	160	65	620	4.3	1.7	3.2	1.3
German	30,000	300	230	350	90	600	6	4.6	7	1.8
33rd Army (32 km)										
Soviet	30,000	114	45	95	37	938	3.5	1.4	3	1.1
German	29,000	210	210	160	100	906	6.5	5	9.3	3.1
43rd Army (32 km)										
Soviet	34,000	146	115	150	85	1,063	4.5	3.5	4.6	2.7
German	29,000	250	200	320	100	906	8	6.2	10	3.1

Conclusion: the sides were almost equal in the number of men, while the enemy enjoyed superiority in equipment (artillery, mortars, and tanks).

The organization of the defense by the Western Front's central armies as of November 16 1941

The defense of the Western Front's center at the start of the second German offensive—November 16 1941—was organized as follows:

1 The 5th Army occupied the right sector. On November 16 the army's forces continued to defend along their previous line, while with part of its forces it carried out limited attacks.

The 144th Rifle Division defended the line Fomkino (17 km northeast of Ruza)-

Vel'kino-Gorbovo-Kolyubakovo-Kryukovo, along a 20-km front. On November 15-16 the division fought to take Redino, Golosovo, and Modenovo.

The 50th Rifle Division defended the line along the northwestern and western outskirts of Tuchkovo-height 212.2 (1.5 km southwest of Mukhino (excluding)-Danilovka-and on to the station 85 km from Moscow, along an 8-km front. On November 16 the division was fighting for Tomshino and Morevo.

The 82nd Motorized Rifle Division occupied the defensive line Trufanovka-Lyakhovo-the woods south to height 223.3 with a single tank brigade along a 7-km front.

Part of the division's forces was fighting to take Brykino.

The 32nd Rifle Division occupied the defensive position Polushkino-Sof'ino-Dyut'kovo-Zhikharevo (excluding)-Myakshevo, along a 15-km front.

Part of the division's forces was fighting for Golovkovo and Radchino.

The army commander's reserve—the 108th Rifle Division (minus a rifle regiment) was located in Zvenigorod, and the 36th Motorcycle Regiment was in the Kubinka area.

Army headquarters was in Kubinka. Lt. Gen. Govorov commanded the 5th Army.

As of November 16th the army commander was apprised of the following:

- that the enemy was not active along the front, but was putting up stubborn resistance to our attacks;
- that the 16th Army to the north was attacking from the morning of November 16 along its right flank, while defending against the enemy attacking along its center and on the left.

2 The center—33rd Army. On November 16 the army continued constructing defenses along its entire front.

The 222nd Rifle Division was defending along the front Myakshevo-(excluding) Naro-Fominsk along an 11-km front.

The 1st Guards Motorized Rifle Division occupied the defensive line Naro-Fominsk- (excluding) Gorchukino along a 5-km front.

The 110th Rifle Division occupied the line Gorchukino-height 195.2 -the forest cutting east of Sliznevo along a front of about seven km.

The 113th Rifle Division occupied the line (excluding) Sliznevo-Ryzhkovo along a defensive front of about nine km.

The army commander's reserve consisted of a rifle regiment from the 108th Rifle Division, located at Kuznetsovo, and the 145th Tank Brigade in Krasnaya Pakhra.

Army headquarters was in Kuznetsovo. Lt. Gen. Yefremov was the army commander.

As of November 16 the army commander was aware that the enemy was not active along the front, limiting his activities to sporadic artillery and mortar fire.

3 The left wing—43rd Army. On November 16 the army's units continued to strengthen their lines, while firing on the enemy's troop concentrations and artillery positions.

The 5th Airborne Corps was defending along the line Inino-(excluding) Kamenka, on a front of about five km.

The 93rd Rifle Division was deployed along the line Kamenka-Kuzovlevo, on a 6-km front.

The 53rd Rifle Division was deployed along the line (excluding) Kuzovlevo-Stremilovo, on a 10-km front.

The 17th Rifle Division was deployed along the line Stremilovo (excluding)-Kormashovka, on an 11-km front.

The army commanders' reserve was the 19th Rifle Division, which was located in Alekseevka, and the 298th Independent Machine Gun Battalion, located in the Dulovo area.

Army headquarters was in Yasenki. Maj. Gen. Golubev was the army commander.

As of November 16 the army commander was apprised of the following:

a) that the enemy was not active, limiting himself to bombing parts of the defensive line and engaging in artillery and mortar fire.
b) on the left, the 49th Army continued to attack throughout the day, while the enemy put up a stubborn defense.

The armies of the Western Front's central sector were not defending along a previously-prepared and fortified line (Volokolamsk, Mozhaisk, Detchino), but in those places where they had managed to delay the enemy's October offensive. It was only in the center of the sector, along the Nara River, that a favorable defensive line existed; along the right flank—the 5th Army, and on the left—the 43rd Army, the defensive lines were not favorably configured for the defending units. The defense was built, in accordance with the importance of the axes, on a normal or broad front; in both cases the defense was positional.

On the whole, the defense consisted of:

a) the divisions' units being arrayed in an almost-linear fashion, and chiefly deployed, because of heavy losses, along the forward edge;
b) a poorly-developed fire system, particularly along the boundaries of the formations;
c) an insufficiently-developed system of engineering defensive structures;
d) a poorly-developed system of anti-tank weapons, covering certain areas.

Rear structure

In its directive no. 022 of October 22 1941, the Western Front command issued the following instructions for organizing the rear services.

Distribution stations for the central sector's armies were designated in the following locations: 5th Army—Orekhovo-Zuevo, 33rd Army—Kurovskoe station, and 43rd Army—Voskresensk. Army supply bases: 5th Army—Fryazevo, Orekhovo-Zuevo, 33rd Army—Gzhel'-Kurovskoe, and 43rd Army—Bronnitsy, Voskresensk.

It was later ordered that the delivery of supplies and equipment from the *front* depots should be carried out by rail to the advanced sections of the army field depots. The delivery of supplies by auto transport should be undertaken only in exceptional cases, and only on the special order of the *front's* military council. The delivery of supplies to the troops from the advanced sections of the army field depots to the divisional terminals should be carried out using divisional transport, reinforcing it with army transport when necessary.

It was suggested by the military council that the armies' existing auto transport should be redistributed so as to guarantee the necessary deliveries to the divisions over 60-70 km. Battalions of horse-drawn transport should be used to strengthen the final leg of the supply chain. The delivery of supplies averaged ¼ of a combat load, ½ of a combat load of fuel, and day's requirement of food and forage over 75 km.

In the Moscow area there was a well-developed road network—railroads, paved and unpaved roads. The roads, despite the Germans' attempts to bomb them, were in good shape by the beginning of the defensive battles along the Nara River. The roads allowed us to carry out any kind of transport radiating from Moscow; the bad weather of autumn had almost no effect on the intensity of transport. However, there were no lateral roads; nor were there a sufficient number of convenient roads bypassing Moscow. This made the delivery of supplies to the front more difficult.

On November 16 the following supplies were available to the armies along the central sector.

Item	5th Army	33rd Army	43rd Army
Rifle rounds	2.3 combat loads	1 combat load	0.4 combat loads
Mortar rounds	0.1 combat loads	1.25 combat loads	0.5 combat loads
Artillery shells	1.2 combat loads	1.4 combat loads	0.98 combat loads
Fuel	0.75 combat loads	2.25 combat loads	2 combat loads
Food and forage	2-3 rations	2.75 rations	3 rations
Supplies in forward depots:			
Ammunition	0.2-2.3 combat loads	0.7-2.8 combat loads	0.1-2.5 combat loads
Fuel	0.5-2.5 combat loads	1.2-3.2 combat loads	1.3-2.9 combat loads
Food and forage	1-3 rations	1.7-2.2 rations	2-4 rations

Conclusions: the armies' supply systems was well organized, the road network guaranteed the necessary deliveries, and the presence of transport enabled their timely delivery. As regards the rear services, there was no threat to the combat effectiveness of the Western Front's central sector in defending the Nara.

German offensive activity on the Nara River

The Germans' second offensive on Moscow began in the middle of November along the right and left flanks of the Western Front.

As early as November 16 heavy fighting was going on along the flanks against the advancing German troops, in the center, along the front of the 5th, 33rd, and 43rd armies, it was quiet: our units continued to fortify their lines and carried out reconnaissance; both armies engaged in periodic artillery and mortar fire.

On November 19 the enemy offensive began along the 5th Army's front. From 1030 these forces were fighting stubbornly to repulse attacks by German infantry, supported by tanks. The enemy managed to push back the 144th, 50th, and 32nd rifle divisions, and they were forced to fail back to a new line.

The German offensive along the 5th Army's front was part of their general offensive against the Western Front's right wing; the right flank of the enemy group, which according to the German command, was to envelop Moscow from the north, passed along the 5th Army's front. In this area the large-scale battle of Istra was waged in November; right-flank units of the 5th Army were drawn into this fighting. Thus in describing the defensive fighting along the Nara River we will not speak of the battles being waged along the army's right flank at the end of November and beginning of December 1941, as these have already been described in detail in the section on the Istra battles (Chapter 3).

One should merely note that the 5th Army, which lay along the shortest route leading to Moscow, played an important role in the city's defense in the autumn and winter of 1941. Standing astride the most important route to Moscow (including the Minsk-Moscow highway), it stood against the enemy and by ferociously counterattacking along its right flank it had changed the situation in its favor by December 3.

At the same time that fierce fighting was going on along the 5th Army's right flank, it was quiet on the 33rd and 43rd armies' front. Their units continued to fortify their lines, improve their defenses, and reconnoiter the enemy position. The enemy was not active, limiting himself to sporadic artillery and mortar fire.

From November 19 the enemy's reconnaissance became more active along the 33rd Army's front. On November 21 the enemy attacked along the axis Biryulevo-Myakshevo, evidently intending to break through to the Naro-Fominsk-Kubinka road, so as to then get into the 5th Army's rear. The enemy's intentions were not realized. The Germans' attacks were beaten back with heavy losses. In this sector the Nara proved to be an insuperable barrier for the enemy. On November 22, the second day, the Germans limited themselves to reconnoitering the Chichkovo area with a small detachment, supported by tanks. The enemy was evidently looking for other routes for his offensive.

During the next few days the Germans more than once bombarded different sectors of our front with artillery and mortars. Behind these bombardments followed infantry attacks, supported by tanks. The enemy conducted a reconnaissance in force, probing for weak spots in our defense. His methodical actions accustomed our units to a certain consistency in repulsing enemy attacks.

During the latter half of November 29, along the 43rd Army's front, there was observed a large concentration of wheeled transport in the Chubarovo area, and crossing equipment in the Gorki area, and infantry in the Ol'khovo area. The enemy evidently was planning to cross the Nara River in this area for the purpose of advancing on Moscow along the Warsaw highway.

The concentration of infantry and wheeled transport was dispersed by our artillery fire and aviation. The enemy's attempt to organize a crossing failed.

On November 30 it was quiet along the front. The enemy was not active. At times he would begin a sporadic fire along a few sectors of the front, predominantly concentrated along our left flank.

The German breakthrough along the Naro-Fominsk Axis

On December 1 there was a sharp change in the situation. On the morning of this day the enemy opened up a powerful artillery and mortar barrage along the entire front of the 33rd Army, except for the sector defended by the 222nd Rifle Division. The enemy, under the cover of this fire and that of his aviation, launched an attack against the army's left flank. At that moment, when the army's attention was focused on this flank, the enemy's motorized units of unknown strength, supported by 60-70 tanks, forced the Nara River near the village of Novaya and, lunging forward, reached the Naro-Fominsk-Kubinka road, after which they continued to attack in the direction of the Minsk-Moscow highway.

In moving forward along the Naro-Fominsk-Kubinka road, the Germans immediately encountered sectors with obstacles; several tanks blew up on mines as they reached the road. This forced the Germans to turn off the road and advance on Akulovo along the road's shoulders and sparse woods, while removing the obstacles. The Germans moved extremely slowly and it was only at 1600 on December 1 that the enemy tanks reached Akulovo. At the same time the head of their motorized infantry column was moving on Malye Semenychi. The enemy was threatening the 5th Army's flank and rear.

At the same time the enemy was bombing Zvenigorod intensely and threatening to break through along this sector. The enemy's "wedges" from Novaya and Zvenigorod were evidently aimed at Golitsyno, where the Germans intended to close their "pincers" around the 5th Army and open the shortest route to Moscow from the west.

But the enemy broke through our defensive front not only at Novaya. Powerful enemy forces that same day attacked south of Naro-Fominsk from the Ateptsevo and Sliznevo, aiming their blow at Mogutovo and Machikhino. Upon seizing these locales, the enemy could attack through Kuznetsovo and reach Naro-Fominsk or Kiev roads and surround, with his Akulovo group, the 33rd Army's right flank.

The 110th Rifle Division was defending this sector and putting up stubborn resistance. A fierce fight broke out in the woods. The insufficiently dense defense of the division's units, as well as the absence of reserves, made it impossible to hold the enemy's attack, and breaking through the division's front he penetrated further to the northeast and at 1600 on December 1 had gotten as far as Sevelovka and Volkovskaya Dacha.

The 113th Rifle Division to the left was fighting at this time with the enemy, who was attacking in the area of Kamenskoe and Klovo. A large enemy group, supported here by 30 tanks, routed the 113th Rifle Division's 1290th Rifle Regiment, which was defending here and moved further in the direction of Sergovka.

The same kind of threat was arising on the army's left flank, as on the right. However, the greater danger was in the area of Novaya and Akulovo.

The situation was saved by the 5th Army's 32nd Rifle Division (Col. Polosukhin, commanding), whose rear had been exposed by the enemy's advance toward Kubinka. Having quickly occupied a defensive position near Akulovo, the division's artillery fire prevented the enemy from emerging from its narrow wooded defile on to the open area before Akulovo. Not being able to go around the numerous obstacles in the woods, and scared of the mined sectors, the enemy tanks bunched up near the road at the exit from the woods toward Akulovo and were fired upon at point-blank range by our artillery and attacked with bottles of flammable material. Aside from the 32nd Rifle Division's various units, the 5th Army staff, thrown into the fighting by automobile from Kubinka, also took an active part in destroying the enemy tanks.

Having lost 35 tanks and the opportunity of breaking through to Akulovo, the Germans turned around, having decided to reach the Minsk-Moscow road by another, roundabout, way. Near the village of Goloven'ki they turned to the east and headed along the road Goloven'ki-height 210.8, through Petrovskoe and Yushkovo, toward Golitsyno. On December 2 the Germans' forward units (478th Motorized Regiment, supported by 12 tanks) occupied Yushkovo and Burtsevo and at the same time continued to bring up their main forces to this area. To secure this move, the enemy, with part of his forces (200-300 motorized infantry, with 15 tanks), fortified their position in the area of height 210.8

The German breakthroughs in the center of our Western Front, although small in scope, could nonetheless have serious consequences. They coincided in time with the enemy's northern group reaching the line of the Moscow-Volga Canal, and the southern group reaching the area of Venev and Mikhailov. The German command was hoping that the successful development of the breakthroughs would disorganize our front, as a result of which the advance of the northern and southern groups would be made easier. It's possible that by breaking through in the Naro-Fominsk area the Germans calculated on attracting our reserves here, which would lessen the Red Army's ability to launch a blow in another place. Thus relatively small breakthroughs in our center could have major operational consequences.

This is the way the Western Front command saw it, taking note of the particular danger of the possibility that the enemy might reach the Minsk-Moscow highway at Kubinka. In a December 2 order by *front* commander Gen. Zhukov, Lt. Gen. Yefremov, the commander of the 33rd Army, was instructed to: "With a group, which is being concentrated in the area of Kokoshkino station and Aprelevka, and consisting of the 18th Rifle Brigade, two ski battalions, one tank battalion, plus another 15 tanks, an anti-tank regiment, with rocket artillery, attack the enemy along the Yushkovo axis. The group is to then swiftly attack in the direction of Goloven'ki and restore the situation.

The blow is to be launched on the morning of December 3.
I am personally entrusting the group's command to you. Report on execution.

Upon receiving this assignment, the 33rd Army's commander decided on the following: by means of a concentric blow from the northeast and southeast, encircle and destroy the enemy's Yushkovo group, while at the same time pinning down his main forces by attacking their flank from the Rassudovo direction toward height 210.8. The group was to then swiftly attack in the direction of height 210.8 and Goloven'ki and liquidate the overly bold enemy and completely restore the situation on the army's right flank.

For this, the 18th Rifle Brigade, operating with the 5th Army's 20th Tank Brigade (six tanks), attacking from Golitsyno, was to launch its blow from the jumping-off point along the line Taraskovo-the woods to the south in the direction of height 203.8 and Yushkovo; the tank group (140th and 136th tank battalions—21 tanks, under the command of Col. Safir), along with two ski battalions, was to operate from the wooded area east of Burtsevo and Petrovskoe, in order to envelop the enemy group from the southeast.

At the same time a second group of tanks (5th Tank Brigade, with 11 tanks, under the command of Lt. Col. Sakhno), with a detachment of infantry 140 men strong, was to attack height 210.8 from the area of Rassudovo, with the task of destroying the enemy in this area and preventing the arrival of his reserves to the Yushkovo group.

The enemy that had broken through to the Yushkovo-Burtsevo area was in a difficult position, because he had expended a significant part of his forces along the way, while at the same time our troops barred the way. However, the 33rd Army's situation at this time was also serious: it had to scatter its forces, while at the same time success against the enemy could only be achieved by concentrating them. In the meantime, one group of the 33rd Army's forces was to prevent the Germans from developing their success near Mogutovo, while another under the army commander was to liquidate the enemy breakthrough in the Yushkovo-Burtsevo area.

The accomplishment of the latter task was complicated by the activities of the enemy's aviation, which during December 2-3 bombed those routes by which our troops could concentrate at the breakthrough area.

Moreover, by means of bombing and strafing, the enemy air force operated against our forces in the area of Taraskovo, Aprelevka, and Alabino.

The main fighting on December 3 occurred in the Yushkovo-Burtsevo area; it continued throughout the night of December 3-4 and all of December 4. The fighting was fierce. Our units operated decisively and with great skill. The enemy, pressed in a vice in the Burtsevo-Yushkovo dead end, was fired upon at close range; having lost a large amount of men and matériel, he was forced to turn back and, with the pitiful remnants of his units, hurriedly fell back to height 210.8, and then to Goloven'ki, and then crossing the Nara, return to his jumping-off position. The enemy's attempt to move up reserves to his units that had broken through to the Yushkovo-Burtsevo area was unsuccessful, because the narrow forest road was under the observation and fire of our aviation.

During the battle the enemy suffered a serious defeat, leaving more than 2,000 dead on the battlefield. The Germans' overall losses reached 7,500 men. Our troops captured the following: 27 knocked-out tanks, two armored cars, 36 guns, 40 machine guns, ten mortars, and a large amount of shells, rifles, wheeled transport, bullets, horses, wagons, and other equipment.

At the same time the enemy was being destroyed in the Yushkovo-Burtsevo area, we were liquidating his breakthrough along the Mogutovo-Machikhino sector.

The 110th Rifle Division, with nine tanks, strained every fiber to prevent the enemy from reaching Mogutovo. However, its forces were not sufficient for this. The enemy captured Mogutovo and Machikhino and drove on Kuznetsovo. However, the advance along the wooded sector was not without its difficulties, and the enemy, having exhausted himself in overcoming them, suffered heavy losses in the fighting and was halted and thrown back by a counterattack by units of the 110th Rifle Division from the area of the Kuvyakino state farm. Having launched a powerful blow against the Germans in the Mogutovo area on December 4, units of the 110th Rifle Division occupied that locale and pursued the enemy in a southwesterly direction. At the same time, a composite regiment of the 43rd Army, operating with units of the 33rd Army in eliminating the enemy breakthrough, knocked the Germans out of Machikhino and pursued them in the direction of Plaksino.

By the morning of December 5, through the efforts of units from the 33rd and 43rd armies, the enemy breakthrough along the line Ateptsevo-Klovo was eliminated; the Germans were thrown back to their jumping-off positions with heavy losses and our troops occupied their former defensive lines.

The enemy had been thoroughly defeated and his threat to reach the direct route to Moscow and split our front into separate parts was eliminated. The 5th Army's victory near Akulovo, and the 33rd Army's at Yushkovo and Burtsevo acquired all the greater significance in that they were the Red Army's first major victories during the Moscow operation. From them begins the turning point: the growing victories of our troops, and the increasing defeats of the enemy.

Conclusions regarding the defensive fighting along the Nara River

The defensive fighting along the Nara River, despite its comparatively small scope, is very instructive.

1. A water barrier, even such an insignificant one as the Nara River, given its proper fortification and the resolute behavior of the troops may prove to be an insuperable barrier to an enemy, even in winter conditions.
2. Despite the ice cover and the possibility of crossing from one shore to another over the ice, the forcing of a river in modern conditions will often be linked to those points, the exits from which will present motor-mechanized equipment the possibility of broad maneuver. Thus the fight for water barriers will be to a significant degree a battle for the crossings.
3. Due to necessity, the armies' defense of the Western Front's central sector was not built upon previously chosen and prepared lines; the defense lacked the necessary depth, a well-developed fire system, and sufficient anti-tank weapons. This created difficulties for the troops of the 5th, 33rd, and 43rd armies. The German breakthroughs at Novaya, Ateptsevo and Sliznevo show that in modern conditions the defensive zone cannot be secure if it lacks sufficient depth and the approaches to it are not subject to heavy fire from our artillery.
4. The following considerations in the elimination of the breakthroughs along the Naro-Fominsk axis deserve attention:
    a) our troops' energetic and skillful actions in quickly dealing with the German units that had broken through;
    b) the good work of the 5th and 33rd army staffs in eliminating the danger;

c) the precise activities of the artillery, which bravely and accurately hit the enemy's tanks and motorized infantry near Akulovo and Yushkovo;
d) the skillful work of our aviation, which prevented the enemy from moving up reserves to the Yushkovo area.

5 Also worthy of notice is the enemy's conduct before December 1: the enemy for some time "accustomed" our units to its barrages and the methodical infantry attacks which followed. During one of these barrages along neighboring sectors, the Germans attacked near Novaya on that portion of the front (defended by the 222nd Rifle Division) where no barrage was being conducted.

6 As regards troop control, of note is the division of command in the 33rd Army into two operational groups—one, headed by the army commander dealt with eliminating the German breakthrough at near Novaya and, the other, headed by the army's military council member and chief of staff, was fighting at the time with the enemy, which had broken through in the area of Mogutovo and Machikhino.

7 It's necessary to emphasize that behind the forward German units attacking toward Moscow, there were no large reserves in the second and follow-on echelons, as a result of which the breakthroughs at Novaya Ateptsevo and Sliznevo were not exploited. This speaks to the excessive self-confidence of the Fascist command and the adventurist nature of its offensive plans.

5

Defensive activities on the Western Front's left wing. The defense of Tula

The 49th and 50th armies' defensive battles from the latter half of October to the beginning of December 1941 unfolded at the same time the German command conducted its first and second general offensives on Moscow. The significance of both armies' defensive actions is quite great. Their overall goal of wearing out the enemy through endless holding actions was achieved. Doubtlessly, the central point of the defense on the *front's* left wing was the heroic defense of Tula. That we held on to the city was the result of the overall efforts of the 50th Army's units and that of the Tula workers, who held their city under the leadership of the party organizations and military command. Here the front and rear fused into a single monolithic whole.

The fighting for Tula acquired an operational-strategic significance, and its stubborn defense broke one of the German pincers that was striving to close to the east of Moscow.

Combat activities on the *front's* left wing took place under the control of the Supreme Commander-in-Chief, comrade Stalin. The Western Front command, under Gen. Zhukov, was a talented executor of the *Stavka's* plan.

The overall result of these combat activities was as follows: the enemy offensive was halted and even as the fighting was going on, the prerequisites for launching a powerful counterblow were being created, followed by our troops' further offensive.

One of the characteristic factors that complicated the situation was the fact that at first the defensive battles were taking place along the boundary between the Western and Bryansk fronts. This placed great demands on the organization of the coordination of both *fronts* and was carried out under the *Stavka's* direct control during the period of the most decisive actions. When it became necessary, because of the situation, to unite the Tula axis with the Western Front, the *Stavka* on November 10 1941 subordinated the 50th Army to the Western Front.

The defensive fighting on the *front's* left wing during the period under review was characterized by a variety of operational-tactical forms and the alternation and combination of some with others. They are described in the present chapter.

The 49th Army's retreat to the Oka River and the defensive battles, October 15-November 10

In the period October 15-20, when the Bryansk Front's right-flank 50th Army was stubbornly withdrawing to the Tula area, the Western Front's 49th Army, following bitter fighting for Kaluga against units of the enemy's 17th, 137th, 52nd, and 260th infantry divisions, was also withdrawing to the east and northeast.

During this period the army's units conducted holding actions along intermediate lines and by October 23 had concentrated on the following sectors:

Two regiments from the right-flank 194th Rifle Division occupied the line Stremilovo-Butyrki-Kalugino-Drakino, covering Serpukhov from the west; the third regiment was in reserve in the Proletarskii area.

In the Glazovo area (three km north of Serpukhov) the firing positions were occupied by the 992nd Anti-Tank Artillery Regiment and the 570th Artillery Regiment, while two regiments from the 60th Rifle Division defended the sector Vyazovnya (seven km east of Vysokinichi)-Troitskoe, while the third regiment defended Tarusa, with a screen to the southeast near Antonovka (ten km southwest of Tarusa) and was observing the line Kresty-Petrishchevo.

The 5th Guards Rifle Division, after being relieved in the Aleksin area by units of the 238th Rifle Division, had been pulled back into the area of the Tarusskaya station for refitting.

The 238th Rifle Division was defending on the eastern bank of the Oka River to the south of Tarusa (along the line from Bunyrevo to Shchukino), repulsing with artillery and mortar fire the enemy's attempts to cross the river.

All the army's intelligence means had uncovered the presence along its front of the 17th, 137th, 260th, and 52nd infantry divisions, and the XLIII Army Corps' 131st and 31st infantry divisions in the Aleksin area along the boundary with the 50th Army.

Thus by October 23 the sector Stremilovo-Kalugino-Drakino, around 35 km, was covered by only two rifle regiments, which undoubtedly created a threat to Serpukhov, enabling the enemy to break through the 194th Rifle Division's comparatively weak screen, all the more so as this sector was on the boundary with the 43rd Army and, as such, served as the axis of the entire left wing of the *front's* defense.

The enemy's breakthrough along this boundary, besides the immediate threat to Serpukhov, could lead to, first of all, to the separation of the *front's* left-wing armies and, second, would enable the enemy the cut the Moscow road, which could not fail to have an effect on our forces' Tula group.

The situation around Serpukhov was evaluated in a timely manner by the *Stavka* and the *front* command; afterwards the right flank was more securely covered. In particular, the 415th and 7th Guards rifle divisions were transferred to the 49th Army from the *Stavka* reserve, while several rifle brigades were also brought up later.

During October 22-23 the enemy's 17th, 137th, 260th, and 52nd infantry divisions were not particularly active along the army's right flank and center; separate groups, supported by intensive artillery and mortar fire, attempted to cross the Oka in the Aleksin area and take the town. All the German attacks were beaten back.

During October 24-25 the Germans strengthened their pressure on the army's right flank, with the objective of breaking through along the boundary with the 43rd Army. Simultaneously, units of the Germans' 260th, 52nd, and 31st infantry divisions attacked in the direction of Tarusa and Aleksin, seeking to capture both towns. The German attacks against Aleksin were once again beaten back; in the Tarusa area the enemy, supported by aviation, which bombed the 60th Rifle Division's artillery on its firing positions, pushed back our forces and by 1600 on October 24 captured Tarusa and continued to advance on Serpukhov.

On orders from the army commander, two regiments from the 60th Rifle Division counterattacked from the Troitskoe area with the objective of throwing the enemy out of Tarusa. However, the counterattack was not successful.

Thus in the period under review the Germans sought to break through the army's center and along both its flanks.

Under these conditions, the 49th Army's commander, Gen. Zakharkin, ordered the commander of the 5th Guards Rifle Division to move up part of his force to the Tarusa area, to the sector Bekhovo-Velogozh, to oppose the enemy which had broken through, while he was to leave for the Serpukhov area with his main body in order to strengthen the army's right flank, where the German-Fascist units were striving to break through our troops' defenses.

During October 24-25 the army's air force carried out a number of strafing and bombing attacks against the enemy's motorized infantry in the area of Tarusa and Petrishchevo, destroying his crossings across the Oka in the Aleksin area, while conducting reconnaissance in front of the 49th Army.

In the following period up to November 1 combat activities along the 49th Army's front were characterized by separate collisions for the purpose of improving the position along the occupied lines. By the end of October the 49th Army was solidly holding the line of the woods east of Burinovo-Voronino-Borovna, and then along the northern and eastern banks of the Protva and Oka rivers as far as Aleksin.

During November 1-10 the following events took place along the army's front. On November 2 the 5th Guards and 60th rifle divisions launched a partial attack along the sector Voronino-Sinyatino-Maleevo, but as a result of a powerful enemy counterattack, fell back 1-1½ km from the aforementioned line. On November 3 the 5th Guards Rifle Division once again attacked and captured Sinyatino, where it destroyed up to a company of enemy infantry. During the night of November 5-6 the division captured Voronino, routing in this area up to two German infantry companies. From the morning of November 7 the division's units occupied Vysokoe, after which they took up defensive positions along the sector Voronino-Vysokoe-Sinyatino.

The 60th Rifle Division, following its unsuccessful attack on Maleevo, had by November 6 reverted to defense along the line Yekaterinovka-Borovna.

During this period the 194th Rifle Division continued to defend along the line (excluding) Borovna-east of Kremenki, and then along the northern bank of the Protva River to Drakino.

By November 7 the 7th Guards Rifle Division was located on the sector Shatovo-Noviki-Dashkovka, where it was preparing a defense.

The 238th Rifle Division occupied its previous defensive position, repulsing various German attempts to force the Oka.

Thus as a result of the 49th Army's defensive actions through November 10 one may note that despite the difficult conditions of withdrawing along the entire front after the fighting around Kaluga, as well as a maneuverable defense along certain sectors, the 49th Army's units held the line of the Oka River, thus placing a limit to the German-Fascist forces' further advance. On the other hand, the maintenance of this line doubtlessly had an influence of the course of the defensive fighting around Tula by depriving the enemy the opportunity of cutting the Moscow road in the Serpukhov area. The elimination of the enemy's attempts to break through to break through to the Moscow road along the Sukhodol axis (southeast of Aleksin), in conjunction with the 50th Army, once again confirmed the great significance of the 49th Army's defensive battles.

The operational situation along the Tula Axis by the end of October 1941. The two sides' plans

The retreat of the 50th Army's units and the disposition of our forces for the defense of Tula

During October the forces of the Bryansk Front, waging defensive battles along various lines, retreated to the east and northeast.

The enemy, having seized Likhvin, Yurino, Kireevskoe, and Sorokino, continued to concentrate troops in the Mtsensk area, where according to prisoner reports the 3rd and 4rth panzer divisions (both from the XXIV Panzer Corps) from Guderian's Second Panzer Army were located, while on October 22 in the area of Kipet' and Nikolo-Gastun', according to prisoner reports, units of two infantry divisions were located.

On October 24 the fighting in the area northeast of Mtsensk, where along the Gorodishche-Mtsensk sector, there was no less than one infantry division and about 110 tanks, was particularly fierce.

The course of the fighting showed that the enemy, in attacking from Belev to the northeast and southeast, intended to get astride our communications in the Chern' area and link up with his Mtsensk group for a further offensive on Tula. Combat occurred in conditions of poor weather, during a period of rains and fog. Visibility usually did not exceed 2-4 km, and the temperature not more than 2-3 degrees centigrade.

The condition of the roads did not allow for the movement of auto transport, while animal-drawn transport moved with difficulty; to a significant degree this determined the development of combat activity along the good roads, particularly along the Orel-Tula road.

As early as October 13 the *front* headquarters in Belev organized a combat sector, with forces of about a single rifle division in strength, with the task of defending the Belev area, the evacuation of matériel, equipment, and transport from the area of Belev, Ul'yanovo, and Bolkhov, and for covering the *front* staff's trains. On October 23 units from five rifle divisions, plus another 1,000 men from other formations, were already subordinated to the Belev sector.

The 50th Army's forces, having suffered heavy casualties, were retreating under enemy blows to the east and northeast; by 1000 on October 25 units of the Belev combat sector passed through the line Chelyuskino-Manaenki.

50th Army headquarters was located in Tula.

The Bryansk Front command, having evaluated the enemy's actions as a pair of concentric blows by motor-mechanized units along the flanks of the *front's* armies from Kaluga to Aleksin and from Mtsensk to Tula, for the purpose of securing an advance on Moscow by means of capturing the Tula area, in an October 25 directive (no. 316) ordered the 50th Army (217th, 258th, 260th, 278th, 279th, 290th, 299th, 173rd, and 154th rifle divisions, the 108th Tank and 31st Cavalry divisions, and formations from the former 26th Army) to fall back by October 30 under the cover of rearguards to the line: Pavshino-Sloboda-Krapivna-Plavsk-Novo-Pokrovskoe-Novosil'-Verkhov'e. They were to organize a rigid defense along the following axes: Serpukhov-Tula—with two rifle divisions; Plavsk-Tula—with three reinforced rifle divisions, and also having not less than a rifle division in Tula. An intermediate line of withdrawal was designated along the line Khanino-Odoevo-Arsen'evo-Chern'-Voroshilovo, to which the troops were to fall back on by the end of October 27.

In order to cover Tula from the west and to secure the right flank and rear of the Belev combat sector along the line Pavshino-Bredikhino, on October 24 the 194th Rifle Division, numbering about 4,500 men, was moved forward from the troops along this sector. Later one this division carried out a very important task—preventing the enemy from crossing over to the eastern bank of the Upa River (in November the division became part of the 258th Rifle Division).

During the fighting waged by the the Bryansk Front's right-flank 50th Army along the line Khanino-Chelyuskino-Manaenki-Chern', it was established by all our intelligence means that by October 26 an infantry division apiece was operating in the areas of Kipet', Nikolo-Gastun', and Nikolo-Gastun'-Belev; in the Likhvin area the concentration of up to an infantry division was noted; on the Gorodishche-Mtsensk sector a single infantry division and 110 tanks from the 3rd Panzer Division were operating; that is, in all on the Tula axis up to four infantry divisions and one panzer division were operating, with the latter operating from Mtsensk along the Orel road to Tula.

The enemy, having seized with his forward units the southern outskirts of Plavsk, on the morning of October 27, and following a powerful artillery, mortar and aviation preparation, attacked the 108th Tank Division's 108th Motorized Rifle Regiment, the 11th Tank Brigade's 11th Motorized Rifle Battalion with up to a battalion of infantry and 18-20 tanks, and at 1800 on October 27 bypassed Plavsk with his armor from the east and west, heading for the Zhitovo and Karamyshevo areas, concentrating in Karamyshevo up to 40 tanks during the night of October 27-28.

Troop control was carried out under difficult conditions, because communications with the 50th Army's headquarters worked only intermittently (both radio and cable); as a result of the washed out roads, communications officers carried out their duties with a great deal of delay.

In order to stabilize the defensive front on the approaches to Tula, the army command established the main defensive line along the southern edge of the woods along the front Solosovka-Yasenki-Smirnoe, which was prepared during October 26-28 by units of the 290th Rifle Division. A forward edge was chosen along the Solova River. Before the arrival of the 290th Rifle Division, the main line was being prepared by a construction battalion, which dug trenches and anti-tank ditches.

In connection with the crossing by the enemy's forward units to the northern bank of the Solova River, the army command moved up to the line Zakharovka-Nikolaevka the 173rd Rifle Division, which had been falling back from the Belev area through Odoevo, with the task of attacking the enemy flank and throwing him back to the south bank of the Solova River. But the enemy took Zakharovka and Nikolaevka by assault. The 173rd Rifle Division fell back to the Goloven'ki area, where at 1600 on October 29 it was once again attacked by tanks carrying infantry and was falling back to the southwestern outskirts of Tula. The activities of the 50th Army's few aircraft were made much more difficult, because the airfields, as a result of the poor weather, were inoperable for takeoff by combat aircraft. In particular, on October 29 no combat or reconnaissance flights were conducted.

During the latter half of October 29 the enemy, accompanied by dive bombers and assault aircraft, broke through the 290th Rifle Division's position in the area of Yasnaya Polyana. About 20-25 tanks broke into the woods to the north of the town and, bypassing our infantry, by 1600 had advanced as far as Kosaya Gora. By this time the 31st Cavalry Division was deployed in the area of Kosaya Gora, following a difficult 80-km march. The enemy's automatic riflemen, carried on tanks (4-5 men on a tank), having dismounted and dispersed along the forest, opened a disorderly fire against the 31st Cavalry Division's position and inflicted significant losses on the division's mountain gun crews, which had been firing on the enemy. Then the Fascist tanks (12-15 tanks and several armored cars) moved on to Tula, on the approaches to which they were repulsed by the 156th NKVD Regiment, but chiefly by artillery fire from by 732nd PVO Regiment.

The army's forces fell back to the north and organized a defense on the immediate approaches to Tula along the line Ratovo-Kharino-Ivanovskie Dachi-Osinovaya Gora.

The activities of our air force were once again made more difficult as a result of the poor condition of the airfields, which prevented the bombers from taking off. Assault aircraft were employed, which attacked the enemy along the Mtsensk-Plavsk road.

The threat of the Germans taking Tula from the south demanded the unification of the immediate control of the troops on the approaches to the city, as a result of which on October 29 the commander of the 50th Army created an auxiliary control organ for himself in the form of the Tula combat sector. Included in the sector's forces were the 217th, 173rd, 290th, 260th, and 154th rifle divisions, the 58th Reserve and 1005th rifle regiments.

At this time the divisions' strengths varied greatly: from 600 to 2,000 and more men, but on the average about 1,000 men. The largest were the 154th and 290th rifle divisions, with more than 2,000 men apiece. The 58th Reserve and 1005th rifle regiments had on the average up to 600 men apiece.

The number of guns and mortars among the units of the Tula combat sector was insignificant; for example, the 154th Rifle Division had two 122mm guns, the 217th Rifle Division 12 guns (nine 76mm and three 152mm), the 58th Reserve Rifle Regiment had eight guns (four 76mm and four 45mm), and the 1005th Rifle Regiment had a single 45mm gun; there were ten mortars (eight in the 217th Rifle Division, and two in the 58th Reserve Rifle Regiment).

Things were no better regarding the availability of heavy machine guns; for example, there was one such machine gun in the 290th Rifle Division, and seven in the 217th Rifle Division. The number of rifles as a proportion of soldiers was as follows: 154th Rifle Division—34%; 260th Rifle Division—56.7%; 217th Rifle Division—62.7%; 290th Rifle Division—73%; 58th Reserve Rifle Regiment—59% and; 1005th Rifle Regiment—74%.

By the end of October 29 the army's forces occupied the following position: the 194th Rifle Division occupied the line Pavshino-Bredikhino station; the 258th Rifle Division defended with part of its forces the northern outskirts of Tula, while the remainder was concentrated inside the city; the 173rd Rifle Division, along with the 58th Reserve Rifle Regiment, continued to withdraw under fire toward Tula; the 290th Rifle Division, after enemy tanks broke through its front along the line Krivtsovo-Smirnoe, was falling back to the Tula area; the 260th Rifle Division was deploying along the southwestern outskirts of Tula; the 217th Rifle Division was in the area of Trufanovo, with the task of reaching the Tula area; the 154th Rifle Division was concentrated in Tula. There was no word from the 299th Rifle Division. It was afterwards learned that this division, as the 50th Army was falling back to the east, passed through the enemy rear in the Plavsk area and emerged in the Stalinogorsk area (40 km southeast of Tula), and then was holding the Dedilovo area. The 31st Cavalry Division fell back to the Tula area, having received instructions to concentrate in Chastnoe (ten km east of Tula).

The enemy, by occupying the woods to the north of Yasnaya Polyana before October 29, guarded the massing of his forces for the further advance on Tula. Many railroad and road bridges were not blown up by our units during their retreat.

The German command's plan for taking Tula

The German command's immediate objective was the capture of Tula, for the purpose of launching a follow-on blow against the flank and rear of our troops defending Moscow.

In order to carry out this assignment, a powerful group of mobile troops—Guderian's Second Panzer Army, was being moving forward along the Tula axis.

Just how seriously the Germans regarded the capture of Tula can be seen from order no. 21 of October 15 to the Second Panzer Army. One of the chief tasks assigned to the army was the rapid breakthrough from Mtsensk through Tula, the seizure of the Tula railroad junction and the important industrial regions along with Tula, Stalinogorsk and Kashira, followed by the encirclement of Moscow from the southeast and the closing of the ring to the east.

For this purpose the Second Panzer Army was reinforced with the LIII Army Corps (112th, 167th, and 56th infantry divisions) and the XLIII Army Corps (31st and 131st infantry divisions).

The breakthrough to Tula and the crossings over the Oka was to be carried out by the reinforced XXIV Panzer Corps, to which were attached the 17th Panzer Division, the *Grossdeutschland* Infantry Regiment, the headquarters of the 792nd Artillery Regiment, and the XLVII Panzer Corps' artillery, an engineering-construction battalion, the 18th Panzer Regiment, and other units, which were brought up through Orel as they were freed up following the fighting.

The plans for the XLVII Panzer Corps depended on the XXIV Panzer Corps' success in taking Tula; the corps was to take Kolomna and create bridgeheads across the Moscow River.

The realization of this plan in October was foiled by our troops' resistance. The fighting in the Tula area became protracted.

The Second Panzer Army was to advance on Tula from the south on November 10, take the city and move to the east with its main forces. It was first of all planned to take the Tula-Venev road, from which it would advance in the direction of the Tula-Serpukhov road and there close the encirclement ring with units of the XLIII Army Corps (131st and 31st infantry divisions), outflanking Tula from the west and northeast.

The XLIII Army Corps had the task of attacking to the northeast, of supporting Gen. Guderian's panzer army's operation and, in conjunction with its tank forces, to encircle the Tula group of Soviet troops between the Upa and Oka rivers south of Aleksin. In this regard, particular attention was attached to the swiftest gaining of the Tula-Serpukhov road and closing it around Kostrovo (22 km northwest of Tula).

Thus the XLIII Army Corps was to carry out its mission by attacking the boundary between the 43rd Army's left flank and the 49th Army's right flank.

The 50th Army's objectives in the overall plan for defeating the enemy's Tula group

In order to defeat the enemy's Tula group, the Bryansk Front command developed an operational plan for its armies for the period November 1-15. The operation's goals were as follows: 1) to destroy the enemy forces which had broken through Plavsk to the Tula area, and; 2) to stabilize the defensive front of the Bryansk Front's armies.

The realization of these goals was foreseen by the plan in three stages.

For the operation the 50th Army consisted of: 217th, 154th, 260th, 258th 194th, 413th, 299th, and 290th rifle divisions, 31st Cavalry Division, 32nd Tank Brigade, 108th Tank Division, 9th Guards Mortar Regiment, 58th Reserve Rifle Regiment, 156th NKVD Rifle Regiment, 1005th Rifle Regiment, 51st Local Rifle Battalion, and a battalion of militia.

The 50th Army was assigned the following tasks by stage: during the first stage (November 1-6), to securely defend Tula by launching a counterblow against the enemy by the 194th Rifle Division from the area of Intyushevo and Khlynovo in the general direction of Mikhalkovo (2.5 km southwest of Tula); by the 413th Rifle Division from the Volokhov area in the direction of Novyi Tul'skii (both locales five and 15 km southeast of Tula) and prepare a shock group for defeating the enemy in the direction of Shchekino and to secure this blow from the north and northwest; during the second stage (November 7-10) to secure the operation from the northwest along the line Khomyakovo-Nekrasovo-Plekhanovo, and with the main forces launch a blow along the road to Shchekino (20 km south of Tula) in order to destroy the enemy group in cooperation with the 3rd Army to the south;

during the third stage (November 11-15) to pursue the enemy and reach the front Pavshino-Sloboda-Krapivna-Plavsk, and there organize a solid defense, with the main forces in the area of Tula and Plavsk, with the reserves in Dedilovo.

The 50th Army was to attack at dawn on November 7. Front aviation's main forces in the first stage were directed at the destruction of the enemy in the Tula area.

Preparing Tula for defense—organising the city's defense

The construction of defensive works on the far approaches to Tula was begun in the first days of October 1941. Defensive works were built near Chern'; along the Oka River on the front Belev-Likhvin- Kaluga; along the Plava River; along the Solova River-Yasnaya Polyana-Solosovka-Yasenki-Smirnoe However, given the enemy advance, the work on these lines was not completed.

Work began on a defensive system around the city on October 20. The civil population of Tula was mobilized for this purpose; the work was supervised by the chiefs of the defensive sectors—the first secretaries of the district party (VKP(b)) committees.

At an October 25 meeting of the provincial party committee, attended by the deputy commander and member of the Bryansk Front's military council, the plan for building defensive works was refined.

In all, three defensive lines were built:

> The first—on the approaches to Tula—consisted of common field fortifications (trenches, mine fields, anti-tank ditches, etc.).
> The second and third defensive lines represented a system of barricades made of wood, concrete slag, scrap metal, and other available materials. The barricades were covered by stakes.

The second line ran, for the most part, along Lev Tolstoy and Technical streets, while the third ran from the railroad bridge to Khomutovskaya Street. Part of the 732nd PVO Regiment's artillery was used for anti-tank defense. Work was carried out non-stop, despite the action of the enemy air force, by whose fire a number of people were killed and wounded.

The city defense committee, created by a decision of the State Defense Committee, under the chairmanship of the provincial party committee's first secretary, comrade Zhavoronkov, took an active part in supervising the construction of the defensive works, the work of the factories repairing and making weapons for the Red Army units, the evacuation of the industrial concerns' equipment and material goods and labor force, the formation of a Tula worker's regiment, and other measures for defending the city. In supporting the army command's measures, the city defense committee undertook the most energetic and emergency measures for repairing tanks, armored trains, the guards mortar units' equipment, cars, and other military equipment. Having mobilized the city's transport, the committee used it to aid the army, sought to restore the permanent communications lines at the request of the 50th Army staff, improved roads in the necessary places, and produced digging implements necessary for engineering work.

By the beginning of the Germans' advance on Tula the Tula worker's regiment had been formed in the city. The formation of combat units from the local workers had begun as early as June 1941, when, according to a decision by the Tula party provincial committee of June 26, destroyer battalions, local militia, and combat squads began to be formed in Tula and areas of Tula province.

Nineteen battalions, with an overall strength of 2,100 men, were created in the city. The battalions were divided into companies, platoons, and sections and immediately began their training, without leaving their work places.

The units' commanders were selected from reserve commanders and political workers, who had distinguished themselves by work in factories and enterprises.

In training the battalions, special stress was put on the ability to fight tanks, throwing anti-tank grenades and bottles with flammable liquid. The battalions' combat instruction continued until October 1941.

According to an October 23 decision by the city defense committee, a Tula worker's regiment was formed from the cadre of the destruction battalions, which was joined by many soldiers from the former militia detachments and worker's combat squads. By October 27 the regiment numbered up to 980 men.

On October 27 the regiment, in accordance with an order of the city defense committee and the garrison commander, took up a defensive position along the southern outskirts of Tula (from height 225.5 to the Voronezh road), to the left of the 156th NKVD regiment, and repelled the first blows by the German tanks and motorized infantry from October 29-31. Later, in December, this regiment became part of the army and maintained by organs of the People's Commissariat for Defense.

As early as the end of August 1941, on the initiative of the Tula railroad junction's leadership, it was decided to build an armored train with their own funds. The party provincial committee supported this initiative and in September 1941 work on the armored train, which was completed in October, was begun. The armored car, christened "Tulyak", was turned over to the army and took part in the defense of Tula.

The enterprises' work in meeting defense needs

In the workshops, remaining in the factories in Tula following evacuation, during the days of the city's defense, a large production and repair base was create for meeting the army's needs. Factory no. 66 repaired rifle weaponry and produced 82mm mortars; factory no. 176 repaired tanks; factory no. 314 fixed small arms, and factory no. 187 made 37mm mortars.

The equipment remaining in the factories after evacuation was repaired and redistributed among the factories, and was supplemented by transferring equipment form small-scale enterprises. The party organizations put all their efforts into gathering worker cadres for servicing the repair and production base.

The following figures are an indication of the enterprises' role in meeting the city's defense needs:

repaired in the period from November-December 1941 were 89 tanks, 49 guns of various calibers, 43 machine guns, and 206 vehicles; built were 21 anti-tank obstacles, 800 mortar-shovels, 3,500 shovels, 726 crowbars, 250 armored rifle shields, seven armored towers, and many other weapons types.

Aside from this, the Tula factories also turned over from their own supplies 20,000 aviation cannon rounds, 90,000 12.7mm armor-piercing rounds, 350,000 rifle rounds, and 500,000 rounds for the TT pistol.

Work was carried out by the party, Komsomol, and social organizations of Tula for collecting warm clothes and skis for the Red Army, as a result of which there were gathered thousands of gloves, felt boots, sheepskin coats, hats, quilted trousers, jackets, towels, and other items.

The partisan movement in Tula Province

In the struggle with the German occupiers, the Red Army was greatly helped by the partisan detachments and diversionary groups formed by the party provincial and district committees, together with the provincial and district NKVD directorates. The formation of these units began in September 1941 and by the middle of October there were already 31 partisan detachments in 30 districts of the province, numbering 806 men, as well as 73 diversionary groups, including 290 men.

The detachments and groups were staffed by volunteers from the workers and intelligentsia. While training the rank and file, they learned how to handle weapons and studied the fundamentals of intelligence work.

The targets of the detachments' and groups' actions were German vehicles, soldiers, supply columns, aircraft forced to make emergency landings, railroad permanent ways, and freight cars. The partisans did not only deliver valuable information about the enemy, but in many cases engaged the enemy in battle and inflicted serious losses. In those areas where the fighting was heaviest the partisans mined the roads in the German rear, and the enemy's tanks and vehicles were destroyed by these mines. Most effective were the actions of small groups and individuals, who infiltrated into the enemy rear and put cable and radio equipment out of action, stole enemy maps and established contact with the intelligence organs of the Red Army's regular units.

During the period October-December 1941 the partisans blew up, burnt down, or otherwise destroyed a lot of the enemy's combat equipment and weaponry; for example, 18 tanks and armored cars destroyed, 164 vehicles with ammunition and fuel, 70 motorcycles, 100 vehicles with ammunition and food, 138 structures, five locomotives, and two trains. Captured were four guns, 17 light machine guns, 21 automatic rifles, 85 rifles, two mortars, 132 vehicles, 100 bicycles, 70 motorcycles, one banner, and 45 men captured. 1,597 enemy soldiers were killed, of which 35 were officers and 61 sergeants.

The partisans of Tula province rendered a great service to the units of the Red Army. In many cases the information gathered by them determined the success of the 50th Army's combat operations, a fact which was noted by the army command in order no. 23 of December 19 1941.

Repulsing the German blow Against Tula from the south

Combat activities in the area to the south of Tula, October 30-November 6. The counterblow by parts of the 50th Army on November 7-8

From October 30 to November 6 the enemy, while carrying out numerous attacks, tried to capture the city by means of a frontal blow from the south. The attacks, begun by the enemy from the morning of October 30, turned into a series of fierce battles, as a result of which by 1200 ten tanks and up to a battalion of German infantry had been destroyed. Not less than a company of motorized infantry attacked along the Stalinogorsk road. About a battalion of infantry, supported by 30 tanks, was operating between the Orel and Stalinogorsk roads.

At 1300 the line Mikhalkovo-Nizhnee Volokhovo was attacked by forces up to an infantry battalion in strength, with tanks. All the enemy attacks were beaten back. It was only toward Volokhovskii that the enemy broke through our lines along the road with 19 tanks, which we engaged in fighting in the village of Rogozhinskoe on the southern outskirts of the city. The remains of the 217th and 154th rifle divisions continued to arrive in Tula on that day. While unloading at the Khomyakovo station, the 32nd Tank Brigade (31 tanks) was already fighting with part of its forces, as a result of which it suffered the following losses: one KV and three T-34s.

Units of the 260th and 290th rifle divisions, the 156th NKVD regiment, and the Tula worker's regiment defended the city from the south. The reserve consisted of a single battalion. The enemy's attempt to take the city on October 30 cost him dearly in men, while 31 tanks were destroyed as well.

The strength of the units manning the Tula combat sector by the end of October 30, following the repulse of the enemy attack, overall numbered about 4,400-4,500 men.

The enemy continued to reinforce his Mtsensk group attacking toward Tula, moving up forces by rail and air. The enemy, using the gullies to collect his infantry, on October 31 attacked eight times in the direction of the city's southern outskirts in strength of up to a regiment of motorized regiment and up to 100 tanks (of which 16 were destroyed), supported by aviation. The 732nd PVO Regiment was particularly effective in dealing with the latter.

In the following days the enemy continued to bring up forces to the Tula region from the south; a particularly large concentration was noted on November 1 in the area of Kosaya Gora, and which was covered by fighters, anti-aircraft artillery, and anti-aircraft machine guns. Between 1000 and 1100 the Germans, in strength up to two infantry battalions and 18 tanks, attempted to attack Tula from the south, supported by aviation, but their four attacks were halted during the course of the day, while units of the 50th Army continued to hold their lines without any material changes; six enemy tanks were knocked out, as well as an armored car, 25 vehicles, while two aircraft were shot down.

The air force attacked the enemy during the first half of November 1 in the area of Tula, Kosaya Gora, and Plavsk, conducting 48 sorties, while during the second half of the day the *front's* air force carried out 90 sorties on the same mission.

Aside from the newly-arrived 32nd Tank Brigade, the 50th Army command was also reinforced with the 413th Rifle Division, which was unloading in Stalinogorsk. The division was organizing the immediate defense of the city and was trying to prevent the enemy from moving to the east of the Orel road. On November 1 16 of the 413th Division's trains had already unloaded, with another four en route (the 413th Division arrived from the Far Eastern Front. By order of the *Stavka* of the Supreme High Command the division was sent to the area of Dedilovo, Uzlovaya station, and Maklets, and immediately entered into the fighting.

The period from November 2-6 was characterized by an increase in enemy activity, primarily to the west of Tula along the 194th Rifle Division's front, as well as an increased reconnaissance in force in the area of Dedilovo. The enemy did not cease his attacks immediately to the south of Tula, but they were carried out with smaller forces than before.

Evidently the loss in tanks inflicted on the enemy during the period October 29-November 1 had an effect on the activity of the German infantry, whose tactics consisted of attacking behind their tanks, as well as the delivery of small parties on the tanks. Taking this into account, the defenders of Tula directed their efforts to first of all destroying the attacking tanks.

Besides this, our aviation became noticeably more active, which also weakened the enemy's first attacks from the south.

Nonetheless, the Germans attempted to deliver blows along the southern outskirts of Tula from a platoon of automatic riflemen to a battalion of infantry in strength, and supported by 3-5 tanks. The resort to night fighting by the enemy on the night of November 2-3 along the 156th NKVD regiment's defensive sector was unsuccessful.

On the 194th Rifle Division's front the enemy, in more than division-sized strength, attacked during the latter half of November 2, attempting to turn the division's right flank and at the same time to capture by frontal attacks the eastern bank of the Upa River in the areas of the crossings at Pavshino and Voskresenskoe. The enemy attacks were beaten back, but the 194th Rifle Division moved up a battalion and two guns to Il'ino in order to secure its right flank.

On November 3 the 413th Rifle Division arrived at and consolidated along the following lines: two regiments along the line Nizhnie Prisady-Dubovka, and the other regiment in Dedilovo. The 32nd Tank Brigade defended the southern outskirts of Tula and its motorized rifle battalion was concentrated in Gorelki as the commander of the Tula combat zone's reserve.

On November 5 the enemy's Orel-Mtsensk group was as follows: the XXIV Panzer Corps (3rd and 4th panzer divisions), the *Grossdeutschland* Infantry Regiment, probably the XLVII Panzer Corps (17th and 18th panzer divisions), and two motorized divisions: according to prisoner reports, the 167th Infantry Division was in the Teploe area (20 km southeast of Plavsk). The 31st Infantry Division was located in the Protasovo area (35 km west of Tula).

Units from the neighboring 49th Army on the right reached the boundary with the 50th Army's right flank on November 5 along the line Belolipki-Spas-Kanino-Pronino.

The stoutness of Tula's defenders prevented the enemy from capturing the city by a frontal blow from the south, while at the same time it offered the 50th Army's units the necessary time to put themselves in order following the retreat, to concentrate reinforcements (the 32nd Tank Brigade and the 413th Rifle Division), to establish communication with the Western Front's 49th Army, and to concentrate the 299th Rifle Division in the Dedilovo area, in all—to establish a strong defense. It was not only the defense of Tula which blocked the enemy's way to the north immediately through the city, but the heavy losses inflicted on his men and matériel on the southern approaches to the city and to the west.

However, the enemy nevertheless managed to concentrate his forces in the area to the south and southeast of Tula, using the woods to the north of Yasnaya Polyana and in the area of Kosaya Gora, where as early as November 5 up to 100 tanks and 160 vehicles had been spotted.

As new forces arrived in the Tula area, the 50th Army command on November 5 managed to create a reserve of two regiments from the 31st Cavalry Division in the Myza area (five km northeast of Tula), as well as the commander of the Tula combat sector in the form of the 290th Rifle Division, which he deployed on November 5 in the center of the city for the defense of its bridges. On November 6 the first stage of the *front* operation ended, and on November 7 the second began—the 50th Army was to launch a blow at Shchekino. At 2200 on November 6 the 50th Army command, in order no. 10, evaluated the enemy's actions as an attempt by units of the XXIV Panzer Corps to take Tula from the south, and by an infantry attack along the Pavshino-Voskresenskoe sector, to reach the Moscow road to the north of Tula. This summation in general corresponded to the general situation.

The following units were designated to launch the attack on November 7: the 413th Rifle Division, in coordination with the 32nd Tank Brigade in the direction of Malaya Yelovaya and Tolstovskii; the 260th Rifle Division along the Gosteevka-Rudakovo axis, with the task of seizing the heights near Maleevka; the 290th Rifle Division in the direction of Strukovo and Kosaya Gora. The army's remaining units were to hold their present positions. 30 minutes was set aside for the artillery preparation.

Having carried out during the night of November 6-7 the necessary regrouping in accordance with their mission and having thrown the enemy out of Nizhnyaya Kitaevka in a night attack by the 58th Reserve Rifle Regiment, the army's units, under cover from the defending 258th Rifle Division (from the northwest) and the 194th Rifle Division (from the west) at dawn on November 7 began their offensive.

But the offensive developed slowly due to the defending enemy's active resistance. The 32nd Tank Brigade was late in reaching its jumping-off point (Bol'syaya Yelovaya), while there was no organization of coordination between the tank brigade and the 413th Rifle Division on the ground; communications worked poorly, and there were no reports from the 413th Rifle Division and the 32nd Tank Brigade to army headquarters. By the end of November 7 the 413th Rifle Division had reached the line Malaya Yelovaya-Tikhvinskoe, but attacked there at 2200 by two battalions of enemy infantry and 25-30 tanks, fell back and by 2400 had consolidated along the line Bol'shaya Yelovaya-Vechernyaya Zarya, with division headquarters in Sergievka.

So as to continue the offensive on November 8, responsibility for the organization of coordination between the infantry and artillery was entrusted to the commander of the 32nd Tank Brigade; this cannot be seen as correct, because this task should have been the direct concern of the army staff.

As a result of the offensive activities that took place on November 8, the 50th Army's forces advanced all the way to Kosaya Gora, occupied Rvy station and Strukovo, and captured Maleevka, Basovo-Shishi, and Krutoe. The situation along the remaining defensive sectors was unchanged. During November 8 the 217th and 154th rifle divisions beat off multiple enemy attacks toward Kitaevka and in the area of the Orel road.

The 50th Army's counterblow did not yield the expected results, because the Fascists, having gone over to the defensive south of Tula, had entrenched and organized a fire system, repelling the 413th Rifle Division's attacks with infantry fire and tanks. The enemy had a small superiority in infantry and a four-to-one advantage in tanks. Finally, the insufficient coordination between the 413th Rifle Division and the 32nd Tank Brigade was also one of the reasons for the failure. Nonetheless, the counterblow by our units played a positive role and significantly activated the defense. The 413th Rifle Division, in acquiring combat experience around Tula, later operated effectively against the enemy and by means of its stubborn defense, prevented him from reaching Tula from the east.

Simultaneous with the 50th Army's offensive, the 3rd Army units to the south also began to attack with a shock group along the axis Teploe (20 km southeast of Plavsk)-Shchekino-Tula, in order to defeat the Germans" Tula group in conjunction with the 50th Army.

The 3rd Army, through its activities, distracted the enemy's 112th and 167th infantry divisions of the LIII Army Corps.

Units of the 3rd Army's shock group, overcoming the enemy's resistance along dispersed sectors during November 7, by November 8 had reached the line: Alekseevka (20 km west of

Bogoroditsk)-the Sverdlovskaya machine-tractor station-Naryshkino and further to the southwest of Vol'chya Dubrava.

The units of the 112th and 167th infantry divisions, which were securing communications through Orel and Tula along the line Sury-Teploe-Pokrovskoe, felt the threat occasioned by the 3rd Army's offensive, not only to the right flank and rear of the Germans' Tula group, but to their main communications as well. The resulting situation forced the Germans to immediately carry out corresponding measures: from the morning of November 9 stubborn fighting broke out in the area of Teploe, from which the enemy had been evicted on November 7 by units of the 6th Guards Rifle Division.

The enemy, having begun his attack on November 9, continued it the following day from the Sury area (30 km east of Plavsk) to the south. Throughout November 10 there was heavy fighting between the 3rd Army and two enemy infantry divisions attacking in the area of Sury, Teploe, and Pokrovskoe. Thus combat activities became more active along a front more than 30 km in length.

Combat activities for eliminating the Germans' breakthrough on the boundary between the 49th and 50th armies

In *Stavka* directive no. 004692 of November 9, the Bryansk Front's 50th army was subordinated at 1800 on November 10 to the commander of the Western Front. On that same day the enemy launched a blow against the boundary of the 49th and 50th armies and broke through in the area of Spas-Kanino, advancing in the direction of Kleshnya and Sukhodol. The 49th and 50th armies were ordered to liquidate the breakthrough by joint flank attacks; at 0130 on November 11 the *front* staff transmitted an order to the 50th Army staff to quickly shift the 31st Cavalry Division to the army's right flank in order to destroy (with units of the 49th Army) the enemy which had broken through in the Kleshnya area.

In a *front* directive of November 10 the 49th Army was assigned the task, together with the 50th Army, of eliminating the enemy breakthrough. The 49th Army commander was ordered to appoint responsible commanders for controlling combat activities, while he was to personally lead those forces appointed for the operation to eliminate the breakthrough. At the same time, according to a *front* order of November 11, the 49th Army's commander was assigned three tank platoons from the 112th Tank Division and two guards mortar battalions, which were being quickly shifted to the army's left flank.

In accordance with the *front* directive, Gen. Zakharkin, the 49th Army commander, assigned the 238th Rifle Division the following mission in order no. 014 of November 10:

> Carry out a regrouping during the night of November 10-11, removing everything possible from the division's secondary sectors and move the units to their jumping-off points to defeat the enemy attacking in the direction of Nikulino and Sukhodol.

The time for the attack was set for 0800 on November 11.

On the morning of November 11, on the 49th Army's left flank, heavy fighting resumed with the enemy units that had broken through in the area of Pronino, Naryshkino, and Nikulino. The enemy, during the latter half of the day, attacked in strength up to a battalion along the sector Gorushki-Boloto and at 1300 occupied Gorushki.

During the night of November 11-12 units from the army's left flank carried out the necessary regrouping so as to launch a decisive offensive on the morning of November 12 and destroy the enemy who had broken through in the area of Kleshya, Man'shino, and Spas-Kanino.

On the morning of November 12 the 238th Rifle Division once again attacked and occupied Sukromna (two km southeast of Kolyupanovo), Danilovka, and Sukhodol. On that day the 50th Army, stoutly holding the Tula and Dedilovo axes, attacked with units from the 258th Rifle and 31st Cavalry divisions the enemy's flank and rear in the direction of Nikulino and Sukhodol.

On the following day, November 13, units of the 238th Rifle Division continued to fight along their left flank, fending off German counterattacks. Particularly stubborn fighting occurred on November 14 in the area of Sukromna and Kolyupanovo, where the enemy managed to push back our units and seize Kolyupanovo.

During November 15-16 units from the 49th Army's left flank, along with the 50th Army's right flank, continued the fierce fighting in the area of Spas-Kanino and Sukhodol. As a result of these battles, the enemy was prevented from reaching the Tula-Moscow road and was forced to go on the defensive on several sectors.

On the 49th Army's right flank the troops attacked in the area of Troyanovo, Semkino, Vysokoe, Yekaterinovka, and Pavlovka, overcoming strong enemy resistance and repelling attacks by the enemy's 137th and 260th infantry divisions. Several locales changed hands several times.

Fighting along the 49th Army's entire front during this period involved intensive air activity by both sides. On November 15 the enemy carried out a series of massive bombing raids against our troops' positions on the army's right and left flanks. During November 16-18 the 49th Army's air force conducted a number of bomber and assault raids and destroyed in Makarovo (six km north of Vysokinichi) an ammunition depot and bombed a large unit headquarters in Vysokinichi. The *front's* air force, assisting the 49th Army, on November 18 bombed and strafed enemy troops in the villages of Chernaya Gryaz', Semkino, and Gosteshevo.

In the days following November 18 there was small-scale fighting on the army's right flank, and on the left flank the 238th Rifle Division went over to the defensive along the line Bunyrevo-Aleksin-Danilovka-Man'shino-Nikulino.

Thus during the period November 10-18 the most important operationally-significant event on the 49th Army's front was the fighting on the left flank against units of the enemy's XLIII Army Corps (131st and 31st infantry divisions), which were seeking to break through to the Moscow road. The offensive operation by the 49th Army's left-flank units to eliminate the breakthrough was conducted in the closest coordination with the 50th Army's right flank, where during this period events developed in the following manner:

The 50th Army's order no 14 of November 13 assigned to the 258th and 194th rifle divisions and the 31st Cavalry Division the task of eliminating the enemy in the area of the Nikulinskie settlements and the White Woods, after which they would consolidate along the line Pronino and west of the Nikulinskie settlements, while the remaining forces were to temporarily assume the defensive along the line Ketri-Upa River-Myasnovo state farm-Mikhalkovo-Osinovaya Gora-Nizhnie Prisady-Zamyatino-Dedilovo-Uzlovaya.

As the result of the fighting the 258th Rifle Division, in conjunction with the 194th Rifle Division, at 0400 on November 15 captured Yesipovo; the 194th Rifle Division was fighting for Glebovo. On the morning of November 16 the 258th Rifle Division, together with the 31st Cavalry Division, was fighting to capture Bizyukino, and the 194th Rifle Division was continuing the battle for Glebovo against strong resistance and counterattacks by the enemy, whose 31st Infantry Division assumed the defensive along the line Bizyukino-Izvol', while the line Sudakovo-Prisady was defended by units from the 3rd and 4th panzer divisions. The SS *Grossdeutschland* Regiment, consisting of five battalions, was also concentrated in this area.

As a result of the fighting on the boundary between the 49th and 50th armies the enemy was halted; he was not able to reach the Moscow road. The 50th Army's right flank was as firm as before; later this played a large role and made it easier for the army's forces to eliminate the German blow in the area to the northeast of Tula.

The defense along the 49th and 50th armies' front, November 20-December 4 1941. The 2nd Cavalry Corps' offensive

Defensive fighting along the 49th Army's front

On the 49th Army's right flank the following combat events occurred on November 10. The German-Fascist command was putting together a group of forces in the area west of Serpukhov, evidently for the purpose of attacking toward Serpukhov and Lopasnya and creating small internal "pincers". Our command, divining the enemy's intentions, planned a countermaneuver. Gen. Belov's 2nd Cavalry Corps was shifted to the area north of Serpukhov, and the 112th Tank Division was concentrated in the Lopasnya area with a large number of tanks. These formations, forming a single group, were to launch a blow against the Germans on a front from Burinovo approximately to Maleevo, on the 5th Guards and 60th rifle divisions' sectors, and upon reaching the enemy lines to push the attack in the direction of Vysokinichi. The 415th Rifle Division, transferred from the *front* reserve, was to attack along the extreme right flank.

The 2nd Cavalry Corps' offensive began on November 14. It was preceded by an enemy attack by troops concentrated for an offensive on Serpukhov. As a result, our offensive and the German blow led to a series of meeting engagements, as a result of which the enemy's plan was foiled; our troops wore him out in the stubborn fighting. However, they themselves suffered significant losses. The 112th Tank Division, which was mainly outfitted with T-26 tanks, was hit particularly hard.

The 2nd Cavalry Corps, the 112th Tank Division, and the troops of the 49th Army's right flank, having repulsed the enemy offensive, were not in a condition to break through the German front and get into their rear. One of the offensive's shortcomings was the poor coordination between the cavalry and tanks, the unfavorable terrain conditions for the T-26 tanks, and the poorly organized troop control. As a result, the 2nd Cavalry Corps and the 49th Army's right flank, which took part in the offensive, went over to the defensive and on November 23 it was planned to pull the cavalry corps behind the Nara River and then to the Lopasnya area.

The 415th Rifle and 112th Tank divisions (the latter minus a tank regiment) remained with the 49th Army. Later the entire 112th Tank Division was transferred to the 50th Army. The 2nd Cavalry Corps, after concentrating in the Lopasnya area (in connection with the worsening situation near Venev), was ordered by the *front* to the Kashira area, from which on November 27 it carried out its blow against units of the Second Panzer Army.

After November 20 the situation along the 49th Army's front was as follows. Our troops on the right flank went over to the defensive on a number of sectors. Units of the 2nd Cavalry Corps were preparing to fall back to the Nara River. On the left flank the enemy continued his attempts to go on the offensive and capture Aleksin. In the center our forces held off the enemy everywhere; there was no active combat here.

On November 21 the *front* command, in connection with the 2nd Cavalry Corps' (later the 1st Guards Cavalry Corps) unsuccessful offensive in the Serpukhov area and the sharp change in the situation along the *front's* flanks, ordered the 49th Army to halt its offensive and assume the defensive. By this time a significant portion of the 49th Army's forces had factually already gone over to the defensive.

In accordance with the *front* directive the 49th Army commander, Gen. Zakharkin, on November 28 issued order no. 015, according to which the army was to continue defending along the line Sidorenki (20 km northwest of Serpukhov)-Vysokoe-Gur'evo-the eastern bank of the Oka River as far as Aleksin-and then Mar'ino-Nikulino, concentrating its main defensive forces in the direction of Serpukhov. The 415th Rifle Division (which had arrived from the Far East by order of the *Stavka* and transferred to the army in the first half of November), was to secure the army's right flank and defend the sector Sidorenki-Burinovskii station and prevent the enemy's tanks and infantry from breaking through in the direction of Burinovo and Kalugino. The division was ordered to prepare anti-tank strong points near Terekhun', the wooded area east of Burinovo, in the woods near the Burinovskii station (two km south of Burinovo), Stanki station (two km northwest of Kalugino), near Kalugino, to construct a switch position along the northern bank of the Nara River along the sector Dubrovka (one km northeast of Sidorenki)-Butyrki, and a rear position along the line Shakhlovo-Kalugino.

The boundary line on the left was (excluding) Raisemenovskoe-Kalugino-height 174.7

The 5th Guards Rifle Division was ordered to defend the line Burinovskii station-Vysokoe-Sinyatino-Borovna and prevent a breakthrough by enemy tanks and infantry in the direction of Kalugino and Shatovo and prepare anti-tank strong points near Voronino, Sinyatino, Nebotovo (one km northeast of Yekaterinovka), Yekaterinovka, Pavlovka, and Shatovo, with an intermediate position along the line (excluding) Noviki-Pavlovka.

The main forces of the 60th Rifle Division, which was the army reserve, were pulled back into the area of Zaokskoe (17 km south of Serpukhov), Dyatlovo, and Savino, while one regiment was to take up defensive positions laong the easten bank of the Oka River along the Pan'shino-Lamonovo sector, relieving the troops there. The 194th Rifle Division was to defend the line Borovna-Gur'evo-Drakino and prevent a breakthrough by enemy tanks and infantry in the directions of Kremenki, Pavlovka, Shatovo, Volkovskoe, and Kalinovo, having prepared strong points near Borovna, north and east of Kremenki and Drakino.

The boundary line was Dashkovka-the Oka River-(excluding) Bol'sunov.

The 238th Rifle Division was ordered to occupy defensive positions along the eastern bank of the Oka River from Lamonovo to Aleksin, and then along the line Svinka (three km south of Aleksin)-Man'shino-Nikulino, paying particular attention to its left flank in order to prevent the enemy from reaching the Tula-Serpukhov road. All the divisions were ordered to maintain mobile reserves in their areas of no less than a rifle battalion in strength.

Front-line defensive works were to be completed by December 1, with the second-line works completed by December 5.

The army's artillery chief was ordered to organize the anti-tank defense of the approaches to Serpukhov from the north, west and south from the weapons in his anti-tank regiments; to organize the artillery's fire coordination along the divisional boundaries and to coordinate with its neighbor to the left—the 43rd Army's 17th Rifle Division, and to keep in the anti-tank defense's mobile reserve no less than three batteries. At the same time he was to prepare a massive artillery bombardment against the areas of Burinovo, Burinovskii station, Semkino, Vorontsovka, Kremenki, and Volkonskoe, and defensive fire along the lines of the Protva and Borovna rivers, and in the divisions' zones. No less than two artillery battalions from the 194th Rifle Division must be ready to support the 60th Rifle Division's rifle regiment defending the sector Pan'shino-Lamonovo.

According to intelligence sources, by November 20 the following enemy units were facing the army: units of the 17th, 137th, and 260th infantry divisions, with tanks, were operating along the sector from Burinovo approximately as far as Tarusa. The 52nd Infantry Division was located south of Tarusa, and in the area of Aleksin, along the boundary with the 50th Army—units of the 131st and 31st infantry divisions, with tanks and other small units.

Thus the attention of the 49th Army's defense was mainly concentrated on the right flank, which had the task of securely covering the Serpukhov axis, and on the left flank, coordinating with the 50th Army and covering the Moscow road from the west and preventing a German breakthrough north of Tula.

Throughout November 24 the enemy, following a powerful mortar and machine gun fire, attempted to attack on the 5th Guards Rifle Division's sector, but was everywhere thrown back. Attempts by the enemy's reconnaissance parties to pierce the forward edge of the 238th Rifle Division's defense ended the same way.

During November 25-26 there were no substantial changes along the army's front; the army's units continued to improve their defensive lines.

On the morning of November 27 German-Fascist units, more than three regiments in strength from the 52nd and 31st infantry divisions, attacked along the entire front of the 238th Rifle Division and captured Bunyrevo, Pogiblovo, Svinka, Surnevo, Yepishkovo (two km west of Mar'ino), and Laderevo. Following a counterattack by our units, the enemy was thrown out of the first two locales, and with heavy losses fell back to the western bank of the Oka River. The enemy was not active along the remainder of the front.

On the morning of November 28 large enemy forces, supported by aviation, resumed the offensive along the 238th Rifle Division's sector, pressing its left flank. The army command subordinated to its commander a battalion of the 5th Guards Rifle Division, reinforced by a battalion from a howitzer regiment.

During November 29-30 the enemy continued to fiercely attack the 238th Rifle Division's position, particularly in the area of the woods north of Abryutino, where he had up to four infantry regiments.

The *front* command once again demanded that the 50th Army commander aid the 49th Army's left flank with the forces of the 258th Rifle Division. At the same time the 340th Rifle Division, whose trains were unloading at Pakhomovo station from the morning of November 30 (the division was formed on the basis of the 47th Reserve Regiment in the Balashov area and was transferred to the Western Front from the *Stavka* reserve) was attached to the 49th Army. Throughout November 30 *front* aviation bombed the enemy's troops and tanks in the Aleksin area. Units from the army's right flank and center continued to stubbornly defend, repelling the attempts by a number of enemy groups to penetrate our position.

By the end of November 30 a turning point had been reached along the 49th Army's left flank. Units of the 238th Rifle Division, having been reinforced, attacked on the morning of December 1 in order to restore the situation. During the period December 2-5 fighting occurred with variable success on both sides, although the offensive initiative remained in the hands of the 238th Rifle Division

The attempt by the enemy's 31st Infantry Division on December 5 to break through to the Moscow road was also beaten back.

The defensive fighting on the 50th Army's front and the offensive by the 1st Guards Cavalry Corps from the Kashira area

Combat activities on the 50th Army's front during this period unfolded in the following manner:

> The enemy, following his unsuccessful attempts to launch a frontal blow against Tula from the south and reach the Moscow road north of Tula, was forced to forego continuing the attacks along these axes and seek to accomplish his mission—the capture of Tula—from another direction.

For this purpose, the enemy chose the Dedilovo-Stalinogorsk axis, from which an offensive on Venev and then onto to Kashira was begun, accompanied by a blow toward Tula from the east and northeast.

The Germans, having by November 18 concentrated the XXIV Panzer Corps' main forces (3rd and 4th panzer divisions) in the area to the south of Tula, and the 17th Panzer and 112th Infantry divisions in the area to the south of Dedilovo and Stalinogorsk, on the morning of November 18, in up to an infantry division and panzer division in strength (80-90 tanks), began their attack from the line Lutovinovo (ten km southeast of Tula)-Kireevka in the direction of Dedilovo and Uzlovaya and by the end of the day had overcome the resistance of the 413th and 299th rifle divisions and captured Dedilovo, developing the attack to the east.

The enemy, having concentrated his chief attention during these days on the Dedilovo axis, was not active along the front's other sectors and went over to the defensive south of Tula. The enemy's forward units, launching a blow on Venev and engaging in heavy fighting with units of his 17th Panzer and 112th Infantry divisions for Stalinogorsk 2, by the close of November 23 had reached the area of Sem'yan' (five km southwest of Venev).

On November 20 the 239th Rifle Division was subordinated to the commander of the 50th Army and as early as November 19 was successfully fighting off attacks by an enemy infantry division and cavalry regiment along the line Zarech'e-Cheremukhovka-Durovka-Vel'mino-Smorodino (the division had arrived from the Far East and during November 17-18 had concentrated in the area of Uzlovaya station, where it was subordinated to the commander of the 3rd Army; on November 20, in connection with the breakthrough on the 299th Rifle Division's front, the 239th Division began to fall back to the north under pressure from German tank units). Following the fighting in the Stalinogorsk area, on November 23-24 the division was encircled by the enemy (up to two infantry divisions in strength, plus tanks), and from 1600 on November 25 began to fall back to the northeast, having lost contact with the 50th Army's headquarters.

The 413th Rifle Division and the 32nd Tank Brigade, having waged stubborn defensive battles on November 20, did not have a continuous front and held Bolokhovka with a single regiment, while another was fighting in the area of Gorki and Dubravo, and the third in the area of Kurakino, faced by up to an infantry division and 40-50 enemy tanks, which were trying to outflank Bolokhovka from the north and south.

East of the 413th Rifle Division, the 108th Tank Brigade, with units of the 299th Rifle Division, was fighting the enemy (up to an infantry regiment in strength, plus 50-60 tanks) along the line Kuz'mishchevo-Shakhovskoe.

As a result of this fighting, the 413th Rifle Division, the 108th Tank Brigade, and the 299th and 239th rifle divisions, having regrouped 6-8 km to the north of the battle zone during the night of November 20-21, occupied a line chiefly along the northern bank of the Shat' River: 413th Rifle Division—along the front Mar'ino-Verkhnee Petrovo; 108th Tank Brigade and 299th Rifle Division (the latter suffered heavy losses on November 19 in the fighting for the Dedilovo area)—Kukui-Urusovo; 239th Rifle Division—Kostornya-Shakhovskoe-Donskoi-Dubovoe. The 31st Cavalry Division was moving up to the Arsen'evo area.

The enemy, having moved up units of the 17th Panzer Division to the Venev area by November 24, had concentrated the forces of two infantry regiments and a panzer division along a 12-15 km front along the railroad and continued to advance on Kashira, and on the 413th Rifle Division's front the enemy limited himself to attempts (unsuccessful) to cross the Shat' River.

As a result of the breakthrough and the Germans' rapid advance to the north, the *front's* military council on November 24 issued directive no. 062/op, which ordered the 2nd Cavalry Corps to make a forced march and concentrate in the area of Chernevo and Zaraisk by the end of November 25, where it would be subordinated to the 50th Army commander.

On November 25 the cavalry corps' mission was refined—to advance to the Ryazan' area and defeat the enemy attacking in a northeasterly direction toward Zaraisk and Ryazan'. On that same day the cavalry corps commander was informed of the *front* military council's decision to make him personally responsible for Kashira, against which the Germans had designated their blow.

The 2nd Cavalry Corps, along with the 112th Tank Division and the 9th Tank Brigade from the Kashira area, having completed its concentration by the morning of November 27, began its attack at 0900 along the front Ivan'kovo-Sorokino-Red'kino-Klishino against the enemy forces, with the tank division and brigade on the flanks. The cavalry corps defeated the enemy in the fighting and forced a significant part of the enemy's shock group to defend and then fall back to the south. The

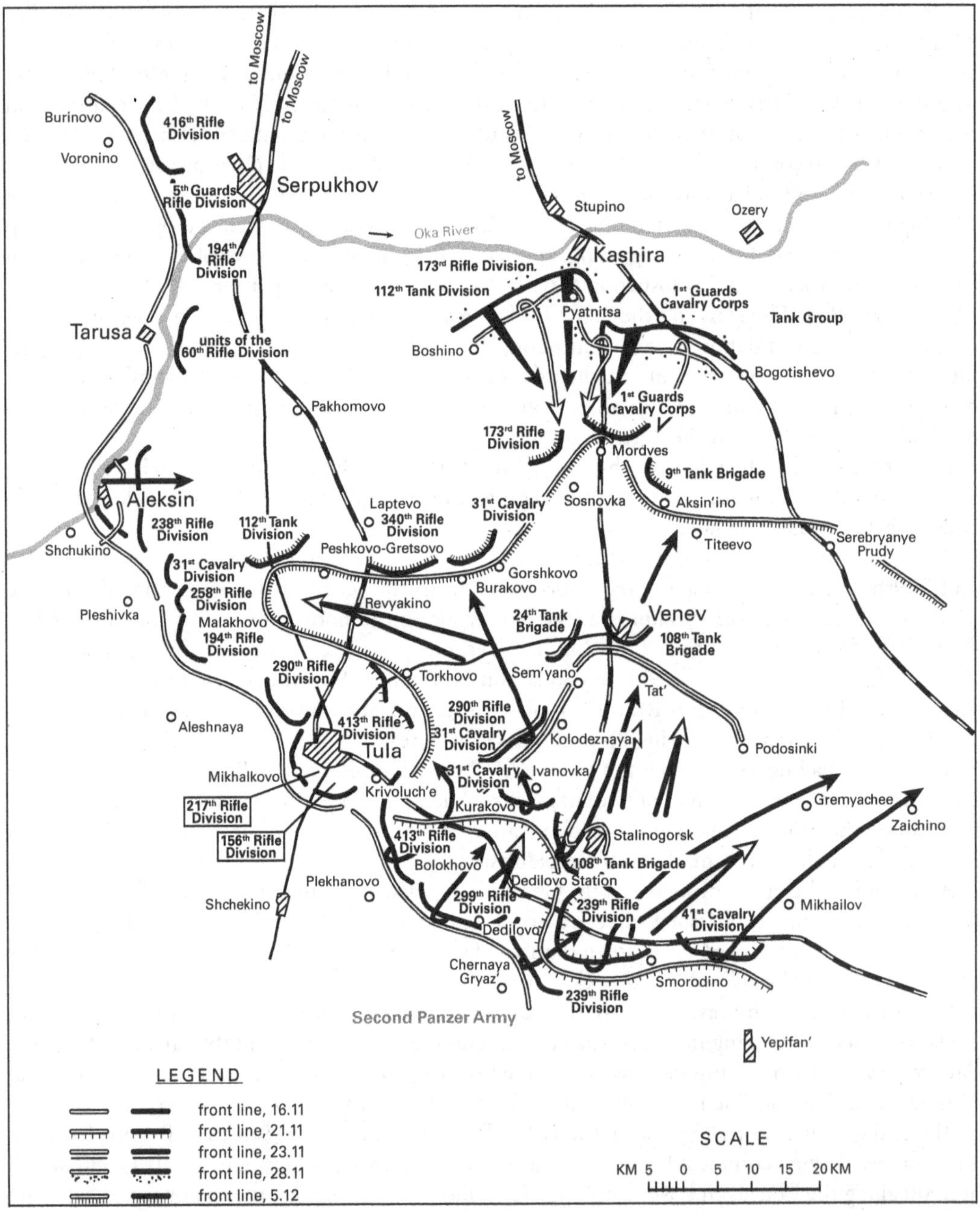

Map 4 The Withdrawal by the Front's Left-Wing Forces in November and the Counterblow by the 1st Guards Cavalry Corps in December, 1941

2nd Cavalry Corps' (afterwards the 1st Guards Cavalry Corps) success brought about the transfer of the Germans' 29th Motorized Division to the line Pryakhino-Tyunezh in order to secure their right flank and rear, over which the reinforced cavalry corps' attacking units were constantly hanging from the north.

During the offensive's first day (November 27) the cavalry corps had by 1600 already achieved a number of successes:

The 5th Cavalry Division took height 210.7, the northern outskirts of Pyatnitsa, and Timiryazevo, and was faced by up to an infantry battalion with tanks, supported by artillery from the south-eastern outskirts of Starodub;

The 9th Cavalry Division, attacking with two regiments from the area of Znamenskoe and Makarovo, captured Ozherel'e and Grabchenki, continuing its attack against an infantry battalion and 8-10 tanks; the cavalry division's remaining forces were moving up along the railroad; the division's artillery had fallen behind because of the horses' exhaustion.

A group of light tanks from two of the 9th Tank Brigade's battalions reached the area of Topkanovo and Ostroga with their forward units, while their main forces passed through Chernevo, while attacking in the direction of Barabanovo. The heavy tanks lagged behind because of the lack of heavy-duty bridges in the Zaraisk area.

The 112th Tank Division was engaged with the enemy's tanks and motorized infantry in the Ivan'kovo area.

The 1st Guards Cavalry Corps (2nd Cavalry Corps), in carrying out its assignment of destroying the enemy's Kashira goup, regrouped on the night of November 27-28 in order to continue the offensive at 1915 on the same day. Throughout November 28 the corps' units occupied the following positions:

The 112th Tank Division in the Ivan'kovo area covered the road to Serpukhov; the 1st Guards Cavalry Division captured the villages of Pyatnitsa and Dudilovo; the 2nd Guards Cavalry Division captured Kokino and Ozherel'e.

By 0500 the tank group had reached the line D'yakovo-Purlovo.

The following enemy group was facing the corps on the approaches to Kashira: in Dudilovo and Pyatnitsa—up to a battalion of motorized infantry and 20-25 tanks. The Germans, being halfway surrounded, stubbornly defended in the Starodub-Pyatnitsa-Rudnevo area on November 28 with forces up to an infantry regiment in strength, with 60 tanks, a part of which were dug in.

The enemy air force's activities sought to disrupt the cable communications of the 1st Guards Cavalry Corps' units throughout November 28; the enemy also stubbornly attempted to counterattack the 2nd Guards Cavalry Division's 136th Cavalry Regiment in the direction of Kokino, with up to two companies of infantry and a small amount of tanks.

During the period November 29-December 3 the cavalry corps, along with reinforcements, attacked and by November 29 the enemy was already falling back to the south and putting up stubborn resistance. With the coming of darkness on November 29 the corps' units, as a result of the fighting in the Kashira area with units of the enemy's 17th Panzer Division, an SS battalion, and a regiment of infantry, had reached the line Blagovo-Barabanovo-Nikulino, and the 112th Tank Division the line Shepilovo-Zhizhelna. The pursuit of the enemy continued on November 30 and in the following days, against stubborn resistance by the Germans, who counterattacked (chiefly with tanks) the 1st Guards Rifle Division from the Konchinka area. The division, after repulsing this attack, consolidated along the line Uvarovka-Rusalkino, while defending Kashira with one regiment.

The 2nd Guards Cavalry Division, having destroyed up to an enemy company, captured Orekhovka, Pavlovo-Vorontsovo, and Kozlovka and, in coordination with the 9th Tank Brigade in taking Marygino, attacked toward Mordves.

In connection with the enemy breakthrough in the Rudnevo area (18-20 km northeast of Tula), units of the 112th Tank Division and the 35th Tank Battalion (the latter's main forces of which were located along the line Borisovo-Pavlovskoe-Odintsovo on December 2), received orders to attack in the direction of Rudnevo in order to destroy the enemy who had broken through there. Throughout December 2 the 173rd Rifle and the 1st Guards Cavalry divisions, the 9th Tank Brigade, along with the 127th Tank Battalion, continued the pursuit, while the 173rd Rifle Division attacked in the direction of Gritchino, the 1st Guards Cavalry Division took Konchinka, the 9th Tank Brigade and the 127th Tank Battalion were fighting for Pryakhino, with their main forces along the line D'yakonovo-Barsuki.

The 2nd Guards Cavalry Division, deployed along the line Selinka-Kozlovka, formed the corps commander's reserve.

On December 3 the 173rd Rifle Division, having taken Zarazy, Khrenovo, and Zhilevo, continued to attack toward Gritchino, faced by up to a battalion from the 63rd Motorized Regiment; by 1800 the 1st Guards Cavalry Division had captured Martem'yanovo and Lashino. The 2nd Guards Cavalry Division, having captured Nemerino with two regiments, attacked toward Mikhailovka with the other regiment and the 9th Tank Brigade. The Germans' forces before the 1st and 2nd guards cavalry divisions consisted of up to two battalions from the 40th Motorized Regiment.

The enemy, continuing his fighting retreat in front of the 1st Guards Cavalry Corps, at 1300 on December 3 attempted to launch a blow against the corps' left flank and in the near rear of the 9th Tank Brigade with motorized infantry in 50 vehicles and with two tanks and penetrated to the Marygino area. A tank battalion was moved up from the D'yakonovo area to Marygino in order to eliminate the breakthrough; the 2nd Cavalry Division was also being concentrated in the area Marygino-D'yakonovo-Kozlovka area to cover the corps' left flank.

The enemy, in order to carry out his plan for encircling Tula from the north near Kostrovo in conjunction with units of the XLIII Army Corps, on December 2 mounted an attack with units of the 3rd Panzer Division to the east of Tula in a northwestern and western direction and that morning the main forces of the 3rd and 4th panzer divisions fought their way to the line Sevryukovo-Revyakino (15 km north of Tula)-Torkhovo-Dorofeevka-Dubki; on December 5 the 31st Infantry Division began its offensive from the west, but was halted along the line of the Nikulinskie settlements by our troops' counterattacks. A critical situation developed to the north of Tula. As a result of the battles here, the Germans were not able to close the ring in order to encircle Tula in the Kostrovo area (on the Tula-Serpukhov road).

The 1st Guards Cavalry Corps, attacking from the south, defeated a significant portion of the Germans' motor-mechanized troops which were most quickly approaching Moscow from the south, halted them and forced them on the defensive, and then to withdraw. While the enemy attempted to take Tula from the northeast the corps hung over him from the north. While eliminating the enemy forces that had broken through in the Rudnevo area, the corps, with its tank units, participated directly in liquidating the enemy in the tensest moment of the battle for Tula and in this way helped the 50th Army's troops hold Tula.

The countermaneuver by the 50th Army and 1st Guards Cavalry Corps

By December 4 the crisis of the battle had been reached. The enemy forces were straining all their efforts so that, having broken through with tanks from the east and infantry from the west, they could close the encirclement ring around Tula near Kostrovo. Along with this, the constantly growing threat to the flank and rear of the Germans' tank group from the 1st Guards Cavalry Corps (from the north) was forcing the Fascists to speed up their efforts to encircle Tula, so as to free up a part of their forces to oppose the offensive by our troops from the northeast.

The troops of the Western Front's left wing also faced the question of holding Tula and its environs as a strong point that steadied the *front's* wing, and as an anvil for the already-prepared blow from the north against the overstretched enemy.

The crisis was resolved in our favor by the efforts of the troops outside of Tula and those immediately near the city. In launching concentric blows, they forced the Germans who had broken through here into a difficult position.

During the period under review the enemy's 3rd and 4th panzer divisions had concentrated in the Rudnevo area (20 km northeast of Tula) and were attempting to reach the northern and eastern outskirts of the city by launching tank attacks against the city along the road from the north and from the Torkhovo area. At 2100 on December 2 the *front* commander ordered the commander of the 50th Army, Gen. Boldin, to destroy the enemy advancing toward Rudnevo: the 340th Rifle Division, transferred from the 49th Army and reinforced by two mortar battalions, was to attack the enemy in the direction of Rudnevo. The commander of the 1st Cavalry Corps was to launch a blow with the forces of the 112th Tank Division toward Rudnevo as well, while the corps' remaining forces were to attack toward Venev. On December 4 the *front* commander demanded that the corps commander help the 50th Army and prevent the enemy from encircling our Tula group by attacking the 17th Panzer Division.

By December 4 the remains of the enemy's 63rd and 40th motorized regiments were thrown back to the Mordves area, while the 29th Motorized Division's 71st and 15th infantry regiments reached the area Marygino-D'yakonovo-Krasnyi Pakhar'. The leading units of the 167th Infantry Division were approaching the Mordves area from the west.

At 1700 on December 4 the corps commander's order no. 096 laid out the tasks for the further offensive (slated to begin at 1020 on December 5). A 20-minute artillery preparation was to be conducted before the start of the offensive. The corps' overall task was to destroy the enemy's 29th Motorized Division and pin down the 167th Infantry Division with a supporting attack from the right.

On December 6 the *front* headquarters once again informed the commander of the 1st Guards Cavalry Corps that the *front's* military council demanded rapid and decisive actions from him.

The 50th Army commander, Gen. Boldin, included the following units in the force assigned to attack Rudnevo from the south: the 740th Rifle Regiment, with nine tanks, the 32nd Tank Brigade (which was concentrated in Medvenka, the 124th Tank Regiment (minus one company) with the third battalion of the 740th Rifle Regiment from the army's right flank (advancing through Malakhovo).

The 510th Rifle Regiment with a company of tanks (eight tanks) from the 124th Tank Regiment was to attack from the Laptevo area along with the 340th Rifle Division.

The 31st Cavalry Division, based in the Gorshkovo area, was operating against the rear of the enemy's Mordves group, disrupting his communications between Venev and Kashira, and securing the left flank of the group attacking from the Laptevo area toward Rudnevo.

Our Laptevo group began its offensive on December 3 from the line Shemetovo-Melekhovka, concentrating its efforts in the direction of Revyakino station (where our armored train was battling enemy tanks) and launched a supporting blow toward Rudnevo and Torkhovo. By 1000 on December 3 the 510th Rifle Regiment had captured the southern outskirts of Kryukovo. The 217th Rifle Division's 740th Rifle Regiment (minus its third battalion), along with a company of tanks, by 1000 had captured Gnezdino and from 1400 was fighting for Kryukovo and meeting heavy enemy resistance.

The 124th Tank Regiment, with a battalion from the 740th Rifle Regiment, and the 112th Tank Division, were on the move. Units of the 1st Guards Cavalry Corps were pushing the enemy's motorized infantry back to the south.

Simultaneous with the attack by our shock groups, the 413th Rifle Division (covering Tula from the east) on December 3 occupied Kolodeznaya with a single regiment and by 1400 was fighting for Dorofeevka, which to a certain degree secured the 740th Rifle Regiment's right flank.

The attack by the enemy's 31st Infantry Division, which began at dawn on December 5 against the 50th Army's right flank, was beaten off on December 6 with heavy losses, as a result of which the situation there remained stable.

Units of the 1st Guards Cavalry Corps, successfully developing their offensive to the south, by December 7 had occupied Mikhailovka, Pryakhino, Darovoe, and Marygino, and by 1500, having broken the enemy's resistance, had reached the line Afanas'evka-Kamenka-Barsukovskie Vyselki settlements-D'yakonovo-the woods north of Stolbovka, and continued to pursue the enemy toward Venev, directly threatening the Germans' rear and flank.

On December 7 the 340th Rifle Division, successfully attacking to the south, occupied Nefedovo, Revyakino station, Fedyashevo, Sukhotino, and Rudnevo, linking up with the 217th Rifle Division's 740th Rifle Regiment in the Sine-Tulitsa area, while the 112th Tank Division occupied Volot'.

The shock groups' actions were secured by the 31st Cavalry Division in the Burakovo area and by the 413th Rifle Division, covering Tula from the east and securely holding the line height 217.2-Glukhie Polyany-Kryukovo-Sine-Tulitsa.

By this time the 10th Army from the Supreme High Command reserve had deployed southwest of Ryazan'. The army received orders to attack on the morning of December 6, launching its main blow in the direction of Mikhailov and Stalinogorsk. It was trying to get into the flank and rear of the Second Panzer Army's forces. The enemy began to withdraw.

Conclusions on the defense of Tula

Tula and the adjacent area, being the main strong point of the Western Front's southern sector, anchored the stability of the entire left wing through its stubborn and active defense. The left wing covered the most important approaches to Moscow from the south, along which the enemy was directing a powerful group of forces, well supplied with equipment.

Thus the significance of Tula in the period under study grew beyond the bounds of the 50th Army's defensive operation and was, in essence, a factor of consequence for the entire *front*.

A German breakthrough along the Tula axis was rife not only with operational, but with strategic consequences as well.

Thus the *Stavka* of the Supreme High Command twice (October 29 and 30) focused the attention of the Bryansk Front commander on the important significance of Tula, which was necessary to hold at any cost, in order to retain not only Tula, but to close off the enemy's path to Moscow from the south.

Amongst several instances of defending cities in the Western Front's area, the defense of Tula may be considered a model, both in the sense of its organization, but in the sense of its final result as well.

The conditions, the course of combat operations, and the results of the defense of Tula in the period from the end of October to the beginning of December 1941, fully illustrated that modern defense, based upon a large inhabited area, can be successful if the fight against the enemy's mobile formations is conducted in a combined fashion, that is, by means of combining fixed defenses along the main axes, with active offensive actions by mobile formations outside the inhabited area, that is, by using the same operational methods and means as the attacker.

In the overall operational formation of the troops defending the city, the securing of the flanks by powerful and active units is of exceptional importance. This imparts stoutness to the defense and makes easier the creation of shock groups for attacking the enemy, even in a very difficult situation for the defense.

The creation of reserves must be of constant concern to the command. Their composition cannot be permanent, and it changes at the expense of the troops in those sectors where enemy pressure is weakening at any given moment.

Conclusions on the 49th and 50th armies' defensive battles on the Western Front's left wing

During the fighting at the end of October and beginning of December 1941, the 49th Army, which together with the 50th Army comprised the Western Front's left wing, was one of the most important links in carrying out the Soviet command's strategic plan at that stage, which sought to exhaust the enemy by means of stubborn defensive battles, thus inflicting an appreciable loss on his men and matériel.

The defensive battles by the left-wing armies at the end of October and beginning of December 1941 may be divided into three basic periods, which, however, differed somewhat for both armies as to their content and did not always coincide in time.

The first period (October 15-30 1941) was characterized by a maneuver defense, when both armies' units were conducting a stubborn holding action and falling back to the line of the Oka River (49th Army) and the Tula area (50th Army), where by that time defensive structures were being built. The given period is characterized by the retreat by the armies' units along a broad front, while conducting holding actions along intermediate lines, so as to secure the withdrawal of men and matériel. Troop control was greatly complicated as a result of the broad front and the gaps between units. There were instances when separate units fell back without unified control, which demanded the manifestation of intelligent initiative by their commanders.

Despite these difficult conditions and enemy pressure, both armies, overall, coped with this task.

The second period (October 30-November 25 1941) was characterized by the enemy's attempt to seize Tula by frontal attacks from the march and to break through toward Serpukhov. The fighting during this period was distinguished by great exertions and stubbornness on both sides (particularly along the 50th Army's flanks and its boundary with the 49th Army, where a counteroffensive was conducted along the Spas-Kanino-Sukhodol axis in order to eliminate the attempts by the German-Fascist troops to break through to the Moscow road). No less heavy fighting during this period occurred on the 49th Army's right flank (along the boundary with the 43rd Army), where the enemy sought to break through our lines and reach Serpukhov, which threatened to separate the *front's* left-wing armies from the center. On the 50th Army's front during the period November 7-8 we launched a counterblow (chiefly with the forces of the 413th Rifle Division and the 32nd Tank Brigade) in the general direction of Kosaya Gora and Shchekino, with the objective of destroying the enemy group in cooperation with the 3rd Army. The 50th Army's remaining forces (the 258th Rifle and 31st Cavalry divisions, along with the 238th Rifle Division and other units from the 49th Army) held Tula and through their active efforts prevented the enemy from breaking through along the boundary between the two armies toward the Moscow road.

The third period (November 26-December 6) was characterized by the preparation and conduct of active maneuver by the *front* command outside of the defended site—Tula. This period concluded with a powerful counterblow by the 1st Guards Cavalry Corps from the Kashira area to the south. This counterblow was launched in conjunction with blows by other groups (the 340th Rifle, 31st Cavalry, and 112th Tank divisions) and the fixed defense of Tula. During the third period the 49th Army went over to a positional defense along the entire front, with the mission of securely covering Serpukhov. Having pinned down the enemy, the 49th Army secured the 50th Army's right flank; active countermaneuver characterized the situation on the front of the 50th Army and the 1st Cavalry Corps to its left.

Thus the 49th and 50th armies' defensive battles were distinguished by a variety of operational-tactical forms, their alternation and combination: maneuver defense and attack on some sectors, with static defense on others, etc. This comprises the originality of the defensive battles on the Western Front's left wing.

Thus the success of modern operational defense, as was shown by the experience of the 50th Army's combat activities, in conjunction with the left flank of the 49th Army and the 1st Guards Cavalry Corps, is founded on stubborn defense against the attacking enemy, while maintaining an organized front, (based in this case on the fixed defense of a large city). At the same time, spare forces, reinforced by *front* reserves, conduct operational maneuver to create groups of forces capable of inflicting a blow against the attacking enemy, having occupied a favorable jumping-off position.

This later on allows us to carry out an operational counterblow against the enemy forces in order to eliminate his offensive activities, or at least restoring the former situation.

6

The Air Force's combat activities

By the beginning of the Moscow operation significant changes had occurred in the aerial situation, which influenced the development of events on the ground and later facilitated the success of our counteroffensive.

These changes will become understandable if we examine the events preceding the Moscow operation.

By the time of the offensive, which began on the Western Front on October 2 1941, the enemy had concentrated 600-700 aircraft. The enemy's air force was used in the same manner as in earlier operations, but on a significantly greater scale. The offensive was conducted on a broad front and pursued strategic goals.

The German offensive was preceded by scrupulous air reconnaissance, which sought by means of aerial observation and photography to uncover the composition of our forces, to determine the shape of the defensive zone, the defense's rear lines, the character of the anti-tank obstacles, and also to determine the condition of the roads and other important targets. Reconnaissance along the important axes was conducted to a depth of 300 km.

The activity of the German air force along those sectors where the enemy launched his main blow increased several times upon the beginning of the offensive and reached (according to incomplete information) no less than 600-700 sorties per day. The enemy aviation's main forces operated along the forward edge and on the battlefield, destroyed crossings, and bombed and strafed the troops' rear areas. Simultaneous with this, the enemy air force operated against targets in our rear. The activity of the Fascist air force during these days reached its height; it weakened only as a result of the worsening weather conditions, or in connection with the regrouping of air units to other airfields.

The German air force suffered a serious reverse in the fighting with our aviation. The enemy was not able to carry out wide-ranging operations against our airfields before the beginning of the offensive, although this had been planned by the German command. The proper camouflage and dispersal of our aircraft, as well as the great activity of our fighters, prevented the enemy from fully uncovering the disposition of our aircraft in order to undermine their resistance. The enemy also lacked the necessary forces for this task. The enemy air force, still in the process of concentrating on the main airfields, suffered heavy losses as the result of strikes by our air force: in September 1941 up to 175 aircraft were destroyed on the ground alone. The Western Front's air force rebased itself to rear airfields, thus conserving its strength.

In the middle of October the enemy, following a regrouping of his forces, continued his operations along the Moscow axis. On October 19 his units took Mozhaisk. At the end of October they were attacking along the Volokolamsk axis, where they once again tried to break through to Moscow. During this time the enemy air force, upon meeting strong resistance not only from the Western Front's air assets, but aviation from the Moscow PVO zone, began to operate in larger groups (in certain cases up to 40-60 planes) in several echelons, under the cover of fighters. These actions were not very successful, because our forces were skillfully masked and hid themselves from enemy air raids.

Our fighter aviation would meet the enemy bombers and engage them in fierce aerial combat, interfering with (and in some cases preventing), along with Moscow's land-based anti-aircraft defense, the bombing of targets on our territory.

In the fighting along the approaches to Moscow, the enemy was unable to maintain his superiority in the air, despite the fact that by November 1 he had increased his air strength; with each day air superiority grew more favorable to us.

The Germans' air activity declined as time went on, in connection with the lessening of combat at the front, the sharp fall in temperature, and the poor weather conditions.

The Germans' second general offensive on Moscow in mid-November once again gave rise to an increase in combat air activities.

In November 1941 the enemy, ignoring his huge losses, developed his offensive along the flanks, attempting from the north and south to cut off the main communications arteries and encircle Moscow.

The enemy suffered great losses in men and equipment due to the incessant blows by ground forces and our air force.

Our aviation, based along the Moscow axis, during this period operated every day and launched assault and bomber blows against the enemy reserves moving up to the front. On the right wing our main air efforts were directed against the area of the Moscow Sea, Klin, and on the left wing in the Venev and Mikhailov area.

The existing conditions restricted our aviation's basing, as a result of which the Western Front's aviation, the aviation assets of the Moscow Defense Zone, National Air Defense (PVO), the High Command Reserve, and operational air groups, were based on airfields in the Moscow area and to the east, as far as the line Zagorsk-Noginsk-Kolomna. Such a concentrated basing of our aviation enabled us to operate in the needed direction along all sectors of the Western Front. Also, the basing of our aviation was significantly protected by the Moscow zone's PVO.

The basing conditions and data on the airfield network for our air force and that of the enemy was listed earlier (in the section "A Short Description of the Theater of Military Activities").

By the second half of November the Red Army's aviation directly involved in the fighting for Moscow, consisted of the following: a) the Western Front's air force; b) Sbytov's group; c) Golovanov's group, and; d) the Moscow zone's PVO aviation.

By the end of November two more air groups had been created from the High Command Reserve: Petrov's group and Kravchenko's group.

In these groups there were about 700 combat-ready aircraft that took part in the fighting.

The number of enemy aircraft along the Moscow axis during this period was 500-700 planes. The correlation of forces in the air during the battle for Moscow was not in the enemy's favor. This enabled us to enjoy air superiority during the period of defensive fighting and the defeat of the Germans at Moscow and to employ part of our PVO fighter aviation for strafing the enemy troops.

The situation demanded the unification of all our air strength deployed along the Moscow axis.

Our main air strength was directed at the main enemy force northwest of Moscow (in the area of Klin, Istra, and Solnechnogorsk), while the remainder was used along the left flank in the area of Tula, Stalinogorsk, and Venev. Petrov's, Sbytov's and Golovanov's groups, PVO air assets, long-range bomber aviation, and the Western Front's air force operated under the control of the Supreme Commander-in-Chief.

The Kalinin Front's air assets and Kravchenko's group operated along the flanks, having the following tasks:

- the Kalinin Front's air force was to prevent the arrival of enemy reserves from Kalinin to the Moscow Sea;

- Kravchenko's group (with part of the Western Front's air assets and the High Command's long-range bomber aviation, together with the ground troops, was to retard the enemy's further advance toward Mikhailov and Venev.
- Petrov's group, based in the Zagorsk area, had the mission of operating along the Dmitrov-Klin axis and, in conjunction with the ground troops, of delaying the enemy on the western bank of the Moscow-Volga Canal and then to assist the Western Front's right flank in its offensive along this axis.
- Sbytov's group, together with the Moscow PVO aviation, operated along the Solnechnogorsk-Istra axis and was based in the Moscow area.

The Western Front's air assets operated according to the situation along the Istra, Mozhaisk, Naro-Fominsk, Serpukhov, and Venev-Stalinogorsk axes.

In this way the air force's main efforts in the second half of November and first half of December were directed at the main enemy group northwest of Moscow (in the area of Klin, Istra, and Solnechnogorsk).

The control of our aviation's main forces in their operations was carried out under the direct leadership of the Supreme Commander-in-Chief. Missions were assigned separately for each group. The rapidly changing situation sometimes forced us to reorient our air assets' activities to a newly-discovered enemy motor-mechanized column. This was, to a significant degree, the result of insufficiently organized intelligence.

A unified command enabled us to concentrate our air strikes in the necessary direction. Massed air actions against enemy forces were quite effective and in many cases slowed down the German offensive in November; in December our aviation cleared the way for our ground troops. Particularly illustrative of this were our air operations along the Klin axis during the critical days of the fighting along the near approaches to Moscow. On November 27 1941 the combined forces of our aviation along the Klin axis carried out 1,525 sorties, dropped 4,798 bombs, fired 1,506 rocket rounds, 5,905 cannon rounds, 48,873 armor-piercing rounds, and 145,900 standard rounds. Around 100 tanks and 600 vehicles were destroyed or put out of action.

The beginning of December was characterized by stubborn holding battles along the entire central axis around Moscow. As a result of this bitter fighting and unremitting attacks from the air, the enemy was severely battered; he assumed the defensive along a number of sectors.

During the period November 26-December 5, when the German-Fascist troops were making their last attempts to break through to the capital, their aviation went all out to assist them (primarily on the northern wing and in the center), bombing and strafing our troops and lines, and along the way to the front.

The Red Army's ground troops and our aviation prepared for the counteroffensive and along some sectors were already attacking the enemy. The enemy's last attempts to break through along the Dmitrov axis in the Yakhroma area, and along the Solnechnogorsk axis in the Kryukovo area, and in the south along the Tula axis, were beaten back. It was clearly felt that a turning point must take place in the fierce fighting for Moscow.

As one can see from the above, our aviation played a great role in repulsing the Fascist troops' offensive on Moscow.

7

Rear organization and matériel-technical supply

In mid-November the Western Front's rear area, with an average depth of 300-400 km, was bordered on the east by the line through Ivanovo-Kovrov-Melenki and then to the south; and along the flanks it was the boundary between the Kalinin and Southwestern fronts.

The boundary between the *front* and army rear zones was designated in a directive by the *front* deputy commander on October 22 (and in a supplement of November 11) as the line Aleksandrov-Orekho-Zuevo-Kurovskoe-Voskresensk-Kolomna-Zaraisk-Ryazan'-Spas-Ryazanskii, with all points within the army zones. A December 3 directive extended the boundary northward as far as Rostov.

The depth of the army and *front* rear zones guaranteed the normal distribution of the necessary facilities for the rear organs, units, and services. A thick network of rail lines and roads, a well-developed industry and agriculture, and large supplies of local resources, helped to create favorable conditions for the organization of the troops' matériel supply. At the same time, a number of circumstances made the organization of the rear and supply more difficult. Of five railroad lines feeding into Moscow from the east and southeast, two of the most important were overloaded with evacuation cargos. Operational shipments and the delivery of the necessary matériel to the Western Front had to be carried out over the three remaining lines.

During the second half of November the delivery of reinforcements increased. At the same time, new units and entire formations were being delivered to the *front*. The situation urgently demanded the maximum securing of the operational shipments. The dispatch of military shipments was carried out without the same demands on the rolling stock as with operational shipment.

Front bases were deployed on the Gor'kii, Moscow-Kazan', and Lenin railroads. The *front's* distribution stations, along with the area directorate chief's distribution stations, were located at the following junction stations: Vladimir, Okatovo, and Ryazan'; field depots were moved forward to the areas of Yur'ev-Pol'skii, Kol'chugino, Undol, and Novye Petushki.

Army distribution stations were located along the boundary of the *front* rear zone, along well-developed railroad stations. Each army received a railroad sector for organizing its supply base: 16th Army—the Zagorsk-Aleksandrov railroad sector; 5th Army—Fryazevo, Orekho-Zuevo; 33rd Army—Gzhel'- Kurovskoe; 43rd Army—Bronnitsy-Voskresensk, and; 49th Army—Kolomna-Peski and Kolomna-Ozery.

The Moscow area has a well-developed road net, although their radial configuration made the organization of our basing, and particularly transport, more difficult. We encountered these difficulties in drawing up rear area boundaries between the armies. The 16th Army's boundary to the left was the line Bel'kovo-Sofrino-Ozeretskoe-Istra-Tarkhanovo; the 5th Army's boundary to the left was the line Lachugino-Molzino-Mytishchi-Khimki-Golitsyno-Maurino; the 33rd Army's boundary to the right was the line Likino-Dulevo-Lyubertsy-Peredelkino-Vnukovo-Golitsyno and then coincided with the 5th Army's left boundary. The 33rd Army's leftward boundary was the line Slobodishche-Bronnitsy station-Podol'sk (the road was used together with the 49th

Army)-Kamenka; the 43rd Army's leftward boundary was the line Peski station-Shugarevo-Proletarskii-Vysokinichi; the 49th Army's leftward boundary was the line Rybnoe-Korovino-Laptevo and then along the operational boundary line to Voronovo.

In order keep Moscow from being overloaded and to free up the Gor'kii highway from army transport, it was necessary to removed both of them from the army rear area (the passage of army transports through Moscow was restricted, while the use of the Gor'kii road was forbidden); it was necessary to do this, although it also made more difficult the organization of depots and transport for the 5th Army.

As a result of the operational and rear situation, a *front* directive of October 19 limited transient supplies in the army field depots and set up the following norms: no more than 75% of a combat load, one refill of fuel and lubricants, two days' helping of food, and in the *front* depots—one combat load, two refills of fuel and lubricants, and 2-3 days' helping of food. In order to further free up the army rear of permanent depots, the armies were authorized to in certain cases not to establish their own depots and instead present claims for the delivery of the necessities directly through the *front* depots to the unloading stations and to the division exchange points by auto transport.

The armies made wide use of their right to request the delivery of the necessary supplies from the *front* depots to the unloading stations, to the division exchange points, and sometimes directly to the troops; nor did they necessarily refrain from setting up their own field depots.

The level of troop supply at the army and *front* depots as of November 12-15, according to the most popular kinds of ammunition, fuel and food was (in terms of combat loads, refills, and helpings) as follows:

Table III/7.1 Level of troop supply at the army and *front* depots as of November 12-15 1941

Type	Army						Front depots
	16th	5th	33rd	43rd	49th	50th	
Rifle rounds	0.2	2.3	1	0.4	1.6	2	0.2
Mortar rounds	0.52	0.1	1.25	0.5	0.87	1	0.8[1]
Artillery shells	1	1.2	1.4	0.98	0.85	4.0[2]	0.9
Fuel	2.4	0.75	2.25	2	2	–	1.7
Food	2	–	–	–	–	–	–

Notes:

1 Only 50mm rounds; there were no others.

2 There should have been 16 combat loads of 76mm division artillery shells.

With the exception of those figures which define the amount of rifle ammunition, all the other indices are approximate. From the table it is evident that the overall supplies at the army and *front* depots varied within the bounds of the norms established for maintaining transient supplies. Also, there were fixed depots under the People's Commissariat for Defense, on the territory of the army and *front* rear, which had large supplies. These supplies played a large role in the *front's* matériel supply during the defensive battles. Thanks to the presence of these depots, shortcomings in railroad supply were not reflected in the troops matériel supply.

Given the daily factual consumption of ammunition at 0.1 of a combat load, the *front* was completely supplied. The only exceptions were all types of mortar ammunition, which were in extremely short supply not only in the army and *front* depots, but in the fixed ones in Moscow as well.

Supplies of fuel, lubricants and food exceeded the established norms. The command also received large mobilization supplies of fuel and lubricants from the Reserve Committee and local depots belonging to the Main Directorate for Oil Supply. Matters were even better with food and forage. State farm and collective farm leaders sought out representatives from the quartermaster service and individuals units in order to turn over food and forage to them. The collective farmers were more than happy to sell their own supplies.

The *front* was fully supplied with transportation means. There were about 8,000 transport vehicles (not counting those vehicles servicing the air force) in the *front's* auto transport units; of these, more than 6,000 were at the disposal of the armies and divisions, with the other 2,000 in the *front's* auto reserve. The High Command's automobile reserve was a great help in large operational movements or mass freight shipments.

The heavy fighting in the second half of November put significantly greater demands on the rear and supply organs than before. If the armies received 420 tons of ammunition per day from the *front* depots in October and the first half of November, during the second half of November the actual expenditure of the chief types of ammunition, listed in table III/7.2, was 450 tons. The expenditure of fuel, lubricants, spare parts rose accordingly; so did the amount of work for the repair and restoration services, and for freight awaiting evacuation. The amount of freight for constructing defensive works increased significantly. The overall amount of ammunition expended in the November battles, and the number of transport vehicles necessary to transport them, is shown in Table III/7.2.

Table III/7.2 The expenditure of the most important types of ammunition, November 16-December 6 1941

Type	Expended in thousands	In combat loads	Needed to transport		
			Rail cars	3-ton trucks	1.5-ton trucks
Rifle rounds	24,000	–	50	275	550
50mm mortars	100	0.37	10	51	102
82mm mortars	92	about 1.0	31	155	310
107- and 120mm mortars	32	3.5	32	160	320
45mm shells	32	0.75	20	100	200
76mm regimental & divisional guns	144	1.5	150	750	1,500
122mm guns	83	3.3	240	1,200	2,400
152mm howitzers	25	2.6	147	735	1470
TOTAL	–	–	680	3,426	6,852

Data from this table, which shows the expenditure of various types of ammunition during the battle, has not only historical significance, but a practical one as well. In analyzing this data one must take into account the extreme shortage (throughout the battle) of mortars, which forced the troops to use artillery fire against targets quite within the range of mortar fire, and to leave unsuppressed the enemy's firing points inaccessible to our artillery.

Workers with the rear and supply directorates were up to the task of supplying the troops' matériel needs. Despite the enemy air force's attempts, by means of systematic raids on railroads, roads, highways, and *front* and army depots, to disrupt our rear and supply, the armies did not suffer any particular shortcomings in ammunition. According to several items, the supplies present at army depots not only did not decrease, but actually grew, which is supported by data about the movement of supplies at the *front* and army field depots (table table III/7.3).

Table III/7.3 Movement of supplies at the Front and Army field depots, November 16-December 6 1941

Type	As of November 16				As of November 22		As of December 6			
	Front depots		Army depots		Army depots		*Front* depots		Army depots	
	In thousands	In combat loads	In thousands	In combat loads	In thousands	In combat loads	In thousands	In combat loads	In thousands	In combat loads
Rifle rounds	12,018.0	–	21799.0	–	29834.0	–	3,493.9	–	53990.0	–
50mm mortars	40.8	0.2	54.5	0.26	40.6	0.23	10.0	0.05	306.0	1.5
82mm mortars	–	–	34.7	0.32	63.0	about 1.0	0.1	0	130.0	1.5
107mm, 120mm mortars	–	–	3.3	0.25	3.0	0.24	0.8	0	20.0	2.0
45mm shells	30.7	0.3	49.2	0.45	112.1	1.0	67.2	0.6	396.0	3.5
76mm regimental & divisional artillery	16.8	0.2	66.0	0.75	117.1	1.4	1.1	0	291.3	3.2
122mm guns	26.5	1.08	16.9	0.75	30.9	1.25	1.1	0	35.9	1.7
152mm howitzers	4.3	0.3	10.9	1.0	5.2	0.5	3.6	0.4	17.4	1.8

By December 6 the supply of ammunition at the army field depots had particularly increased. This increase basically came about at the expense of the *front* depots, the supplies of which decreased, although the *front's* overall provision of ammunition by December 6 was significantly greater than in mid-November. The rear and supply organs, working in extremely difficult conditions, were able to satisfy the troops' day-to-day demands and to prepare the material base for the Red Army's counterblow.

The *front* was completely supplied with fuel. The transient fuel supplies of the most popular brands were always more than the established norm at the *front* and army depots. The movement and volume of work for supplying the front with fuel in November may be seen in table III/7.4.

Table III/7.4 The condition of Front supplies of the most important fuel types from November 1-December 1 1941

Name	(in tons) As of Nov. 1	Arrived in November from factory	From main Oil Supply Directorate	To the troops	As of Dec. 1	
					In tons	In re-fuelings
KB-70[1], B-70, B-59	639	2,226	631	2,718	861	14.0
Auto fuel	2,241	15,605	5,069	20,609	2,566	2.6
Diesel fuel	475	478	839	981	791	8.0
Ligroin	261	518	184	361	657	55 days
Tractor fuel	551	1,343	1,078	1,368	1,447	33 days

Note:

1 Cracking fuel.

In all, it was necessary to deliver from the factories more than 25,000 tons of fuels and lubricants in November.

Besides ammunition, fuel, fuel and forage, a large amount of engineering equipment, uniforms, and tank equipment was delivered. The overall volume of freight deliveries to the front was 20 trains per day. The scope of supply shipments was relatively small; although one must consider that in November it was necessary to carry out these deliveries in extremely difficult and complex conditions. The massive evacuation, operational shipments, the necessity of organizing these shipments' movements along new lines greatly increased the difficulty of the military communications organs' work.

It was particularly necessary to overcome many difficulties in transporting freight to the armies and troops. It was particularly necessary at this stage to deliver supplies on time and namely those supplies which the troops needed. The rear organs did not always cope with this. Given the presence of sufficient overall matériel supplies, in certain cases the troops did experience shortages, chiefly in ammunition, and to a lesser degree in fuel. With the exception of the mortar shortage (which the *front* often lacked), shortages in all other categories were caused by late deliveries and the inability to shift supplies. This led to a situation in which some units were short of this or that article, while other units had them in abundance. For example, the level of supply for two armies, which were in almost identical situations, was quite different: in the 49th Army there were 0.2 combat loads (1,900 shells) of 76mm divisional artillery shells, while the 50th Army had 16 combat loads (42,000 shells). There were breakdowns in supplying the troops with certain kinds of food; for example, sugar (less so with fats). By the way, in the latter half of October the 33rd Army had 18 helpings of fats and 22 of sugar in its field depots; in the 49th Army there were 14 helpings of fats and 20 of groats.

A similar situation prevailed with fuels and lubricants. The chiefs of the *front's* and army fuel supply sections sought to disperse their supplies by using the numerous fixed bases of the machine-tractor stations and the Main Oil Supply Directorate, so as to move them closer to the troops and thus reduce the distance to be covered by auto transport. However, they did not carry this useful initiative to its conclusion and failed to ensure the timely replenishment of the depots' railhead sections with the most popular brands of fuels and lubricants. It was necessary to dispatch trucks to other depots for other lubricants and fuel brands.

The Supreme High Command, so as to unburden Moscow, excluded the city and its immediate outskirts from the army and *front* rear area; in the meantime a portion of the freight, distributed among the armies at the *front* distribution stations, could reach their distribution stations only through the Moscow junction. As a result, a backup in freight cars, destined for various armies, occurred at the Moscow junction. This required the adoption of special measures.

New problems arose with the regulation of freight distribution. The freight distributed at the Moscow station was to be shipped back to the army distribution station, which was obviously inexpedient. This was not done, because the troops received a significant portion of their supplies from fixed depots around Moscow. So as not to scatter the supplies, those freight cars which had arrived in Moscow were unloaded in near the fixed depots, or sent to unloading stations.

The intensity of the fighting and the frequent changes in the operational situation, made the organization of the delivery of supplies significantly more difficult. There were numerous instances in which sharp changes in the operational situation forced us to reroute freight trains which were already en route to their formations. In such situations, the previously-compiled plan for matériel-technical supply played the role of a reference point in resolving numerous questions which arose as the result of rapid changes in the situation.

The lack of circular highways near Moscow also created problems in organizing deliveries. It was necessary to use routes which were sometimes insufficiently prepared or completely unprepared for auto transportation.

During the November defensive operation auto transport's task was made simpler by the widespread use of transport by railroad to the unloading station (in certain cases, to the artillery's firing positions), which factually cut out the army road sectors from the mix, and army auto transport worked together with troop transport in its supply sphere. Nevertheless, in certain situations there was a shortage of transport equipment and the maneuver of matériel resources became more difficult.

In conclusion, it should be pointed out that the *front's* troops entered the November fighting completely outfitted with equipment. The workers of the rear and supply directorates were successful not only in meeting the day-to-day requirements in a complex rear and front situation, but they were able to prepare the matériel base for the Red Army's decisive counteroffensive.

8

The role of defensive lines and the Moscow Defense Zone in the defeat of the Germans at Moscow

The Supreme High Command's plan for creating a multi-layered defensive system for Moscow

As early as the beginning of the war the creation of a new defensive line between the Vyaz'ma defensive line and Moscow was foreseen, the so-called Mozhaisk defense line.

An order by the *Stavka* of the Supreme High Command (no. 00409) of July 18 1941 planned to construct the main defensive position along the line Kushelevo-Yaropolets-Koloch' station-Il'inskoe-Detchino, and a rear defensive position along the line Nudol'-Lake Trostenskoe-Dorokhovo-Borovsk-Vysokinichi. By the creation of the Mozhaisk defense line it was planned to close the far approaches to Moscow along the Volokolamsk, Mozhaisk, And Maloyaroslavets axes, that is, at a remove of 120-130 km from Moscow.

The 32nd, 33rd, and 34th armies, which formed part of the Mozhaisk defense line, began their construction duties on July 22, but eight days later these armies received new orders and the building of the defensive system was halted.

In August, following the German seizure of Smolensk, the threat to Moscow became more real and the construction work on the Mozhaisk defense line was resumed, while it was decided to extend the line along the flanks: a) on the main position: on the right flank—to the Moscow Sea and the Volga Reservoir, which would secure the northern flank with a large water obstacle; on the left flank—Polotnyanyi Zavod-the east bank of the Ugra River to where it flows into the Oka River, which would cover Kaluga; b) on the rear defensive position: on the right flank—to Klin; on the left flank—southeast of Kaluga.

Also, on August 8 the Red Army's Military-Engineering Directorate issued an order for the construction of a second rear defensive position along the line Khlebnikovo-Skhodnya-Nakhabino-Krasnaya Pakhra-Domodedovo.

It was then decided to build intermediate defensive positions along the most important operational axes in the following areas: 1) Teryaeva Sloboda-Volokolamsk; 2) Mozhaisk-Vereya; 3) Maloyaroslavets; 4) Solnechnogorsk; 5) Istra; 6) Zvenigorod; 7) Kubinka; 8) Naro-Fominsk; 9) Kamenka.

Thus according to the plan of the *Stavka* of the Supreme High Command, the defense system for the approaches to Moscow was to consist of *three continuous defensive zones*, separated from each other by a distance of 30-60 km, and between these zones—*intermediate defensive lines* along the most important operational axes (emphasis in the original). The depth of the fortification preparation for the defense of Moscow was to reach 120-130 km.

The Mozhaisk Defensive Line's role

Four fortified area directorates—Volokolamsk, Mozhaisk, Maloyaroslavets, and Kaluga—were established to organize the work on the defenses.

It was planned to complete all the defensive works by November 15-25 1941, while the most important work—that on the main defensive position, 330 km in width—was to be completed by October 15-25 (for various sectors). However, the pace of construction increased only at the end of September and the beginning of October, when the Germans, having broken through the Vyaz'ma defense line, were approaching the Mozhaisk defense line.

By the time the German forces reached the Mozhaisk defense line, that is, by October 10-15 1941, the defensive works along this line had not been completed. The following data shows the degree of readiness (in percentages) of the main defensive zone's defensive works.

Table III/8.1 Readiness of main defensive zone's works, Mozhaisk Defense Line

Works	Volokolamsk Fortified Area	Mozhaisk Fortified Area	Maloyaroslavets Fortified Area	Kaluga Fortified Area	Overall readiness
Concrete Pillboxes	36	47	60	0	38.9
Wooden Pillboxes	13.5	103	80	1	42.5
Anti-tank Ditches	80	70	190	31	86.3
Scarps	50	45	48	no information	–
Barbed Wire Obstacles	no information	13	5	no information	–

As the table indicates, by the beginning of the fighting the main defensive position was not fully ready and the plan had not been fulfilled. The Kaluga fortified area was completely unprepared. Communications equipment in the fortified areas and in the units of the Moscow defense line did not guarantee troop control on such a broad front.

According to the plan of the Moscow Military District command, 25 divisions from the Western Front's retreating units were to occupy the Mozhaisk line. However, with the breakthrough along the Bryansk Front, the Western Front's troops were unable to systematically withdraw to the Mozhaisk line and occupy the positions. Thus in order to organize the defense along the Mozhaisk line, the *Stavka* of the Supreme Commander-in-Chief transferred rifle divisions and specialized units from its reserve with the mission of preventing a breakthrough by enemy tanks and infantry to Volokolamsk, Mozhaisk, Maloyaroslavets, and Kaluga.

During October 10-12 the Mozhaisk defense line was occupied by 45 battalions. The length of the Mozhaisk defense line's front (from the southern bank of the Moscow Sea to Polotnyanyi Zavod) reached 220 km, that is, an operational density of one battalion per five km; the defensive's tactical density was even lower. As a result, the defense line was intermittent and lacked depth. A number of sectors (for example, along the right flank: Dorino-Maksimovo, about 22 km) was not occupied at all by our troops and the defense as of October 10-12 had no mobile reserves. Nor were there any troops along the planned Kaluga fortified area.

With such a defense, it was extremely difficult to hold up the enemy's offensive, all the more so as the troops of the Western and Reserve fronts had not yet occupied their defensive positions (with the exception of the Volokolamsk combat sector). Nevertheless, the Mozhaisk defense line played a certain role in holding up the Germans' brisk advance.

The enemy, after breaking through the Western Front, directed his main blows during the period October 10-19 against the weakest parts of the Mozhaisk line's main defensive position—along the boundaries between the fortified areas. By this time those troops sent out to defend the

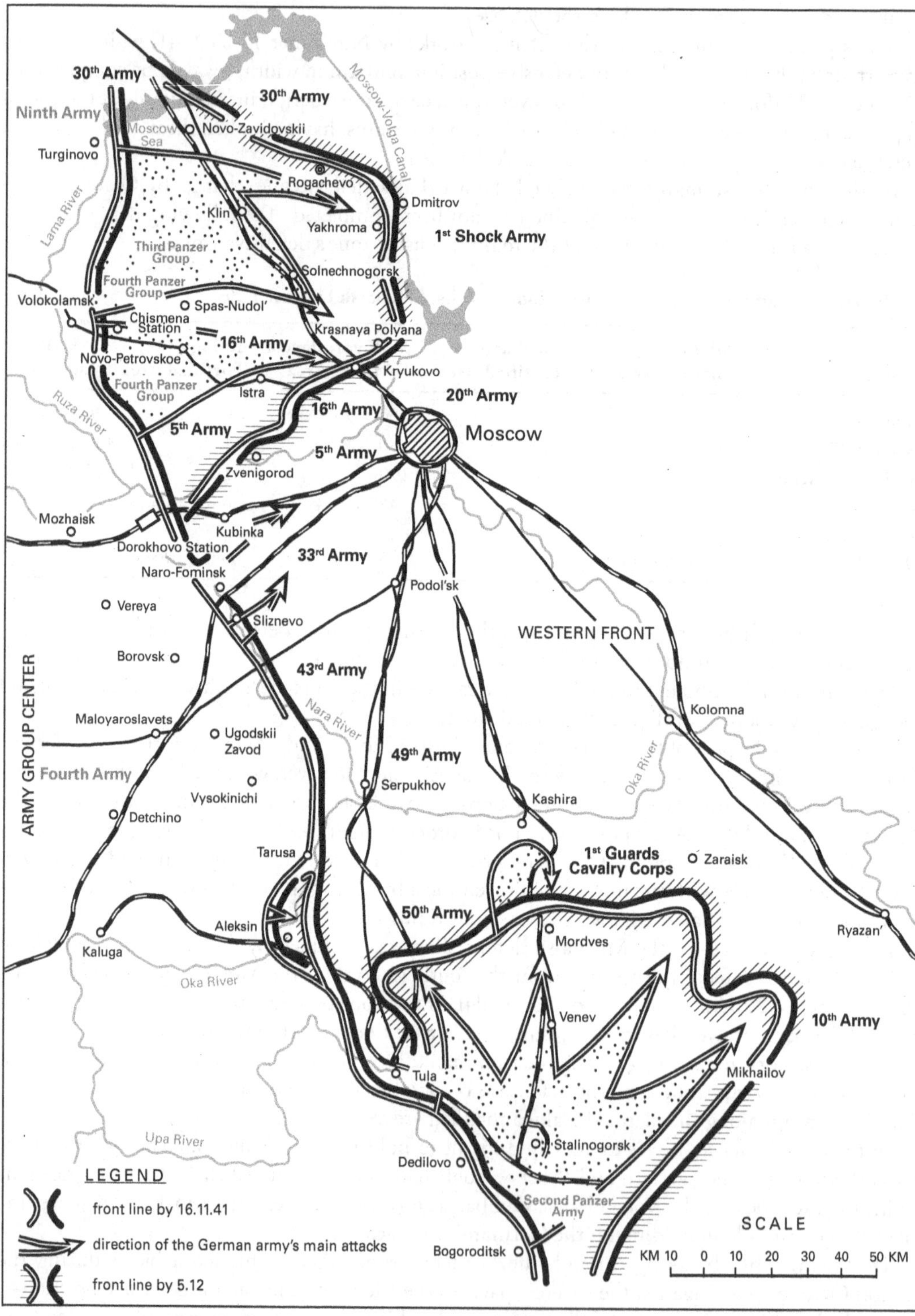

Map 5 The Germans' November Offensive on Moscow in 1941

area had only just occupied their assigned positions and had not had time to acclimate themselves; certain units (for example, the 1083rd Rifle Regiment and units of the 110th and 112th rifle divisions) had not been able to reach their designated areas by the start of the fighting and their collisions with the enemy took the form of a meeting engagement. Nonetheless, the troops occupying the Maloyaroslavets combat sector, relying on the prepared line, fought the enemy during October 10-19 in conditions under which the enemy had turned both their flanks. The troops of the Mozhaisk fortified area's combat sector were holding two enemy infantry divisions and one panzer division in battles lasting October 12-19. The troops of the Volokolamsk combat sector, while fighting along the main defensive position on October 12-25, stubbornly held the German offensive, and on the fortified area's left flank (on the Vysokovo-Prozorovo sector), from which the enemy was launching his main blow, he was able to penetrate into our defense only to a depth of ten km.

Conclusions

The fighting on the Mozhaisk defense line, which lasted 7-9 days (and 10-12 days on the Volokolamsk sector), showed that although the enemy had not been halted on the Mozhaisk line, the speed of his advance had been reduced and that he had lost time for his "lightning" blow against Moscow.

During this time the troops of the Western and Reserve fronts were able to fall back, put themselves back in order and occupy new defensive positions. Simultaneously, these 7-9 day battles gave the High Command the opportunity to move new reserve units up to the far approaches to Moscow's defense and won time for organizing the defense of the near approaches to Moscow.

Preparing a platform for defeating the enemy on the approaches to Moscow

With the withdrawal of Soviet troops from the Mozhaisk line's main defensive position, the threat to the capital increased. An October 19 decree by the State Defense Committee declared Moscow and the adjacent area to be in a state of siege. In accordance with this move, the fortification of defensive lines on the near approaches to Moscow was begun.

The question of creating a Moscow regional defensive system, which had been raised in August, now demanded immediate action. The course of events meant that the Mozhaisk defense line's second rear position was turning into the *outer belt of Moscow's defense*, the construction of which was planned approximately along the line Khlebnikovo-Nakhabino-Krasnaya Pakhra-Domodedovo station. However, in view of the possibility that the enemy might outflank Moscow from the north and south, it became necessary to strengthen the flanks of the outer belt of Moscow's defense (emphasis in the original). Based on these considerations, the chief of the General Staff, on instructions from the *Stavka*, issued an order on October 9 to construct *field flank security lines* for the defense of Moscow along the line: in the north, along the eastern bank of the Moscow-Volga Canal and then along the eastern bank of the Volga River to the south as far as Serpukhov, and then along the Oka River (emphasis in the original).

At the end of October the Moscow Military District's military council adopted a plan for the immediate positional defense of Moscow. This plan foresaw: 1) a security zone running parallel to the outer belt; 2) a main defensive zone in the shape of a half-circle; 3) a second defensive zone in the shape of a ring closed around Moscow, and; 4) a defense inside the city in the shape of circular and radial obstacles and fortifications.

The depth of the Moscow area defensive system (not counting the remaining parts of the Mozhaisk defense line) is illustrated by the following data (in km).

Table III/8.2 Depth of the Moscow area defensive system

Axis	Outer belt	Security zone	Main defense zone	Secondary defense zone	Depth of the Moscow defensive zone
Dmitrov	3-4	4-5	6	4	21-22
Solnechnogorsk	2-3	4-5	6.5	8	25-26
Volokolamsk	2-3	8-9	7	8	30-32
Mozhaisk	4-5	14-15	4.5	4.5	30-31
Podol'sk	3-4	18-19	6	4	38-39
Kashira	4-5	16-17	5.5	5.5	34-35
Average Depth	3-4	11-12	5-6	5-6	26-27

The capital's entire multi-layered deeply-echeloned defensive system became known as the *Moscow defense zone* (emphasis in the original). According to the plan of comrade Stalin, the Supreme Commander-in-Chief, the system was to become a platform for concentrating and deploying reserves brought up from the deep rear. This was necessary so as to hold on to the Soviet capital, wear out and bleed white the Hitlerite army and inflict a crushing blow on it.

Natural, economic and strategic conditions facilitated the construction of such a platform. For example, there are a lot of water obstacles in the outer defensive belt: reservoirs and rivers, as well as a large number of gullies, which were being outfitted as anti-tank obstacles by building escarps and counterescarps; a number of wooded areas, which if blocked, could serve as anti-tank and anti-personnel obstacles; the presence of heights that commanded the surrounding countryside and which were used as firing points; many inhabited areas with buildings, which could be used for setting up firing points and outfitted as strong points.

A characteristic feature of the main defensive zone was the presence of a large number of inhabited areas and separate buildings, which could successfully be used to set up firing points and strong points. The firing points constructed commanded the terrain immediately in front of them, in the tactical sense. There were few natural anti-tank and anti-personnel obstacles along this line; they needed to be built. However, the abundance of different building materials in these areas for the construction of military-engineering structures made up for this shortcoming. Finally, a peculiarity of the second defensive zone was the presence of continuous structures, which could be used for defensive purposes. Streets leading into the city begin at the circle rail line. Thus it was necessary to block the entrances to the town with artificial obstacles.

Of no small importance for the Moscow platform were the roads and transport. The Moscow railroad junction's thick and multi-branched rail net, well-made paved and dirt roads, as well as the presence of an enormous engine and boxcar park and automobile transport, enabled us to deliver construction materials and workers, and to concentrate troops and supply them with ammunition, food, and forage. According to data from the staff of the Moscow defense zone, during the period October-December 1941 1,126 trainloads were transported by the Moscow railroad junction, of which 370 trainloads contained freight being evacuated, while the other 756 contained operational shipments. During the period August-December 138,000 tons of artillery and quartermaster stores and 77,000 troops were transported by the Moscow Military District's auto transport section alone, which involved 71,500 vehicles.

The readiness of the roads and transport for military shipments played its role in the expansion of defensive construction and preparation of a platform for the concentration and deployment of the Red Army's forces, and created favorable conditions for carrying out troop maneuver, which in the final analysis had an influence on the successful defeat of the German troops around Moscow.

The defensive construction of the entire system of the Moscow-area defense, and within the capital itself, began on October 15-16. The most important task was the *obstacle work*, particularly on the roadways leading to Moscow (emphasis in the original). As a rule, the enemy employed well-made roads for launching his blows. Thus the paved roads, bridges and other road structures were mined in the course of 2-3 days. By the beginning of the German army's November offensive Moscow was reliably surrounded a belt of obstacles. This told on the course and speed of the Fascist advance on the capital: the Fascist command had to renounce its favorite method—the development of the breakthrough by tank units along the roads; the enemy was forced to the so-called tactic of "slicing off the edges," which was reflected in the battles for Klin and Solnechnogorsk.

The arrival of cold weather and the hardening of the earth in the fields and country roads facilitated the maneuver activities of the German tank formations. However, this was met b y the State Defense Committee's wise decision to construct forest obstacles in front of the defensive lines and along the avenues of the enemy tank units' like advance.

During December an unprecedented amount (in scope) of work in constructing obstacles, was carried out through the efforts of the mobilized population (mostly women), which is evident from the following data:

Table III/8.3 Construction of obstacles, December 1941

Province	Obstacle width in kilometers	Obstacle depth in meters	Obstacle area in hectares
Moscow	1053.8	From 50 to 1,000	41,565
Ryazan'	274.8	From 30 to 1,000	9,920
Ivanovo	37.6	From 50 to 1,000	1,700
Total	1,366.20	From 30 to 1,000	53,185

Forest obstacles were also set up by the troops in front of their positions. Also, the local population constructed obstacles along those sectors of open terrain favorable to enemy airborne landings and by digging up the area with ditches and planting poles in the ground.

Thus by means of carrying out obstacle construction, the defensive lines around Moscow were reliably reinforced, which led to a situation in which the opportunities for the enemy's maneuver were sharply restricted.

The construction of defensive lines in the Moscow area—trenches, anti-tank ditches, escarps, counterescarps, stakes, anti-tank obstacles, command and observation posts, machine gun and artillery firing points, and other structures—continued according to plan to the end of 1941.

The hardest work involved the creation of an outer defensive zone for Moscow. Of 36 construction sectors, two were completely finished by November 16; work continued on the remaining sites, but a large number of structures was already operational; by December 6 work on another 18 sectors had been completed, and by December 31 the work was finished on the remaining 16 sectors.

According to incomplete data, 325 km of anti-tank obstacles (not counting minefields), 256 km of anti-personnel obstacles, up to 3,700 firing points, of which 1,500 were of reinforced concrete, 1,275 earth and wood firing points, and 37,500 metal obstacles were built along the Moscow lines and in the city itself.

The Moscow-Volga Canal and the Moscow-Oka river basin was used for defensive purposes, particularly as concerns controlling these systems' water level. The Germans were often faced with the flooding of the countryside and the destruction of their crossings by the unexpected release of water during the fighting on the Yakhroma River and near the Istra Reservoir.

The defense of Moscow was built according to the principle of long-term defensive junctions.

The participation of the workers of Moscow and Moscow province in defending the city against the German aggressors was a mass phenomenon.

165,000 people were engaged in defensive construction, in plus 85,000 making forest obstacles, for a total of 250,000 inhabitants of Moscow and Moscow province, of which 75% were women. The civilian population expended the following number of man-days in carrying out the work:

On the construction of Moscow-area lines	more than 1,717,000
On the construction of defensive works inside the city	679,000
On the construction of forest obstacles	1,657,000
TOTAL	more than 4,000,000

The civilian population worked enthusiastically, despite the -35 degree (Celsius) December frosts. The chief of the 5th Moscow Rifle Division's engineering service wrote:

> Thousands of housewives, leaving their children with their grandmothers, went out to defend their native city; thousands of students dropped their studies and joined the labor front. Here were mothers with children, grandmothers with their grandchildren; here entire families worked. Each one of these wanted to do what he could for the defense of his native city. Muscovites, who previously had no experience with shovels or crowbars, carried out their work norms by 120-150% and for 2-3 weeks did not leave their positions to return home.

The construction of defensive positions and obstacles around Moscow enabled us to concentrate and deploy large forces from the Moscow defense zone here; the construction work played an important role in preparing a springboard for the Western Front's counteroffensive and the defeat of the Fascist troops around Moscow.

The deployment of of the Moscow Defense Zone's forces and their role in defeating the Germans around Moscow

The difficult situation along the Western Front by the end of the first half of October demanded the closing of the near approaches to Moscow with fresh forces. There were no available reserves nearby at the time, so the Moscow party committee called upon its members to come to the capital's defense. By October 16, literally in the space of 2-3 days, 25 communist battalions, with an overall strength of 10,000 men, were formed in Moscow's 25 districts from volunteers. The battalions were formed into two rifle regiments, and at the end of October they were used to form the 3rd Moscow Communist Rifle Division.

The district destruction battalions, formed in the same way at the beginning of the war from Moscow residents, became the 4th and 5th Moscow communist rifle divisions at the end of October, while the 2nd Moscow Rifle Division was formed from mobilized Muscovites. There were up to 40,000 Muscovite workers in these four divisions, among which 46% were communists of members of the Komsomol.

On October 17-18 the Moscow units were transferred outside the city to take up their positions in the suburbs. They covered the most important routs leading to Moscow: the Kiev and Minsk highways, and the Kaluga, Volokolamsk, Leningrad, and Dmitrov roads.

As a result of the failure of the Germans' October offensive, the situation enabled us to use these divisions on defensive construction around Moscow. At the same time, units of the Moscow divisions carried out reconnaissance on the front line and took part in combat against the enemy. This was a real force, ready at any price to hold the German troops on the capital's outskirts.

On the Western Front's right wing at the end of November, following the seizure by Fascist troops of the towns of Klin, Rogachevo, Solnechnogorsk, and the forcing of the Moscow-Volga Canal in the Yakhroma area; the capture of Gorki, Krasnaya Polyana, Vladychino, and the fighting for the village of Kievo, the enemy had come up against the outer belt of the Moscow defenses in the area of Khlebnikovo. Artillery fire could be heard in Moscow.

But by this time the concentration of the Supreme High Command's reserves from the deep rear was already underway. On November 27, on comrade Stalin's order, an operational group was hurriedly created under Col. Lizyukov, consisting of the 28th and 43rd rifle brigades, a company of KV tanks, and two guards mortar battalions, in the Moscow defense zone. The *Stavka* of the Supreme High Command ordered the group to: "By means of stubborn defense along the line Khlebnikovo-Cherkizovo, prevent the enemy from breaking through to Moscow." On that day the group, on orders of the commander of the Moscow Military District, having occupied the line Ivakino-Cherkizovo-Uskovo, entered the fighting and barred the enemy's path to Moscow.

To the right of Lizyukov's group, the 2nd Moscow Rifle Division (minus the 2nd Rifle Regiment), with the mission of covering the Rogachevo-Dmitrov axis, together with the attached 311th Machine Gun Battalion and the 15th Guards Mortar Battalion, occupied a defensive line northeast of Khimki. On November 29 the 40th Rifle Brigade was ordered to: "Immediately leave for the area of Krasnogorsk, Nakhabino, and Dedovsk and take up the defense along a prepared line, with the mission of preventing the enemy's tanks and infantry from breaking through in the direction of Krasnogorsk." (order no. 29 of the Moscow Defense Zone staff, of November 29). Consequently, by the end of November the most dangerous north and northwestern defensive sectors were covered, thanks to the timely arrival of units from the Supreme High Command reserve and their inclusion into the troops of the Moscow Defense Zone.

From November 20 through December 2 the concentration and deployment of the forces of the 20th, 60th, and 24th armies was carried out.

At dawn on December 2 the reformed 20th Army attacked with the mission of surrounding and destroying the enemy in the area of Krasnaya Polyana, Vladychino, and Kholmy. By this time the 20th Army had left the control of the Moscow Defense Zone and was subordinated to the Western Front; on December 11 it took Solnechnogorsk.

The 60th and 24th armies, still part of the Moscow Defense Zone, received the following orders from the Moscow Defense Zone's military council.

60th Army—to occupy and defend the prepared line along the front Tarasovka-Klyaz'ma Reservoir-Nakhabino-Perkhushkovo; to cover in particular the Solnechnogorsk, Istra and Kubinka axes. By means of a positional defense of the outer belt of Moscow's fortifications, prevent the enemy from breaking through to Moscow, and to destroy him in front of the forward edge and be ready to operate in a northwestern direction.

To the right was the 20th Army and to the left the 24th Army was defending, while to the front were the Western Front's 16th and 5th armies.

24th Army—to occupy and defend the prepared line along the front Davydkovo (ten km southwest of Odintsovo)-Krasnaya Pakhra-Domodedovo, and then to the northeast to the Moscow River; to cover in particular the Naro-Fominsk, Kaluga, Tula, Kashira, and Kolomna axes. By means of a positional defense of Moscow's outer defensive belt, to prevent the enemy from breaking through to Moscow, to destroy him in front of the forward area and be ready for operations, depending up the situation along the northwestern, western and southwestern axes.

In front, along the line Zvenigorod-Naro-Fominsk-Nara River were the Western Front's 5th, 33rd, and 43rd armies.

In conclusion, at the beginning of December 1941 the troops of the Moscow Defense Zone defended with the following forces: a) 60th Army, consisting of the 329th Rifle and 11th Cavalry divisions, six rifle brigades, the 323rd Machine Gun Battalion, and the 2nd Moscow Rifle Division;

the 24th Army, consisting of two rifle divisions and eight rifle brigades, and the 40th Rifle Brigade, along the outer defensive belt; b) 3rd, 4th, and 5th Moscow Rifle and the 332nd Rifle divisions, nine artillery regiments, eight artillery battalions, five machine gun battalions, seven flamethrower companies, three companies of canine tank destroyers along the main defensive zone, and; c) two rifle divisions, four rifle brigades, a special sailors' detachment, a rifle battalion from the Moscow Defense Zone military council, a cavalry squadron, a motorcycle battalion, and three armored trains, in reserve.

In all, these units numbered:

Men	about 200,000
Guns of various calibers, not including anti-aircraft artillery	850
Mortars	870
Heavy machine guns	1,450
Light machine guns	2,600

The saturation of the Moscow Defense Zone with the above-listed weapons enabled us to guarantee the reliability of the city's defense.

Thus on comrade Stalin's initiative, and under his constant observation, in a short time there was concentrated a new 200,000-man army of the city's defenders along the near approaches to Moscow. The 60th and 24th armies, having deployed in the rear of the Western Front's forward units, were a mighty reserve for the Western Front when it launched its counteroffensive.

Aside from the troops' of the Moscow Defense Zone main mission—to defend Moscow's outer belt through a positional defense and prevent the enemy's breakthrough to the capital—they also carried out reconnaissance activities in the zone dividing the Moscow Defense Zone from the Western Front's forward units, as well as combat by being transferred beyond the bounds of the outer defensive belt in order to reinforce the Western Front's units along the most threatened axes.

The terrain within a 60-80 kilometer radius of Moscow was under the observation of the Moscow Defense Zone's intelligence organs. Reconnaissance activity increased at the end of November, when the enemy began to infiltrate between the lines of the Western Front's armies. This was particularly noticed along the *front's* right flank—along the Leningrad and Volokolamsk roads; here the reconnaissance detachments were in constant contact with the enemy.

With the enemy's approach to the towns of Klin, Rogachevo, and Dmitrov, the Moscow Defense Zone's staff formed detachments of 1,200-1,500, men for active operations with the Western Front's units, the mission of which was to prevent the enemy from breaking through to Moscow. As a result of the fighting near Klin on November 22-24, the Klin detachment destroyed up to 500-1,000 German officers and men, knocked out three tanks, suppressed a mortar battery, 8-10 vehicles with infantry, and two anti-tank guns. The Rogachevo detachment destroyed 13 tanks, three mortars, and scattered up to three companies of infantry. The Dmitrov detachment prevented the Germans from crossing the canal in the Pochinka area and covered the approaches to Dmitrov. These detachments, in delaying the German offensive, also secured the planned withdrawal by the Western Front's units to new lines.

At the end of November units of the 2nd Moscow Rifle Division, through an active defense, were holding off the enemy in the area of Ozeretskoe, Myshetskov, Vladychino, Krasnaya Polyana, Katyushki, and Kievo, until the arrival of from the reserve of units of the 20th Army.

During the Western Front's counteroffensive some units from the Moscow Defense Zone took part in offensive operations.

Combat activities by the air force during the defense of Moscow were conducted by an air group from the Moscow Defense Zone, consisting of 95 planes on October 5 and 78 planes on October

25. According to available data, from October 5 1941 through February 15 1942 the air group spent 112 combat days and 67 combat nights, carrying out 6,000 combat sorties.

The air group's combat activities were quite active in character: they were conducted along the Western Front's seven most important axes: Klin, Volokolamsk, Mozhaisk, Naro-Fominsk, Yukhnov, Serpukhov, and Tula. Frequent air attacks forced the enemy to leave the main roads and travel along country lanes, and to disperse, which restricted the maneuver of his tank and motorized units.

The results of the air operations for 112 days are shown by the following enemy losses:

> Destroyed: 155 enemy aircraft, 392 tanks, 13 tankettes, 20 armored cars, 4,580 motor vehicles, 2,261 other vehicles 197 guns, and 199 anti-aircraft machine guns.
> Destroyed and scattered: up to 17 infantry regiments, up to 950 cavalrymen, up to 100 motorcyclists.
> Destroyed: four formation headquarters.
> Blown up: 22 depots, 41 fuel containers, six bridges and crossings, one train.
> The losses for the air group during the same period were: 27 pilots, 32 aircraft.
> The group conducted aerial reconnaissance to a depth of 150 km.

Anti-aircraft defense

The PVO troops were of great significance in the defense of Moscow and the Moscow Defense Zone. The enemy sought to undermine the combat capability of the Soviet Union's capital by attacks from the air. However, his plans were foiled.

The enemy, in October and especially November, sharply increased the number of his raids on Moscow: in October there were 31, and 41 in November, and the raids began to be conducted not only at night, but in the daytime. However, thanks to the activities of our anti-aircraft artillery and fighter aviation, which formed part of the PVO system for Moscow and the Moscow Defense Zone, of the 2,018 enemy planes that took part in raids during October, 1,783 reached our anti-aircraft's fire zone, while only 72 made it as far as the city. The results for November were even worse for the enemy: of 1,953 enemy aircraft, 1,891 entered the anti-aircraft fire zone, of which only 28 reached the city, which accounts for 1.4% of those Fascist aircraft which took part in the attacks on Moscow. This is testimony to the enormous significance of the anti-aircraft artillery, particularly its defensive fire, which blocked like a fiery wall the enemy aircrafts' path to Moscow and scattered them.

In December the number of enemy raids on Moscow fell sharply (to 14). The number of aircraft taking part in raids also fell (to 200), and only nine planes made it to the city.

The lessening of enemy air activity, even in good flying weather, shows that the enemy was giving out (this is also shown by the fact that old-model bombers had appeared among his aircraft), that he was unable to adjust to winter conditions, and that he had encountered difficult obstacles in the form of defensive fire from anti-aircraft artillery, aimed fire from anti-aircraft machine guns, and from fighter aviation: night flights began to be carried out by single aircraft and at high altitudes.

Beside the tasks of the direct defense of Moscow and covering the Moscow zone, the PVO troops—fighter aviation and anti-aircraft artillery—carried out the mission of covering the Western Front's forces and operating with them, which aided the success of the *front's* units in defeating the enemy around Moscow. Of the greatest significance here were the assault actions of the PVO's fighter aviation. In November and December fighter aviation's assault blows were massive in character and directed against the enemy's main groups. At the same time, the Moscow Military District's air force attacked these groups, which further increased the massed air attacks and ensure the ground troops' success.

The PVO's anti-aircraft artillery and anti-aircraft machine guns, which took part in joint operations with the Western Front's forces, were detailed for operations against the enemy on the ground, particularly in those areas where the threat of a breakthrough by tanks arose: on November 12-13 in the direction of Borovsk and Maloyaroslavets; November 23-December 12 along the Solnechnogorsk and Istra axes. Anti-aircraft anti-tank groups delayed the offensive of the enemy's motor-mechanized troops with their fire and secured the forward advance of our units, while covering the infantry from the air. Our 85mm and 76mm anti-aircraft guns showed themselves to be an effective means of fighting the enemy's tanks and infantry.

During enemy raids on Moscow in the final quarter of 1941, the number of enemy aircraft shot down and destroyed, chiefly by fighter aviation (not counting those enemy planes that were shot down but managed to land on enemy-occupied territory) was as follows:

Table III/8.4 Enemy aircraft destroyed during raids on Moscow, October-December 1941

Month	Number of aircraft	As a percentage of all aircraft participating in the raid
October	278	13.2
November	198	10.1
December	91	45.5

Our PVO losses were insignificant. We lost six men killed, 15 wounded, and 12 anti-aircraft guns destroyed among those anti-aircraft units defending the most important targets in the Moscow zone. In the first six months of the war the losses among all the PVO's forces were: 131 killed, 161 wounded. On the other hand, the Fascist vultures made up for it by destroying the defenseless civilian population and their homes. As a rule, once the enemy had entered our anti-aircraft artillery's zone, he carried out a disorderly bomb run and dropped his ordnance, so as to get away as quickly as possible. His attempts to reach a lower altitude for precision bombing were unsuccessful as a result of the high density of anti-aircraft machine guns around the targets. Thus those targets in Moscow and the Moscow zone did not suffer at all from the enemy's air bombings.

The organization of Moscow's help for the front

With the movement of the front to the east, many industrial areas that supplied weapons and ammunition were cut off from Moscow, while supply from the country's eastern regions fell behind the speed of combat operations. Thus Moscow and the Moscow industrial area were becoming the main source for mobilizing available resources, the repair and production of weaponry and ammunition for the troops defending the capital. Here one must also take into account the fact that that industry having a defensive significance had by October been evacuated (or was being evacuated) from Moscow; the equipment, raw materials, and skilled labor had been moved away. As a result of this situation, enormous difficulties arose in the regulation of military production. However, the Muscovites were able to cope with this task.

First of all, 263 older-model guns, which had been designated for melting down, were unearthed; these were transferred to the artillery regiments of the Moscow rifle divisions that were being formed, as well as to PVO units. Also discovered were 1,600 old heavy machine guns; in the Osoaviakhim organizations up to 100 light machine guns and more than 1,500 rifles of various models. These had to be repaired and retooled.

The chief repair base was the scientific-production workshops and the large enterprises, where the equipment that remained after evacuation was gathered. Here guns, mortars, rifles, and pistols were repaired. Of those vehicles gathered from "automobile graveyards" during November and December, 529 were repaired and transferred to the forces of the Moscow Defense Zone, while overall 2,450 vehicles, 296 tractors, and 60 motorcycles were repaired. The repair of tanks, armored cars, and armored trains was organized.

The chief task, which consisted of organizing the production of weaponry and ammunition in Moscow, was also carried out in a timely way. Non-evacuated equipment was used for building new factories. The Moscow workers and engineering-technical staff displayed a great deal of inventiveness, skillfully adapting the available equipment for work and organizing production, which resulted in overfulfilling the plans. Soviet patriots gave all their strength and knowledge, striving to secure the defeat of the German troops around Moscow. P.A. Gorkin, an old Moscow metal worker, and his son adapted the available machine tools for rounding artillery shell casings and rifling, without leaving their shop for days at a time. A factory, which received an order for grenades, prepared in a single day the material specifications for this type of production and within two days had finished working out the technical process and by the end of October was already overfulfilling the norm. At another factory the workers quickly developed the technology for producing a flammable substance for incendiary bottles and within 48 hours had outfitted a casting shop. Ten small enterprises were co-opted for producing bayonets. A cooperative for making locks for women's purses began to produce parts for anti-tank grenades. A cooperative which used to put out glass beads and Christmas tree decorations, organized the production of flammable bottles. Students from Moscow's higher technical-education establishments, under their professors' guidance, organized the production of anti-tank rifles, aluminum moulds for bombs and frames for mini-obstacles in their study shops. Almost all the enterprises (all the way to factories for making children's toys) rapidly switched over to military production. All Moscow worked for the front.

Conclusions

1 The construction of a multi-layered defensive system around Moscow and the timely deployment of the Moscow Defense Zone's forces allowed us, first of all, to carry out the assignment of holding the near approaches to the capital; nowhere was the enemy able to break through Moscow's external defensive belt, not to mention the main defensive zone; secondly, to secure the Moscow-area bridgehead for preparing a counteroffensive.

2 A nearly 200,000-man army of warriors deployed along the Moscow bridgehead, ready to defend their capital to the last drop of blood. These troops stoutly defended all the most important operational axes and, should the enemy Germans break through the Western Front, possessed sufficient forces and weapons to destroy the enemy.

Thus the troops of the Moscow Defense Zone were a powerful second echelon for the Western Front's armies and turned into a solid support for the *front's* troops.

3 Under the cover of the Moscow Defense Zone, reserves for the Western Front were concentrated—the 20th and 1st Shock armies, and tank and cavalry formations, which secured the successful counteroffensive by the troops of the Western Front's right wing. At the same time the forces of the Moscow Defense Zone constituted in the hands of the Supreme High Command a powerful reserve, which, if necessary, was employed in the *front's* armies (Col. Lizyukov's group, the Klin, Rogachevo, and Dmitrov detachments, and other units).

4 A correctly organized anti-aircraft defense system played an exceptional role in the defense of the Soviet Union's capital and the military targets in the Moscow zone against the enemy in the air. Thanks to the skillful employment of all the PVO's weapons, and in particular the anti-aircraft

artillery's defensive fire, the most important targets in Moscow did not suffer from air raids by the Fascist vultures during the period June 22-December 31 1941.

5 Under the leadership of the Moscow city party committee, the workers of Moscow and Moscow province—male and female workers, male and female collective farmers, engineering-technical workers, housewives, students and professors, communists and Komsomol members—showed their loyalty to the socialist Motherland, not in word, but in deeds. They actively participated in the building of fortifications and obstacles for the Moscow-area defensive lines; they rapidly organized defensive-production help for the front and, as true sons of their homeland, stood with weapons ready for the defense of the capital of the Soviet Union.

6 The very idea of creating the Moscow Defense Zone, for creating a bridgehead for defeating the German troops around Moscow, and the idea's realization—belongs to the great commander of our time, comrade Stalin.

Comrade Stalin personally and ceaselessly followed the course of the construction of fortified lines and the deployment of fresh forces for backing up the Western Front's forces through his General Staff and the Moscow Defense Zone's military council; Moscow's magnificent anti-aircraft defense and that of the Moscow zone are the product of his attention; it was through his orders that the Western Front's forces switched from defense to the offensive and that the *place and time for going over to counterblows*, as the course of the fighting showed, was determined with great precision (emphasis in the original). It was namely here—on the approaches to the outer belt of Moscow's defenses—that the enemy was hit with an unexpected and crushing blow, after which the offensive initiative passed to the Red Army.

9

Party-political work among the Western Front's troops during the defensive fighting for Moscow

In the overall complex of measures for defeating the Germans around Moscow, an important place is occupied by party-political work. Military commissars, political organs, and party organizations politically aided the troops' fulfillment of the *front's* command' combat orders through their work.

The fighting around Moscow was characterized by a high degree of maneuver, intensity, and rapid changes in the tactical situation. The party-political apparatus had to take note of the changes in the tactical situation in a timely manner and influence the course of combat activities in our favor.

In the conditions of fierce defensive fighting for Moscow, the Western Front's commissars, political organs, and party organizations were confronted with an extremely important task: to employ all means to strengthen the units' combat capabilities, to achieve such a high combat and moral steadfastness among the troops that would enable them in the shortest time possible to halt and defeat the Fascist troops streaming toward Moscow.

It was in accordance with this task that the political organs and party organizations carried out their work.

First of all, it was necessary make it clear to each soldier, commander and political worker the great danger in the situation on the front and to make sure they clearly understood their responsibility for the fate of Moscow.

Using the entire system of party-political work, the commissars and political organs aided the mobilization of the rank and file around the historic decree of the State Defense Committee of October 19, which placed the defense of the approaches to Moscow on the troops of the Western Front.

The Western Front command issued an appeal to the soldiers, commanders and political workers, in which it emphasized in a no-holds-barred way the danger overhanging the Motherland and called upon the *front's* troops to defend Moscow from the Hitlerite bands with their last drop of blood.

> Comrades, the appeal read. In this hour of mortal danger for our state, the life of each soldier belongs to the homeland.
>
> The Motherland demands from each of us the maximum exertion of strength, bravery, heroism, and steadfastness.
>
> The Motherland calls upon us to stand like an immovable wall and block the way of the Fascist hordes to our beloved Moscow.
>
> Now, as never before, what is needed are vigilance, iron discipline, the ability to organize, decisiveness in action, an unbending will to victory, and a readiness to sacrifice oneself. There can be no place in our ranks for pusillanimous whiners, cowards, panic mongers, and

> deserters. Leaving the battlefield without the sanction of one's commander is treason and betrayal of the Motherland.
>
> Soldiers, commanders, and political workers!
>
> You are putting your life on the line for the honor and freedom of our people. Let us even more closely rally around the Communist Party (of Bolsheviks), around our commander, the great Stalin and destroy the Fascist slime.

The decree by the State Defense Committee and the appeal by the Western Front command were met by the troops with great enthusiasm. The soldiers, commanders, and political workers welcomed the decree of the State Defense Committee at meetings and swore to triumph or die in the battle with bloody Fascism.

Comrade G. Arshinov, a gun commander, brilliantly expressed the overall attitude of the soldiers and commanders:

> All our feelings, all our thoughts, are directed toward you, Moscow. We will defend you to the death.

Propagandizing the historical mission, placed by the State Defense Committee on the troops of the Western Front, was carried out from day to day. It was explained to the soldiers and commanders in slogans, posters, in conversations, and in lectures that the people and the Motherland had entrusted namely them with the great cause of defending Moscow and place upon them the obligations:

> Halt the enemy! Hold Moscow! This is the Motherland's order.

The question of defending Moscow was directly related to the Red Army's overall tasks in the Patriotic War:

> In holding Moscow, we will hold up the honor of our Motherland, the pride of our people!
>
> In holding Moscow, we will at the same time set in motion the rout of the Hitlerite army.

Alongside the agitation and propaganda work regarding the defense of Moscow, the commissars and political workers took a very active part in realizing the command's organizational measures that were directed at increasing the troops' combat capabilities and strengthening the front.

The *front's* political directorate continuously shifted large groups of political workers (up to 150-200 men) to those sectors of the front that were under the heaviest enemy attack. These workers, often headed by the chief of the Political Administration himself, or his deputy, were endowed with wide-ranging rights and powers and undertook the most decisive measures to restore the situation at the front and to put shaky units back in order, etc.

Workers from the *front's* political directorate and the armies' political sections were sent to the divisions to assist the command in withdrawing the units in an organized manner to new defensive positions established by order of the *front* or army. In some cases, the political organs' representatives led our units out of encirclement. The *front's* political directorate and the armies' political sections also did a great deal of work in fulfilling the *front* military council's orders for forming combat detachments and reserve regiments from those soldiers and commanders who had emerged from an encirclement, and from the remains of units that had suffered heavy losses. Usually this work was carried out at temporarily created formation points. This demanded of the political workers a high degree of vigilance and the ability to quickly size people up. There was no time for a prolonged study of people or a careful examination of the situation and their previous actions. Alongside this, it was necessary to carry out enormous organizational and agitation-propaganda work, in order to best prepare the troops for being sent to the front.

During the critical days of October, the *front's* military council ordered the immediate formation of a rifle division out of the rank and file of rear-area air units. The *front's* political directorate sent a group of its workers to the airfield service battalions in order to explain the military council's order and to personally take part in the selection of soldiers for the division. The entire work of selecting and dispatching the troops to the front was completed in the course of three days.

These measures enabled the *front* command to strengthen and reinforce the defending troops with new units at the expense of "internal resources."

In order to realize the order of the *front's* military council to remove weaponry from rear units and dispatch it to the front, the *front's* political directorate commandeered 15 of its workers and a group of political workers from the reserve. In the course of several days, one group of political workers alone removed 1,212 rifle, nine light machine guns, and one heavy machine gun from the rear units and sent them to the front.

Also the *front* political directorate and the armies' political sections detached the most experienced workers, who had proven themselves in battle, for preparing newly-arrived divisions for combat. They would begin this work while the division was still heading to the front. By way of example, one may cite the 82nd Motorized Rifle Division. As soon as the *front's* political directorate learned that the division was being subordinated to the Western Front command, 20 political workers were sent to meet it. On the way to the front, the *front's* political workers examined the division's command-political element, learned the condition of the rank and file's overall degree of combat and political preparation, the degree to which the units were supplied with weapons and clothing, etc. At the same time, the representatives of the *front's* political directorate acquainted the soldiers and commanders with the situation at the front, with the German troops' tactics, and the methods for fighting them. Upon the division's arrival at the front, conversations and were conducted and political information shared with the entire rank and file, in which the October 19 decree by the State Defense Committee and the appeal by the Western Front command was explained in detail to the soldiers, commanders, and political workers. In the majority of units party meetings were conducted, which included reports by commissars on the tasks of communists and Komsomol members in battle.

On October 26 the division was committed into battle along the Mozhaisk axis.

The results of this political work were evident from the first day. The division's units demonstrated great bravery and stubbornness in the battles with the enemy.

The *front's* political directorate, along with commandeering its own workers, every day sent out hundreds of communists sent by the party Central Committee. They were sent to units in the capacity of political workers and regular soldiers—political soldiers. The newly-arrived political soldiers imparted new strength to units that had grown tired and worn down in the continuous fighting. Being constantly among the units and constituting the backbone of the party organizations, the political soldiers exerted the party's influence on the masses of Red Army soldiers, rallied them around the party of Lenin and Stalin and inspired them up by the example of their own fortitude and bravery in order to ruthlessly exterminate the Fascist headhunters. When necessary, the political organs dispatched large groups of political soldiers in order to immediately restore the combat capability of a unit or formation. Such was the case, for example, with the 113th Rifle Division. In later October the division was unable to withstand the enemy's fierce pressure and started to fall back in disorder, without having received permission to do so. In order to quickly restore order in the division, a group of political workers and political soldiers was immediately dispatched, and they were able to restore the division's combat capability to such a degree so that during the remainder of the entire campaign it defeated the Germans no worse than the Red Army's other divisions.

A significant place in the political organs' activity in strengthening the troops' combat capability was taken up in propagandizing combat experience and in quickly inculcating proven methods and means of combating the enemy's equipment and soldiers. Thanks to this work, the Western Front's forces were more successful in parrying the enemy's blows and in beating off his attempts to encircle them, and quickly mastered the art of combating the enemy's tanks. The latter was one of the most important in eliminating the superiority in tanks that the enemy had managed to create against our Western Front. The resolution of this task was practically carried out simultaneously along two avenues: by organizing special destruction detachments in units and by propagandizing the experience of combating enemy tanks.

By means of personal agitation and the conduct of propaganda in print, the following slogans were popularized: "A brave soldier is not afraid of a tank," "The enemy's armored hordes will not break through where tank destroyers are fighting bravely."

The *front's* political directorate issued in a large press run several leaflets, booklets, and brochures on fighting enemy tanks. Concerning this aspect of his work, division commissar Lestev, in an article written on the eve of his death, pointed out that the first leaflet only called upon the soldiers not to fear the enemy's tanks and to fight them and then, as they accumulated experience, succeeding leaflets and booklets contained a concrete description of the ways and means of destroying enemy tanks. *Front*, army, and division newspapers daily told of fearless soldiers and commanders who had distinguished themselves in destroying enemy tanks and transmitted their experience to the *front's* entire rank and file. The materials contained in these newspapers were accompanied by illustrations, in which arrows indicated the most vulnerable places of the enemy tanks and means of hitting them with various types of weaponry.

In one of the best divisional newspapers (the 11th Guards Rifle Division's "For the Motherland"), the section on "feats" contained a description of how Red Army rifleman Voronovich destroyed two Fascist tanks. Afterwards Voronovich personally related in the division's units how he managed to knock out the German tanks. The straightforward tales of this simple soldier had a great effect on those soldiers who heard him. They were clearly convinced that each soldier may just as successfully destroy the enemy's tanks.

By a decision of the *front's* military council, in October a great deal of work was carried out in organizing detachments and groups of tank destroyers in all the rifle units and formations. The *front's* political directorate and the political sections of the armies and divisions, rendered practical assistance to the units' command in creating destruction detachments, in selecting their rank and file, and in supplying them with weapons.

The organization of the destruction detachments was carried out quite intensively and successfully. In a few days 72 destruction detachments were created in the 16th, 33rd, and 43rd armies, of which 26 were subordinated to battalions, 26 to regiments, and 20 to divisions and armies. The destruction detachments were staffed with tested and experienced Red Army men, chiefly drawn from volunteers. They were commanded by experienced and brave junior officers and NCOs who had displayed initiative. The following data for the 33rd Army gives an idea as to the percentage of communists and Komsomol members in the destruction detachments: of 663 soldiers and commanders who served in 24 destruction detachments, 166 were members or candidate members of the VKP(b), and 151 members of the Komsomol, or about 48% of the total.

Hundreds of German tanks, armored cars and vehicles were destroyed or put out of action by the brave destroyers. A single destruction detachment from the 32nd Rifle Division, under the command of Sgt. Konovalov, destroyed 12 Fascist tanks in a single battle. The brave destroyers let the tanks advance to close range and then attacked them with anti-tank grenades and bottles with flammable liquid.

The same sort of work as the creation of destroyer detachments was conducted by the Western Front's political organs and political apparatus for organizing and outfitting companies and groups of automatic riflemen. The best soldiers, who had proven themselves in the fighting with the German-Fascist invaders, were selected for these companies and groups of submachine gunners. Military commissars and political section chiefs directly carried out the selection of the rank and file. Particular attention was given to selecting experienced and decisive commanders for these units, as they were entrusted with very responsible tasks. The automatic riflemen successfully operated in all aspects of battle and inflicted great losses on the enemy, primarily destroying his troops.

All the organizational and agitation-propaganda measures directed toward strengthening the troops' combat capabilities were closely intertwined with an enormous amount of educational work, which the political organs and party-political apparatus in the units carried out. The political organs and party organizations worked on inculcating into the entire rank of file of those forces defending the approaches to Moscow the most important qualities—fearlessness and stubbornness in battle with the enemy, the willingness to sacrifice oneself, and contempt for death. Work on inculcating these qualities was carried out by means of encouraging and popularizing heroic feats and rewarding those who distinguished themselves in battle, and by ruthlessly combating cowards, panic mongers and unreliable elements.

"He who bravely defends the Motherland has a right to life," was the slogan put forward by the Western Front's soldiers and commanders, who had been valorously fighting for the Soviet capital. Like hot steel they burnt out every manifestation of faint-heartedness and cowardice, panic mongering and treason. They treated cowards and panic mongers and those who abandoned the battlefield as traitors to the Motherland, just as the 28 heroic guardsmen who covered themselves with immortal glory and who shot the 29th, who tried to surrender.

The example of the 28 soldiers of the Panfilov guards division, who fought off several attacks by 50 Fascist tanks and who, at the price of their own lives, held off the enemy's rabid pressure until their own units came up, is the most outstanding example of stubbornness in battle and contempt for death shown by the Western Front's forces in the battle for Moscow.

Each one of the 28 guardsmen proved that "one man in the field is a soldier" if he's a Soviet soldier. Hero Komsomol member Sosnovskii proved that in practice. During the fighting he noticed that the Fascists were laying down flanking fire with a machine gun and holding back our unit's advance. At a bound he threw himself on the German pillbox and covered the machine gun's barrel with his chest, pressing it to the ground. A machine gun burst tore the fearless warrior apart. However, his dead body blocked the embrasure and kept the Fascist machine gun from firing.

The soldiers of 6th Company of the 6th Motorized Rifle Regiment (1st Guards Motorized Rifle Division) were distinguished for their bravery and valor in the fierce fighting for Naro-Fominsk. Having been cut off from their company, a platoon under political leader comrade Tsitsyura continued to carry out its orders. The platoon burst into the center of town and threw the Germans out of their fortified houses and captured it.

Over eight days a handful of brave men waged a sustained fight against the German troops who filled the town. The platoon's soldiers knocked out a German tank, destroyed its crew, and destroyed several groups of German soldiers who were trying to approach the tank. Through a series of fearless sorties they killed the Fascist automatic riflemen, who had established themselves in homes and on the streets. It was only on the morning of November 1 that political leader Tsitsyura led his heroic platoon, consisting of 30 men, out of the town and linked up with his unit.

It was namely of such soldiers, who fought so heroically, like the 28 guardsmen, like Komsomol member Sosnovskii, like political leader Tsitsyura and his brave soldiers that comrade Stalin spoke about on the 24th anniversary of the great October socialist revolution:

> … in the fire of the Patriotic War new Soviet soldiers and commanders, pilots, artillery men, mortar operators, tank men, infantrymen, and sailors are being forged, and have been forged, and who will tomorrow turn into a terrible storm for the German army.

It was such soldiers, commanders, and units which formed the foundation of the Western Front's troops. The Fascist hordes, streaming toward Moscow, broke their teeth on them. For their bravery and valor, their heroism and contempt for death, they were the first to receive the honorary title of guards.

The fight for the title of guards unit or formation took place on the field of battle. By means of their glorious combat feats and valorous deeds, the regiments and divisions earned and justified in later battles the guards banner. The political organs and party organizations raised the fight for the guards title to a great political height as a matter of honor for each regiment and division.

Units and formations were tested several times in battle before being awarded the title of guards. And it was only those which had truly skillfully and bravely fought and inflicted heavy losses on the enemy, manifesting examples of bravery and valor, discipline and organization that were honored with the title of guards and the guard's banner.

The awarding of the guard's title and the guard's banner caused an unusual amount of excitement amongst the entire units' and formations' rank and file. The transformation of a unit into a guards unit multiplied the strength of the soldiers, commanders, and political workers and inspired them to new heroic feats for the glory of our Motherland.

The soldiers, commanders and political workers expressed their thoughts and feelings at the moment they received their guard's banners in letters and appeals to the Red Army's great leader and commander—comrade Stalin.

> We have the historic mission," wrote the soldiers, commanders, and political workers of the 1st Guards Tank Brigade to comrade Stalin, "of defending Moscow blocking the path of the Fascist aggressors, destroying their forces, and once and for all teach them to encroach upon our Motherland. Today we are receiving the Red Banner from the government…
>
> Today we swear that the title of guards, which the soldiers, commanders, and political workers of our brigade are being awarded, we will further justify, inflicting crushing blows on the Fascist aggressors. Upon receiving the Red Banner we will fearlessly go where it is hardest: despite the dangers, we will not give in to panic, will not tremble before the enemy, and will put all our efforts toward holding and destroying him.
>
> We will bravely and valorously carry out our duty before the Motherland and honorably justify the high title of guards.

The close proximity of Moscow told, to a significant degree, on the political unity of the Western Front's troops and their combat capabilities. The consciousness that they were defending the Soviet capital increased their strength tenfold and raised their steadfastness and fury in battle. The Western Front's units were connected by a thousand threads to Moscow. They received reinforcements, ammunition and weapons from Moscow. The Moscow city party committee was particularly solicitous of the 1st Moscow Guards Motorized Rifle Division. Hundreds of volunteers from Moscow, communists and Komsomol members, who had undergone combat training in the communist battalions and destroyer detachments of the city's districts, were sent to the division. Some divisions, operating within the Western Front, had earlier been formed as militia divisions from Moscow's workers. These units' political organs and party organizations established direct communications with the capital's district party organizations and enterprises. In letters to the front it was communicated how Moscow was helping the front, how the capital's workers were preparing to rout the enemy.

> We have transformed our Moscow into an unassailable fortress," wrote the secretary of the Leningrad district committee, comrade Titov, to the soldiers of the 11th Guards Division, "and should it be necessary, will fight for each street, each building, and each handful of our dear Muscovite earth. Be just as stalwart and brave, comrades, each at his post.

Blue and white collar factory workers from the Leningrad, Frunze, Sverdlov, Krasnaya Presnya, October and other districts of Moscow, systematically maintained communications with the *front's* divisions and regiments. They sent the units letters and presents and sent delegations to the front.

In speaking before the soldiers of the 11th Guards Division, a delegate from the Leningrad district, a worker from the 1st Stalin Factory, D.P. Voronin, said:

> We not only brought you presents, but an order from the residents of Moscow. Moscow is living a combat life. Everybody is working with redoubled energy. The workers are not leaving their benches for even a minute, even during bombing raids. After all, each minute represents a shell or grenade. We are supplying you with everything and demand only one thing: not a step back.

The arrival of delegations of Moscow workers at the forward positions inspired the soldiers. They really felt that Moscow was fighting alongside them on the front. This raised the feeling of responsibility of each soldier for the fate of Moscow.

When the Bashkir soldier Sharipov received a present from the workers of Moscow not long before a battle, on said with some agitation:

> Moscow is helping me; Moscow is sending me a present. I'll fight for Moscow and will not spare myself, and will not spare my life.

* * *

The Western Front's forces met the 24th anniversary of the Great October Socialist Revolution in an atmosphere of continuing bloody battles. At the price of extreme exertion, the soldiers and commanders were holding back the pressure from the attacker, wearing out and destroying his forces and equipment. However, despite his colossal losses, the enemy continued to slowly advance on Moscow. Our units fell back with a sharp pain in their heart. Not everyone sufficiently correctly understood the reasons behind their retreat. Some soldiers began to be plagued by doubt as to the success of the struggle.

And at just that moment, just when it seemed that there was no force capable of taming the Fascist beast, when the German generals were already celebrating and tasting victory, and the cannibal Hitler was wrapping up his final preparations for a triumphant entry into the Soviet capital; at that moment in Moscow, at a solemn meeting of the Moscow Soviet, dedicated to the 24th anniversary of the Great October Revolution, the leader of the peoples, the commander of the Red Army, comrade Stalin, spoke.

More than two thousand of the meeting's participants and together with them the entire country, the entire Red Army, heard the leader's wise and clear report.

In his report, comrade Stalin answered all the questions which at that moment were agitating the soldiers and commanders. They learned of the reasons behind our army's temporary setbacks and received an exhaustive program for struggling for victory over the German-Fascist aggressors.

Comrade Stalin's report and his speech during the Red Army's parade caused an enormous political swell in the *front's* units and formations. The rank and file was literally transformed. The troops cheered up. They forgot about being tired and came to believe even more in their strength and began to appraise the enemy's success differently.

In all the *front's* units and formations, depending upon the combat situation, meetings and gatherings were held, as well as individual and group conversations, dedicated to comrade Stalin's report and speech. All the speeches were infused with passionate love and fidelity to our Bolshevik party and great Stalin. The soldiers, commanders, and political workers thanked comrade Stalin for his report and vowed to fully carry out his instructions.

Comrade Titov, an army scout from the 2nd Independent Guards Mortar Battalion, declared at a meeting:

> It was with great joy that I listened to comrade Stalin's report. The leader's report is an action program for destroying the enemy. Thanks be to our great Stalin for his clear, simple and accessible report.

The Western Front's forces answered the leader's call—"Death to the German occupiers!"—with concrete combat deeds.

On November 8 the rank and file of the 24th Mortar Battalion destroyed 24 of the enemy's vehicles and 450 infantrymen, as well as a mortar battery.

Machine gunner Petrenko, having acquainted himself with comrade Stalin's report and speech, promised to destroy in the first battle no less than 15 Fascists. In a battle on November 14 he fulfilled his promise, destroying up to 40 German soldiers and officers. Although he was wounded three times, comrade Petrenko did not leave the battlefield and went to the dressing station only after our units had accomplished their mission and captured the village of Sinyatino.

The political enthusiasm among the troops found its manifestation in the growth in the ranks of the party and Komsomol. The best of the best soldiers and commanders linked their life to the life of the party. The thoughts of those soldiers who joined the party during these days were expressed by comrade Belousov, a soldier from the 108th Artillery Regiment: "The appeal of the great leader—to bravely and stoutly fight the enemy until his final defeat—is directed most of all to the communists. I answer for that appeal with combat deeds and consider it impossible to further remain outside the ranks of the VKP(b). I will not shame the title of communist and will fight the enemy until he is destroyed and driven from Russian soil." In the 49th Army's units alone from November 7 through November 10, 101 requests were submitted for admission into the party. On November 11 the 43rd Army's party organizations received 39 requests to join the party and 12 to join the Komsomol.

In joining the party, the Red Army's soldiers and commanders took upon themselves the entire heavy responsibility for the defense of Moscow. They now went into battle not just as soldiers, but as soldier-communists, leaders of the masses.

The work around comrade Stalin's report took on enormous scope. The *front's* political directorate received about a half-million copies of *Pravda*, with the text of comrade Stalin's report and speech and saw to it that these papers were immediately delivered to all units. Also, comrade Stalin's report and speech were printed in the *front* and army newspapers and reproduced in several million leaflets and brochures. Special issues of newspapers and combat leaflets, dedicated to the leader's report and speech, were issued in the units and formations. All the party workers, from the *front's* political directorate all the way down to company political leaders, inclusively, were occupied in propagandizing the content of comrade Stalin's report and speech. Lectures, political classes, political information, collective and individual discussions, all forms of propaganda and agitation, were used so as to relay the content of comrade Stalin's historic addresses to the *front's* soldiers and commanders.

Alongside the propaganda and study of comrade Stalin's report, the political organs and party organizations took charge of the soldiers' and commanders' combat enthusiasm in order to carry out at any cost comrade Stalin's call to "Destroy all Germans to the last man, who have entered the territory of our Motherland as occupiers." Personal accounts for each soldier were opened in the companies, where the number of Germans destroyed in combat was noted. For example, the rank and file of the 12th Rifle Regiment undertook the task of destroying as many Fascists as possible. Individual soldiers tried to destroy up to 50 Fascists. The soldier Rubtsov, of the 258th Rifle Regiment, killed five Fascists in a single day. Soldier Gavrilov, of the 1289th Rifle Regiment, killed 12 Fascists, and Jr. Lt. Makhorin, from the same regiment, killed 18. A movement began among the snipers to join the 100 club. Each heavy machine gun crew sought to destroy no less than 500 Fascists.

In response to comrade Stalin's appeal to "reduce the German superiority in tanks to nothing," the *front's* soldiers and commanders undertook to master new methods of fighting the enemy's tanks with even greater energy, particularly as regards destroying tanks with anti-tank rifles. New groups of tank destroyers were formed from the best volunteer soldiers.

In such a way the *front's* forces answered comrade Stalin's report and speech with concrete acts.

Comrade Stalin's historic speech had a decisive significance for the political enthusiasm of the soldiers and commanders at the front, which was immediately reflected in the course of our troops' combat activities. Comrade Stalin's report and speech determined the presence of all the prerequisites for a new phase in the war and the rout of the German occupiers around Moscow. Now no one doubted any longer that the enemy would be halted and routed. A sharp turning point was reached in the consciousness and attitudes of the soldiers and commanders. The *front's* troops were receiving reinforcements and they were politically preparing for going over from an active defense to a decisive offensive against the enemy.

10

The results of the defensive battle on the Western Front

On the threshold of a new stage in the war

The defensive battle around Moscow took place in a definite historical situation and in concrete political and strategic conditions. Only after having grasped these conditions can one correctly understand and evaluate the development of the operational events around Moscow, which were linked to the overall situation on the theater of war and to a great degree were conditioned by it. Comrade Stalin, in his order on the 24th anniversary of the Red Army, pointed out:

> In the first months of the war, in light of the unexpectedness and surprise of the German-Fascist attack, the Red Army was forced to fall back and abandon a part of Soviet territory. However, in falling back, it wore out the enemy's strength and inflicted heavy blows on him. Neither the Red Army's soldiers, nor the peoples of our country, doubted that this withdrawal was temporary and that the enemy would be halted and then routed.

By the end of November—beginning of December 1941 realistic conditions for changing the overall course of military activities on the Soviet-German front in favor of the Red Army began to appear. By this time it was no longer a case of accidental and temporary reasons, which conditioned the Germans' opening successes, but rather permanently operating factors—the strength of the rear, the state of the army's morale, the quantity and quality of divisions, the army's weaponry, and the command element's organizing capabilities, that is, the fundamental political, economic, and military reasons, which were starting to starting to exert a decisive influence on the war. As regards these basic factors, which influence the course of military activities as a whole, the Soviet Union had undoubted advantages over Hitlerite Germany.

The enemy, as a result of the preceding five-month struggle on the Soviet-German front, had suffered enormous losses and was exhausted and weakened. The conditions of the theater of war had also changed: the German-Fascist troops, having advanced deep into the Soviet Union, found themselves surrounded in a strange and hostile country. Their communications stretched back 1,000 km; they were being attacked by Soviet aviation and partisans. The occupation of the temporarily-conquered territory, protecting communications, and the struggle with the partisans entailed an extra expenditure of troops. The difficulties of insuring the German occupiers' regular supply and reinforcements, as well as the timely movement of forces to threatened sectors constantly increased. The German-Fascist command still possessed large forces and superiority in equipment, which enabled them to carry out active operations along some axes. However, in examining the sides' situation in the larger strategic sense, one can conclude that the German offensive on the Soviet-German theater of war had already reached its culmination point for the 1941 campaign. The German offensive was already on the downward slope of the strategic curve and in places was already beginning to give out. In such a situation a setback, even in some battles, can be an extremely unfavorable circumstance, entailing serious consequences often going beyond the bounds of the initial setbacks. An operational setback here can have great strategic consequences.

Comrade Stalin, the great commander of our time, thoroughly examined the emerging situation, weighed the chances of victory, and determined the time when the Red Army could go from active defense to a counteroffensive. Our blows against the Germans near Rostov-on-Don, near Tikhvin, and along other sectors of the enormous front, visibly showed that the Red Army was already beginning to seize the initiative along certain axes and in places was successfully defeating the enemy. The great battle around Moscow unfolded on the threshold of a new stage in the war, at its possible turning point.

In this way, the German command's operational plan for seizing Moscow (which has been described earlier) was being carried out in strategic conditions more favorable for the Red Army than during the first part of the way. And if the subsequent rout of the Germans at Moscow was the turning point in the further development of the 1941 campaign on the Soviet-German front, then this victory was prepared by the entire preceding five-month course of the war.

However, the favorable strategic situation facilitated the achievement of operational success and its further exploitation, although it itself did not predetermine victory on the battlefield. It was necessary to win the battle against an experienced and skillful enemy in those cruel and bitter battles which resounded in the Moscow area's fields and forests in late autumn 1941. In order to achieve a victory over the hated enemy, it was necessary to defeat him directly in battle. This was not an easy task.

In November the situation around Moscow was extremely serious and crucial. A terrible danger hung over Moscow and the Soviet Motherland. Only by means of exerting all one's forces could such a dangerous enemy be halted and defeated. The German-Fascist armored hordes, in overcoming our troops' valorous resistance, were surging toward the Soviet capital. The entire multimillion country, while holding its breath, followed the course of the great battle around Moscow. *Pravda*, the central organ of our party, with fiery words raised the masses for the struggle against the aggressors and planted in them confidence in our final victory. Here are some of *Pravda's* editorial headlines and slogans which appeared during the alarming days at the end of November.

> November 21—"The Patriotic War gives birth to heroes." Now there is no more important task than the task of beating the enemy.
> November 22—"Stoutly defend our Moscow." Not a step back! Don't let the enemy reach the capital!
> November 24—"Not a hint of carelessness, raise higher vigilance and organization!" It's necessary to halt the enemy at any cost, to defend Moscow and in this way begin the defeat of the Hitlerite army.
> November 25—"Crush the enemy's military might!"
> November 27—"The enemy's defeat must begin at Moscow."

The Western Front's troops fought heroically. They understood the great historic responsibility that lay on their shoulders. The leader's call to "hold every inch of Soviet territory, to fight to the last drop of blood for our cities and villages, and to manifest bravery, initiative and gumption peculiar to our people," met a resounding response among the broad masses of soldiery. It found remarkable expression in the immortal words of one of the 28 hero-guards, political leader Klochkov-Diev: "Russia is big, but there's no place to fall back on. Moscow is behind us."

The soldiers realized not only the great military significance of the battle, but its enormous political significance. Moscow is the heart and brain of the Soviet Union. The heroic struggle of our people for its independence, honor, and freedom is linked to Moscow. It was near Moscow that the motley detachments of the Polish-Lithuanian grandees met their end; here, for the first time, the glory of Napoleon was dimmed. From Moscow spring the sources of the great Russian national culture and statehood. In the most difficult minutes, the peoples of our country turned their faces toward Moscow, which poured into them confidence and faith in their strength and inspired them to self-sacrificing and creative work and heroic feats. Moscow is the foundation of the fraternal family of peoples—the Union of Soviet Socialist Republics. Stalin works in Moscow. From here come his orders to destroy the beastly enemy. Our country's fraternal unity of peoples and their readiness to defend their Moscow to the last were beautifully expressed in a letter by the Uzbek people to comrade Stalin:

> The enemy at Moscow will not chop off heads.
> Our Moscow has many defenders:
> The Kazakh and Turkmen, Belorussian and Georgian,
> The Ukrainian, Russian, Tadzhik, as one,
> They will begin to strike the enemy hordes,
> With fire and sword they will shoot and hew...

In the battle for the capital of our country all the most dear and valuable for Soviet man organically came together: the Motherland, Moscow, and Stalin. The fighting against the Fascist aggressors was particularly fierce and prolonged. The newspaper *Red Star* wrote that "The earth becomes sticky when Moscow is behind your back." The battle was for every inch of Soviet earth.

The operation's turning point

During the period from November 15-16 through December 5 the German-Fascist troops of Gen. von Bock's Army Group Center carried out an offensive operation, striving by means of concentric blows to encircle and defeat the forces defending Moscow and capture the capital. The theory and practice of the concentric offensive operation had long ago been worked out in the German army. This operational form has a number of definite advantages (along with certain shortcomings),[1] which in a favorable situation, make it preferable to other offensive forms. The troops are in a favorable jumping-off position for the operation's beginning. By means of a simple forward movement, they come out on the enemy's flank and rear. The latter (unless he takes timely countermeasures) may soon end up in an unfavorable situation, being tied down from the front and flanked on both sides; his communications are threatened. As the concentrically attacking groups approach each other and the internal space decreases, the defender's situation quickly worsens and he may end up being encircled.

The defender's chief measures for countering the encirclement consist of delaying the advance of the enemy's tank wedges (by adopting positional and maneuver defense, as well as withdrawing troops from under the enemy blow along the threatened sectors) and separately attacking the enemy's groups.

For the side operating along internal lines, one needs swiftness in making decisions and energetic actions, along with forces possessing the necessary strength, quality and mobility, in order to attack the separate enemy groups ("wedges") with powerful counterblows and prevent them from linking up. It's very good if one has a part of one's forces (a reserve) beyond the designated encirclement ring in order to win the enemy's flank oneself. Otherwise, the encirclement ring might close. A similar form for conducting concentric operations was widely used by the Germans, both on

1 The transfer of efforts from one of the front's sectors to another is made more difficult, as is the organization of cooperation between the separately attacking groups, and others.

our front and on other fronts on various scales. One could say that it is their favorite operational method in the current war and has become a cliché.

The German command, in carrying out its operational plan at Moscow, had evidently calculated that their flank shock groups, including the great mass of motor-mechanized formations (11 tank and four motorized divisions), supported by infantry divisions, could quickly defeat the opposing forces of the Red Army along the Western Front's wings and break through further into the operational depth and close the encirclement ring to the east of Moscow. They also calculated that the German center, including their main infantry forces, could at the start pin down our central armies along the shortest approaches to Moscow from the west and prevent them from maneuvering against the offensive along the wings, and then (as the turning blows along the flanks developed) break through our front and reach Moscow, having deprived the Red Army's forces of the opportunity of rendering organized resistance. However, as we know, this did not come to pass on either of the flanks or in the center, despite all the efforts of a perfidious and skillful enemy.

The German-Fascist troops in the north, having come down on the Western Front's right wing with two tank armies (groups), forced our 30th, 16th, and 5th armies to fall back to the east as a result of 20 days of bloody fighting. The Germans managed to advance 80-90 km and even reach the Moscow-Volga Canal north of Moscow. However, the Red Army's operational front was not broken through. As was the case 20 days before, the enemy was faced with the Red Army's impregnable wall. Instead of the expected operational breakthrough and the defeat of our right wing and those reserves concentrating under its cover, the front line was only deeply indented. Our armies fell back slowly under pressure from the enemy's superior forces, inflicting losses on him and counterattacking; but no matter how much the enemy advanced, they encountered a renewed front along every new line. Front faced front everywhere and there was no operational breakthrough anywhere. At the battle's decisive moment the Supreme High Command's strategic reserves (1st and 20th armies) entered the fighting on the right flank and changed the correlation of forces in the Red Army's favor. As a result of this, as well as the great losses suffered by the Germans, the operational situation of their strongest northern shock wing began to worsen and by December 5 had become unfavorable.

An advance into the enemy's position is advantageous if it lead to the defeat of part of the enemy's combat order and the formation of a breakthrough, splits the front and enables one to maneuver in the operational depth and attack the enemy's flanks, to destroy isolated parts of his combat order, and encircle him from the rear. Such an advance, when fed by reserves, yields great advantages to the attacker.

But if a strong and active opponent is not defeated and his front not broken and, as a result of the offensive only a dent has been made in the front, if a "bubble" has formed facing the enemy, if the attacker does not have sufficient reserves nearby, then in such a case circumstances may turn out unfavorably for him. There's no breakthrough, but there is a "sack," inside of which his forces are in an unfavorable operational-tactical situation. If the defender has preserved his forces (or received reinforcements), and if he's sufficiently active and bold, then he may put the attacker's forces in the "sack" in a difficult condition for continuing the fight.

The Western Front's right wing was forced to cede the enemy significant territory, but it was not routed and did not fall apart under the enemy's fierce pressure; but being supported in a timely manner by the High Command's strategic reserves, played to the full its responsible role in the Moscow operation. The right-flank 30th Army, having bent back its left wing, nevertheless held on its main zone and then, reinforced with newly-arrived divisions, hung over the German troops' flank from the north. The High Command's reserve armies (1st and 20th) entered the battle in the area between the 30th and 16th armies, right where the Germans were driving their wedge. The 5th Army was holding its positions near Zvenigorod and further to the southwest along the Moscow River, flanking the enemy from the southeast. In this manner, the Germans' northern shock group, which was striving to break through the front and outflank and encircle the Red Army's Moscow group, was itself factually outflanked around Moscow from three sides. This group, lacking the strength for a further advance and forced to go over to the defensive found itself in an operational "sack," and faced by a powerful and active enemy. It's both difficult and unfavorable to defend in such a situation. The Red Army's forces counterattacked and inflicted heavy losses on the enemy, all the time grasping the initiative from his hands. As a result, the Germans' northern group (the strongest and most dangerous) ended up in a difficult operational situation.

The operational situation was no better for the Germans along the opposite, southern, wing. Guderian, as is known, at first wanted to get to Moscow through Tula. But the hero-city halted the Germans. It was our defense's strong point and for the subsequent offensive along the Western Front's left wing. All of the enemy's attempts to encircle and capture Tula were eliminated, although at times the situation was extremely dangerous. The Germans, unable to seize Tula, were forced to go around it. Their Second Panzer Army moved to outflank Tula from the east along the boundary between two *fronts*. The panzer army managed to penetrate into the operational depth and, as the German command planned, to find space for maneuver. However, in the final analysis this only worsened the enemy's situation, because the Western Front's left wing forces remained organized in this difficult situation. The front around Tula and north of the city held, despite the fact that the Tula area was almost completely surrounded by Fascist troops. All of the Germans' attempts to defeat it by combined blows from the front and rear were repulsed. The 1st Guards Cavalry Corps arrived in time from Kashira and launched a counterblow. From Ryazan' in the east the 10th Army, from the High Command Reserve was deploying, and occupied a favorable operational position on the flank of the German forces. Tula also became more active and began to threaten the flank and rear of the German troops that had penetrated the area to the north and east of the city. Guderain, who had earlier planned to attack through Kashira and Kolomna in order to close the encirclement ring around our forces to the east of Moscow, found himself in an operational encirclement at the beginning of December: from the west—the Tula fortified area and its continuation along the Red Army's front to the north; from the east—the 10th Army in the Ryazan' area; from the north the 1st Guards Cavalry Corps was successfully attacking from Kashira.

Thus in the course of a vicious battle the sides' correlation of forces and operational situation on the Western Front's left wing changed. The armored fist, with which the Germans wanted to launch a crushing blow through Tula to Moscow, was forced to unclench and spread its "fingers" toward Ryazan', Zaraisk, Kashira, Laptev and Tula. The Germans' offensive along the Western Front's left wing collapsed.

Vivid and troubling events were occurring along both of the Western Front's flanks. They played the main and decisive role. In a way, they leave our center armies in the shade. The role of our center, which did not move, at first glance seems less noticeable, but was nevertheless significant. Without a solid center, it would have been impossible to successfully withstand such a prolonged battle on the flanks and to carry out such a large-scale operation successfully. The center armies (5th, 33rd, and 43rd) blocked the shortest routes to Moscow. They met and repulsed the blow by the enemy's infantry groups, reinforced with tanks. A stable center was a reliable base for the entire maneuver along the flanks and guaranteed their flanks and the entire front operation's unity. In order to correctly understand the center's important role in the Moscow operation, it is sufficient to imagine how the situation would have become more difficult for the Red Army if the center had buckled at the same time the Western Front's wings were falling back to the east under enemy pressure.

However, the wave broke against the shore. Our center stood fast. It held the line of the Nara River and destroyed those few enemy units which succeeded in breaking through, and kept our front from splitting. And it was this very important circumstance, when under the enemy's fierce pressure the Western Front, although it bent back along the flanks and curved, as if gathering its forces for a counterblow against the hated enemy, it remained whole and solid, with all its parts cooperating and capable of launching even more powerful and crushing blows—it was this important circumstance no small credit is due to our valorous central armies. The defense of the Nara River is a positive example of an operational defense, both on the scale of an army, and of the entire *front*. Both German flank wedges were separated by our broad and solid center; they were isolated and could not cooperate operationally with each other. The German center was not in a condition to accomplish its mission. The Western Front's center armies carried out their mission in the Moscow operation.

Conclusions

As a result of their November offensive, the Germans managed to advance deeply on both the Western Front's flanks. In the north they reached the line Moscow-Volga Canal-Krasnaya Polyana-Kryukovo-north of Zvenigorod; to the south the line of the Tula-Moscow road, as well as the area of MIkhailov, Mordves, and Venev.

The Germans were sure of the success of their offensive on Moscow. The German information bureau wrote at the beginning of December that "... the German offensive against the Bolsheviks' capital has moved so far forward that one can already make out the inner part of Moscow through a good pair of binoculars." In Berlin on December 2 there was an order to leave blank spaces in the newspapers for news about the capture of the Soviet capital.

But the Germans obviously underestimated the Red Army's resistance and the presence of its powerful and deep reserves. This was a huge miscalculation by the German command.

During the struggle on the approaches to Moscow the Red Army's strength and might grew, while that of the German armies fell, their divisions melted away, and their equipment broke down. As a result of 20 days of non-stop fighting, the Germans lost (according to incomplete data) about 55,000 men killed. During that same time our troops destroyed or captured (not counting aviation) 777 tanks, 534 vehicles, 178 guns, 119 mortars, and 224 machine guns, etc.

Instead of the concentrated and purposeful blows by armored groups along the Klin-Solnechnogorsk and Venev-Kashira axes, the enemy was forced to wage an intense battle from the Moscow Sea to Tula and Mikhailov along a 350-km front.

The Supreme Commander-in-Chief of the Red Army, while concentrating the reserve armies (1st, 20th, and 10th) and directing large reserves to the 30th Army, sought to deploy them behind the Western Front's flanks, countering the Germans' maneuver with his own active countermaneuver, so as to prevent them from taking Moscow in their tank pincers. The reserve armies, according to the Supreme High Command's plan, were not for being expended in the defensive fighting or plugging gaps along various sectors of the broad front. The reserve armies were supposed to oppose the attempt by the Germans to encircle Moscow with their tanks and to win the enemy's flanks, and to create a superiority of forces along the most important axes and prepared for a general counteroffensive. We have seen what an important and decisive role was played during the course of the Moscow operation by the High Command's forces and equipment of all kinds (reserve armies, separate divisions, brigades and other units, aviation, and material resources), which were fed into the Western Front.

By December 6 the Hitlerite troops' second general offensive on Moscow had misfired and burnt itself out. The grandiose plan to seize Moscow and rout the Red Army had collapsed. By this time the Western Front had achieved superiority in forces and the operational situation along the main axes and went from defense to a counteroffensive.

The defensive stage of the Moscow operation demanded an enormous exertion of all forces and means, not only from the combat units, but from staffs, directorates, and many institutions as well. The maneuver character of the fighting along a broad front, plus the Western Front's bulky organizational structure (up to 11 armies and operational formations), put exceptional demands on the precision and organization of troop control by the Western Front's military council and staff. The very volume of was extremely large and varied. The armies were not united into groups (along the wings, for example), and all the armies (at first six, and then ten armies) were directly subordinated to the *front* command, which gave each of them a concrete mission and carefully monitored its fulfillment. Control of the armies was very firm and strict and highly centralized. Despite the difficult situation, troop control was established and functioned without significant breakdowns. This was facilitated by: the developed road and communications net in the Moscow area; the high qualifications and hard work of the *front* command and staff, which were able to organize the enemy's repulse in a very difficult situation and prepare his subsequent defeat.

The Red Army's heroic struggle in defending each inch of Soviet territory against the German-Fascist aggressors lasted 20 days. As a result of this struggle, the correlation of the sides' force changed and the double envelopment by the Germans of the flanks of our Western Front, which had the mission of closing the encirclement ring to the east of Moscow, was transformed into two operational "sacks," from which he found it difficult to escape from. The blow against our center was also successfully repulsed. Nowhere were the Germans able to smash a hole in Stalin's defense around Moscow. The Red Army was aided by the commitment of new operational-strategic reserves, which had been created in a timely way in the country's depth and which were moved up by Stalin's hand precisely to that area where the operation's fate was being decided, where they were needed most of all. The German-Fascist forces were forced to assume the defensive in unfavorable conditions, having no reserves.

The decisive turning point in the events, which had been gathering steam around Moscow in the first days of December, a turning point which a great country was passionately wishing for, straining its strength in work and battle, had at last arrived.

Part IV

The Red Army's counteroffensive on the Western Front and the defeat of the German-Fascist troops around Moscow (December 6-December 24 1941)

1

Changes in the operational-strategic situation during the Red Army's battle on the approaches to Moscow. The Red Army's counteroffensive and the beginning of the German forces' defeat

During the first days of December the battle on the approaches to Moscow entered its decisive phase. The German-Fascist command, despite the large losses and lack of reserves, was attempting at all costs to break through to the Soviet capital and seize it, no matter what, before the onset of the hard frosts. In connection with the uninterrupted 20-day fighting, in many German divisions there retained no more than 50-60% of their authorized strength. However, the fascist command stubbornly drove its forces forward, evidently unaware of the Red Army's concentration of large reserves around Moscow, or underestimating their role. One of the communications from the German Fourth Army during the latter half of November stated that "We should not expect significant reserves around Moscow at the present time."

But the Red Army's resistance grew. There was fierce back-and-forth fighting in the north—along the Klin, Solnechnogorsk, Istra, and Zvenigorod axes.

Upon approaching the line Dmitrov-Yakhroma-Krasnaya Polyana, the Germans met an unexpected blow by the new armies—1st and 20th, which had completed their concentration by this time.

On December 4 the right wing's reserve armies, breaking the enemy's stubborn resistance, gradually expanded their counterblow along the Dmitrov and Solnechnogorsk axes. The enemy was forced to go over to the defensive on a number of sectors. In the following days the neighboring 30th and 16th armies joined in the offensive.

In the south the Germans attempted to carry out a turning maneuver north and northeast of Tula. Our troops successfully prevented a breakthrough by the Second Panzer Army into the operational depth and the envelopment of our left flank and before long were themselves squeezing the Germans into a vise between strongly-held Tula and the 10th Army (transferred from the Supreme Command Reserve), attacking from the Ryazan' direction. To the north, blocking the direct route to Moscow, the 1st Guards Cavalry Corps was developing its counterblow from the Kashira area.

The commitment of three new armies from the Supreme Command Reserve into the *front* battle at the decisive moment ensured the Red Army's necessary superiority in forces. It created the conditions for going over to a decisive counteroffensive along both wings. The participation in the battle of the Moscow Defense Zone's forces and those of the Supreme High Command (air, PVO, and others) increased the Western Front's strength. The Red Army also enjoyed a superior operational position by this time. The German wedges were not able to make any breaches in our front, but were only able to make deep indentations. Now they were forced in the north to scatter their efforts along a large bulge in the front, from the Moscow Sea to Dmitrov and then to Zvenigorod. In the south the enemy was not only unable to take Tula, but was forced under pressure from our forces to scatter his divisions along different axes. The advantages of an overall superiority in forces and a flanking position along both wings were in the Red Army's favor. During the fighting in the early days of December on the snow-covered fields and forests around Moscow the initiative began to incline more and more in the Red Army's favor. The Germans approached to within 25 kilometers from the northwest, but with that their offensive capabilities were exhausted. The Red Army began to gain the upper hand over the fascists in the cruel fighting; with each day, with each hour, it more and more overcame the hated enemy.

The German forces, no longer having either free reserves or a superiority of force, and having lost their favorable operational situation, went over to the defensive on various sectors of the front and then, under pressure from our troops, began a partial withdrawal on Klin and Solnechnogorsk. In the south, after the initial fighting along the Kashira axis against the 1st Guards Cavalry Corps, and in connection with the beginning of the 10th Army's offensive, the Germans also went over to the defensive and before long, waging holding actions, began to fall back on Stalinogorsk.

Thus almost simultaneously there occurred following: the beginning of our right wing's offensive, the counterblow by the 1st Guards Cavalry Corps, the activation of our left wing with the commitment of the 10th Army, the elimination of the Germans' attempts to break through north of Tula (in the Laptevo and Revyakino areas) and along the Naro-Fominsk axis. The German command suddenly found itself with several axes and sectors along a broad front, all of which demanded the immediate commitment of significant reserves in order to parry our counterblows. But the Germans lacked the necessary reserves for this. Their main forces were spread along a line and their lateral movement along the front was difficult and would take time, while the throwing in small reinforcements was unable to save the overall situation. The troops, operating along separate axes and having gotten into a difficult situation, found themselves isolated and left to their own devices.

The right-wing armies (30th, 1st, 20th, and 16th) were waging offensive battles against the Third and Fourth panzer armies of generals Hoth and Hoeppner, reinforced with infantry divisions. In the center our 5th, 33rd and 43rd armies were defending against the Germans' IX, XII, XX, and XII army corps; our forces were occupying and rebuilding in some areas defensive lines previously abandoned. On the left wing, the 49th and 50th armies, the 1st Guards Cavalry Corps, and the 10th Army were battling the XIII and XLIII army corps and General Guderian's Second Panzer Army, resisting their attempts to encircle Tula and launching counterblows against the Germans along different axes.

The shape of the front, especially along the wings, took on a winding and queer shape. The overall length of the front was 600 km, and with the addition of the various small twists and turns reached 700 km, or approached the length of the entire English-French front during the First World War.

Overall the Red Army deployed along the Western Front 57 rifle and motorized divisions (three rifle brigades are equivalent to a single rifle division), seven tank divisions (three tank battalions are the equivalent of a tank brigade, and three tank brigades are the equivalent of a tank division), and 15 cavalry divisions. The combat strength of these troops was about 380,000 men, 1,935 field guns, 550 tanks, and 750 aircraft.[1]

1 In the Western Front's combat units and formations, as of December 1, there were about 520,000 men (not counting the armies' and *front's* support troops and rear services).

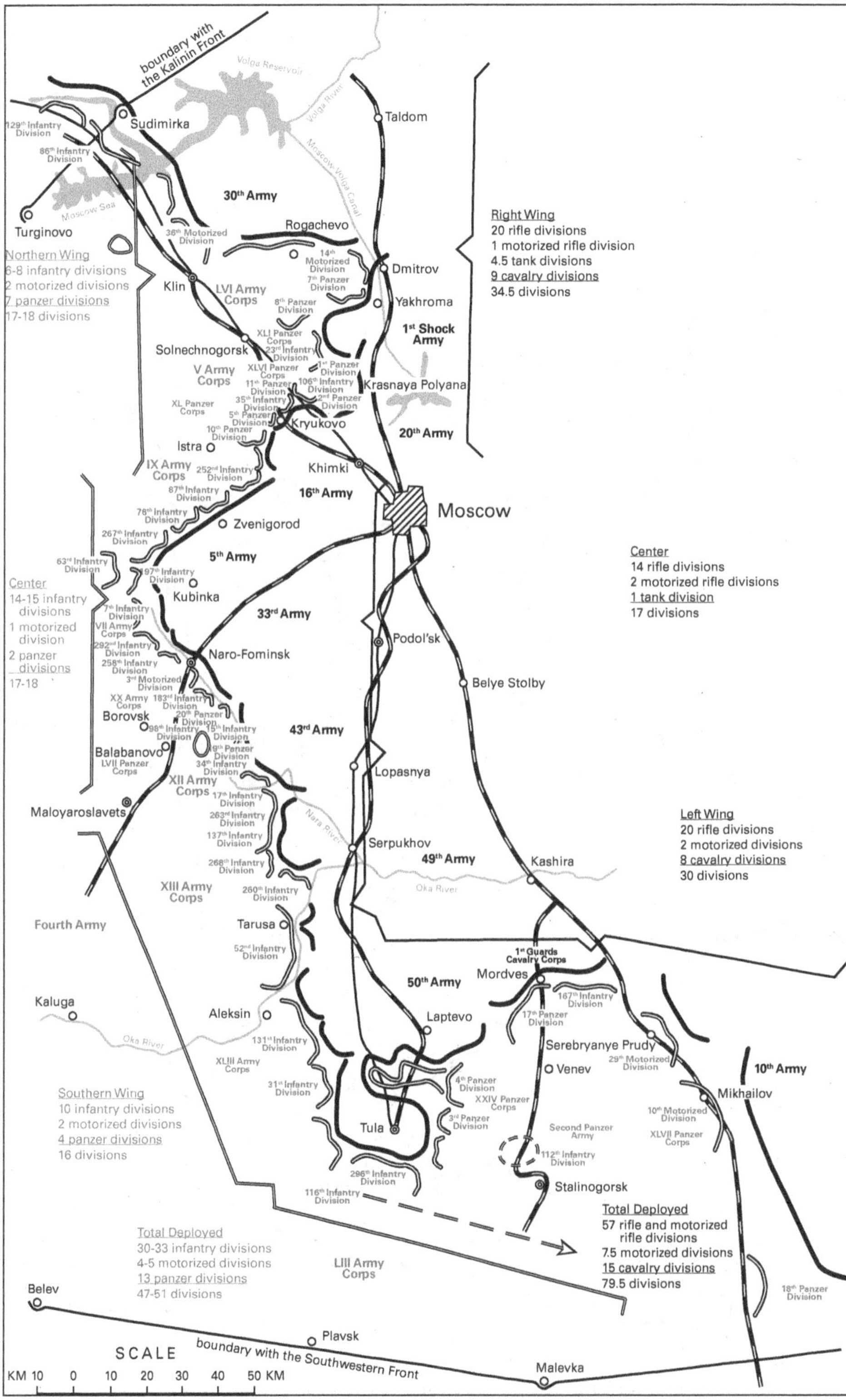

Map 6 The Situation by December 6

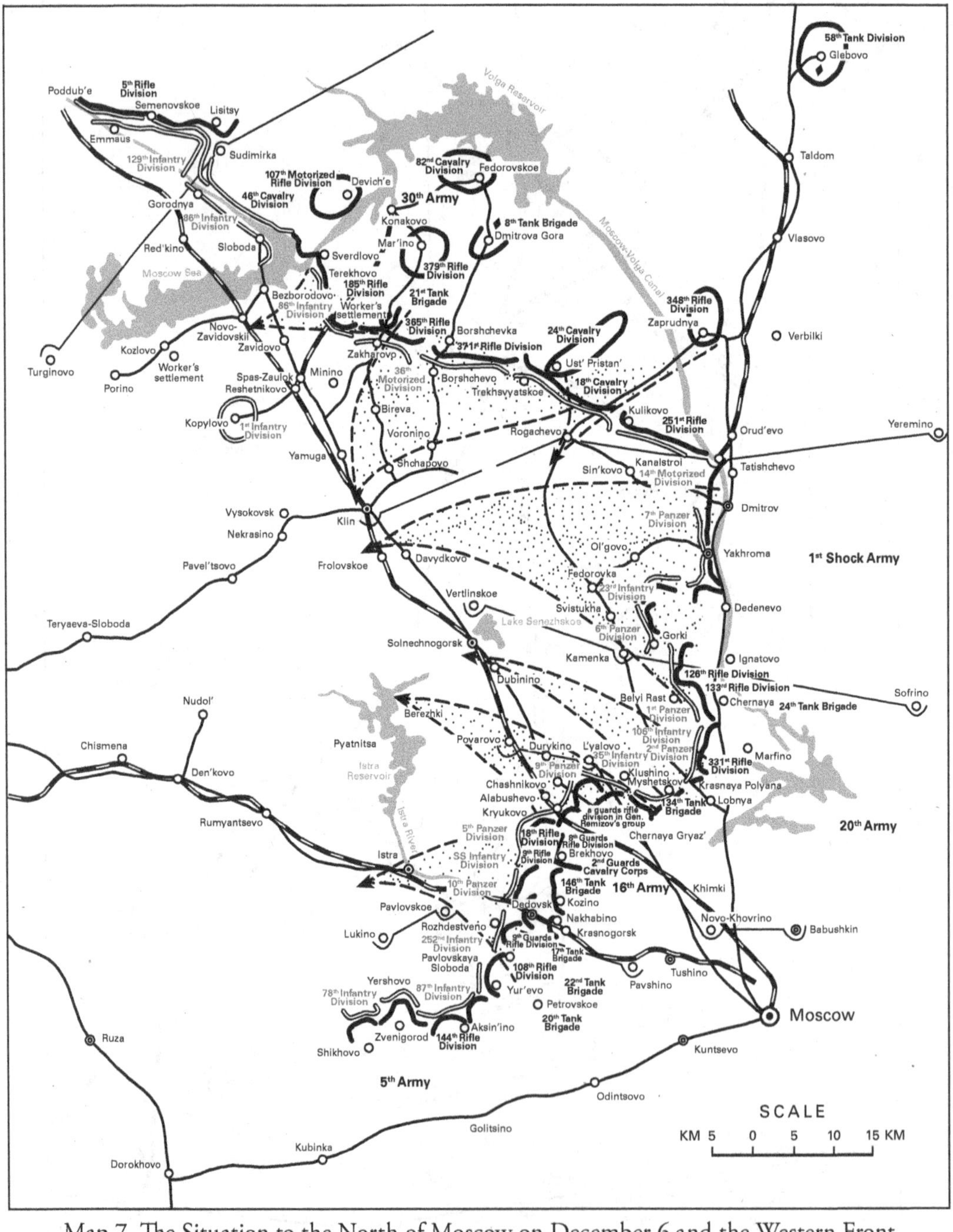

Map 7 The Situation to the North of Moscow on December 6 and the Western Front Command's Plan

The opposing enemy forces were determined to consist of 30-33 infantry divisions, 4-5 motorized divisions, and 13 panzer divisions. Their combat strength was set at 240,000 men, 1,700 field guns, 900 tanks, and 600 aircraft.

Thus the Western Front enjoyed a superiority of 1½ over the enemy in the numbers of men, a near equality in artillery, was inferior in the numbers of tanks, and had a small superiority in the number of aircraft.

The front's density varied. The densest grouping of forces was along the right wing, where we had an overall continuous operational front. The greatest density was along our 16th Army's sector: one rifle division per three km, and about 20 guns and 20 mortars per km. The Germans in this area had one division for every five km, and 12 guns and 10-15 mortars per km of front. There was no continuous operational front along the left wing and the troops fought along separate axes. The smallest density was along our 50th Army's front, where a single rifle division occupied a front of 17 km.

Table IV/1.1 The correlation of forces along the Western Front by December 6 1941 – German Forces

Formation name	Number of formations	Combat strength					
		Men	Field guns	Anti-tank guns	Mortars	Tanks	Planes
XXVII Army Corps	2-3 infantry divisions	22,000	170	150	300	20	–
LVI Army Corps	1 motorized division 1 brigade						
XLI Panzer Corps	1 infantry division 1 motorized division 2 panzer divisions	18,000	120	100	190	110	–
V Army Corps	1 infantry division 2 panzer divisions	13,000	90	80	140	120	–
XLVI Panzer Corps	2 infantry divisions	22,000	150	140	250	130	–
XL Panzer Corps	3 panzer divisions						
IX Army Corps	7-8 infantry divisions	40,000	320	280	550	130	–
VII Army Corps							
XX Army Corps	2 infantry divisions	20,000	135	120	230	50	–
LVII Panzer Corps	1 motorized division 1 panzer division						
XII Army Corps	4-5 infantry divisions 1 panzer division	27,000	220	200	400	40	–
XII Army Corps	4-5 infantry divisions	25,000	200	180	350	–	–
XIII Army Corps							
XLIII Army Corps	3 infantry divisions	15,000	120	110	220	–	–
XXIV Panzer Corps	1 infantry division	18,000	115	110	170	240	–
XLVII Panzer Corps	3 panzer divisions						
	1 infantry division 2 motorized divisions 1 panzer division	20,000	120	110	200	60	–
TOTAL	47-51 divisions	240,000	1,760	1,580	3,000	900	600

Table IV/1.2 The correlation of forces along the Western Front by December 6 1941 – Red Army

Formation name	Combat strength					
	Men	Field guns	Anti-tank guns	Mortars	Tanks	Planes
30th Army	40,000	190	70	130	35	–
1st Shock Army	28,000	145	35	490	50	–
20th Army	29,000	130	65	410	60	–
16th Army	55,000	320	190	480	125	–
5th Army	35,000	250	70	140	90	–
33rd Army	26,000	115	60	110	40	–
43rd Army	35,000	180	80	180	50	–
49th Army	40,000	250	100	350	40	–
50th Army and Belov's Group	40,000	130	40	200	60	–
10th Army	60,000	225	60	450	–	–
TOTAL	388,000	1,935	770	2,930	550	750
(57 rifle and motorized rifle divisions; 7 tank divisions, 15 cavalry divisions)						

Note: The figures for the sides' combat strength and correlation of forces were arrived at by compiling and studying data from several sources.

On December 6, in accordance with the Supreme Commander-in-Chief's instructions, the Western Front's forces, according to the decision of its commander, Gen. Zhukov, launched a counteroffensive against the Germans' flank shock groups. Our right-wing armies were to carry out an offensive toward the areas of Klin and the Istra Reservoir, so as to defeat the enemy here, by overwhelming him from the north. In the south our 50th Army, 1st Guards Cavalry Corps, and 10th Army were attacking Guderian's Second Panzer Army along converging axes east of Tula, striving also to encircle and defeat it. Combat activities unfolded successfully.

A December 9 directive (no. 086/op) by the Western Front's military council stated the following:

> The main task of the Western Front's forces consists of defeating as quickly as possible the enemy's flank groups, capturing his equipment, transportation, and weapons, and moving swiftly forward to outflank his flank groups, to finally encircle and destroy all the enemy's armies facing our Western Front.

In the battles that followed the enemy's resistance was broken and he began to fall back, abandoning his weapons, burning his transport, and covering his path of retreat with the corpses of his men and horses.

On December 12 the Western Front's military council reported to comrade Stalin:

> On December 6 1941, the *front's* forces, having worn out the enemy in the preceding fighting, went over to a decisive counteroffensive against his shock flank groups. As a result of the offensive under way both of these groups have been defeated and are rapidly retreating, abandoning their equipment and weapons, and suffering enormous losses.
>
> After the start of the offensive, during December 6-12 our units have taken and liberated from the Germans more than 400 inhabited areas. During December 6-10 we have captured 386 tanks, 4,317 motor vehicles, 704 motorcycles, 305 guns, 101 mortars, 515 machine guns, and 546 automatic rifles. During that same time our forces have destroyed, not counting air actions: 271 tanks, 565 motor vehicles, 92 guns, 119 mortars, and 134 machine guns. A huge

amount of other weaponry, ammunition, uniforms, and other property has been captured. The Germans have lost 30,000 killed on the battlefield during this time.

The Western Front's subsequent goal (in cooperation with the Kalinin Front) consisted of encircling and defeating the remaining German forces (the Gzhatsk-Vyaz'ma and Yukhnov enemy groups) opposing the Western Front. The operational plan of the Red Army command (reflected in the Western Front's directives during December 13-24) called for the rapid advance of both wings: the right wing to the line Zubtsov (on the Volga River)-Gzhatsk, and the left wing to the line Polotnyanyi Zavod-Kozel'sk, with the center echeloned back approximately along the line Mozhaisk-Maloyaroslavets. Thus it was planned to create a situation by which the forward position of the advanced wings would favor the encirclement of the central German groupings main forces.

In the course of the first two weeks (December 6-19) the offensive of the Western Front's armies unfolded in the following manner:

1 the right wing (1st, 20th, and 16th armies) advanced 70-90 km, with an average daily advance of 6-7 km per day;
2 the center (33rd and 43rd armies) did not move at all;
3 the left wing moved forward unevenly: its northern part (49th Army) advanced slightly, but along the flanking southern wing the pace of our advance was growing: the 1st Guards Cavalry Corps advanced at a rate of 8-9 km per day, while the 10th Army advanced 12-15 km per day, as a result of which 160 km were covered.

The accomplishment of these objectives by the Western Front's armies, reinforced by reserves from the Supreme High Command, is examined in succeeding chapters.

In the dark days of early December, when the Western Front was waging a fierce struggle along both of its wings, attempting to wrest the initiative from the enemy, both neighboring fronts—the Kalinin and Southwestern—acting on orders from the Supreme Commander-in-Chief, were adopting measures for activating their flanks next to the Western Front, so as to render aid and ease its situation.

The Kalinin Front, in accordance with a *Stavka* directive of December 1, was to attack with the forces of 5-6 divisions along the front Kalinin-Sudimirka (30 km southeast of Kalinin) to the south in order to reach the line of Milulino-Gorodishche and Turginovo, and then to get into the rear of the Germans' Klin group. The boundary line between the Kalinin and Western fronts ran along the line: Kalyazin-Sudimirka-Turginovo (all within the Western Front).

In order to carry out the directive, the Kalinin Front during December 2-4 prepared for the offensive along its left wing, regrouped its forces, concentrating along the sector of the forthcoming offensive five of the most combat-ready divisions, while strengthening its defenses along the remainder of the front, stretching from Kalinin westward in the general direction of Selizharovo. On December 5 the Kalinin Front's forces forced the Volga and after a battle seized a bridgehead southeast of Kalinin (in the area of Emmaus and Semenovskoe) 5-6 km in width and about three in depth. The German brought up their nearest reserves and counterattacked. On December 6 our forces in the Kalinin area beat off the enemy's counterattacks and in the following days overcame the enemy's resistance and moved along the right bank of the Volga River south and southeast of the city.

On the *front's* right wing and center our forces held their former positions.

Further events unfolded gradually. On December 14 our forces waged local offensive actions along the right wing, while on the left they continued to successfully pursue the offensive against the enemy's Kalinin group, attempting to surround it. On December 16 the forces of the Kalinin

Front's left wing, having inflicted a defeat on the forces of the Ninth German Army, captured Kalinin. The left flank reached the northwestern shore of the Moscow Sea.

By this time, in connection with the overall shift in the situation in the Moscow area in our favor and the developing withdrawal of the German troops, the *Stavka* considered that the objective of the Western Front's right wing could be achieved without the participation of the right-flank 30th Army. Thus the 30th Army was transferred to the Kalinin Front at 1200 on December 16. The new boundary between the *fronts* was as follows: Rogachevo-Reshetnikovo station-Kotlyakovo-Bol'shie Ledinki-Pokrovskoe (all within the Kalinin Front). The 30th Army, by attacking to the west and northwest, was to seize the Staritsa area with its left wing, and with its right block the withdrawal routes of the enemy's Kalinin group.

In the first days of December the Southwestern Front was engaged in stubborn fighting on its right wing along the Yelets axis. On December 6 the *front's* right wing was successfully carrying out a counterblow against the German group that had captured Yelets. The front ran along the line from Kurkingo to Yefremov and Yelets (both places under enemy control) and further to the south. The boundary line between the *fronts* ran along the line Ryazhsk-Malevka-Belev-Dyat'kovo (all inside the Western Front). On December 9 our forces, attacking along the Yelets axis, defeated two German divisions and captured Yelets.

The Southwestern Front's right wing subsequently pursued the defeated enemy units toward Verkhov'e and Livny. To the north our offensive unfolded along the Yefremov axis, where we were moving forward. By December 16 the front line along the right wing ran from Volovo to the south, then eight km west of Yefremovo and then to Livny. We managed to carry out our subsequent advance in December primarily on the right flank, in the direction of Chern', in conjunction with the successful offensive by the Western Front's left flank.

Thus the Southwestern Front, in accordance with the overall course of events, also moved its right wing to the west, although it nonetheless lagged behind and remained echeloned behind the Western Front's left flank.

2

The offensive by the Western Front's right wing. The defeat of the enemy's Klin-Rogachevo Group. The fighting in the area of the Istra Reservoir. The arrival of the Red Army's forces at the line of the Lama and Ruza rivers

The situation on the Western Front's right wing

In the beginning of December the forces of the Western Front's right wing occupied defensive positions along the near approaches to Moscow. The right-flank 30th Army was defending along the line: Volga River-the northern part of the Moscow Sea northeast of Rogachevo, with its front facing southwest. In accordance with an order of the Supreme Commander-in-Chief, the 1st Shock and 20th armies occupied the line: the eastern bank of the Moscow-Volga Canal-Dmitrov-Yakhroma-Ignatovo-south of Krasnaya Polyana, and then to the south; the 16th Army was defending along the line Kryukovo-Dedovsk and to the south.

With the arrival of the enemy along the line Moscow-Volga Canal-Krasnaya Polyana-Kryukovo-Rozhdestveno, an immediate threat to the capital arose, with the possibility of Moscow being turned from the north and northeast.

Despite losses in personnel and equipment, the German command stubbornly sought to carry out Hitler's order "to take Moscow at any cost before the onset of winter."

However, the attacking troops of the enemy's left wing had already committed and expended in battle their available reserves before reaching Moscow and lacked the men and equipment to launch a final blow.

At the same time, as the enemy approached Moscow, he began to feel the growth of our forces. This growth was due to the commitment of two newly-formed armies (1st Shock and 20th) and the reinforcement of the 30th and 16th armies with new formations and units.

The measures undertaken by the Supreme Command played an enormous role in inflicting a powerful counterblow against the overstretched enemy.

The sides' situation and correlation of forces

By the start of the counteroffensive the disposition of both sides' forces was as follows:

> The 30th Army occupied a defensive front of 80 km and was completing its regrouping and concentration of new reserve formations. By order of the *Stavka*, during the period December 2-5 three rifle divisions (348th, 371st, and 379th) arrived to reinforce the 30th Army. A large part (2/3) of these forces was concentrating in the center and on the left flank along a 40-45 km front. Against our 30th Army the Germans had deployed units almost evenly along the entire front; from November 30 they went over to the defensive, and were strengthening their position.
>
> The 1st Shock and 20th armies during December 1-3 were attacking with the greater part of their forces along a 50-60 km front. Their main forces were concentrating along the armies' right flank. The enemy was stubbornly defending along the entire front and in places counter-attacked, with his main forces in the areas of Yakhroma and Krasnaya Polyana.
>
> The 16th Army was defending stubbornly along the entire front, with its main forces along the right flank and in the center. The enemy was trying to attack along a number of sectors, particularly in the Kryukovo area.

The correlation of the sides' forces is shown in the table following.

In comparing both sides' disposition of forces, it is necessary to note the following.

1 The 30th Army occupied a favorable operational situation in relation to the enemy's main group operating against the 20th and 16th armies, insofar as it hung over its left flank and rear and threatened to launch a blow in the direction of Klin and further to the south and thus cut off the communications of the Third and Fourth panzer groups, which were already worn out in the preceding fighting.

2 The concentration of the 1st Shock Army's dense group along a 30-km front and the 20th

Army's right-flank units along a 10-12 km front yielded an average operational density of about five km to a single rifle division. Such a density must be recognized as quite favorable for conducting an offensive operation.

As far as the concentration of equipment was concerned, the 16th Army's sector was the most favorable.

The Western Front commander's decision for the counteroffensive

When the situation began to sharply change in our favor, the Germans calculated on holding the line achieved during their offensive and to improve their positions so as to keep Moscow in a state of immediate threat. However, under the powerful blows of our attacking units, the enemy was forced to retreat in disorder, abandoning equipment and weapons; the German command sought to halt its beaten forces along the line Terekhovo-Klin-Istra Reservoir-Istra-the Nara River, and then along the line of the Lama and Ruza rivers.

In accordance with the developing situation, the commander of the Western Front made the decision for a counteroffensive and issued his orders to the armies of the right wing:

a) the 30th Army (directive no. 7387 of December 3), in conjunction with the 1st Shock Army, was to launch a decisive offensive on the morning of December 5. The main blow was to be launched in the direction of Borshchevo, outflanking Klin from the north. Auxiliary blows were to be launched toward Novo-Zavidovskii and Rogachevo; December 3-4 was to be spent preparing the operation; the Kalinin Front will attack on the right; on December 3 the 1st Shock Army will attack on the left in order to capture Fedorovka.

b) the 1st Shock Army was to launch a decisive offensive on the morning of December 3, having as its immediate objective the capture of the Ol'govo area and reaching the line Yakhroma-Ol'govo-Svistukha; it was to subsequently take Fedorovka and attack toward the southern outskirts of Klin; to the left the 20th Army would attack with the objective of taking Krasnaya Polyana.

c) the 20th Army, in conjunction with the 16th Army, was to complete the elimination of the Krasnaya Polyana enemy group and during December 7 to reach the line of the Ozeretskii state farm (three km north of Krasnaya Polyana)-Myshetskoe, where it was to regroup in order to further attack Solnechnogorsk. The 16th Army would attack to the left with part of its forces.

d) on December the 16th Army's right flank and center, in conjunction with the 20th Army, was to go over to the offensive with the objective of capturing the area of L'yalovo and Kryukovo, with the subsequent objective of attacking on the morning of December 8 along the entire front. The 5th Army would defend on the left.

In this way the *front* command tasked its right-wing armies with launching a powerful blow against the main German group, acting along converging axes, in order to cut off the enemy's communications and to encircle and destroy him.

Table IV/2.1 The correlation of forces along the Western Front's right wing by December 6 1941 – German forces

Formation name	Number of formations	Combat strength					
		Men	Field guns	Anti-tank guns	Mortars	Tanks	Width of front
XXVII Army Corps	2-3 infantry divisions	22,000	170	150	300	20	80 km
LVI Army Corps	1 motorized division						
	1 brigade						
XLI Panzer Corps	1 infantry division	18,000	120	100	190	110	30-40 km
	1 motorized division						
	2 panzer divisions						
V Army Corps	1 infantry division	13,000	90	80	140	120	20-30 km
	2 panzer divisions						
XLVI Panzer Corps	2 infantry divisions	22,000	150	140	250	130	25 km
XL Panzer Corps							
TOTAL		75,000	530	470	880	380	155-175 km
6-7 infantry divisions 2 motorized divisions 7 panzer divisions 1 brigade							

Table IV/2.2 The correlation of forces along the Western Front's right wing by December 6 1941 – Red Army

Direction of army	Combat strength				
	Men	Field guns	Anti-tank guns	Mortars	Tanks
1. Klin					
30th Army	40,000	190	70	130	35
5 rifle divisions					
1 motorized rifle division					
4 cavalry divisions					
2 tank brigades					
1st Shock Army	28,000	145	35	490	50
2 rifle divisions					
8 rifle brigades					
1 tank brigade					
1 cavalry division					
2. Solnechnogorsk					
20th Army	29,000	130	65	410	60
2 rifle divisions					
3 rifle brigades					
2 tank brigades					
3. Istra					
16th Army	55,000	320	190	480	125
5 rifle divisions					
4 rifle brigades					
4 tank brigades					
4 cavalry divisions					
TOTAL	152,000	785	360	1,510	270
14 rifle divisions 1 motorized rifle division 9 cavalry divisions 15 rifle brigades 9 tank brigades					

Note: The correlation of forces by combat arm: infantry—2:1; field artillery—1.5:1; anti-tank artillery—1:1.2; mortars—1.7:1; tanks—1:1.4. That is, in infantry, field artillery and mortars our side had superiority; in anti-tank artillery and tanks, the enemy had the advantage.

The counteroffensive by the *Front's* right-wing armies

On the northern flank the German forces were occupying a defensive position. By December 6 the 129th and 86th infantry divisions were carrying out defensive works along the line Novo-Semenovskoe-Sloboda-Terekhovo; the 36th Motorized Division and an SS brigade were consolidating in the areas of Zavidovo and Rogachevo; the 14th Motorized and 7th Panzer divisions were fighting west of Dmitrov and Yakhroma; the 23rd Infantry and 6th Panzer divisions were in the area southeast of Fedorovka; the 106th Infantry and 1st and 2nd panzer divisions were operating in the sector of Belyi Rast, Krasnaya Polyana, Klushino; the 35th Infantry Division and 11th and

5th panzer divisions were fighting along the Kryukov line; an SS division and the 10th Panzer Division, together with units of the 202nd Infantry Division, were grouped along the Istra axis.

On December 4 on certain sectors, and on December 5 along the greater part of the front, the Germans were forced to go over to defensive fighting (from Novo-Semenovskoe to Kryukovo, inclusively).

Many of the enemy's divisions had suffered heavy losses (50-60%) in the 20 days of heavy fighting on the approaches to Moscow. According to a number of documents and prisoner interrogations it was established that 30-60 men (out of 100-120) remained in many companies. In the 106th Infantry Division's 240th Infantry Regiment only 600 men remained; in the 35th Infantry Division's companies 50-60 men remained; the 6th Panzer Division lost almost all its tanks in the November-December fighting, with the tank companies numbering 30-35 men, with 600-700 men in the regiments.

In carrying out the Western Front command's orders, the 30th, 1st and 20th armies went over to the offensive on the morning of December 6, overcoming the enemy's stubborn resistance.

General Lelyushenko's 30th Army (46th Cavalry, 107th Motorized, 185th, 365th, and 371st rifle divisions, the 8th and 21st tank brigades, the 379th and 348th rifle divisions, and the 18th, 24th, and 82nd cavalry divisions), attacking along the entire front, was concentrating its main forces in the center and along its left flank, launching its main blow against Klin (365th Rifle

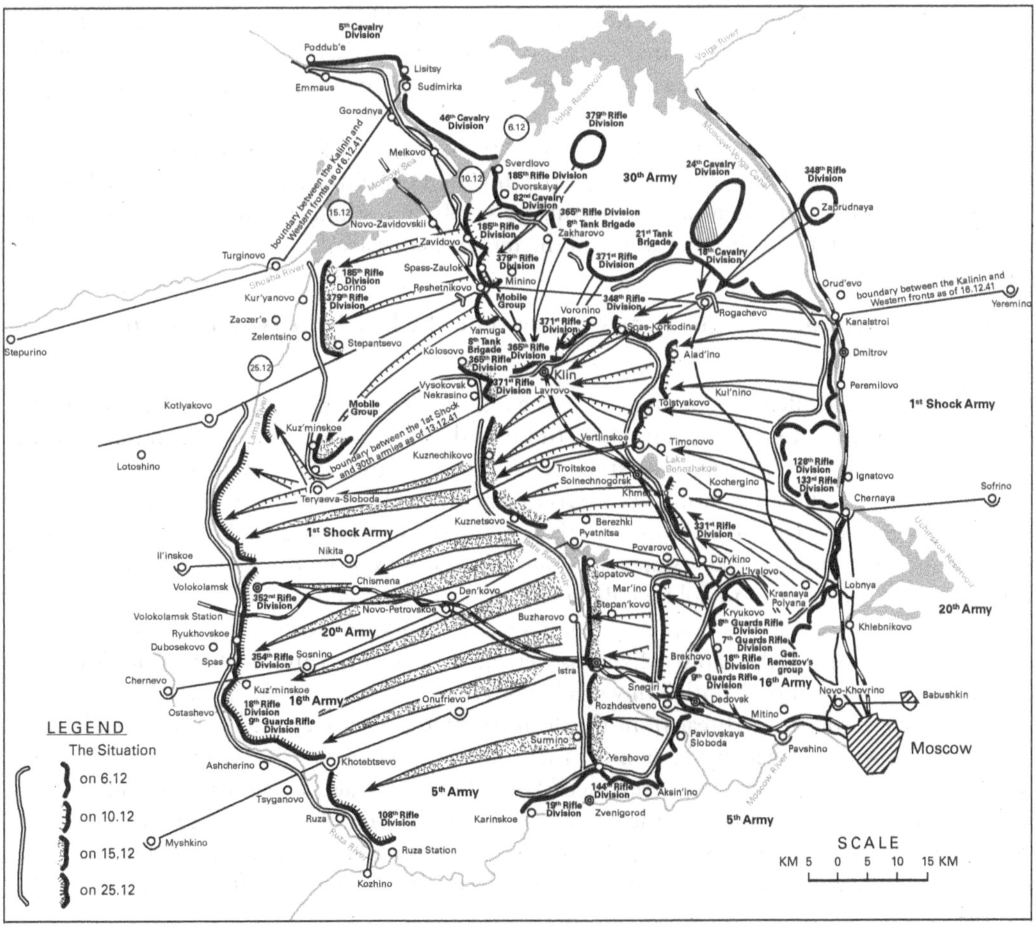

Map 8 The Offensive by the Right Wing's Armies, December 6-25, 1941

Division and 8th Tank Brigade, the 371st Rifle Division and 21st Tank Brigade) and an auxiliary blow (348th Rifle and 18th and 24th cavalry divisions) toward Rogachevo. By the end of the day, overcoming the enemy's stubborn resistance, the troops took the area of Borshchevo, occupied a number of inhabited areas, and were further attacking toward Birevo and Sloboda (12-15 km north of Klin).

Gen. Kuznetsov's 1st Shock Army, with the greater part of its forces (29th, 50th, 44th, 56th, 71st, and 55th rifle brigades, and the 133rd and 126th rifle divisions) was engaged in fierce fighting, overcoming the enemy's stubborn resistance, and by the end of December 6 had captured Podolino, Pochinki, the eastern part of Yakhroma, and Kovshino; the army's units were concentrating the main forces along the right flank and in the center in the Yakhroma area. The fighting for the inhabited areas on the army's right flank in the Yakhroma area was especially fierce. At the same time the Germans were becoming active against the army's left flank.

The larger part of the 20th Army's forces (64th and 35th rifle brigades, 331st and 352nd rifle divisions) on this day were engaged in heavy fighting for Krasnaya Polyana, where the enemy was putting up stubborn resistance, and even counterattacking along some axes. Simultaneously, the enemy was entrenching and putting up obstacles in the area of Belyi Rast. The 20th Army's main forces were concentrating in the direction of Krasnaya Polyana, the southeastern outskirts of which units of the 331st Rifle Division, the 28th Rifle Brigade, and two tank brigades reached by the end of December 6 and where they were engaged in heavy fighting.

The 16th Army's forces under Gen. Rokossovskii on December 6 continued to carry out defensive works along their front, prepared for the offensive and carried out an energetic reconnaissance of the enemy; the enemy was not particularly active and consolidated in the areas occupied by him.

Thus during December 6 the right-wing armies attacked along a 120-km front, launching blows with the 30th, 1st Shock and 20th armies in the direction of Klin, Fedorovka, Krasnaya Polyana, and Solnechnogorsk. The enemy, while putting up stubborn resistance along a number of sectors, began a partial withdrawal in front of the 30th, and 1st Shock armies.

The development of the right-wing's offensive to the line Klin-Istra Reservoir, December 7-11

On December 7 the offensive continued. On the right flank, under the blows of the 30th Army's forces, the enemy's 86th Infantry and 36th Motorized divisions began a slow withdrawal to the southwest. Units of the 7th, 6th, and 1st panzer and 14th Motorized and 23rd Infantry divisions, were involved in stubborn fighting with our attacking units against the 30th Army's left flank and the center of the 1st Shock Army, especially along the line Dmitrov-Yakhroma, and in some places launched counterattacks. Along the Solnechnogorsk axis the enemy was fiercely engaged with the 20th Army's forces to hold the Belyi Rast and Krasnaya Polyana areas; along the Istra axis the Germans were stubbornly defending along the line Kryukovo-Rozhdestveno against the 16th Army; the 252nd and 87th infantry divisions were holding Anosino and Yershovo (four km north of Zvenigorod) in front of the 5th Army's right wing.

Taking into account the threat from the 30th Army, the enemy created in a number of areas strong points with earthen firing points. These fortifications were discovered near Varakseno (northeast of Novo-Zavidovskoe), Arkhangel'skoe, Eldino, Shetakovo, Zakharovo, and Sloboda, and especially near Rogachevo. To the north of Klin, in the Rogachevo area, significant German air strength was operating. Opposing the offensive by our 365th Rifle Division and 8th Tank Brigade toward Zakharovo and Bortnikovo, groups of 6-18 enemy aircraft bombed and strafed our troops.

During December 7 the 30th Army's 365th and 371st rifle divisions, supported by the 8th and 21st tank brigades, attacked in the general direction of Klin, and the 348th Rifle and 18th and 24th cavalry divisions attacked toward Rogachevo.

By 0600 on December 8 the army's units had captured a number of settled areas. The arrival of the 365th Rifle Division and the 8th Tank Brigade in the Birevo area created a direct threat for the Yamuga area, and the capture by the 371st Rifle Division and 21st Tank Brigade of Sokovo and Muzhevo, west and southwest of Sloboda and the further advance in a southwesterly direction presented the opportunity of cutting the Leningrad road northwest of Klin and the Klin-Rogachevo road. This circumstance was favorably reflected on the 30th Army's offensive operation. During December 7 and the first half of the following day the enemy desperately defended the Rogachevo defensive strong point and supported his ground troops with air attacks.

The 1st Shock Army, in conjunction with the 30th and 20th armies, continued to attack with its right flank in a northwesterly direction, and to the west with its center toward Fedorovka (20 km southwest of Dmitrov). During the second half of December 8 the army captured Yakhroma, Stepanovo, and Zhukovo (seven km southwest of Yakhroma). The Germans put up a stubborn resistance, particularly in the area of Fedorovka, Kamenka, and Ol'govo (seven km northeast of Fedorovka), and were regrouping their forces. During December our reconnaissance unearthed the movement of vehicles with troops along the Rogachevo road.

The commander of the 20th Army, in his order no. 05/op, laid out the army's objectives:

1 in conjunction with units of the 16th Army, finish eliminating the Krasnaya Polyana enemy group on December 7 and reach the line Ozeretskii state farm-Myshetskoe (four km southwest of Ozeretskii) and regroup in preparation for subsequent offensive activities;
2 the army's right flank (64th Rifle and 24th and 31st tank brigades) is to hold its position and prevent the enemy from breaking through toward Chernaya and Marfino;
3 the army's center (331st Rifle Division, 134th Tank Battalion, 7th Independent Guards Mortar Battalion, and the 1st and 2nd battalions of the 517th Artillery Regiment) are to envelop the enemy in the Krasnaya Polyana area from the north and south and, together with the 28th Rifle Brigade, complete the encirclement and destroy him, and then reach the line Ozeretskii state farm-height 196.6;
4 the left wing (28th Rifle Brigade, 135th Tank Battalion, 15th Independent Guards Mortar Battalion) is to bypass Krasnaya Polyana from the west and close the encirclement ring and, together with the 331st Rifle Division, destroy the enemy in Krasnaya Polyana and then take Myshetskoe;
5 the reserve (35th Rifle Brigade, with armored trains nos. 53 and 55) was ordered to defend the line Sukharevo (eight km northeast of Sukharevo)-Kievo and prevent the enemy from breaking through to Khlebnikovo.

The 352nd Rifle Division was to concentrate in the area of Sukharevo, Shlokhovo, and Marfino in order to continue the offensive to the west.

The 20th Army attacked on the morning of December 7, concentrating its efforts on the right flank and in the center; heavy fighting broke unfolded for Krasnaya Polyana. By the end of the day the 64th Rifle Brigade had taken Belyi Rast, continuing the offensive toward Nikol'skoe. On the rest of the front the troops fought stubborn battles all day, and the 331st Rifle Division, together with the 28th Rifle Brigade and 134th Tank Battalion continued street fighting in Krasnaya Polyana.

The 16th Army attacked on the morning of December 7 with the greater part of its forces.

The previous evening, December 6, Gen. Rokossovskii reported to the *front* commander that, in accordance with his orders, the 16th Army would attack at 1000 on December 7 with the following objectives:

1. Remizov, with part of his forces, is to attack from the area of the Children's Colony and Klushino (eight km northeast of Kryukovo), with the object of taking Verevskoe and Zhilino, while the remaining forces are to hold the Klyaz'ma River along the sector Shemyakino-Klushino, securing the army's right flank.

2. The 7th Guards Rifle Division is to attack with the objective of taking L'yalovo and by the end of the day to consolidate along the line Klushino-L'yalovo (excluding)-Chashnikovo (four km southwest of L'yalovo) (exclusively).

3. The 354th Rifle Division is to take Matushkino (three km west of Alabushevo) and by the end of December 7 is to reach the line Chashkino-Alabushevo-Andreevka (exclusively).

4. The 8th Guards Rifle Division, with the 1st Tank and 17th Rifle brigades, is to take Kryukovo and by the end of December 7 to reach the line Andreevka-Gortovka (4-5 km west and southwest of Kryukovo).

5. The 18th Rifle and 9th Guards Rifle divisions are to hold their present positions on December 7 and prepared for an offensive on December 8.

In accordance with this, the 16th Army's forces waged fierce offensive battles on December 7 for Klushino, L'yalovo, Nikol'skoe, Matushkino, Kryukovo, and Rozhdestveno.

The Germans put up fierce resistance along the entire front (particularly in the areas of Matushkino, Kryukovo, Kamenka, and Rozhdestveno), and on certain sectors carried out counterattacks with infantry and tanks.

Gen. Remizov's group (145th Tank Brigade, 282nd Rifle and 523rd Artillery regiments) attacked Valdychino and, following an artillery barrage along the enemy's front line, part of its forces crossed over to the northern bank of the Klyaz'ma River and was involved in the fighting for Vladychino.

The 7th Guards Rifle Division attacked toward L'yalovo and Nikol'skoe, but was halted by the defense's fire.

The 354th Rifle Division was involved in heavy offensive fighting for Matushkino, but was not successful.

The 8th Guards Rifle Division was involved in street fighting for Kryukovo by the end of the day.

The 18th Rifle Division was operating in the Dedovo area, where up to two enemy infantry battalions, with 12-15 tanks, were located.

The 9th Guards Rifle Division was involved in heavy fighting for Rozhdestveno, which involved bayonet attacks. The Germans, having consolidated in the houses and employing rifle-machine gun and mortar fire on the attacking units, defended fiercely. The division was unsuccessful.

It follows that the offensive's first day did not yield any particular success for the 16th Army.

As a result of the fighting on December 6-7 by the armies of the *front's* right wing, the enemy began to withdraw to the west. The following men and matériel were captured: 200 automatic rifles, many rifles, 46 guns, 80 mortars, 227 automobiles, two motorcycles, and two automobiles with uniforms, eight tanks, 12 cars, and a large amount of other property. More than 5,800 enemy officers and men were killed.

Taking into account the developing situation and the beginning of the German withdrawal, the Western Front commander ordered his forces to defeat the enemy's flank groups as quickly as possible, to capture his equipment, transport, weapons, and to swiftly advance to envelop his flank groups, and to completely encircle and destroy all of the enemy's armies. The *front* commander also forbade frontal attacks against the enemy's rearguards and fortified positions, having pointed out that small blocking forces should be left behind to deal with rearguards and fortified positions, meanwhile swiftly bypassing them and advancing as deeply as possible along the enemy's route of withdrawal.

The *front* commander ordered the formation within the armies of several shock groups, consisting of tanks, automatic riflemen and cavalry, to be sent into the enemy rear in order to destroy his fuel stocks and artillery transport.

Gen. Dovator's 2nd Cavalry Corps was removed from the 16th Army on December 7 and transferred to the 5th Army.

On the morning of December 8 the *front's* right-wing armies, overcoming the enemy's stubborn resistance, continued their offensive.

The 30th Army's forces in the center and left flank continued to carry out their orders to take Klin and Rogachevo. On the right flank the 107th Motorized Rifle Division, having pushed back the enemy and crossed the Moscow Sea over the ice, reached the northern edge of Bezborodovo (five km northeast of Novo-Zavidovskii), and by the end of the day was engaged in fierce fighting with the 86th Infantry Division's right-flank units to take the village; the enemy's 36th Motorized Division was engaged in heavy defensive fighting along the line (excluding) Shetakovo (five km east of Novo-Zavidovskii)-Minino-Berezino against the 185th and 379th rifle and 82nd Cavalry divisions. The Germans had along this line a fortified zone with earthen firing points. During the second half of the day the enemy air force bombed our units (185th and 365th rifle divisions) in the area of Iskrino and Pervomaisk (3-5 km south of Sverdlovo) with 18 bombers, and in the Borshchevo area with 16 bombers.

In the center the 30th Army by midday had achieved significant successes: the 371st Rifle Division, along with the 21st Tank Brigade, having captured a number of settlements, was involved in heavy fighting near Shevelevo and Yasenevo (five km northeast of Klin). By reaching this area the division could cut the Klin-Rogachevo road, cutting off the Rogachevo group's withdrawal route to the west to Klin, while enveloping Klin from the northeast.

Taking into account the increasingly unfavorable situation in the Klin area, the enemy units defending Rogachevo (14th Motorized and 7th Panzer divisions) ceased their resistance and began retreating to the southwest. At 1600 on December 8 Rogachevo was taken after a fight by units of the 348th Rifle Division, while the 24th and 18th cavalry divisions captured at 1630 Kochergino, Zhirkovo, and Sofrygino (three km west of Rogachevo) after heavy fighting. The 14th Motorized Division's 118th Motorized Regiment was completely destroyed in the Rogachevo area.

Units of the 14th Motorized Division, which had been defending Rogachevo, fell back on Klin. At the same time the enemy was undertaking measures to securely hold the Klin area, by moving up tank units and organizing the area's anti-tank defense.

The 1st Shock Army's forces, attacking in accordance with the army commander's decision, in the general direction of Fedorovka, were overcoming the enemy's fierce resistance along the entire front. Units of the enemy's 6th and 7th panzer and 23rd Infantry divisions, while putting up fierce resistance, by the end of December 8 were thrown out of a number of settlements. As a result of this fighting, by the end of the day the 1st Shock Army had reached the line: Sin'kovo-Kindyakovo (seven km northwest of Fedorovka)-Fedorovka-Gul'nevo, having established contact with the 20th Army's 64th Rifle Brigade in Nikol'skoe (eight km north of Ozeretskoe). Particularly heavy fighting for Fedorovka against the enemy's 6th Panzer Division fell to the lot of the 56th Rifle Brigade. As a result of stubborn resistance by the enemy, who had created a number of obstacles and carried out destruction as he withdrew, the 1st Shock Army's advance was quite slow and the pace did not exceed 6-8 km per day.

The 20th Army's units were faced by the enemy's 106th Infantry and 2nd and 1st panzer divisions, which were stubbornly defending in the area of Belyi Rast and Krasnaya Polyana, partially regrouping their forces to the north so as to strengthen the resistance to the 1st Shock Army's attacking units.

The 20th Army commander's order no. 06/op ordered his forces to destroy the Fascists in the Krasnaya Polyana area by launching a blow with the right wing in the direction of Belyi Rast and Rozhdestveno (eight km west of Belyi Rast). The army's objective of the day was to reach the line height 239.6-Nikol'skoe-Vladychino. The army's main forces were concentrated along the left flank and in the center.

The enemy, taking into account the unfavorably developing situation (the 30th and 1st Shock armies hanging over him from the north), was withdrawing to the west and northwest. At 0300 on December 8 the 331st Rifle Division and the 28th Rifle Brigade captured Krasnaya Polyana after two days of fighting. During the day the division's units cleaned out Krasnaya Polyana of small groups of automatic riflemen and continued attacking in the direction of the Ozeretskii state farm and Myshetskoe. By the end of the day units of the enemy's 23rd and 106th infantry and 1st Panzer divisions had been completely thrown out of Belyi Rast, Ozeretskii and neighboring villages by the 20th Army's actions. The *front* commander ordered the commander of the 20th Army to station tanks and anti-tank guns in these locations, so as to prevent the enemy from restoring the situation through counterattacks. The enemy continued to withdraw toward the west along the entire front. A prisoner from the 23rd Infantry Division testified that the division suffered heavy losses on December 8 from our artillery fire and air attacks and also had a large number of frostbite cases. A few companies had as few as 25 men.

The *front* commander, in evaluating the developing situation, as early as December 7 ordered the commander of the 1st Shock Army to "continue the offensive by all means, move tanks and automatic riflemen forward, destroy the enemy's rearguards by maneuvering against his flanks and to break into the enemy's combat order…" The most important and basic task put forward by the Western Front commander was to not let the enemy escape and to completely defeat him.

On the 16th Army's front as early as December 8 the first results of the offensive, begun the previous day, were becoming evident. Gen. Remizov's group had taken Vladychino (six km southwest of Krasnaya Polyana), where it inflicted heavy losses on the enemy's 240th Motorized Regiment.

The 7th Guards Rifle Division, after fierce fighting, drove two battalions of German troops out of L'yalovo, who then began to fall back toward Zhilino and Nikol'skoe.

The 354th Rifle Division, following heavy fighting, captured Matushkino (three km north of Kryukovo).

The 8th Guards Rifle Division occupied Kryukovo and Kamenka as the result of night fighting.

The 18th Rifle and 9th Guards Rifle divisions were fighting along their previous positions.

On December 9, following fierce fighting with the forces of the 16th Army along the line Alabushevo-Kryukovo-Dedovo-Rozhdestveno, the Germans, covered by powerful rearguards, began to gradually fall back to the west and northwest. The German withdrawal was evidently linked to the fact that on this day the 30th Army's forces reached Klin from the north and threatened a flank attack into the entire German northern group.

In connection with the enemy's withdrawal, the 16th Army began pursuing him in the general direction of the Istra Reservoir and Istra.

As the 16th Army drew closer to the Istra Reservoir the question was raised as to the army's further disposition of forces. The natural line demanded the creation of two groups (north and south of the reservoir) and the detachment of sufficiently strong reserves, which was done.

The 16th Army commander created two shock groups for operating against the flanks and rear of the enemy: the first consisted of the 145th Tank Brigade, the 44th Cavalry Division, and the 17th Rifle Brigade, for a blow in the direction of Zhilino, Mar'ino, and Sokolovo (15 km north of Istra) and further to the north; the second consisted of the 9th Guards Rifle Division, 17th Tank Brigade, the 36th and 40th rifle brigades, and the 89th Independent Tank Battalion, for a blow against Istra and then to the north.

Both groups attacked on the morning of December 10.

On December 9 the 7th and 8th guards rifle divisions were pulled back into the army reserve: the first into the area of Bol'shie Rzhavki, and the second into the Kryukovo area (on December 14 both divisions were put into the *Stavka* reserve).

The *front's* right-wing armies operations during this period reveal the following:

1 The concentration of large reserves along the line of the Moscow-Volga Canal (1st Shock Army) and along the line Chernaya-Marfino-Khlebnikovo (20th Army), along with the strengthening of the 30th and 16th armies, had begun to yield a large-scale result. By the end of the counteroffensive's third day there was noted a gradual, then a more hurried, withdrawal by the enemy along the entire front.
2 The 30th and 1st Shock armies' main efforts were directed at inflicting a blow against the left flank and rear of the main enemy group attacking Moscow. The 20th Army was attacking in the direction of Solnechnogorsk, with the task of defeating the opposing enemy group and throwing it back to the west.
3 The 30th Army's position overhanging the enemy's communications and its energetic advance on Klin created a threat to the main German group. The German command was forced to adopt measures to extract the Third and Fourth panzer groups' main forces out from under the blows of the 30th and 1st armies. The German command also focused all its efforts in order to hold off the pressure by the 20th and, particularly the 16th armies, as a breakthrough of the enemy front by the 16th Army threatened him with encirclement in the area of Klin, Solnechnogorsk and the Istra Reservoir. The Germans sought to hold on to the area of Klin, Solnechnogorsk and Istra as long as possible in order to pull out their main mass of equipment and personnel.
4 The Supreme High Command's decisive measures, the insistent and active leadership of the Western Front commander and the commanders of the 30th, 1st, 20th, and 16th armies prevented the enemy from carrying out an orderly withdrawal. The blows delivered by our forces in conjunction with the combat operations of our air force, not only forced the enemy to make a hurried withdrawal, but also forced him to incur heavy losses in personnel during the process of withdrawing, and also to abandon his equipment—tanks, armored cars, trucks, vehicles, and other valuable property.

The 30th Army's offensive battles on its right flank during December 9-11 were intense. The enemy's 86th Infantry and 36h Motorized divisions put up strong resistance. Our troops could not at first move forward and it was only after fierce two-day fighting that by the end of December 11 units of the enemy's 36th Motorized Division were ejected from Varakseno and Arkhangel'skoe, which were occupied by our 185th Rifle Division. Fighting unfolded on the eastern outskirts of the villages of Eldino and Vysokovo (six km southeast of Novo-Zavidovskii).

In the 30th Army's center and left flank our troops during December 9-11 continued to attack, forcing the enemy to pull back to the west and southwest. By the end of December 11 the army's units had reached the line Koromyslovo-Staroe Melkovo-Varakseno-Vysokovo-Zhukovo-the southeastern part of Reshetnikovo-Yamuga-Golyadi-Pershutino-the western and northern outskirts of Klin-Maidanovo-Bol'shoe Shchapovo-Spas-Korkodino.

The course of the offensive operation for these three days showed that the enemy was putting forth all his efforts to halt our blow in the direction of Klin and sought to secure the roads leading to the west and southwest. It was especially important for the Germans to secure movement along the following main routes: a) Klin-Teryaeva Sloboda; b) Klin-Solnechnogorsk; c) Solnechnogorsk-Spas-Nudol'-Volokolamsk; d) Istra-Novo-Petrovskoe-Volokolamsk, and remove his personnel and equipment out from under the blow. Thus the 30th Army's task was to continue an energetic offensive and quickly take Klin and block off the withdrawal routes to the west and southwest for the enemy's retreating units.

The 1st Shock Army's offensive during these three days unfolded a little more slowly due to the stubborn resistance put up by the enemy. The Western Front commander ordered the commander of the 1st Shock Army to "decisively pursue the enemy from Fedorovka in the direction of Lake Senezhskoe to the Klin-Solnechnogorsk road and thus cut up the retreating enemy forces into two groups and destroy them in detail."

The 1st Shock Army was ordered: to reach the Klin-Solnechnogorsk road more quickly and, in conjunction with its neighbors, destroy the Fascists. The slow advance of the 1st Shock Army's units and the 29th Rifle Brigade's loss of contact with the enemy, who had managed to slip out from under the blow along this sector of the front, occasioned the Western Front commander's repeat order to force at all costs the army's advance in order to reach the Leningrad highway between Klin and Solnechnogorsk with its main forces by the morning of December 10. The forward units were ordered to cut the highway as early as the previous night, and the 29th Rifle Brigade was ordered to immediately establish contact with the enemy and by the morning of December 10 to take Davydkovo (eight km southeast of Klin), in order to envelop Klin from the south.

The enemy in front of the 1st Shock Army continued to defend stubbornly. On the right flank the 29th Rifle Brigade was only able to reach the line Dubrovka-Pochinki by the end of December 10, where it was engaged with a motorized regiment from the 6th Panzer Division. Along the remainder of the front the units attacked slowly, overcoming the enemy's resistance, which was particularly heavy in the inhabited areas and along road junctions.

Thus the 1st Shock Army was slightly tardy in carrying out its assigned tasks. While waging continuous battles along the entire front, on December 11 the army's forces had reached the line Zolino-Borozda-Vorob'evo-Tolstyakovo (ten km north of Solnechnogorsk)-Zagor'e (north of Lake Senezhskoe)-Rekintsy-Dubinino, having cut the Leningrad highway in two places (Borozda and Dubinino) and having established closed contact with units of the 20th Army in the Solnechnogorsk area.

On December 9 air reconnaissance established the continuous movement of automobiles in two lanes along the Klin-Teryaeva Sloboda road. Unfortunately, the poor weather conditions on December 9-10 limited our air actions. Nonetheless, the 23rd Air Division bombed enemy automobile and troop columns moving northwest along the Leningrad highway (in the area of Peshki and Solnechnogorsk) and inflicted heavy losses on them. The enemy, while withdrawing, set up obstacles and mined the roads, houses and other objects.

The 20th Army commander, in order to destroy the Solnechnogorsk group, issued order no. 08/op, which contained the following instructions:

a) the 64th Rifle Brigade, along with the 24th Tank Brigade, is to pursue the enemy along the road to Timonovo and, upon linking up with the forward detachment on the Leningrad highway north of Solnechnogorsk, prevent the enemy's Solnechnogorsk group from withdrawing, as well as the arrival of his reserves from the north and northwest;

b) the 35th Rifle Brigade and the 31st Tank Brigade are to reach the area of Redino, with the task of attacking Solnechnogorsk in order to envelop it from the north;
c) the 331st Rifle Division, 134th Tank Battalion, 7th Independent Guards Mortar Battalion, and the 517th Artillery Regiment's 2nd Battalion are to reach the area of Skorodumki, Snopovo (five km south of Solnechnogorsk) by the end of the day for a blow from the southwest;
d) the 28th Rifle Brigade, 135th Tank Battalion, and the 15th Independent Guards Mortar Battalion are to reach the area of Obukhovo and Ozhogino (three km southwest of Solnechnogorsk) for delivering a blow from the southwest and securing the army's left flank.

During December 9-10 the 20th Army continued to pursue the enemy, who was retreating to the west and southwest, seeking to cut off his route of retreat with its right-flank units. The enemy was falling back rapidly, abandoning his weapons and other equipment. For example, in Belyi Rast he left behind several corpses, a heavy tank, four anti-tank guns, as well as heavy and light machine guns. He lost heavily in men and matériel in the fighting for Krasnaya Polyana; in his hurried withdrawal from Krasnaya Polyana to Myshetskoe the enemy abandoned along the road up to 15 vehicles and 50 motorcycles.

It was clear that the enemy, under the blows of the units of the 30th, 1st, and 20th armies, was forced to undertake a hurried retreat, instead of an organized withdrawal.

At 1400 on December 10 the enemy's rearguards were thrown out of a number of inhabited areas and the army's main forces reached the line Shikhovo-Red'kino (nine km north of Belyi Rast)-Kochergino-Khougvino-Yesipovo-Radomlya, with a group of forces on its right flank and fighting the enemy's covering units.

On December 11 the commander of the 20th Army ordered the army to take Solnechnogorsk and by the end of the day reach the line Misirevo (three km south of Klin)-Mikhailovskoe-Troitskoe-Timofeevo (two km northwest of Pyatnitsa) and be ready to continue the offensive to the west.

In order to carry out this assignment, the 64th Rifle Brigade, along with the 24th Tank Brigade and the 133rd Rifle Division, were ordered to reach the line Misirevo-Mikhailovskoe, securing the army's right flank;

The 331st Rifle Division and the 134th Tank Battalion were to reach the area of Troitskoe, Gorki, and Dudkino; the 28th Rifle Brigade and 135th Tank Battalion, in conjunction with the 16th Army's 354th Rifle Division, were to destroy the opposing enemy and take the villages of Berezhki and Pyatnitsa (on the northeastern bank of the Istra Reservoir), and throw a forward detachment to the western bank at Melechkino and Timofeevo;

The 35th Rifle Brigade was to reach the area of Moshnitsy and Golovkovo (four km northwest of Solnechnogorsk), securing Solnechnogorsk from the northwest; the 31st Tank Brigade was to reach the area of the rest home northeast of Solnechnogorsk and be ready to: a) for an offensive in conjunction with the 331st Rifle Division; b) to coordinate with the 35th Rifle Brigade in case of a possible enemy attack from the northwest; the 352nd Rifle Division and the 7th Independent Guards Mortar Battalion were to concentrate in Solnechnogorsk.

In this fashion the 20th Army sought to get astride the Leningrad highway as quickly as possible with its right flank and completely capture Solnechnogorsk; the 20th Army's left flank, in coordination with the 16th Army's right-flank units, were to reach the area west and northwest of the Istra Reservoir, with the task of helping the 16th Army to force this line. This was necessary, as the enemy was trying to hold off the 16th Army's offensive by means of strong rearguards and tanks.

Continuing the pursuit to the west and northwest, the 20th Army's forces went around Solnechnogorsk from the north and south. On the morning of December 11 the 31st Tank Brigade's forward units were reconnoitering the enemy's positions on the southeastern outskirts of the town. By 1400 the 35th Rifle Brigade was fighting in Rekintsy. A group, consisting of the 64th Rifle and 24th Tank brigades, bypassing Solnechnogorsk from the north, reached the highway north of the town and forced the Germans to abandon the town; the Germans did not have time to burn it down. Only a few covering forces were left in the town (automatic riflemen on vehicles). Simultaneous with the actions of this group, the 31st Tank Brigade at 1400 broke into Solnechnogorsk. By the end of December 11 the 64th Rifle Brigade had reached as far as Osipovo, where it was engaged in fighting.

In this area we captured two tanks, 30 motor vehicles, four anti-tank guns, rifles, light machine guns, and other military equipment. Our left-flank units (331st Rifle Division) captured 41 motor vehicles in the Peshki area.

The enemy, covering the withdrawal of his main forces (23rd Infantry and 1st Panzer divisions) and taking heavy losses, hurriedly fell back to the west in the direction of Nudol', trying to more quickly reach the Volokolamsk road. The Germans strained in front of the 1st Shock and 20th armies to avoid the encirclement of their worn-out units by our troops and their complete defeat. However, the situation was developing unfavorably for the Germans, because as a result of the arrival of the 30th Army's units in the Klin area and the 30th and 1st armies hanging over the left flank and rear of the Third Panzer Group, a dangerous situation was being created which threatened its path of retreat to the west. On December 11 air reconnaissance noted the rapid movement of columns of motor vehicles to the west and southwest along the following roads: 1) Klin-Teryaeva Sloboda; 2) Solnechnogorsk-Nudol'; 3) Istra-Novo-Petrovskoe.

In the areas southeast of Klin a large amount of automobile transport was noted, moving in disorder in different directions. According to the testimony of prisoners, there were incidents when German officers abandoned their units and sought escape in flight; in these cases the units were commanded by sergeants and corporals.

By the end of December 11 the 20th Army's forward units were fighting in the area of the Leningrad highway. The 31st Tank and 35th Rifle brigades were fighting on the outskirts of Strelino. The 331st Rifle Division, having bypassed Peshki from the north, was attacking toward Savel'evo and Snopovo; the 28th Rifle Brigade reached the line Rostovtsevo-Dudkino; the 352nd Rifle Division in the second echelon was moving to the Peshki area. In this fighting we seized four tanks, 13 motor vehicles, seven mortars, 13 guns, and many other trophies.

By the end of December 11 the 16th Army had reached the line Kurilovo-Lopotovo (on the eastern bank of the Istra Reservoir)-Maksimovka-Istra. The Germans, in falling back, set fire to the inhabited areas, mined the roads, and destroyed the bridges; in the village of Novoe they poisoned the wells, as a result of which horses in the 44th Cavalry Division were poisoned, and in Akishevo they poisoned the inhabitants' potatoes.

Reconnaissance data showed that the Germans, in falling back toward the reservoir, planned to use it as a convenient defensive line.

Our air force—the 47th Air Division—during December 11 conducted reconnaissance of the area of Solnechnogorsk, Klin, Teryaeva Sloboda, and strafed concentrations of enemy troops in Teryaeva Sloboda.

On December 11 the Western Front staff established operating zones for the armies' further offensive. The 30th Army continued to fight for Klin with the 1st Army. The 1st Army, enveloping Klin from the south with its right flank, directed its center and left wing toward Teryaeva Sloboda. The 20th Army was advancing on Nudol' and the 16th on the Istra Reservoir and Istra.

The defeat of the enemy's Klin-Rogachevo Group, December 12-16

On December 12 the offensive by the 20th and 1st Shock armies continued. The enemy, covering himself with rearguards, sought to remove his units out from under our troops' flank blows. The Germans' Zavidovo group, covering the Third Panzer Group's retreat from the north, during the day fought in the area of Bezborodovo (on the Leningrad highway, near the Moscow Sea), Novo-Zavidovskii, and Zavidovo. On the morning of December 12 the 30th Army's forces attacked along the right and left flanks. In the army's center they repulsed enemy counterattacks from the areas of Vysokovsk and Klin.

By 1300 the 185th Rifle Division capgtured Bezborodovo, Mokshino, and Kabanovo and was attacking toward Novo-Zavidovskii; the 379th Rifle Division captured Zavidovo, Spas-Zaulok, and Reshetnikovo; by 1200 a detachment was removed from the division and assigned the task of attacking toward Voroshilovskii (ten km southwest of Novo-Zavidovskii) and cutting off the retreat route of the enemy's Zavidovo group to the west toward Kozlovo and Kur'yanovo.

A mobile group (82nd Cavalry Division, a composite regiment from the 107th Motorized Rifle Division, a tank battalion, and the 2nd and 19th ski battalions) was fighting with its right column near Kopylovo, overturning small enemy units, while with its right column it took Semchino and continued to attack toward Borikhino and Pavel'tsevo (20 km northeast of Teryaeva Sloboda).

The 365th Rifle Division and 8th Tank Brigade were attacked from the area of Vysokovsk and Klin by motorized infantry (14th and 36th motorized divisions), supported by 40 tanks and aviation. The counterattack forced the division to pull back to the southern edge of the woods north of Golyadi, Polukhanovo, and Maidanovo.

The 371st Rifle Division and 21st Tank Brigade continued fighting along the line Selyukhino (6-10 km northeast of Klin)-Maloe Ivantsevo Shchapovo, having repulsed the enemy's counterattack from the woods south of Selyukhino; Gen. Khetagurov's group (348th Rifle, 24th and 18th cavalry divisions), continued the offensive and captured Melenkami and Sokolovo and continued to attack toward Klin. Thus the units of the 30th Army's center and left flank were hanging directly over Klin from the north and northeast, halfway encircling this area.

Events on the 1st Shock Army's front, as was noted, developed more slowly. This brought about repeated and insistent instructions from the Western Front command, demanding rapid and decisive actions from the commander of the 1st Army. The *front* commander, in order to achieve complete cooperation between the 1st and 20th armies, on the morning of December 12 transferred the 55th Rifle Brigade to the 20th Army. The 46th Cavalry Division was also transferred to the Kalinin Front.

Along the 1st Shock Army's front the enemy was covering himself with units from the 36th Motorized, 23rd Infantry, and 6th Panzer divisions along the line Akulovo-Yelino (ten km southeast of Klin)-Chepchika, while withdrawing his main forces to the west.

During the first half of December 12 the army's units continued attacking and were fighting along the line Sokolovo (ten km northeast of Klin)-Naprugovo-Akat'evo-Leonidovo-Zagor'e (on the northern bank of Lake Senezhskoe), and meeting stubborn resistance.

The 55th Rifle Brigade, operating south of Lake Senezhskoe (outside the 1st Shock Army's attack zone) by 0900 had reached the southern outskirts of Solnechnogorsk and was fighting the enemy, helping the 35th Rifle Brigade (20th Army) in cleansing the city of small groups of automatic riflemen. On the morning of December 13 the army continued attacking along the entire front, aiding the 30th Army in completing the encirclement of the Klin group.

On the 30th Army's front the enemy's Zavidovo group, covering the withdrawal of Hoth's Third Panzer Group from the north, could not withstand the blow by our forces from the west, north and south and, having suffered heavy losses, was rapidly falling back in a westerly direction along the road to Dorino, and from Kopylovo to Stepantsevo.

The 185th Rifle Division, attacking along the southern shore of the Moscow Sea, captured Voroshilovskii, Chistyi Mokh, and Kleshchevo and continued to pursue the retreating enemy; to the south the 379th Rifle Division captured Kopylovo; the mobile group captured the area of Krutsy, Komlevo and Vasil'kovo (20 km west of Klin) and continued the pursuit.

The 365th Rifle Division attacked from the line Golyadi-Madanovo toward Klin, beating off counterattacks by infantry and tanks; the 8th Tank Brigade, having broken the enemy's resistance, reached the line northeast of Lavrovo-Vasil'evo (three km southwest of Klin). In the Klin area, where the remains of the enemy's Rogachevo group (36th and 14th Motorized, 1st Panzer divisions) had concentrated, seeking to break out of the encirclement, put up stubborn resistance, counterattacking with infantry, supported by tanks and aviation.

The 371st Rifle Division, having crushed with two regiments the fascists' resistance in the Praslovo area and to the west, broke into the northern outskirts of Klin; another of the division's regiments was fighting along the front Maloe Ivantsevo Shchapovo-Plyuskovo.

The 348th Rifle Division was operating along the front Zolino-Opritovo; the 18th and 24th cavalry divisions, having thrown the enemy back from Borisoglebsk and Pustye Melenki, reached the Borozda area, from which it continued to attack toward Klin from the southeast.

The enemy (14th and 36th mechanized, 1st Panzer divisions) were fighting fiercely along the line Golyadi-northern outskirts of Klin-Opalevo. His situation in the almost-surrounded town of Klin was becoming critical.

On this day the 47th Air Division bombed and strafed the Germans' retreating troops and motor columns in the area of Klin, Solnechnogorsk, Teryaeva Sloboda, and Pavel'tsevo.

During December 13 the 1st Shock Army's right-flank units were engaged in combat, cooperating with the 30th Army's center and left flank; the 1st Shock Army's main forces were concentrating in the direction of Klin.

The 29th Rifle Brigade was attacking in the direction of Klin. The 50th Rifle Brigade was attacking in the direction of Pustye Melenki and Borozda; the 84th Rifle Brigade was attacking toward Davydkovo and Akulovo; the 47th Rifle Brigade was attacking in the direction of Dulepovo, Pokrov, and Frolovskoe, with the objective of attacking Klin from behind the 84th Rifle Brigade's left flank. The army's remaining units were carrying out their previous assignments.

The developing situation demanded energetic measure for defeating the Germans. The Western Front commander on December 13 issued the following order to his right-wing armies:

To the commanders of the 30th, 1st, 20th, 16th, and 5th armies No. 0130/op
Copy: to the chief of the General Staff Very important
13.12.41. 1:500,000 map.

1 The enemy, waging stubborn rearguard battles, continues to retreat to the west.

2. The immediate task of the *front's* right-wing armies is to complete the defeat of the retreating enemy by means of a continuous pursuit and by the end of December 18 to reach the front Stepurino-Ramen'e-Shakhovskaya-Andreevskoe-the headwaters of the Ruza River-Ostashevo-Ashcherino-Vasyukovo-Kliment'evo-Oblyanishchevo-Gribtsovo-Maurino.

3 I order:

a) The 30th Army commander, having surrounded Klin with part of his forces, is to reach with his main forces on December 16 1941 the line Turginovo-Pokrovskoe-(excluding) Teryaeva Sloboda and to securely anchor the *front's* right flank. The boundary line: from the right—as before as far as Turginovo, then approximately (excluding) the Shosha River; from the left—as before as far as Klin, and then (excluding) Teryaeva Sloboda-(excluding) Knyazh'i Gory.

b) The 1st Army commander is to assist the 30th Army with part of his forces in encircling Klin from the south, and with his main forces reach the front Teryaeva Sloboda-Nikita on December 16.

The boundary line from the left is, as before, as far as Vertlinskoe, then to Troitskoe-Nikita-Volokolamsk-Romantsevo.

c) The 20th Army commander is to reach the front Kolpaki-Davydkovo-Novo-Petrovskoe with his main forces by December 16.
The boundary line is, as before, as far as Pyatnitsa, then to Novo-Petrovskoe-Sosnino-Chernevo.

d) The commander of the 16th Army is to reach the front (excluding) Novo-Petrovskoe-Skirmanovo-Onufrievo with his main forces on December 16.
The boundary as far as Istra is as before, and then along the line Onufrievo-Khotebtsevo-Myshkino.

e) The 5th Army commander is to reach the front Fafonikha-Ozernaya River-Tabolovo-Ruza-Tuchkovo with his main forces on December 16.
The boundary as far as Maurino is as before, and then to Novo-Nikol'skoe-Kolychevo.

4 The army commanders are personally responsible for reaching the indicate objectives on time. The army commanders are to establish objectives for the divisions for each day, indicating which lines should be reached by the divisions, and very sternly demanding that the division commanders carry out their tasks.

5 The *front's* air arm will support the armies' offensive.

6 The pursuit should be pushed vigorously, without breaking contact with the enemy. Powerful forward detachments should be widely used for seizing road junctions and bottlenecks, and for disorganizing the enemy's march and combat formations.

7 I categorically forbid frontal attacks against the enemy's fortified strong points. The forward echelons, are not to get bogged down and, bypassing them, leaving their destruction of these strong points to the following echelons.

8 I demand the precise organization of cooperation along the boundaries with neighbors and that they assist one another, without reference to formal boundaries.

9 Report receipt and orders issued.

Zhukov Bulganin Sokolovskii

With this order the commander of the Western Front demanded that the main forces of the *front's* right wing reach the line Turginovo-Teryaeva Sloboda-Novo-Petrovskoe-Ruza-Tuchkovo by December 16. The armies were overcome enemy resistance in the course of three days and advance 25-30 km in winter conditions.

Aside from the main order, taking the situation in the Klin area into account, the Western Front commander issued the commanders of the 30th and 1st Shock armies special instructions:

Very important

Army commanders Lelyushenko and Kuznetsov
No. 090/op, 13.12.1941

I order:

1 Part of the armies' forces are to operate along your joint flanks. On December 13 the complete encirclement of the Germans in the Klin area is to be carried out, along with their capture. The remaining forces are to decisive and uninterruptedly continue to carry out their orders, pursuing the retreating enemy.

2 Propose surrender to the Germans in Klin, using aircraft, envoys under a flag of truce, and loudspeakers, promising to spare them. If not, then destroy them to the last man.
Fulfillment of these orders is the personal responsibility of the army commanders.

Zhukov. Bulganin.

The 30th Army commander, in carrying out the *front* commander's orders to encircle Klin, sent forward a composite detachment from the mobile group, with the task of cutting off the enemy's columns retreating from Vysokovsk. Also, our aviation carried out 150 sorties to destroy the Germans' retreating groups. During December 6-13 the army captured: 150 tanks and armored vehicles, 356 machine guns, 186 guns, 168 mortars, 1,200 automatic rifles, 35,000 shells, 25,000 mortar shells, 1,056 motor vehicles, 3,000,000 rifle rounds, and 540 km of telephone cable. Up to 15,000 Germans were killed and wounded.

The *front* command confirmed to the 30th Army commander that with the elimination of the enemy in Klin a delay had set in, which might unfavorably influence the development of the success of the right-wing armies. It was pointed out that the *Stavka* demands the immediate elimination of the enemy in Klin and his rapid defeat to the west of Klin, so as not to allow him to consolidate somewhere along lines in the area of Teryaeva Sloboda or Volokolamsk.

Air reconnaissance reported that the Germans were pulling back their forces from the Klin area to Teryaeva Sloboda. The army commander repeatedly demanded that the road to Teryaeva Sloboda be cut to prevent the Germans' retreat along it, and ordered that a cavalry group consisting of the 18th and 24th cavalry divisions be thrown into the area of Teryaeva Sloboda and Volokolamsk with the task of preventing the enemy from consolidating in this area and to completely rout him.

The 1st Shock Army continued its offensive to the west and southwest, while simultaneously squeezing the encirclement ring around Klin. The 30th Army's right-flank units (185th and 379th rifle divisions, the mobile group) by the end of December 14 and the night of December 14-15 were continuing the offensive and, pushing back the Germans, reached the line Kozlovo-the worker's settlement-Volovnikovo-Vasil'kovo (12 km northwest of Vysokovsk). The enemy continued to put up stubborn resistance, covering the retreat of its northern group's main forces retreating in a westerly and southwesterly direction to Volokolamsk.

The mobile group (82nd Cavalry Division, the 107th Motorized Rifle Division's composite regiment, 2nd and 19th ski battalions) from the Dyatlovo area (13 km northeast of Teryaeva Sloboda) continued moving toward Teryaeva Sloboda, with the objective of cutting the road and blocking the enemy's route of retreat to the west.

The troops in the center (365th Rifle Division, 8th and 21st tank brigades, the 371st and 348th rifle divisions) sought to complete the encirclement of Klin, waging stubborn fighting against the enemy along the line Borisovo-Golyadi-Polukhanovo-Malanino and the southwestern outskirts of Klin, near the road to Vysokovsk (one km west of Pershutino and Lavrovo). The Fascists repeatedly counterattacked, supported by tanks and aviation, but all the attacks were beaten off with heavy losses for the enemy.

However, the 1st Shock Army's units gradually moved forward, meeting the enemy's stubborn resistance, and were not able to fully coordinate their actions with the 30th Army, as a result of which it proved impossible to completely encircle Klin. It should be added that Vysokovsk had still not been taken by this time (and was not even blocked). Thus the Germans could keep the Vysokovsk-Klin road under observation and fire from this area. The fighting for Klin continued with unrelenting force on both sides.

The 371st Rifle Division, having captured Maloe Ivantsevo Shchapovo and Gubino, was engaged in fierce fighting on the eastern outskirts of Klin, with its right flank near the southern outskirts of Maidanovo, and its left 1½ km west of Kirp.

At the same time units of the 348th Rifle Division, having completed by the end of December 14 stubborn fighting with the enemy's Voronino group (having partially destroyed it, and partially thrown it back to the southwest), reached the eastern outskirts of Klin.

The 30th Army's left flank (24th and 18th cavalry divisions) attacked the southeastern outskirts of Klin from the Borozda area. The enemy, while holding off our troops' offensive, was defending fiercely, employing automatic riflemen and putting up obstacles. Particularly heavy fighting was underway near Praslovo, on the western outskirts of Klin, and near the western outskirts of Akulovo and Borozda.

The 1st Shock Army's right-flank units (29th, 84th, and 47th rifle brigades), although late, assisted the 30th Army in encircling Klin from the south and southeast. During the latter half of December 14 the 29th Rifle Brigade was engaged in fierce fighting on the eastern outskirts of Klin; the 84th Rifle Brigade, having captured Akulovo, continued its attack on Borodino; the 47th Rifle Brigade captured the northwestern edge of the woods south of Sokhino and was attacking toward Lavrovo; the remaining units of the 1st Shock Army continued to carry out their assigned tasks.

The following German forces were operating in Klin and the immediate area: the 14th Motorized and 1st Panzer divisions, the 900th SS Brigade, 36th Motorized Division, the 138th Engineering Battalion, and other units, or 18,000 combat troops, 150 tanks, and up to seven artillery battalions.

Our troops, attacking around to bypass Klin from the west, met powerful enemy counterattacks. They were unable to completely close the encirclement ring from the west; the Klin-Vysokovsk road still remained open to the Germans. By the end of December 14 the attempts by the German garrison to widen its gateway to the west increased. With the onset of darkness, a part of the enemy's forces was able to break out of the encirclement to the west, although with heavy losses.

The fierce fighting by units of the 30th Army in the Klin area and the arrival of the 1st Shock Army's right-flank units at the southeastern outskirts of the town ended with the fall of Klin. At 0200 on December 15, following several days of heavy fighting, units of the 30th Army's 371st Rifle Division entered Klin. The first unit to enter the town was the 1263rd Rifle Regiment under the command of Col. Reshetov. By 0700 the 371st Rifle Division's other two regiments had entered the town. Prisoners were taken and a lot of equipment captured. The remains of the Klin garrison filtered into Vysokovsk in a southwesterly direction. Upon capturing Klin, the troops continued to pursue the enemy.

The Third Panzer Group's main forces fell back toward Volokolamsk and to the north. The covering units were fighting along the line Kozlovo (on the southern shore of the Moscow Sea)-Chernyatino-Vasil'kovo and to the southeast. The enemy's transport columns fell back along the road to Teryaeva Sloboda and further to the west.

By the end of December 15 our troops had reached Vysokovsk and Pavel'tsevo; the mobile group reached Kurbatovo (eight km northeast of Teryaeva Sloboda). The 30th Army's main forces were directed at moving the mobile group as quickly as possible to the road near Teryaeva Sloboda, in order to cut the enemy's escape route.

The 1st Shock Army's forces continued to pursue the enemy to the southwest and during the latter half of the day, as the result of combat collisions along various sectors of the front, had reached the line Gonchakovo-Kuznechikovo-Trunyaevka (11 km south of Vysokovsk)-Karavaevo.

The 30th and 1st Shock armies' offensive activities on December 15 were supported by Gen. Petrov's air group, which had been ordered to destroy the enemy's forces within the following bounds: to the right—the Moscow Sea; to the left—Klin (excluding)-Volokolamsk, with particularly attention paid to the Klin-Teryaeva Sloboda-Suvorovo road, with its branches to Lotoshino and Volokolamsk.

Thus ended the operation by the 30th and 1st Shock armies to take Klin. During December 9-15 the forces of both armies captured the following amounts of equipment: 82 tanks, 18 armored cars, 750 automobiles, 80 guns, 120 mortars, 250 machine guns, 800 automatic rifles, up to 10,000 shells, 2,000,000 rifle rounds, etc. The operation in the Klin area was characterized by the following:

1 The most important activities occurred along the boundary of the 30th and 1st Shock armies. This circumstance demanded the precise organization of cooperation between the two armies. The *front* staff directly controlled operations and concentrated the forces of both armies to encircle Klin. As a result of the delay by units of the 1st Shock Army in moving forward, which was caused by the enemy's stubborn resistance, the brunt of the fighting for encircling Klin fell to the 30th Army (chiefly its center and left flank). The 30th Army's encirclement operation lasted seven days, beginning on December 8 and ending on December 14. One must admit that operations unfolded with insufficient speed, the reasons for which are as follows: a) the harsh winter conditions (heavy frosts had begun and a thick snow had fallen); b) a shortage of good rods in the direction of Klin from the north and northeast, which was reflected in the units' speed and maneuverability; c) the 1st Shock Army's slow advance, against which the enemy put up a stubborn resistance with two tank and two infantry divisions, using engineering obstacles (mining the roads, blowing up bridges), and burning down villages.

2 A complete encirclement as a result of our offensive on Klin was not achieved, because Vysokovsk was not taken by our forces; the Klin-Vysokovsk road was constantly under fire from the enemy's artillery and mortars. This made it difficult to move our troops forward and made it impossible to close the encirclement ring with a sufficient number of units on the western side; as a result, the remains of the Klin garrison were able to filter through to the west and southwest.

On December 16 the 30th and 1st Shock armies continued to pursue the Third Panzer Group.

The 30th Army, while pursuing, and in connection with the new situation, was subordinated to the commander of the Kalinin Front at 1200 on December 16.

The following boundary was established between the Western and Kalinin fronts: Rogachevo-Reshetnikovo station-Kotlyakovo-Bol'shie Ledinki-Pokrovskoe (all within the Kalinin Front). The Western Front commander ordered the commander of the 1st Army to take over the sector south of the boundary with the Kalinin Front. The task assigned to the 1st Shock Army remained as before, but the army was ordered to make its main effort in the direction of Teryaeva Sloboda, Yaropolets, Ramen'e and Knyazh'i Gory.

The boundary to the left, with the 20th Army, remained as before as far as Nikita, and then Ivanovskoe-Shakhovskaya-Kuchino (all within the 1st Shock Army). During December 16 and the night of December 16-17 the army's units continued to attack along the entire front, pursuing the enemy, who was retreating to the west.

The 84th Rifle Brigade, which had been thrust forward, by 0800 on December 17, was fighting to take Petrovsk. The 50th, 47th, 56th and 71st rifle brigades fought for and captured the villages of Bogaikha, Zakharovo, and Vlaskovo (all 20-25 km east of Teryaeva Sloboda). The enemy in front of these brigades was falling back to the line Ivanovskoe-Aksenikha.

The 29th Rifle Brigade reached the area of Yazykovo (nine km south of Klin); the 44th Rifle Brigade the area of Kuznechikovo; the 46th Rifle Brigade reached Torbeevo and Ozeretskoe (20 km east of Dmitrov); the 62nd Rifle Brigade reached the area of Kudrino and Vas'kovo (20 km southeast of Dmitrov); the 41st Rifle Brigade reached Khot'kovo. Units of the 1st Shock Army were concentrating their main forces along the right flank and in the center, trying to cut the enemy's escape route as quickly as possible.

The 20th Army's offensive battles in the area of the Istra Reservoir, December 12-17

On December 12 the 20th Army's forces were fighting west of Solnechnogorsk and near Obukhovo, where the enemy was putting up stubborn resistance, although by the end of the day he was nevertheless pushed out of these places. By the end of December 12 units of the 20th Army had reached the line Subbotino (four km west of Solnechnogorsk)-Obukhovo-Berezhki (12 km southwest of Solnechnogorsk)-Pyatnitsa, where communications were established with the 16th Army's right-flank units (the 354th Rifle Division, whose right flank was located in Lopotovo). The army commander's reserve—the 352nd Rifle Division—was concentrated in Solnechnogorsk.

During December 13 the 20th Army's forces, overcoming the resistance of the enemy's 23rd and 106th infantry divisions, covering the retreat of the main forces, had advanced on the right and left flanks a little bit, and had moved forward somewhat in the center.

On the morning of December 14 the main forces were concentrating along the right flank and in the center, in the general direction of Gorki, Nikol'skoe, and Kuznetsovo, along the northern bank of the Nudol' River, in order to deliver a flank blow against the enemy in a southwesterly direction. For this purpose, the 64th Rifle Brigade and the 331st Rifle Division, (together with Remizov's newly-arrived group—17th Rifle Brigade, 44th Cavalry Division, 145th Tank Brigade) occupied the line Zamyatino (nine km northwest of Solnechnogorsk)-Loginovo and sent forward a forward detachment to Troitskoe and Kuznetsovo. The 28th Rifle Brigade was preparing to force the Istra Reservoir along the line Berezhki-Pyatnitsa, cooperating with the 16th Army's right-flank units.

Having received orders to bring up the army's main forces to the front Kolpaki-Davydkovo-Novo-Petrovskoe, the 20th Army commander issued the following orders to his forces.

The 64th Rifle and 24th Tank brigades were to pursue the enemy in the direction of Kut'ino (12 km southeast of Teryaeva Sloboda) and by the end of December 14 their main forces were to reach the area of Nikolaevka, Skripyashchevo, and Khokhlovo (ten km northeast of Nudol'-Sharina); by the end of December 16 they were to reach Savino.

The 331st Rifle Division, the 134th Tank Battalion, and the 31st Tank Brigade were to pursue the enemy in the direction of Nudol'-Sharino and by the end of December 14 were to reach the area of Koren'ka and Podzhigorodovo with their main forces, and by the end of December 15 the Denezhkino area.

The 35th Rifle Brigade was to pursue the enemy in the direction of Den'kovo and by the end of December 14 reach Antipino, and by the close of December 15 Bodrovo (seven km south of Nudol'-Sharina).

The 28th Rifle Brigade was to pursue the enemy in the direction of Davydkovo and by the close of December 14 reach the area of Maloe Ivantsevo, Ushakovo and Leonovo; by the close of December 15 to reach Rybushki.

The 55th Rifle Brigade was to reach Yekaterinovka by the close of December 14, and Stepan'kovo by the close of December 15, securing the army's right flank.

The 352nd Rifle Division, which comprised the second echelon, was to reach the area of Gorki, Khrenovo, and Pogorelovo on December 14 and by the close of December 15 Koren'ka and Tiliktino.

Despite all our efforts, as a result of the enemy's extremely stubborn resistance, the 20th Army's forces were not able to reach the designated line and by the close of December 14 they were 8-10 km from it. On the morning of December 15 the *front* commander ordered the commander of the 20th Army to explain the reasons for his troops not carrying out the order to reach their objectives for the day. The army commander reported:

> The slow advance by the 20th Army's forces is caused by the following reasons: first, the enemy is putting up stubborn resistance along the line of the Katysha River from Troitskoe to the Istra Reservoir, and has organized a defense along that line; second, in retreating, the enemy is blowing up the bridges, mining the roads, and putting up obstacles, as a result of which our offensive through the woods must be carried out extremely slowly, overcoming the snow, dismantling his obstacles, and bringing up artillery and ammunition; third, the military council personally organized an attack by units of the 64th Rifle Brigade and led a battalion into the attack, which at 2130 on December 14 broke through the enemy's defense and captured Troitskoe, destroying up to two companies of infantry and capturing five anti-tank weapons and motor vehicles.

The 20th Army's forces, cooperating with the 1st Shock Army, as well as the 16th Army, which at that time was fighting to capture the Istra Reservoir, lagged behind somewhat in their advance, as a result of the Germans' stubborn resistance. This could not but influence the course of the operation by the Western Front's right wing, as it enabled the enemy to put himself in order and erect obstacles.

During December 15-16 the 20th Army's forces continued to wage stubborn offensive battles along the entire front. On the left flank the 28th Rifle Brigade at 0500 on December 15, having forced the northern branch of the Istra Reservoir, captured Melechkino and continued to attack to the southwest. To the south the 20th Army's forces also forced this water line.

On December 17 the army's forces were approaching the line Semenkovo-Klimovka-Denezhkino (seven km north of Novo-Petrovskoe)-Prechistoe-Rybushki-Rumyantsevo. The 352nd Rifle Division was concentrated in the area of Shapkino and Stegachevo in reserve.

In the fighting of December 13-16 the 20th Army captured 79 guns, 113 motor vehicles, 20 motorcycles, 16 mortars, 102 motorcycles, 300 barrels of fuel, a large number of mortar rounds, stores and vehicles, and other property stolen by the Germans. Many enemy soldiers and officers were killed. The 20th Army later was concentrating its main efforts along the road to Volokolamsk. Testimony by prisoners established that the enemy was pulling back his forces north of Volokolamsk to the line of the Lama River. To the south our air reconnaissance on December 15 noted the movement of the enemy's automobile columns, retreating along the Volokolamsk-Ryukhovskoe road.

The 16th Army's offensive fighting for the Istra Reservoir, December 12-17

On December 12 units of the 16th Army's left wing, continuing to pursue the enemy, reached the Istra River (where they were met with powerful fire from the enemy on the river's western bank), while units of the right wing reached the reservoir.

The Germans, in retreating to the reservoir's and river's right bank, destroyed all the existing crossings, blew up the reservoir's dike, and organized a powerful fire resistance along its entire western bank.

Attempts to force the Istra River on the march did not yield positive results. For example, during the daylight hours of December 12 the 18th Rifle Division was fighting for a crossing along the line Buzharovo (seven km north of Istra)-Nikulino, faced by up to a regiment of infantry with tanks. The division's repeated attempts to force the river were repulsed by enemy fire from the opposite shore, after which our units were forced to consolidate on the eastern bank, in order to prepare for a crossing on the next day.

The same situation held on the 9th Guards Rifle Division's front. Following unsuccessful attempts to force the river, the division was forced to remain on the eastern bank in the area of Istra, which had been occupied by us as early as December 11.

One should note that one of the reasons for the first failures to cross the river was that the units' artillery (particularly reinforcement artillery) began to noticeably fall behind our forces from the beginning of the offensive, as a result of which the Germans' fire resistance on the western bank of the river was not suppressed at first.

On the morning of December 13 the army's units resumed their offensive and during the day fought, while at the same time erecting crossings from materials at hand. However, a crossing did not take place that day.

By the close of December 13 the following situation had developed on the 16th Army's front.

Gen. Remizov's group (which had been bypassing the reservoir from the north), having broken the enemy's resistance, reached the line Gorki (12 km southwest of Solnechnogorsk)-Terbeevo, thus creating a threat to envelop the German units located on the reservoir's western bank. During the day's fighting the group's units routed the enemy's 111th Infantry Regiment/35th Infantry Division, killing up to 500 Germans and capturing six heavy guns, 20 horses with artillery harnesses, motorcycles, radio stations, and other military equipment. Also, the group's tanks destroyed nine anti-tank guns and four 75mm guns.

Isolated companies of the 354th and 18th rifle divisions managed to cross over to the reservoir's western bank, but these companies were thrown back to their jumping-off points by German counterattacks (the two division's were faced by up to two infantry regiments with tanks). The 9th Guards Rifle Division, under the cover of its forward units, prepared a forcing in the Istra area.

More fortunate were the actions on the army's left flank, where the 36th Rifle Brigade crossed a battalion over to the river's western bank and was attacking in the direction of Yabedino (five km west of Istra)-Telepnevo, and Maj. Gen. Katukov's group (1st Guards and 17th tank brigades, 89th Independent Tank Battalion, and the 40th Rifle Brigade) crossed the river in the area of Pavlovskaya Sloboda and by the close of the day was fighting for Lukino (eight km south of Istra).

The emergence of this enveloping group south of Istra (much as the emergence of Gen. Remizov's group from the north) was creating an encirclement threat for the Germans on the reservoir's western bank.

The emergence of these groups to the reservoir testifies to the fact that the flanks of the Germans' Istra group were unable to hold off for long the 16th Army's offensive.

Because the water from the reservoir was released by the Germans before their withdrawal, the ice was lowered a few meters and the western bank of the reservoir was also covered by a layer of water to a depth of 35-40 centimeters. The reservoir's western bank had been mined by the Germans. The operations of the attacking troops were necessarily made more difficult in these conditions and the defender had the opportunity of using his available firepower.

Despite these difficulties, two battalions of the 18th Rifle Division managed to cross to the western bank of the Istra River during the night of December 14-15 under enemy fire in the area of Nikulino (three km north of Istra); the remaining units of the division began crossing under their cover.

The 9th Guards Rifle Division, the forward units of which had crossed the river in the area of Istra, was fighting for Il'ino (five km west of Istra) and Yabedino, covered by fire from a regiment from the eastern shore of the river.

Gen. Katukov's group, having routed up to two enemy infantry companies in Telepnevo (seven km southest of Istra), reached the Volokolamsk road north of this point and continued pursuing the Germans toward Yadromino and Rumyantsevo.

Because Gen. Remizov's group by this time had reached the Shchekino area (five km west of the northern part of the reservoir), the enemy was forced to begin withdrawing in a westerly direction.

The Germans' defense along the line of the reservoir was quite stubborn. For example, the area of Rakhmanovo and Soskino (seven km northwest of Pyatnitsa) was occupied by units of Remizov's group only after repulsing repeated German counterattacks. In this battle the group captured 13 light guns, nine heavy and 14 anti-tank guns, 26 machine guns, 40 motor vehicles, eight motorcycles, 126 bicycles, and killed up to 250 Germans.

The 354th Rifle Division attacked toward D'yakovo twice and on December 14 two companies reached Armyagovo (both places are on the reservoir's western bank), but coming under organized German fire, were forced to pull back with heavy losses to their jumping-off position.

Thus the Germans along the line of the reservoir (as had been assumed) attempted to put up serious and prolonged resistance to our troops. However, on December 15 their defense on this line was pierced and the flanks enveloped. The arrival on the enemy's flanks of generals Remizov's and Katukov's mobile groups, which were bypassing the reservoir from the north and south, were of decisive importance.

Also, the 5th Army's 108th Rifle Division, which was attacking from the Petrovskoe area in the direction of Lake Trostenskoe, was of material significance, as it was very important that the 16th and 5th armies' adjoining flanks simultaneously attack to the west. This cooperation during the offensive was factually realized and both adjoining flanks helped each other in inflicting coordinated blows against the retreating enemy.

On December 15 the major water line along the Istra axis was overcome by units of the 16th Army, as a result of which it became possible to begin developing further operations toward Volokolamsk.

On December 16 troops of the 16th Army were pursuing the Germans along the entire front and its mobile units by the end of the day had reached the line Novo-Petrovskoe-Rumyantsevo-Yadromino (ten km southeast of Novo-Petrovskoe)-Novo-Dar'ino (12 km west of Istra).

While retreating, the Germans abandoned equipment and ammunition and burned down inhabited areas, carrying out Hitler's order to create a "zone of dead wasteland."

During December 16-20 the troops successfully pursued the enemy, captured a large amount of matériel, and reached the Ruza River (north of the town of Ruza).

In the space between the Istra and Ruza rivers the Germans attempted to delay their retreat along the line Chismena (17 km west of Novo-Petrovskoe)-Pokrovskoe-Sychevo, were pushed out. After a short period of resistance, they abandoned the remaining lines and retreated further to the west. The enemy suffered his greatest losses during this period. The most important equipment captured by our forces is shown in the following table.

Table IV/2.3 German equipment captured by the Red Army, Istra Reservoir area, December 16-20 1941

Units	Captured equipment		
	Motor vehicles	Guns	Tanks
9th Guards Rifle Division	199	9	9
Gen. Katukov's Group	451	18	40
18th Rifle Division	192	24	15
354th Rifle Division	130	13	30
TOTAL	972	64	94

These figures testify to the fact that while retreating to the west of the reservoir the Germans lost a large amount of equipment; they are a graphic refutation of the German press's fantasies about the supposedly "organized" withdrawal to new positions. It is clear that the withdrawal was not an organized one, but rather a hurried retreat under the blows of our forces, which in some areas became a rout.

The 16th Army's operations during the period under study enable us to make a few operational-tactical conclusions:

1 The 16th Army's December offensive began in conditions, in which the enemy, having expended his reserves, was forced to switch from the offensive to the defensive. This enabled the Western Front command, having concentrated significant forces along the 16th Army's sector, to take the initiative in its own hands and began a counteroffensive. The army's counteroffensive had as its goal the destruction of the Fascists' opposing forces and the emergence of our forces on the Istra River. Thus the command's efforts were directed at capturing that water barrier that could yield a material influence on the course of further operations.
2 A sufficiently high density of troops along the 16th Army's front enabled its command to inflict a series of consecutive blows by both the army's flanks, as a result of which this peculiar "shaking up" of the defending enemy's front had a positive result and the army was able to continue its further offensive.
3 The presence of the Istra Reservoir in the army's zone of operations had an effect on the disposition of its forces. The shock groups, created in accordance with the army commander's order no. 053/op, directed their efforts at first along diverging, and then converging, axes. Such a directing of the blows secured the success of the operation, one of the goals of which (along with the main goal of destroying the enemy) was to overcome a serious water barrier. The emergence of two flank groups north and south of the reservoir forced the German command to quickly fall back to the west in order to preserve the remains of his men and equipment.
4 As was mentioned above, the attempt by the 16th Army to force the Istra Reservoir from the march was not successful; the reasons were as follows: first of all, the Germans defended stubbornly; second, they destroyed all the crossings and blew up the dike; third, our artillery fell behind our units. However, it should be noted that the forcing of the reservoir dragged out for three days, as a result of which measures were not taken in a timely manner to secure the crossings. This made it easier for the Germans to withdraw and organize a defense along the Ruza River.
5 The energetic pursuit of the enemy to the Ruza River aided the army's relatively swift arrival at that line. However, this pursuit suffered from the same shortcoming as the pursuit to the line of the Istra.: in approaching the Ruza, the units were not able to break through the Germans' defensive line on the march and were forced to wage extended fighting.

The offensive by the right-wing armies west of the Klin-Istra Reservoir line and their emergence on the line of the Lama and Ruza rivers

On the basis of intelligence information and prisoner testimony, one could assume that the German command had decided to consolidate on the line of the Lama and Ruza rivers and delay there our offensive for an extended period.

The Western Front commander, in his order no. 0112/op of December 16, laid out the following tasks for the *front's* right-wing armies:

> … to unceasingly continue pursuing the enemy and by the close of December 21 reach the line (excluding) Bol'shie Ledinki-Pogoreloe Gorodishche-Kuchino-Mikhalevo-Myshkino-Borodino-Simbukhovo…

In accordance with this, the armies are ordered:

1 The 1st Shock Army's main forces are by the close of December 18 to reach the line Alaevo-Ramen'e-Shakhovskaya, solidly securing the *front's* right flank. The boundary line on the right is as before; on the left it is the same as before as far as Nikita, then Il'inskoe-Shakhovskaya-Kuchino-Pesochnaya.
2 The 20th Army, having taken Volokolamsk, is to reach by the close of December 18 with its main forces the line (exclusive) Shakhovskaya-Andreevskoe-Chernevo. The boundary line on the left is the same as before as far as Chernevo, and then to Zlatoustovo.
3 By the close of December 18 the 16th Army's main forces are to reach the line Ostashevo-Ashcherino-Tsyganovo. The boundary line on the left is as before as far as Myshkino, and then including Gzhatsk.

The 5th Army's right-flank units must reach the line of Vasyukovo by the close of December 18.

The *front* commander also demanded:

a) to more actively employ mobile detachments to seized road junctions, bridges, and tactically-valuable lines;
b) to broadly employ ski detachments in moving across open ground;
c) to establish uninterrupted troop control, rationally using all communications means, the most important being radio.

Thus the *front's* right wing was supposed to try and overwhelm the enemy from the northeast.

On the morning of December 17 the right wing's armies continued pursuing the retreating enemy. The enemy was hurriedly withdrawing the remains of the Third and Fourth panzer groups to the line of the Lama and Ruza rivers, covered by rearguards. During December 17-20 the fighting on the 1st, 20th and 16th armies' front took on the character of an uninterrupted pursuit of the Germans. The enemy, in retreating, widely employed automatic riflemen on motor vehicles and obstacles, particularly in inhabited points and on road junctions. The Germans, while retreating, abandoned their weapons and auto transport on a number of sectors.

The 1st Shock Army was faced by covering units from the 106th and 23rd infantry divisions, which put up stubborn resistance to the attacking troops. In connection with the 1st Shock Army's broadening front (as a result of the 30th Army's transfer to the Kalinin Front), the commander of the 1st Army move up one brigade apiece to the army's flanks; the sector inherited from the 30th Army was to be covered by the 29th Rifle Brigade, while the main forces, consisting of four brigades (84th, 47th, 50th, 71st rifle brigades) were to attack in the general direction of Teryaeva Sloboda, Suvorovo, and Shakhovskaya; the 56th Rifle Brigade was to secure the army's left flank and cooperate with the 20th Army's 64th Rifle Brigade; the 44th Rifle Brigade constituted the reserve.

The troops were given the assignment of moving up forward detachments of December 17 to the Lama River and with their main forces reach the line Kharlanika-Golubtsovo. On December 18 the forward units were to arrive at the line Dorozhaevo-Shakhovskaya, while the main forces attacked toward Yaropolets and Ramen'e.

By the close of December 17, overcoming resistance by the enemy's rearguards, the troops reached the line (excluding) Nagornoe-Vysochkovo-volosevo, although they were unable to throw out a forward detachment to the Lama River. In the fighting we captured 14 guns, two tanks, four armored cars, 133 motor vehicles, and other equipment. On December 18th the 1st Shock Army's forces continued attacking along the entire front.

The 20th Army commander directed his forces' main efforts toward taking Volokolamsk, as detailed in his order no. 012/op: in cooperation with its neighbors to the right (1st Shock Army) and left (16th Army), by the close of December 17 to take Volokolamsk and by the end of December 18 to reach with its main forces the line (excluding) Shakhovskaya-Andreevskoe-Chernevo. The capture of Volokolamsk was entrusted to Gen. Remizov's group. However, as a result of the enemy's stubborn resistance (units from the 106th Infantry and 2nd and 5th panzer divisions), the day's objective was not achieved. Gen. Remizov's group (131st and 145 tank, 17th Rifle, and 24th Tank brigades) by the end of the day were occupying Den'kovo, and from the morning of December 18, in conjunction with Gen. Katukov's group (1st Guards and 17th tank brigades, 89th Independent Tank Battalion) of the 16th Army was fighting during the day with the enemy in the area of Chismena. The 20th Army's other units continued to carry out their assigned tasks.

During December 17-18 the 16th Army's forces continued to pursue the retreating enemy (units of the SS infantry division, 152nd Infantry and 10th Panzer divisions) , while the 16th Army's major efforts were directed at capturing, in conjunction with the 20th Army, Volokolamsk and destroying the opposing enemy forces. At 2100 on December 17 Gen. Katukov's group attacked from the line Den'kovo-Rozhdestveno, together with Gen. Remizov's group, to the west, with the task of taking Volokolamsk. The 16th Army's offensive continued all of December 18. The enemy, mining the inhabited areas, roads, and forest edges, withdrew to the west and northwest.

As a result of the fighting, the 16th Army's forces on December 17 captured 162 motor vehicles, six anti-tank guns, one heavy gun, eight tanks, eight motorcycles, 50,000 rifle rounds, and much other equipment.

However, along a number of sectors on the 20th Army's and particularly the 16th Army's front, the German rearguards stubbornly delayed our troops' offensive with engineering obstacles and organized fire. For example, in the Goryuny and Danilkovo area the Germans, with a strength of up to two battalions, three mortar batteries, and a battalion of artillery and tanks, put up stubborn resistance to generals Remizov's and Katukov's groups. After a stubborn fight, the enemy's units hurriedly fell back in the direction of Volokolamsk, abandoning up to 30 tanks and suffering heavy losses in personnel.

During the latter half of December 19 Gen. Remizov's group, in conjunction with Gen. Katukov's group, was fighting to take Volokolamsk. Units from Gen. Remizov's group, together with units from the 64th Rifle Brigade, occupied Pushkari, continuing the offensive on Volokolamsk from the north and from Chentsy from the northeast. The enemy's 106th Infantry Division and 5th Panzer Division stubbornly tried to hold the area of Volokolamsk and the road to Suvorovo in the north, and to Spas-Ryukhovskoe in the south.

By the close of December 19 Gen. Katukov's group was fighting on the approaches to the town, developing the blow from the area of Yadrovo and Yazvishche.

During the daylight hours of December 20 the 1st Shock Army's right-flank units, continuing to pursue the enemy, reached the Lama River: the 29th Rifle Brigade was fighting for Pokrovskoe; the 84th Rifle Brigade had reached Shilovo while fighting; the 47th Rifle Brigade captured Suvorovo, and the 56th Rifle Brigade occupied Verigino and was attacking toward Maleevka and Yefremovo.

On December 20 the Western Front commander, Gen. Zhukov, issued his order no. 0116/op, in which the right-wing armies were ordered to continue an unceasing offensive and by the close of December 27 to reach the line Zubtsov-Vasyutina-Zlatoustovo-Gzhatsk-Kiselevo-Mikhailovskoe-Medovniki.

In accordance with this order, the armies were assigned the following tasks:

1 The 1st Shock Army, firmly securing the *front's* right flank, was by the close of December 22 to reach with its main forces the line (excluding) Zheludovo-Pogoreloe Gorodishche-Kuchino. A mobile group was to take Sychevka and Novoduginskaya by the close of December 27. The boundary line on the right was Rogachevo-Reshetnikovo-Kotlyakovo-Zubtsov (all points within the 1st Army); the boundary on the left was, as before, as far as Pesochnaya, and afterwards to Pomel'nitsa station.

2 By the close of December 22 the 20th Army's main forces were to reach the line (excluding) Kuchino-Bol'shoe Krutoe-Mikhalevo.
A mobile group, cooperating with the 16th Army, was to take Gzhatsk on December 25. The boundary on the left was the same as far as Zlatoustovo, and then to Novoduginskaya.

3 By the close of December 22 the 16th Army's main forces were to reach the line Panyukovo-Astaf'evo-Galyshkino. The boundary on the left was the same as far as Gzhatsk, and then to Meshcherskaya station.

Thus all the armies of the *front's* right wing had the task of advancing further to the west and overcoming the defensive line along the Lama and Ruza, where the Germans sought to halt our offensive, in order to win time and firmly consolidate and hold the area of Rzhev, Gzhatsk and Vyaz'ma.

The *front* commander, in his order, once again demanded that commanders at all levels "take the enemy's fortified points, bypassing them, and not to slow down the forward movement of the combat order's forward echelons…"

At 0600 on December 20 units from the 20th Army—64th Rifle Brigade and Gen. Remizov's group—in conjunction with Gen. Katukov's group, captured Volokolamsk, having ejected the remnants of the 106th Infantry and 5th Panzer divisions from the town. A large amount of equipment was captured in the town. Upon the capture of Volokolamsk, the *front* command ordered that Gen. Remizov's group be transferred to the 1st Shock Army, and Gen. Katukov's group to the 20th Army. Both groups, following the fall of Volokolamsk, continued to attack and by the close of December 20 captured the village of Spas-Pomazkino and continued to develop the success in a westerly direction.

By the close of December 21 and the first half of the following day the 1st, 20th, and 16th armies had reached the line of the Lama and Ruza rivers. The 1st Shock Army's forces reached the line Marmyli-Telegino, and then along the Lama River. They encountered organized resistance by the enemy's 14th Motorized and 23rd and 106th infantry divisions along the line Zvanovo-Plaksino-Lama River-Yaropolets. Units of the 20th Army reached the Lama River and on December 22 were carrying out a partial regrouping. During December 21-22 the enemy was engaged in stubborn fighting in the area of Ivanovskoe (up to two infantry battalions from the 106th Infantry Division, reinforced by tanks), Timkovo (units of the 35th Infantry Division), and Ryukhovskoe (35th Infantry and 11th Panzer divisions). Simultaneously, the 16th Army's forces were engaged in stubborn fighting with the enemy defending the line Spas-Ryukhovskoe (units of the 5th Panzer Division)-Ostashevo-Ivan'kovo-Glazovo-D'yakovo (two infantry regiments from the SS division and units of the 252nd Infantry Division).

On December 23 the right-wing armies continued fighting along the entire front. Units of the 1st Shock Army were engaged in the most stubborn fighting against the enemy along the army's flanks. However, despite all the troops' efforts, the offensive here was unsuccessful.

On 1200 on December 23 the 20th Army's forces went over to the offensive, with orders to break through the enemy's defense along the Volokolamsk axis (Timkovo, Khvorostinino and to the south). The offensive was not developed as a result of the enemy's strong defense. By the evening of December 23 the army's forces were regrouping toward the right flank for the purpose of resuming the offensive on the morning of December 24.

During December 23 the 16th Army also continued fighting; simultaneously the army was carrying out a regrouping of its forces to the right flank for the purpose of resuming the offensive on December 24.

On the morning of December 24 the forces of the right flank once again attacked. The 1st Shock Army was launching blows along both flanks. The 20th Army had concentrated its main forces along its right flank for the purpose of taking Mikhailovka, Timkovo; the 16th Army was attacking along the entire front.

The enemy was putting up strong resistance, firmly holding the defensive line and repulsing our offensive with fire and counterattacks. Fighting continued throughout the day, but did not bring much success. The troops only captured isolated points—Plaksino, Pagubino, and Kolyshkino. During December 25, as a result of the enemy's counterattacks, the places were retaken by him.

The difficult winter conditions, the short day, deep snow, and deep frosts (minus 25-35 celsius) made the operations of the attacking troops more difficult and limited them. The enemy's organization of a powerful fire defense, his creation of strong points (particularly in populated areas), his widespread employment of automatic riflemen, the mining of some sectors, the erection of obstacles in the woods in front of the defensive zone, and, finally, the actions of his air force against our troops, made the attacking troops' operational-tasks more difficult.

The combat operations of the *front's* right-wing armies along the line of the Lama and Ruza rivers became drawn out.

Operational-tactical conclusions

1 The German command, which had counted on routing our right wing by the consecutive blows of two panzer groups, reinforced by infantry formations, as a result of its offensive, had placed this group under our crushing blow.

On December 6 the counteroffensive by the right-wing armies of the Western Front began. The right wing's offensive operation was built upon the calculation of inflicting a powerful blow against the main enemy group (Third and Fourth panzer groups), in order to overcome this group with our right wing and rout and destroy it. As a result of the measures taken by the Supreme Commander-in-Chief, the Western Front's right wing was reinforced with reserve armies (1st Shock and 20th), as well as new reserve units and formations, which became a part of the 30th and 16th armies.[1] The active operations of the right wing forced the enemy to assume the defensive along the entire front. Taking advantage of the fact that the enemy's Fourth Panzer Group was pinned down along the 16th Army's front, the Western Front command launched an attack with

1 In all (together with the 1st Shock and 20th armies), eight rifle divisions, three cavalry divisions, 15 rifle brigades, nine artillery regiments, and a number of other units.

the forces of the 30th, 1st Shock, and 20th armies, for the purpose of launching a blow at Klin and Solnechnogorsk and destroying the enemy operating along this axis. The 16th Army operated in the direction of the Istra Reservoir. The Germans facing the right-wing armies were forced at first to go over to a gradual, and then a hurried retreat to the west and southwest.

Our troops, in routing the enemy and overcoming his resistance, advanced 70-100 km and by December 20 had reached the line of the Lama and Ruza rivers, where they encountered the Germans' organized defense. Our armies' attempts to break through the enemy's defense from the march did not yield significant results and they were forced to halt before this fortified line.

The line of the Lama and Ruza rivers was a serious obstacle for the right wing's armies, which demanded in the beginning the conduct of a series of local battles (December 20-25) in order to improve their position, and then the organization of a thorough preparation for breaking through the enemy's defensive zone.

As a result of the Germans' defeat and retreat before Moscow, we captured 314 tanks, 517 guns, 35 armored cars, 67 mortars, 451 machine guns, 400 automatic rifles, 3,960 motor vehicles, 841 motorcycles, 1,044 bicycles, 15 radio stations, 1,529 rifles, a million rifle rounds, and 35,000 shells (not counting those that were destroyed by our air and artillery).

The right wing's offensive was conducted in difficult climatic conditions: the frosts grew worse (During the last third of December the frosts went down to 35 degrees below zero Celsius), the snow cover deepened and we had to move predominantly along the roads. The beginning scope of the operation, which was being conducted for the purpose of encircling and completely destroying the enemy, was, in fact, somewhat scaled down. The tasks laid out by the Western Front commander for the right-wing armies on December 18, 21 and 27 were not carried out by the indicated deadline. With the arrival of our units along the line of the Lama and Ruza rivers, our offensive was delayed, because the enemy managed to organize a stubborn defense. It later became necessary to organize a breakthrough of this fortified zone.

2 The counteroffensive by the right-wing armies consisted of two consecutive stages:

The first stage, lasting from December 6 to 16 involved the start of the offensive, the enemy's defeat and the fighting for Klin, Solnechnogorsk, the Istra Reservoir, and Istra.

The second stage, from December 17 to 25, involved offensive battles west of Klin, Solnechnogorsk, and Istra, the continuation of the pursuit of the enemy and reaching the line of the Lama and Ruza rivers.

The offensive operation by the *front's* right wing developed basically along three operational axes: a) the 30th and 1st Shock armies delivered their blows toward Klin and then toward Teryaeva Sloboda; b) the 20th Army attacked in the general direction of Solnechnogorsk and Volokolamsk; c) the 16th Army, attacking toward Istra and to the north, destroyed the opposing German forces.

The 30th Army's objective consisted (in conjunction with the 1st Shock Army) of landing a deep blow against the enemy's communications, cutting the Leningrad road and the withdrawal routes of his Rogachevo group and routing the Fascists in the direction of Klin and Teryaeva Sloboda.

The 1st Shock Army's objective (in conjunction with the 30th Army) was the destruction of the enemy's Klin group and continuing the offensive to the west. The 20th Army was to destroy the enemy's Solnechnogorsk group and, continuing the offensive to the southwest, take Volokolamsk. The 16th Army's task consisted of, in conjunction with the 20th and 5th armies (to the left), defeating the opposing enemy forces, taking the line of the Istra Reservoir and Istra, and continuing the offensive to the southwest.

3 The winter conditions significantly influenced the course of operations of both sides.

The German forces, in withdrawing, were not able to widely employ their mobile units, due to the deep snow cover in the area of operations. A part of the enemy's heavy tanks could overcome the snow cover, but even they were forced to stick to the well-trodden winter roads, while their combat activities unfolded in close cooperation with the infantry. One may say the same about our attacking tank units.

As concerns our rifle units, they were unable to move with the necessary speed, because they were attacking in the open in the snow. Thus the overall speed of the offensive declined. The deep snow cover undoubtedly influenced the maneuver of artillery (particularly heavy artillery), which was also one of the reasons for the slowdown in our troops' advance.

Our ski battalions (overall) hardly ever operated as ski units as a result of their insufficient ski training; they were often employed as rifle battalions.

Under the harsh winter conditions, given the presence of a deep snow cover, an enemy defending and withdrawing from line to line, is capable of (as combat experience shows), relying on inhabited points, of deploying his fire resources and using his equipment (tanks along the roads) against the attacker, in order to delay his advance and win time for the organization of a solid defense along one of the rear lines.

4 The extended period of the counteroffensive, which was complicated by a series of circumstances, in harsh winter conditions demanded a great deal of skill and uninterrupted troop control on the part of the *front* and army commands and their staffs.

The number of formations (divisions and brigades) in the armies varied from three to 15; the largest army was the 16th. As of December 6 this army included five rifle and four cavalry divisions, four rifle and four tank brigades, for a total of 17 formations; also, the 16th Army included a large amount of artillery: three artillery regiments from the High Command Reserve, two artillery regiments, a large-caliber howitzer regiment, seven anti-tank artillery regiments, and eight independent guards mortar battalions. Naturally, given the large number of formations that made up the army, the complex organization of troop control was called for and a number of problems arose in its work.

Independent of the number of formations making up this or that army in the right wing, troop control in retreat and the offensive was complex and painstaking. Thus the appearance of new sectors of the front demanded the rapid adoption of new decisions. It was necessary to transmit these decisions to the troops, using all means of communication. Cable communication broke down, and so radio and communications officers in aircraft, motor vehicles, and motorcycles were employed for transmitting orders. Also, troop control was carried out by means of personal contact, visits to the units, and telegraph-telephone conversations with the commanders. It should be noted that despite significant difficulties, troop control during the counteroffensive (particularly that of the Western Front command and staff) was at a high level; this is supported by data.

During December 6-25 the commander of the Western Front issued several operational orders for all the *front's* forces and an entire series of specific orders and instructions to the individual armies; also, the *front* staff issued orders in the command's name.

The army commanders issued orders almost daily, usually assigning objectives for each day.

5 During the fighting along the western and northwestern approaches to Moscow, a most important role was played by large reserves, which were located at various distances from the front line and which enabled the command to transfer them to the battlefield or line of deployment quite rapidly, despite the winter conditions. The significance of the operational-strategic reserves was particularly apparent during the deployment and commitment into battle of two new armies (1st Shock and 20th), by order of the Supreme Commander-in-Chief, and which began the

counteroffensive at the moment the enemy's flank shock group reached the Moscow-Volga Canal, which marked the crisis of the defensive battle along the northwestern approaches to Moscow.

The reserves at the disposal of the armies received, as a rule, their assignments within the boundaries of the armies they were attached to, and where they were sometimes pinned down by the enemy (30th and 16th armies). In such cases the *front* command would throw in additional forces, in order to achieve the necessary result.

6 One should also note the great significance of the capture of Klin and the defeat of the Klin-Rogachevo enemy group had for the overall successful development of the right wing of the *front's* counteroffensive. The German group defending Klin had the task of holding the area as long as possible, in order to retain the road junction for a retreat to the west and southwest. The 30th and 1st Shock armies launched concentric blows against the enemy's Klin group from the north and east, which later led to its encirclement.

As a result of the defeat of the enemy's Klin group, the forces of the 30th and 1st Shock armies were able to continue the offensive.

However, it should be pointed out that the prolongation of the operation to take the area of Klin and the Istra Reservoir, in the final analysis, enabled the enemy to win time and organize a stubborn defense along the line of the Lama and Ruza rivers.

One of the methods employed by the German command, and not without success, for holding up our offensive involved placing a group of automatic riflemen on motor vehicles in an inhabited area or any other convenient local feature, which would fire and sometimes force our units to deploy into their combat order, after which it would fall back on motor vehicles to the next convenient line.

7 The operational density of the right-wing troops was approximately as follows: one division for every seven km for the Red Army, and ten km for an enemy division. The tactical density varied along different axes. The greatest density of equipment was in the 16th Army: 16-20 guns and 20-25 mortars per kilometer of front.

The German troops' initial disposition of their combat order during their offensive on Moscow was carried out according to the standard formation of wedges: tank units, automatic riflemen on motor vehicles or motorcycles, anti-tank artillery, motorized infantry, divisional artillery, the motorized infantry's main forces with tank cover, and finally, infantry transported on motor vehicles or on foot. But the gradual increase in the number of tanks, automatic rifles, anti-tank rifles, and mortars by our side, as well as our aviation's bombing and strafing activities (which destroyed enemy equipment), forced the Germans to change their tactics and adopt such combat formations more carefully.

Our troops' combat formations in winter conditions basically represented the combat formations of infantry units with attached tanks and artillery (reinforcement artillery, anti-tank, and anti-aircraft). Thus during the December offensive the infantry, reinforced with modern weapons, constituted the basis of the combat formations and pursued its activities according to the principles of the combined-arms battle. Also, the infantry's actions were combined with the activities of tank raids, which consisted of automatic riflemen and attached anti-aircraft and anti-tank artillery, which enabled the troops to achieve the necessary maneuverability and in some sectors caused panic in the ranks of the retreating enemy (particularly during the pursuit). These tank raids during the offensive were particularly successful along the boundaries of the enemy's formations and his open flanks.

Under winter conditions a significant part of the automatic riflemen (except for those engaged in tank raids) and rifle units must be able to operate on skis.

8 The troops' rate of advance depended on a number of conditions.

The German troops, during the November offensive, which was undertaken in more favorable conditions: winter had not yet arrived; there was no significant snow cover, advanced 80-100 km in 20 days along the Volokolamsk-Klin-Dmitrov axis, with an average daily rate of movement of 4-5 km.

Despite the fact that the German shock group consisted primarily of motor-mechanized formations (the 1st, 2nd, 5th, 6th, 7th, 10th, and 11th panzer, and 14th and 36th motorized divisions), supported by artillery and air power, the Germans could not achieve a higher rate of advance. Our forces (30th and 16th armies) waged fierce delaying actions and inflicted severe losses in men and equipment on the enemy.

During the fighting the Red Army was supplied with powerful fire weapons (anti-tank and anti-aircraft artillery, anti-tank rifles, mortars and, finally, independent guards mortar battalions). This enabled the command to strengthen our fire resistance to the Fascist invaders. Our aviation, through its bombing and strafing activities, held up the movement of the enemy's tank and infantry and inflicted losses on him. At the same time the Red Army's forces began to better adapt themselves to the terrain and entrench, thanks to which they became less vulnerable to enemy fire; they also learned to wage a more stubborn defense. Thus the rate of advance for the Germans' tank units fell. It should also be noted that the enemy's equipment was being significantly worn out by this time. All this led to a situation in which the German command's calculations for its armored units' rapid advance in November-December 1941 were not justified.

The rate of advance of the Red Army's troops in December 1941 (despite the difficult winter conditions and the presence of a deep snow cover) reached an average of six km per day (it should also be taken into account that infantry accounted for the great mass of troops in the offensive); such rates of advance must be recognized as quite satisfactory. In the table below are shown the rates of advance for the armies of the Western Front's right wing from December 6-25 1941.

Table IV/2.4 Rates of advance for the armies of the Western Front's right wing, December 6-25 1941

Armies	Average width of attack front (in km)	Rate of advance along the main axis (in km)				
		06/10/2012	11-15/12	16-20/12	21-25/12	Average
30th	About 60	3.5	6	Subordinated to Kalinin Front		
1st Shock	About 30	6	6	9.5	2	6
20th	About 25	6	6	10.5	–	5.5
16th	About 20	1	4.5	About 12.0	2	5

The width of the armies front contracted upon reaching the line of the Moscow-Leningrad railroad: a) for the 30th Army—to 30-32 km; b) for the 1st Shock Army—to 14-15 km; c) for the 20th Army—to 14-15 km, that is, the front shrank by almost half, which enabled us to echelon the armies' combat orders in depth.

By 20-21 December the advance of the 1st Shock, 20th, and 16th armies ended along the line of the Lama and Ruza rivers, where our units met the enemy's organized defense. This circumstance explains the very low rate of the offensive's advance during December 21-25.

9 In withdrawing, the enemy employed tanks in small groups of 5-10 tanks (sometimes more) in close cooperation with the infantry. These small groups of tanks mainly operated along the roads; the enemy avoided moving into the forests. The Germans sought in the fighting to launch

rapid attacks, after which the tanks took cover behind the infantry; the tanks also operated from ambushes, inhabited areas, and other means of cover. As a rule, the German tanks did not get into open fighting with our tanks and usually withdrew, attempting to get around their flanks, or fired upon them from a hiding place.

As regards our tank units, during the right wing's counteroffensive the tanks were usually attached to rifle and cavalry divisions and rifle brigades. For the most part, tanks were employed in small groups (as infantry support tanks) in close coordination with rifle units.

It is necessary, however, to point out that the problems of coordinating with the infantry and artillery were insufficiently worked out. This was confirmed by a number of examples from the fighting. Aid to the tanks by the infantry and artillery during the fighting was often insufficient. During the offensive the tanks did not have artillery accompaniment attached to them, in order to suppress the enemy's anti-tank defense, or it was attached in insufficient amounts. The accompaniment of tanks by artillery fire was also practiced insufficiently, as a result of which almost the enemy's entire anti-tank defense remained untouched. Coordination between tanks and aviation during the right wing's counteroffensive was not achieved. Our aviation, operating against the enemy's troops and rear, carried out assignments laid down by the *front* command.

But in those places where the combined-arms command allowed the tank troops time to prepare for the offensive and correctly organized its coordination with the infantry, artillery, and air, the tank units rendered a great service to the infantry in battle and suffered insignificant losses in equipment.

Under winter conditions the offensive was conducted by small groups of tanks, launching quick attacks, in which the tanks, breaking into the enemy's line, inflicted heavy losses on him; later they deployed in ambushes and through their flanking fire would clear the way for the attacking infantry.

According to data from the Western Front staff, the overall tank losses in December-January are as follows (in percentages):

From anti-tank and medium-caliber artillery	65
From heavy-caliber machine guns	5
Blown up on enemy minefields	10
From enemy aviation	0[2]
From enemy tanks	15
Technical breakdowns	5
TOTAL	100

Thus the greatest tank losses were due to enemy artillery fire.

The experience of the fighting showed that our tank formations and units have the capability to wage active and successful operations against German troops, on the condition that they cooperate with the infantry and aviation and are supported by artillery during the offensive.

10 Among the armies of the *front's* right wing as of December 6 there were nine cavalry divisions, that is, about 25% of the overall number of formations. The enemy did not have large cavalry formations. Our superiority in cavalry enabled the army commands to employ it actively on some axes and achieve significant results.

The presence of large wooded areas favored the cavalry's operations, because they offered shelter from enemy tanks and aviation. Our cavalry widely used the forests; its combat activities during

2 There were no losses due to enemy aviation, because the tanks were painted white.

the counteroffensive confirms the possibility of employing large cavalry masses in a favorable operational situation, even along axes with a large number of enemy troops. The practice of joint activities of the cavalry and infantry showed that reinforcing a cavalry corps (division) with one or two tank brigades and a rifle division (on motor vehicles) enables us to carry out active operations on the flanks and rear of the enemy.

11 During the counteroffensive by the *front's* right-wing armies the question arose about taking Inhabited areas (transformed by the Germans into strong points or centers of resistance). Climatic and tactical conditions forced the German command to cling to these inhabited areas and employ engineering means to turn these places into a defensible condition. This was done so as to hold off the pressure or our attacking units. A typical example of this is the fortification and defense of Kryukovo, Krasnaya Polyana, and Klin by the Germans; the buildings in these inhabited areas were turned into concrete or wood and earth firing points, while the scrupulous defense of these towns' streets was organized as well. Thus the Western Front commander energetically and insistently demanded the troops' rapid advance to turn the enemy groups' flanks and forbade the waging of frontal battles with the enemy's covering units, as well as frontal attacks against the enemy's fortified areas.

12 The right-wing armies' complement of artillery during the offensive was as follows:

Armies	Artillery Units
30th	108th and 542nd artillery regiments, 540th Anti-Tank Artillery Regiment, 29th and 30th independent guards mortar battalions
1st Shock	701st Artillery Regiment from the High Command Reserve
20th	517th Artillery Regiment from the High Command Reserve
16th	2nd Guards, 39th and 138th artillery regiments from the High Command Reserve, the 523rd and 528th heavy artillery and 544th Howitzer regiments, 1st and 2nd guards, 533rd, 610th, 768th, and 863rd anti-tank artillery regiments, the 13th, 17th, 28th, 30th, 31st, 35th, 37th, and 26th independent guards mortar battalions, and the 871st Anti-Tank Artillery Regiment.

The number of guns at the beginning of December was as follows:

30th Army	190 field guns	70 anti-tank guns
1st Shock	145 field guns	35 anti-tank guns
20th Army	130 field guns	65 anti-tank guns
16th Army	320 field guns	190 anti-tank guns
TOTAL	785 field guns	360 anti-tank guns

The greatest density of artillery was on the 16th Army's front. The large number of artillery pieces here was due to the presence of a large enemy tank group (Fourth Panzer Group) along the army's front, and also by the fact that the 16th Army stood athwart the most direct approach to the capital. When the army attacked on December 7 the enemy, who at first put up significant resistance, began to fall back to the west under the powerful action of our artillery and the pressure of our units.

The actions of the 16th Army's artillery (which are the most instructive) may be divided into three periods.

The first period includes the fighting for the line Klushino-Kryukovo-Snegiri-Rozhdestveno (December 6-9); in accordance with the offensive's first objectives, the artillery was regrouped in order to achieve a sufficient density of fire along the attacking divisions' sectors, while the greatest density was created in the center and on the left flank. The independent guards mortar battalions played a great role in inflicting a blow against the enemy before his retirement. The number of these units on the 16th Army's sector during the most important period reached ten. The mortar battalions inflicted large losses in men and equipment through their fire and in a number of cases caused panic and confusion. The appropriate effectiveness was achieved in those cases when the enemy was not in shelters.

The second period includes the fighting east of the Istra Reservoir and the fight for this area (December 10-15). With the beginning of the advance, the artillery was regrouped, taking into account the assignments and the presence of transport in the regiments. In winter conditions the artillery and guards mortar battalions fell behind the forward rifle units; the chief difficulty in moving forward lay in the enemy's blocking and mining of the roads (given the lack of equipped detours). The fighting here came down to supporting the actions of those units fighting to take the reservoir.

The third period includes the beginning of the pursuit of the enemy to the Ruza River to our arrival at this line (December 15-25). The enemy's hurried retreat obliged our troops to speed up their pursuit. The divisional artillery in winter conditions fell behind the infantry. The artillery's combat activities mounted to supporting those units attacking the enemy's fortified inhabited areas and lines.

If the 16th Army's combat order was significantly supported by artillery during the offensive, the same cannot be said of the other of the right wing's armies. The enemy's defense represented a series of centers of resistance, scattered along the front and in the rear and, as a rule, anchored on inhabited areas or commanding heights. The winter conditions limited the combat activities of tanks and aviation; the artillery and mortars were the chief means of suppressing the enemy's defense. The enemy configured for defense not only an inhabited area as a whole, but also individual buildings for stubborn defense. The standard methods of artillery support did not always yield the desired results. Thus it was necessary to switch over from an artillery preparation to the "artillery offensive," that is, to the uninterrupted accompaniment of the enemy's attack by the artillery (fire and on wheels) until the enemy's defense was broken through throughout the entire depth.

13 As can be seen from the above, the fighting on the approaches to Moscow, at the end of November and beginning of December, was filled with fighting for the initiative and the alternation of defensive and offensive battles. In certain cases these turned into meeting battles. The largest meeting battle between two operational groups in these distinctive conditions was the battle of the 1st Shock and 20th armies along the line Dmitrov-Yakhroma-Krasnaya Polyana against the attempts by the German-Fascist troops to break through.

The Third Panzer Group and units of the Fourth Panzer Group (1st, 2nd, 6th and 7th Panzer, the 14th Motorized and 106th Infantry divisions) at the end of November 1941, faced by the retreating units of the 30th and 16th armies, upon reaching the line of the Moscow-Volga Canal (in the area of Dmitrov, Yakhroma, and Krasnaya Polyana), unexpectedly met a rebuff from the new reserve armies (1st Shock and 20th). The enemy sought to force the Moscow-Volga Canal in the area of Dmitrov and Yakhroma and cross to the eastern bank in order to outflank the capital from the northeast. The enemy's attempt to cross on November 29 in the Dmitrov area was eliminated by a counterattack by units of the 1st Shock Army; the Germans' attempt (7th Panzer and 14th Motorized divisions) to cross the canal in the Yakhroma area on November 28 at first were successful. Having pushed back units of the 29th Rifle Brigade, the enemy took Peremilovo and Bol'shie Semeshki, but was thrown back to the western back with heavy losses by a counterattack by units of the 1st Shock Army. In the area of Belyi Rast and Krasnaya Polyana the German offensive encountered the active actions of the 20th Army, which had launched a counteroffensive with its right wing and center (64th Rifle Brigade, 331st Rifle Division, 28th Rifle and 24th Tank brigades). In the fighting on the near approaches to the capital, lacking superiority in forces to develop the success, the enemy was forced to abandon the offensive for the defensive, at first along individual sectors, and then along the entire front. In the following days the initiative passed completely to the 1st Shock and 20th armies and they began to push back the enemy, who was forced to retreat and suffer a defeat.

Thus one can say with confidence that the combat activities of both sides on the 1st Shock and 20th armies' front from November 20 through December 4 were characteristic of a meeting battle. It later turned into an operational defense and withdrawal for the Germans and into an offensive battle and pursuit for the troops of the Western Front's right wing.

3

The situation in the center. Our forces' attempts to breakthrough the Germans' defensive line along the Ruza, Moscow and Nara rivers

At the same time that defensive fighting was continuing along the Nara River, the radio broadcast a message from the Sovinformburo[1] to the effect that:

> On December 6 1941 the forces of our Western Front, having exhausted the enemy in preceding battles, went over to a counteroffensive against his shock groups. As a result of this offensive, both of these groups have been routed and are rapidly withdrawing, abandoning equipment and weapons and suffering enormous losses.

By the close of December 11 the situation on the 5th Army's right flank was as follows. As a result of the counteroffensive by the 108th, 144th, 19th, and 329th rifle divisions, the defensive front of the enemy's 252nd, 87th, 78th, and 329th infantry divisions was pierced; our units, breaking down the enemy's resistance, had reached the area of Lokotnya and Kolyubakovo by the close of the day indicated.

By this time the enemy had been exhausted in the Western Front's center—along the Nara River. After the defeat suffered around Yushkovo and Mogutovo, the enemy no longer undertook active operations here and had gone over to the defensive and began to vigorously dig in, erecting a powerful defensive line in the occupied territory.

On the Western Front's central sector our armies lacked superiority in equipment. However, the situation which had arisen by the middle of December 1941 around Moscow was such that it was becoming more difficult for the Germans to hold their center along the occupied line, at the same time as their flanks continued to fall back.

The German troops' morale had fallen; the unit commanders sought in vain to raise it by referring to past victories. The soldiers were suffering horribly from the cold; their food supply was poorly organized; in the trenches abandoned by the Germans we found such notes: "Farewell, Moscow," "We will never see Germany again," and "Down with Hitler!" and others. However, as the experience of the preceding battles showed, the Germans continued to put up stubborn resistance to our offensive.

1 The Sovinformburo (Soviet Information Bureau was the official Soviet news agency during the Great Patriotic War.

At the same time the morale of the Soviet troops, in view of the Red Army's victories, was high; this factor, in light of the ongoing events, had great significance in inflicting a defeat on the enemy in the Moscow operation.

The orders by the Western Front command for the start of the counteroffensive

In connection with the situation, the Western Front command on December 13 1941 issued orders to the central sector's armies (5th, 33rd, and 43rd) to go over to a counteroffensive.

The *front* command's plan called for a blow by our armies to pin down the enemy in the center and to prevent him from maneuvering in the direction of the flanks; nor was the possibility excluded of later splitting the Fascist front against Moscow into two separate parts.

The *front* command's directive nos. 0103/op and 0104/op to the center's armies laid out these tasks:

> The 5th Army, which in conjunction with the 16th Army was to pursue along its right flank the retreating enemy and by the end of December 18 reach the line Vasyukovo-Klement'evo-Oblyanishchevo-Gribtsovo-Maurino, having reached by December 16 the line Safonikha-Ozernaya River-Tabolovo-Ruza-Tuchkovo. The boundary line on the left as far as Maurino was as before, afterwards it was to pass through Novo-Nikol'skoe and Koloch' station.
>
> The 33rd and 43rd armies," directive no. 01014/op stated, were to "launch an attack in the direction of Ateptsevo, Balabanovo, and Maloyaroslavets. By the close of December 18 the armies are to reach the line: Tashirovo, Mishukova, Balabanovo, Tarutino, Komarovo-Chernaya Gryaz'...
>
> a) The commander of the 33rd Army is to launch an attack at dawn on December 17 with no less than four reinforced rifle divisions from the line (excluding) Naro-Fominsk-Kamenskoe in the direction of Balabanovo and Maloyaroslavets and defeat the enemy, and by the end of December 18 is to reach the line Tashirovo-Mishukova-Balabanovo.
>
> The boundary line on the left is Dyatlovo-Balabanovo-Uvarovskoe-Stupino.
>
> b) The commander of the 43rd Army is to regroup his forces and create a group on the right launch an attack at dawn on December 17 in conjunction with the 33rd Army in the direction of Romanovo and Balabanovo, and by the end of December 18 reach the line (excluding) Balabanovo-Vorob'i.
>
> The boundary line on the left: Burinovo-Maloyaroslavets-Medyn'.

All armies were ordered:

1 The armies commanders were made personally responsible for the timely arrival of their forces along the indicated lines.
2 The armies' offensive will be supported by the *front's* air assets.
3 The pursuit is to be waged vigorously, without losing contact with the enemy, broadly employing mobile forward detachments for seizing road junctions and narrows, and for disorganizing the enemy's march and combat orders.

Head-on attacks against the enemy's fortified resistance points were categorically forbidden; the leading echelons were urged to go around such points, leaving their destruction to the second and other echelons.

The necessity of the precise coordination with neighbors and the rendering of aid to each other were particularly singled out. In this case it was suggested "to strive to encircle and destroy the enemy, without being bound by formal boundary lines."

The armies' fulfillment of the *Front* commander's order

5th Army

When the *front* commander's orders were received, combat activity along the 5th Army's sector was unfolding as follows. The army's right flank, along with units from the 16th Army's left flank, were attacking the German-Fascist troops, which were falling back to the west at this time under the blows of the Red Army. Securely maintaining its position in the center and along the left flank, the army was moving its right wing further and further toward the west, throwing back the enemy's forward units and seizing occupied territory and equipment. The enemy was putting up stubborn resistance and using enemy means to delay our advance along previously-prepared defensive lines.

In order to disrupt the enemy's defense system and upset his planned withdrawal of troops, and also to disorganize the German-Fascist units' rear, the *front* commander ordered the inclusion of Gen. Dovator's 2nd Guards Cavalry Corps into the 5th Army. The corps was tasked with carrying out combat operations in the enemy rear.

On December 10 the corps (3rd and 4th guards cavalry divisions, along with the attached 20th Cavalry Division and the 1st Independent Cavalry Regiment) had concentrated in the woods north of Kubinka in readiness to carry out its assignment.

On December 13, following a series of quick blows against the enemy's points of resistance, the 5th Army's right-flank and center divisions (108th, 144th, 19th, 329th, and 50th) once again went over to the offensive. The enemy put up stubborn resistance along the entire front of the attacking units. Fierce fighting broke out, which in view of the enemy's powerful defensive structures and his weapons, began to drag on. It proved to be extremely difficult to eject the enemy from his defensive line; this demanded great efforts and could cause unnecessary losses.

Under these conditions, the commander of the 5th Army employed the 2nd Guard Cavalry Corps. On December 13, along the boundary between the 19th and 329th rifle divisions, it passed through the front of our units and, along a forlorn and roadless forest sector, while overcoming the deep snow cover and the enemy's resistance, began to advance along German-occupied territory.

It seemed unlikely that the cavalry could successfully attack in such conditions. Nonetheless, on the first day the corps's forward units covered a distance of 15 kilometers and reached the line Spasskaya-Lokotnya, with its second echelon along the line of the Moscow River. The most difficult sector had been overcome; this raised the possibility successful activities by the 2nd Guards Cavalry Corps and the army's right-flank divisions, which, taking advantage of the enemy's confusion, were approaching the line: Davydovskoe (15 km north of Zvenigorod)-Surmino-Novo-Aleksandrovskoe-Spasskaya-Lokotnya-Kolyubakovo-Kryukovo. At the same time units of the 82nd Motorized Rifle and 32nd Rifle divisions on the army's left flank occupied, as before, a defensive line along the line Krutitsy-Asakovo-Dyut'kovo-Myakshevo. The army's front resembled a bulge, with its right part thrown back toward the east. The center of the bulge was pointed to the northwest, although according to the *front* commander's order the army's front should basically be turned toward the west.

The army commander's decision was set forth in two orders: no. 023 of December 15, and no. 024 of December 17.

The first of these ordered:

1 The enemy, continuing to put up resistance, is being thrown back by our units to the north, northwest, and west.
2 A shock group, consisting of the 19th, 329th, and 336th rifle divisions, is continuing to attack, turning with its main forces from the line Terekhovo-Vel'kino-Gorbovo-Lyzlovo to the west in the direction of Ruza.

The successful activities of Gen. Dovator's cavalry group in the enemy rear aided the turn of the army's right-flank divisions to the west. At 1500 on December 14 this group advanced into the Terekhovo area, where it seized enemy artillery and mortar batteries. By the end of the day the group was fighting in the area to the north of Terekhovo, advancing in the direction of Lake Trostenskoe. The group was trying to cut off the routes by which the Fascist troops were falling back and creating panic in their rear. The 5th Army's right flank, taking advantage of this, successfully advanced, throwing back and destroying the opposing German units.

By December 17 Dovator's cavalry group had reached the area of Lake Trostenskoe, having destroyed German units in its path and capturing equipment: 50 guns, 17 heavy machine guns, 45 light machine guns, 136 automatic rifles, a large quantity of rifles and ammunition, 204 trucks and 46 cars, 30 motorcycles, and much other equipment. The group's successful actions eased the advance by the army's right flank and its reaching the line Onufrievo-Zagor'e-Vishenki-Vorontsovo-Khrushchevo.

The front of the army's right flank was ahead of the left-flank divisions—82nd and 32nd. In light of this, the 5th Army commander issued an army order (No. 024, of December 17) for the development of the offensive. The order stated:

1 In destroying the enemy group along the Ruza-Zvenigorod axis, unit's of the army's shock group are approaching Ruza. The enemy, while putting up stubborn resistance, is pulling his forces back to the west.
2 The 5th Army, while regrouping its forces and continuing its uninterrupted pursuit of the retreating enemy along its right flank, simultaneously is going over to the offensive along its left flank.

In accordance with the tasks assigned to separate divisions, the army was by the close of December 18 to reach the line Maloe Ivantsevo-Gorki-Vatulino-Kozhino-Yeskino-Lyakhovo-Yakshino-Kryukovo, in readiness with the next effort to reach the line indicated by the *front* commander (Vasyukovo-Klement'evo-Oblyanishchevo-Gribtsovo-Maurino).

The mobile tank group (20th Tank Brigade, 136th Independent Tank Battalion) was ordered to launch a blow on December 18 in the direction of Ruza and Klement'evo and by the end of the day to occupy the Klement'evo area.

In an army order (just as in the case of the *front* order) head-on attacks were forbidden, vigor was demanded in pursuing the enemy, while the necessity of cooperating with neighbors was noted.

In carrying out the army commander's order, the 5th Army's right-flank units continued to pursue the enemy, who was putting up increasing resistance as our units approached the Ozernaya and Ruza rivers, upon which the enemy had erected a strong defensive line. The town of Ruza had been turned by him into a major strong point.

On December 20 the 19th and 329th rifle divisions forced the Ruza River and captured Komlevo, Gorki, and Syt'kovo. The 336th Rifle Division, along with the 20th Tank Brigade and 136th Independent Tank Battalion, in conjunction with the 108th Rifle Division, broke into Ruza and became involved in street fighting, destroying the enemy's automatic riflemen and repulsing their counterattacks.

On that day the 50th Rifle Division and the 60th Rifle Brigade, advancing along the south bank of the Moscow River, captured Krasotino, Kozhino, and the settlement named after Kaganovich. The 82nd Motorized Rifle and 32nd Rifle divisions, having broken through the enemy's defense and overthrown the defenders in their path, reached the line Krymskoe-Bolkino-Maurino.

On that day the 2nd Guard Cavalry Corps, having defeated the enemy in the area of the villages of Novaya and Lyzlovo, was moving forward toward the army's right flank. On the way to Zakhryapino, the group encountered strong enemy forces. Fierce fighting developed, in which the commander of the 2nd Cavalry Corps, Maj. Gen. and Hero of the Soviet Union Dovator, was killed during a reconnaissance.

The loss of the outstanding commander of the cavalry group was extremely heavy for it. Gen. Dovator's group, while under his command, had carried out a great deal of work, aiding the successful offensive by the 5th Army's right flank through its valorous actions. Operating against the enemy rear in conditions of winter and a lack of roads, it gave an example of the combat employment of cavalry.

Subsequently, the group continued its activities against the enemy rear and before long was transferred to the 16th Army, where its combat employment was more efficacious according to the overall situation.

Meanwhile, the following was transpiring along the 5th Army's front:

On December 21 the 108th Rifle Division, along with the 37th Rifle and 22nd Tank brigades, forced the Ruza River; during the second half of the day these units were fighting along the line Palashkino-Maloe Ivantsevo.

Having reached the western bank of the Ruza River, the 5th Army had achieved a great success in pursuing the retreating enemy. However, the 15-day fighting pursuit, through deep snow and hard frosts, had weakened the army's right-flank units; the personnel and equipment losses were large. The divisions, having reached the western bank of the Ruza River, encountered the enemy's fortified line here.

On December 21 the Germans carried out powerful counterattacks along the western bank of the Ruza River. They forced the 108th Rifle Division, the 37th Rifle and 22nd Tank brigades, and the 19th Rifle Division and the 18th Rifle Brigade to fall back to the eastern bank of the Ruza River, and the 50th Rifle Division and 60th Rifle Brigade to the northern bank of the Moscow River. The fighting in Ruza also failed to yield success, and the 336th Rifle Division and the 20th Tank Brigade and 136th Independent Tank Battalion were forced to abandon the town and fall back to the east in order to put themselves in order. The offensive by the 82nd Motorized Rifle and 32nd Rifle divisions were also halted and their units returned to their jumping-off positions.

The army's offensive was unsuccessful. Until it could be reinforced with men and matériel, and its units put in order, there was no sense in resuming the offensive. This could bleed the army and put it out of action for a long time. The army commander made the decision to halt the offensive for the time being.

The army's right-flank units consolidated along the eastern bank of the Ruza River and on the northern bank of the Moscow River. The left flank remained in its previous positions.

33rd Army

The *front* commander's order tasked the 33rd Army with breaking through the enemy front along the Naro-Fominsk-Kamenskoe sector (exclusively), with the main blow directed at Balabanovo and Maloyaroslavets, having in its shock group four rifle divisions.

The projected breakthrough zone was defended by units of the enemy's 3rd Motorized, 183rd Infantry, 20th Panzer divisions, and part of the 15th Infantry Division. The defensive line had been prepared for two months. It had a line of strong points with fully-developed trenches, dugouts, and communications trenches. On certain sectors a groups of strong points formed centers of resistance.

Among the anti-personnel obstacles was barbed wire (thrown together or erected as a fence) and tension or pressure mines. Anti-tank obstacles, primarily mines, were widely used.

Strong points and centers of resistance had, as a rule, a well-organized system of mortar and machine gun fire. As strong points, the Germans used inhabited areas, the spaces between of which were filled by snow trenches and walls and which were usually enfiladed by flanking fire from machine guns and mortars.

The 33rd Army commander resolved his assignment as follows:

a) he placed in the first echelon: in the shock group—the 1st Guards Motorized Rifle Division, the 110th, 338th, and 113th rifle divisions, and in the pinning group—the 222nd Rifle Division; the shock group's front was 16 km in width, and that of the pinning group 14 km.
b) in the second echelon—the 201st Rifle Division (behind the shock group's right flank).

The correlation of forces and weapons along the breakthrough front was as follows:

Table IV/3.1 Soviet forces and weapons along the 33rd Army's breakthrough front, December 1941

Unit	Total				Per kilometer			
	Men	Guns	Mortars	Tanks	Men	Guns	Mortars	Tanks
1st Guards Motorized Rifle Division	The figures below are for the entire group.							
110th Rifle Division								
338th Rifle Division	About 22,000	120	60	50	1,375	7.5	3.7	3
113th Rifle Division								
201st Rifle Division								

Table IV/3.2 German forces and weapons along the 33rd Army's breakthrough front, December 1941

Unit	Total				Per kilometer			
	Men	Guns	Mortars	Tanks	Men	Guns	Mortars	Tanks
3rd Motorized Division	The figures below are for the entire group.							
183rd Infantry Division								
20th Panzer Division	About 17,000	About 70	About 120	30-40	1,063	4.3	7.5	2
15th Infantry Division (partially)								

Note 1. According to our intelligence, the enemy's units were one-third to a half of their authorized strength.
Note 2. Our units at the start of the breakthrough were seriously understrength, following the fighting along the Narev River.

The 33rd Army commander's order for the offensive read as follows:

> The 33rd Army (222nd Rifle Division, 1st Guards Motorized Rifle Division, 110th, 338th, 201st, 113th rifle divisions), in conjunction with the 43rd Army, is to launch a blow at dawn on December 18 1941 in the direction of Balabanovo and Maloyaroslavets, with the task of defeating the enemy and by the end of the day reaching the line Tashirovo-Mishukova-Balabanovo.

There then followed the assignments for the shock and pinning groups and orders for the combat support of the attacking troops. "The chief of the army's armored troops," it was stated in paragraph 10, "is to set aside ten tanks from the overall number for each division (except the 222nd Rifle Division) for coordination with the infantry." Paragraph 11: "The artillery is to be ready at 2300 on December 17. Adjustment of fire for 30 minutes; the artillery preparation is to be from 0830 to 0930. The beginning of the attack is at 0930. Missions; 1. To suppress the centers of resistance in the areas of Kotovo, Yelagino, Ateptsevo, Sliznevo, Chichkovo. 2. Suppress the enemy's artillery in the areas of Aleshkovo, Kotovo, Rozhdestvo, Pavlovka."

In carrying out the army commander's orders, units of the 33rd Army attacked on the morning of December 18, following an hour-long artillery preparation.

The 1st Guards Motorized Rifle and 113th Rifle divisions were able to cross the Nara River. The 1st Guards Motorized Rifle division occupied the barracks two km southwest of Naro-Fominsk; the 113th Rifle Division was fighting in the woods and bypassing Chichkovo from the northwest. At the same time the 338th Rifle Division occupied Sliznevo on the eastern bank of the Nara River. Such were the results of the offensive's first day. The enemy put up stubborn resistance and prevented the attacking units from developing their success. The 110th Rifle Division was completely unable to move forward on the offensive's first day.

On December 19 there were no significant changes in the situation of the 33rd Army's units. During the night of December 18-19 the 110th Rifle Division crossed the Nara River and captured Yelagino from the march. Bitter fighting broke out with the enemy, who began to bring up reserves. As a result of counterattacks by superior forces, units of the 110th Rifle Division abandoned Yelagino and were forced by the morning of December 19 to return to their jumping-off position.

Having determined the most important enemy strong points—the 75-kilometer station, Yelagino, Ateptsevo, and Chichkovo—the 33rd Army's units subsequently sought to attack by going around these points. By the close of December 20, despite the commitment into the fighting of the reserve 201st Rifle Division, the offensive was developing poorly and the army's units remained approximately in those places from which they began their offensive.

The task assigned by the *front* command was not carried out. The difficulties which arose during the offensive reduced the army's efforts to naught.

43rd Army

According to the *front* commander's orders, the 43rd Army, in conjunction with the 33rd Army, was to launch a blow in the direction of Romanovo and Balabanovo and by the end of December 18 reach the line Balabanovo-Vorob'I (inclusively).

The breakthrough front was defended by units of the enemy's 15th Infantry (partially), 19th Panzer, and 34th Infantry divisions. The enemy's defense here was the same as the one before the 33rd Army.

The army's neighbor to the right (33rd Army) had a similar assignment to that of the 43rd Army. The neighbor to the left (49th Army) was to break through the enemy front in the direction of Kuz'mishchevo and Vysokinichi.

The 43rd Army commander sought to break through the enemy's defense in the following manner:

a) the first echelon—the shock group—93rd Rifle Division, 5th Airborne Corps, 26th Tank Brigade and the pinning group—53rd and 17th rifle divisions; the shock group's front was ten km in width and that of the pinning group 22 km;
b) the second echelon—298th Machine Gun Battalion—was behind the shock group's left flank.

The correlation of forces along the breakthrough front was as follows:

Table IV/3.3 Soviet forces and weapons along the 43rd Army's breakthrough front, December 1941

Unit	Total				Per kilometer			
	Men	Guns	Mortars	Tanks	Men	Guns	Mortars	Tanks
			The figures below are for the entire group.					
5th Airborne Corps								
93rd Rifle Division	About 15,000	111	127	50	1,500	11	13	5
26th Tank Brigade								

Table IV/3.4 German forces and weapons along the 43rd Army's breakthrough front, December 1941

Unit	German troops							
	Total				Per kilometer			
	Men	Guns	Mortars	Tanks	Men	Guns	Mortars	Tanks
			The figures below are for the entire group.					
15th Infantry Division (partially)								
19th Panzer Division	About 9,000	50	100	50	900	5	10	5
34th Infantry Division								

Note. The combat strength of the enemy and our units was approximately what it was along the 33rd Army's front.

The army's tasks, as laid out in the order of the army commander (no. 41/op) of December 15 1941, was formulated as follows:

> The 43rd Army, continuing to defend with a portion of its forces along the previously-occupied line, at dawn on December 18 is to attack, and in conjunction with the 33rd Army, is to defeat the enemy's opposing units, launching its main blow along the right flank along the front (excluding) Kamenskoe-the ford one km west of Inino in the general direction of Romanovo and Balabanovo, and by the end of December 18 is to reach the front Balabanovo-height 181.0, along the Balabanovo-Vorob'I road.

The order for the 43rd Army's offensive, just like the *front* commander's order, contained the following: it forbade carrying out frontal attacks against the enemy's fortified points of resistance; orders to pursue the enemy vigorously and not to allow his retreating units to break contact, and a demand to closely coordinate with neighbors and observe the necessity for surprise while attacking.

At dawn on December 18 the 43rd Army, following an hour-long artillery preparation, went over to the attack. The 93rd Rifle Division, having crossed the Nara River and overcoming the enemy's fire resistance, by the end of the day had reached the eastern edge of the woods southwest of Mel'nikova, having captured height 208.3 and blockaded Romanovo. The 5th Airborne Corps, having suffered heavy losses from the enemy's mortar and machine gun fire, by the end of the day had taken height 189.2 and Nikol'skie Dvory. At the same time the 26th Tank Brigade had concentrated in Sergovka, in readiness to develop the shock group's success. The 53rd and 17th rifle divisions were defending the line Inino-Stremilovo-Kormashevka.

During the night of December 18-19 the 93rd Rifle Division and the 5th Airborne Corps were subjected to fierce enemy counterattacks. The 93rd Rifle Division beat off these attacks, while the 5th Airborne Corps was forced to abandon Nikol'skie Dvory and fall back to the Nara River.

December 19 brought no success to the army. Its units were putting themselves in order following the unsuccessful fighting and were preparing to continue the offensive from the morning of December 20.

On December 20 the 93rd Rifle Division began its attack on Romanovo, and the 5th Airborne Corps on Nikol'skie Dvory. The fighting for these points became drawn out and the advance by our attacking units halted. The army was not able to carry out its mission, just as its neighbor to the right. The 43rd Army proved not capable of breaking the enemy along his main line of resistance.

The reasons behind the unsuccessful offensive operations by the armies of the Western Front's central sector

In all the central sector's three armies the offensive failed to develop; the armies' forces did not achieved their assigned tasks and were partially forced to return to their jumping-off points.

One of the reasons for the lack of success was that the attacking units lacked a decisive superiority in men in their attack zones. The enemy resisted stubbornly. In this case, success could only be achieved by the troops' skillful and decisive actions.

It was namely in the troops' activities that the Western Front command noted a number of serious shortcomings that lowered the results of their combat efforts. These shortcomings were primarily in the area of troop control during the battle.

While agreeing with the army commanders' reports regarding the great difficulties in the offensive (winter, no roads, over deep snow, in hard frosts, and over mined and obstacle terrain), the *front* command nonetheless saw the chief reason for the offensive's lack of success not in these factors, but in unsatisfactory troop control. In *front* directive No. 0120/op of December 23 and in the *front* commander's order No. 0137/op of January 1 1942, it was pointed out that the headquarters are located far from the troops and lack continuous and reliable communications with them, as a result of which troop control falls behind the developing situation and guidance is late.

Formation commanders and their subordinate regimental commanders often do not carry out reconnaissance of the main axes of the offensive, as a result of which some battalion and even regimental commanders do not know where the artillery observation posts for the supporting artillery are located, while the commanders of the artillery battalions do not know the rifle battalions' and regiments' missions. As a rule, as pointed out in the *front* order, rifle battalion and regimental commanders do not know what tanks have been attached to them, or what tanks are operating in their attack zones. Tanks are assigned hazy missions and in haste. The tank attack is not supported by our artillery fire. The artillery's work in the offensive is limited to the artillery preparation, after which the tanks and infantry are left to their own devices and suffer heavy losses. Despite direct orders, there were instances of head-on attacks, which led to heavy losses.

The *front* commander proposed eliminating the above-mentioned shortcomings. The troops and the command were supposed to review their work methods on the basis of reconnaissance conducted against the enemy and to prepare for new offensive actions. This took up more time in the 5th Army, which had the greatest number of losses, while less time was needed in the 33rd and 43rd armies. The renewal of the offensive in the two latter armies coincided with the general offensive by the Western Front's flank armies.

Rear organization

The *front* directive (No. 027) of December 22 1941 pointed out: the field depots of the Western Front's central armies are to be deployed in the following areas:

> 5th Army—Kuntsevo, Golitsyno; a branch in Dorokhovo; the Moscow highway as the delivery artery;
> 33rd Army—Vnukovo, Krekshino; a branch in Bekasovo; the Naro-Fominsk road as the delivery artery;
> 43rd Army—Podol'sk, Domodedovo; a branch in Kamenka; the Warsaw highway as the delivery artery.
> The main railroads for the delivery of supplies during the offensive were:
> 5th Army—Moscow-Kubinka;
> 33rd Army—Moscow-Naro-Fominsk;
> 43rd Army—Moscow-Naro-Fominsk.
> Paved and dirt roads:
> 5th Army—Moscow-Kubinka;
> 33rd Army—Moscow-Naro-Fominsk'
> 43rd Army—Moscow-Podol'sk-Maloyaroslavets.
> Conclusion: the existing network of railroads and paved roads in the armies' of the Western Front's central sector zone of activity enabled us to normally carry out supply and the movement of bases forward, as far as the troops' advance to the line Gzhatsk-Yukhnov.

On December 15, the beginning of the offensive by the Western Front's central sector armies, their supply bases contained the following supplies: ammunition—1.5-2 combat loads; fuel—two refills; food—6-7 rations and four rations of forage. There was a shortage of hay, which was almost completely absent in the combat units.

Conclusions

The operations carried out by the Western Front's central sector armies in December 1941, despite their unsuccessful outcome, are to a certain degree instructive.

1 They show that sometimes, depending on the situation, it will be necessary to attack without a decisive superiority in forces. However, such an offensive must be particularly well organized. The commander of the Western Front in December 1941 (according to the situation that had arisen) was justified in ordering the Western Front's central-sector armies to undertake an offensive, although at the time they lacked a superiority of force over the enemy.

2 An offensive against an organized defense, even under especially favorable conditions, should not be conducted without corresponding reconnaissance of the enemy and preliminary reconnaissance of the direction of the main blow. This relates in particular to an offensive against a fortified zone. The 5th Army's failures on the western bank of the Ruza River and the southern bank of the Moscow River are to a significant degree explained by the hurried offensive against the enemy's defensive zone, which at the time had not been reconnoitered.

3 In the offensive and breakthrough of the enemy's defensive zone the correct formation of the combat order has great importance. In this case, the operational formation of the 33rd Army before the offensive and the equal distribution of tanks among all the divisions cannot be considered

fortunate. The shock group's front was wide (16 km) and the distribution of tanks by division led to a dispersal of forces.

4 The artillery support of the attacking troops during the offensive along the Nara River was organized in an old-fashioned way. The artillery preparation, conducted in the course of a definite time and along a broad front, cannot be justified under modern conditions. The disengagement of the artillery from the attacking infantry enables the enemy to attack our infantry with his artillery and mortar fire and foil its offensive.

Instead of an artillery preparation, it is necessary to practice an artillery offensive, gathering a bunch of artillery pieces along the most important sectors and accompanying the attacking units with artillery fire on wheeled transport throughout the entire depth of the offensive.

1. Troop control and the organization of cooperation between the combat arms and supply services play an important role in the offensive. Shortcomings in troop control were one of the major reasons behind the failure of the Western Front's central-sector armies to develop their offensive.
2. During an offensive in winter conditions a series of difficulties arises, which were not known in summer: the advance through deep snow without roads, frostbite, difficulties with communications, breakdowns in ammunition and food supply, and others. All of this should be taken into account when organizing an offensive and setting out missions for the troops.

4

The offensive along the *Front's* left flank. The Tula Offensive Operation. The offensive's development toward Vysokinichi, Kaluga and Belev

The situation on the Western Front's left wing

By December 7 1941 the general situation on the Western Front's left wing was developing as follows.

As a result of the fighting and countermaneuvers by our 50th Army and 1st Guards Cavalry Corps, General Guderian's Second Panzer Army and its attached infantry divisions began to fall back to the south and southwest. Under the threat of encirclement, the Second Panzer Army's main forces (3rd, 4th, and 17th panzer, the 167th Infantry, and 29th Motorized Infantry divisions, plus the SS *Grossdeutschland* Infantry Regiment) were retreating to the area of Venev and further behind the Shat' River, evidently with the intention of organizing a defense along this line. To the northwest of Tula the enemy was stubbornly hold the Aleksin area. On the Don River, along the sector from the southern bank of the Stalinogorsk Reservoir to Granka, the Germans had quickly erected fortifications for the purpose of delaying the offensive by Soviet troops from the east and securing the retreat of their units. As it was subsequently learned, the banks of the Don River were partially escarped and iced over. Full-blown trenches, girded by several rows of barbed wire had been dug in places, and wood and earthen firing points constructed.

On December 7 the armies of the Western Front's left wing occupied the following positions: 49th Army—the woods east of Burinovo-Voronino-the eastern bank of the Protva River-Podmoklovo, and then along the eastern bank of the Oka River as far as Sotino, from which the army's front swerved to the southeast and passed through Nikulino to the boundary with the 50th Army. Defensive fighting continued along the 49th Army's right flank and in the center, while the left flank, in conjunction with the 50th Army's right flank, was preparing to attack the enemy's Aleksin group. The 50th Army's front ran along the line (excluding) Nikulino-Nekrasovo-Mikhalkovo-Krivoluch'e-Kolodeznaya-Gorshkovo. While preparing for an offensive to the south, the 50th Army's left-flank divisions, in conjunction with the 1st Guards Cavalry Corps, was engaged in stubborn fighting with the Second Panzer Army east of Tula up to December 7. By December 7 units of the 1st Guards Cavalry Corps had reached the line Sosnovka-Borzovka-Aksin'ino-Petrovo, preparing to continue their offensive in the direction of Venev.

According to a *front* directive of December 5, the 10th Army, transferred to the Western Front from the High Command reserve, was to launch its main attack from the start line Zakharovo-Pronsk in the direction of Mikhailov and Stalinogorsk and an auxiliary attack from the area of Kolomna and Zaraisk, through Serbryanye Prudy in the direction of Venev and Kurakovo.

By December 7 the 10th Army, with a strength of six rifle and one cavalry divisions in the first line, and two rifle and two cavalry divisions in the second line, reached the line Serebryanye Prudy-Dmitrievka and east of the railroad line Serebryanye Prudy-Mikhailov-Ranenburg as far as the boundary with the Southwestern Front. The Southwestern Front's 61st Army to the left was to attack to the west, with its 346th Rifle Division on the right flank south of Skopino.

By December 7 the overall situation on the Western Front's left wing was characterized by the cessation of the enemy's offensive attempts along the decisive axes and his desire to pull his men and matériel out from under the Red Army's blow, and the beginning of the Western Front's left-wing armies' general offensive.

The area's peculiarities and climatic conditions, having an effect on the course of combat operations

The area in which the fighting unfolded during the period of the Tula offensive operation, embraces terrain having the following dimensions: from north to south (along the line of Mordves, 30 km south of Kashira, Malevka, along the boundary with the Southwestern Front)—110 km; from east to west (from the Paveletskaya railroad to the line of the Upa River)—130 km. Thanks to the open plain-like terrain, there are favorable conditions for the operation of tanks. The presence of water obstacles (Don, Upa, Pronya rivers, and others), which flow in a north-south direction and are parallel to the attack front, could not be a serious obstacle in winter conditions for single or small groups of light tanks. Heavy and medium tanks demanded the creation of special planking and the construction of new or use of existing bridges. The presence in this area of gullies with steep slopes was an obstacle for all types of tanks.

The presence of small wooded areas to the east and southeast of Tula was conducive to cavalry operations. To the west of Tula, particularly along the line Dubna-Voronovo and almost the entire sector of the 49th Army, the terrain is more wooded, which aided the Germans in waging defensive actions, while at the same time favoring the troops of the left wing in bringing up and concentrating reserves. Villages are encountered quite often; the Germans used them for creating strong points, which dovetailed with the enemy's tactical methods for conducting defense.

The main lateral railroads serving the forces of the *front's* left wing were: Moscow, Ryazan', and the Paveletskaya railroads, and during the fighting to the west of Tula—the Dzerzhinskaya railroad. They were the main communications for the *front's* left-wing armies. The Moscow-Serpukhov-Tula road played an important role. In the period preceding our offensive, the Germans sought to cut the road north of Tula, complete the encirclement of our Tula group and cut off its supply.

The comparatively deep snow cover (in places reaching 50-80 cm) created difficulties for the attacking troops. Snowstorms, hard frosts (up to -35 degrees Centigrade), and snow drifts (especially during the second half of December and the beginning of January) made the troops' advance difficult, forcing them to clear the roads. For the most part, the same conditions (with the exception of a more wooded terrain situation) characterized the terrain and meteorological situation during the offensive to the west of Tula during the second half of December 1941 and in January 1942.

The sides' plans

As is known from the preceding chapters, the German command's plan (as far as it concerned the troops of the southern wing) consisted of ach to achieving a breakthrough and deep envelopment in the general direction of Kolomna and reaching the east of Moscow and, uniting with the troops of the northern wing, close the encirclement ring. A spinoff task while fulfilling this plan was to be the seizure of Tula as an important strong point in the path of the movement of the southern wing of the German armies on Moscow.

Following the failure to take Tula from the march through a head-on blow, the German command changed the axis of the movement of its troops on the right wing and flung separate groups to the northeast (toward Ryazan'), to the north (toward Kashira), and northwest (toward Revyakino), striving first of all to finish our Tula group and then continue the offensive in the former direction—toward Moscow.

The successful countermaneuver by the 50th Army and 1st Guards Cavalry Corps, and the beginning of the 10th Army's offensive, forced the German command to renounce this plan and adopt the decision to pull back its men and equipment, in order to save them from defeat by our forces.

In this regard, a captured document from the XLIII Army Corps staff, which was in the Tula area, stated:

> ...When on the night of December 5-6 the 31st Infantry Division moved out it was hit during the attack by an unprecedented frost of -35 degrees Celsius. As a result, men and weapons were put into extremely difficult circumstances. At the same time *the enemy attacked in unexpected strength* (our emphasis).
>
> ...We took heavy losses in men and matériel, which prevented us from consolidating possible success.
>
> Simultaneously, the then committed against us new tank forces, particularly north of Tula, which continued to increase. The army was forced to break off operations and pull back its forces to the jumping-off position.[1]

The German offensive along the Stalinogorsk-Mikhailov axis led to the same results, when their units, encountering the counterblow of the 10th Army, began to fall back to the southwest, and seeking to delay along intermediate lines. As the course of events showed, these lines were: the Oka River for defending against the 49th Army; the Upa River and the line of strong points from Tula to Shchekino against the 50th Army; the Shat' River and the fortified points of Stalinogorsk, Uzlovaya, Dedilovo, and others, against the 1st Guards Cavalry Corps, and; the Don River to the south of the Stalinogorsk Reservoir, the line Uzlovaya-Bogoroditsk, and the line of the Plava River from Plavsk and to the north, against the 10th Army.

Evidently with the intention of securing the withdrawal of their forces to these lines, the Germans during the entire period of the Tula operation and immediately before it, continued to strengthen their Aleksin group (according to data from the Western Front on December 14 1941).

The plan of the Western Front command as regards the left-wing armies flowed from the *front's* overall task—the defeat and destruction of the enemy forces advancing on Moscow. One of the most important components of this plan was the commitment, by *Stavka* order, of the fresh 10th Reserve Army along the *front's* left turning wing, for the purpose of encircling and destroying, in conjunction with the 50th Army and 1st Guards Cavalry Corps, Gen. Guderian's Second Panzer Army.

In accordance with this overall plan, a *front* directive (No. 093/op) of December 10 tasked the 49th Army with encircling and destroying the enemy group operating between the Oka and Upa rivers in the Aleksin area. For this purpose, the 49th Army received from the 50th Army the 173rd and 340th rifle divisions, with 20 tanks, which were by December 12 to concentrate in the area

1 Cited from a description by the Western Front staff—"The Rout of the Germans near Moscow."

of Il'ino, Obidimo, and Burkovo, from which they were to launch their main blow in the overall direction of Shchukino, with a supporting blow in the direction of Morgen Rot, Surnevo, and Kishkino.

According to a *front* directive of December 8, the 50th Army, the main forces of which were located in the Tula area, was ordered to prepare a lightning blow to the south and southeast, for the task of reaching the area of Shchekino and Retinovka. The enemy's forces, deployed to the southwest of Tula, were to be thrown back to the western bend of the Upa River.

The mission of the 1st Guards Cavalry Corps, together with the attached 173rd Rifle Division, was as before—to swiftly attack to the south and southwest.

The 10th Army, transferred from the *Stavka* reserve, was instructed in *front* directive no. 0044/op of December 5, to attack from the line Zakharovo-Pronsk, with its main blow in the direction of Mikhailov and Stalinogorsk. One rifle division was to launch a supporting blow from the area of Kolomna and Zaraisk through Serebryanye Prudy in the direction of Venev and Kurakovo. The army's immediate objective was the defeat of Guderian's Second Panzer Army and the capture of the area of Stalinogorsk and Uzlovaya station by the close of December 10. In order to secure the juncture with the Southwestern Front's 61st Army, the 10th Army was ordered to move up no less than a division in the direction of Pronsk and Yepifan', in order to capture Yepifan' by the close of December 10. The army's offensive was to be supported by a special plan, following its coordination with the *front's* air chief.

Thus the cornerstone of the Western Front command's plan was the idea of concentric blows against the main forces of Guderian's Second Panzer Army in the area of Tula, Venev, Stalinogorsk, Dedilovo, and Shchekino, and their destruction.

The following goals of the operational plan were to be achieved: first of all, by the defeat of the main forces of the German-Fascist troops' southern wing attacking toward Moscow and, which presented an immediate threat to the Western Front's left wing; secondly, the creation of favorable prerequisites for the actions of our left-wing armies to the west.

The grouping of the sides and the correlation of forces (ground and air)

According to available information, the grouping of the German-Fascist forces by December 7 1941 was as follows. Units of the XII and XIII army corps were operating in front of the 49th Army along the line Burinovo-Tarusa and then to Aleksin. Units of the XLIII Army Corps and the XXIV and XLVII panzer corps from Guderian's Second Panzer Army were operating in front of the 50th Army and Gen. Belov's cavalry group along the line Nikulino-Verigino station-Shchekino-Dedilovo-Uzlovaya-Venev. Units of the 10th and 29th motorized and 18th Panzer divisions, which were part of the XXIV and XLVII panzer corps, were engaged against the 10th Army in the area of Uzlovaya, Stalinogorsk, Serebryanye Prudy, Mikhailov, and Yepifan'.

The correlation of forces is shown in the following tables.

From an analysis of the data showing the correlation of forces, it is obvious that while we were superior to the enemy in men, our left-wing armies were inferior in tanks and artillery. As regards operational densities, here it is necessary to add that in the conditions of the left wing's armies fighting along a broad and broken front (particularly in the 50th and 10th armies), the correlation is not shown.[2]

2 The correlation in the number of troops, in tanks and mortars, is shown in the overall table of the correlation of forces on the Western Front as of December 6 1941.

Table IV/4.1 Correlation of forces on the Western Front's left wing (49th, 50th, 10th Armies, and 1st Guards Cavalry Corps) as of December 7 1941 – German Forces

Unit	Army & Panzer Corps	Army	Total
263rd and 268th infantry divisions	XII Army Corps	Fourth	5 infantry divisions
52nd and 137th infantry divisions, 260th Infantry Division (in reserve); Guns (field and anti-tank) 380	XIII Army Corps		
31st and 131st infantry divisions	XLIII Army Corps	Second Panzer	Up to 4 infantry and 2 panzer divisions
296th Infantry Division, SS *Grossdeutschland* Regiment (three battalions), 3rd and 4th panzer divisions; Guns (field and anti-tank) 350	XXIV Panzer Corps		
167th Infantry Division, 17th Panzer Division; Guns (field and anti-tank) 125	XLVII Panzer Corps (17th and 18th panzer and 29th Motorized divisions	Second Panzer	1 infantry and 1 panzer divisions
10th and 29th motorized divisions, 18th Panzer and 112th Infantry divisions; Guns (field and anti-tank) 240	XXIV and XLVII panzer corps	Second Panzer	2 motorized, 1 panzer and 1 infantry divisions

Table IV/4.2 Correlation of forces on the Western Front's left wing (49th, 50th, 10th Armies, and 1st Guards Cavalry Corps) as of December 7 1941 – Soviet Forces

Unit	Army	Total
5th Guards, 415th, 60th, 194th, and 238th rifle divisions; Guns (field and anti-tank) 350	49th (70-km front)	5 rifle divisions
258th, 290th, 217th, 154th, 413th, and 340th rifle, 31st Cavalry, and 112th Tank divisions, 11th, 32nd, and 108th tank brigades and the 35th and 127th tank battalions; Guns (field and anti-tank) 120	50th (100-km front)	6 rifle, 1 cavalry, 1 tank divisions, 3 tank brigades, 2 tank battalions
1st and 2nd guards cavalry divisions, 173rd Rifle Division and 9th Tank Brigade; Guns (field and anti-tank) 50	A group from the 1st Cavalry Corps (about 40-km front)	2 cavalry and 1 rifle division, 1 tank brigade
239th, 322nd, 323rd, 324th, 325th, 326th, 328th, and 330th rifle, 41st, 57th, and 75th cavalry divisions; Guns (field and anti-tank) 285	10th (about 100-km front)	8 rifle and 3 cavalry divisions

Table IV/4.3 Density of forces on the Western Front's left wing as of December 7 1941

Our Forces	The Density Correlation of our Troops and the Enemy's		
	Enemy Forces Opposite	Correlation	
		Our Forces	Germans
49th Army			
1 rifle division on a 14-km front	1 infantry division on a 14-km front	1	1
5 guns per km of front	up to 5.5 guns per km of front	1	1.2
50th Army			
1 rifle division and 1 cavalry division on a 14-km front	1 infantry division on a 25-km front	1.8	1
1 tank division on a 45-km Front	1 panzer division on a 50-km front	1	1
Less than 1 gun per km of front	up to 3.5 guns per km of front	1	3
A group from the 1st Guards Cavalry Corps			
1 rifle division and 1 cavalry division per 13 km of front	1 infantry division per 40 km of front	3	1
1 tank brigade per 40 km of front	1 panzer division per 40 km of front	1	3
more than 1 gun per km of front	more than 3 guns per km of front	1	3
10th Army			
1 rifle and 1 cavalry division per 9 km of front	1 motorized and 1 infantry	4	1
	division per 35 km of front		
	1 panzer division per 100 km of front	–	–
2.8 guns per km of front		1.1	1

The tactical density along the main axes was completely different. For example, on the 50th Army's sector to the southwest and south of Tula it was as follows. During December 10 along the line Berniki-Sudakovo-Petelino (the Tula area), having an overall frontage of 18 km, defensive fighting was being waged by units of the 296th and, presumably, the 112th infantry divisions, which amounted to 8-10 km per division and corresponded to the normal defensive sector for a German division. As regards the 50th Army, the same sector was occupied by up to four rifle divisions (258th, 290th, 217th, and 154th), which yielded up to 4-4.5 km per division. Another example: according to intelligence data from December 13, on the 49th Army's sector along the line Ryzhkovo-Burinovo-Maleevo-Drakino, extending 25-30 km, units of the 137th, 263rd, and 268th infantry divisions and, presumably, the 260th Infantry Division, which had been put into the reserve in the Vysokinichi, which yields a frontage of 6-8 km per division. Four of the 49th Army's divisions were attacking along this line, which yielded from six to seven km per division.

The quoted calculations should be regarded as deeply tentative, as under maneuver conditions along a broad front the number and composition of the forces involved changed often.

The composition of the sides' air forces immediately along the left wing, by the beginning of the Soviet counteroffensive, was determined by the following data. Out of the overall strength of the German-Fascist air force, the enemy could use against the *front's* left-wing armies up to 300 aircraft (25th, 26th, and 27th bomber, and 21st and 52nd fighter squadrons), deployed on their main bases in the areas of Maloyaroslavets, Kaluga, Yukhnov, and Kirov. In certain cases, evidently, air power from other, more distant airfields was thrown into the fighting.

The 49th, 50th, and 10th armies and 1st Guards Cavalry Corps did not have their own air assets. The offensive actions of the left-wing armies was supported by an independent air group of the Red Army Air Force, which by December 13 had the 2nd Mixed Air Division (assault, dive bomber, and short-range bomber regiments), deployed at the Noginsk and Monino airfields.

Besides this, there were also thrown into the fighting units of the Western Front's 77th Mixed Air Division, deployed on airfields around Podol'sk, and air regiments from the 6th Air Corps from the Moscow PVO Zone, which were deployed on airfields in Podol'sk, Lipitsy, Kashira, and Ramenskoe. Subsequently, (mostly in the 50th and 10th armies' zones) long-range bomber units from the High Command Reserve, based on the Sasovo and Kirsanovo airfields, took part.

The operation's matériel-technical support

The condition of the left-wing armies' rear services was as follows. The 49th and 50th armies had a rear directorate and supply organs, personnel and equipment for its army bases, as well as sufficient transport equipment.

Supplies of ammunition, fuel, food and fodder in the 49th and 50th armies, according to data for December 2, were as follows: 49th Army—ammunition (including rifle rounds) 1-2 combat loads; fuel—two refuelings, and food and four days' supply of food and forage; 50th Army—ammunition (only mortars and artillery shells) two combat loads, two refuelings, and four days' supply of food and forage.

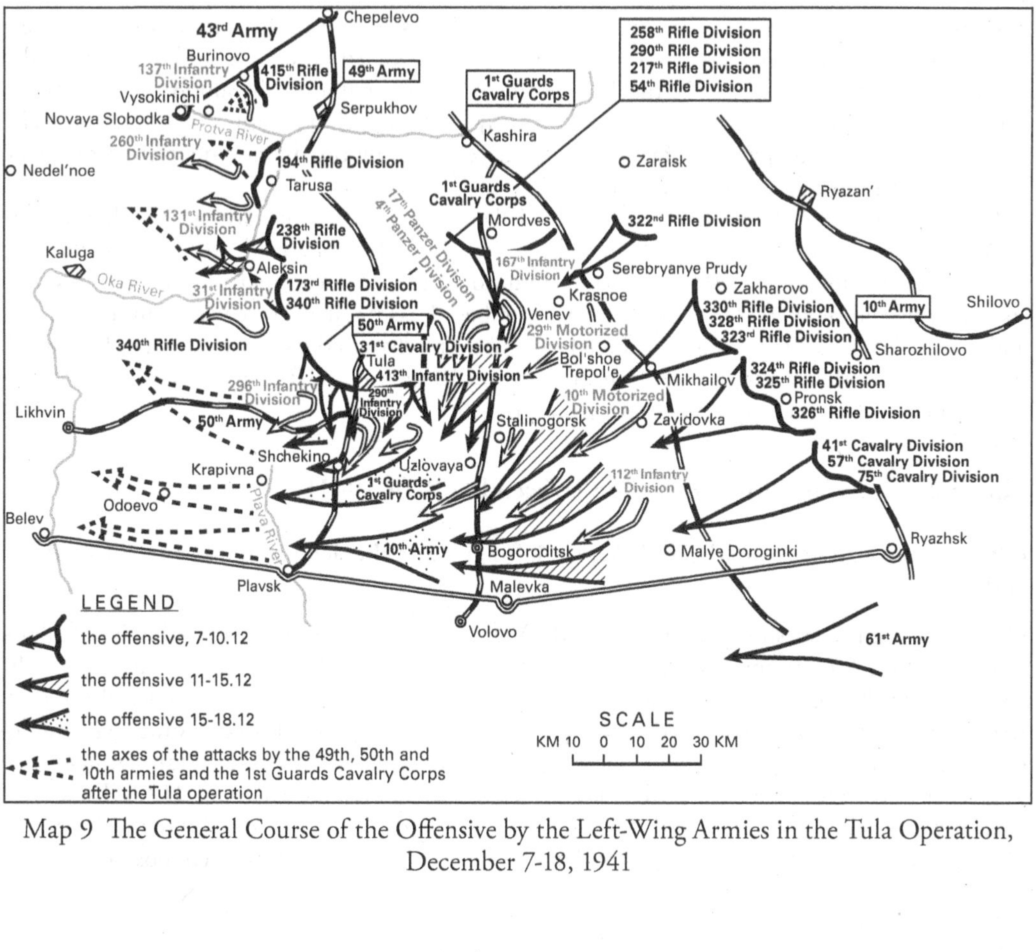

Map 9 The General Course of the Offensive by the Left-Wing Armies in the Tula Operation, December 7-18, 1941

In a worse position was the 10th Army, which by the beginning of the operation was only just creating rear and supply organs and had little in the way of transportation equipment, particularly in its divisions. Up to December 16 the army lacked its own base, while army supplies were absent. There were two auto battalions numbering overall 528 vehicles and a horse-drawn battalion with 394 vehicles and sledges. The situation was particularly bad in the divisions, where instead of the authorized 230 vehicles, some divisions had only ten. The 10th Army's matériel supply situation was made more difficult by the fact that the army, being operationally subordinated to the Western Front, was for the purposes of supply in the care of the main directorates.

According to rear directive no. 025, of December 3 1941, the 49th Army had its bases in the areas of Voskresensk, Bogdanovka, and Khoroshevo railroad stations, and the army depots' forward branches in the areas of the Sharapova, Okhota, and Tarusa railroad stations.

The 50th Army's bases were the Kashira, Stupino railroad stations, and the army depots' forward branches were in the Tula area.

The 10th Army lacked its own base and was supplied from the High Command's bases, located at the Shilovo and Ryazan' railroad stations. The 1st Guards Cavalry Corps was supplied by the 50th Army and, in certain cases, from the *front's* Moscow bases.

Thus the condition of the 49th and 50th armies' rear services supported their offensive. The presence of supplies in Tula compensated for the certain remove of the 50th Army's bases. As concerns the 10th Army, the condition of its rear services throughout the operation was quite critical.

Overall, the rear services coped with the task of materially supplying the attacking troops, particularly as the supplies of ammunition in the 49th and 50th armies were solidly reinforced by December 17 and they were better supplied than on December 6. The same was true of the situation with fuel and lubricants. The supply situation was eased by the proximity of the army's rear services and the bases of the *front* and High Command. Local stores of food and forage were also employed. Matters were worse in the 10th Army, where interruptions in supply were observed. This was made worse by the poor work of the army's rear supply apparatus. To a certain extent, this poor work was compensated for by the initiative shown by the division quartermasters, who fleshed out the shortages from local sources.

In describing the rear services' work in the Tula and succeeding operations, one should keep in mind the winter conditions in which these actions unfolded. The rear's work was made more complicated by difficulties with transport in conditions of the armies' rapid advance. As a result of snow storms and snow drifts, army units in a number of cases failed to receive ammunition, fuel and food at the proper time and were forced to limit themselves to the supplies at hand. In general, in connection with the winter conditions, the armies of the *front's* left wing encountered difficulties throughout the entire course of the operation.

The first stage of the Tula Operation (December 7-14 1941)

Offensive operations along the 49th Army's left flank and the defense along its right flank and center

One of the 49th Army's main tasks during the December 4-7 period was employing its left-flank units to aid the 50th Army toward Revyakino (north of Tula), for the purpose of destroying the enemy group that had broken through to that area. In his orders to the commander of the 49th Army, the *front* commander noted the importance of carrying out this task, ordering him "to organize communications and fire cooperation and secure normal supply to Boldin's units in the Tula area." This goal was pursued by the unification of the 340th Rifle and 112th Tank divisions under a single command and their direction in the direction of Revyakino and Kostrovo. During December 4-6 the army's right-flank units continued to fortify their positions in the

Serpukhov area and fought defensive battles. During this period the enemy was not particularly active along the army's right flank and center, while both sides exchanged periodic artillery, mortar and machine gun fire and sent out reconnaissance groups.

On the army's left flank in the Aleksina area units of the 238th Rifle Division, on the night of December 4-5, attacked the German-Fascist units along the sector Savino-Kaznacheevo-Morgen Rot and occupied these places. From December 6 the 238th Rifle Division was waging defensive battles along its entire front, beating off enemy attempts to attack from the Aleksin area, where the Germans had quite a strong group.

The movement of this group into the boundary between the 49th and 50th armies, to the northwest of Tula, could once again create a threat to the latter and impede the unfolding of the fighting along the Shchekino axis. On the other hand, the 50th Army's planned turn from the southern to the west and northwest insistently demanded the liquidation of the enemy's Aleksin bridgehead and the cleansing of the Oka River's western bank in this area. Also, the defeat of the Germans' Aleksin group would ensure more favorable possibilities for the 50th Army's offensive on Kaluga.

In furtherance of Gen. Zhukov's, the commander of the Western Front, directive no. 093/op of December 10 1941 (which demanded the encirclement and destruction of the enemy group operating between the Oka and Upa rivers during December 13-14), the commander of the 49th Army, Gen. Zakharkin, created an independent operational group. The group consisted of the 238th Rifle Division and the 340th and 173rd rifle divisions, transferred from the 50th Army on December 10. Order no. 1, issued to the operational group on December 12 1941, laid out the following general tasks:

- the main blow is to be made by the forces of the 340th and 173rd rifle divisions toward Pleshivka and Shchukino;
- a supporting blow is to be made by the forces of the 238th Rifle Division and the 20th Guards Mortar Battalion in the direction of Bunyrevo and Aleksin, for the purpose of encircling and destroying the enemy's Aleksin group in conjunction with the divisions launching the main blow.

Within the confines of this overall task, the divisions, according to order no. 1, were assigned the following immediate tasks: the 238th Rifle Division was supposed to attack with its right flank in the direction of Kashcheevo and Aleksin, and with its center and left flank toward Shelepino and Surnevo (3 km southwest of Shelepino), with the mission of reaching the line Kashcheevo-Shelepino by the end of December 15 and to subsequently continue the attack toward Aleksin. The task of securing the division's right flank was entrusted to a specially-selected detachment consisting of a reinforced company, which would be thrown onto the Oka River's western bank in order to get into the rear of the enemy's rear on the western outskirts of Aleksin. The 173rd Rifle Division was to attack the Germans along the front (excluding) Pronino-height 210.3 and by the close of December 14 reach the line Belolipki-(excluding)-Lomintsevo and to subsequently attack the southern outskirts of Aleksin. The 340th Rifle Division and the 36th Guards Mortar Battalion, and an independent tank battalion, having destroyed the enemy, by the close of December 14 were to reach the line Lomintsevo-(excluding)-Dudnevo (3 km south of Lomintsevo) and then attack toward Shchukino.

The start of the offensive was planned for 0700 on December 14.

As can be seen from the operational group's tasks, the 49th Army command had the mission of encircling and destroying the group of German troops in the area to the east and southeast of Aleksin and then continuing the offensive to the northwest in conjunction with the army's right flank and center.

The fighting along the operational group's front developed in the following manner. Carrying out the order of the army command, the operational group's units on the morning of December 14 opened their attack and during the day fought: the 238th Rifle Division in the first half of the day took Bunyrevo and Pogiblovo (1 km northeast of Bunyrevo) and, having surrounded Botnya, were fighting for Goryanovo (1.5 km southwest of Kaznacheevo). The 173rd Rifle Division took Pronino and was attacking toward Yesipovo (0.5 km west of Pronino). The 340th Rifle Division was fighting for Glebovo and Skorovarovo (2 km south of Glebovo). Along all the operational group's sectors the enemy put up stubborn resistance, bringing up tanks and reserves from the depth. The presence of the enemy's 131st and 31st infantry divisions were confirmed by our intelligence. Air reconnaissance and observation noted the accumulation of tanks in Aleksin (up to 120 vehicles) and in Myshega. The same means confirmed the movement toward the front of a large number of vehicles (up to 500), tanks and carts. During the second half of December 14, as a result of his counterattacks, the enemy forced units of the 238th Rifle Division to abandon Bunyrevo and Pogiblovo.

During December 15 units of the 238th Rifle Division, beating off numerous counterattacks by the German-Fascist troops, were stubbornly fighting along their previous line. In the Botnya area the enemy employed flamethrowers against our attacking units.

The offensive by the 173rd and 340th rifle divisions developed successfully and by the end of December 15 the 173rd Rifle Division had taken Spas-Kanino (3 km northwest of Pronino) and was fighting for Stupino and Berezovka (both locales 5 km west of Pronino), while the 340th Rifle Division captured Popovka and was attacking toward Zakharovka. During the night of December 15-16 the army's left-flank units consolidated these areas and were preparing to continue the offensive from the morning of December 16.

Along the 49th Army's remaining sectors during this period, the following events transpired. On the army's right flank the 415th Rifle Division was defending its position as before, while the 5th Guards and 60th rifle divisions were conducting a partial attack in the direction of Vorontsovka (20 km west of Serpukhov), Novaya Vyazovnya, and in the direction of Ostrov. Units from the army's center were fighting on the western bank of the Oka River. Our intelligence was establishing the presence of a concentration of enemy forces in the Vysokinichi area.

Thus as a result of the fighting along the 49th Army's front during the period described, one can note the following: first of all, the strengthening of the enemy in the area of Vysokinichi for the purpose of holding that area; secondly, the stubborn defense by our forces of the army's extreme right flank and its increased activity; third, the enemy's continuing strengthening in the Aleksin area and his stubborn resistance for the purpose of holding this bridgehead.

The Offensive by the 50th Army in Conjunction with the 1st Guards Cavalry Corps and the 10th Army to the South, for the Purpose of Defeating the Germans' Second Panzer Army

As a result of the preceding battles, the troops of the 50th Army by the morning of December 8 had reached the line Ploshchanka-Fedorovka-Mikhalkovo-Novo-Tul'skii-Kolodeznaya, and were preparing to continue the offensive. Units of the 1st Guards Cavalry Corps to the left by that time had reached the front Studenets-Isakovo-Prichal', having captured these villages.

The overall front of the 50th and 10th armies and the 1st Guards Cavalry Corps by December 8 resembled a horseshoe, with its internal side pointed toward the enemy, while the Germans' Second Panzer Army's main forces were located in the Venev-Dedilovo-Stalinogorsk area, thus creating favorable conditions for the *front's* left-wing armies for launching a concentric blow. The 50th Army, in particular, had the possibility of launching a blow from the Tula area to the south and southeast to cut off the retreat route of the enemy's 3rd, 4th, and 17th panzer and 167th Infantry divisions and an SS regiment toward Shchekino and Dedilovo.

Taking the situation into account, the *front's* military council on the morning of December 8 1941 issued the following directive to the 50th Army:

> In connection with the retreat by Guderian's group to the south and the arrival of Golikov's[3] army in the Gagarino area (10 km south of Mikhailov), prepare a swift blow to the south and southeast in order to reach the area Shchekino-Retinovka. The enemy along the Mikhalkovo-Aleshnya sector is to be thrown back to the Upa River.[4]

It was ordered to begin the offensive on the morning of December 8 1941.

In accordance with the *front* directive, the commander of the 50th Army, Gen. Boldin, that same day made the following decision. As the army's main objective was the enemy group in the Kosaya Gora-Yasnaya Polyana-Shchekino area, the army's main forces would be concentrated to destroy this group. For this purpose the army's center divisions (290th, 217th, and 154th) were to, operating along converging axes, surround the enemy in the Kosaya Gora-Yasnaya Polyana area and then reach the area laid out in the *front* directive. The right-flank 258th Rifle Division, while throwing back the enemy to the western bend of the Upa River, was to secure the mission's completion by the army's center divisions. The left-flank 413th and 340th rifle divisions, along with the task of securing the blow in the direction of Shchekino, were to attack toward Dedilovo, cutting off the retreat route of the Germans' Venev-Dedilovo-Stalinogorsk group, against which the blows by the 1st Guards Cavalry Corps and 10th Army were being aimed. Thus the plan and decision by the 50th Army commander corresponded with the idea of the *front* command.

In the spirit of the above decision, the army's forces, in order no. 35 of December 8, were given the following tasks:

a) the 258th Rifle Division, along with a battery from an independent guards mortar battalion, with a covering force along the long Man'shino-Ketri, is to launch a blow in the direction of Aleshnya and Voskresenskoe, with the task of by the close of December 8 of taking Aleshnya and then reaching the western bend of the Upa River along the Pavshino-Sloboda sector.
b) the 290th Rifle Division is to attack with all its forces in the direction of Kharino-Kosaya Gora and by the end of December 8 reach the line of the Odoevo road, having captured Khopilovo and Dement'evo (both locales 8 km southwest of Tula).
c) the 217th Rifle Division, with a battery from an independent guards mortar battalion, is to attack with all its forces in the direction of Mikhalkovo, Kosaya Gora, and Shchekino and by the close of December 8 take Kosaya Gora and Tolstovskii (3 km southeast of Kosaya Gora).
d) the 154th Rifle Division, while holding the defensive line along the southern outskirts of Tula to the village of Novo-Tul'skii with two regiments, is to attack with one regiment in the direction of Krutoe and Prilepy (6 km southeast of Krutoe) and by the close of December 8 to occupy the line Krutoe-Krasnaya Upa (4 km east of Krutoe).
e) the 413th Rifle Division, along with the 156th NKVD Regiment, the 112th Tank Division, and an independent guards mortar battalion, is to launch a blow in the direction of Prisady station and Dedilovo and, together with the 340th Rifle Division, is to destroy the enemy on the northern bank of the Shat' River and by the close of December 8 is to occupy the line Ozerki (3 km west of Prisady station)-Mar'ino (2 km north of Prisady station).
f) the 340th Rifle Division,[5] together with the 131st Tank Brigade and an independent guards mortar battalion was to launch a blow in the direction of Novoselebenskoe together with the 413th

3 Filipp Ivanovich Golikov (1900-80) joined the Red Army in 1918 and later rose to be chief of military intelligence. During the Great Patriotic War he commanded an army and fronts and was also involved in repatriating Soviet citizens from Germany and other countries. Following the war, Golikov headed the armed forces' Main Political Administration.

4 File from the General Staff's operational directorate, no. 132 (top secret), p. 167.

5 On December 10 the division was subordinated to the 49th Army and operated as part of the army along the

Rifle Division and destroy the enemy on the northern bank of the Shat' River and by the close of December 8 reach the line Zabusovo-Treshevo.

g) the 31st Cavalry Division is secure the army's left flank and by the close of December 8 is to take Kryukovo (3 km north of Arsen'evo) and then, having taken Arsen'evo, to cut off the enemy's route of retreat from Venev to Bolokhovka. The division was ordered to conduct reconnaissance in the direction of Uzlovaya, 2nd Stalinogorsk, and Venev. A rifle regiment and a tank battalion remained in the army's reserve with the task of covering the Venev-Tula road.

According to the order, the offensive by the army's units unfolded as follows.

The 258th Rifle Division, attacking in the direction of Aleshnya, during the first part of December 9 captured Ploshchanka and Pommogalovo (3 km west of Fedorovka). The German-Fascist units, striving to delay the division's attack, repeatedly launched counterattacks from the Izvol' area toward Zanino (1 km northeast of Ploshchanka). In the center and along the 258th Rifle Division's left flan the German also put up stubborn resistance.

The 290th Rifle Division, attacking in the direction of Khopilovo (2 km west of Kharino), encountered the most powerful resistance along the line Fedorovka-Yamny-Maslovo (2 km southeast of Yamny). The division's units on December 8 waged street battles in Yamny, expelling the Germans' units holed up there.

The 217th Rifle Division was attacking in the direction of Kosaya Gora. On the night of December 8-9 the division's units captured Nizhnee Yel'kino and Pirovo (both locales 2-3 km north of Kosaya Gora). Units of the Germans' 296th Infantry Division defended along the front of the 290th and 217th rifle divisions.

Approximately the same situation prevailed along the sectors of the army's remaining divisions.

The 50th Army, overcoming the stubborn resistance of units of the 296th Infantry Division and the *Grossdeutschland* Regiment, by the close of December 10 had reached the front Aleshnya-Koptevo-Tat'evo (2 km northwest of Kharino)-Prudnoe (2 km east of Kharino)-Petelino-Teploe (7 km east of Novo-Tul'skoe).

On the morning of December 11 the *front's* military council, in pursuit of previous-assigned tasks, issued a new directive (no. 094/op), according to which the 50th Army was to:

a) by a blow in the direction of the Udarnik state farm (3 km northwest of Kharino), Shevelevka, Solosovka (8 km southwest of Kosaya Gora), Trosna (2 km west of Shchekino), take the road junction in the area of Samokhvalovka, Retinovka, Ozerki (2 km southeast of Shchekino).
b) by a blow from the Krutoe-Mar'ino sector (2 km north of Prisady station) in the direction of Nizhnie Prisady (2 km northwest of Prisady station), Gora Uslan', and Bol'shaya Mostovaya (6 km east of Retinovka), reach the same area.
c) securely tie down the enemy along the front Strukovo-Skuratovo (both locales 7 km south of Tula.

Thus the *front* command, in directing both of the army's flanks in a southerly direction, while holding the enemy in the center, had in mind cutting off the retreat route of the enemy's group to the south of Tula, in order to cut off and destroy it.

According to the same directive, the 1st Guards Cavalry Corps to the left was to, in conjunction with the 50th Army, attack in the direction of Dedilovo, Zubarevka, Zhitovo, with the mission of preventing the withdrawal of the enemy's Tula group to the south.

In accordance with the *front* directive, the 50th Army command that same day issued order no. 38, according to which the divisions' tasks were slightly changed. The same axes of attack were

Aleksin axis.

retained, although the deadlines for reaching the indicated areas were pushed back a little. Along with this, the more or less correctly determined main enemy group (296th Infantry Division and the *Grossdeutschland* Regiment) in the Shchekino area forced the army to concentrate its main forces on destroying this group.

The 258th Rifle Division's tasks basically remained unchanged—a blow in the direction of Aleshnya and Voskresenskoe, with the immediate task of reaching the line Baboshino-Dyagilevo.

The 290th Rifle Division was to reach the line Intyushevo-Zaitsevo on December 11, and by the end of December 12 the line Kurakovo-Trufanovo station.

The 217th Rifle and the 112th Tank divisions were assigned the immediate task of capturing Yasnaya Polyana on December 11 and by the end of the day capturing Shchekino.

The 154th Rifle Division was to direct its main forces along the front Lomintsevo-Plekhanovo (2 km east of Lomintsevo), with the task of capturing both locales by the close of December 11.

With the arrival of the 217th and 154th rifle divisions in the Shchekino area the defeat of the German-Fascist group in that area was to be complete.

In accordance with this, the boundaries of the 290th and 217th rifle divisions were slightly changed. The 413th Rifle Division was by the close to December 12 to reach the line Dolgoe-Panino (both locales 2 km west of Dedilovo), having first taken Bolokhovka. It was in this composition that the army continued its offensive from December 11.

In the latter half of December 11 the 258th Rifle Division, while overcoming the enemy's resistance along its right flank and center, reached the line Merlinovka (2 km east of Pavshino), Baboshino-Loshach'e-Goroden'ki (both locales 3-5 km east of Baboshino), having captured these areas. The activities of the German 31st Infantry Division were noted in this area. By the close of December 12 units of the 258th Rifle Division reached the Upa River along the Porech'e-Sloboda (3 km northeast of Voskresenskoe) sector, while its forward detachments had reached Voskresenskoe, cutting the Odoevo road in this area. In subsequent days the division's main forces began regrouping in the western and northwestern directions, so as to carry out new tasks.

After December 15 a turn to the northwest by the army's remaining divisions begins. This turn in a new direction was occasioned by the interests of the *front* operation; it had basically been completed by December 18 and immediately following a regrouping was realized as the 50th Army's Kaluga operation.

The 290th Rifle Division, overcoming the resistance of the Germans' 296th Infantry Division, advanced forward while fighting and by the end of December 13 had reached the line Intyushevo-Pyatnitskoe. Both villages had been transformed by the Germans into strong points and stubborn fighting was necessary to capture them. After December 13 the 290th Rifle Division, having taken these villages, began to regroup to the west. Units of the 217th Rifle Division were fighting with mixed success along the approaches to Kosaya Gora, where the enemy put up his most ferocious resistance, especially along the line Sudakovo-Ivanovskie Dachi (both locales 1-2 km north and northeast of Kosaya Gora). The fighting along this line continued until nightfall; during the night the division's units put themselves in order for a subsequent attack. In subsequent days until December 14 the division's units reached the line Ugryumy (3 km west of Yasnaya Polyana)-Yasnaya Polyana-Ovsyannikovo (4 km northeast of Yasnaya Polyana), capturing these locales.

The offensive by units of the 154th Rifle Division developed mostly along the Upa River in a southeasterly direction. The enemy's most serious resistance was offered by units of the 296th and 112th infantry divisions and the SS regiment near Bolshaya Yelovaya (3 km southwest of Novo-Tul'skii) and Petelino, having turned them into strong points.

Following heavy fighting, the Germans resistance near Bolshaya Yelovaya and Petelino was crushed and on December 14 the 154th Rifle Division, attacking toward Lutovinovo (8 km west of Bolokhovka), reached the line Krutoe-Vechernyaya Zarya, Sergievskoe (the latter two locales

2-6 km east of Krutoe). By that time the 413th Rifle Division to the left had taken Podosinki, Zamyatino, and Krutoe (all 5 km southwest of Bolokhovka). The division had to fight the hardest along the Shat' River along the sector from Prisady station to the east.

The 340th Rifle Division during this period was resubordinated to the commander of the 49th Army and sent to the area of Obidimo and Yakovlevo (6-7 km northwest of Tula), to operate on the 49th Army's left flank against the enemy's Aleksin group. The 173rd Rifle Division, which had been removed from the control of the commander of the 1st Guards Cavalry Corps and transferred to the 49th Army, was being regrouped in the same direction. The 31st Cavalry Division, which had been covering the army's left flank, without meeting serious enemy resistance reached the area Ivrovka-Kuchino-Ol'khovka (all locales 4 km west of Arsen'evo) and had concentrated in this area.

In tabulating the results of the 50th Army's combat activities during the first stage of the operation, it's necessary to note that despite the decisive offensive by our troops, the majority of the units were unable to reach the designated lines in the time indicated, as laid out in army order no. 38. The actual pace of the offensive proved to be slower (an average of 1 ½ -2 km per day). This can be explained by the fact that, first of all, the army's units went over to the offensive following extensive preliminary fighting and were tired; secondly, the offensive was conducted under winter conditions, and; third, (and most important), under conditions in which the enemy put up powerful resistance, particularly on December 13, along the following lines: a) Zaitsevo-Pyatnitskoe, covering the Tula-Odoevo road; b) Sudakovo-Ivanovskie Dachi, 1-2 km north and northeast of Kosaya Gora, covering the Tula-Orel road; c) Bolshaya Yelovaya-Petelino, covering the Tula-Dedilovo road. The object of these activities was to cover the withdrawal of the Germans' main forces to the south and southwest.

General Belov's group, following fierce fighting for Mordves, continued attacking toward Venev. Units of the German-Fascist 17th Panzer, 167th Infantry, and 29th Motorized divisions conducted a fighting withdrawal along the cavalry corps' front.

On the morning of December 9 the 1st Guards Cavalry Division, in conjunction with the 173rd Rifle Division, seized Venev and, pursuing the enemy, in the first part of the same day reached the line Terebush-Lopatino. The 173rd Rifle Division was left in Venev, and then from there was transferred to the 49th Army's left flank for an offensive against the Germans' Aleksin group. The corps was reinforced with the 322nd Rifle Division from the 10th Army.

By that time the 2nd Guards Cavalry Division, together with the 9th Tank Brigade, reached the area of Medvedki and Gati, with the mission of attacking toward Stalinogorsk-2. In the first part of December 10 the 2nd Guards Cavalry Division's forward detachments reached Stalinogorsk-2 and engaged the enemy defending it. By this time the corps' main forces had reached the line Pozhilki-Mikhailovka (10 km south of Venev)-Urusovo.

The fighting for Stalinogorsk lasted about two days.

The commander of the 2nd Guards Cavalry Division, having left behind two regiments for attacking the enemy from the front and pinning him down, threw his other two regiments around Stalinogorsk-2 from the west and northeast. The cavalry regiment and 9th Tank Brigade, which were attacking from the east, were forced to advance across the ice, while a number of tanks and a battery of guards mortars broke through the ice and sank. As a result of these turning movements, the 2nd Guards Cavalry Division took Stalinogorsk-2 on the night of December 10-11 and by the morning of that day had concentrated in the same area, having advanced a cavalry regiment in the direction of Stalinogorsk-1 as a forward detachment.

Following the capture of Stalinogorsk-1, Gen. Belov's cavalry group, in carrying out *front* directive no. 095, began to turn to the southwest. The Germans' 17th Panzer, 167th Infantry, and part of the 29th Motorized divisions unsuccessfully sought to delay the corps' advance. It was for this reason that the enemy blew up the dam on the Shat' River in the area of Verkhnee Petrovo (3 km southwest of Arsen'evo) and Prokhorovka (3 km north of Stalinogorsk-1). However, these attempts to halt our offensive failed to yield a result. Units of the cavalry corps, in encircling separate enemy groups and bypassing some of his strong points, continued their pursuit. In places (for example, the 1st Guards Cavalry Division in Kukuya) this involved street fighting.

As a result of our cavalry's successful operations, the Germans' resistance on the line of the Shat' River was broken and by 1600 on December 13 the cavalry corps, with the 322nd Rifle Division echeloned to the right rear, had reached the line Lipnya-Berezovka-Ogarevka-Shakhovskoe-Pashkovo (all locales 8-10 km west and southwest of Stalinogorsk-1), having taken these places. Forward units of the 2nd Guards Cavalry Division were involved in fighting along the approaches to Uzlovaya station.

Combat operations along the 10th Army's front (December 7-14)

General Golikov's 10th Reserve Army, which had been transferred to the *front*, on December 6 reached the line: 322nd Rifle Division—Klemovo-Okun'kovo-Rybkino (5 km east of Okun'kovo); 330th Rifle Division—was fighting to bypass Mikhailov from the north; the 328th Rifle Division was fighting to the east of Mikhailov; the 323rd Rifle Division was attacking toward Mikhailov from the southeast from a line to the north of Slobodka; 324th Rifle Division—Slobodka-Pecherniki; 325th Rifle Division—Pecherniki-Berezovo; 326th Rifle Division—Durnoe-Semenovskoe; the 41st Cavalry Division was moving from the Vysokoe area to Katino; the 239th Rifle Division remained in the army reserve, with the task of reaching the area Durnoe-Telyatniki (2 km northwest of Durnoe) by the end of December 6; the 57th Cavalry Division, while remaining in the army reserve, was by the end of December 6 to reach the area Mamonovo-Bulychevo; the 75th Cavalry Division was located in Ryazan' and after December 6 was transferred to the army's left flank. The army staff's operational group, followed by the entire 10th Army staff, at first located in Shilovo, moved to Starozhilovo. The 10th Army's neighbor to the left—the 346th Rifle Division of the 61st Army (Southwestern Front)—was deployed along the Skopino line.

In accordance with a *front* directive of December 5, the army commander that day issued order no. 002,[6] according to which the main forces of the Germans' 29th and 10th motorized divisions were determined to be in the areas of Serebryanye Prudy and Mikhailov. To the south were noted units of the 18th Panzer Division, while later units of the 112th Infantry Division were discovered operating along the 10th Army's front.

The army was to launch its main blow in the general direction of Mikhailov along the front Zakharovo-Pronsk. The 322nd Rifle Division had the mission of attacking in the direction of Serebryanye Prudy and, having captured the latter, by the close of December 6 ready to continue the attack toward Venev; the 330th, 328th, and 323rd rifle divisions were tasked with taking Mikhailov. The remaining divisions were aimed toward Stalinogorsk, while the 41st Cavalry Division was to be moved in the direction of Yepifan'.

The 10th Army's forces, in carrying out their task, by the close of December 7 had captured Serebryanye Prudy and Mikhailov and had reached the line Yeliseevka-Mochily-Kurlyshevo-Bol'shaya Doroginka-Gagarino station to the south. The enemy's 29th and 10th motorized and 18th Panzer divisions, plus other small infantry units, conducted rearguard actions along the army's front. The Germans did not put up particularly strong resistance against the 10th Army's left flank. The 41st Cavalry Division, while fighting along the line Nyukhovets-Bogoslovo-Petrushino (all locales 15 km northeast of Yepifan'), was opposed by the Second Panzer Army's 40th Communications Regiment. According to data from the *front* staff, Guderian's headquarters was located in this area. Given

6 File from the General Staff's operational directorate for the Western Front, no. 130 (top secret).

more decisive and rapid actions by the 41st Cavalry Division, it would have been possible to capture Guderian's headquarters, which the *front* command communicated to the commander of the 10th Army. The offensive by the army's left-flank units unfolded slowly and lagged behind that of the right flank. At the moment the right-flank divisions (322nd, 330th, 328th, 323rd, and 324th) were along the line Yeliseevka-Mochily-Kurlyshevo-Bol'shaya Doroginka, the left-flank divisions were moving echeloned behind them. For example, the 325th Rifle Division was located 8-10 km behind, while the 326th Rifle Division was only advancing on Gryaznoe (near Gagarino station). The 41st Rifle Division was located on the same meridian as the 326th Rifle Division.

This circumstance forced the *front* command to repeatedly point out the offensive's slow pace and demand its increase. At the cost of the extreme exertion of our forces, it was necessary to prevent the enemy from withdrawing. The *front* headquarters demanded that mobile detachments be immediately thrown deep to the west in order to cut off the enemy's retreat routes. On the morning of December 8 this demand was once again repeated and it was communicated that the enemy was swiftly falling back on Stalinogorsk under the blows of the 50th Army and 1st Guards Cavalry Corps.

On December 10 and 11 the *front* command, in directives nos. 94 and 95/op, categorically confirmed the 10th Army's mission: to continue the offensive and, in conjunction with Gen. Belov's group, develop the blow on Plavsk, with the immediate objective of reaching the front Bogoroditsk-Kuzovka by the end of December 11.

In the spirit of these directives, commander of the 10th Army Gen. Golikov, on the morning of December 11 issued order no. 06, according to which the first-echelon 330th, 328th, 324th, 323rd, and 326th rifle divisions were to reach the line Uzlovaya station-Bogoroditsk-Kuzovka by the end of December 11 and the morning of December 12. The army headquarters' operational group was in Mikhailov.

During December 8-10 the army's units continued their offensive along the indicated axes. By the close of December 11 the 330th Rifle Division was fighting enemy detachments covering the withdrawal along the line Khlopovo-Rogachevka, from which it was preparing to attack to the south. The 328th Rifle Division, having arrived at the Don River along the Bobriki-Mikhailovka sector, encountered powerful resistance and during the latter part of December 11 was engaged in combat. The 41st Rifle Division, overcoming the resistance of those German units covering the withdrawal, had reached the Don River along the Bol'shaya Kolodeznaya-Khmelevka sector (both locales near the southern end of the Stalinogorsk Reservoir), but under the enemy's powerful artillery fire, suffered losses and was forced to fall back to the Ivan'kovo area. Only during the latter half of December 12 was enemy resistance along the Don River broken and units of the 328th Rifle Division by December 13 had reached the line Bobriki-Mikhailovka. By that time the 330th Rifle Division to the right, having thrown back the enemy units, had occupied the glen southeast of Urvanki.

On the army's left flank the 324th Rifle Division on December 13 occupied Lyutorichi (on the Don River) after fighting and was moving to the west. On the same day the 323rd Rifle Division, have broken the resistance by units of the 10th Motorized Division and, evidently, separate units of the 112th Infantry Division, had occupied Yepifan'.

The 326th Rifle Division, overcoming the resistance by small groups of Germans, was moving to the line Kamenka-Klinovoe, which it had occupied by the end of December 14. After this the division attacked to the west. The 239th Rifle Division, in the army's second echelon, on December 13 reached the area Sukhanovo-Buchalki-Krasnoe.

The 57th and 75th cavalry divisions (transferred from Ryazan' to the army's left flank) moved extremely slowly; in the latter half of December 13 the 57th Cavalry Division was in the area of Valshuta, Katino, and Churiki (8 km northeast of Bogoslovo), while the 75th Cavalry Division was arriving in the area of Samodurovka.

As a result of the 10th Army's offensive from December 7 to 13, the following should be noted: 1. The army began its offensive along a broad front (up to 80 km) in conditions in which the divisions were scattered in areas far from each other. This situation increased the demands placed upon the communications service, which was called upon to secure the uninterrupted control of the formations. However, the communications service failed to cope with this task. For example, during December 8-9 the army command, as a result of poor communications, did not know where the army's units were. No small part was played by the fact that the 10th Army was insufficiently equipped with communications equipment. By the way, the absence of a sufficient amount of communications equipment told upon the control of the army's units in subsequent operations.

At the same time that the offensive by the army's right flank was being conducted at a more or less rapid pace (the 330th Rifle Division covered an average of nine km per day from December 7 through the 13th), the left-flank divisions attacked comparatively slowly, which undoubtedly negatively told upon the fulfillment of the *front's* directive no 095/op of December 11.

In totaling up the results of the first stage of the Tula offensive operation, it is necessary to note the chief feature in the operations of the *front's* left wing—the beginning of the German defeat and the transformation of the offensive against the defending enemy to his pursuit. This was basically one of the first and most tangible successes by the forces of the Western Front in the battle for Moscow. In the operational sense, the counteroffensive by the left-wing armies, which was conducted over 5-6 days, represented a concentric blow along converging axes, with the necessary coordination of the armies among themselves. The realization of such a maneuver under snowy winter conditions and sharp frosts once again speaks to the daring nature of the plan by the *Stavka* and the Western Front command and the combat capabilities of our troops. The connecting link between the 50th and 10th armies was the group of the commander of the 1st Guards Cavalry Corps. The character of our cavalry's actions during the first stage of the Tula operation (as was the case during its second stage)—the combination of mounted activities alongside dismounted ones, alongside close tactical cooperation with the attached rifle units and tanks. The horse, in this case, served as a means of more rapid maneuver.

In the cavalry group's tactical actions methods of wedging separate cavalry regiments between the enemy's rearguards were widely employed, as well as the envelopment and encirclement of German separate strong points and troops.

The second stage of the Tula Operation (December 15-19 1941)

The highly worn out units of the enemy's Second Panzer Army continued their retreat to the south and southwest, behind the line Dedilovo-Shchekino, and then on to Bogoroditsk and Plavsk, losing weapons, equipment, and personnel. According to testimony by prisoners, of the 6,000 men in the *Grossdeutschland* Regiment only about 2,000 remained. The same enemy units were active along the front of our left-wing armies as on December 7. Along certain axes these units had been reinforced by units from the rear. This was particularly the case in the Aleksin area, where the reinforcement of the XLIII Army Corp's left flank with infantry and tanks was noted. This demonstrated once again the German command's desire to hold on to the Aleksin bridgehead.

The left-wing armies continued their offensive basically in the same grouping as had been the case in the first stage of the operation. Only in the 50th Army toward the close of the first stage, as we have seen, a partial regrouping of units from the right flank to the west, and then the northwest, had begun.[7]

7 Aside from this, as was noted above, the 340th and 173rd rifle divisions had been transferred from the 50th

The Southwestern Front's 60th Army to the left had by the close of December 13 reached the line Mikhailovskoe-Rakhmanova-Bol'shaya Mokhovaya-Zalesskoe-Yefremov, with the task of continuing the offensive to the west.

The development of the 49th Army's offensive in the center and left flank, while tying down the enemy on the right flank (December 15-19)

The 49th Army's tasks during the period following December 14 were laid out in *front* directive no. 0104/op of December 13, according to which the 49th Army was to "destroy the enemy's Aleksin group during December 14-15 and develop the success in the direction of Nedel'noe. On the morning of December 15 the group, consisting of one rifle division and four rifle brigades, plus reinforcements, is to launch its main blow from the starting line Iskon'-Tarusa (exclusively) in the direction of Kuz'mishchevo and Vysokinichi." According to the same directive, a supporting attack was to be launched by the army's right-flank divisions. By the close of December 18 the army's main forces are to reach the front Komarovo-Chernaya Gryaz'-Nedel'noe-Akhlebnino. The directive established the boundary line with the 50th Army as (excluding) Titovo-Akhlebnino-Kaluga-Pletnevka.

In accordance with the *front* directive, the commander of the 49th Army on December 15 issued order no 016/op, according to which the army was to go over to a general offensive from the morning of December 16, launching its main blow with its center (194th and 133rd rifle divisions,[8] the 19th, 26th, 30th, and 34th rifle brigades,[9] and the 18th and 23rd tank brigades) in the direction of Saltykovo and Gostishchevo. The army's right wing (415th, 5th Guards, and 60th rifle divisions) were to launch a supporting attack with part of their forces in the direction of Novaya Vyazovnya, with the task of reached the line Novaya Vyazovnya-Troitskoe, while the 415th Rifle Division, through the active operations of some of its detachments, was to tie down the enemy and prevent him from transferring his reserves to the south.

The left-flank divisions (238th, 173rd, and 340th) were to complete the destruction of the German's Aleksin group and develop the success to the northwest toward Petrishchevo.

The artillery was tasked with preparing to fire against the southern part of Volkovskoe, Saltykovo, and Bol'sunovo (2 km south of Saltykovo) and assisting the army's shock group in capturing and holding a bridgehead on the western bank of the Oka River along the indicated axes. Along with this, the artillery was to prevent the enemy's movement from the direction of Tarusa, Kuz'mishchevo, and Seliverstovo.

Both tank brigades were attached to the 194th and 133rd divisions of the shock group and were to carry out missions assigned by the division commanders.

The air assets supporting the offensive (an independent air group) were assigned the tasks of covering the army's shock group, to assist it in carrying out its tasks and preventing the arrival of enemy reserves to the battlefield from the south and west.

As can be seen from the tasks assigned to the divisions, the fundamental idea of the offensive was built around a concentric envelopment of the enemy's group in the corner formed by the confluence of the Oka and Protva rivers and the overwhelming of the enemy forces in the area of Tarusa. The army commander's plan was confirmed by the *front* command, and it was ordered to

---

Army to the 49th Army, of which the former was subsequently resubordinated to the commander of the 50th Army.

8 This was transferred from the 1st Army in the Solnechnogorsk area.

9 All the rifle brigades were attached to the 49th Army from the High Command Reserve and from other parts of the front.

begin carrying it out according to the timetable. However, the actual course of events turned out somewhat otherwise.

On the morning of December 16 the army's units began to carry out their assigned tasks. The enemy put up resistance everywhere; this was particularly stubborn on the right flank, along the Troitskoe-Kuz'mishchevo sector, and on the left flank, along the Naryshkino (3 km east of Belolipki)-Popovka, employing previously-prepared positions.

On December 16 the 5th Guards and 60th rifle divisions moved forward somewhat and during the following day fought unsuccessfully in the wooded area to the west and southwest of the line Vysokoe-Maleevo.

The 194th Rifle Division also moved forward and by 1200 on December 17 had occupied Novoselki and Yershovo (3 km southeast of Ostrov) and was fighting for Troitskoe, which had been turned by the enemy into a strong point. During the first half of December 19 this defense was overcome and the division attacked in the direction of Gosteshevo.

The 133rd Rifle Division and the 26th and 19th rifle brigades were fighting on the western bank of the Oka River along the line Saltykovo-Tarusa. The town of Tarusa was taken by the 19th Rifle Brigade on December 19.

Enemy units which had been located on the south bank of the Protva River, were withdrawing to the Vysokinichi area, where groups of forces were evidently being created to hold this area. According to intelligence data, units of the 260th and 52nd infantry divisions were operating along the line Tarusa-Troitskoe, while to the north of the Protva River the 263rd, 137th, and 268th infantry divisions were fighting. Along the Aleksin axis, units of the army's left flank, having broken the German-Fascist troops' resistance along the line Bunyrevo-Naryshkino-Popovka, reached the Oka River at 1530 on December 17, captured Aleksin and were developing the success to the northwest. The 173rd and 340th rifle divisions reached the sector Fomishchevo-Shchukino, and on December 19 crossed over to the western bank of the Oka River and were attacking to the west. The German-Fascist units, abandoning their equipment, were withdrawing under the cover of rearguards, to the west and northwest.

In the combat actions of the 49th Army just covered, one may note the following: first, the army's assumption of the offensive along the entire front, with the exception of its extreme right flank (415th Rifle Division); secondly, the enemy's most stubborn resistance was encountered along the 5th Guards and 60th rifle divisions' sectors, which was assisted by the wooded terrain, and; thirdly, the overall successful carrying out of their tasks by the divisions of the center and left flank, with the diversion of the 17th and 340th rifle divisions from their designated axis of advance (particularly the 340th Rifle Division) to the northwest and west. The latter occurred as a result of the fact that a significant part of the Aleksin group of enemy forces withdrew to the southwest (the Titovo-Vysokoe-Stolbovo area), from which area during the Kaluga operation they formed a threat to the 50th Army, hanging over its right flank.

The development of the 50th Army's offensive in conjunction with the 1st Guards Cavalry Corps and the 10th Army to the south, with the mission of destroying the withdrawing troops of the enemy's Second Panzer Army

In the period after December 13 the 50th Army's missions remained essentially unchanged. According to *front* directive no. 0104/op of December 13, the army, in conjunction with the 1st Guards Cavalry Corps, was to continue the offensive in the direction of Shchekino, with the task of destroying the enemy's Tula group, and by the close of December 15 reaching the line Plastovo-Zhitovo with its main group of forces.

During the second half of December 14, and during the course of December 15-16, combat activities on the 50th Army's front essentially developed along two axes—the western and southern, and on the approaches to Shchekino. Units of the 258th Rifle Division, having broken the Germans' resistance along the Upa River, in the Pavshino area, by 1100 on December 16 had reached the line Berezovo-Krasnaya Zarya-Ivanovka (all locales 10 km southwest of Pavshino), having captured these locales.

In the following days, the division's offensive developed according to the army's new plan to the northwest. The 290th Rifle Division had concentrated its main forces in the Verigino-Voskresenskoe area by December 16 and was in readiness to carry out the army's new missions. The 217th Rifle Division, with the 32nd Tank Brigade, attacking from the Vorob'evka-Baburino-Yasenki area (all locales 3 km north of Shchekino), was fighting for Shchekino. Units of the enemy's 296th Infantry Division, together with a large amount of automatic weaponry and mortars, occupied prepared positions in the Shchekino area and were rendering stubborn resistance. The 154th Rifle Division was attacking from the line Smirnoe-Panarino (both locales 1-2 km northwest of Lomintsevo)-Lomintsevo in the direction of Shevelevka (4 km east of Shchekino). By December 17 the 154th Rifle Division had been pulled out of the fighting and concentrated in the area 5 km south of Tula (Tat'evo-Khopilovo-Dement'evo), in order to carry out the army's new tasks. The 413th Rifle Division, was attacking from the line Podosinki-Zamyatino-Krutoe, occupied on December 14, toward Kosov and Shchekino (both locales 3 km southwest of Lomintsevo), where it encountered stubborn resistance by the Germans, who were occupying previously-prepared defensive positions in strength of up to two infantry battalions and 15 tanks.

Thus during the course of December 15-16 the center of the 50th Army's combat operations was the area of Shchekino station, which the enemy sought to hold in order to secure its troops' withdrawal.

On the morning of December 15, in accordance with orders from the *front*, which was demanding that the army turn its main forces to the northwest, the 50th Army command laid down new tasks for its troops. According to the army's order no. 39/ op of December 15, the army's right flank and center were to assist the 49th Army in destroying the enemy's Aleksin group, while the left flank and part of the army's center (413th and 217th rifle divisions) were to, in conjunction with the 1st Guards Cavalry Corps, complete the rout of the enemy's group in the area Shchekino-Zhitovo, after which these divisions would turn to the west. The 31st Cavalry Division was to secure the army's left flank, operating along the boundary with the 1st Guards Cavalry Corps.

The army order laid out lines for the divisions and the dates they should be attained. The echeloned character of this formation can be explained by two reasons: first, the necessity of eliminating the Shchekino-Zhitovo enemy group and, secondly, the lagging behind of the neighboring 10th Army, which demanded the securing of the army's left flank against the enemy's Likhvin-Cherepets group.

During the second half of December 16 the army's divisions, in carrying out their orders, attacked to the south and southwest. The 258th Rifle Division encountered the most stubborn enemy resistance in the Andreevskoe area (7 km northwest of Pavshino) and pulled back its right flank toward Pavshino. The 290th Rifle Division continuing fighting with one regiment for Suprut. The 217th Rifle Division continued fighting for Shchekino, from which the two regiments of the 154th Rifle Division were attacking from the Shevelevka area (4 km east of Shchekino station). The 413th Rifle Division was continuing the fight along its previous position. By the close of December 17 the 50th Army, having captured Shchekino with its 217th Rifle Division, had reached a line west of Plastovo-Gur'evka-Suprut-Shchekino.

During the night of December 17-18 the army's units were putting themselves in order and preparing for further attacks.

During the succeeding days the 50th Army carried its offensive along the Kaluga axis, by which time some of its units were already fighting.

Combat along the front of the neighboring group of Gen. Belov's 1st Cavalry Corps unfolded as follows.

According *front* commander Gen. Zhukov's directive no. 0106/op of December 13, the group, in conjunction with the 50th and 10th armies, was to destroy the enemy in the Dedilovo-Shchekino-Bogoroditsk (excluding) and by the end of December 16 was to concentrate in the area Krapivna-Danilovka (10 km south of Krapivna).

Based upon the *front's* orders, Gen. Belov deployed his units as follows:

a) along the right flank the 322nd Rifle Division was attacking to the southwest from the line Lipnya-Berezovka (3 km southeast of Lipnya);
b) in the center the 1st Guards Cavalry Division was attacking in the direction of Dedilovo;
c) on the left flank the 2nd Guards Cavalry Division, along with the 9th Tank Brigade, was fighting with part of its forces for Uzlovaya station, while pushing its remaining forces to the west in conjunction with the 1st Guards Cavalry Division.

At dawn on December 14 the 2nd Guards Cavalry Division, following stubborn fighting, captured Uzlovaya station and began to pursue the Germans to the west. One cavalry regiment was sent forward with tanks to cut the Tula-Orel road in the Zhitovo area.

However, it proved impossible to carry out this assignment immediately, as a result of the enemy's resistance.

On the morning of December 15 the 1st Guards Cavalry Division took Dedilovo after fighting. The 322nd Rifle Division, having taken Bykovo, continued attacking toward Plekhanovo (15 km northwest of Dedilovo).

The cavalry group's offensive continued with minor interruptions at night. On the morning of December 16 the cavalry group reached the Upa River along the sector Dubrovka (2 km north of Gory Uslan')-Kurovo-Smirnovka. In the Kurovo area units of the 1st Guards Cavalry Division encountered powerful resistance by the enemy's 399th Infantry Regiment, against which it was fighting.

On December 17 the *front* commander, in his directive no. 7989, assigned the cavalry corps the task of reaching the area Krapivno-Arkhangel'skoe-Umchino by the end of December 18. The *front's* directive essentially repeated the task assigned to the corps the evening before in directive no. 112/op.

That same day Gen. Belov reported to Gen. Zhukov his decision to move to the designated area on the night of December 17-18, basically leaving the grouping of his units unchanged.

Intelligence and fighting determined that the remains of the units of the 167th Infantry and 17th Panzer divisions, and, evidently, the 10th Motorized Division, were pulling back before the corps.

On the night of December 17-18 units of the cavalry group began moving to the designated area and by the morning of December 18 had reached the line Zhitovo-(Sorochinka (exclusively).

Thus one may note the following combat activities on the 50th Army's front during the period December 13-17: first, the task of defeating the Shchekino-Zhitovo enemy group, which had attempted to hold the area of Shchekino and Zhitovo and thus cover the Tula-Orel road, had basically been achieved; secondly, while still in the process of completing the Tula operation, the latter began to grow into the 50th Army's Kaluga operation, which found expression in the army's regrouping from the Shchekino (southern) axis to the northwest.

The 1st Guards Cavalry Corps and the 10th Army during this period still had to complete the Tula offensive operation, whereupon it was necessary to begin the new Belev-Kozel'sk operation, particularly as the 1st Guards Cavalry Corps, which was operating along the boundary between the 10th and 50th armies, as we shall see later on, also took a certain part in the Kaluga operation.

The development of the 10th Army's offensive in the Bogoroditsk-Plavsk direction until its arrival at the line of the Plava and Upa rivers and the capture of Plavsk

The *front's* directive no. 0106/op of December 13 laid down the following task for the 10th Army: with its main group of the army's left flank, and launching its main blow in the direction of Bogoroditsk, Plavsk, and Arsen'evo (35 km west of Plavsk), and in conjunction with the 1st Guards Cavalry Corps, it was to destroy by the end of December 16 the enemy in the area Uzlovaya-Bogoroditsk-Plavsk, with its main forces reaching the line Zhitovo station-Plavsk.

The army's left boundary remained unchanged.

As can be seen from the directive, the blow by the army's main forces was aimed to the southwest for the purpose of more deeply enveloping the enemy forces north of the Bogoroditsk parallel.

On the morning of December 14 the 10th Army's troops resumed their offensive and by the end of the same day had reached the front: 330th and 328th rifle divisions had crossed the Uzlovaya-Bogoroditsk railroad along the sector Bibikovo (2 km south of Uzlovaya)-Pritony and were attacking to the west. To the left of the 324th Rifle Division, along the Bogoroditsk-Tovarkovo sector, the 323rd Rifle Division was moving forward in fighting. The 326th Rifle Division, echeloned to the rear, was attacking. The latter's offensive was delayed by the resistance of the German-Fascist infantry from the Kaganovich-Mokhovoe area. By that time the 325th Rifle Division had concentrate in the area of Yepifan' and to the south, with the mission of reaching the area of Kaganovich by the morning of December 16.

The army's three cavalry divisions, actually acting separately from one another, were moving to the southwest: the 41st Cavalry Division, bypassing Bogoroditsk from the south, was attacking Plavsk with the task of capturing it. The 57th and 75th cavalry divisions were only concentrating in the area Starya Gat'-Matveeka (11 km south of Yepifan'). Such a situation forced the army command to unite on December 17 all three cavalry divisions into one group under the command of Gen. Mishulin. The group operated on the army's left flank along the boundary with the Southwestern Front and had the task of attacking in the direction of Plavsk. This measure should be seen as expedient, but against the overall course of events along the 10th Army's front, did not yield any great results.

In the following days until December 19 the 10th Army's offensive developed as follows. By the end of December 17 units of the 324th Rifle Division crossed the Upa River along the Naumovka-Myasnovka sector, and the 323rd Rifle Division's forward units reached Rzhavo. The 326th Rifle Division by that time had passed Sukhoi Ruchei. The cavalry divisions, lagging behind a little, were located as before on the army's left flank, moving on Plavsk and to the south.

The distribution of enemy forces in front of the army remained basically unchanged. The German-Fascist 167th and 112th rifle, and the 29th and 10th motorized divisions resisted stubbornly and were falling back on Plavsk and Odoevo. The retreat was being covered by the powerful fire of 150mm batteries.

By the close of December 19 the 323rd Rifle Division's main forces (two regiments) had taken Plavsk in fighting and were developing the blow to the northwest. Gen. Mishulin's cavalry group, during December 18 was fighting in the area of Teploe (10 km southeast of Plavsk), where it was trying to encircle the enemy. By this time the neighboring 1st Guards Cavalry Corps had occupied the line Prishnya-Staraya Krapivenka-Staryi Khutor (6 km south of Staraya Krapivenka) and, in conjunction with the army's right flank, was moving toward the Plava River.

With the arrival of the units of the 10th Army and 1st Guards Cavalry Corps along the Plavsk meridian and the line of the Plava River, one must consider the second stage of the Tula operation for the 10th Army and 1st Guards Cavalry Corps to be completed. Subsequent combat operations along the *front's* left wing were broken up into a series of partial, consecutive operations (the 49th Army's offensive on Vysokinichi, as well as the Kaluga and Belev-Kozel'sk operations).

In the 10th Army's combat operations during the period under consideration in the second stage of the Tula operation, one may note the following highlights. First of all, the army's offensive basically came down to frontal, head-on blows without any attempts to bypass and envelop a number of the enemy's strong points. This circumstance forced the *front* command to repeatedly point out to the army commander (as well as to the commanders of other armies) the necessity for more decisive actions, combined with the extensive employment of flanking and enveloping actions, using the gaps between the strong points, in particular those which were not subject to the enemy's enfilading fire. Secondly, despite the fact that the 10th Army's overall rate of advance during the entire operation was greater than 12 km per day (significantly greater than in the 50th and 49th armies), according to the *front* command's plan, which sought to encircle the Second Panzer Army's main forces, this rate should have been increased. The 1st Cavalry Corps, operating along the boundary of both armies, was, unfortunately, also unable to develop a faster pace of attack at this stage, chiefly due to the resistance put up by the enemy along a series of lines. As a result of this, the *front* command was forced in directive no. 0102/op of December 13 to note "the 10th Army, by its passivity and systematic inability to fulfill orders to occupy forward lines and places, is foiling the *front's* operational plan and enables the enemy to withdraw his units and equipment..."[10] Besides this, the *front* command demanded from that the army command an accounting of the reasons for the offensive's slow pace. Third, the unification of the three cavalry divisions into a single group was, in principle, correct, although as a result of their differing combat and technical equipping (the 57th and 75th cavalry divisions were particularly badly equipped), the mobile group did not play a particular important role and was later disbanded and its divisions were transferred to the 1st Guards Cavalry Corps.

Overall conclusions on the Tula Offensive Operation

The role and significance of the Tula Offensive Operation in the Western Front's overall operation

The operation by the Western Front's left wing unfolded along one of the front's most important operational directions—the Tula direction—and according to its scope was an operation by a group of armies, connected by the unity of the operational plan and goal. During the course of combat activities the 49th Army's left flank took part, carrying out in conjunction with the 50th Army's right flank, the mission of defeating the enemy's Aleksin group. The way this group hung over Tula from the northwest was creating a threat to the 50th Army's right flank, which could hinder the development of its offensive to the south of Tula. Thus the *front* command devoted special attention to the fighting along the Aleksin axis. The main forces of the 50th Army, 1st Guards Cavalry Corps, and the 10th Army were fighting to destroy the enemy's Second Panzer Army, which also included a number of infantry divisions (112th, 167th, 296th and, evidently, the XLIII Army Corps' 31st and 131st divisions). The defeat of these German-Fascist troops on the Tula bridgehead was acquiring great significance for the battle of Moscow, being a part of the overall rout of the enemy forces by the Western Front's armies and their successful advance to the west. Despite certain shortcomings in the operation's conduct, already noted by us, this task was, on the whole, resolved successfully. For the left-wing's armies the prospect of resolving a new and important *front* task was opening up—in conjunction with the *front's* center and right wing, to defeat the German-Fascist troops' central group.

10 This excerpt from the order is taken from the "Western Front Combat Log for December 1941," p. 89.

Peculiarities of the Tula Operation

One of the peculiarities of the Tula operation is that it grew immediately out of the operational defense that the troops of the Tula axis had been conducting before this. Thus, for example, the 49th Army as early as the operation's first stage had been waging an active defense along its right flank and in the center, while the army's extreme right flank defended during the second stage. On the left flank, against the Aleksin bridgehead (in conjunction with the 50th Army's right flank), active offensive operations were being conducted in the interests of the operation as a whole. Here there was no pause between the defensive activities being conducted earlier along this sector and the offensive; one operational activity proceeded from another. We see almost the same picture on the front of the 50th Army, which during the period preceding the operation, had been forced to withstand attacks by powerful forces of the German-Fascist troops' right wing, which were attacking toward Moscow. Thanks to the measures taken by the *Stavka* and the *front*, during the course of the defensive fighting the power of resistance was increasing, which enabled the 50th Army to go over to the offensive in the overall group of the left-wing's armies. As regards the 1st Guards Cavalry Corps, which was one of the most important links in our counterblow along the Tula axis, even before the start of the general offensive, it was conducting active operations since November 27 in the Kashira area. By its blow, the 1st Cavalry Corps made it possible to avoid the premature commitment of the 10th Army before its operational concentration and deployment could be completed. Thus as early as the period of the defensive operation along the Tula direction an offensive had begun along one of its sectors, this was a precursor of the future general offensive by the front's left wing and of the entire Western Front.

The 10th Army, committed from the *Stavka's* strategic reserve, entered the operation in a different manner. Its offensive was proceeded by a period of operational concentration and deployment, followed by a period of preparatory measures and planning (out of contact with the enemy), which had not been completed before the start of the operation.

During the course of the Tula operation, there arose the necessity for a number of local regroupings in accordance with the situation and the command's plan. The resubordination of the 340th and 173rd rifle divisions to the 49th Army was necessary for the purpose of more rapidly defeating the enemy's Aleksin group. The subordination of rifle divisions to the 1st Guards Cavalry Corps was also due to the situation, which demanded that the cavalry be reinforced by infantry, because the corps, in the majority of cases, was forced to fight dismounted and the horse served as a means for more rapid maneuver. And, finally, the most visible example of a regrouping carried out during the course of the fighting, was the 50th Army's regrouping by orienting it to a new operational direction. In the description of the operation we devoted sufficient attention to this question and explained the reasons for turning the 50th Army from the southwest to the northwest.

Let's sum up briefly. First of all, a peculiarity of the Tula offensive operation was that it grew immediately out of a defensive operation, without a significant space in time. Secondly, defensive fighting was still being conducted along certain sectors during the course of the offensive along a broad front. Third, local regroupings were carried out during the course of the offensive, which found their most colorful expression in the regrouping of the 50th Army, which was conditioned by the maneuver character of the fighting along a broad front and the complexity of tasks facing the troops of the Western Front's left wing.

The operation's Scope and depth, the offensive's pace, problems of coordination, control and communications

The overall scope of the operation along the front and in depth is expressed in figures, which we provided while describing the area of military operations, that is about 110 km in a north-south direction and about 130 km from east to west. As to time, the operation last 10-12 days, during which fighting was almost continuous. The pace of the armies' offensive varied. For example, this was no more than one km per day for the operation as a whole for the 49th Army's right flank and center. During the operation's second stage this figure increased and the operation's pace reached 3-4 km per day (taking into account the divisions' deviation from the designated axis in order to outflank and envelop certain of the enemy's strong points). The left flank's units, overcoming the enemy's resistance on the Aleksin bridgehead, in general attacked at the same speed. If you count the regrouping of the 340th and 173rd rifle divisions (taking into account the time spent by the divisions in transit), then the offensive's pace increased to 6-8 km per day.

The 50th Army's advance (taking into account its regrouping to the northwest) over ten days was 25-30 km, which amounts to 2.5-3 km per day. The 1st Guards Cavalry Corps came to 100-120 km, or 8-10 km per day.

The 10th Army's offensive pace was the most rapid, varying between 12 and 13 km per day.

Questions of coordination in the Tula operation, as an operation involving several armies, were extremely important. The main factor here was the assignment of objectives to the army by the *front* command, and which were directed at achieving a single objective. For example, the decisive factor in this matter on the Aleksin direction was the coordination of the 49th Army's left flank with the 50th Army's right flank, which the *front* command pointed out more than once. On the Shchekino and Stalinogorsk axes this cooperation was achieved by directing the 50th Army's offensive to the south and southeast, the 1st Guards Cavalry Corps to the southwest, and the 10th Army to the west and southwest. There also appear to have been cases of the army commanders agreeing among themselves as regards problems arising during the offensive as one of the forms of coordination.

An important role was played by instructions from the *front* command regarding the movement of the army commander's command post to a distance of 10-15 km from the front line, as well as the location of the army headquarters no further than 25-30 km which made troop control significantly easier. It's necessary to note that the army staffs basically coped with this task, with the exception of those incidents already mentioned. This maneuver operation also revealed those difficulties encountered by an army command having control of up to ten troop formations and more (the 10th Army had 11 divisions). Thus, for example, the 10th Army commander later raised the question of the necessity of the constant or temporary unification of separate divisions into groups or corps.

The operation's development toward Vysokinichi, Kaluga and Belev

By December 18 the armies of the Western Front's left wing, continuing to fight the enemy, were located along the following lines. The 49th Army, defending along its right flank, with its center and left flank continued to attack in the direction of Vysokinichi and Petrishchevo from the line Troitskoe, west of Tarusa and Aleksin. The 50th Army was attacking to the northwest and west from the line Vysokoe-Dubna-Voskresenskoe. A group from the 1st Guards Cavalry Corps and the 10th Army, developing the offensive to the west, were approaching the line Prishnya-Staraya Krapivenka-Plava River-Plavsk, and to the south.

With the conduct of the Tula operation, the offensive by the left-wing armies actually never stopped. In accordance with the *front* command's overall operational plan, this offensive continued and, developing to the northwest and west, resulted in an offensive by the 49th Army on Vysokinichi and Nedel'noe, the 50th Army on Kaluga, and the 1st Guards Cavalry Corps and 10th Army on Belev and Kozel'sk.

The development of the 49th Army's offensive in the direction of Vysokinichi and Nedel'noe

Having suffered a defeat along the Protva River from Troitskoe to its mouth and further along to the Oka River as far as Aleksin, the German-Fascist units, for the most part, began to fall back, approximately to the following areas: from Troitskoe and to the south—to the Vysokinichi area; from Tarusa—to Nedel'noe, and; from Aleksin—to Kaluga and to the area 30-40 km southwest of Aleksin (Makarovo, Stolbova, Titovo, Pozdnyakovo).

Intelligence data revealed the following enemy forces: units of the 263rd, 137th, and 268th infantry divisions, as well as units of the 260th Infantry Division (the main forces of which were evidently located in the Vysokinichi area during this period) occupied the front from Burinovo to Tarusa. Units of the 52nd Infantry Division were placed from Tarusa to Aleksin. Along the Aleksin axis units of the XLIII Army Corps' 31st and 131st infantry divisions were falling back in fighting.

On the northern bank of the Protva River the enemy continued to hold his position from Ostrov (2 km west of Troitskoe) to Vorontsovka and on to Burinovo. Due to the forested character of the terrain and the Germans' stubborn defense, the attack by the army's right flank was unsuccessful. Overall, the successful resolution of the 49th Army's shock group's tasks and the elimination of the enemy's Aleksin bridgehead by the left wing's units during the Tula operation demanded the setting of new objectives for the 49th Army for the purpose of further developing its offensive.

On the night of December 18-19 the *front* chief of staff informed the 49th Army: in connection with the shock group's successful advance, the *front* commander orders part of the forces of the 5th Guards and 60th rifle divisions were to move laterally south of the Protva River, for the purpose of reinforcing the shock group's right flank in order to get as quickly as possible into the rear of the enemy's Vysokinichi group.

In furtherance of the *front* directive, the 49th Army commander, Gen. Zakharkin, that same day issued order no. 018/op, according to which:

> the 49th Army, while tying down the enemy along the Burinovo-Maleeva (2 km east of Vorontsovka) sector with part of its forces (415th and 5th Guards rifle divisions), is to continue the offensive with the remainder of its formations with the objective of eliminating the enemy's Vysokinichi and Aleksin groups and, employing forward mobile detachments, is by the end of December 19 1941 to reach the line Chernaya-Gryaz'-Nedel'noe-Stepanovskoe-Fetin'ino-Akhlebnino.

In accordance with this order, the 415th and 5th Guards rifle divisions were to tie down the enemy through the actions of detachments and prevent him from throwing his reserves to the south. Subsequently, the 5th Guards Rifle Division would be sent into the reserve north of Tarusa. The 60th Rifle Division was given the objective of capturing Vysokinichi by the end of December 19. The 194th Rifle Division was to operate in the direction of Gosteshevo and Novaya Slobodka, bypassing Vysokinichi from the south and by the close of December 19 was to take Nikonovo and Karpovo with its main forces, while its forward detachments were to take Novaya Slobodka. To the left the 26th Rifle Brigade was being directed to the line Lopatino-Filippovka, with the objective of capturing both locales with its forward detachments on December 19, and with its main forces to reach the area of Volyntsy (3 km southwest of Vysokinichi). The 133rd Rifle Division and the 30th Rifle Brigade to its left had the objective of by the close of December 19 reaching the line Filippovka-Nedel'noe-Kudinovo with its forward detachments, while their main forces were to take the line Altukhovo-Durovo-Pozdnyakovo. The 19th Rifle Brigade was tasked with, having destroyed the enemy southwest of Tarusa, by the end of the day concentrating in the area Isakovo-Latynino-Kresty.

The left-flank 238th and 173rd rifle divisions, attacking to the northwest at that time, were to reach the line Latynino-Bogorodskoe-Yel'kino with their main forces. The 340th Rifle Division, upon reaching the Ferzikovo area, was to be transferred to the 50th Army. The army staff's command post continued to be located in Buturlino.

As can be seen from the above, the 49th Army's overall objective was the concentric envelopment of the enemy group in the Vysokinichi area by units of the right flank (excluding the 415th Rifle Division) and launching a blow by its left-flank divisions to the northwest. During the latter part of December 19 the army's forces, while overcoming enemy resistance, would have to cover 10-20 km over wooded territory (the latter figure is for the forward detachments).

The army's matériel-technical provision as of December 18: rifle shells—1.4 combat loads; artillery shells (all calibers)—1.5 combat loads; mortar rounds—1 combat load; fuel—1.5 refills; daily rations, plus supplies from field depots—3.5. It follows that the army's ammunition, fuel and food supplies were satisfactory. Aside from this, the presence in the 49th Army's operational zone of the Moscow-Serpukhov road guaranteed the delivery of supplies from *front* bases and that of the High Command. The basing of the army's rear services was the same as of December 7.

The offensive by the 49th Army's units from December 19 unfolded in the following manner. On the morning of December 19 units of the 415th, 5th Guards, and 60th rifle divisions continued

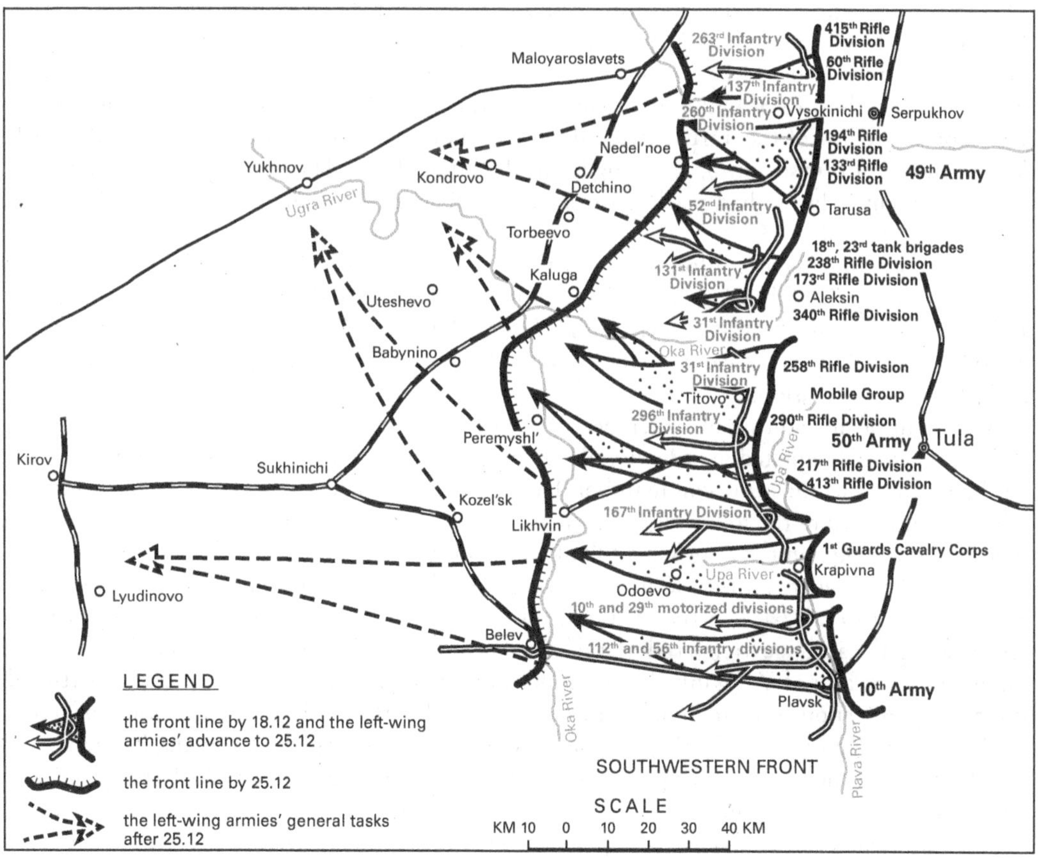

Map 10 The Overall Offensive by the Left-Wing Armies, December 18-25, 1941

fighting along the line Burinovo-Voronino-Maleeva-Borovka (4 km southeast of Vorontsovka, encountering heavy resistance from the Fascists, who were relying on a developed system of forest defense. The 194th Rifle Division was attacking toward Gostishchevo. In the Troitskoe area a large enemy unit was routed, evidently belonging to the 268th Infantry Division. By the close of December 19 and all of December 20 the division was fighting for Ostrov, surrounding it from the north and south. The enemy put up stubborn resistance, relying on previously-prepared defensive positions.

The 133rd Rifle Division and the 26th Rifle Brigade continued fighting to take the line Radenki (2 km north of L'govo)-L'govo. Having blocked the latter point, our units (a rifle regiment) was attacking toward Titovo (2 km west of L'gov). The 30th Rifle Brigade was attacking toward Boltanogovo (4 km southwest of L'gov). The 19th Rifle Brigade was advancing to its designated area.

The 238th Rifle Division, encountering strong resistance from the German-Fascist units, advanced with great difficulty to the line indicated by the army order. Only by the close of December 20 did the division capture Petrishchevo and was continuing to attack toward Kareevo. The 173rd Rifle Division reached the area of Semeikino and Bogimovo only by the morning of December 21, having taken these two locales.

During December 20-22 the 49th Army's forces, carrying out the army commander's December 19 order, were fighting in the following areas: 415th Rifle Division and two regiments from the 60th Rifle Division were defending along the line Burinovskii station (3 km south of Burinovo)-the woods north of Ostrov. The 5th Guards Rifle Division was being pulled back into the army reserve to the area of Saltykovo-Bol'sunovo (both locales 6-8 km north of Tarusa). The 194th Rifle Division, as before, was waging an unsuccessful fight for Ostrov and Galchatovka (1 km south of Ostrov). The 133rd Division and the 26th and 30th rifle brigades continued to fight for the line of fortified points Radenki-L'govo-Boltanogovo. The 34th Rifle Brigade, from the army reserve, was fighting in the area of Lytkino-Khomyakovo. The 238th Rifle Division was crossing with its main forces the line of the Tarusa River along the Pimenovo-Lotrevo sector (both locales 10-12 km northwest of Petrishchevo), attacking in the direction of Nedel'noe. The 173rd Rifle Division, following night fighting, had reached the area of Lobanovo, Kamenka, and Maksimovo by the morning of December 23.

According to intelligence information, by the morning of December 25 the enemy forces were operating along the following lines: 137th Infantry Division—Semkino-Vorontsovka; 268th Infantry Division—Maleeva-Ostrov; 260th Infantry Division—Ostrov-radenki-L'govo-Zavorovo; 52nd Infantry Division—Zavorovo-Khomyakovo-Kresty-Shul'gino, and further units of the 131st and 31st infantry divisions.

As a result of the fighting of December 19-23 it was determined that we would not be able to achieve the lines designated in order no. 018 by the deadline, due to the enemy's strong resistance. In these conditions the army command on December 22 adopted a new decision, the essence of which comes down to the following. The enemy, relying on a system of powerful strong points, is holding his position on the army's right flank and center.

On the army's left flank the Germans, having been defeated by our units in the Aleksin area, are continuing to fall back to the west and northwest. It is necessary, while holding down the enemy along the army's extreme right flank, that the units of the center surround and destroy the Germans in the area of Vysokinichi. To simultaneously develop the blow by the army's left-flank units in the direction of Detchino, with the objective of cutting off the enemy's route of retreat to the west and northwest. In this manner, the idea of encircling the Germans in the area of Vysokinichi and their deep envelopment in the direction of Detchino lay at the heart of the 49th Army commander's decision.

The army command's decision corresponded to the situation. Despite the somewhat prolonged fighting against the enemy's Vysokinichi group, the outcome of this battle was clear. The units of the army's center had the task of defeating the enemy's Vysokinichi group. The arrival of the 50th Army in the Kaluga area and the fighting for the city indicated to the 49th Army command that the enemy was tied to this area and, thus that he would have to secure his left flank. All of this, evidently, gave the 49th Army command the right to direct its left-flank divisions significantly deep than had been indicated in order no. 018. The realization of this maneuver would have created double prerequisites: on the one hand, the enemy group in the area of Nedel'noe and Bashmakovka would be outflanked, while on the other the arrival in the Detchino area would ease the 50th Army's defeat of the Germans' Kaluga group.

According to this decision by the army commander, on December 22 order no. 019/op was issued, according to which the 415th Rifle Division was to, while carrying out combat reconnaissance in the direction of Vysokinichi, securely defend its position; the 60th 194th, and 133rd rifle divisions and the 26th and 30th rifle brigades were to continuing carrying out the missions laid out in order no. 018. The 34th Rifle Brigade was to attack from the area eight km west of Tarusa to the northwest and, by the end of December 23, reach the area Andreevskoe-Antonovo-Lopatino (all locales 8 km west of Vysokinichi) and from there turn toward Vysokinichi for a joint blow with a group of units attacking from the east.

The 19th Rifle Brigade received the assignment of developing the offensive toward Nedel'noe, from which it was then to operate in the direction of Lopatino, assisting in the encirclement of the enemy's Vysokinichi group.

The 238th and 173rd rifle divisions were to continue pursuing the enemy and by the close of December 23 reach the line Afanas'evo-Detchino-Torbeevo with their main forces.

The 5th Guards Rifle Division, as was stated, was to be put into the army reserve north of Tarusa, from where it was to operate according to the situation: either with a group of units from the army's center, or with the shock group (238th and 173rd rifle divisions) from the army's left flank. As the further course of the fighting showed, the 5th Guards Rifle Division was later transferred to the army's left flank for the purpose of developing its offensive.

In accordance with the *front* command's repeated instructions, the army command demanded in its own order that commanders at all levels avoid head-on attacks against the enemy's fortified areas and seek to bypass these places. It was ordered to more decisively employed mobile detachments to block the enemy's path of retreat in order to encircle and destroy his forces. These orders were necessary, because in a number of cases head-on attacks took place, besides which slowness and indecisiveness were displayed in employing ski troops and other mobile detachments.

During the period from December 23-27 events on the 49th Army's front developed as follows.

Up to December 24 the 415th Rifle Division was defending its former position. From December 24 the division went over from the defensive to the offensive and, operating in individual detachments, was slowly moving forward. The enemy's resistance along the division's sector began to weaken. Developing the offensive, units of the 415th Rifle Division on the first half of December 26 reached the line Kurkino (2 km north of Troyanovo)-Troyanovo-Makarovo, where they once again encountered stubborn German resistance. Having taken Makarovo in the latter half of December 28, the division was attacking to the west.

Units of the 60th Rifle Division slowly, in fighting, moved forward and on December 25 reached the area of Verkhnyaya and Nizhnyaya Vyazovnya (4 km east of Vysokinichi) and occupied the indicated points. In the latter half of December 26 the 60th Rifle Division entered the fighting against the enemy on the approaches to Vysokinichi. Bypassing Vysokinichi from the north and northeast, by the morning of December 27 the division, following stubborn fighting, captured it and began to develop the offensive to the west.

The 194th Rifle Division, having crossed the wooded area to the south of Vysokinichi, on December 27 was developing the offensive in the direction of Ivanovskoe (3 km west of Vysokinichi).

Small units covering the enemy's withdrawal were operating in front of the division. By this time the 133rd Rifle Division had captured Stekhino and Utkino (5 km southwest of Vysokinichi) and was attacking in the direction of Antonovo (6 km west of Vysokinichi).

Upon capturing the area Boltanogovo-Zavorovo (3 km northwest of Tarusa), the 30th Rifle Brigade was to be put into the second echelon behind the 238th Rifle Division. Units of the 238th Rifle Division, successfully advancing in the designated direction, on December 24 reached the line Nedel'noe-Bashmakovka, where stubborn fighting once again broke out.

The 173rd Rifle Division by this time was only approaching Maslovo, advancing slowly. The *front* command, taking into account the 238th Rifle Division's exposed forward position, on December 24 demanded that the army command immediately transfer the 173rd Rifle Division and the 19th Rifle Brigade to the line of the 238th Rifle Division.

The 5th Guards Rifle Division and the 23rd Tank Brigade, following a difficult march along poor and snow-covered roads, by the close of December 24 had concentrated in the Petrishchevo area with the mission of moving on the morning of December 25 to the Nedel'noe area, where it was to constitute the shock group's (173rd and 238th rifle divisions) second echelon.

During December 25-27 the main fighting along the 49th Army's left flank unfolded in the Nedel'noe area. The enemy, in holding on to this area, evidently considered it the key to the Maloyaroslavets-Kaluga railroad and to the line of strong points along the railroad from Afanas'evo to Detchino and Torbeevo.

The opportunities for bypassing Nedel'noe and Bashmakovka were not fully taken advantage of by the army and division command, which was one of the reasons that some of our units got bogged down around Nedel'noe.

In first half of December 26 the 173rd Rifle Division reached the line Bol'shaya Luga-Pnevo-Rakhmanovo (4 km southeast of the line Detchino-Torbeevo), but as a result of a powerful enemy counterattack and intensive fire, withdrew its right flank to Dol'skoe (7 km southeast of Detchino).

As a result of the fighting along the 49th Army's front during December 19-27, one may note the following : first of all, the objective of capturing the Vysokinichi area was, for the most part, successfully carried out by the units of the right flank and center; secondly, a new center of stubborn enemy resistance had appeared in the Nedel'noe-Bashmakovka area, which the German-Fascist units sought to hold so as to prevent the arrival of our units along the line of the Maloyaroslavets-Kaluga railroad; third, the offensive unfolded in poor weather conditions (snow drifts) and over wooded terrain, which slowed down the offensive's pace.

In the period following December 27 the 49th Army attacked in the direction of Detchino and Kondrovo and west, with the objective of defeating and destroying (together with the 43rd and 50th armies) the Germans' Myatlevo-Kondrovo-Yukhnov group. The 49th Army's new operation consisted in carrying out this assignment.

The 50th Army's Kaluga Operation

The situation on the 50th Army's front and that of its neighbors by the beginning of the operation

At the same time that the 10th Army and the 1st Guards Cavalry Corps' group were reaching the line Prishnya-Staraya Krapivenka-Plava River-Plavsk, and further south, the units of the 50th Army's right flank were attacking to the west and northwest. On December 18 the 258th Rifle Division's center captured Vysokoe, its right flank was fighting for Khovanskaya (4 km southeast of Titovo), and its left flank was fighting for Lobzha.

The resistance by the German-Fascist units in these areas continued to grow.

The 290th Rifle Division, having left a regiment to occupy Krapivna, by this time had reached the line Drokovo-Biketovka (6 km south of Drokovo). The army's remaining units continued to regroup. The 49th Army's neighboring 340th and 173rd rifle divisions on the right were on the western bank of the Oka River in the Aleksin area, from which they were developing the offensive to the northwest (173rd Rifle Division) and west (340th Rifle Division).

The enemy's formation on the Kaluga axis as of December 18 was as follows.

The area of Zabelino-Titovo-Stolbova-Makarovo was being defended by the 31st Infantry Division. Also observed here were small units of the 296th Infantry Division. In Kaluga the remains of the 131st and 137th infantry divisions were concentrating, as well as other small units transferred from the rear and other sectors of the front.

Units of the 296th and 167th infantry divisions were operating in the Odoevo area and to the northwest, near Likhvin and Cherepet'.

Units of the 19th Panzer Division, as well as the *Grossdeutschland* regiment, which had suffered heavy casualties, were located in the second line.

The sides' plans by the beginning of the operation

As is evident from the distribution of enemy forces, the German command sought to remove its units from out of the way of the Soviet forces' blow, to delay our offensive on the approaches to Kaluga and then along the line of the Oka to Belev and further to the south. Under the cover of this line, it was evidently hoped that they could bring up reserves, carry out the necessary regrouping and hold on for the winter. It is likely that the formation of groups in the Likhvin-Cherepet' area and to the southeast of Kaluga (in the Zabelino-Titovo-Stolbova-Makarovo) area, as well as the erection of fortifications in the Kaluga area itself was subordinated to this idea. According to our intelligence[11] it was noted that in Kaluga the civilian population had been mobilized and captured Red Army soldiers brought in to carry out defensive works around the city.

According to the *front* command's directive no. 112/op of December 16 1941, the 50th Army received the task: by the end of December 18 to reach the front Pozdnyakovo-Stolbova-Drokovo with its main forces. The boundary line as far as Odoevo was as before, and further excluded Likhvin.

Simultaneously the *front* command ordered the 50th Army commander, Gen. Boldin, to form a maneuver group for striking toward Kaluga from the south in conjunction with the 49th Army.

In pursuance of the *front* directive, the 50th Army command on the morning of December 17 issued order no. 40, according to which the army was to continue the offensive to the west.

As Kaluga was part of the operational zone of the 49th Army's left flank, the latter's task was to take the city by a blow from the east.

In accordance with the orders of the *front* commander, Gen. Zhukov, the commander of the 50th Army created a mobile group, which was to, in conjunction with the 49th Army, take Kaluga through a surprise attack from the south. It originally followed from this that the 50th Army was supposed to help the 49th Army. However, as we will see later, the course of combat activities led to a situation whereby the task of capturing Kaluga was carried out independently by the 50th Army, with the indirect assistance of its neighbor to the right—the 49th Army, and its neighbor to the left—the 1st Guards Cavalry Corps.

The mobile group was made up of two regiments of the 154th Rifle Division, the 112th Tank Division, two batteries of a guards mortar battalion, and a flamethrower-incendiary company. Aside from this, from the morning of December 18 the mobile group was strengthened by the

11 Intelligence report of the Western Front headquarters no. 210, of December 19 1941.

addition of the 31st Cavalry Division, a Tula worker's regiment, the 131st Tank Battalion, and other small units, while the command of the mobile group was entrusted to the 50th Army's deputy commander, Gen. Popov.

According to the order, the mobile group was to secretly concentrate by the end of December 18 in the wooded area in the area Zyabki-Alekseevskoe-Zelenino-Yurovo (the three latter locales are 5-7 km west and south of Zyabki), from which by means of a surprise attack at dawn on December 20 they were to take Kaluga from the south. The mobile group was to depart from its jumping-off point along the line Zaitsevo-Kharino-Pyatnitskoe no later than 2200 on December 17 and move by night marches along the axis Zaitsevo-Voskresenskoe-Dubna-Khanino-Zyabki-Muzhach'-Kaluga.

From the north the operations of Gen. Popov's mobile group would be secured by the 258th Rifle Division, which having destroyed the enemy, was to reach on December 20 the front Akhlebnino-Zyabki-Pleshkovo.

From the southwest and south the mobile group's maneuver was to be secured by the 290th Rifle Division, which had the assignment of reaching the area of Khanino and to the west on December 19 and having thrown mobile detachments toward the Oka River along the sector Korekozevo-Gerasimovo (5 km north of Cherepet').

The 217th and 413th rifle divisions' objectives remained basically unchanged.

Thus the newly-created mobile group had the assignment of suddenly breaking through the enemy's line and reaching Kaluga from the south. In taking Kaluga a wedge would be driven between the right flank of the German Fourth Army and the left flank of Guderian's Second Panzer Army.

Gen. Popov's group had to overcome a distance of more than 80 km, while piercing the enemy's line to a depth of 40-45 km. The group was to move at a speed of more than 30 km per day.

It's necessary to note that the moment for this group's operation was well timed. It coincided in time with the defeat of the enemy group in the Tula area and the arrival of the main forces of the *front's* left-wing armies to the west of the city. Under winter conditions and the enemy's continuing resistance, such a decision is instructive and the successful fulfillment of the designated maneuver by the mobile group is proof of the high combat qualities of the Western Front's troops and the skill in commanding them.

The Operation's matériel-technical support

According to the *front's* rear directive no. 026 of December 16, the 50th Army's field depot was to be deployed in the Tula area. The 1st Guards Cavalry Corps, which was supplied by the 50th Army, was supplied predominantly from the same base. Mobile supplies among the troops were to be brought up to norms by December 20 according to orders placed by the army commander, while the delivery of stocks and property from the *front* depots was to be carried out by rail (and only in exceptional cases by auto transport) to the railhead army depots. By means of distributing auto transport among the troops and the employment of horse-drawn transportation battalions, division supply was to be guaranteed for 60-70 km. On the average, ¼ of a combat load, ½ of a fuel refill, one day's food ration, and ½ of the daily forage requirement would be delivered over 75 km.

According to *front* directive no. 027 of December 22, the army's rear service boundaries were established as the line Kashira-Tula. An army supply base was to be located in the Tula area, with a branch in Aleksin. It was ordered to create supplies along dirt-road sectors in the area of Krosna (23 km east of Kaluga) and Makarovo. The supply route was Tula, Aleshnya, Gryaznovo (7 km southwest of Titovo), and Makarovo (depending on the army's forward advance). In order to supply the 1st Guards Cavalry Corps, the army was augmented for 5-6 days with 150 motor vehicles, with 50 of them to carry fuel. The main road was Moscow-Serpukhov-Tula. Railroad basing was mainly carried out toward Tula at the expense of delivery from Moscow. As the army moved forward, the chief railroad communication was to be the line Tula-Kozel'sk, with the Tula-Kaluga line as an auxiliary one. The army base in Tula supplied the army before the arrival of its units at the line Kaluga-Kozel'sk, after which it was switched to Cherepet'. In this way normal supply and evacuation were ensured.

By December 21 the *front* transfer base and the 50th Army's base were located at Khanino station. There were no supply structures. The Khanino station's anti-aircraft defense consisted of one battery.

On December 18 the 50th Army disposed of the following ammunition, fuel and food supplies: 1.5 combat loads of mortar rounds, different types of artillery shells—1-1.5 combat loads, 1.3 refuelings, 10,275,000 rifle rounds, and four day's rations. Aside from this, there was also up to one combat load and one fuel load in the army field depots. Thus there was sufficient ammunition, fuel and food to conduct the operation.

However, the delivery of supplies in winter conditions, particularly over dirt roads, was made difficult in a number of cases, which could not but be reflected in the supply of units as they moved rapidly forward.

Aviation support for the operation was mainly conducted according to that of the Tula operation. The basing for aviation supporting the left-wing armies' combat operations remained unchanged. The 50th Army's offensive would be supported by the same air formations as during the Tula operation. The increase in air power on the Sasovo and Kirsanovo airfields should be noted. A portion of the air assets was subsequently transferred to the Tula area in January 1942, where it began its combat activity.

The operation's first stage (December 17-25 1941). The completion of the 50th Army's regrouping and the offensive along a new operational direction up to the arrival at the line of the Oka River and the beginning of the fighting for Kaluga

The 50th Army's Offensive after the occupation of the jumping-off point by the Mobile Group until its arrival at the southern outskirts of Kaluga

By the close of December 17 units of the mobile groups had concentrated in the area designated by the army order and during the night of December 17-18 moved out along the route Voskresenskoe-Dubna-Khanino. Units of the 154th Rifle Division moved in the first echelon, with the 31st Cavalry and 112th Tank divisions in the second. The group's night march was carried out in secret, out of contact with the enemy.

By 1400 on December 19 the units of the mobile group, while destroying small groups from the Fascists' 296th Infantry Division, reached the wooded area in the Pleshkovo-Lisovo-Butyrki area (all locales 3-5 km north of Khanino), from which, following a short bivouac, they continued their movement toward Kaluga. By 2000 of the same day the group, using the woods for cover, crossed the line Mitinka-Alekseevskoe (10 km northwest of Khanino), aiming for the southern approaches to Kaluga. While continuing to move in the designated direction, by the close of December 20 the mobile group had reached the line Puchkovo-Nekrasovo-Sekitovo (all locales 2 km south of Kaluga), and under the cover of night began to prepare a blow against Kaluga from the south.

Thus the mobile group, in the course of three and a half days, covered about 90 km and basically was successfully able to carry out the first part of its assignment—to quickly reach the southern approaches to Kaluga.

However, on the army's right flank events developed differently. Units of the 258th Rifle Division, overcoming the stubborn resistance of the enemy's 31st Infantry Division along the Titovo-Lobzha sector, advanced extremely slowly. In the area Titovo-Stolbova-Gryaznovo-Makarovo the

German-Fascist troops had prepared an all-round defense on time, having transformed inhabited areas and the approaches to them into strong points with a well-organized system of mortar and artillery fire. Our head-on attacks against these strong points were unsuccessful and led to excessive losses. The division command resorted to the method of surrounding separate points and blocking them.

On the morning of December 21 the 258th Rifle Division, continuing to fight on its right flank in the area of Men'shikovo-Verkhovoe (3 km northwest of Titovo), and with its left flank and center was encircling the enemy group in the area of Kut'kovo (3 km southwest of Titovo)-Stolbova. By the close of December 21 units of the 258th Rifle Division had captured the listed locales and were developing the offensive to the northwest. The German-Fascist units put up especially stubborn resistance from the Gryaznovo area, holding the division's offensive with the support of artillery, mortars, and tanks.

By this time the *front* command, taking into account the slowing of the offensive by the 50th Army's right flank, once again transferred the 340th Rifle Division to the army. The division had the task of assisting the 258th Rifle Division. By the morning of December 21 the 340th Rifle Division took Srednyaya station and Pushkino after a fight (8 km west of Aleksin), having moved one regiment forward to assist the 258th Rifle Division in the direction of Pozdnyakovo.

The 290th Rifle Division, attacking to the west, reached the line Drokovo-Biketovka (6 km south of Drokovo) after fighting, having moved one regiment forward to take Krapivna. By the close of December 18 the division, having crushed the enemy's resistance, took Butyrki, Bogdanovo (both locales 3 km northeast of Khanino), and Khanino station and had begun the fight for Khanino. The latter's garrison consisted of units from the 248th Infantry Regiment.

During the first half of December 19 the division's units, having thrown the enemy out, captured Khanino and were developing the offensive to the northwest of it. Upon reaching the line Polevoi-Masalovo-Glubokoe (5 km west of Khanino), the 290th Rifle Division was attacked by the enemy from the Likhvin area and temporarily went over to the defensive. The army's remaining divisions, having completed their regrouping, by December 20 had reached: 217th Rifle Division—the line Zhitnya-Markovo-Andreevka (all locales 4-7 km south of Khanino), ready to continue the offensive to the west; 413th Rifle Division, while continuing to move in the direction specified in army order no. 39, reached the line Sizenevo-Nikol'skie Vyselki; the 32nd Tank Brigade, while in the army commander's reserve, was located in the area Zaitsevo-Pyatnitskoe.

The neighboring 1st Guards Cavalry Corps to the left, while continuing to pursue the remains of the enemy's *Grossdeutschland* Regiment, and of the 3rd Panzer and 167th Infantry divisions, by the morning of December 20 had captured Krapivna and Arkhangel'skoe. The corps subsequently was developing the offensive to the west from these areas.

Thus in the course of the 50th Army's offensive during December 17-21 the following operational-tactical situation developed.

The army's right flank (340th and 258th rifle divisions) was being pinned down by an enemy group from the area of Gryaznovo, Verkhovoe, and Stolbova and was moving forward slowly.

On the army's left flank the 290th Rifle Division, as a result of the enemy's pressure from the Likhvin area was forced to temporarily go over to the defensive. The 217th and 413th rifle divisions were moving echeloned to the rear and left.

Simultaneously, an operational success was achieved along the army's center. The mobile group had surged forward and advanced 20-25 km ahead of the army's front and reached the approaches to Kaluga. The mobile group's success, first of all, was weakening the enemy's defensive strength against the army's right flank, and, second, correspondingly was influencing the firmness of his position along the Oka River.

The blow by the 1st Guards Cavalry Corps that followed to the left in the direction of Odoevo, its capture on December 22, and the development of the offensive to the Oka River, removed the threat from Likhvin and Cherepet', having exerted a favorable influence on the outcome of the Kaluga operation.

The start of the Mobile Group's Battle for Kaluga and the offensive's continuation by the 50th Army's remaining divisions

On the morning of December 21 the 50th Army's mobile group began its attack on Kaluga, operating from three directions: from Puchkovo, from Nekrasovo, and from the direction of Sekiotovo through Romodanovo (2 km north of Sekiotovo). The first units to break into the town from the southeast were from the 31st Cavalry Division, the 154th Rifle Division's 473rd Rifle Regiment, and tanks from the 112th Tank Division. The enemy put up stubborn resistance; units of the 20th Panzer Division, transferred from the Mozhaisk area, took part in the fighting. There were also reinforced units from the 137th Infantry Division, a motorcycle battalion, and other small German units. Our troops, having burst into the city, were soon cut off by the enemy and became involved in street fighting while surrounded. The fighting continued all day and the army headquarters had no information about the battle's progress.

Along the front of the army's remaining divisions by this time the following combat events had been taking place. The neighboring 340th Rifle Division on the right continued attacking to the west along the north bank of the Oka River with two regiments. One regiment, while bypassing Dugna in fighting from the south, was attacking as before in the direction of Pozdnyakovo. During the first half of December 23 the 340th Rifle Division's main forces reached the line Komola-Polivanovo (5 km southeast of Komola), with its left-flank regiment along the southern bank of the Oka River.

The 258th Rifle Division, moving forward under heavy fighting, by 1100 on December 23 was bypassing Makarovo from the northeast. Each inhabited area had to be taken in fighting.

The 290th Rifle Division, following a temporary defense along the line Polevoi-Masalovo-Glubokoe, went over to the attack on the morning of December 21, having thrown its forward detachments to the eastern bank of the Oka River along the sector Korekozevo-Golodskoe-Dobroe. The enemy was not particularly active; a local counterattack by small groups from the area of Cherepet' and the area of Ushatovo and Ageevo (4-6 km northeast of Cherepet') was successfully repulsed.

By December 24 the 217th Rifle Division had reached the eastern bank of the Oka River along the sector Korekozevo-Golodskoe-Mekhovo and was preparing to attack toward Peremyshl'. The latter had been transformed by the enemy into a powerful strong point and was defended by units of the 137th Infantry Division and small units from other German units.

The 413th Rifle Division was fighting for Odoevo with one regiment, while its main forces were developing the offensive in the direction of Okorokovo. By the morning of December 21 two regiments of the division had occupied the line Govorenki-Novo-Arkhangel'skii-Apukhtino (all locales 4-10 km north and northwest of Odoevo), having occupied these locales. One of the 413th Rifle Division's regiments was continuing the fight for Odoevo. The presence of Odoevo on the division's left flank, occupied by the remnants of units from the enemy's 112th and 167th infantry divisions, was hindering its movement to the west.

In the case at hand, the maneuver by Gen. Belov's 1st Guards Cavalry Corps on Odoevo and its capture by the end of December 22 had great significance.[12] The corps subsequent arrival at the Oka River (south of Likhvin), to the west of Odoevo would put it on the flank of the enemy's

12 The capture of Odoevo by the 1st Guards Cavalry Corps is fully narrated in the description of the Belev-Kozel'sk operation.

Likhvin-Cherepet' group, forcing it to lessen its pressure on Khanino. Besides this, the maneuver would free up the 413th Rifle Division for a movement to the west and would enable us to transfer one of the 217th Rifle Division's regiments to the area of Vorotynsk station for the deep envelopment of Kaluga from the southwest and west and to transfer all of the 290th Rifle Division in the direction of Pushkino for the fight for Kaluga from the southeast. The removal of this threat to the 50th Army's left flank made it easier for the 258th Rifle Division to carry out its assignment to combat the enemy group in the Makarovo area and enabled us to send the division to the Romodanovo-Zhelybino (6 km west of Kaluga) area in order to envelop Kaluga from the west.

The development of the offensive by the 50th Army's units up to December 25

In the period following December 22 combat activities on the 50th Army's front were developing as follows. Taking into account the hitch in the right flank of the army's movement toward Kaluga, the *front* command, in an order of December 24, ordered the 50th Army commander to direct the 340th Rifle Division along the Kaluga-Tarusa high road with the objective of enveloping Kaluga from the northeast.

In accordance with the new assignment, the 340th Rifle Division, overcoming the enemy's resistance in strength of up to two infantry regiments, reinforced with artillery and mortars, during December 23-24 was attacking to the west and somewhat to the northwest. By the close of December 25 the division had reached the line of Zhelyabuzhskii station-Nekrasovo-Ivashevo-Novoloki (all three locales 8-16 km south of Zhelyabuzhskii station), having captured these places.

One of the 258th Rifle Division's regiments continued fighting in the area of Zabelino and Makarovo; the division's other two regiments were moving into the area southwest of Kaluga: one regiment passed through Yelovka on the morning of December 24, while the other passed through Zyabki at noon on the same day. Both regiments' movement took place without any serious collisions with the enemy.

Units of Gen. Popov's mobile group continued stubborn street fighting in Kaluga. In the course of December 22 alone up to 500 Fascist soldiers and officers were killed and several enemy aircraft were shot down. During December 23-24 the street fighting continued. The remains of the enemy's 131st and 137th infantry divisions[13] put up stubborn resistance. During the course of these two days up to 1,900 German-Fascist soldiers and officers were killed. The 154th Rifle Division's 437th Regiment, while breaking through to the units cut off in Kaluga, killed up to 200 Germans while taking the Puchkovo strong point (2 km south of Kaluga).

Units of the 290th Rifle Division, having concentrated by the end of December 22 in the area Koshelevka-Novoselki-Pleshkovo (all locales 8-9 km north of Khanino), moved out from there on the morning of December 23 with the mission of reaching the eastern outskirts of Kaluga for a blow against the city in conjunction with the 340th Rifle Division.

By the morning of December 24 the 290th Rifle Division captured Akhlebnino and Nikol'skoe in fighting and during the day was fighting for Pushkino. By the end of the day the division, having crushed the Germans' resistance, captured Pushkino and was moving into the Turynino area.

The 217th Rifle Division during December 24-25 was waging a stubborn fight for Peremyshl', which it captured by the end of December 25. During the night of December 25-26 this division, while pursuing the enemy's isolated units, was moving to the northwest.

13 This division's rear services and other units were evidently at this time along the 49th Army's sector in the area of Peremyshl'.

The 413th Rifle Division, after Gen. Belov's 1st Guards Cavalry Corps had captured Odoevo, was attacking in the direction of Cherepet' and Likhvin, meeting hardly any resistance. The remains of the enemy's 296th Infantry and 29th Motorized divisions were operating in the latter area. Defending along the Oka River, the Germans were putting up stubborn resistance, trying to hold this line. Intelligence noted the enemy's transfer of part of his reserves to the Peremyshl'-Likhvin sector, so as to delay our offensive. The enemy's transfer of reinforcements to strengthen the Kaluga axis was simultaneously noted. On the army commander's orders, the commander of the 413th Rifle Division, by avoiding head-on attacks, had encircled Likhvin with two regiments and moved the third toward Gordikovo. Units of the 413th Rifle Division, following stubborn street fighting, crushed the enemy's resistance and on December 26 occupied Likhvin. Upon capturing Likhvin, the 413th Rifle Division continued to develop the offensive to the northwest.

Thus the 50th Army's combat activities in the operation's second stage unfolded in basically two directions: a) in Kaluga itself and along the approaches to the city from the east, southeast and southwest and, b) along the Oka on the sector Peremyshl'-Likhvin. Both axes represented a single whole for the enemy. The enemy's main task was to delay our offensive along this line.

The character of the 50th Army's activities, from the point of view of the operation's further planning, was quite colorfully expressed in the army commander's bold decision to direct his left-flank divisions (413th and 217th) in the general direction of Uteshevo (36 km west of Kaluga) for a deep envelopment of Kaluga from the southwest and west and in directing, in accordance with the orders of the *front* commander, the 340th Rifle Division to bypass Kaluga from the northeast so as to attack it from that direction. The fight for Likhvin by blocking it with units from the 413th Rifle Division is deserving of attention, as is the 258th Rifle Division's elimination using the same method of certain enemy strong points in the area of Makarovo, Titovo, Stolbova, and Gryaznovo.

At this stage the control by the army commander of the mobile group presented significant difficulties. From his command post (at first deployed in Khanino and then moved along the axis Khanino-Yelovka-Kaluga) the army commander did not always find it possible to follow the course of the developing events in order to direct them toward the proper goal.

The departure of the army's chief of staff for Kaluga at the height of the fighting for the town was correct, although on the condition that the necessary personnel are left at army headquarters to command the army's other units.

In the period following December 25 the army conducted the second stage of the Kaluga operation, the completion of which coincided with the beginning of a new stage in the *front* operation. The 50th Army, in conjunction with the 43rd and 49th armies, and the 1st Guards Cavalry Corps, began to carry out the *front's* order to surround and destroy the enemy's Myatlevo-Kondrovo-Yukhnov group.

The 10th Army's and 1st Guards Cavalry Corps Belev-Kozel'sk Operation

The situation on the 10th Army's and neighbors' front by the beginning of the operation

After the 10th Army's arrival at the Plava River and the occupation of Plavsk there were no significant changes in the army's distribution of forces. The army's troops, continuing to pursue the enemy, by the end of December 20 occupied the following positions: the 328th Rifle Division was moving on the sector Korenevka-Bulandino (13 km southwest of Krapivna), which it reached on December 21; the 323rd Rifle Division, following the capture of Plavsk, occupied its assigned zone along the sector Krekshino-Volkhonshchino, from which it was moving into the area Chastye Kolodezi (6 km west of Krekshino).

The 326th Rifle Division was concentrated in the area of Plavsk:

The 239th Rifle Division was on the march and by the close of December 20 its main forces' leading units were passing through Sorochinka;

The 324th Rifle Division, moving in the army's second echelon, was concentrated in the area Lyapishchevo-Polozovo-Rzhavo, and the 330th Rifle Division in the area Ivanovka-Skorodumovo-Spasskoe;

The 41st Cavalry Division from the morning of December 20 was fighting for Kamynino, to which the 57th Cavalry Division was arriving during the second half of the day;

The 75th Cavalry Division had by 1200 on December 20 passed through Ponomarevo and Urusovo (7 km south of Plavsk on the Plava River).

The neighboring 1st Guards Cavalry Corps on the right by this time had cleared the line of the Plava River along the sector Krapivna-Danilovka and was moving to the west with the objective of taking Odoevo.

The Southwestern Front's neighboring 61st Army to the left, while attacking to the west had reached by December 20 the line Teploe (20 km southeast of Plavsk)-Ogarevo-Milyuki-Arkhangel'skoe, having along its right flank and the boundary with the 10th Army, the 142nd Independent Tank Battalion, the 91st Cavalry and 348th Rifle divisions, which were fighting near Teploe. As before, the 10th and 29th motorized divisions and the remains of the 112th Infantry Division were operating along the 10th Army's front; according to certain reports, units of the 56th Infantry Division were here as well. These enemy groups, while hanging on to intermediate defense lines, were falling back to the west.

In essence, the German-Fascist command's plan remained unchanged. Having suffered a defeat along the lines Stalinogorsk-Yepifan', Dedilovo-Bogoroditsk, and Krapivna-Plavsk, the enemy was withdrawing his troops to the Oka River, seeking to consolidate along it and halt our offensive. The most powerful defensive position along the Oka River was the town of Belev, which the enemy sought to hold at all costs. The Germans' desire to hold Belev was for the purpose of threatening the Western Front's extreme left flank with an attack and to improve the position of its Kaluga group. Besides this, Belev covered the Orel axis from the north and northeast.

The operation's matériel-technical supply

The *front* command's directive no. 026 of December 16 ordered that food supplies in the army depots be raised to seven day's rations, ammunition to 1-1.5 combat loads, and fuel and lubricants to 1.5-2 refills.

It was not possible to determine in what particular area this directive was carried out, although it seems that during December 16-20 the army was still receiving replenishment in ammunition, although there do not appear to have been particular problems in this regard, particularly during the first period of the operation. Besides, in directive no. 027 of December 22 to the *front's* supply organs, it was ordered that branches of its depots should be opened in the Tula area, which also improved the supply situation for the 10th Army. By the start of the operation an army base was deployed in the area of Uzlovaya station and Dedilovo, with railhead field depots in the area of Yasnaya Polyana and Shchekino.

For the purpose of saving fuel, the delivery of supplies and property from the *front* depots was to be carried out along the railroad up to the railhead branches of the army depots. Delivery by auto transport at this stage was allowed only by special permission of the *front's* military council.

It was ordered that deliveries from the railhead branches of the army field depots should be carried out by division transport, for which the army command was supposed to redistribute the existing auto transport among the units, using the same supply calculations at the division level as had been the case before the Tula operation. It was difficult to carry out this demand in the 10th

Army, because instead of the authorized 922 motor vehicles in the army, by December 25 there were only 507 motor vehicles. A weak area in the army's rear services was the shortage of personnel in the army base directorate and the field depots, which were staffed at the expense of the rear directorate, which undoubtedly made organization and delivery more difficult.

The operation's first stage (December 20-26 1941). The Battle for Belev and the attack on Kozel'sk

The development of the offensive by the 1st Guards Cavalry Corps and the 10th Army up to the arrival at the line of the Oka River

After the 50th Army's turn to the west and northwest and the arrival of the 1st Cavalry Corps and 10th Army's main forces at the Plava River, the Western Front's left wing had the general task of rapidly attacking to the west, defeating the opposing German-Fascist units, having deprived them of the opportunity of consolidating along intermediate lines and holding on to the most important railroad junctions and belt roads and communications.

In the operational zone of the 10th Army and the cavalry corps the most important road and railroad junctions were: Kozel'sk, Sukhinichi, Kirov, and Lyudinovo. The Sukhinichi railroad junction and the Vyaz'ma-Bryansk belt road, which the German-Fascist troops relied on, were acquiring particular operational importance. The rapid attainment of these communications arteries by the Western Front's left wing was dictated by the overall situation.

With the loss of Sukhinichi the enemy would be deprived of a very important base for his forces, and with the cutting by our forces of the Vyaz'ma-Bryansk railroad the operational link of the two main German-Fascist groups operating against the Western and Southwestern fronts would be disrupted. However, the realization of the main objective without the elimination of the Germans' Belev and Kozel'sk defensive centers would be more difficult. The Belev defense area, located along the boundary between the Southwestern and Western fronts represented a serious danger and threatened the 10th Army's left flank.

Thus the operations for capturing the Belev and Kozel'sk areas were becoming an independent operation, although an auxiliary one in relation to the overall task of the Western Front's left-wing armies—reaching the Warsaw highway and the Vyaz'ma-Bryansk lateral road.

According to the *front* directive, the 1st Guards Cavalry Corps had the mission of launching a rapid blow and forcing the Oka River along the sector Likhvin-Belev and then, turning its main forces to the northwest, take Yukhnov on December 28 and cut off the enemy's path of retreat from Kaluga and Maloyaroslavets. The capture of Kozel'sk was essentially an incidental objective, which would secure the blow in the direction of Yukhnov. The corps was subsequently to operate toward Vyaz'ma. The 10th Army, upon capturing Belev, was to reach the Kozel'sk area on December 27, from whence it would throw out mobile detachments toward Sukhinichi and carry out deep reconnaissance in the direction of Kirov and Lyudinovo.

The cavalry corps plan was laid out by the commander, Gen. Belov, to the *front* commander on December 20. It consisted of four stages: the first stage (December 20-22)—preparatory measures while on the move, with the incident capture of Odoevo; second stage (December 22-24)—the forcing of the Oka River along the sector Likhvin-Belev; the third stage (December 24-27)—getting into the enemy's rear in the area of Yukhnov and Mosal'sk, while capturing Kozel'sk along the way, and, finally; the fourth stage—fighting the enemy in the Yukhnov area. This plan was basically confirmed by the *front* command.

Thus the corps commander's plan (its first and second stages from December 20 through 24th) was calculated to a depth of up to 65 km (from the line Krapivna-Plavsk to the Oka River along the sector Likhvin-Belev), which would yield an average daily rate of advance of more than 20 km.

The highest rate of advance and depth of penetration into the enemy's line would come during the third stage (December 24-27). The cavalry corps blow during the third stage was calculated to a depth of more than 100 km (from the line Likhvin-Belev to Yukhnov), which would yield an average daily rate of advance of more than 25 km.

Consequently, given the wintry conditions and the resistance from an active enemy, the cavalry corps was faced with carrying out a difficult task.

The plan of the 10th Army commander, Gen. Golikov, consisted of quickly seizing Belev and a subsequent offensive—pursuing the enemy in the direction of Sukhinichi (through Kozel'sk) and then to Kirov and Lyudinovo.

Air support for the operation by the 10th Army and 1st Guards Cavalry Corps would be provided by the same air formations as was the case during the Tula operation, with the subsequent rebasing of some air units to the Tula area.

In accordance with the *front* directives and the plans drawn up by generals Belov and Golikov, the offensive by the cavalry corps and the 10th Army would continue. However, the deadlines for carrying out these plans changed in accordance with the situation.

Just as in the 50th Army's Kaluga operation, the offensive by the 10th Army and 1st Guards Cavalry Corps in the Belev-Kozel'sk direction actually developed non-stop upon the completion of the Tula operation and grew immediately out of it. All regroupings, the issuing of orders, and operational preparations were conducted while the operation was developing, alongside the achievement of incidental tasks.

The offensive by the cavalry corps and the 10th Army after December 19 unfolded in the following manner.

The cavalry corps, having moved out at the close of December 19 from the previously-occupied line of Prishnya-Staraya Krapivenka and southwards, during December 20 attacked in a westerly direction, overcoming the resistance by the remains of the 167th Infantry and 3rd Panzer divisions, and the *Grossdeutschland* Regiment. By the close of December 20 the corps had reached the line two km west of Krapivna-Umchino-Arkhangel'skoe and had begun preparing to attack in the direction of Odoevo, with the task of taking it by the close of December 21.

The offensive by the 1st Guards Cavalry Corps for the purpose of taking Odoevo began on the morning of December 21 in the following formation. The 1st Cavalry Division was attacking along the right flank from the Zherdevo area in the direction of Chantsevo and Zhemchuzhnikovo, with the task of taking Odoevo from the east.

The 2nd Guard Cavalry Division was attacking from the line Umchino-Terenino (both locales 3 km south and southeast of Krapivna) in the direction of Bashevo, Nikol'skoe, and Obalduevo, with the task of taking Odoevo from the south.

The 322nd Rifle Division, which was on the guards cavalry corps left flank, had the task of attacking from the Akhangel'skoe area to the west, securing from the south the maneuver by the 2nd Guards Cavalry Division. The cavalry group's headquarters was in Prudy.

Gen. Belov's attacking group encountered stubborn enemy resistance all along the front. As a result, our units, successively throwing the Germans out of the inhabited areas, moved forward while fighting throughout December 21. No less stubborn fighting took place during December 22. By the close of December 22 the 1st Guards Cavalry Division, by a blow from the east, and the 2nd Guards Cavalry Division, by a blow from the south and southwest, captured Odoevo, ejecting from the town units of the Germans' 112th and 167th infantry divisions. The 322nd Rifle Division by this time had reached the area of Zhestovoe.

Following the capture of Odoevo, units of the 1st Guards Cavalry Corps pursued the retreating enemy to the west and by 1600 on December 24 reached the eastern bank of the Oka River along the sector Kipet'-Moshchena-Gorbunovo. During this period the group was reinforced by the 41st, 57th, and 75th cavalry divisions, which up until December 23 had comprised an independent group under a single command, but as a result of its small numbers and poor armament the group did not play a significant role. Thus the *front* command considered it necessary to transfer all three divisions to the group of the commander of the 1st Guards Cavalry Corps.[14]

During the latter half of December 24 all three cavalry divisions (41st, 57th, and 75th), after fighting the remains of the enemy's 112th Infantry Division along the line Pokrovskoe-Belyi Kolodez', moved out to the area Krutoe-Romanovo-Rakhleevo (25 km southeast of Belev), having fallen behind the cavalry corps main units by 10-12 km.

It should be added here that the march of the corps itself after the capture of Odoevo was carried out under conditions of relatively weak enemy resistance. A critical shortcoming in the organization of the group's offensive by the corps commander was the fact that during the period of its advance following December 24 communications between the corps and the 50th and 10th armies was often lost, as was the case with the *front* as well.

During the December 21-24 period units of the 10th Army, while overcoming the resistance of small enemy rearguard units, reached by the latter half of December 24 the following areas:

324th Rifle Division—the area Krasnokol'e-Sonino-Kostino (all locales 8-10 km southwest of Odoevo). There were almost no enemy units along the division's front, because at this time units of the 1st Guards Cavalry Corps were located ahead.

The 330th Rifle Division, upon approaching the line Yamontovskii-Arsen'evo station, was fighting the remains of the 112th Infantry Division and, it was assumed, units of the enemy's 56th Infantry Division. Behind the 330th Rifle Division along the Ryazantsevo-Astapovo road (2 km north of Arsen'evo station), the 326th Rifle Division was moving up. The 239th Rifle Division was concentrated in the area Odoevo-Krupets-Brusna (both locales 5 km northwest and west of Odoevo), with the task of arriving the following day at the Oka River in the area of Moshcheno. The army's remaining units, being echeloned, were located behind.

During the offensive by the 10th Army and the 1st Guards Cavalry Corps from December 20 to the 24th the corps reached the Oka River and began fighting with those enemy units covering the withdrawal. The 10th Army's units, having fallen behind by 10-15 km, were echeloned back to the left. This situation can be explained, first of all, by the fact that the Southwestern Front's neighboring 61st Army to the left had fallen behind and forced its neighbor to the right to divert its attention to its left flank, where the remains of the Germans' 112th Infantry Division were resisting. In particular, the 61st Army's right-flank 342nd Rifle Division was fighting the enemy by 1200 on December 26 along the line Belyi Kolodez'-Chermoshny, and it was only by the end of that day that it began to arrive at a line approximately to the south of Arsen'evo. The 61st Army's remaining divisions at that time were echeloned behind the 342nd Rifle Division. Second, this situation is explained by the conditions of attacking in the 10th Army itself, whose rear service condition was not very good. The most singular combat episode during the period under review was the capture by the 1st Guards Cavalry Corps of Odoevo. This, as we saw, favorably influenced the 50th Army's offensive.

The beginning of the fighting for Belev

The *front* command, in its directive no. 125/op of December 24 mentioned previously, assigned the 10th Army the following task: to reach with its main forces by the end of December 27 the area of Kozel'sk, while at the same time pushing forward mobile detachments in the direction of

14 In a directive by the *front* commander of December 20 all three cavalry divisions (just as the 322nd and 328th rifle divisions) are mentioned as being attached to the cavalry corps, although their actual attachment to Gen. Belov's group was carried out only during this period (December 23).

Sukhinichi for the purpose of capturing that town. Simultaneously, the 10th Army was to carry out deep reconnaissance in the direction of Sutoki, Kirov, and Lyudinovo.

After the arrival of the 1st Guards Cavalry Corps units along the line of the Oka River and the 10th Army along the line Krupets-Krasnokol'e (7 km southwest of Odoevo)-Arsen'evo station, their subsequent offensive was to develop as follows.

During the night of December 24-25 the corps' main forces were regrouping to the western bank of the Oka River for the purpose of continuing the offensive to the northwest. The 1st Guards Cavalry Division, having crossed the Oka River on December 25, was fighting with an enemy engineering battalion and other units along the line Likhvin station-Peskovatskoe (3 km west of Likhvin station)-Myzhbor, where up to a company of Germans was destroyed.

At 1500 on December 25 the 2nd Guards Cavalry Division crossed with its main forces near Nikolo-Gastun' (1 km north of Moshchena), while its forward detachments were fighting along the line Senino 1-Sergeevka. The 75th Cavalry Division was subordinated to the commander of the 2nd Guards Cavalry Division and was attacking in the direction of Senino-2 (1 km south of Senino-1).

By the end of December 25 the 57th Cavalry Division had concentrated in the area of Nikolo-Gastun', Moshchena, Blizhnyeye Rusanovo, having been subordinated to the commander of the 1st Guards Cavalry Division.

The 9th Tank Brigade was in Krapivna, where it was putting itself in order and repairing its equipment.

The 41st Cavalry Division remained in the corps commander's reserve and was in the Kipet'-Pereslavichi area.

The 332nd Rifle Division had begun fighting the enemy on the approaches to Belev, while the 328th Rifle Division (both divisions were part of the 1st Guards Cavalry Corps) was moving toward the Oka River from the area Bogdanovo-Streshnevo.

The *front* headquarters knew nothing about the 10th Army's situation during the night and day of December 25 as a result of a communications disruption. The radio worked intermittently and it proved impossible to restore communications by aircraft due to the snowstorm and snowfall. Only by the morning of December 26 did it become known that the army's divisions were continuing to attack to the west, with the mission of reaching the line Gorki-Kudrino-Maslovo-Rovna. By the close of December 26 the 10th Army's units had reached the following lines:

239th Rifle Division—Kryukovka-Zenovo (both locales on the west bank of the Oka River, north of Belev)-Moshchena;

324th Rifle Division—Kudrino-Snykhovo;

330th Rifle Division—Georgievka-Gorbunovo-Barovka (on the eastern bank of the Oka River, northeast of Belev);

The 325th Rifle Division was moving to the line Kurakovo-Temryan', having in front the 322nd Rifle Division, which was beginning the fight for Belev; by December 27 the 325th Rifle Division, together with the 323rd and 326th divisions, was concentrated in the army's second echelon in the area Semenovskoe-Boloto-Pustynovka-Streshnevo (all locales 15 km east of Belev).

On the morning of December 27 the fighting began for Belev, which had been transformed by the enemy into a powerful fortified defensive area with a well-developed system of obstacles, and packed with a large amount of artillery, mortars, and machine guns. The approaches to the city were mined along a number of sectors.

With the arrival of units of the 1st Guards Cavalry Corps and the 10th Army at the Oka River and to the west along the sector to the north of Belev, the first stage of the Belev-Kozel'sk operation was coming to an end. The enemy had been thrown back from the line of the Oka River north of Belev, but was holding on stubbornly to the town, covering the Orel axis. Simultaneously, the Germans, while falling back to the west, were trying to hang on along other defensive positions (at Kozel'sk, Sukhinichi, and others).

Seen in this light, the arrival of the 10th Army and 1st Guards Cavalry Corps to the west of the Oka River had a positive effect not only on the operation's of the left wing's armies, but of the entire *front*, creating favorable prerequisites for achieving the *front* operation's subsequent tasks.

The left-wing armies, in concluding the tasks set out by the *front* for the period of the counteroffensive was simultaneously getting ready to carry out new *front* assignments as a whole. This was one of the characteristic features of the operations conducted during the defeat of the Germans around Moscow. This feature was dictated by the situation which had come about on the front and which demanded an unremitting offensive.

Conclusions regarding the operations of the left wing 's armies during December 6-25 1941

With the arrival of the Western Front's left-wing armies along the line west of Sukhinichi, east of nedel'noe and Kaluga and then south along the Oka River as far as Belev, an important period in the *front* operation—the counteroffensive—was coming to a close.

The overall results of the left-wing armies' counteroffensive are as follows. During the period December 6-25 the armies, while fighting a powerful enemy in conditions of a snowy winter, covered the following distances. 49th Army—40-60 km (the latter figure is for the left-flank divisions), with an average daily rate of advance of 3-4 km. if one takes into account the fact that the army's center began its offensive on December 19 (the army's extreme right flank began it on December 24), and the left flank on December 14, then the rate of advance rises to 5-6 km per day. The 50th Army, taking into account its attack toward Shchekino during the Tula operation, advanced about 110-120 km to the line Kaluga-Likhvin, for an average daily rate of advance of 5-6 km.

The 1st Guards Cavalry Corps, having begun the offensive from the area south of Mordves, from December 6 to 25th covered a distance of about 200 km, which yielded a daily rate of advance of 8-10 km.

The 10th Army, operating along the Western Front's turning flank, attacked the most rapidly. In 20 days the 10th Army covered a distance of about 220 km, which yielded an average daily rate of advance of 10-12 km.

During the period under review the *front's* left-wing armies had to dislodge the enemy in heavy fighting from the following defensive lines and drive him from very important strong points: on the 49th Army's front from the line of the Oka and Protva rivers and from the Vysokinichi area; on the 50th Army's front from the area Kosaya Gora-Yasnaya Polyana-Shchekino, from the bend of the Upa River and further from the line of the Oka River from Kaluga to Likhvin. The most powerful enemy strong point in the 50th Army's zone of operations was Kaluga, the battle for which was decided only on December 30. The 1st Guards Cavalry Corps encountered the most powerful enemy resistance along the line Stalinogorsk-Shat' River, and then Dedilovo-Uzlovaya, and on the Plava River from Krapivna to the south. In moving from the line of the Plava River to the west the most serious fighting was for Odoevo and on the Oka River along the sector Kipet'-Moshchena.

The 10th Army drove the enemy out of Mikhailovo, threw him back from the Don River from the southern shore of the Stalinogorsk Reservoir to Yepifan', andovercame his resistance along the line Uzlovaya-Bogoroditsk-Plavsk, and the Plava River north of Arsen'evo station, and finally, from the line of the Oka River near Belev, the outcome of which was decided only on December 31.

During the operations along the Tula axis the troops of the Red Army, having liberated from the enemy several hundred inhabited areas, captured from the Germans the following equipment (not counting a large amount of military equipment destroyed): 54 tanks, 179 guns, about 300 motor vehicles, 104 mortars, 185 machine guns, about 1,000 rifles, about 2,000 shells, about 500,000 rounds of ammunition, more than 6,000 mortar rounds, more than 400 bicycles and motorcycles, six aircraft, and other equipment.

With the arrival of the *front's* left-wing armies at the line west of Vysokinichi, east of Nedel'noe and Kaluga and then to the Oka River as far as Blev, combat operations continued, remaining as bitter and active as before and being, in essence, a new stage in the *front* operation.

5

The Air Force's combat activities

The Germans began their operation to seize Moscow, lacking air superiority. The enemy was not capable of suppressing the Western Front's aviation, the complete destruction of which the German information bureau repeatedly announced.

Our forces' withdrawal to Moscow and the commitment of the Moscow Defense Zone's men and matériel into the fighting along the front brought about a significant increase in the combat strength of our air force immediately taking part in the operation, as well as our aviation's air superiority. In the first half of December the correlation of forces in the air was 1.3 to 1 in our favor (750 aircraft to 550).

By the beginning of the Red Army's counteroffensive our air strength was being partially reinforced from the High Command Reserve, while retaining approximately the same composition as before. Air groups, PVO air assets and those of the Western Front continued to be based in the same areas and had as their chief task cooperating with the ground forces along the same axes as during the defensive fighting for Moscow.

In particular, the Western Front's air assets carried out the following assignments in December: a) the destruction of the enemy's personnel and equipment; b) preventing the arrival of enemy reserves to the front; c) disrupting the enemy's communications; d) destroying railroad junctions and bridges along the main routes for the arrival of reserves and ammunition supply, and; e) covering the *front's* offensive. In the battles for Moscow our aviation was one of the important factors which made it possible to halt the Germans' further advance and inflict a defeat upon them.

The first local operation in the defeat of the Germans was the destruction of the enemy group in the area Petrovskoe-Akulovo-Tashirovo (the area north and northeast of Naro-Fominsk). After this the pursuit of the enemy began to the north of Moscow in the direction of Klin, and to the south of Moscow in the direction of Stalinogorsk.

In December our aviation, continuing to work under high stress, directed mass blows against the enemy's retreating units on the right flank along the Leningrad road from Kryukovo to Klin and along the roads leading west in the direction of Teryaeva Sloboda and Volokolamsk.

Long-range bomber aviation, in launching its blows against railroad junctions and roads, was simultaneously during the day bombing the Germans' retreating units on the left flank.

The enemy sought to evacuate his equipment as quickly as possible, particularly tanks. The roads to Klin and Teryaeva Sloboda were literally packed with retreating cars and other vehicles, and tanks. Our aviation's activities were so effective that following the Red Army's capture of Teryaeva Sloboda and Klin the road between these locales was covered with the bodies of German soldiers, vehicles and tanks destroyed by our aviation during the defensive battles for Moscow and during the Red Army's counteroffensive.

The offensive by our left-wing armies was supported by the 2nd Mixed Air Division, which was based at the Noginsk and Monino air junctions. Besides this, the Western Front's 77th Mixed Air Division and regiments from the 6th PVO Air Corps periodically took part in the fighting. The air units' actions aided the success of our offensive to a great degree.

From November 22 to December 22 our air assets operating along the Moscow direction carried out 6,450 sorties, of which 4,543 sorties (or 70%) were directed at enemy forces. In all, including PVO aviation, 11,944 sorties were carried out. 2,369 tons of bombs were dropped, and 8,360 rocket rounds and 132,605 other shells were expended.

As a result of our aviation's activity, there was destroyed, damaged and put out of action (according to approximate calculations) about 600 tanks, more than 5,000 motor vehicles, about 100 guns, and a large amount of enemy infantry.

The activities of the Germans' aviation after December 5 1941 (in connection with our troops going over to the offensive and the beginning of the enemy's withdrawal) were somewhat different. The German air force, while continuing to carry out active reconnaissance, directed its chief blows against our attacking troops, for the most part along the front line, for the purpose of disorganizing our combat formations, to delay our offensive, and to cover the retreat of his troops against blows by our aviation. During this period attacks against targets in our rear became an exception; enemy air operations against our airfields ceased. The enemy's air force were not strong enough to cope with all its tasks during this decisive period for the ground troops and thus directed its main efforts toward easing the withdrawal of its troops.

Besides this, the hard frosts and deep snow cover, and the difficulties of employing equipment in winter, as well as the lack of preparedness for servicing aircraft in winter conditions, also led to a decrease in enemy air activity. The number of his aircraft operating against the Western Front gradually fell off. Large losses forced the German command to remove some units to the deep rear in order to refit and retrain.

By the end of 1941 the myth of the German air force's "invincibility," just like the army's, was finally swept away.

Our air force played a large role in repulsing the offensive by the Fascist troops on Moscow and in their defeat during the counteroffensive.

In accordance with the development of the operational situation, the air force's efforts were directed at resolving those tasks which the command considered to be the most important at the given stage.

Of the 11,944 sorties carried out by our air force during the period from November 22 to December 22 1941, 5,510 were carried out against enemy forces, 4,164 were for covering targets and troops and for air escort, 162 were for attacks against airfields, and 674 against railroads; the remaining sorties were carried out in pursuit of other tasks.

Alongside this, one must note that the all-out offensive by the ground forces was not accompanied by a similar offensive against the German air force, despite the presence of favorable conditions for this. Such conditions were: our air force's moral and, to a certain extent, numerical superiority, and the German air force's insufficient preparation for operations in winter conditions.

An organized battle for air superiority by means of destroying enemy aircraft on their airfields was not carried out. This enabled the German command to withdraw its air assets into the rear and preserve their strength, which told later in the course of our offensive. This enabled the enemy to carry out aerial reconnaissance, which the German command could use in organizing its defensive operations.

Our air force, in seeking to achieve the most important and immediate tasks, upon which our victory on the battlefield depended, was unable to simultaneously exert a powerful influence throughout the entire depth of the enemy front (by means of disrupting supply deliveries and preventing evacuation, etc.).

Along with this, the fluid operational situation demanded great flexibility in air control. Our air force often had to act "on call," based upon the day's demands, and even on the demands of the moment, in order to achieve the greatest effectiveness in its actions.

6

Rear area organization and supply

In the beginning of December the level of the Western Front's matériel supply (see table IV/6.3) was higher than in the middle of November. The Western Front had among the more commonly-used kinds of ammunition 2-3 combat loads, 5-6 fuel refills, and 10-12 days' rations. The greater part of these supplies (4/5 of the ammunition, and 2/3 of the fuel and food) were located in the army bases.

Such a distribution of supplies was favorable in case of an offensive. Alongside this, the insufficient and rapidly-expiring supplies from the *front* bases in the first days of December (by December 6 1941 supplies of the more common types had diminished to 0.1-0.2 combat loads, 0.6 refills of gasoline, and 1.5 day's supply of flour) troubled the *front* command.

The *front's* rear directorate, in its report of December 6, signaled Moscow about the threatening exhaustion of supplies in its bases. "The delivery of ammunition, fuel, food, and forage according to the center's orders is proceeding extremely slowly and does not satisfy the armies' growing needs."

The depth of the *front* and army rear areas and the location of their bases fully satisfied the task of materially supporting an offensive operation.

The Western Front's rear and supply by the start of the offensive were organized in accordance with rear directive no. 025 of December 3 1941. The *front's* rear boundary remained as before. Only the 49th Army's boundary, because of the enemy's advance in the direction of Ryazan' and Kashira, had to be changed: the army rear supply boundary was moved somewhat back, and the *front* distribution station was switched from Ryazan' to Kustarevka station (75 km east of Shilovo), and on December 8 was moved to Sasovo station (50 km east of Shilovo).

Larger changes were instituted in the majority of the armies' rear organization. However, these came about not because of the rear's restructuring in accordance with new operational tasks, but due to the radical changes in the basing conditions, the transfer of newly-formed armies to the *front*, and the disruption in the organization of the 50th Army's rear.

The 30th Army's right rear boundary followed the *front's* operational boundary, while the left was along the line Moshnino-(excluding) Rogachevo-(excluding) Tatishchevo, and further along the army's operational boundary. The army was allotted the railroad sector Ryazantsevo station-Moshnino for organizing its basing purposes. It was ordered to deploy an army base in the area of Berendeevo station and the field depots' forward branches in the area of Savelovo and Taldom.

The 1st Army's boundary on the left was the line Kirzhach-Ashukino-Chernaya, Kamenka. The railroad section Aleksandrovka-(excluding) Sofrino was set aside for basing purposes; it was ordered to deploy the army base in the area Aleksandrov-Buzhaninovo-Zagorsk.

The 20th Army's boundary on the left was (excluding) Sonino-Ivanteevka-Chernaya Gryaz' and then the army's operational boundary. The army received the railroad sector Sofrino-(excluding) Moscow for its basing purposes. Before this base was organized the army was supplied from the *front* depots located in Moscow.

The 16th Army's left-flank boundary ran along the line Gorodishche-Noginsk-Lukino-Babushkin-Pavshino-Rozhdestveno, and then along the army's operational boundary. The army was allotted the railroad sector Mamontovka-(excluding) Moscow, and the Mytishchi-Monino branch line basing purposes. The army was ordered to deploy an army base with a small amount of supplies along the sector Shchelkovo-Bolshevo. The army was authorized to receive all necessary supplies from the *front's* Moscow depots, using its own auto transport to deliver them.

The 5th Army's right-flank boundary was the line Pavlovskii Posad-Zheleznodorozhnyi-Kapotnya-Troparevo-Nemchinovo; the left-flank boundary was Zaponor'e-Il'inskoe-Biryulevo-Vnukovo, and further along the army's operational boundaries. These boundaries, the presence of which complicated the rear organization of not only the 5th Army, but the neighboring armies as well, were necessary so that Moscow could be removed from the army rear area.

The army received the following railroads sectors for organizing it basing: Orekhovo-Zuevo-Zheleznodorozhnaya station-Lyubertsy; Bronnitsy-Kratovo-Butovo-Podol'sk, and Vnukovo-Alagino. The army was ordered to deploy a base along the sector Kurovskoe-Gzhel' and its field depots' forward branches along the railroad sectors Rastorguevo, Domodedovo and Butovo-Podol'sk.

The 43rd Army's left-flank boundary was the line Stepanshchino-Vel'yaminovo-Lopasnya, and then along the army's operational boundary. The railroad sectors Voskresensk-Bronnitsy, Domodedovo-Vel'yaminovo, and Podol'sk-Lopasnya were set aside for organizing the army's basing. The army was ordered to deploy an army base along the sector Voskresensk-Bronnitsy, and its field depots' forward branches along the sectors Domodedovo-Vel'yaminovo-Podol'sk-Lopasnya.

The 49th Army left-flank boundary (together with the 50th Army) was the line (excluding) Stupino-(excluding) Priluki-(excluding) Shul'gino. The army was allotted the railroad sectors Khoroshevo-Voskresensk-Zhilevo-Mikhnevo (together with the 50th Army) and Lopasnya-Serpukhov-Shul'gino for organizing the army's base. The army was ordered to deploy a base in the area Khoroshevo-Voskresensk-Bogdanovka, with its field depots' forward branches in the areas of Mikhnevo-Zhilevo and Sharapova Okhota-Tarusa.

With the 10th Army's rear-area subordination to the Western Front and its arrival on the line of the 50th Army, a *front* rear order of December 8 designated the 50th Army's left-wing rear boundary as the line (excluding) Spassk-Ryazanskii-(excluding) Mikhailov-(excluding) Uzlovaya station. The 50th Army was allotted the railroad sector Kolomna-Ryazan', along with the railroad branches to Ozery and Zaraisk for the organization of its basing.

The army was ordered to deploy a temporary base with a small amount of supplies in the area Stupino-Kashira, with the field depots' forward branches in the Tula area. Actually, the army received the greater part of its supplies along the Kursk railroad and the Serpukhov road; the field depots' forward branches were the army's base.

Until the middle of December the 10th Army did not have its own base, but was supplied from the field depots' forward branches toward Sasovo station.

Auto transport had been wearing out over the fall and a part of the vehicles was in need of or actually undergoing repairs. Besides this, as a result of the *front's* rapid numerical growth the shortage of auto transport was felt, mainly ZIS-5 vehicles and fuel canisters. The availability of *front* auto transport by the beginning of the operation and in its middle stage is shown in the table below.

Given the *front's* average daily needs in matériel supply, the weight of which was determined at 8,000-10,000 tons, the existing auto transport with a lift capacity of 40,000 tons, was fully capable of guaranteeing the timely delivery of everything necessary to the troops. The army bases' proximity to the front and the presence of a well-developed network of railroads and roads simplified and eased the supply problem.

In a modern operation, particularly an offensive one, auto transport is necessary not only for the delivery of matériel supply to the troops. During an offensive the volume of operational tasks reaches significant proportions; a growing numbe of vehicles are siphoned off to service repair-reconstruction work. Alongside this, with the movement of the troops forward they become more removed from their army bases, the delivery and evacuation lines become longer, and the delivery conditions become worse. In order to guarantee the uninterrupted supply of the attacking troops and the rapid restoration of the roads on territory liberated from the enemy, it is necessary to calculate and prepare additional transportation means.

Table IV/6.1 Availability of Technical State of the *Front's* Auto Transport as of December 6 and 15, 1941

					Undergoing Repairs			
Vehicle Type	**Authorized**		**Present**		**Major Repairs**		**Routine Repairs**	
	by 12/6	by 12/15	by 12/6	by 12/15	by 12/6	by 12/15	by 12/6	by 12/15
GAZ-AA	19,042	24,119	18,905	19,857	444	538	1,388	1,169
ZIS-5	20,435	23,503	10,595	11,327	139	329	632	615
Fuel tanks (various types)	2,445	2,689	1,228	1,557	11	–	37	45

If the *front's* supply of transportation means at first was favorable, one cannot consider their distribution among the armies and divisions to have been rational. For example, the 43rd Army, with a shallow rear and favorable road conditions, had about 4,000 supply vehicles (of these 770 were in army transport; the 30th Army, with its extended supply lines and worse supply of division auto transport, had by November 27 136 and by December 12 250 motor vehicles in its army transport. The 16th Army's auto transport situation was even worse, with only 156 motor vehicles in its army transport, of which only 13 were ZIS-5s.

As a result of the incorrect distribution of auto transport means, these vehicles were not used to full capacity in some armies, while in others the existing auto park could not meet the ongoing demands. A December 5 report from the 16th Army's rear service reported: "The lack of authorized vehicles in the 8th Guards Rifle Division, 49th and 40th rifle brigades, the 354th Rifle Division, and the 36th Rifle Brigade is resulting in breaks in supply, particularly of ammunition and food." There was a shortage of army transport in order to cope with the delivery of army cargoes and to render assistance to the divisions.

The *front's* auto reserve (about 2,000 vehicles) had the task of transporting supplies along *front* roads, guaranteeing operational deliveries and, if necessary, to assist the armies in deliveries. However, there were so many who wished to take advantage of the *front's* auto reserve that the auto-road section could not satisfy all the demands.

By the start of the offensive the *front* had four road-exploitation regiments, one road-exploitation battalion, and an independent traffic control company. Of these only the 5th Road-Exploitation Regiment, at the disposal of the *front*, and the 30th Army's 41st Road-Exploitation Regiment were more or less up to strength. The 50th Army's road-exploitation regiment shows up as an active unit for the last time in a report of December 1 1941.

The *front* was also insufficiently supported by road building units. There were only six battalions of these: two each in the 43rd and 49th armies, and one each in the 16th and 5th armies. Besides this, the NKVD's highway and road directorate, which was servicing the Western Front, there were three road construction and two bridge construction battalions.

As a result of the insufficient amount of road-exploitation units with the *front* and armies during the period under consideration, there were no fully-outfitted military roads. The best roads within the army boundaries were declared by a rear service order to be military-automobile roads. Traffic regulation posts were ordered set up along these roads, although this was often not carried out.

The influence of winter conditions on the organization of the rear and supply told later. In December there were no major snow drifts, but the hard frosts from the middle of the month made the organization of deliveries more difficult; while fueling vehicles it was necessary to first of all heat the water and oil and protect vegetables and bread from the cold. Even greater difficulties arose in evacuating the sick and wounded in empty vehicles. It was necessary to construct rest stops along the evacuation route to warm those being evacuated and to supply auto transport units with special blankets and sleeping bags.

Preparation for securing the auto transport's work in delivering and evacuating in winter conditions began in early autumn. The *front's* fuel supply sections and medical services carried out a great deal of work in this regard. The necessary supplies were prepared beforehand, instructions issued, and their study by the commanders and drivers was organized. All of this guaranteed later on the rapid solution of problems that arose.

Preparation for the matériel support of the offensive was carried out by the Supreme High Command and the main directorates. This was caused by the operational and rear situation that had arisen at the end of November—the presence in close proximity to the front of the Defense Commissariat's large depots with large amounts of matériel, Moscow's enormous resources, which supported not only the Western Front. Life fully bore out the correctness of this decision: to concentrate the preparation for the material support of the offensive in the hands of the main directorates. Nevertheless, this expedient, although it helped to keep the coming operation a secret, should not become a hard and fast rule. A number of difficulties in supplying the attacking troops, as we will see below, were a result of the lack of preparation by the *front* and army rear apparatuses for the offensive.

From the end of November the flow of reinforcements and additional units to the front increased. New armies were created in immediate proximity to the front. At the same time, a sharp change in the composition of forces was taking place. The greater number of these forces was sent to the wings, as were the newly-created armies. As a result of this, the fighting's center of gravity at this time shifted to the front's wings.

The distribution of weaponry at the disposal of the *front* in the first days of December is shown in the table below.

Table IV/6.2 The Distribution of the Western Front's Weapons by the Beginning of the Counteroffensive

Weapons	Right Wing	Center	Left Wing
Rifles	136,500	116,400	125,900
Mortars	1,670	552	1,081
Division and regimental artillery	472	230	430
122mm guns	99	38	66

One the basis of this data one may draw a conclusion as to the wings', having an active mission, important role—taking the enemy pincers in Soviet pincers. Along with this, the center armies, covering the shortest routes to Moscow, also demanded constant concern as to their supply.

Despite the fact that the rear workers devoted a lot of attention to the matériel support of the flank armies, this was insufficient to guarantee them a superiority compared with the center armies. Data about the condition of the armies' matériel supply fully confirms this.

Table IV/6.3 Matériel supply of the center and flank armies by December 5 1941

Type	On hand in combat loads, refueling, and food rations		
	Right flank armies (30th, 1st, 20th, and 16th)[1]	Center armies (5th, 33rd, and 43rd)	Left flank armies (50th, 10th, 49th, and 1st Guards Cavalry)[2]
Rifle rounds	1.8	1.8	1.7
Mortar rounds	1.2	2.8	2.6
Artillery rounds	1.4	2.5	2.1
Fuel	2.3	2.5	2
Food	4.5	6	4.5

Notes:

1 It was impossible to find data on the 20th Army's materiel supply. The supplies at the 1st Army's field depots are not counted.

2 It was impossible to find data on the materiel supply of the 20th Army and 1st Guards Cavalry Corps.

This tablet shows that by the start of the offensive the center armies were slightly better supplied than the ones on the flanks. The concern of the rear workers as to the matériel supply for the center armies was completely understandable. They covered the shortest routes to the Motherland's capital.

In conclusion, it should be said that the main directorate's measures for preparing for the forthcoming offensive and the presence of large supplies in the defense commissariat's Moscow depots, and Moscow's rich industrial and transportation resources guaranteed the counteroffensive as far as matériel was concerned. Along with this, the extremely insufficient supplies in the *front* bases negatively told (as we shall see below) on the work of supplying the attacking troops.

The depth of the *front* and army rear areas and the composition of the material means satisfied the demands of the offensive operation. Given the presence of a well-developed road network, the supplies located in the defense commissariat's depots were a maneuver reserve of material means which could be swiftly delivered to any of the *front's* wings.

The shortage of road-exploitation and road-repair units with the *front* proved to be a weak spot in the forthcoming counteroffensive, as was the absence of the precise calculation of the increase in the *front's* transportation means in accordance with the units' advance.

The greatest difficulties in organizing supply and delivery could have arisen in the 30th and 10th armies, which were poorly supplied with auto transport, while at the same time they had the longest supply lines over dirt roads.

The Western Front's offensive, which began on December 6, presented the rear workers with large and difficult tasks. It was necessary to restructure the rear work on the march and seek out necessary additional matériel means for satisfying the troops' increasing demands.

The *front's* rear, along with the energetic assistance of the main directorates, coped with its mission. During the offensive's first days measures were adopted to increase the arrival of supplies at the *front* bases and move them closer to the troops.

On orders from the chief of the rear services, the *front* quartermaster drew up a plan for deploying by December 13 forward branches of the *front's* food depots in case of the troops' advance, with six days' food rations in the following areas: Skhodnya station—for supplying the 30th and 1st armies, Nakhabino station for supply the 20th and 16th armies, and Odintsovo station for supplying the 5th Army.

It was planned to concentrate the food supplies for the 49th, 50th, and 10th armies in the Moscow area, with shipment to the armies carried out by special trains to Lukhovitsy station and Tula station.

During the organizing for the counteroffensive's supply, not only were supplies maneuvered around, but the rear organizations and transport units as well.

On the initiative of the *front's* road section, a part of the vehicle reserve was transferred closer to the *front's* left flank, which was in a less favorable situation as regards the organization of deliveries.

During the counteroffensive the volume of rear work increased significantly, and the situation and conditions changed as well. It was necessary to supply the *front's* troops somewhat more than was planned. Along with this, during the course of the troop supply work it was necessary to make some changes in the previously-adopted plan for distributing the most popular types of ammunition. Corrections were made in accordance with the armies' operational tasks and with the situation. The work carried out by the *front's* rear is shown in the following table.

An insufficient amount of transport and the absence of maneuver supplies of mortar shells and rounds for regimental and divisional artillery in the *front* depots caused great difficulties in supplying the troops with these needs. There were days when there were absolutely none of the more popular types of ammunition at the *front* command's disposal. A rear report of December 19 finished with the following conclusion: "There are absolutely no mortar shells and rounds for regimental and divisional artillery in the *front* depots."

The Main Artillery Directory came to the rescue at these critical moments, directing ammunition to the front from its Moscow-area depots, or directly from the factories in the Supreme High Command Reserve's motor vehicles. Shipments were often dispatched to the formation, and sometimes directly to the unit in need. For example, in the critical time around December 5, 3,000 bottles of flammable liquid were sent directly from the factories to the 64th Rifle Division. Rifle and machine gun rounds, hand grenades, and 122mm howitzer shells were sent from the factories and Moscow-area depots on 36 vehicles were sent to the 331st Rifle Division. On the same day shipments for the 35th, 17th, 336th, and 338th rifle divisions were sent, according to the orders placed with other directorates.

Table IV/6.4 The ammunition supply plan and its realization (in combat loads)

Weapon type	Right flank armies		Center armies		Left flank armies	
	Planned for 12/1-12/20	Delivered 12/6-12/20	Planned for 12/1-12/20	Delivered 12/1-12/20	Planned for 12/1-12/20	Delivered 12/6-12/20
Rifle rounds	0.88	0.77	0.5	0.7	0.8	1.2
50mm mortars	0.25	0.5	0.2	0.3	0.3	0.6
82mm mortars	1.5	1.5	0.36	0.7	2.2	0.85
120mm mortars	0.45	–	0.32	–	0.5	–
76mm guns	0.8	0.6	0.25	0.3	0.6	0.45
122mm guns	2	2.6	5	4.3	3.6	4.2
152mm guns	1.6	2.3	0.95	1	1	0.5

These facts; and more can be cited; testify to the flexibility of our rear and supply apparatus and its ability to renounce standard operating procedures in the interests of the cause, and to concentrate its entire efforts to supplying the troops along the decisive sector of the battle and to find the necessary means and corresponding methods for delivering them to the troops.

The situation which had arisen around Moscow in the beginning of December forced, in certain cases, the central directorates to take on the direct supply of formations, and sometimes units. However, one should not abuse this method. At the same time, no fewer shipments were sent to certain formations by order of the main directorates during more quite periods. This rendered a great service to the *front*, although it seriously overloaded the main directorates and interfered with their carrying out their main task, which was of greater significance.

The weight of ammunition actually delivered to the armies was on the average about 1,000 tons per day. This was not that great for the *front*, although in certain cases there were difficulties in delivering ammunition, particularly after December 15, when the main mass of these supplies was delivered. These difficulties were caused, for the most part, by snow drifts and, in certain cases, by the poor organization of delivery.

With the increase of men and matériel at the front the workload in the rear and the delivery routes increased, the need for well-outfitted roads and the introduction of transportation schedules for them was increasingly felt. Due to the poor organization of traffic control on December 13 the 340th Rifle Division was late in concentrating in its arrival area by 12 hours. This operational transfer was basically foiled. The 5th Guards Rifle Division ended up in an even worse situation. During the division's transfer of December 22 the Serpukhov-Volkovskoe road was deeply covered in snow, and "a traffic jam" developed, "as a result of which," as the army order stated, "the 5th Guards Rifle Division's concentration was delayed by five hours and because its units were forced to move during the daytime, and suffered needless losses in killed and wounded due to enemy air activity."

The question of attaching road-exploitation units to the *front* was put before the *front* more than once. However, only now, having experience in organizing delivery in conditions of an offensive operation, the *front* made realistic calculations. For the organization of military-vehicle roads, the *front* required one road-exploitation regiment per army and for each *front* military-vehicle road.

The *front* military council, in order to relieve the roads and free up vehicle transport for maneuvering equipment, and for operational transfers, ordered that stocks and ammunition, etc., be delivered from the *front* depots to the armies' field depots' railhead branches by railroad. Auto transport could only be used for this purpose by special authorization of the *front's* military council.

The unequal distribution of vehicle transport among the divisions led to its irrational employment and made the delivery of supplies more complicated. In order to eliminate this, the *front* ordered the armies' military councils to redistribute the existing automobile transport, so as to ensure that it was possible to deliver to each division daily ¼ of a combat load, ½ of a refuel, one day's rations, and ½ day's fodder supply to a distance of 60-70 km.

With the bringing up of divisional auto transport to full strength, the divisions were order to carry ou the delivery of troop supplies from the armies' field depots railhead branches using their own resources. In exclusive cases, units from horse-drawn transport battalions were authorized to be attached to them.

The importance and timeliness of these orders cannot be disputed, although the situation demanded the reinforcement of the flank armies with automobile transportation means, as their delivery conditions were particularly difficult.

According to comrade Stalin's orders, on December 14 1941 the 805th Auto Battalion from the Supreme High Command's auto reserve was attached to the 10th Army, and the 775th Auto Battalion to the 30th Army.

Simultaneously, in order to reduce the delivery distance along dirt roads, the *front* rear supply chief orderd that the armies' field depots' railhead branches be moved forward by December 20: 1st Army—to the area of the Klin and Solnechnogorsk stations; 20th Army—to Kryukovo and Povorovo; 16th Army—Nakhabino and Istra; 5th Army—Golitsyno and Kubinka; 33rd Army—Vnukovo and Aprelevka; 49th Army—Sharapova Okhota and Serpukhov; 50th Army—Tula, and; 10th Army—Uzlovaya, Tula, and Shchekino.

The 43rd Army's field depot's railhead branch remained as before.

On December 20 the heads of the supply directorates were ordered to increase the supplies in the army depots to seven days' food rations, one combat load of ammunition for rifles and machine guns, and 1.5 for artillery shells, 1.5 refills for combat vehicles, and two refills for transport vehicles. At the same time, mobile supplies within the units should be brought up to norms.

These orders had important consequences. The employment of army auto transport at the troop supply stage was reduced. Fewer shipments began to be made by auto transport at the army stage. If in October and the first half of November more than half of the ammunition was delivered by auto transport, then during the counteroffensive 2/3 of this material was delivered by rail transport.

One should not the concern by the *front's* military council over the timely repositioning of the *front* depots. Simultaneously, the army commanders were ordered to bring up their army and troop rear services closer to the front. This was a correct measure. The timely bringing up of the rear services and equipment during an offensive is one of the important conditions for ensuring the troops' supply. This truism, which is no less the case in our time, was not understood by all.

A 16th Army rear order of December 16 mandated that before the troops reach the line Novo-Petrovskoe-Kostrovo, the division rear services were forbidden to cross over to the western bank of the Istra Reservoir and beyond the line Povarovo-Rozhdestvenskoe. This led to the division rear services falling behind the troops by 30-35 km.

The delay in bringing up the rear services behind the attacking troops led to their falling behind as early as the period under consideration. The 229th Rifle Division's ammunition fell behind so far that "it was recognized," as stated in a report by 10th Army's assistant chief for artillery supply, "that it was more expedient to transfer them by railroad to the army's field depot and to supply the division with a combat load from a branch of the army field depot.

One of the reasons for the rear services' falling behind (particularly the armies' bases and medical services) was the slow railroad repair. For this reason on December 22 the 10th Army's depots were 100-150 km from the troops. It was necessary to deliver along damaged and country roads 400-500 tons daily, which accounted for the army's daily consumption. The delivery situation worsened as a result of the snow drifts, the absence of an organized army snow-removal system for the roads, and the untimely snow removal from them. In such conditions the existing auto transport (1,260 trucks) was unable to cope with delivery. The army command turned to the *front* with a request to restore the Tula-Kozel'sk railroad sector and to reinforce the army's transport with *front* means.

Things were no better in the 50th Army. There was an adequate supply of foodstuffs in the army's depots, but because of their distance from the front and the shortage of auto transport there were breakdowns in supplying unit. In order to avoid supply breakdowns the army quartermaster created mobile detachments, which delivered the most necessary articles—bread, meat and concentrates, to the divisional supply points.

As a result of the successful offensive by the Western Front's units, there arose the problem of quickly repairing the railroads, and the paved and dirt roads. The existing railroad and repair-restoration units, according to the *front's* calculations, guaranteed the restoration of 7-8 km of roads per day in winter conditions; actually, the sectors we were able to restore were even fewer. The bitter frosts, short days, and difficulties with bringing up construction materials, created enormous difficulties, which had to be overcome by the repair-restoration and railroad units; in the meantime, according to these same calculations, it was necessary to restore 10-12 km or roads per day in order to ensure the uninterrupted supply of the attacking units.

According to calculations made by the *front's* auto-road section, two road-construction and one bridge-construction battalions per army and for each *front* road were required to ensure the timely restoration and repair of the paved and dirt roads, in all 28 road-construction and 14 bridge-construction battalions.

During the counteroffensive the volume of supply work increased significantly. For purposes of comparison, let's take the expenditure of the most popular types of ammunition during the Western Front's defensive battle from November 16 through December 6 and compare it with expended during the counteroffensive from December 6 through the 22nd.

Table IV/6.5 The expenditure of the most important types of ammunition in the defensive and offensive battles

Weapon type	Expenditure in defensive fighting, 11/16-12/16		Expenditure in offensive fighting 12/6-12/22	
	In thousands	In combat loads	In thousands	In combat loads
Rifle rounds	24,000	about 0.4	33,600	0.66
50mm mortars	100	0.5	237	1.04
82mm mortars	92	0.9	182	1.35
107mm, 129mm mortars	32	2.6	25.6	2.15
45mm rounds	82	0.5	104	0.86
76mm regimental & divisional guns	144	1.2	185.6	1.4
122mm howitzers	72	2.2	73.6	2.3
122mm guns	11	2.0	11	2.0
152mm guns	25	2.0	16	0.75

From the table it is clear that the expenditure of ammunition during the offensive was significantly greater than during the defensive fighting.

The table shows the proportion of the different kinds of ammunition in defensive and offensive operations in the specific conditions which existed around Moscow at the end of 1941. For greater clarity let's take the expenditure of the most important types of ammunition in the defensive and offensive operations per weapon (for the same period of time).

The expenditure of rifle-machine gun rounds in the defensive operation relative to their expenditure during the offensive is 1:1.5. The expenditure of the remaining types of ammunition is as follows: 50mm mortar rounds—1:2.4; 82mm mortar rounds—1:1.75; 107mm and 120mm mortar rounds—1:0.8; 45mm artillery rounds—1:2; 76mm regimental and division artillery rounds—1:1.1; 122mm artillery rounds—1:1.2, and; 152mm artillery rounds—1:0.8.

In analyzing this data, it is necessary to take into account the peculiarities of the situation which had arisen in the beginning of December on the Western Front. The enemy had not succeeded in consolidating along the line achieved by him, as a result of which the expenditure of ammunition in the first days of the counteroffensive was less significant than one could have expected. No less influential were the winter conditions, which made it more difficult to move heavy weapons (152mm guns) and deliver round for the 107mm and 120mm mortars.

During the offensive the precise planning of supply and delivery of matériel in general, was extremely important. At the same time, the delivery of shipments from the *front* bases to the army ones, and from the latter to the troops (as the deputy rear service's commander pointed out on December 18) was often carried out without any kind of planning through the issuance of individual orders. The delayed arrival of reports, their unclear and incomplete description of the rear situation, made the rear services' work more difficult and led to haste. Only this can explain the frequent instances of deliveries to units and formations of matériel they did not require, the dispatch of auto transport to the depots for shipments that weren't there, etc. On December 17 the 796th Auto Battalion sent 17 motor vehicles to haul supplies from depot no. 1,389 in Solnechnogorsk, but the supplies weren't there and the motor vehicles, having stood in place for 11 hours, returned to their unit, having failed to carry out their assignment.

Having noted the irregular nature of this situation, the deputy *front* commander for rear services demanded in his directive that the chiefs of the supply directorates think through the question and issue the necessary instructions to their subordinates for compiling reports that sufficiently fully and clearly describe the rear's condition and to ensure their regular and timely receipt. The directive demanded that orders be sent in time to the supply organs and that the work be planned.

Conclusions

The *front's* matériel means and the supplies located in the defense commissariat's supply depots in the Moscow area ensured that the *front* could carry out its offensive tasks. The exhaustion of the supplies in the *front* bases by December 6 and their slow renewal caused a number of difficulties in the supply of the attacking units.

The most difficulties were encountered while organizing delivery to the troops. These difficulties were caused by a shortage of road-exploitation and repair-restoration units, the influence of winter conditions, the not completely rational distribution of transportation means, and defects in the organization of delivery. The lack of full-strength auto-transport units also told in a negative way as the troops moved further from their bases.

During the counteroffensive the problem of planning the rear's work for the matériel supply of the attacking troops became acute. Without this, as experience showed, it's impossible to organize the interaction of numerous rear sectors and supply organs and achieve the purposeful and economic employment of the existing means. The directives and instructions, issued by the *front* rear directorate and the central organs, demanded a radical improvement in the planning of work for matériel supply.

In conclusion, it should be said that despite the serious difficulties that arose, the *front* supply apparatus, along with the energetic aid of the center, materially aided the Red Army's counteroffensive. Breakdowns in supply did not interfere with the troops' operational-tactical activities.

7

Party-political work among the troops of the Western Front during the offensive operation around Moscow

The tasks of party-political work

In the beginning of December the military-political situation at the front changed fundamentally. The Red Army won a series of important victories over the Hitlerite hordes. The news that the troops of the Southern Front had taken Rostov and defeated Gen. Kleist's group flew around the world. Troops of the 4th Army occupied Tikhvin, eliminating the Germans' attempt to completely surround the city of Leningrad. Units of the Southwestern Front at the same time drove the German aggressors out of Yelets, inflicting upon them heavy losses in men and matériel.

During these days the troops of the Western Front wrote a new and brilliant page in the history of the Soviet people's struggle with German fascism. By December 6 the *front's* troops, reinforced with fresh reserves and equipment and upon comrade Stalin's order, went over to a counteroffensive, which was primarily directed at the enemy's shock flank groups. Within three days the Western Front's military council reported the successful operations along the front's northern and southern sectors and called upon the Red Army rank and file, its commanders and political workers, to increase the pressure on the enemy.

The appeal read as follows:

> Comrade soldiers and commanders! Use the situation at hand and don't let the enemy recover. Act decisively and boldly. Ruthlessly destroy the Fascist aggressors. We will smash the Hitlerite hordes and bury them in the snows and forests around Moscow.
>
> Death to the German aggressors!
>
> For the Motherland! For Stalin! Forward to victory!

The workers of the *front's* political directorate, the armies' political sections, and the unit political workers visited the soldiers in their dugouts and trenches and explained the content of the military council's appeal and those tasks faced by the *front's* troops. The entire rank and file greeted the appeal with great enthusiasm. Private Afanas'ev, of the 479th Rifle Regiment's destruction detachment, who had distinguished himself in battle, stated: "Comrade Stalin picked a good time for the decisive offensive and destruction of Hitler's marauding army."

On the approaches to Moscow the Western Front's troops began the complete rout of the Hitlerite army. The German command's boasting plan, which saw the encirclement and seizure of Moscow, collapsed shamefully. In breaking the enemy's resistance, our armies successfully moved forward to the west.

The Western Front's assumption of the offensive demanded from the political workers greater flexibility in the organization of party-political work. The main task, which now determined the content of the entire range of party-political work, was the necessity of the all-round development of the troops' offensive spirit, so as to complete the rout of the Germans, which had begun in the fighting around Moscow.

Party-political work was carried out along the following basic lines:

a) explain that the Germans' defeat around Moscow was the beginning of the complete rout of the German-Fascist army and that the rapid offensive by our forces and the unceasing pursuit of the enemy accelerates the liberation of millions of Soviet people groaning under the yoke of the Fascist aggressors;
b) the strengthening of the burning hatred for the Fascist monsters and the inculcation of ruthlessness toward the German occupiers;
c) the inculcation of a feeling of pride in the Red Army's combat successes and the mobilization of the rank and file to strive for the honorary guards title;
d) the propagandizing of combat experience and the instruction of the troops in the art of waging offensive operations in winter (the ability to surround and destroy the enemy's men and matériel, break through his defense, blockade inhabited areas, consolidate in captured inhabited areas, to repel enemy counterattacks, to pursue him, and to not relinquish the initiative).

Political support for carrying out the combat mission

The offensive operations significantly complicated and broadened the work of the commissar and political apparatus in the units and formations. The commissars and political organs now had to help the commander more in drawing up operational-tactical plans, in the organization of the battle, and ensuring that combat orders were carried out. The work over the combat order occupied one of the main places in party-political work.

One can basically divide the political work over the offensive combat order into three stages:

a) the transmission of the order to the rank and file and the conduct of a series of preparatory measures ensuring its fulfillment;
b) work while carrying out the combat order;
c) compiling the results of the battle.

In order to completely and in good time carry out the command's combat order, the commissars and political organs noted beforehand those measures that had to be carried out by stages.

Experience showed that in those areas where the work for ensuring the political support of the combat order was planned, the results were always positive. Just the opposite was true where the political organs underestimated the importance of planning the work for carrying out the combat order, and there were serious shortcomings in realizing it.

How the political organs' work in the offensive was planned and how the political preparation of the offensive battle should be carried out may be seen by the example of the work of the commissar and the political section of Maj. General Panfilov's 8th Red Banner Guards Rifle Division, which formed a part of the 16th Army. In the newspaper *Red Star* of January 20 1942, the division's military commissar, Regimental Commissar comrade Yegorov shared his experience of planning the political preparation of the offensive battle in carrying out the division's combat order to take the village of Kryukovo.

At 1800 on December 6 the division received an order to go over to the offensive at 1000 on December 7, with the mission of taking the village of Kryukovo. There remained only 13 hours for preparatory work. But this time proved to be quite sufficient in order to think through and realize a number of measures, which should ensure the fulfillment of the combat order.

The division commissar, first of all, defined the content of the political preparation for the offensive. It was established that Kryukovo was a strong point in the enemy's resistance. Here was concentrated a large number of mortars, the cross-fire of which enfiladed all the approaches to the village. Thus in one of the discussions, outlined in the plan, the troops and commanders were reminded of the danger they would be subjected to if they delayed in the range of the mortar fire, and that the most reliable means of guaranteeing themselves against mortar fire was the rapid and unbroken movement forward. It was further established that there were up to 50 enemy tanks in Kryukovo, which had been concentrated in this place for operations against our troops. Therefore a second discussion was dedicated to explaining the methods of fighting enemy tanks.

So that the soldiers would fight with all their heart, it was necessary before the start of the offensive to ignite their hatred for the German aggressors. For this purpose, the political section's planned called for time to read newspapers reports of German atrocities in Rostov, of German reprisals against innocent civilians and captured Red Army soldiers.

Besides this, the men and officers were informed that they were carrying out comrade Stalin's personal order and that the people's commissar would be following their actions. This gave them renewed strength and caused an exceedingly offensive upsurge and desire to justify as much as possible the high confidence bestowed by comrade Stalin.

Having determined the content of political work for the preparatory period for the offensive, the division commissar compiled a plan of organizational measures for ensuring that the combat order was carried out. According to this plan, the political preparation for the offensive began by convening an instruction meeting of the political section's workers. One question was discussed at the meeting: the forthcoming offensive and the political workers' tasks. At 2000 an instruction-meeting of company political leaders was called to discuss the question of their tasks in preparing for the forthcoming offensive.

During these hours the agitators were briefed on the theme: "The reliable guarantee against being hit by the enemy's mortar fire is the offensive—the rapid and determined movement forward."

At 2030 collective readings of newspaper materials on the Germans' barbarities in Rostov was conducted, and within an hour discussions with the rank and file on moving forward under mortar fire were discussed.

The next day, at 0800 on December 7, political information meetings were conducted on the topic: "What the experience of the division's past battles shows." At 0830 regimental discussion of the party activists were conducted, with the agenda: "On the forthcoming offensive and the Communists' tasks." At the same time Komsomol activists were conducting battalion meetings on the same topic.

At 0900 company meetings were conducted. The content of the meetings:

> Today we are going into battle according to the personal order of comrade Stalin. The plan for today's offensive, in which the 8th Guards Division is participating, has been drawn up in detail by the people's commissar himself. Guards soldiers may die, but they will carry out Stalin's mission. Today Kryukovo must once again become Soviet.

In this manner the combat task, in the interests of military secrecy, was communicated to the troops only an hour before the start of the offensive. However, the skillful and well thought-out preliminary work by the party-political apparatus among the divisions' rank and file enabled us to prepare it for the forthcoming offensive in a timely manner.

The second half of the plan for organizational-political measures consisted of a listing of personal assignments for each worker of the division's political section.

The deputy chief of the political section was sent to the 1075th Rifle Regiment, and the political section's instructors to the 1073rd and 1077th rifle regiments, with the task of helping the company political leaders prepare political information and meetings before the battle and to personally conduct discussions with tank destroyers, and to check just how much the troops' equipment satisfied the conditions of prolonged fighting in the field at temperatures of -28 degrees Celsius.

Other political workers were dispatched to the division's rear, in order to help the rear commanders in supplying the offensive's matériel-technical needs (the organization of meals, the uninterrupted delivery of munitions, the evacuation of wounded, etc.).

The chief of the political section visited a unit that had just arrived and which consisted of men who hadn't been under fire, in order to share with them the 8th Guards Division's combat experience.

The leadership and control over the plan for fulfilling the offensive's political preparation was concentrated directly in the commissar's hands. He was in charge of the political sections postings of its workers, he received communications from the units, and he issued all instructions.

The large amount of political work conducted by the party-political apparatus ensured the successful realization of Stalin's order. As a result of the fierce fighting, which lasted nearly a day, the 8th Guards Division captured the village of Kryukovo.

Similar work on fulfilling the combat order was carried out in the 133rd Rifle Division, which formed part of the 49th Army. Before carrying out every combat assignment, the political section composed a plan for politically supporting the offensive battle. The plan laid out practical measures which were to be carried out during the preparation period for the offensive and during the offensive itself. Here is the plan for politically supporting the achievement of the combat order for taking the village of Kurdyukovka.

> The main task. By means of broadly explaining the significance of the Red Army's successes and relaying to the rank and file the tasks contained in the division command's combat order no. 01, make sure that the inhabited locale Kurdyukovka is taken at any cost.
>
> Carry out the following practical measures:
>
> 1 A short briefing with the units' political workers to lay out the tasks in connection with carrying out order no. 01, and explain:
> a) the significance of capturing the village of Kurdyukovka and cutting the road and railroad;
> b) the significance of bypassing the enemy's Detchino group's from the left flank and getting into the enemy's rear.
>
> 2 The distribution of the party-political apparatus's forces in the regiments, so that there would be a representative in each battalion.
>
> 3 Short party and Komsomol meetings in smaller units, dedicated to the question of the vanguard role of communists and Komsomol members in the battle for the village of Kurdyukovka.
>
> 4 The dispatch of communits to platoons (and to small units with new reinforcements) for the purpose of preventing the slightest attempt at cowardice and panic mongering.
>
> 5 The issuing of "combat pages" in the smaller units, featuring those who have distinguished themselves in battle (after capturing the village of Kurdyukovka).
>
> 6 A meeting of citizens in Kurdyukovka (after its capture), dedicated to questions of elections to local organs and rendering aid to the Red Army's attacking units.
>
> 7 Securing the correct reception and evacuation of wounded.

The measures laid out in this plan were carried out fully. The command's order was realized—the division took the village of Kurdyukovka.

The work of political leader Kazantsev (19th Rifle Division) may serve as an example of the skillful political support for carrying out a combat order in a small unit.

In the first half of December 1941 political worker Kazantsev's company was ordered to attack. There was little time left before the offensive's beginning. Nonetheless Kazantsev managed to gather the communists and Komsomol members in his dugout and explained to them the situation and the company's combat task. Following the meeting the communists and Komsomol members dispersed to their platoons and sections and conducted discussions with the soldiers about the coming offensive battle. Communists Fil'chenko, Likhvarev and Pestov reminded the soldiers about certain of the enemy's perfidious methods, and recounted in particular the example of how in one of the battles a group of Fascist automatic riflemen penetrated into the rear of Dement'ev's unit and attempted to create the impression that they had encircled them so as to sow panic among the rank and file. But this maneuver failed to work. The soldiers of Dement'ev's units quickly destroyed the Fascist automatic riflemen. Through this example the agitators reminded the men and commanders of the necessity of being vigilant and to see through the enemy's tactics in a timely manner, to manifest initiative and resourcefulness, and to act bravely and decisively. Before the attack "combat pages" were issued, which were read in the sections. Handwritten instructions on "How to Act in the Offensive" were distributed in the platoons.

At dawn the company entered the fighting. The enemy opened heavy mortar and machine gun fire on the attackers. However, the soldiers did not waver. The company continued to move forward.

The company political leader, observing the battle, noticed that some of the soldiers from the new intake were attacking recklessly, running at full height, and not using breaks in the enemy fire. The political leader immediately ordered the corporals and NCOs and agitators through a liaison to explain to the troops how to rush the enemy's positions. This was carried out by the time a new line was reached.

During the offensive the section of Junior Sergeant and Komsomol member Yemel'chenko distinguished itself. It destroyed two enemy machine gun sites in a decisive attack and killed about 20 Fascists, thus securing the timely advance of the entire platoon forward. The agitators immediately told about the exploits of the troops in Yemel'chenko's section and called upon all the rank and file to follow their example. By a rapid move forward, the company kicked the Germans out of their positions and carried out their mission.

The modern offensive battle demands the most careful preparation, but even given this one often encounters unexpected situations in the process of carrying out the combat order, which cannot always be foreseen in drawing up a plan. Besides this, the large amount of weapons in the enemy units, and the hard frosts, in which our armies had to attack, demanded of the entire rank and file an enormous concentration of strength and will, stoutness and persistence in carrying out orders. In those places where the work connected with the combat order was carried out properly, no difficulties could weaken our troops' offensive *elan*.

The 173rd Rifle Division's 1313th Rifle Regiment and an obstacle detachment received the division commander's order to attack toward the village of Red'kino. Before departing for the line of attack indicated in the order, the obstacle detachment's commissar gathered the political leaders and their assistants, explained the task to them and warned them that the detachment would have to use a road that was under German fire. The political leaders conversed on this matter with the rank and file.

The work carried out yielded the desired result. When the detachment had approached the line in question and the enemy opened a heavy fire, there was no confusion in the detachment. That night the detachment attacked the village of Red'kino. In a short but hot battle the village was captured by our soldiers.

Comrade Stalin's instructions to the *front's* commanders and political workers had an enormous significance for the troops carrying out their orders. Comrade Stalin's name inspired the men and commanders to overcome any obstacles during their offensive operations. The political workers used each of the leader's words and each of his instructions for developing the troops' offensive surge and for their outstanding fulfillment of their orders.

At the end of November 1941 Gen. Belov's cavalry corps was ordered to eliminate the enemy that had broken through toward Kashira. At night comrade Stalin called Gen. Belov to the telephone. A conversation of historical importance for the corps took place. After a series of organizational question, comrade Stalin said:

> Comrade Belov! Recommend your cavalry divisions for the guards title. You fought very well in Ukraine and are fighting well around Moscow.

The corps's political workers immediately passed on to the future guards cavalrymen the content of comrade Stalin's conversation with Gen. Belov. The explained to the rank and file and commanders the significance of Stalin's praise and the responsibilities which the title of guards lays upon each cavalryman. They had to justify the great Stalin's praise by launching new mortal blows against the enemy. An enormous political rise was noted in the corps units. An offensive surge seized everybody. The Germans' offensive on Kashira was beaten back. The red cavalrymen themselves went over to the offensive and consecutively took Mordves, Venev and Stalinogorsk. The enemy, having lost several divisions and a large amount of equipment, was thrown back.

The work on the combat order is wrapped up by a summation of the combat results. This concluding phase of the work has no less significance than the political preparation of the offensive and the political support of the battle itself. The results of the battle must be evaluated. Even in those instances when a unit immediately receives a new assignment, the commissar and political workers have to make sure that the lessons of the past battle are communicated to the rank and file, so as to prevent a repetition of past mistakes and to use the acquired experience in carrying out a new combat task.

The results of a battle are summarized in various forms. The 230th Rifle Division command summarized the battle's results in special orders. These contained an evaluation of the units' actions and indicated measures for further improving the combat work of the division's rank and file. The command issued orders in which were summarized the results of combat activities during January 14-22 1942, and the results of the fighting around Kaluga. After a battle, as a rule, party and Komsomol meetings were conducted, in which the behavior of communists and Komsomol members in the battle was discussed and the new tasks of the party and Komsomol organizations were planned.

Meetings, political information sessions, the agitators' conversations with the rank and file, and the issue of papers and combat pages were dedicated to summing up the results of combat activities. All of these forms were employed for popularizing the most effective methods of fighting the enemy and the most distinguished soldiers and commanders.

If on a whole the commissars and political organs of the Western Front conducted a large and all-round deal of work for politically supporting the combat orders, then certain political sections failed to adjust themselves in accord with the offensive's conditions.

In the beginning of December the 329th Rifle Division received an order from the 5th Army's military council to march to its jumping-off point for an attack. The political section and the units' political apparatus did not take timely steps to ensure that the order was carried out on time, which led to a disruption of the schedule d movement. The troops' feeding and resting was poorly organized on the march route. Discipline on the march was poor. As a result of all of this, the division arrived late at its jumping-off point.

On January 30 the 882nd Rifle Regiment was given the task of capturing the edge of the woods north of Kostino and cutting the Chernevo-Bol'shaya Srednyaya road. Despite the fact that there was sufficient time to prepare for carrying out the order, no political work was carried out with the rank and file, and the order was not conveyed to them. The unsatisfactory political work in the regiment told in its combat operations. The regiment, having suffered heavy losses, fell back to its starting point.

The political support of the combat order is the most responsible part of the commissars' and political organs' work and the chief content and basic forms of political work in the offensive are subordinated to it. The quality of the work by the military commissar and the political apparatus should be, first of all, evaluated on the basis of how the given unit or formation carries out the command's combat orders.

Party work during the offensive

With the beginning of the Western Front's offensive operations the organizational and educational work by the party organizations became apparent. If during the defensive period all of the party work was basically directed at supporting the vanguard role of the communists and Komsomol members in the battle, who were obligated through personal example of fortitude and bravery to inspire the non-party rank and file and prevent manifestations of panic and disorganization, then under conditions of the offensive party work acquired a more multifaceted character. Party and Komsomol organizations now were more concerned with ensuring that the combat orders were carried out and in maintaining an offensive *elan* in the *front's* rank and file. At the head of the agenda for the party and Komsomol bureaus and meetings, as a rule, stood questions connected with carrying out the command's combat orders to attack.

Thus in the sections of the 418th Rifle Division in January 1942, meetings were conducted dedicated to the question "Concerning Certain Results of Our Units' Offensive Operations and the Party Organizations' Tasks in Supporting the Further Offensive." In the 146th Tank Brigade's units in December 1941 company party meetings were conducted, in which the results of combat operations were analyzed and the party organizations' latest tasks were discussed. A discussion was held with the Komsomol activists regarding the formation's combat operations.

Besides the political work around the combat orders, on the initiative of the party and Komsomol organizations the condition of the troops' weapons and equipment was checked and the necessary measures were taken for making them combat ready.

On the initiative of the 1140th Rifle Regiment's party organization the readiness of the unit's weaponry for battle was verified. In order to remove dirt and thick lubricants, which could cause delays in firing in the cold, rifles, automatic rifles, and machine guns were cleaned with kerosene; the coordination of units was tested. This timely preparatory work ensured the weapons' flawless work during the offensive battle.

Under the conditions of an offensive the demands on intraparty work increased. The composition of party and Komsomol organizations can undergo significant changes, even in the course of a single battle. A large number of communists were often put out of action. New rank and file and commanders who had distinguished themselves in the fighting against the Fascists took their place in the party. This new intake of communists was in need of serious educational work. It was necessary to arm the young communists with the ideas of Leninism, to inculcate in them a feeling of responsibility before the party not only for their conduct, but also for the conduct of that collective in which they were fighting, and to steel them for new battles.

To an even greater extent this relates to party and Komsomol cadres, the composition of which often changes during the course of an offensive. Young communists and Komsomol members come to take up leadership posts, often lacking experience in organizing party and Komsomol work. They all are in need of assistance, both in the sense of methodological habits of party work, and in the sense of ideological and political maturation.

Finally, going over to the offensive placed before the party and Komsomol organizations the task of inculcating in the men and commanders those new qualities which ensure the troops' offensive *elan*. This task was resolved under the leadership of the units' commissars and political organs.

The experience of party and Komsomol work in the Western Front's troops in December 1941 and January 1942 showed that it is not necessary to employ any kind of special forms of intra-party and Komsomol work for the period of the offensive. In the conditions of the offensive, those same forms that were employed during the defensive fighting remain vital, namely: general party and Komsomol meetings, party meetings with delegates, meetings of party activists, party and Komsomol instructions, and group and individual conversations with communists and Komsomol members, etc.

To be sure, the proportion of each of these forms changed somewhat at this stage. For example, group and individual conversations occupied a greater place in the work of the party and Komsomol organizations than, say, general meetings. But this in no way means that the role and significance of party meetings under conditions of the offensive is reduced. Quite the opposite, their role increases and the demand for them grows. Party and Komsomol meetings were and remain a most important school for the Bolshevik education of communists and Komsomol members. By means of party and Komsomol meetings, provided they are well organized, young members and candidate members of the party and Komsomol are more quickly included in the general life and work of the organization as a whole; they are inculcated with a feeling of responsibility before the party collective for carrying out those combat tasks that are laid upon communists by the units' commanders.

The preparation and conduct of party meetings under the conditions of an offensive are linked to greater difficulties than in the defensive. Nonetheless, many party organizations, overcoming these difficulties, scrupulously prepared for the party meetings. For example, the party bureaus for the 290th Rifle Division's units gathered the company party organizers and political leaders two-three days before the party meeting and discussed the matter of the agenda and the preparation of the communists for the meeting. After this, the members of the party bureaus, party organizers, and political leaders conducted corresponding work with each communist.

The party meeting in the 909th Artillery Regiment was well prepared. Here the communists also familiarized themselves with the agenda two days before the meeting and were able to prepare to address the meeting. The party bureau secretary issued instructions to the party bureau's members on questions connected with the agenda. At one of the party meetings the question of creating full-blooded party organizations and eliminating shortcomings in accepting new members into the ranks of the VKP(b) was discussed. After the party meeting the work of the lower-level party organizations improved noticeably. Some communists began to receive from the battery party organizers assignments, the fulfillment of which they were periodically called to account for. The demands placed on communists increased significantly.

The party meeting in the 12th Guards Rifle Division's 991st Rifle Regiment was conducted at a high ideological level. The party meeting discussed the problem of the party organization's tasks in connection with the division's renaming as a guards unit. All the addresses were distinguished by their efficiency and deep knowledge of the party organization's situation, and were suffused with the desire to justify the confidence of the party and government, which had conferred the guards designation upon the division.

The party bureaus of the 154th Rifle Division's units organized their work well. At the party bureaus' meetings questions of the communists' vanguard role were discussed, as well as intraparty work in the lower party organizations. The specificity and purposefulness of the party bureaus' work told accordingly in the work of the sections' party organizations. For example, before the units' attack on the city of Kaluga, party organizer comrade Dedkov (292nd Independent Communications Battalion) gathered the communists and discussed with them the question of how best to carry out the combat order to capture the central telegraph station in Kaluga. After the meeting the communists communicated the order's contents to the section's rank and file. The troops, inspired by the communists, overcame the enemy's fire resistance and captured the most important communications junction—the telegraph station. The order was carried out with honor. For their exemplary fulfillment of the combat order, five men were nominated for government decorations.

Party and Komsomol organizers began to be found more often among the rank and file of their section, where they strengthened their individual work with communists and Komsomol members and improved their educational work among those accepted into the party and Komsomol.

Thus the overwhelming majority of party organizations were able to rapidly and correctly restructure its work in accordance with the conditions of our troops' offensive operations. However, in some units and sections during the offensive the weakening of party-political and educational work was observed.

Certain party organizations limited themselves to admitting people into the party. They did not devote much attention to problems of combat and educational work.

In the majority of the 30th Rifle Brigade's sections during offensive operations party meetings were not conducted at all. Among the main shortcomings of some meetings were a lack of purpose and specificity in the questions under discussion and in the decisions adopted. For example, among the decisions by the party meeting of the 564th Artillery Regiment's first battalion was the following formula: "To achieve by all means purposefulness in party-political work, which would support the realization of those tasks by the battalion and by the regiment as a whole."

The overall improvement in intraparty work under offensive conditions and the Red Army's successes was reflected in the growth of the Western Front's party and Komsomol organizations. Comparative data for November and December 1941, and January 1942, are witness to a significant growth of the party and Komsomol ranks during the period of the *front's* offensive operations.

In November 1941 811 applications were submitted for membership in the VKP(b), and 3,341 candidate member applications; in December 1941 the corresponding figure was 1,665 and 5,651, and in January 1942 the figure was correspondingly 2,190 and 6,459.

However, despite the significant growth in the party and Komsomol organizations of the *front's* units, the losses suffered by the party and Komsomol organizations in the fighting were not fully covered. The weakest area was the growth of party organizations in the rifle units. In seven of the 1111th Rifle Regiment's rifle companies, in four of the 1109th Rifle Regiment's rifle companies, and in three of the 1113th Rifle Regiment's rifle companies—all in the 330th Rifle Division—for December 1941 and January 1942 not a single man was admitted into the party. Particularly noticeable was the weak growth of party organizations through the admission of the rank and file and corporals and NCOs. A directive by the Main Political Directorate on the creation of full-bodied party organizations in companies was not carried out in a number of units and formations.

Among the shortcomings in the work for admitting people into the party was slowness in filling out the paperwork for applicants and delays in reviewing materials in the division party commissions.

A study of the composition of those admitted into the party during the offensive shows that the best people, who had distinguished themselves in the fight against German fascism, were joining the party and the Komsomol. The men and commanders, in their applications to the party organizations, expressed their desire to go into battle as communists and fight to their last drop of blood for the cause of the party of Lenin and Stalin.

Communists and Komsomol members stand in the vanguard of the struggle against the German-Fascist aggressors. They display examples of selfless heroism and resilience in battle and a readiness to sacrifice their lives, inspiring through their fearlessness and toughness the non-party soldiers and commanders. They take part in the most dangerous undertakings—in reconnaissance, into the enemy rear, in destroyer groups, and volunteer to carry out the most important tasks for the sake of speeding up the larger victory over Fascism.

During the attack on Kaluga the 2nd Squadron's runner, candidate member of the VKP(b), comrade Ponomarev, particularly distinguished himself. He crossed the Oka River nine times under the enemy's heavy mortar and machine gun fire, delivering the regimental commander's orders and instructions to the sections.

Jr. Lieutenant and Komsomol member, comrade Tarasov (217th Rifle Division) is known as a combat commander. Once comrade Tarasov, together with a group of soldiers, captured a mortar and several score mortar rounds in fighting near the village of Sudakovo. The captured mortar was immediately turned against the Germans. Tarasov commanded: "Open fire on the Fascists with their own Fascist mortar and Fascist mortar rounds!" The enemy couldn't take it. The village was captured. The combat commander was nominated for a government medal.

Our party and Komsomol activists offer an example of bravery and valor on the battlefield. The other party and Komsomol members try to emulate them.

One could always see party organizer comrade Kuz'michev (50th Rifle Division) at the head of the attack. In battle he taught the troops how to better aim against the retreating Fascists, which cover is better to use while running, etc. Comrade Kuz'michev, after the end of a heated battle, conducted a discussion with the troops. Just then the section commander entered the dugout and announced that the section had been given the assignment to carry out a night-time reconnaissance in the enemy rear. Comrade Kuz'michev was the first to volunteer, followed by all the soldiers. Private Volkov said "We're ready to go through fire and water with communist Kuz'michev. With him any, even the most difficult assignment, will be carried out."

The communist soldiers are the pride of every unit and section. They cement the ranks of men and commanders. By their personal example, they support our troops' offensive *elan* and inspire them to completely defeat the enemy.

Agitation and propaganda work among the troops in the Offensive

Our troops' offensive and the accompanying combat and political enthusiasm among the masses exerted an extremely favorable influence on the unfolding of agitation-propaganda work in the units.

The overall animation of agitation-propaganda work among the Western Front's troops during the offensive operations was also connected with the receipt of the directive by the Red Army's Main Political Directorate "On the Elimination of Slackness in Oral Propaganda and Agitation." The discussion of the directive aroused the *front's* political organs and party organizations. It reminded every communist that his sacred duty is to carry our party's ideas to the masses.

At meetings of the party workers and at party gatherings conducted in all the units and formations in connection with the directive's appearance, concrete measures for improving the state of oral propaganda among the rank and file were outlined. The realization of this directive occasioned a turning point in all agitation-propaganda work in favor of sharply increased the proportion of oral agitation and propaganda. Propaganda in the form of a lively and understandable word occupied the commissars' and political organs' attention. It became more concrete and purposeful and began to respond in a timelier manner to the troops' and commanders' needs and requests.

The skillful use of different forms of agitation and propaganda applicable to the combat situation made it possible for the commissars and political organs to constantly exert ideological-political influence on the units' entire rank and file and to mobilize its attention and forces for the best fulfillment of its combat tasks.

A large place in oral propaganda was occupied by lectures, reports, and discussions on general political, military, and military-historical themes. For example, in the 1st Shock Army's 71st Rifle Division more than 400 discussions, reports, and lectures were conducted during a 15-day period in December. Lecturers and instructors from the 20th Army's political section read 14 lectures and reports for the command element in the second half of January, and 11 for agitators and the troops, while the workers of the 20th Army's units during the same period read about 150 lectures and reports. The troops listened with especial attention to reports and lectures about the Great Patriotic War and the international situation. These were usually accompanied by a mass of notes with additional questions, which testified to the high troops' high educational level. By way of example, one can quote a few of these questions to the 49th Army's lecturers: "How can one economically base the inevitable doom of German imperialism?", "What is the essence of Japanese aggression's southern and northern variations?", "What is the position of Turkey and Sweden in the present war?", "Is the appearance of a pan-Slavic federation possible following the defeat of Germany?", "What Germany's oil and food resources?", "May one expect a social explosion in Germany in the near future?", When and where will a second front be opened against Hitlerite Germany?", "What will be the state structure of a future Germany," "Who in the British cabinet in against the USSR?", and "Won't the war in the Pacific have an effect on military deliveries to us?", etc.

Along with reports and lectures on general political subjects connected with the Great Patriotic War and international events, lectures and reports were also made for the purpose of acquainting the rank and file with the experience of modern war: fighting in winter conditions; operations by ski troops with automatic rifles; the organization of breaking out of an encirclement; capturing enemy strong points; means and methods for blockading concrete and wood-earth firing points; attacking in forested and broken terrain in winter; cooperation between tanks and artillery; attacking an inhabited locale at night, etc.

Given this scope of oral propaganda the political organs did not limit themselves only to employing their permanent lecturers, but also summoned the most prepared political workers and commanders to deliver reports and lectures. Within the divisional and army political sections groups of non-staff lecturers were formed, consisting of 10-15 men. Among these non-staff lecturers were a number of unit and formation commanders. Commanders from the 49th Army headquarters also took part in this work.

Lectures and reports earned their full "right of citizenship" under the conditions of offensive operations. The work practice of the Western Front's political organs proved the viability and expediency of these forms of oral propaganda in the units during the offensive, even in the difficult conditions of winter fighting. However, despite the comparatively large amount of lectures and reports read, they are nonetheless episodic in character and thus cannot satisfy all the rank and files' needs, nor can they keep even with the units' combat life, and are even more so incapable of orienting the troops and commanders in a rapidly-changing situation and direct them toward carrying out their most immediate concrete combat tasks.

It is for these reasons that other forms of oral propaganda—discussions, political information, are so important. By means of conducting short group and individual discussions in the trenches and dugouts, etc., one can quickly encompass all the men and commanders. A lively discussion and personal contact make it possible to quickly inform each soldier and commander of the latest news and crystallize the combat tasks in accordance with the changed situation.

This political work of enormous importance was carried out by thousands of political workers, most of all by the political leaders of companies, batteries and squadrons, as well as by tens of thousands of lower-level agitators. Taking into account the fact that the overwhelming majority of these are young political workers lacking sufficient experience, the Western Front's commissars and political organs attached great significance to raising their ideological-theoretical level and inculcating them with the skills of agitation-propaganda work. For this purpose, seminars for political leaders, party and Komsomol organizers, and agitators were conducted with the divisional and regimental political sections, without taking them away from their work in the sections. The 16th Army's political section, for example, suggested that the divisions' political sections conduct short-term seminars from December 12, organizing studies of not more than 2-3 hours per day. And the seminars were conducted, despite the fact that the 16th Army was at the same time carrying out offensive operations on the Western Front's right wing.

In the regiments of the 50th Army's 340th Rifle Division, which was attacking on the *front's* left wing, similar seminars were conducted in the second half of January. In connection with the fact that the seminars were conducted in conditions of the units' unbroken military activity, the seminar participants were summoned to their studies in order; the company political leaders, battery leaders, and deputy political leaders were summoned first, followed by party and Komsomol organizers.

The commissars and political organs devoted special attention to the selection of lower-level agitators and their training for work with the rank and file.

Groups of agitator-discussants and agitation collectives were created in all units and sections. They were selected from the section's combat activists, from the best soldiers and commanders—party and non-party Bolsheviks. The following data give an idea of the composition of the agitators: by the end of January the 47th Rifle Brigade numbered more than 140 agitators, of which 61 were communists and 59 were Komsomol members, 69 were from the rank and file, and 52 were corporals and NCOs. 94 agitators had a higher and secondary education. The 50th Rifle Brigade had 102 agitators, of which 53 were communists and 31 members of the Komsomol. Special lectures and reports were read for the lower-level agitators, as well as thematic seminars and instructive meetings conducted.

The agitators' work was concrete in character. They linked discussions on general political or military topics with facts from the section's and unit's life and with the combat tasks and skillfully combined the narrative visual aids. Thus their agitation and propaganda were on target and actual.

Soldier-agitator comrade Inkin was conducting a discussion on how to better carry out comrade Stalin's instructions for destroying the German-Fascist aggressors. Before long they went into battle. Noticing that his neighbor's machine gun had jammed, comrade Inkin crawled over to him, fixed the machine gun and began himself to shoot. On the battlefield remained 53 dead German soldiers and officers, the greater part of which had been shot by comrade Inkin. During the attack comrade Inkin was the first to break into the village of Prudnoe, destroying the Fascists. The soldiers speak of him with affection: "With Inkin there's no difference between word and deed. He showed us how to understand and carry out comrade Stalin's report."

Agitator Zubtsov, from the 475th Rifle Regiment's eighth company, was carrying out a discussion about the anti-tank grenade, characterizing it as a powerful and terrible weapon for destroying enemy tanks. During the discussion he instructed the troops on the practical way to employ the grenade in battle, so as to achieve the best results. The troops listened to his discussion and tried to master the methods shown, as they saw that Zubtsov knew grenades through and through and masterfully uses them in battle. The troops listed with great attention to the discussion by agitator Zadorozhnyi about the rifle as a soldier's foolproof personal weapon. They knew he was a sniper and his accurate fire had killed many Fascists.

Agitation-propaganda work in all its forms and manifestations exerted an immediate influence on the development of the troops' offensive *elan* and mobilized the Western Front's commanders and political workers to carry out the command's combat orders.

Before the attack on the village of Dorokhi the 843rd Rifle Regiment's political workers and lower-level agitators conducted a discussion with the troops on the subject of "street fighting and attacking separate buildings." The sections were given precise instructions as to what streets and buildings they were to attack. Thanks to this preparation, the soldiers operated bravely and decisively, skillfully attacking separate structures and ejecting the Fascists from them.

The 194th Rifle Division's political workers and agitators told the troops how not far from the frontline the village of Strelkovka was being held by the Germans, the birthplace of the Western Front commander, Gen. and comrade Zhukov. Having learned this, the troops and commanders strengthened their pressure on the enemy, so as to more quickly liberate the village of Strelkovka from the Fascist aggressors and report the joyful news to the *front* commander.

After the capture of the village of Udinsk by the 133rd Rifle Division's 418th Rifle Regiment, the units, although tired after the battle, were ordered to continue the offensive toward the village of Vekishino. The enemy put up strong resistance, delaying the offensive along this sector. At this time one of our planes flew by and dropped over our lines the latest communiqués from the Soviet Information Bureau about the course of the German defeat around Moscow. The political workers and agitators quickly communicated the joyful news to each soldier. They soldiers, having forgotten how tired they were, threw themselves into battle with renewed energy. Despite the strong enemy fire, they surrounded Vekishino and drove the enemy from it. Developing their success, they continued to pursue the enemy and before long captured a second inhabited area—the village of Kochergino.

Approximately the same thing happened after the arrival of units of the 55th Rifle Brigade in the city of Solnechnogorsk. The troops were very tired after the stubborn fighting. However, it was necessary to pursue the enemy and deprive him of the opportunity of consolidating along a new line. At that moment the latest communiqué arrived from the Soviet Information Bureau about one of our victories. This communiqué quickly made the rounds of all the soldiers and so inspired them that they overcame their exhaustion and with renewed strength continued their attack.

Simultaneously with the improvement in oral propaganda and agitation, the commissars and political organs did not lessen their attention to such an important means of political work as printed and visual propaganda. In the *front*, army, and divisional print organs, in many posters, slogans, leaflets and brochures, the units' and sections' combat life was highlighted and the *front's* combat tasks propagandized, while the best soldiers and commanders who had distinguished themselves in the battles with the Fascists, were popularized.

The magazine "Front Humor," published by the *front* political directorate, was the object of the rank and file's special love. Appearing in the units, the magazine creates an upbeat attitude, arousing laughter and a merry exchange of opinions apropos of the witty and accurate caricatures, satirical articles, ditties, and sayings contained in it.

Newsletters were published in many units and sections: "The Regiment's Best People," "Combat Notes," "The Regiment's Combat Day," "An Album of our Victories," etc. The newsletters briefly described the mission being pursued by the unit or section during the preceding day and told about the soldiers and commanders—heroes of the day, who had distinguished themselves in carrying out orders, while relaying combat experience and explaining new combat tasks.

A noticeable role was played by mass-agitation work in raising the combat spirit of the Western Front's troops. Divisional clubs were the organizing center of the mass-agitation work. Constantly moving with the units, they were in direct contact with the soldier masses and used every opportunity in the combat situation to organize the rest of their units' rank and file. The showing of movies, the organization of Red Army amateur presentations, holding concerts, the distribution of literature, posters, and slogans, etc.—was the divisional clubs' main work.

In showing movies, the clubs exerted direct assistance to the command and the troops in resolving the unit's combat tasks. The 194th Rifle Division's 616th Rifle Regiment received on December 15 the movie "Fighting the Enemy's Tanks." Before the film was shown, discussions were held in the sections on the topic of "The Experience of Combatting Enemy Tanks in our Regiment." Viewing the film by our regiment's troops and commanders enriched them with new experience in combating Fascist tanks. The showing of this film was particularly useful for the troops of the regiment's destruction detachment, who viewed the film separately.

The film "The Red Army's Parade on Red Square on November 7 1941" caused a particularly big combat and political surge in the units. The appearance of comrade Stalin on the screen was met with stormy greetings and enraptured shouts in honor of the great leader and was accompanied by an harmonious army "Hurrah." Five showings of this film were arranged in the 185th Rifle Division's units, while more than 800 soldiers and 200 civilians watched it. During the film's showing in the 237th Rifle Regiment the regiment's military commissar made a speech and told the assembled troops and commanders about the results of the regiment's latest combat operations and about the Germans' defeat on the approaches to Moscow. In a number of units, following the showing of this film, meetings were held in which the men, commanders, and political workers expressed their love and devotion for comrade Stalin and their complete readiness to carry out all his instructions.

Among the other forms of mass-agitation work carried out by the divisional clubs, concert ensembles and agitation brigades, organized by some divisional political sections, were particularly popular. The 173rd Rifle Division's concert ensemble worked well and fruitfully. In January 1942 alone the ensemble put on 60 concerts, entertaining up to 3,000 soldiers, commanders, and political workers.

The agitation brigade of the 11th Guards Division's club enjoyed the deserved love of the division's soldiers, commanders, and political workers. The agitation brigade consisted of only six people, among which were two singers, two readers, one dancer, and a bayan player. In the four months of its existence, this small collective gave more than 150 concerts, conducted 46 meetings and discussions, organized 75 evenings of army amateur presentations, helped to put out 36 "combat leaflets," and five artistically laid-out wall newspapers.

The agitation brigade performed before the troops in dugouts, huts and often in the woods, in gullies, and in the open air, despite the frost. The agitation brigade's performances created a happy and joyful attitude among the soldiers, commanders, and political workers. The political leader of the 1306th Rifle Regiment's third company gave the following assessment following one of the brigade's concerts: "The soldiers and commanders will remember the unusual 45 minutes, during which the brigade's concert, under the leadership of comrade Levitskii, continued. The frost ceased to freeze and our faces broke out in smiles."

Once the brigade gave a concert in an independent guards anti-aircraft battery on the same day the gunners had shot down three aircraft. The agitation brigade made a deal with the battery's gunners that in the future they would give a new concert for every plane shot down. Laughing, the soldiers told the brigade's artists: "Now you'll have to perform for us often."

The Western Front's political directorate's agitation vehicles also did good service. Each one of these vehicles contained a political worker-propagandist as chief, a reader, a bayan player, and a movie operator. Besides this, there were female singers in two vehicles.

In two months the agitation vehicles completed two trips among the troops (each trip lasting 10-12 days) and at the same time conducted 263 reports and discussions, 255 concert performances, and 278 film showings. More than 70,000 people were serviced during these trips.

Thanks to their possession of a radio, the agitation vehicle brigades had the opportunity to use the latest news and communiqués from the Soviet Information Bureau in the performances and could quickly communicate the news to the units.

The agitation vehicles literally followed the attacking troops, servicing them at stops (in the second echelon), while they serviced the 44th Cavalry Division during intervals in the attack two km from the enemy. The agitation vehicles often arrived in inhabited areas from the enemy two or three hours after their occupation by the Western Front's troops.

One should also note radio broadcasts as an important form of mass-agitation work systematically carried out by the Western Front's political directorate.

The programs and transcripts of "The Front Speaks" radio broadcasts were carefully prepared by the Western Front's political directorate. In them the success of the *front's* troops in the defeat of the German-Fascist occupiers, the heroic feats of the troops, commanders, and political workers were highlighted. Articles and essays, letters from the front, satirical articles and poems, stories and songs were part of every broadcast's program, while the textual material alternated with the musical and song material. The broadcasts were often done from forward positions or from inhabited areas recently liberated by our troops, and were broadcast through the Moscow radio stations.

Work among the population and partisans in territory liberated from the enemy

A great deal of work was carried out by the Western Front's political organs among the local population and partisans. Its volume increased significantly in connection with the *front's* assumption of the offensive. The political organs now had to resolve complex and responsible tasks among the local population liberated by the Red Army from the German-Fascist yoke.

Basically, the work among the local population was conducted along the following lines:

a) first of all, it was necessary to tell the population the truth about our country and relate to it the contents of comrade Stalin's historic addresses, and to unmask the Fascist propaganda's lies about the Red Army and Soviet power;
b) then it was necessary to help our punitive organs in revealing and unmasking among the local population of traitors who had been serving the Fascists and carrying out anti-Soviet work;
c) to restore the work of Soviet organs, party and Komsomol organizations, and collective farms;
d) to mobilize the population for the rapid elimination of the consequences of the German-Fascist robber occupation and render aid to families which had suffered the most from the German brigands;
e) to get the population to render assistance to our troops waging offensive battles (cleaning roads, taking care of the wounded, quartering troops, etc.).

In almost all the inhabited areas liberated by our troops, the political section's workers carried out meetings among the local population. For example, after the occupation of Volokolamsk (December 20), the 331st Rifle Division's political section organized a meeting of the civilian population with the division's troops, commanders, and political workers. The meeting took place next to the scaffold where eight of our Motherland's glorious patriots had been hanged. The meetings participants swore to help the Red Army in every way to destroy the German aggressors.

In the first half of December 1941, in the Zavidovo and Klin areas liberated from the Germans, the 30th Army's political workers conducted meetings of the party activists, and the calling of a session of the district and rural soviets of worker's deputies was prepared. Meetings were conducted in all the collective farms, during which was discussed the problem "On the Restoration of the Collective Farm and the Preparations for the Spring Sowing." Along with the district party and soviet organs, the political section's workers were busy selecting and distributing collective farm and soviet cadres. Wide-ranging agitation-explanatory work was conducted among the local population. The political workers conducted 14 meetings and 24 discussions. More than 2,000 leaflets were distributed containing the text of the Soviet Information Bureau's communiqué "On the Failure of the Hitlerite Plan for Surrounding and Seizing Moscow."

Among the population of the Smolensk province's Dzerzhinskii district the 49th Army's political section conducted meetings with the local population in all the district's villages, in which the workers greeted the Red Army as their liberator.

In just a month the workers of the army's political section, together with the district organizations in the Dzerzhinskii district carried out 75 reports and discussions, which reached 3,903 people. In this period the district's population was shown more than 20 films.

On January 25 1942 a report was read on the current situation for the workers of the Troitskaya paper factory. The workers, in their addresses, thanked the Red Army and promised to devote all their strength to restoring the factory as soon as possible.

The local population joyfully greeted our troops and aided their successful advance in every way. During the fighting for Stalinogorsk the city's inhabitants formed a volunteer detachment, which bravely fought alongside the cavalrymen for their city.

Shura Moskovtseva, a resident of the village of Maloe Ivantsevo, performed a glorious deed. Our tanks, motor vehicles, and infantry were moving along a road to the village, which had just been cleared of Germans by units of the 19th Rifle Division. The columns were approached a ford. The patriot Shura Moskovtseva, who had noticed the previous evening that the Germans were mining the road and ford, ran toward the tanks amidst the explosions of shells, in order to warn the troops about the danger that threatened them.

She made it in time to the lead tank. The tank halted. The sappers were sent forward and found and disarmed 80 German mines. This is the way Soviet patriots, risking their lives, help the Red Army in their liberation struggle against German fascism.

Alongside the work among the population liberated by the Red Army, the political organs carried out work among the population and partisans in those areas temporarily occupied by the Germans.

Leaflets and appeals called upon the population of the occupied areas to be strong, to sabotage all the measures by the German authorities, to prevent the Germans from shipping stolen property, to help our units operating in the enemy rear, to join the partisans' ranks, and to assist our troops' advance.

One may judge about the scope of the spread of various agitation literature among the population of the occupied areas by the following data: in December 1941 and January 1942 the 16th Army's political section distributed 55,400 copies, while the 50th Army in December 1941 alone distributed 40,000. On the whole, our agitation penetrates well beyond the front line and strengthens the population's morale forces and mobilizes it for the further struggle against the German aggressors.

New tasks arose for the political organs involving work among the partisans. With the beginning of the Western Front's offensive, a new stage in the partisan struggle began. Partisan detachments quantitatively increased. Their military tasks increased significantly. Now the partisan detachments were to act in support of our units' offensive. They began to receive concrete combat assignments from the Western Front command. Thus during the offensive the activities of the partisan detachments became more organized and better planned. The political organs' task consisted of embracing the cadres of the partisan detachments with its political-educational work; by relying on the existing partisan detachments, to fan the flames of the partisan war in every way, to help them in swiftly carrying out their combat assignments, as dictated by our forces' offensive operations.

The political organs were also involved in selecting and outfitting small groups of 3-5 men, which were dispatched to the enemy rear to carry out specific missions. From the city of Tula alone during December 2-20, 143 groups numbering 459 men, were thrown into the enemy's rear. During December 20-31 eight groups numbering 47 men were thrown into the rear from Dubna and Khanino.

The partisan detachments, through their active operations, inflicted enormous losses on the German forces and rendered a priceless service to the Western Front's attacking units.

Work on demoralizing the enemy forces

With the Western Front going over to the offensive, work among the enemy's forces became particularly topical and acquired a significantly greater scope. Having been hit hard around Moscow, the Germans began to quickly fall back to the west. In these conditions it was necessary to increase the enemy troops' decline in combat ability with the corresponding political work, so as to always and everywhere remind them that their bloody cause is doomed, and that their resistance only strengthens the pressure by the Red Army and increases the losses among the German troops, and that the wisest decision for them is to turn against their reactionary officers and go over to the Red Army.

Printed propaganda occupied first place in the work among the enemy troops. During December 1941 and January 1942 24,767,000 copies of leaflets, newspapers, magazines, posters, and brochures were distributed throughout the Western Front. The distribution of printed matter was carried out by reconnaissance sections, as well as *front* and army aviation. The leaflets, as a rule, were scattered along the roads along which the German troops were retreating, in inhabited locales, and along the edges of woods in the enemy rear.

The content of the agitation work among the enemy forces changed completely and it became more offensive in character. The German troops were informed that they were surrounded and they received offers to drop their weapons and surrender.

When the Germans were kicked out of Klin and began to fall back in panic, our airplanes dropped a large quantity of leaflets and "Christmas presents" in German, issued by the 30th Army's political section. In them our troops and commanders promised the Germans a good "Christmas reception" with the aid of fire from Soviet guns and machine guns, and with the assistance of crackling Russian frosts.

On the 49th Army's sector in January 1942 leaflets were distributed among the enemy about the encirclement of the Germans in Kondrovo and Polotnyanyi Zavod, caricatures on the subject of the German divisions' defeat around Moscow, and an appeal to the troops of the 17th, 52nd, 131st, 137th, 260th, and 267th infantry divisions to surround.

As a rule, these distributed leaflets were the first experiments at waging oral propaganda on various sectors of the Western Front. On December 9 the 33rd Army's political section organized along the 1st Guards Motorized Rifle Division's sector a radio broadcast for the enemy's troops. A transmitter was set up not far from the German soldiers' trenches. The broadcast began with music by German composers. Then Ludwing Meyer, a German corporal in the 29th Infantry Regiment's fourth company, who had voluntarily surrendered, spoke and called upon the German troops to join the Red Army. The radio broadcast ended with the singing of the "Internationale."

In December 1941 the 49th Army conducted six radio broadcasts and two radio broadcasts in January 1942. These broadcasts were carried out 350-400 meters from the enemy positions. The broadcast program was as follows: "Stalin About the Prospects of the German-Soviet War"; "The Appeal of Prisoner of War Otto Naumen to the Soldiers of the 131st Infantry Division's 434th Infantry Regiment"; "The Appeal by Four Prisoners of War from the 268th Infantry Division to Their Unit's Troops"; "A Communique Regarding our Troops' Defeat of Generals Kleist and Shmidt and the Occupation by Units of the Red Army of Tikhvin, Yelets, and Kalinin and the Complete Failure of the Hitlerite Plan for Encircling Moscow." The broadcast lasted 20 minutes. According to our observers, when the German troops heard the broadcast they began to leave their dugouts. The enemy did not open fire during the broadcast. An immediate result of the broadcast was that eight German soldiers—neighbors of Otto Naumen, went over to the Red Army.

The forms of work among the enemy's troops employed by the Western Front's political organs were extremely varied. On the whole, however, all the work was directed at demoralizing and undermining the German-Fascist soldiers and weakening the Hitlerite army's combat effectiveness.

Thus the work among the enemy troops was one of the important elements in the political support of the Western Front's offensive operations.

In the previously-described account of party-political work during the period of the Germans' defeat around Moscow, only the most important aspects of the work by the commissars and political organs of the Western Front was highlighted, and even then only insofar as it touched upon the strengthening of the troops' combat effectiveness and the political support for carrying out combat orders.

The experience of the political organs' work during the defensive fighting for Moscow and in the offensive period shows once again what a mighty means of ideological-political influence on the masses party-political work is and the great role it played in the defeat of the Germans around Moscow.

The correct use of the varied forms of party-political work, the employment of methods of convincing and, in certain cases forcing, gave the commissars and political organs the opportunity to support the achievement by the troops of the historical task of defending Moscow in the most difficult conditions and in the tensest period the Great Patriotic War.

8

An overall view of the December fighting

As a result of the German-Fascist leadership's miscalculations in the area of war planning in general, and in the waging of operations along the Moscow direction, the plan for seizing the capital of the Soviet state failed. The Germans approached to within 25 km of Moscow from the northwest in the beginning of December and could already have bombarded the city with long-range artillery. But at this point their offensive capabilities were exhausted. During the fierce 20-day battle on the approaches to Moscow, the Germans lost their advantages in forces and the operational situation. They were forced to shortly go over to the defensive in unfavorable conditions, being outflanked on both wings by the Red Army's forces and then, under our units' growing pressure, they began their hurried retreat.

The secret concentration of the reserve armies, the correct determination of the moment for going over to the offensive, and the correct selection of the axes for the main blows along the flanks aided the Red Army's success during these days of crisis around Moscow. These events, as well as the preceding and accompanying circumstances, have already been highlighted by us.

The immediate objective of the Red Army command in the beginning of December consisted of using the favorable moment for assuming the offensive along both wings and, by means of concentric blows, to defeat the Germans' flank groups. This led to the Red Army's successful battles in the area of Klin and the Istra Reservoir, which concluded with the defeat and retreat of the remains of the northern German shock group (Third and Fourth panzer groups, which lost almost all their tanks). Simultaneously, our counteroffensive in the south was unfolding, where the enemy's Second Panzer Army suffered a defeat in the area of Tula, Venev, and Stalinogorsk, and also began to hurriedly retreat to the southwest, pursued by our forces.

In a December 9 directive by the Western Front's military council, it was pointed out that the main mission of the Western Front's troops consisted of defeating as quickly as possible the enemy's flank groups and capturing his equipment, transport, and weapons and by rapidly moving forward to envelop his flank groups, to finally encircle and destroy the enemy armies facing the Western Front.

The Red Army's forces, in carrying out the assigned tasks, developed the offensive and inflicted blow after blow. In the period since the beginning of the Germans' second offensive on Moscow (from November 16) through December 10 we captured and destroyed (not counting our air actions): 1,434 tanks, 5,416 motor vehicles, 575 guns, 339 mortars, and 870 machine guns. The Germans' losses during this period amounted to 85,000 men killed.

Subsequently the Red Army command's operational plan was further developed in the *front's* directives (nos. 0103 and 0104 of December 13, no. 0112 of December 16, no. 0116 of December 24, and no. 0125, and others), which were issued on the basis of instructions by the Supreme Commander-in-Chief. The plan foresaw (in conjunction with the Kalinin Front) the encirclement and rout of the opposing German-Fascist forces by means of an advance by both wings of the Western Front and their envelopment of the enemy's forces.

By December 18 the *front's* armies were to reach the line Stepurino (22 km southeast of Staritsa)-Shakhovskaya-Ashcherino-Gribtsovo (20 km east of Mozhaisk)-Maurino-Balabanovo-Tarutino-Nedel'noe-Zhelyabuzhskii-Khanino-Odoevo-Arsen'evo. According to the directive issued on December 16, the *front's* armies were to reach by December 21 the line Bol'shie Ledinki (8 km south of Staritsa)-Pogoreloe Gorodishche-Mikhalevo-Mozhaisk-to the west of Borovsk-Ugodskii Zavod-Maloyaroslavets-Pletnevka (10 km west of Kaluga)-Likhvin.

The objectives issued to the armies on December 20 foresaw the right wing's arrival by the end of December 27 at the line Zubtsov-Gzhatsk, and that of the left wing to the line Polotnyanyi Zavod-Kozel'sk. Meanwhile, the center was attacking more slowly than the wings and by this time was supposed to be approximately along the line Mozhaisk-Maloyaroslavets. In this fashion it was planned to create a situation in which both wings would move forward and that there would be an opportunity to outflank the entire central (Gzhatsk-Vyaz'ma-Yukhnov) enemy group.

However, as we have seen, life made some significant changes to this plan. The fighting in the areas of Klin and the Istra Reservoir on December 11-15, although they ended in the Red Army's victory, nevertheless delayed our troops' offensive and enabled the German command to win time for organizing a solid defense along the line of the Lama and Ruza rivers. It was on this line that the offensive by the Western Front's right wing was forced to temporarily halt. It was necessary to prepare a breakthrough of the defensive zone, which we were unable to take on the march. The fighting here at the end of December and beginning of January was drawn out.

On the southern wing (particularly on the *front's* left flank) operations developed the entire time in more maneuverable conditions and at a faster pace. At first the Germans sought to get out of their turned position; our troops pursued them. Subsequently, the enemy was nowhere able to linger along intermediary lines and organize a stubborn defense. This was made easier by the fact that the enemy troops' retreat from the Tula area was carried out along diverging axes: units of the German Fourth Army were falling back on Kaluga and Yukhnov, while the Second Panzer Army was falling back on Orel. Even such a favorable defensive line as the Oka River between Kaluga and Belev was, following a series of battles, overcome by our forces at the end of December. As a result, a favorable condition arose for the subsequent and immediate offensive by the left wing to the west and northwest, in accordance with the plan for the *front* operation. Here our troops moved forward rapidly and to a great depth.

The center, against which the Germans had heavily dug in, having occupied these positions for about two months, at first secured the internal flanks of the Western Front's two enveloping wings and then, on December 18 went over to the offensive on its own for the purpose of breaking through the Fascists' defense along the Naro-Fominsk axis. The first offensive here (as we saw) was not crowned with success, but the Red Army's troops tied down the enemy forces in these operations and prevented them from maneuvering them against our active wings. Finally, in these battles our central armies amassed the necessary experience in organizing an offensive, which they employed as early as the end of December.

The Western Front's neighbors were also engaged in active operations. The Kalinin Front in the second half of December was developing the successful offensive by its center along the Staritsa axis. The boundary line with the Western Front ran along the line Rogachevo-Reshetnikovo station-Kotlyakovo-Sychevka (all within the Kalinin Front).

The Southwestern Front's right wing (from December 25—the Bryansk Front) continued in the last ten days of December to attack along the Mtsensk, Orel, and Livny axes. As a result of the fighting here, our troops moved significantly forward (from 50-75 km, depending on the position as of December 16) and captured the towns of Chern' and Livny. The boundary line between the Bryansk and Western fronts was as before: Ryazhsk-Malevka-Belev-Tyat'kovo (all within the Western Front).

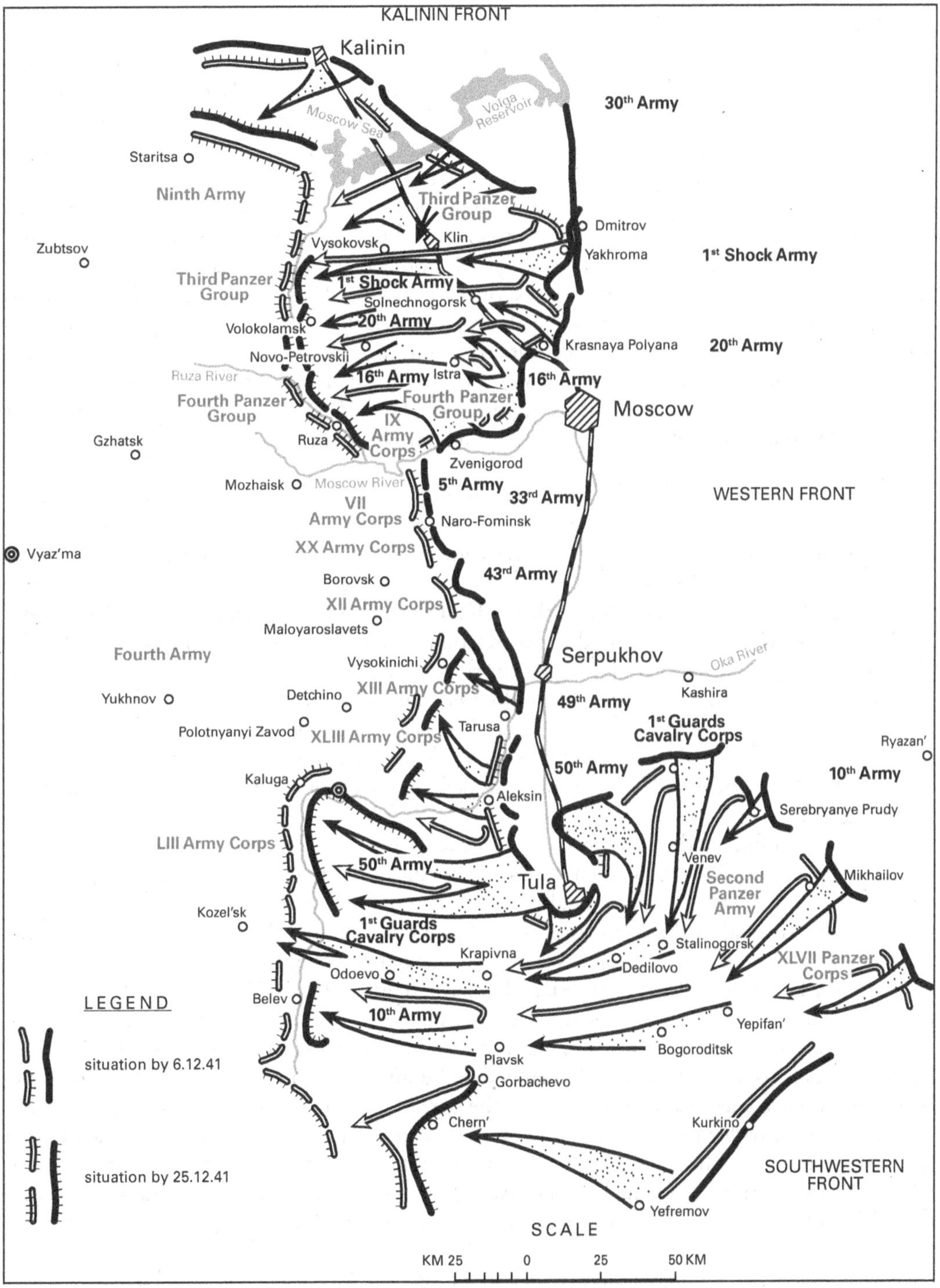

Map 11 The Western Front's Counteroffensive in December, 1941

The December period of the Western Front's operations under review (to be exact, December 6-24) includes as its most important moment the assumption of the offensive by both our wings and the defeat of the Germans' flank shock groups. Thus the Red Army's chief operations during this period were offensive ones. But this was not a usual offensive operation, created in the relatively quiet period of a preparatory period without serious interference by the enemy. Our blow was organized in a period of a combat storm, matured in the process of a cruel struggle with the Germans and in a rapidly-changing situation. This was our counteroffensive, that is an offensive as a reply to the enemy's offensive and which was an outgrowth of a previous defensive situation.

The Western Front's counteroffensive in December was linked to the previously-conducted active defense and in many ways arose from that operational situation in which the Red Army found itself by the end of the defensive battle around Moscow. Our assumption of a general offensive along both wings, as we have seen, was preceded and accompanied by extremely stubborn and fierce battles with an experienced, powerful and shrewd enemy, who had as his goal the defeat of our troops and the breakthrough to Moscow. By no means did the Red Army in these battles limit itself to defensive actions. It not only repelled the enemy attacks, but counterattacked against him, seeking to halt the enemy and grab the initiative from him. The starting point with the bulge-shaped front line, from which our troops went over to the offensive, was created as a result of the fierce struggle of two sides in the preceding defensive period, as well as the result of the correct operational foresight by the Red Army High Command (the concentration and composition of the reserve armies according to place and time).

The goals and tasks of our counteroffensive were positive in nature and sought the defeat of the enemy forces and developed consecutively in accordance with the changing situation. The counteroffensive was conducted by significantly greater forces in comparison with the preceding defensive phase, because (besides the Western Front's earlier seven armies) three new armies from the Supreme Command Reserve (more than 100,000 men, 600 guns, and 100 tanks) and other formations took part, which changed the correlation of forces in our favor. The counteroffensive began with a new composition of forces and the sides' new situation in comparison with the defensive battle; insofar as the shape of the front by that time had changed significantly and the Red Army's large new operational-strategic reserves had been committed to the battle. The defeat of the Germans' flank groups, which had been hanging over Moscow, created favorable conditions for our subsequent offensive for the purpose of defeating all those Germans forces opposing the Western Front.

Within the confines of the *front* operation under consideration (December 6-24), full of various types of military activities and content, the most notable military events took place on the *front's* wings, which were connected by a solid center. Active operations during this period developed, for the most part, within the confines of the wings. One could say that here we had (within the confines of a unified large operation) two offensive operations by groups of armies: the northern group (30th, 1st, 20th, and 16th armies), and a southern group (49th, 50th, and 10th armies, and the 1st Guards Cavalry Corps). To be sure, this was not in the full sense an operation by a group of armies (such groups were not organizationally created), and the *front* command directly controlled all the armies and assigned to each of them a definite mission according to goal, place and time. Nonetheless the armies of both wings, given the overall goal on a *front* scale, were operationally united (particularly during the first period of the counteroffensive) by a local goal, which flowed from the overall goal. The tasks, which were carried out by these armies were quite closely linked with each other within the confines of the given wing and were directed toward an overall object (the defeat of the northern or southern German shock groups). Orders by the *front* command during this time were usually issued separately for one or the other wing, while each wing was responsible for carrying out a definite operational task. This was one of the characteristic features of army control during this stage of the *front* operation. Subsequently, as the entire *front* became more active, the operational independence of the wings disappears in the overall course of the *front* offensive operation and we no longer see sharply delineated operations along the wings.

In December period's army operations we see a great deal of variety. Here we find the maneuver offensive operations by the 30th, 16th, 50th and other armies; a peculiar meeting battle (which grew into an offensive against an opponent on the defensive) along the 1st and 20th armies' front; the 10th Army's operational pursuit to a great depth; operational defense and an attempt to break through the enemy's fortified front by our center armies. In the first period (when the enemy had not yet been broken) one may observe the closer unification and linkage of two-three armies' operations for the resolution of a single overall task, for concentrating efforts along a single axis, or an offensive against a single object (the 30th, 1st, and 20th armies' operations during December 8-15 in the area of Klin and Solnechnogorsk; the offensive by the 50th Army, 1st Guards Cavalry Corps, and the 10th Army against the Second Panzer Army to the east and southeast of Tula). The enemy subsequently began to withdraw and his resistance grew weaker. The army's now have the opportunity of operating with lesser dependence on each other and carrying out independent tasks, each along its own operational axis (for example, the 49th Army in the direction of Vysokinichi and Detchino, the 50th Army toward Kaluga and Peremyshl', and the 10th Army on Belev).

The operational forms in which the fighting on both sides unfolded varied. In the process of the operation's development, they changed and transitioned from one kind into another (sometimes even during a single stage of a *front* operation), nevertheless maintaining a certain connection and continuity. For example, the Germans (employing their hackneyed operational methods) tried to envelop and encircle Moscow from both sides, attacking from the flanks with their two shock groups. This attempt ended with both German wedges, having exhausted their offensive capabilities, had to go over to the defensive in conditions in which each of the wedges was outflanked by the Red Army's forces and sought to escape from the situation by a retreat. If one attempts to brief characterize the turning point of the Moscow operation in the sense of operational forms, then one can say that here the German wedges fell into previously-prepared pincers, from which they were able to extricate themselves with great difficulty and heavy casualties.

The Western Front's offensive unfolded as two coordinated blows, which were launched by both wings (with a stoutly defending center) for the purpose of defeating the enemy's flank groups. The peculiarity of employing this operational form consisted of, by the way, of developing our counteroffensive from those areas of the broad front to where the Germans had been directing their main blow (from the flanks).

The Red Army began its counteroffensive with operations along outer operational axes on a scale of each wing. The subsequent defeat and retreat by the German flank groups led to a situation in which these concentric offensives grew into a pursuit of the enemy along parallel axes. The success achieved on the wings made it possible to advance them more rapidly than in the center. From this arises the question (which, as we have seen, found its expression in the directives of the Western Front command) of moving both wings forward for the purpose of enveloping all the German forces facing the Western Front. Thus from external operational axes on a scale of each wing separately the Western Front, by operations along parallel axes, sought in the second half of December to move to a concentric offensive on a *front* scale (external operational axes within the confines of the entire *front*).

The offensive battles alternated with defensive ones at different periods and along different sectors of the front. The tension and activity on both sides and the desire to snatch the initiative from the enemy's hands, sometimes led to meeting collisions of various scales. For example, the Germans' reserve shock group, moving on Dmitrov and Krasnaya Polyana, sought with part of its troops to force the Moscow-Volga Canal and bypass Moscow from the northeast, while another part was to take the Soviet capital directly.

A meeting blow by the 1st and 20th armies was launched against the Germans along the line of the Moscow-Volga Canal-Krasnaya Polyana, which grew into an offensive for the purpose of defeating the opposing German-Fascist forces. The specific development of combat operations (described in the appropriate chapter) was such that there were almost no meeting engagements, or that only limited ones took place. Before long the Germans went over to the defensive and our armies began to attack the defenders, and then the retreating enemy. However, insofar as both sides during the period November 29-December 4 pursued positive, active goals and were assigning their troops offensive tasks and sought to reach those areas behind the enemy's lines, this period of combat operations should be viewed as a meeting battle in peculiar conditions (a non-typical instance of a meeting battle).

Thus the December period of the *front* operation was full of combat events quite different in their content and form.

As we have seen, the question of reserves played an enormous role in the course of the operation. In the final analysis, the fate of the battle at the gates of Moscow was decided in our favor by the reserve armies and other reserves, which the Supreme Commander-in-Chief, displaying great foresight and prudence, formed and concentrated in a timely manner along the necessary axes (predominantly along the Western Front's flanks) and committed into the fighting at the moment of the battle's crisis. Large-scale and intense modern operations demand the presence of large reserves at the disposal of the high command. This is necessary in order to control the development of the battle and operation in the desired direction and to, in essence, to direct the course of events. The German-Fascist command underestimated the Red Army's powers of resistance and its reserves. It deployed its troops in a line, thus securing a broad offensive front and the power of the first blows. However, when these blows did not yield the desired results for the Germans, they were forced to (no longer having free reserves) go over to the defensive and then to retreat under the Soviet troops' increasing blows.

The Red Army had received by the moment of the decisive fighting not only reinforcements in men, but also in powerful fire means (mortars, guards mortar battalions, artillery, anti-tank rifles, etc.). This enabled us to organize a more stubborn fire resistance, which caused serious losses to the enemy's tanks and men, and then to seize the initiative.

It should also note the maneuver of men and equipment along the front, which the Red Army command resorted to in the tense December fighting. This maneuver of forces along the front was very effective (the transfer of the 1st Guard Cavalry Corps to the Kashira area, the strengthening of the Kaluga group's forces, and other measures). In special emergency situations we even practiced moving small sections (for example, a platoon from each regiment or division), in order to reinforce the bloodied units along an important axis, or to close a breach in the front. The maneuver of combat equipment (artillery, tanks, etc.) along the front during was also practiced, depending on the situation.

So as to strengthen the mobility of our reconnaissance and forward detachments in winter, and to create mobile groups, the *front* command asked for 20 ski battalions.

The conditions that had come about at the end of December enabled us to more rationally fill out our units and formations, which had suffered heavy losses in the preceding battles. Thus the Western Front's military council made the decision to remove ten rifle divisions and an airborne corps to the reserve for refitting. In order to do this, the Western Front requested 70,000 rank and file, corporals and NCOs, of which 25% were armed.

As we noted earlier, the Western Front's troop control was precise, strict and highly centralized. Despite the *front's* bulky organizational composition (ten armies and Belov's group, which were directly subordinated to the *front*), no intermediary instances (groups of armies) were created between the *front* and the armies. The *front* commander directly assigned tasks to each of the armies.

The character of the defensive fighting (in which the initiative belonged to the enemy) laid its imprint on the methods of troop control. During this period general orders and directives gave way to local orders and separate commands to one or the other of the armies. And this was perfectly understandable. With the beginning of our counteroffensive on the wings, in connection with the necessity of planning the operations of several armies, alongside local orders to separate armies, there appear directives to armies on one wing or another, planning and organizing the operations of a group of armies. Finally, when the center went over to active operations, the practice of issuing overall directives on a *front* scale was reborn. Alongside this, telephone conversations and visits to the units were employed. Thus we can note a variety and flexibility in the methods of expressing the command's will, depending upon the goal and the concrete situation.

The harsh and snowy winter hindered the troops' activities. The troops were primarily forced to operate along the roads and the enemy, while retreating, sought to destroy and mine the roads and inhabited areas. Our troops advance slowed under these conditions and their maneuver was constricted. This was described at length in the description of combat operations.

Our troops' political-morale condition during the counteroffensive was higher than the enemy's. Combat feats and heroism grow even more and come to embrace 200,000-250,000 men.

The great battle around Moscow represents one of the most outstanding and inspiring pages in the history of the Great Patriotic War. It will undoubtedly go into world military history as one of the deathless examples of fortitude in battle, bravery and military art, and which was crowned by the Red Army's and it's leadership's great victory over the German-Fascist troops.

The entire world was struck by the unexpected turn of events around Moscow. Foreign newspapers asked in confusion: How did this happen? The "invincible" Germany army, which was always attacking, had almost reached the gates of Moscow and, suddenly, for no apparent reason, ran back, abandoning its weapons and carpeting its path of retreat with thousands of corpses. Foreign newspapers could not explain this and wrote about the "miracle before Moscow."

But we know how it happened. We struck the Germans around Moscow with the entire might of the Red Army, with the entire aroused strength and hatred of the people. The Germans could not withstand this and rolled back. As we have seen, there was no "miracle" here. However, there was the grand patriotism of the Soviet people, the bravery and skill of the Red Army, and comrade Stalin's wise leadership.

This gave us victory over the Germans in the great battle of Moscow.

Part V

The offensive by the Western Front's troops from the line of the Lama, Ruza, Nara, and Oka rivers (December 25 1941—January 31 1942)

1

The Overall Situation on the Western Front at the Beginning of January 1942

Following the December defeat of the German-Fascist troops near Moscow the remnants of the enemy's defeated flank groups were falling back to the west, striving to delay on convenient defensive lines.

One such defensive line, which the Germans reached during the second half of December, was the line of the Lama, Ruza, Moscow, and Nara rivers, and then along the Oka toward Kaluga and Belev, and then south along the Zusha River.

The Germans' defense was based upon a system of strong points and centers of resistance in the inhabited areas, on road junctions and other important sectors. They employed previous defensive structures here for creating field fortifications with wooden and earthen firing points.

Fortifications were unearthed further in the depth around Shakhovskaya, Sereda, Mozhaisk, Maloyaroslavets, Detchino, and points south. Another defensive line was planned by the Germans east of Rzhev and Gzhatsk (the Gzhatsk defensive line), then to the south along the Ugra and Oka rivers.

The enemy was putting up stubborn resistance along the occupied line and evidently wanted to hold out here until the spring. Evidence of this is found in captured orders from the German-Fascist command, the hurried transfer of various units and formations from the depth in order to organize a defense, as well as the Germans' fortification of a defensive line east of Gzhatsk, and the stubborn several-day fighting for Kaluga and Belev, when our troops were forcing the Oka between these two locales.

The Germans' main groups were located along the Gzhatsk axis, as well as in the areas of Medyn', Kaluga, and Yukhnov.

At the end of December the Western Front's armies were carrying out their previous assignments to use both the *front's* wings to envelop the German forces facing the Western Front. The left wing was moving quickly forward, while the right halted briefly along the line of the Lama and Ruza rivers.

The *Stavka's* instructions of January 7 called for the defeat of the enemy's main forces located along the Moscow strategic direction by the joint forces of the Western and Kalinin fronts.

In order to carry out this task, the Kalinin Front, having carried out a regrouping, was to attack with its main forces in the general direction of Vyaz'ma. The Western Front, while conducting an offensive with its right flank along the Gzhatsk axis, intended to attack toward Vyaz'ma with its center armies and part of its left wing (5th, 33rd, 43rd, and 49th armies, and Belov's group). The successful achievement of these tasks by both *fronts* should lead to the encirclement and defeat of the greater part of the central group of the German armies.

In the Kalinin Front's directive no. 057/op of January 8 1942, it was stated that the *front's* troops, having carried out their regrouping, are continuing an energetic offensive, launching their main blow in the general direction of Sychevka and Vyaz'ma. These forces had the task by the close of January 11 of reaching the area of Sychevka, cutting the Gzhatsk-Smolensk railroad and road west of Vyaz'ma, depriving the enemy of his main communications and, together with the Western Front's forces, of encircling and then capturing or destroying the Germans' Mozhaisk-Gzhatsk-Vyaz'ma group of forces.

The Western Front commander, Gen. Zhukov, in his directive no. 0141/op of January 6, assigned the breakthrough along the Volokolamsk-Gzhatsk axis to the 20th Army. The 33rd Army in the center was to attack toward the west and turn Mozhaisk from the south. "The immediate task of the 43rd, 49th and 50th armies," as stated in the Western Front's directive no. 0152/op of January 8 1942, "is to encircle and defeat the Kondrovo-Yukhnov-Medyn' enemy group and develop the blow to the northwest for the purpose of encircling and completely defeating the Mozhaisk-Gzhatsk-Vyaz'ma enemy group."

Thus it was planned to defeat the main German forces by means of a concentric offensive by two *fronts* toward Vyaz'ma. As regards the Western Front, the most rapid results could evidently be expected from an offensive toward Vyaz'ma by our center armies and those of the left wing's northern part. The right wing had almost not moved from December 20 and was encountering stubborn enemy resistance. The left-flank 10th Army was spread out along a broad front, having advanced since the start of the offensive about 350 km in winter conditions; by the middle of January the army was near the limit of its offensive capabilities.

The overall course of the fighting along the Western Front's right wing is as follows. At the end of December the *front's* right-wing armies (1st, 20th, 16th), while continuing to attack, sought to break through the Germans' defense along the line of the Lama and Ruza rivers. The offensive was conducted along a broad front and each of the right wing's armies was launching a blow along its own separate sector, employing its available men and matériel.

However, by this time the enemy had already managed to prepare his defense and consolidate along the appointed line. The German command, by transferring from the depth all sorts of composite and reserve units, as well as divisions brought up from the occupied areas, was able to organize a solid defense along this line by the time his forces falling back from Moscow reached the Lama and Ruza rivers.

This defense was basically created on the basis of fortifications and positions constructed earlier by our forces and the German troops along both banks of the Lama and Ruza rivers.

The attempt by the German command to use the old positions operationally was completely natural, as the wintery conditions did not enable him to build in time new defensive lines necessary for consolidating the retreating troops. The German command, pointed out in its orders:

> The overall combat situation insistently demands that the rapid withdrawal of our units be halted and that a stubborn defense be mounted on the line of the Lama River...
>
> **The positions along the Lama River must be defended to the last man.**
>
> I hold the commanders personally responsible for carrying out this order by our leader and supreme commander, with iron energy and ruthless decisiveness. ... The current crisis must be and will be overcome. The question is one of our life and death.[1]

Hitler, in his order, demanded that the troops not retreat a single step and that they should defend to the last extremity.

The German command, by its actions toward the retreating troops, managed to halt them by the beginning of January and the fighting along the Western Front's right wing took on an

1 From an order by the commander of the 23rd Infantry Division.

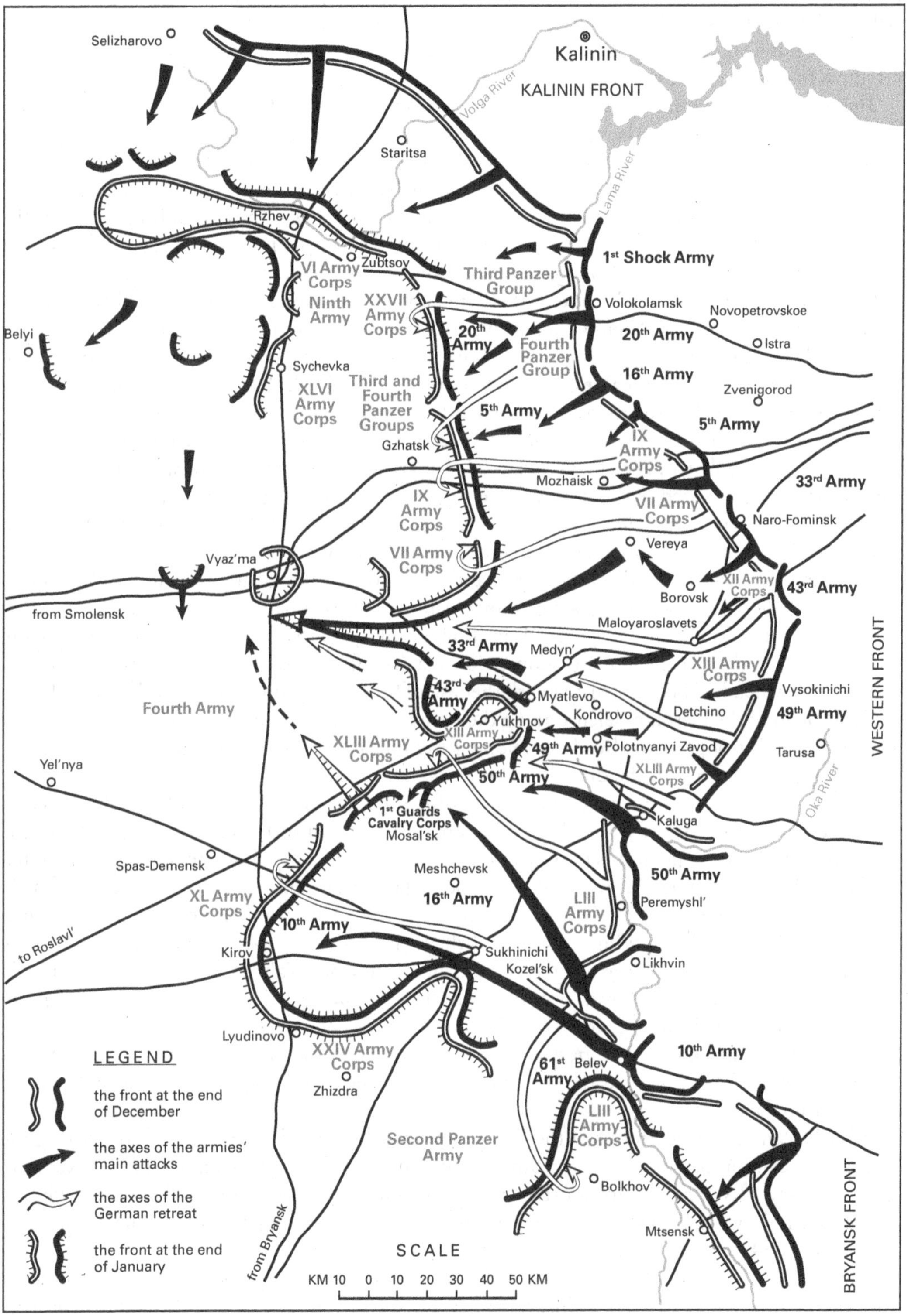

Map 12 The Western Front's Offensive in January, 1942

extended character. The initiative remained in the hands of the Red Army, which was imposing its will on the enemy. Nonetheless, along certain axes the Germans were not only putting up serious resistance, but were carrying out active operations as well (expressed in counterattacks and even in attempts to encircle our units).

The forces of the Western Front's right wing, having reached the Germans' fortified lines, were forced to halt. After putting their units in order, concentrating equipment and carrying out a series of regroupings, they began their planned offensive against the defending enemy.

However, the men and suppression weapons available in each army were insufficient to independently carry out an operational breakthrough and develop it into the depth. If prior to this the right wing's armies, while attacking along a broad front, had pursued the retreating units or fought an enemy who had hurriedly taken up the defense and had not yet had time to successfully consolidate his position, now along the line of the Lama and Ruza rivers they encountered the enemy's timely organized and hard defense. Here new offensive methods were demanded. It was necessary to carefully prepare and skillfully organize a breakthrough, having concentrated large amounts of men and suppression matériel along a narrow front, so as to smash through the Germans' defense and then develop the breakthrough into the depth and along the flanks.

However, evidently this was not immediately recognized. In all three of the right wing's armies at the end of December and the first ten days of January multiple attacks against the enemy's fortified positions were carried out, but they failed to yield any kind of significant successes as a result of the Germans' stubborn defense. The battles conducted here enabled us to accumulate a certain amount of experience and gather additional information about the enemy.

In connection with this, the *front* command gave up on further attempts to break through the German defense by the right wing's three armies along a broad front and decided to adopt a method for breaking through fortified positions using one army along a narrow front, having concentrated in this army men and suppression matériel from the other armies. As a result, the 20th Army, which had been entrusted with the task of breaking through, successfully carried out a breakthrough of the German defense along the Lama and in the second ten-day period of January the right wing's troops were already developing the operational breakthrough and pursuing the retreating German units in the direction of Gzhatsk.

In the center of the Western Front a successful offensive was also unfolding. The Western Front's rapid advance at the end of December and the first half of January was favorable for the development of active operations in the center. As a result of this fighting, the Red Army liberated Maloyaroslavets on January 2 and took Borovsk on January 4. The troops continued to advance to the west from these locales. Our subsequent offensive along the Medyn'-Myatlevo axis had already encountered the growing resistance of the Germans' Medyn'-Kondrovo-Yukhnov group, which was covering the Warsaw highway and the route from Kaluga to Vyaz'ma. Fighting in the area of Myatlevo, Kondrovo, and Yukhnov became prolonged and continued throughout January. To the north of this area the offensive by our center was subsequently eased by the successful breakthrough by the *front's* right-wing armies along the Volokolamsk-Gzhatsk axis and the German withdrawal to the Gzhatsk defensive line, which began in the second ten-day period of January.

After December 25 the troops of the Western Front's left wing had the task of completing the offensive operations begun in the preceding period. The 49th Army, which had captured Nedel'no along the way, was attacking toward Detchino. The 50th Army was fighting for Kaluga with its center and right wing forces, while its left-flank divisions were attacking in the general direction of Uteshevo (20 km west of Kaluga).

The 1st Guards Cavalry Corps, which had been divided into two groups, attacked with one in the general direction of Yukhnov, while the other was aimed at Kozel'sk, with the task of capturing it by December 27.

The 10th Army continued the fight for Belev with part of its forces, while the remainder advanced in the direction of Kozel'sk and to the south.

Thus at the end of December the Western Front's left wing was advancing without a pause and was forcing the Oka between Kaluga and Belev, while attacking to the northwest in the direction of Yukhnov, and to the west in the direction of Sukhinichi and Kirov.

However, the enemy evidently did not want to give up his defensive line along the Oka; he stubbornly sought to hold Kaluga and Belev as strong points along our offensive's flanks. To the north of Kaluga the Germans were holding the Detchino area. The fighting for these towns was stubborn and continued several days. Kaluga was finally occupied by our troops only on December 30 and Belev on December 31.

Subsequently operations by the *front's* left wing developed along the following axes: Kondrovo-Yukhnov, and Sukhinichi-Kirov. The defeat of the enemy's Kondrovo-Myatlevo-Yukhnov group and reaching the Vyaz'ma-Bryansk railroad and the Warsaw highway were the immediate missions.

The development of the offensive along the Western Front's left wing occurred in opposite succession to that of the right wing. There, as we saw, our troops had no significant successes during the first ten days of January, while the main advance occurred during the second half of January as a result of the successful breakthrough by the 20th Army. Here, on the contrary, the troops of the Western Front's left wing advanced rapidly during the end of December and first half of January and nearly reached those lines on which the end of January found them.

Thus, Meshchovsk was taken in the beginning of January and there was fighting for Sukhinichi, where the German garrison was hanging on stubbornly. On January 7 our forces took Serpeisk and were fighting for Mosal'sk. On January 9 the Red Army entered Lyudinovo, followed the next day by Kirov. Stubborn fighting was occurring with a large German group along the Yukhnov axis.

The operations of the Western Front's armies occurred in this overall operational situation in the first half of January.

The Situation of the Neighboring *Fronts*

During the last days of December the Kalinin Front was attacking along the Rzhev axis, striving through enveloping blows from the north and east to cut off the retreat route of the enemy's Staritsa group to the southwest. During December 27-30 the *front's* troops liberated 146 inhabited locales and captured the following equipment: 197 guns, 182 machine guns, 415 automatic rifles, 3,890 rifles, 520 motor vehicles, and other items. On January 1 our troops occupied Staritsa and continued pursuing the Germans retreating on Rzhev and Zubtsov.

On January 5 the Kalinin Front's forces were already attacking the enemy defenders along a line 15-20 km north and northeast of Rzhev and Zubtsov. The next day our units, having advanced to the west of Rzhev, cut the Rzhev-Velikie Luki railroad in the area of Chertolino station. In the following days the Red Army continued to attack toward Rzhev and Zubtsov, enveloping this area from the east, north, and west.

On January 12-13 our units, which were developing the blow in the direction of Sychevka, advanced 8 km from the northwest to this area, having reached the rear of the Germans' Rzhev-Zubtsov-Sychevka group and halfway surrounded it.

On January 15 the Kalinin Front's right wing captured Selizharovo and was pursuing the retreating German units to the south and southwest. Our forces subsequently moved forward successfully in the direction of Velizh and Belyi, having deeply penetrated into the German lines. On the Kalinin Front's left wing the enemy was stubbornly and actively defending the area of Rzhev, Zubtsov, and Sychevka and was solidly holding on here, despite the fact that he had been surrounded on three sides by the troops of the Red Army.

At the end of December the Bryansk Front's right-wing forces, having encountered the organized resistance and counterattacks by the enemy along the Bolkhov and Mtsensk axes, went over to the defensive.

During the first days of January our units repelled German counterattacks and were fighting to take Mtsensk. However, this did not yield decisive results. On January 4-6 the troops of the Bryansk Front's right-flank 61st Army were regrouping their forces, seeking to use the forward position of the Western Front's left-flank 10th Army to pass through the latter and gain the flank and rear of the Germans' Bolkhov group. For this purpose the 61st Army, having left a covering force from the east along the line of the Oka, was transferring its divisions to the north and then through the Belev area to the western bank of the Oka.

On January 7 these forces, having completed their regrouping, attacked from the area west and southwest of Belev, launching a blow against the flank and rear of the enemy's Bolkhov group, defending the western bank of the Oka.

During January 8-10 fierce fighting continued; our troops moved forward somewhat, but without important results, as a result of the Germans' stubborn resistance. On January 13 the 61st Army was subordinated to the Western Front. The boundary line with the Bryansk Front was the line Ryazhsk-Malevka-L'govo-Belye Berega station (all within the Western Front).

The Bryansk Front's right wing subsequently occupied its former position in front of Mtsensk and to the south. There were no important developments along this sector of the front during January.

2

The enemy facing the Western Front in January 1942

An overall evaluation of the enemy's situation at the beginning of January 1942

The Ninth and Fourth German armies, consisting of 14 corps, several independent divisions and groups, as a result of their December defeat around Moscow, were falling back to the west under the blows of the of the Western and Kalinin fronts' troops. While withdrawing the enemy waged stubborn, holding defensive battles, and along a number of sectors would counterattack with the support of tanks and aviation.

By the beginning of January the Germans along their northern wing and in the center, by dint of enormous efforts and desperate resistance, had managed to half the Western Front's offensive and occupy a favorable defensive position, which ran along the western bank of the Lama, Ruza, and Nara rivers as far as Bashkino (10 km southwest of Naro-Fominsk) exclusively, and then to the west of Borovsk and Maloyaroslavets toward Detchino, before turning to the south, west of Kaluga.

Along his southern wing the enemy, under pressure from the 50th and 10th armies, was falling back to the west and northwest, stubbornly fighting along the intermittent and broken line Zubovo (30 km southeast of Yukhnov)-Dolgaya (10 km south of Yukhnov)-Yukhnov-Mosal'sk-Meshchovsk-Sukhinichi-Maklaki (28 km southwest of Sukhinichi)-Klintsy (excluding)-Belev.

The German command, in its offensive on Moscow, as a result of the operation's successful development, did not plan for the possibility of a deep withdrawal. According to the available data, although deep rear lines were planned, they were not sufficiently prepared beforehand and the command of the central army group and the commanders of the Ninth and Fourth armies did not have reserves available to occupy the new defensive line and absorb the retreating forces.

During the withdrawal the insignificant available reserves were employed by the German command to restore the situation, but could not save it. As a result, the enemy was not able to carry out a systematic withdrawal and create powerful shock groups out of its reserve units and formations.

The main operational directions and the enemy's disposition of its forces in the defense

The most important operational directions for the enemy facing the Western Front in the first half of January were as follows:

1 The Volokolamsk-Gzhatsk direction (against the 1st, 20th, and 16th armies) was the most serious and dangerous on the Germans' left wing. Gzhatsk was the junction for the roads leading to Rzhev, Vyaz'ma, and Yukhnov; as to its military-geographical situation, it covers the most convenient roads to Vyaz'ma and then to Smolensk. Gzhatsk formed the top of the triangle of the enemy's defensive position, the base of which were Rzhev and Vyaz'ma. The capture of the Gzhatsk

junction would disrupt the Germans' defensive system and enable us to outflank the Vyaz'ma center of resistance from the north.

2 The Mozhaisk direction (against the 5th Army) was important for the enemy, because it offered the shortest distance to Gzhatsk.
3 The Medyn' direction (against the 33rd and 43rd armies) led directly to Yukhnov and offered the possibility for the deep envelopment of the Vyaz'ma center of resistance from the southeast and south.
4 The Yukhnov direction (against the 49th and 50th armies) covered the shortest routes from the east and southeast to Roslavl' and Vyaz'ma; it had great operational significance for the enemy.
5 The Sukhinichi direction (against the 10th Army) also had great significance. Sukhinichi is a railroad junction in which lines from Smolensk, Roslavl' and Bryansk come together, which facilitates the transfer of men and matériel.

During the second half of January, as a result of the Western Front's successful offensive, the most threatening operational directions for the enemy were:

1 The Novoduginskaya direction (against the 20th Army), as the shortest direction, offered the possibility of enveloping the Gzhatsk center of resistance from the north. The subsequent removal of the 1st Army from the Western Front (the 1st Army was transferred to the Northwestern Front) undoubtedly influenced the development of the operation by the 20th Army, which having alone occupied the 1st Army's former sector, had to carry out a subsequent offensive along a 35-km front (instead of a 20-km one). By this time the enemy, by moving up new reserves and occupying favorable lines, had strengthened his defense.
2 The Gzhatsk direction (against the 5th Army) led directly to Gzhatsk. However, with the departure of the 16th Army to the Western Front's southern sector, the 5th Army's front increased to 50 km (instead of the previous 20 km), which also influenced the course of the subsequent offensive. The enemy, taking into account the importance of this direction, significantly raised his defensive capabilities by the commitment of new reserves from the deep rear.
3 The Yukhnov-Vyaz'ma direction (against the 33rd, 43rd, 49th, and 50th armies) offered the possibility of deeply outflanking the Vyaz'ma fortified region from the southeast and south. The enemy attached great significance to the retention of the Yukhnov center of resistance and had concentrated in the Yukhnov area parts of eight divisions along a 75-km front.
4 The Spas-Demensk direction (against the 10th Army and Gen. Belov's group), threatened the Yukhnov-Vyaz'ma enemy group with a deep flanking movement. Along this direction the enemy sought to retain the Sukhinichi strong point; subsequently, by maneuvering his reserve units, gathered from various divisions and composition detachments, the Germans stubbornly maintained their defense line, covering the Yukhnov-Roslavl' paved road.
5 The Bryansk direction also led to an important communications junction. Along this direction the enemy fought stubbornly, trying to win time for strengthening the defensive line in front of the 61st Army and the arrival of reserves from the deep rear.

The German command distributed its forces in accordance with the importance of this or that operational direction. The main mass of the enemy's combat formations were located in the first line during the December retreat and the defensive fighting. However, by the beginning of January this was no longer the case; a significant number of combat formations had been withdrawn to the second line. At the same time a certain increase in the overall number of formations facing the Western Front was occurring. If in the beginning of January the Ninth and Fourth German armies facing the Western Front numbered 43 divisions, then by January 15 this number had increased to 48.

Depending on the situation, the enemy sought, by maneuvering along the front and from the depth, to secure the most important of the threatened operational directions with the necessary forces.

The defense's operational density was expressed by the following data:

Thus during the course of January, despite the increase in the length of the front, the defense's average operational density remained almost unchanged. The width of the defensive front for a division in the first line increased on the average from 13 to 18 km; consequently, the density of the enemy's first-line defense decreased. This can be explained by two reasons: 1) the enemy on the right wing and in the center was falling back to stronger defensive lines; 2) by the end of January the number of reserve divisions had increased from 8 to 15.

Table V/2.1 German defensive dispositions and density of defense

The front	Width of Ninth and Fourth Army fronts	Number of divisions	Average operational density of defense
January 5—the line of the Lama, Ruza and Nara rivers, then Detchino-Mosal'sk-Sukhinichi-Belev	470 km	43 divisions, with 35 in the first line and 8 in reserve	one division to 10.9 km
January 15—the line Of the Lama, Ruza Rivers-Mozhaisk-Medyn'-Polotnyanyi Zavod-Yukhnov-Kirov-Zhizdra-Mtsensk	550-585 km	48 divisions, with 38 in the first line and 10 in reserve	one division to 12 km
January 25—the line Vasil'evskoe (15 km west of Knyazh'i Gory), then along the Gzhatsk defense line-Yukhnov-Kirov-Sukhinichi-Zhizdra-Mtsensk	615 km	49 divisions, with 34 in the first line and 15 in reserve	one division to 12.5 km

The tactical density of the enemy's defense along different sectors varied. The German divisions occupied denser sectors along the shock directions.

By January 5 the maximum defensive density along the Volokolamsk-Gzhatsk and Mozhaisk directions had reached one division for eight km; the minimal density was on the Sukhinichi direction, where it was one division for 33 km of front.

On January 15 the maximum defensive density was along the Yukhnov direction: one division for 6 km; on the Volokolamsk-Gzhatsk direction it was one division for eight km; the minimal tactical density was along the Spas-Demensk direction, where it was one division for 29 km of front.

By January 25 the maximum tactical defensive density had shifted to the Novoduginskaya direction: one division for 5.8 km; the correlation along the Gzhatsk direction remained unchanged—eight km per division; along the Spas-Demensk direction the density remained minimal, but even more rarefied: one division per 38 km of front.

The weak saturation of the defensive front of the German Fourth Army's southern wing enabled the 50th and 10th armies and Gen. Belov's group to conduct a rapid offensive; here there was no continuous front as was the case with the Ninth Army in the north. The front line here curved and was sporadic. During the fighting the Germans were forced to throw in independent units and composite detachments, pulling them out of their divisions and even special units.

The enemy's disposition of forces at various stages of the defensive battle varied and depended on the developing situation at the front and the importance of the operational direction. In supplement 1 (see the end of the book) the Germans' order of battle is laid out by period. From this it follows that by January 5 the strongest enemy group was operating along the Volokolamsk-Gzhatsk (13 divisions) and Mozhaisk (ten divisions) directions. On January 15 the densest were the Volokolamsk-Gzhatsk (13 divisions) and Mozhaisk—seven divisions against the 5th Army, and Yukhnov (six divisions) directions. By January 25 large enemy groups were concentrated along the Novoduginskaya (nine divisions) and Gzhatsk (11 divisions) directions.

The enemy constantly sought to oppose the Western Front's right wing and adjacent units from the center with his largest forces, which offered the possibility of delaying our advance.

This happened because the Germans took account of the danger of the Western Front's right wing handing over their left wing, as well as the breakthrough and movement into their rear of the Kalinin Front's forces to the west of the line Rzhev-Sychevka. In these conditions the German command decided to stubbornly attempt to hold the area Rzhev-Gzhatsk-Vyaz'ma-Sychevka.

As can be seen from the order of battle, the main mass of the German troops defending in the first line consisted of infantry divisions. On January 5 there were 25 infantry divisions in the first line; on January 15—29 infantry divisions, and; on January 25—28 infantry divisions. The basis of the tank divisions' defense was primarily the motorized regiments. Along the more important operational directions (Volokolamsk-Gzhatsk, Mozhaisk, Sukhinichi) groups of 15-30 tanks were employed.

Motorized divisions in the defense were employed like infantry formations. The army reserve's divisions concentrated at various depths from the front line and, as a rule, were located in inhabited areas that had been adapted for defense as centers of resistance, with wooden-earth firing points, barbed-wire obstacles, ice walls, etc. (Gzhatsk, Mozhaisk, Vereya, Yukhnov, Zhizdra), or as hurriedly fortified strong points (Sereda, Porech'e, Troitsa, Kondrovo, Polotnyanyi Zavod, Sukhinichi, and others).

The troops' combat structure and a description of the enemy's divisions

The combat structure of the Germans' Ninth and Fourth armies on January 5, according to operational direction, can be seen in table V/2.3.

From the table it is clear that the enemy sought to secure the two most threatening operational directions against the large forces of the Western Front's right-wing and center armies (1st, 20th, 16th, and 5th) with its most powerful group of forces, which included 65,700 men (48% of total forces), 463 field guns (47% of divisional field artillery), and 175 tanks (97% of available tanks).

Along the Yukhnov direction the Germans, not having sufficient forces and equipment, defended along a broad front, having grouped here up to 25% of all their forces, except for tanks (3%).

By January 5 units of the Second Air Fleet—the VIII Air Corps, the headquarters of which was located in Smolensk—were operating against the Western Front. The aviation's combat composition included 270 bombers, 95 fighters, and 35 reconnaissance aircraft, or some 400 planes.

Until the end of January there were no sharp changes either in the number or basing of the VIII Air Corps. The airfields were mostly located west of the line Pogoreloe Gorodishche-Gzhatsk-Yukhnov. The number of planes on the airfields varied from eight to 12. Aviation operations were primarily carried out by small groups tasked with covering their withdrawing troops. The Fascist aviation simultaneously bombarded our units along the front line and carried out reconnaissance of our rear sites.

It is clear from the next table that the enemy concentrated more than a quarter of his infantry and artillery along a 50-km front along the most threatened Gzhatsk direction. Despite the increase in the overall number of divisions from 43 (January 5) to 49 (January 25), the number of men fell due to the losses the Germans suffered in the defensive fighting and the subsequent retreat.

By January 25 the enemy disposed of nearly the same number of artillery pieces and tanks as he had on January 5; this happened due to the arrival from the rear of several new divisions, as well as the partial restoration of the artillery and tanks lost in the previous fighting.

It is also clear from the table that in comparison with the enemy's combat composition on January 5, all the operational directions had a small number of tanks, except the Novoduginskaya one. The operational importance of this direction, as the shortest route to deeply enveloping Gzhatsk from the north, was clear to the enemy and was thus secured with a more powerful tank group.

One may reduce to the following the combat characteristics of the German army's formations operating against the Western Front, according to various sources as of January 1942.

The tank formations (2nd, 4th, 5th, 6th, 7th, 10th, 11th, 19th, and 20th panzer divisions) had been operating on the Eastern Front since the beginning of the war, except for the 2nd and 5th panzer divisions, which had been transferred to the Eastern Front in October 1941. During the fighting on the Eastern Front all the panzer divisions had suffered heavy losses and had been repeatedly (two or three times) been replenished with men and equipment. Equipment losses in the enemy's panzer divisions are characterized by the following data: on the average the authorized strength of a panzer division included from 150 to 200 tanks; by the beginning of the offensive on Moscow the majority of the panzer divisions was almost completely fitted out with equipment; as a result of the October-December fighting, the overall number of tanks in all nine divisions in the first half of January numbered 250-300 tanks. Part of them was at the front, while part of them had been sent to the rear for repairs. A short combat description of the panzer divisions in the first half of January 1942 is shown in tables V/2.4a and V/2.4b.

The data show that: 1) the panzer divisions' heavy losses during the October-December fighting around Moscow as a result of the Western Front's crushing blows; 2) the German command was forced to employ the overwhelming part of its panzer divisions, which still retained their combat capability in defense as infantry units, dispersing the tanks into small groups in close coordination with the infantry; 3) the decline in the German panzer divisions' combat capabilities, caused by combat misfortune and heavy losses in men and matériel.

Table V/2.2 Distribution of German forces, January 1942

Operational direction	Width of defensive front (in km)	Combat troops	Field guns	Tanks
Volokolamsk-Gzhatsk (against the 1st, 20th, and 16th armies)	75	34,100	230	135
Mozhaisk (against the 5th Army)	50	31,600	233	40
Medyn' (against the 33rd and 43rd armies)	65	25,300	168	–
Yukhnov (against the 49th and 50th armies)	180	33,760	252	15
Sukhinichi (against the 10th Army)	100	11,500	96	10
TOTAL	470	136,260	979	200

Table V/2.3 The combat composition of the German Ninth and Fourth armies as of January 25 1942

Axes (according to calculations)	Width of defensive front (in km)	Combat troops	Field guns	Tanks
Novoduginskaya (against the 20th Army)	35	14,395	115	98
Gzhatsk (against the 5th Army)	50	31,500	239	10
Yukhnov-Vyaz'ma (against The 33rd, 43rd, 49th, and 50th Armies)	200	31,500	242	33
Spas-Demensk (against the 10th Army)	215	24,500	228	12
Bryansk (against the 61st Army)	115	12,050	105	18
TOTAL	615	113,795	929	171

Table V/2.4a A short combat description of the enemy's panzer divisions during the first half of January 1942

Panzer division	Estimated personnel strength	Tanks	Guns
2nd	1,500-2,000	50 (out of 200)	–
4th	About 2,000	58 (out of 150) By January 15 20 remained	0
5th	About 2,500	20	24
6th	3,000	By the beginning of January it had lost all of its tanks	18
7th	2,400	50 (out of 150)	–
10th	1,000	10	–
11th	In the November and December fighting the division lost a large amount of motorized infantry and almost all its tanks. On December 30 the remaining tanks were transferred to the 5th Panzer Division.		
19th	1,500	4 (out of 200)	24
20th	3,000	60 (out of 200)	6
TOTAL	17,400	252	72

Table V/2.4b A short combat description of the enemy's panzer divisions during the first half of January 1942

Panzer division	Combat capability	Additional data
2nd	The regiment's remaining personnel was used as infantry. Average combat capability.	From January 20 the 3rd Panzer Regiment was resting in Karmanovo (south of Sychevka)
4th	Average combat capability.	On January 15 moved to Bolkhov for rest and refitting.
5th	Not very capable; its political-morale condition is low.	–
6th	Not very capable.	Its motorized regiments noted northwest of Sychevka.
7th	Capable	–
10th	Not capable	Was not noted in combat in January and was located in the reserve as infantry.
11th	Not capable	The remnants of the motorized regiments were used as infantry in the first defensive line.
19th	Average capability	Used as an infantry division.
20th	Capable	Used as a reserve division in the January fighting.

Conclusions

Of nine panzer divisions, five were capable, two not very capable, and two not capable.

Table V/2.5 Combat characteristics of the enemy's motorized divisions

Motorized divisions	Personnel strength (estimated)	Field guns	Additional data
3rd	2,100	24	Took part in the Battle of Moscow. On the Eastern Front since the beginning of the war.
10th	2,500	32	
14th	3,000	10	
25th	about 2,000	15	
29th	about 2,000	24	
36th	1,600	20	
TOTAL	13,200	125	

The motorized divisions, despite their heavy losses (from 60 to 70%) in men and artillery, suffered in the preceding fighting, generally retained their combat capability. These divisions either occupied various sectors of the front in the January fighting along various defensive sectors of the German Ninth and Fourth armies, or were held in reserve.

Combat Description of the Infantry Divisions

The overwhelming majority of infantry divisions (32 out of 38) were transferred to the Eastern Front at the end of June, in July, and in the first half of August 1941. Six divisions (35th, 63rd, 208th, 211th, 213th, and 216th infantry divisions) were transferred to the Eastern Front in December 1941, and in the beginning of January 1942, from Belgium and France. Of the overall number of divisions, seven infantry divisions were cadre formations, while the remainder (31) was formed upon mobilization in the army's divisional districts.

As a result of the heavy losses suffered during the war, all these divisions changed their personnel several times, which could not help but be reflected in their condition. However, the overwhelming number of infantry divisions still retained their combat capability by the beginning of January. Only certain divisions (the 52nd, 56th, 197th, and 267th infantry divisions), which had suffered heavy losses in the preceding fighting (particularly in December 1941), had lost their combat capability.

Besides this, the harsh winter (with temperatures falling to -35 Celsius), lice, diseases, the shortage of warm clothing, war weariness, the not always adequate supply of food, etc., had an influence on the troops' political-morale condition and the decline in discipline. According to prisoner testimony, there were instances when officers (so as not to arouse the troops' discontent) were forced to countermand previously-issued orders. In certain divisions, in connection with the arrival of replacements, the officers promised the soldiers that those units operating in the winter (56th Infantry Division, etc.) would be relieved and that a spring offensive would eliminate all difficulties. One must admit that such agitation in January 1942 still exerted an influence on a certain portion of the Hitlerite army. Alongside of this in instances involving outright dissatisfaction amongst the soldiers (197th and 267th infantry divisions), harsh repressions were immediately employed. Thus the combat capability of the enemy's infantry divisions by the beginning of January was as follows:

Table V/2.6 Combat characteristics of the enemy's infantry divisions

Infantry divisions	Overall combat description	Percentage of divisions
35th, 63rd, 208th, 211th, 213th, 216th	Arrived on the Eastern Front by January 1942. These divisions retained their combat capability. They were almost completely outfitted with mean and equipment.	15.70%
7th, 15th, 17th, 23rd, 31st, 34th, 85th, 107th, 112th, 131st, 134th, 137th, 183rd, 230th, 252nd, 255th, 258th, 263rd, 268th, 296th, SS Infantry Division	Arrived on the Eastern Front in June-August 1941. Suffered significant losses in men and materiel. Were reinforced several (2-3) times and by January 1942 had been partially reinforced. Divisions contain 60-70% of their authorized strength.	55.20%
78th, 87th, 98th, 106th, 167th, 260th, 292nd	Arrived on the Eastern Front in June-August 1941. Suffered major losses and have been reinforced several times. By January they had received insignificant reinforcements. Retain up to 50% of Authorized strength and little equipment. Their combat capability is not high.	18.50%
52nd, 56th, 197th, 267th	On the Eastern Front since the beginning of the war. As the result of heavy losses, war weariness and other reasons, the troops' morale is low. The divisions are not combat capable.	10.60%
38 divisions total		100%

It should be added that during the October-December fighting one could not the increasing break up of regiments due to heavy losses. Some divisions had two regiments each, instead of three, and the regiments had two battalions each.

The overall character of the enemy's defense

The general principles of the German Ninth and Fourth armies' defense against the Western Front's forces basically corresponded to the tenets contained in their manuals. In connection with the wintry conditions and the altered character of the fighting, the structure of the enemy's defense contained a number of peculiarities.

During the offensive on Moscow, the German command was planning a series of defensive lines in the rear. In some places (for example, behind the Ugra River), our intelligence uncovered the enemy's entrenching work even before our counteroffensive. By the beginning of January 1942 the overall contours of a defensive line had been determined in the immediately rear of the German Ninth and Fourth armies, along the line Rzhev-Gzhatsk-Vyaz'ma, and then on to Bryansk. The German command was attempting, covering with powerful rear guards with tanks, to hold our troops' attack, so as to enable its main forces to consolidate along the line of the Lama, Ruza, and Nara rivers, and then along the line Maloyaroslavets-Sukhinichi-Belev. The defense along the northern sector was partially based on the old trench line, ours and the Germans', which had been constructed as early as the time of the October fighting along both banks of the Lama and Ruza rivers.

Based on captured orders for the enemy formations (23rd Infantry Division), it is evident that the positions on the Lama River and to the south were to be defended to the last man. Similar orders were contained in Hitler's order, which demanded that the troops "hang on to each inhabited point, not to retreat a step..."

The defensive line, which the Ninth and Fourth armies were "hanging on" to, as of January 5 basically ran along the western (in places, the eastern) bank of the Lama, Ruza, and Nara rivers, and along a line of the inhabited areas. The enemy was waging a fixed defense along his northern wing and in the center; along the southern wing he was waging holding actions, at times launching counterattacks.

The enemy's defensive system during this period was built according to the principle of organizing strong points and centers of resistance, the basis of which, in wintry conditions, were the inhabited points. Each formation's defensive position consisted of company strong points and battalion centers of resistance, with intervals between them. The latter were covered by a system of flanking and enfilading fire from machine guns, mortar batteries, and automatic riflemen; here and there the intervals were filled in with snow trenches and snow (doused in water) walls.

Cooperation between the enemy's fire structures in the company strong point system was created by powerful machine gun, automatic rifle, and mortar fire along the main axes. A company strong point basically had 2-3 platoon defensive areas and, in its turn each platoon defensive area had 2-3 firing points. The rear was the most weakly defended area in the strong point.

The depth of a battalion resistance center was 1.5 km and that of a company strong point 500-750 meters. The enemy's infantry divisions in the defense occupied an 8-10 km front along the most important and dangerous axes; along the less threatened axes this rose to 12-15 km. However, there were instances of a defensive front of up to 20 km (98th, 258th, the 31st and other infantry divisions). In such instances the divisions were reinforced with either artillery or an infantry unit from another formation. The above-examined fire system was quite broadly complemented by field engineering fortifications.

Firing points were housed in stone or wooden structures, adapted for defense, as well as in specially constructed wood and earth snow points and in snow trenches. The great majority of the enemy's structures were, according to their construction, light field structures. The enemy widely employed the practice of cold-proofing dugouts located along the main communications arteries. The Germans, with machine guns and automatic rifles, would sit it out until the moment of our attack; with the start of the attack they would run out and occupy their positions in the nearby trenches and firing points.

The enemy's company strong points were often located on raised areas; the terrain in front of the front line was well scanned, which made it possible to organize fire. The firing points were sometimes located on the reverse slopes, at a distance of 150-200 meters from the crest, while strong points with all-round fields of fire were often encountered. The enemy widely employed several reserve positions for his weapons; machine gunners, automatic riflemen, and certain guns, moving from one position to another, created the impression of a large force at the defender's disposal.

The enemy outfitted large inhabited points and cities as resistance centers, while the defensive system was build on the strong points' close fire coordination. The approaches to the resistance centers and the intervals between the strong points were covered by an obstacle system. The roads leading to the strong points and resistance center were mined. The Germans widely employed mining in defense. For example, in January the Western Front's engineering units destroyed more than 7,300 anti-tank and anti-personnel mines in different parts of the defensive line. Within the inhabited areas mines were laid on the streets, squares, in government buildings, houses, and in courtyard structures. For example, in abandoning Naro-Fominsk, the Germans mined the textile factory, the square in front of the Lenin monument, and the area of the worker's barracks (100 mines); in Medyn' the ditches along Kirov Street were mined, as were all exits from the town (183 mines).

A weekly developed barbed wire network, chevaux-de-frise, hard-to-spot obstacles of smooth wire, wire fences on stakes, and other means, were also employed between the strong points.

Groves located in the defensive depth were transformed into anti-tank (PTO) areas, which were girded with a line of trenches and covered by anti-tank guns.

An anti-tank ditch was sometimes dug along an axis subject to tank attack. The enemy in defense often employed "surprises" of various types.

While conducting the defensive battle, the enemy would shift the center of gravity to the retention of the tactical defensive zone, using for this purpose the strength of his previously-prepared fire system. He sought, by the concentrated rifle and machine gun fire, and fire from artillery, mortars, and automatic rifles, to destroy the attacking units before they could reach the front line. In the case of a breakthrough of the forward position and our units' rupture into the depth of the defensive position, the Germans counterattacked with regimental and divisional reserves along the flanks of the tactical breakthrough, aiming their blow at the center of the of the breakthrough. Under favorable conditions, when the attacking troops were weakened and disrupted, counterattacks were launched in front of the forward defensive line. In those cases of a deeper penetration by the attacking units into the defensive zone and the threat of a breakthrough of the tactical zone (to a depth of 6-8 km), corps and army reserves would counterattack. In this fashion the first defensive line's formations, which were occupying the defensive zone, were to do their utmost to hold off the attack and, only when they had exhausted their resources, were deeper reserves committed. A second defensive zone was located 8-10 km behind the first. This defensive zone was non-contiguous and included separate strong points or resistance centers, which were partially occupied by corps reserves.

The German Ninth and Fourth armies' third defensive line was located 18-20 km from the front line. It ran along the line Knyazh'i Gory-Shakhovskaya, Sereda-Porech'e-Mozhaisk-Vereya-Medyn'-Kondrovo-Polotnyanyi Zavod-Yukhnov; the enemy held a non-contiguous defensive line before the 50th and 10th armies, waged defensive battles along a broad front and, evidently, lacked a previously-prepared and fortified line.

Inhabited points such as Shakhovskaya, Sereda, Porech'e, Mozhaisk, Kondrovo, Polotnyanyi Zavod, and others, were transformed into strong points, with snow trenches, light dugouts, and wood and earthen firing points between them. The intervals between the strong points (just as in the first defensive line) were enfiladed by flanking fire from all kinds of weapons; the enemy erected artificial ice walls along the most threatened axes before the 20th, 16th, 5th, 33rd, and 49th armies. In the area of Medyn' the retreating Germans did a good job of destroying the Maloyaroslavets-Medyn' paved road; almost all the bridges were blown up and a part were mined. The enemy places a large number of obstacles on the parallel roads. The inhabited points east of Medyn' (Aduevo, Il'inskoe, Podsosino, and others) were fortified as company strong points. The enemy managed to block the passageways, block with wire, and mine a significant part of the forest paths. This, to a significant degree, made the operations of our attacking units more difficult, and it required a lot of time, forces, and equipment to overcome these obstacles.

The Ninth and Fourth German armies' army reserves were located along the indicated line: the 106th and 85th infantry divisions, the remains of the 10th Panzer Division (which was being refitted), the 107th and 230th infantry and 20th Panzer divisions. Army Group Center's first main rear defensive line ran along the line Ostashkov (140 km northwest of Rzhev)-Belyi-Yartsevo-Yel'nya-Bogdanovo-Zhukovo-Bryansk. Field fortifications were being constructed along this rear line.

The overall defensive system in January included the defensive line Rzhev-Gzhatsk-Vyaz'ma-Zanoznaya station (30 km north of Kirov). This line was being heavily fortified with a system of strong points and resistance centers. In the Gzhatsk area in the beginning of January Army Group Center's reserves were concentrated—the 63rd and 255th infantry divisions were located 80-90 km behind the front line.

On January 15 the enemy's overall defensive system along the northern wing remained almost unchanged. In the center the German forces were waging defensive battles along the line Vereya-Polotnyanyi Zavod-Yukhnov, and on the southern wing, along the line Zanoznaya station-Ol'shanitsa-Zikeevo-Melekhova-Fedinskoe-Mtsensk.

By this time the defense represented a strengthened and developed system of strong points and resistance centers.

The German command, which had the task of holding the Rzhev-Gzhatsk-Vyaz'ma triangle at all costs, was feverishly erecting field fortifications here and was concentrating the forces of the Third and Fourth panzer groups and some infantry divisions (from the V, VII, and IX army corps). By the middle of January the enemy had strengthened his resistance by increasing the number of first-line divisions, seeking to delay the rising pressure of the Western Front's armies.

By January 25 the Ninth and Fourth armies' overall defensive system represented a more developed network of fortifications. The first-line divisions were waging stubborn defensive battles along the line Vasil'evskoe (12 km southeast of Pogoreloe Gorodishche)-Tresely-Batyushkovo station-Azarovo-Vyazishcha-Koshnyaki station-Plyuskovo (25 km southwest of Kondrovo)-Yukhnov-Zimnitsy (6 km southeast of Fimino)-Podpisnaya station (7 km southwest of Kirov)-Sukhinichi-Polyudovo (10 km northeast of Zikeevo)-Ktsyn'-Ploskoe-south of Belev and on to Mtsensk.

The Germans, along their northern wing and partially in the center, had managed, relying on a more developed system of strong points and resistance centers, to retard the further advance by the 20th, 5th, and 33rd armies. This was facilitated by the circumstance that the Western Front's right wing had sent part of its forces to another direction. The Ninth and Fourth German armies' overall length of front increased, compared with the beginning of January, by almost 150 km, but the enemy managed to bring up new reserve divisions, pull back some units from the front and create quite powerful reserves along the main and most threatened operational axes, particularly along the Gzhatsk axis (four infantry, one motorized, and one panzer divisions).

The 197th Infantry Division, having lost its combat capability, was being pulled back to the Gzhatsk area to put it in order. The remains of the 52nd and 56th infantry divisions occupied secondary sectors and were included as parts of other divisions; the 267th Infantry Division was being pulled back to the Vyaz'ma area for refitting.

The Germans, along their southern wing against the 10th and 61st armies, continued to wage holding actions along a broad front; in the Sukhinichi area the enemy's Zhizdra group—208th Infantry Division, 35th Panzer Regiment (4th Panzer Division), and the 691st Column (up to a battalion of infantry)—was fighting stubbornly, trying to break through and link up with the garrison in Sukhinichi.

The formation of the Germans' operational defense included the following: 1) a tactical defense zone 6-8 km deep (sometimes 10 km); it included division and corps reserves, while the latter also formed the second defense line; 2) an army reserve zone from 18-20 km from the front line; this zone constituted the third defense line and represented a combination of strong points and resistance centers with connecting fields of fire; 3) an army group reserve zone from 60-80 km from the front line, which was also being fortified by a broken system of strong points and which was occupied along the most important axes by troop formations, and, finally; 4) a reserve was deployed in the area of the first rear defensive line (the area east of Smolensk), usually in a junction of a well-developed road net at a distance of 150-200 km from the front line.

However, one should keep in mind that the Germans had few reserves and that basically everything hinged on the defense of the tactical zone.

Communications routes

By the beginning of January 1942 the enemy, by means of great exertions, had managed to alter the gauge of a portion of the railroad to the European standard. In the Ninth and Fourth German armies' zone both lines of the Minsk-Smolensk-Vyaz'ma railroad had been altered, and one line along the railroad sectors: 1) Vyaz'ma-Mozhaisk; 2) Smolensk-Roslavl'-Bryansk; 3) Bryansk-Orel.

However, in order to exploit these lines it was necessary to transfer from Germany not only rolling stock, but railroad workers as well. The rolling stock which arrived was badly outdated in construction and worn out, and was distinguished by its variety; the rail service locomotives were primarily German, while at the same time the overwhelming part of the wagon park had been gathered from the occupied European countries.

The altered railroads' capacity was small: it did not exceed 20-25 pairs of trains along the double rail lines per day, and about 15 trains on the single-line railroads. The reasons for this involve the quite low technical condition of these roads, shortages in bridges, and the absence of interstation communications and heavy equipment, electric stations, and water supply. Besides this, frequent partisan attacks also told, which is why along a number of sectors the movement of trains was carried out at less than an around-the-clock pace.

The German armies had sufficient paved and dirt roads in the front-line zone. The main rear routes were: 1) Mozhaisk-Gzhatsk-Vyaz'ma-Smolensk; 2) Maloyaroslavets-Medyn'-Yukhnov-Roslavl'; 3) Orel-Bryansk-Roslavl'-Smolensk. The maneuver of troops along the front was conducted over the lateral routes: a) Rzhev-Zubtsov-Gzhatsk-Yukhnov-Sukhinichi-Zhizdra; b) Rzhev-Vyaz'ma-Mosal'sk-Meshchovsk-Lyudinovo; c) Sychevka-Dorogobuzh-Yel'nya-Roslavl'.

During their withdrawal, the German troops in the front-line zone used auto transport to a significant degree, despite the great difficulties in exploiting it in winter, a shortage of fuel, and the enormous losses in trucks.

The German Command's plan

The German forces' operational situation in January was difficult. The German command sought by every means to put its retreating forces in order and delay the Red Army's offensive. Hitler, in his order, laid out the following:

> The current situation demands from us to hang on to each inhabited point, to not retreat an inch, to defend to the last round and grenade.
>
> Each inhabited point occupied by us must be transformed into a strong point. It must not be surrendered to the enemy under any circumstances, even if it has been surrounded by the enemy.
>
> If the higher command nonetheless orders that an inhabited point be abandoned, it is necessary to burn everything to the ground and to blow up the ovens in the houses.

In December the 216th Infantry Division, and in January the 208th, 211th, and 213th infantry divisions, were transferred from France. These divisions suffered from a shortage of officers, a poorly-trained rank and file, and a shortage of weapons. Aside from those divisions transferred from the deep rear, army group reserves (63rd and 255th infantry divisions) and separate units from other sectors were transferred. These reserves were used to restore the situation along the German's threatened operational axes. Besides this, the remains of some divisions (52nd, 56th, 197th, and 267th) were formed into regiments, and the remains of regiments into battalions, and attached to more healthy formations.

The panzer divisions' remaining equipment was partially used at the front, and partially pulled back to the rear for immediate restoration.

At the same time groups of reservists from the rear were hurriedly brought up to fill out the most battered divisions that still retained their combat effectiveness. Composite groups and detachments (the Chevalier and Kuno groups, for example) were created during the fighting.

The German command's plan in the beginning of January was to at all costs halt the further retreat by the exhausted and bloodied units of the Ninth and Fourth armies, which were being squeezed by the Kalinin and Western fronts, to occupy an advantageous defensive position, and to win time in order to prepare the defensive line Rzhev-Gzhatsk-Vyaz'ma-Zanoznaya-Bryansk. The enemy broadly employed separate resistance points (Yukhnov, Sukhinichi) along the most important threatened axes and waged holding actions along other sectors of the front.

The greatest concentration of retreating Fascist troops was observed in the areas of Sychevka, Gzhatsk, and Vyaz'ma, and in the Yukhnov area.

Conclusions

1 The overall situation and condition of the German troops facing the Western Front in January 1942 was unfavorable for the former. Having suffered heavy casualties, the enemy was no longer capable of active operations. The initiative was in the Red Army's hands.

2 In the January fighting the enemy, taking into account the threat of having both his flanks turned, attempted to hold along his northern wing and center along a series of intermediate lines, withdrawing his main forces to the west, first to the line of the Lama, Ruza, and Nara rivers, and then to the line Rzhev-Gzhatsk, and then to the south. On his southern wing the enemy sought to prevent the advance of our units to the Maloyaroslavets-Roslavl's paved road, so as to secure the withdrawal of his main forces. It should be noted that despite the difficult fighting conditions, the enemy, by means of an enormous exertion of men and matériel, the maneuver of certain formations, bringing up reserves from the deep rear, and finally, at the price of great losses in men and matériel, managed to restore its forces' combat capability and for a quite lengthy period of time to secure the line along the Lama and Ruza rivers and to the south.

In this way, the enemy won about three weeks of time and put the Rzhev-Gzhatsk-Yukhnov line into a stronger condition.

3 As a result of the large losses suffered by the Ninth and Fourth German armies in December and January, and the insufficient reinforcements, the German command was forced to resort to breaking up individual regiments and reducing certain divisions into two-regimental ones, and transforming three-battalion regiments into two-battalion ones. However, their combat sectors remained almost without change, which could not but result in the overall weakening of the defense.

Beside this, by the beginning of January, the German divisions' and regiments' organizational-authorized strength condition no longer corresponded to those full-bodied divisions that in June 1941 perfidiously invaded the USSR. The forces of the Ninth and Fourth German armies, instead of the authorized 300,000 men, had only 142,000. The situation was even worse with the panzer divisions' tank park: instead of 1,350 tanks in eight panzer divisions in the first half of January, there remained only 252 tanks. Finally, instead of 1,960 authorized guns in the divisional artillery, there were only 979 guns. This means that the Ninth and Fourth armies suffered 50-55% losses in infantry and artillery in the preceding fighting. The panzer divisions lost 81.5% of their tanks. At the end of January, as a result of the difficult defensive fighting and a large number of frostbite cases, the losses in men and matériel increased even further.

4 The political-moral situation of the German forces facing the Western Front in January is characterized by the following data;

a) the difficult operational situation that had arisen for the Germans at the front;
b) the harsh winter, with frost that reached 30-35 below zero Celsius, the troops' lack of warm clothing, lice, their tired and exhausted condition, which undermined their faith in Germany's rapid victory.

All of this brought about a reduction in the German forces' combat capability.

3

Attempts to break through along the Western Front's right wing at the end of December and beginning of January

The state of the Germans' defense in January was characterized in the preceding chapter.

This kind of defensive lines had to be overcome by the *front's* right-wing forces, which included the 1st Shock, 20th, and 16th armies.

As was already mentioned above, the Germans, besides the construction of new defensive structures, were first of all using the existing ready fortifications along various lines. For example, they outfitted their position along the Lama River by using the structures built there by our troops before their November retreat (the Uzorovo-Novinki sector).

As regards the sides' correlation of forces, this time the Red Army enjoyed overall superiority. The correlation of forces along certain axes and sectors varied at different periods. These data are presented later, in the corresponding parts of the narrative.

At the end of December and beginning of January the right-wing's armies continued to carry out the task, previously laid down by the *front* command, of destroying the enemy along the line of the Lama and Ruza rivers and subsequently advancing in the direction of Gzhatsk and Vyaz'ma, which in the *front* commander's directive no. 016/op of December 16 1941, was expressed as follows:

1 The enemy continues to fall back in front of the *front's* right and left-wing armies, while defending in the center, striving to prevent a breakthrough of his defensive zone.

2 The immediate task of the *front's* armies, while continuing their non-stop offensive, is to reach the front Zubtsov-Vasyutina-Zlatoustovo-Gzhatsk by the end of December 27…

3 I order:

a) To the commander of the 1st Army—while continuing to securely hold the *front's* right flank, is to reach the front (excluding) Zheludovo-Pogoreloe Gorodishche-Kuchino with its main forces by the close of December 22. A mobile group is to capture Sychevka and Novoduginskaya by the close of December 27.

The boundary line to the right is Rogachevo-Reshetnikovo-Kotlyakovo-Zubtsov (all excluding),[1] and on the left as before as far as Pesochnaya, and then as far as Pomel'nitsa station.

1 On December 22 the boundary line between the Kalinin and Western fronts ran from Kotlyakovo to Sychevka.

b) To the commander of the 20th Army—the army's main forces are to reach the front (excluding) Kuchino-Bol'shoe Krutoe-Mikhalevo by the close of December 22. A mobile group, coordinating with the 16th Army, is to take Gzhatsk on December 25.
The boundary line on the left is as before as far as Zlatoustovo, and then to Novoduginskaya.
c) To the commander of the 16th Army—the army's main forces are to reach the front Panyukovo-Astaf'evo-Galyshkino by the close of December 22.
The boundary on the left is as before as far as Gzhatsk, from which it includes Meshcherskaya station...

By this time the fighting along the *front's* right wing began to powerfully reflect the character of the actions of the enemy, who had assumed a stubborn defense along the line of the Lama and Ruza rivers, and who was bringing up fresh forces in order to more securely seal the Gzhatsk axis.

Attempts by the 1st, 20th, and 16th armies at the end of December to smash this defense were not successful and our forces remained on the lines they had reached by the end of December. Powerful fire from all kinds of weapons, wooden and earthen fortifications, counterattacks, and aviation were all employed by the enemy against our attacking forces. Part of the reason for the armies' actions during this period can be explained by the fact that the troops continued by inertia to attack directly against the enemy's fortifications. Gen. Zhukov, in his directive no. 016/op, indicated this shortcoming to the army commanders in the following manner:

> In a number of cases frontal attacks against the enemy's fortified inhabited points continues, which only leads to excessive losses and the slowing of the offensive.
>
> I order to strictly require that commanders at all levels to seize the enemy's fortifications, bypassing them and not delaying the advance of the forward echelons.

Aside from this, the army's numbers at this point were not large—during the December fighting they had suffered significant losses, which noticeably weakened them.

The nature of the enemy's defense demanded great persistence from the armies and in the offensive.

The right-flank 1st Shock Army was stubbornly attacking units of the Third Panzer Group, which was defending the line Maleevo-Kruglovo-Gavrilovo-Brenevo-Chekchino.

The German forces operating against the army were holding the Lotoshino area, covering the valley of the Lob' River from the northeast near Maleevo, the area of Lake Krugloe, while further on their defensive line ran along the eastern bank of the Lama River as far as Alfer'evo.

The most important axes of this sector: a) Maleevo-Lotoshino (the valley of the Lob' River), b) Shubino-Vorob'evo (the valley of the Gorodnya river), and c) Suvorovo-Lotoshino (the high roads)—were covered sufficiently securely by them. The area of Brenevo, Chekchino, and Shubino, where the front protruded toward our forces, was being held the most securely. The Germans, as was confirmed by all intelligence means, occupied the following position in front of the army:

The Third Panzer Group's troops were defending the following lines: 36th Motorized Division—Maleevo-Kruglovo-Gavrilovo; 2nd Panzer Division—Brenevo-Chekchino-Matveikovo; 53rd Motorized Regiment—Telegino-Shilovo; 23rd Motorized Division—Yaropolets-Alfer'evo.

In the depth, in the Vorob'evo area, units of the 14th Motorized Division and the remains of the 7th Panzer Division were noted, while the headquarters of the Third Panzer Group was in the area of Knyazh'i Gory.

In all, up to four divisions were facing the army.

The strength of both sides at this time was approximately equal—the German forces and the 1st Army's units, as a result of the ceaseless fighting, had suffered heavy losses. Each side's operational density was as follows: one division for nine km (taking three rifle brigades as one division), and 3-4 guns per kilometer of front.

The arrival of the 62nd, 44th, and 46th rifle brigades at the Lob' River and Lake Krugloe, and the concentration of the 55th, 56th, and 71st rifle brigades in the Vladychino area enabled the army commander to organize an offensive along intersecting axes for the overall goal of taking the Lotoshino area.

The insufficiency of forces and the desire to support at least the first blow to break through the German defense forced the army command to keep all its formations in a single line. Along with this, the army's left wing was holding a front 6-8 km northwest of Volokolamsk, which made it necessary to cover this axis with sufficiently strong units in order to parry possible enemy counterattacks for the purpose of taking Volokolamsk.

In connection with the fact that units of the Kalinin Front (30th Army) were to the north, the command attached particular significance to operations along the Lob' River (as is known, the Germans often organize counterblows along the operational boundaries of formations).

Consequently, the army's right and left wings, aside from their combat missions, essentially had the second and responsible task of securing the boundary with the Kalinin Front and covering the Volokolamsk axis (the boundary with the 20th Army).

The subsequent offensive by both of the army's wings at the end of December was not successful.

The 1st Army commander, in summing up the army's actions over the last days of December, reported to the *front* military council:

> The attacks conducted by the army's units during 12/27-1/1/42 did not achieve the desired results. The units, being unable to suppress the enemy's defensive fire system, suffered heavy losses. For example, we lost 612 killed and wounded on December 30, and up to 400 on December 31. The attempt to break through along the front Gavrilovo-Brenevo was also unsuccessful and the units suffered heavy losses from enemy fire.
>
> The reasons behind the unsuccessful attacks are:
>
> 1. The enemy's fixed defense, with powerfully developed fire system, and his stubborn counterattacks.
> 2. A shortage of suppression means both in the brigades, as well as in the immediate army artillery, especially howitzers.
> 3. Losses and the unbroken six-day location in the field considerably wore out the troops.

Despite this situation, the army continued the offensive during the subsequent days of January.

For example, on the night of January 1-2 the 62nd Rifle Brigade's night attack once again drove the enemy out of Terebetovo (abandoned by the brigade on January 1) and continued fighting his separate groups, which were withdrawing to Maleevo and Karlovo as a result of the brigade's attack.

From the morning of January 2 the units were fighting along their former lines, without having any kind of significant success.

The latest attack was schedule for January 4.

The commander of the 1st Army ordered:

> 1. On January 4 the main group of the 1st Shock Army's right flank is to consecutively take Brenevo, Kruglovo, the Brenevo paved road, Gavrilovo, and Maleevo, and by the end of the day is to reach the line Maleevo-Gavrilovo-height 155.1-Chekchino.

The Germans (in response to our attacks of January 1-2) carried out a series of counterattacks on the night of January 2-3 against the army's center, but were beaten back by our fire.

In order to fix the location of the enemy's defense, particularly its forward edge, small groups of scouts and automatic riflemen were sent out on the night of January 2-3. That same night the 62nd Rifle Brigade beat off a German attack from Maleevo, and the 50th Rifle Brigade one from Plaksino.

There was no activity on the day of January 3; our forces were putting themselves in order, continuing their preparations for the attack. There was local fire along some sectors in order to improve the jumping-off positions. The units' strength by this time was extremely weak. For example, the 29th Rifle Brigade contained: in its first battalion—180 men, in its second battalion—33, and in its third battalion 60, which together with special subunits amounted to 849 men; the 55th Rifle Brigade had in its first battalion—88 men, in its second—104, and in its third—92 men, or up to 700 men in all. The 84th, 47th, 56th, and 50th rifle brigades were in an analogous position.

The army attacked at 1030 on January 4 with the objective of taking the villages of Kruglovo, Gavrilovo, and Brenevo. This attack, which was met by heavy enemy fire, was not successful and was resumed on January 5.

The 41st Rifle Brigade, supported by two tanks and an army artillery group consisting of the 1st, 5th, and 38th guards mortar battalions and the 701st Artillery Regiment, and supported by the 46th and 50th rifle brigades and the support of the 29th Rifle Brigade's artillery, went into the attack following an artillery preparation. Under the enemy's heavy artillery fire, the brigade's units reached the barbed wire obstacles on the northern outskirts of Brenevo at 1600, but were not able to advance further. Having lost 420 killed and wounded during the attack, the brigade returned to its jumping-off position.

Simultaneously the 46th Rifle Brigade was attacking along the shock group's left flank, but as a result of heavy mortar and artillery fire, and from tanks buried in the ground, did not advance. The attack by the brigade's units was also made more difficult by the presence of minefields, which were located on the approaches to the enemy's positions.

Consequently, the army's attempts to break through the Germans' defensive line during this period were barren of results.

Following the offensive battles of January 4-6 the army's units continued to wear out the enemy through the actions of reconnaissance groups, as these groups predominantly operated at night. Our intelligence confirmed that the most fortified lines were the eastern and western banks of the Lama River, with the depth of the defense back to Spas-Pomazkino.

Along with this intelligence work, the troops were preparing for an offensive by the *front's* right wing, which it planned to commence along the sector held by the neighboring 20th Army.

The offensive here developed like the 1st Army's offensive.

At the end of January and the beginning of January stubborn fighting was waged along the 20th Army's front to improve our positions, or for the jumping-off position for conducting local attacks, which were directed toward a single operational goal—the breakthrough of the enemy's defensive zone. However, attempts by the 20th Army to attack along the entire front, given the limited resources it possessed at the time, did not lead to positive results. As early as December 23 the *front* commander was ordering the army commander:

> Contrary to the orders by the *front's* military council to break through the enemy's defense along a narrow front, the 20th Army is attacking along the army's entire front and, as a result, is not having any success.
>
> I order the breakthrough to be carried out in the area of Volokolamsk station, with the advance of the shock group to the area of Khovan' and Dubrovino…

Local regroupings of forces, which were carried out by the army commander in accordance with this directive, did not guarantee the achievement of the stated mission. The insufficiently precise organization of the battle also negatively influenced the army's successes. *Front* order no. 0137/op of January 1 1942, pointed out:

> ... as a result of the poor organization of the battle, the units mill about, do not achieve success, and suffer heavy losses...
>
> ... there was no reconnaissance of the main offensive axes by the army commanders and the formation commanders...
>
> ... the commanders of the formations and regimens, along with the commanders of attached reinforcements, also failed to carry out reconnaissance of the terrain, limiting themselves to conversations at headquarters...

The army remained along its former line up to January 1 and was unable to carry out a breakthrough to the west.

On January 1 the army continued the attack with its right wing, with heavy fighting along the entire front.

Units of Remizov's group repelled three enemy attacks toward Zubovo and Timonino, where the Germans began to display activity.

The army's forces tried to capture the village of Sidel'nitsy. Some units managed to break into its streets. However, as a result of the battle, the village remained in enemy hands.

During the night of January 1-2 the army continued to wage heavy fighting, which were particularly stubborn along its right flank; units of the enemy's 6th Panzer Division tried to restore the defense along the Lama River by counterattacking in the direction of Sidel'nitsy, Zakhar'ino, and Timonino.

Katukov's group, along with the 352nd Rifle Division's 1162nd Rifle Regiment, the 1160th Rifle Regiment's first battalion, and the 64th Rifle Brigade, waged a fierce fight for Birkino (up to 40 enemy men and officers were killed in this fight), but had not success.

By 1200 on January 2 the 331st Rifle Division had captured Khvorostinino, having cleared it completely of enemy automatic riflemen. Katukov's group continued to attack toward Birkino along with units of the 331st Rifle Division, but these attacks also failed to yield a result.

On January 3 the fighting continued along the entire front, particularly along the right flank for the same points—Timonino and Birkino. On this day the movement of enemy reserves to the front on Spas-Pomazkino and Zubovo was noted. In connection with our units' activity, the enemy's aviation began to increase its activity and at 1400 on January 3 it bombed and strafed the army's forces in the areas of Tim'kovo and Ivanovskoe. Besides this, the areas where our troops were concentrated—Volokolamsk and Vozmishche, were taken under machine gun fire.

On January 4 units of Kautkov's group and the 331st Rifle Division occupied Birkino, and at 1400 on January 5 Katukov's group took Anan'ino, while continuing the offensive toward Aksenovo and Zubovo (up to a battalion of German infantry was destroyed in Anan'ino). On that same day the 331st Rifle Division was fighting on the outskirts of Posadinki (this point and Ludina Gora were defended by two battalions of the 35th Infantry Division).

Thus on January 4-5 some of the army's units achieved insignificant success along some axes. Subsequent attempts to develop the success did not yield a result. For example, on January 6 the 35th Rifle Brigade attempted to attack Posadinki and Ludina Gora, but this attack was also unsuccessful due to the enemy's strong resistance.

The same was true of the offensive by the 16th Army, which according to the *front* command's initial plan, was to break through the enemy's defense along the Gzhatsk axis.

According to the decision by the army commander, Gen. Rokossovskii, the army was to launch a blow with its right flank and by the end of December 24 its main forces were to take the line Vnukovo-Baboshino-Milyatino, while a cavalry-mechanized group was to launch a blow against the enemy's flank and rear toward Prozorovo, Lisavino, Staraya Tyaga, with a subsequent advance on Gzhatsk.

The forces along the breakthrough sector were distributed as follows.

The 16th Army's shock group, consisting of the 354th Rifle Division, the 40th Rifle and 146th Tank brigades, at 0900 on December 24 was to break the enemy's defensive front along the Chertanovo-Ostashevo sector and reach the Ruza River, and to subsequently launch a blow against the enemy flank and occupy Terekhovo and Fedos'ino, cutting off his path of retreat to the west and southwest.

The 2nd Guards Cavalry Corps was to enter the breakthrough along the Chertanovo-Ostashevo sector, in order to launch a blow toward Prozorovo, Lisavino, and Staraya Tyaga.

These actions were unsuccessful as a result of the Germans' stubborn defense and at the end of December the 16th Army's front was characterized by fruitless attempts at an offensive by the army's units against the enemy defending the line of the Ruza River.

The army was faced by the 5th Panzer Division (reinforced by the remains of the 11th Panzer Division and the 327th Reserve Infantry Battalion) along the line Ryukhovskoe-Chertanovo-the grove west of Kuz'minskoe; the *Das Reich* SS Division along the line Kolyshkino-Kukishevo, and; the 252nd Infantry Division along the line Apukhtino-Palashkino.

The presence of these divisions along the army's front was confirmed by prisoners and a multitude of documents.

The enemy waged an active defense. Along certain sectors the Germans launched counterattacks with groups of automatic riflemen, which were thrown back by us to the western bank of the Ruza River.

By this time the combat strength of the army's units was extremely small. According to a report by Gen. Rokossovskii to the *front's* military council, "as a result of the lengthy and fierce fighting, the 40th and 49th rifle brigades suffered heavy losses and had only a few dozen soldiers in their rifle battalions."

The army, continuing to carry out its mission of breaking through the enemy's defensive zone for the purpose of encircling the Germans' Mozhaisk group, made persistent attempts to attack along the entire front. However, the small size of the units, the wintry conditions, and the stubbornness of the German defense, did not enable the army's troops to realize their offensive along the western direction.

The units' actions during this period were chiefly organized according to the method of gradually gnawing into the defense by means of seizing the enemy's individual dugouts and strong points. The forces operated in small shock groups against firing points and resistance centers and conducted methodical artillery fire against the revealed targets.

As was the case with the other armies, the overall course of the offensive during this period was as follows: the units conducted an offensive battle for 1-2 days and then (depending on the results of the battle) the troops either consolidated along the captured lines, or remained in their former position and readied themselves to resume the offensive.

Beginning on January 1 the army's forces carried out combat reconnaissance and a fire battle against the enemy along their former lines, preparing for the latest offensive. The Germans continued to hold the line Chertanovo-Ovinishche and then along the western bank of the Ruza River as far as Palashkino. During this day the enemy fired on our army's columns with artillery, mortar and machine gun fire, while bringing up infantry from the northwest to the areas of Stanovishche and Ostashevo.

On January 2 part of the army's forces waged intense offensive battles along the entire front, encountering the Germans' stubborn resistance. The next day (January 3) there was particularly stubborn fighting along the sector Novoe Kolyshkino-Ovinishche-Tepnevo (the army's right wing). However, all the army's attempts to improve its situation were unsuccessful.

In connection with this, the *front* command was faced with the necessity of regrouping forces on the right wing in order to break through the enemy's defense along a narrower sector. The 16th Army's forces evidently could not carry out this assignment. In some of its divisions the remaining regiments were grouped into a single composite battalion (354th Rifle Division). The 18th Rifle Division, operating with the 18th Rifle Brigade, suffered heavy losses in the attacks that day, losing 172 men killed, 493 wounded, and seven cases of frostbite. On January 5 the 354th Rifle Division, along with the 146th Tank, and the 40th and 49th rifle brigades, could muster only 377 riflemen and 13 tanks (of these, three were medium, and ten light).

On January 4 the 16th Army commander received a directive from the *front* military council on preparations for breaking through the enemy's defense along the 20th Army's sector. In accordance with this directive, a number of units designated for strengthening the 20th Army, prepared to move to new concentration areas in the 20th Army's zone.

The subsequent days of fighting along the army's front did not bring about any significant changes.

In this way the offensive by the 1st, 20th, and 16th armies at the end of December and beginning of January was not successful and by the first ten days of January the right wing's front basically remained unchanged. The left wing of the Kalinin Front was basically in the same position and the offensive by its left-wing units had not yielded positive results.

4

The offensive by the central armies from the line of the Nara, Ruza, and Moscow rivers and the development of the operations (December 25 1941-January 17 1942)

The failures of the beginning period of offensive operations by the armies of the Western Front's central sector in December were the foundation for the restructuring of offensive methods in the spirit of the orders issued by the *front* commander. In a short time a great deal of work was carried out for improving troop control, the cooperation of the different combat arms in the offensive battle, the employment of artillery in the offensive, and the issuing of missions to the tanks. In the 5th Army this work coincided in time with the brining up to strength of its units and knocking them together for a new and forthcoming offensive.

The offensive that was carried out in the second half of December (although unsuccessful) yielded valuable information about the enemy; it defined his defensive system and revealed the tactics of the enemy units.

The offensive of the 33rd and 43rd armies

In connection with the successful offensive by the left-wing armies of the Western Front and the forward movement of the 50th Army and Gen. Belov's group along the Yukhnov axis, the situation improved for operations by the 33rd and 43rd armies. The offensive by the Western Front's left wing was enveloping the German forces facing these armies; on the other hand, combat reconnaissance of the enemy revealed information about him that strengthened our hope for the success of new operations.

Thus the offensive by the 33rd and 43rd armies was continued, despite the lack of success in the first days. On the night of December 23-24 the troops of the 33rd and 43rd armies, although they changed their grouping somewhat, once again launched an offensive along the same axis against the enemy's fortified zone. The Germans resisted, which was particularly stubborn in the areas of large inhabited points. However, the enemy's stubbornness this time was crushed by the even greater persistence of the attackers, who by skillfully bypassing strong points and blocking them with second echelons, moved forward step by step, overrunning the Germans. The rate of advance was not great—at first 2-3 km per day; the offensive resembled the gnawing through of the enemy's defense,, but this gnawing through yielded the attacking units territory that had previously been occupied by the enemy and inflicted losses on him in men and matériel.

The Germans felt the growing successes of the 33rd and 43rd armies and, not hoping to retain the line of the Nara River, began to pull troops back from here to the rear—to the area of Balabanovo, Borovsk, and Maloyaroslavets. On December 25 the armies' shock groups were already at the line: 33rd Army—Rozhdestvo-Dedeneva-Iklinskoe; the 43rd Army—Aristovo-Alopovo.

At this time the enemy continued to hold several strong points (Narö-Fominsk and the 75-km station), which were in the rear of the attacking forces. The 75-km station changed hands several time in fierce fighting and, finally, was securely taken by us. On December 26 our troop captured Naro-Fominsk.

After Naro-Fominsk the problem of Balabanovo arose, from which the enemy as early as December 25 had begun withdrawing his forces in the direction of Borovsk. The evacuation of Balabanovo, which was uncovered by our intelligence, increased the rate of advance of the 33rd and 43rd armies' units. Balabanovo would open the way to Borovsk and Maloyaroslavets, thus its capture acquired great significance.

On December 28 units of the 33rd Army's shock group (which also included the 43rd Army's 93rd Rifle Division) reached the front Koryakovo-Dobrino-Staroe-Mikhailovskoe. At this time the 43rd Army's 5th Airborne Corps overthrew the opposing German units with a headlong blow and on December 28 broke into Balabanovo. To its left, the 53rd Rifle Division reached the front Orekhovka-Bol'shoe Litashevo, and the 17th Rifle Division captured Mikhailovka and Boevo.

Thus the mission, laid down by the *front* commander, was fulfilled. The units reached the designated line. The opportunity was now open for the subsequent offensive toward Borovsk and Maloyaroslavets.

Thus following the capture of Balabanovo the armies' efforts were directed at the capture of the following: the 33rd Army—Borovsk; the 43rd Army—Maloyaroslavets.

On December 31 units of the 33rd Army, pushing aside the enemy along its path, reached the front Cheshkovo-Koryakovo-Inyutino-Yermolino. It was planned to envelop the German group in the Borovsk area. Fearful of being encircled, the enemy was hurriedly withdrawing his forces from Borovsk further to the west.

At the same time, the 43rd Army's units, overcoming the Germans' resistance, were crossing the line of their strong points—Belkino-Pyatkino-Anisimovo-Spas-Zagor'e-Gorodenki and were directly approaching Maloyaroslavets, which, just like Borovsk, was being hurriedly evacuated by the Germans.

The fighting along the approaches to Maloyaroslavets raged during January 1-2 1942. At 1400 on January 2, following heavy fighting, the 53rd Rifle Division, along with the 26th Tank Brigade, took Maloyaroslavets. At the same time the 5th Airborne Corps took Ivanovskoe and Piskovo, while the 17th Rifle Division reached the area southwest of Maloyaroslavets.

The 43rd Army now had the opportunity of attacking toward Medyn' along the Warsaw highway.

On January 2 the 33rd Army's 113th and 93rd rifle divisions became involved in fighting on the approaches to Borovsk. Units of the 93rd Rifle Division penetrated into the town, where street fighting began, which continued all the night of January 2-3 and all day of January 3. The enemy, well supplied with firepower, put up stubborn resistance, trying to save from defeat those units which were withdrawing from Borovsk at the time.

On January 3 the 93rd Rifle Division's 129th Rifle Regiment occupied Sov'yaki and Krasnoe, thus cutting off the retreat routes to the northwest; on the night of January 3-4 the 201st Rifle Division occupied Red'kino, straddling the road from Borovsk to Mityaevo; the roads leading from Borovsk to the south had already been cut by our units. The street fighting in Borovsk was taking place in the center of the town.

In the night of January 3-4 the remains of the enemy's undefeated units abandoned Borovsk and in small groups, suffering casualties, infiltrated through our units to the west. At 0600 on January 4 the town was in our hands. The 33rd Army's operation developed further in a new direction—against the enemy's large strong point of Vereya.

The 5th Army's offensive

Returning to the 5th Army, in the first days of January 1942 we find it along its previous positions along the eastern bank of the Ruza River along the northern bank of the Moscow River. The army's units had consolidated along this line following the unsuccessful December offensive. The 5th Army, having been reinforced with men and matériel, was preparing for a new offensive.

The 5th Army commander was aware that the enemy was rapidly fortifying the western bank of the Ruza River and the southern bank of the Moscow River; the Ruza River was outfitted as a strong center of resistance.

At the same time the 16th Army on the right was attacking and on January 2 its left flank (9th Guards Rifle Division) reached the front Danilkovo-Zakhryapino; to the left the 33rd Army was fighting for Borovsk; its right flank was slowly but surely advancing in the direction of Simbukhovo.

It was not expedient to advance directly on the Ruza; such an attack would be a frontal one and, in connection with the enemy's defensive works along the western bank of the Ruza River, could have led to new sacrifices. Insofar as the 33rd Army's right flank (222nd Rifle Division) had by this time moved forward somewhat and had reached the front (excluding) Maurino-Cheshkovo, there was opening before the 5th Army the opportunity of beginning the offensive by moving its left flank in the direction of Dorokhovo, for the purpose of enveloping those enemy units that's facing the 5th Army's center. Following the capture of Dorokhovo, the attacking units could move along the southern bank of the Moscow River and the western bank of the Ruza River, thus getting into the rear of the enemy group in the area of the town of Ruza.

In the capacity of a shock group, the 5th Army commander chose the 32nd Rifle Division, assigning it the task of breaking through the enemy front along its front and developing the success in the direction of Yastrebovo. On the army's right flank at this time the 108th 19th, 329th, and 336th rifle divisions were to demonstrate.

The 32nd Rifle Division's breakthrough of the enemy's defensive zone was planned along the front Bol'shie Semenychi-Myakshevo-Lyubanovo; in accordance with this, the 82nd Motorized Rifle Division was to lengthen it front as far as (excluding) Bol'shie Semenychi.

The correlation of forces along the 32nd Rifle Division's breakthrough front is presented in the following table.

The course of combat operations

On the night of January 5-6 the 32nd Rifle Division, following the relief of its right-flank units by the 82nd Motorized Rifle Division, attacked from the line Bol'shie Semenychi-Lyubanovo. Cooperating with the 222nd Rifle Division, the 32nd Rifle Division's units were overcoming the enemy's powerful fire resistance and were moving slowly forward. At 1330 on January 6 the division was counterattacked by Fascist infantry, supported by powerful artillery and mortar fire. As a result of the counterattack by superior forces, its units were forced to return and occupy their jumping-off position. The division lost 110 men killed and 185 wounded.

On January 7 the 32nd Rifle Division repeated its attack against the enemy's defensive position. The latter, disposing of a highly developed system of engineering structures, once again put up resistance to the attacking units, not only counterattacking along some axes, but also trying to infiltrate groups of automatic riflemen into the depth of the attacking units' combat order.

Nevertheless, by 2300 on January 7 the 32nd Rifle Division had captured the first line of the enemy's trenches; during the night of January 7-8 it was consolidating along the captured line, preparing for continuing its offensive on the morning of January 8. During January 8-9 the division's offensive continued to develop successfully. By the end of January 9 the 32nd Rifle Division, reinforced by the 36th Motorcycle Regiment, was already pursuing the enemy, who was hurriedly falling back toward Maurino and Simbukhovo, from the line of the children's home (one km southwest of Bol'shie Semenychi).

The division had achieved success; the enemy front had been pierced and his scattered units were withdrawing to the west and southwest. It was necessary to develop the success by having the army's left flank go over to the offensive. On January 9 the 5th Army commander ordered his troops:

1 As a result of the successful breakthrough by the 32nd Rifle Division of the enemy's defensive position," we read in his order no. 01 of January 9 1942, "the latter has begun to fall back on his left flank in a generally westerly direction.
2 The army's left wing is pursuing so as to prevent the enemy from breaking contact and in order to follow up and capture the Dorokhovo junction.
The same order instructed the army's artillery chief: "To organize at 1630 on January 9 1942, and during the night of January 9-10, the artillery softening of the Dorokhovo area and the roads leading to the west.

Table V/4.1 Correlation of forces along the 32nd Rifle Division's breakthrough front, 5/6 January 1942

Units	Overall				Per kilometer			
	Men	Guns	Mortars	Tanks	Men	Guns	Mortars	Tanks
5th Army								
32nd Rifle Division and 36th Motorcycle Regiment	about 5,000	48	47	45	1,000	about 10	9.4	9
Germans								
508th Infantry Regiment/ 292nd Infantry Division	about 1,300	20	50	–	260	4	10	–

In carrying out the army commander's order, the 82nd Motorized Rifle Division, attacked in the night of January 9-10 and by 0700 on January 10 its forward units had occupied Yakshino, Boldino, and Vyglyadovka. The division continued the attack, cooperating with the 32nd Rifle Division. The latter, pursuing the enemy, by the end of the day reached the front Shubinka-Rodionchik.

On January 11 the 108th Rifle Division, which was concentrated in the Kryukovo area (two km northwest of Maurino), was transferred by auto transport to the army's left flank. The 82nd Motorized Rifle Division, which was disorganizing the Germans' defense with small detachments, was attacking toward Dorokhovo.

On January 12 the 50th Rifle Division, having encircled the enemy in Beloborodovo and the Kaganovich collective farm, attacked; that day the 82nd Motorized Rifle Division captured Trufanovka and Anashkino. The 108th Rifle Division, which had gone over to the attack, reached the front Yastrebovo-Novo-Arkhangel'skoe. The 32nd Rifle Division, along with the 36th Motorcycle Regiment, was fighting the enemy in the area of Simbukhovo.

On January 13 the 50th Rifle Division captured Dubrovka and the 82nd Motorized Rifle Division Kapan', while the 108th Rifle Division reached the front Mishinka-Stroganka. Dorokhovo was being enveloped by our units.

In the night of January 13-14 the enemy, pressed from three sides by Soviet troops, abandoned Dorokhovo. The 82nd Motorized Rifle Division broke into this fortified site on the enemy' heels. On the morning of January 14 Dorokhovo was completely in our hands. Following its occupation, the opportunity presented itself for a blow in the direction of Mozhaisk into the rear of the enemy group defending Ruza.

The divisions of the army's left wing and center were aiming for Mozhaisk and while moving forward were to cut off the routes to it from Ruza. Only the 19th Rifle Division was left facing Ruza, while two other divisions (329th and 336th) advanced toward the left flank, increasing the force of the army's attacking wing.

On January 16 this wing's forces reached the front Tovarkovo-Lyskovo-Aleksandrovo-Kozhukhovo. At the same time the 16th Army's 9th Guards Rifle Division had advanced to the southwest from the line Danilkovo-Zakhryapino. The enemy's Ruza group was being enveloped by our units. Finding themselves faced with the threat of a possible encirclement, the Germans on the night of January 16-17 abandoned Ruza and began to withdraw to the west. At 1130 on January 17 units of the 5th Army's 19th Rifle Division occupied Ruza and reached the western bank of the Ruza River. The 5th Army received a new assignment—to take Mozhaisk.

Conclusions

In the operations of the Western Front's central sector armies in the second period of their offensive against the defending enemy, it is necessary to note the following:

1 The failures of the first days did not break the offensive will of the 33rd and 43rd armies' units. Having taken into account the *front* commander's reprimands and having restructured their work methods, before long they had the opportunity to achieve their goals with fewer difficulties than before. The success of the offensive by the *front's* left wing (50th Army and Gen. Belov's group) gave them the opportunity not only to improve their position, but also to achieve definite successes in a new offensive. This is instructive in the sense of employing the favorable situation that had arisen at this time along another sector of the Western Front.

2 The 5th Army commander acted correctly in temporarily halting the attack by his units, by refitting them and putting them in order. The offensive, organized by him along the army's extreme left flank, must be recognized as very expedient. It was through this attack that the army was breaking through the enemy's front along its weak sector and, following the breakthrough by its left-flank divisions, the army reached the flank of the enemy's large resistance center—Dorokhovo. Continuing the offensive in the former direction would possibly not have yielded a positive result and would have led to new and heavy losses.

3 The breakthrough sector on the enemy's front, which had been well chosen by the 5th Army's commander, afforded the prospect of no less fortunate maneuvers by separate divisions for the purpose of liquidating the enemy's strong points and resistance centers. As a result of the breakthrough achieved by the 32nd Rifle Division, their followed the envelopment of Dorokhovo and its abandonment by the enemy under threat of encirclement by our troops. Before long a similar threat arose to the German garrison in Ruza, as a result of which they were forced to abandon the town.

We see the same thing in the 5th Army' neighbors—the 33rd and 43rd armies. Both armies at first were aiming for Balabanovo. As soon as Balabanovo was occupied by our forces there appeared new objectives for these armies: for the 33rd Army—Borovsk and Vereya, and for the 43rd Army—Maloyaroslavets and Medyn'.

Skillfully directed operations exclude frontal attacks against the enemy, reduce losses during the offensive, and more quickly lead to the goal—the destruction of the enemy's men and matériel and the liberation of territory seized by the Germans.

5

The offensive by the left-wing armies on Detchino, Kozel'sk and Sukhinichi and the end of the fighting for Kaluga and Belev (December 25 1941-January 5-9 1942)

The situation along the left wing as of December 26 1941

After December 25 the armies of the Western Front's left wing faced the task of completing the offensive operations begun in the preceding period. By December 26 the situation on the *front's* left wing was as follows.

The right flank of Gen. Zakharkin's 49th Army was fighting to the northeast of Nedel'noe, while the center and left flank continued fighting for Nedel'noe, attacking the line Detchino-Torbeevo. The enemy was stubbornly resisting along this line. By December 26 the 137th, 263rd, 260th, 52nd, and 131st German infantry divisions were facing the 49th Army. It was known from various sources that the Germans in the Nedel'noe area had committed separate unit of the 17th Infantry Division into the fighting, which were trying to halt the attack by our 238th Rifle Division.

Gen. Boldin's 50th Army and Gen. Popov's mobile group continued the street fighting in Kaluga, while the remaining force enveloped the city from the north and southeast, while simultaneously attacking (with their extreme left flank) in the direction of Uteshevo. As before, units of the 31st, 131st, 137th, and 296th infantry, and 20th Panzer divisions, and other smaller units faced the army.

Gen. Belov's 1st Guards Cavalry Corps, which had crossed the Oka River on December 25 along the sector Kipet'-Moshchena, was attacking with its main forces (1st Guards, 57th, and 41st cavalry divisions) toward Yukhnov, while two divisions (2nd Guards and 75th cavalry divisions) were advancing on Kozel'sk, with the mission of taking it on December 27.

The right-flank divisions of Gen. Golikov's 10th Army were on the western bank of the Oka River and were attacking toward Kozel'sk and to the south; the army's center and left flank was fighting for Belev.

Units of the enemy's 296th and 112th infantry, and 10th and 29th motorized divisions were withdrawing in front of the 1st Guards Cavalry Corps and the 10th Army. The 216th Infantry Division was operating in Kozel'sk, while units of the Germans' 296th and 112th infantry divisions were stubbornly holding the Belev area.

Thus the German-Fascist troops had been thrown back from the Oka River and Kaluga as far as Belev, but they continued to stubbornly hold both towns, attempting to halt our further advance. The Germans evidently subordinated to this goal the attempt to hold around Nedel'noe and the line of the railroad along the sector Afonasovo-Detchino-Torbeevo. The retention of this railroad sector would enable the enemy to secure Kaluga from being enveloped by the 49th Army's forces from the north.

Combat activities on the 49th Army's front until its units reached the Kaluga-Maloyaroslavets railroad (December 27 1941-January 9 1942)

During the period from December 27 through the 31st the troops of the 49th Army's right flank continued their attack and were fighting along the following lines:

The 415th Rifle Division encountered the heaviest enemy resistance along the Alozha River (one km west of the line Troyanovo-Makarovo) and after crossing it our offensive developed more successfully. Having captured together with units of the 60th Rifle Division the village of Chernaya Gryaz', the troops by the morning of December 30 had reached the line Dubrovka-Durakovo-Pursovka (five km west of Chernaya Gryaz') and were attacking to the west. By order of the *front* command, on December 31 the 415th Division was transferred to the 43rd Army and operated on its left flank.

By this time the 60th Rifle Division was being put into the *front* reserve in the area of Troyanovo, Makarovo, Maleeva, Semkino, from which, according to *front* command order no. 36 of January 3 1942, it was being commandeered together with the 26th Rifle Brigade to Serpukhov for inclusion into the Supreme High Command Reserve.

By this time the 194th Rifle Division, having overcome the enemy's mine obstacles and the resistance of his units covering the retreat, reached the line Kan'shino-Vasil'chinovka. This division subsequently continued to attack to the west. The 133rd Rifle Division, which up to December 29 had been attacking to the northwest through Chausovo and Tishkovo (six km southwest of Vysokinichi), was turned to the southwest upon reaching the Filippovka area and by December 31 had concentrated in the Verkhovaya area. This was due to the necessity of strengthening the Detchino axis and the turn by the army's main forces toward Kondrovo.

The 26th Rifle Brigade, together with the 19th Rifle Brigade, was attacking toward Nedel'noe. On the morning of December 30 units of the 238th Rifle Division and the 19th Rifle Brigade took Nedel'noe in fighting. The 238th Rifle Division, having left behind a part of its forces to clean up the Nedel'noe area of the enemy, launched an attack toward Voznesen'e (four km southwest of Nedel'noe). The 19th Rifle Brigade was attacking in the direction of Altunino. In the following days the brigade developed the blow toward Mikheevo (two km north of Detchino), while the 238th Rifle Division, transferred to the army's left flank, arrived after fighting at Torbeevo, where it encountered strong Germans resistance.

Also successful at this time were the actions of the 5th Guards Rifle Division, two regiments of which, together with the 34th Rifle and 23rd and 18th tank brigades, on December 30 reached the line Ozhogino-Vorob'evo and to the south, where they fought off a number of enemy attacks. Units of the 5th Guards Rifle Division had to fight along the indicated line under conditions where the enemy had cut them off from their rear supply and part of its artillery. A blow by the 30th Rifle Brigade from the Potopkino area in the direction of Ushakovo broke through the Germans' blocking position, and the 5th Guards Rifle Division's transport, artillery and part of its headquarters, which were located in Verkhov'e got out. The arrival of the 5th Guards Rifle Division and its attached units to the line Ozhogino-Vorob'evo had a positive influence on the outcome of the fighting by our units in the Nedel'noe area.

The 173rd Rifle Division, which was located in the area of Asorgino, Gur'evo, and Makarovka, to which it had withdrawn on December 28 as a result of an enemy counterattack, received the assignment of restoring the previous situation and capturing Detchino. The division began to immediately carry out its assignment.

During the January 1-9 1942 period combat activities along the 49th Army's front unfolded in the following sequence: the 194th Rifle Division, in cooperation with the 49th Army's 415th Rifle Division, overcoming enemy minefields and obstacles, was moving forward and following a series of battles reached (January 4) the line Afonasovo-Starosel'e, having captured these points. On January 5 the *front* command subordinated the 194th Rifle Division to the 43rd Army, where it operated on its left flank.

The 5th Guards Rifle Division, which had been directed to the west, up to January 9 was stubbornly fighting along the railroad line on the Vorob'evo-Mikheevo sector (three km north of Detchino) and was advancing with difficulty. The enemy was putting up stubborn resistance. In the Vorob'evo area the German-Fascist units undertook a "psychological" attack with forces up to a battalion in strength, which cost them dearly. The guards division met the attack and inflicted a crushing blow on the Germans; the enemy battalion was destroyed; up to 200-300 corpses of men and officers were left on the field.

Up to January 4 the 5th Guards Rifle Division, together with the 30th and 34th rifle and 23rd Tank brigades were fighting along the railroad line north of Detchino, and by January 9 had reached the area of Motyakino, Vasisovo, and Mikheevo, from which, according to the army command's new plan, the division was to operate with the 43rd Army in the direction of Kondrovo, for the purpose of destroying the enemy group concentrated there. The 18th Tank Brigade (which up until this time had been operating with the 5th Guards Rifle Division) was transferred to the 43rd Army and directed toward Maloyaroslavets. The army's remaining forces were involved in heavy fighting along the line of the railroad on the Detchino-Torbeevo sector.

The enemy was stubbornly holding his line and had concentrated there a large amount of artillery and mortars, with the mission of keeping our units away from Polotnyanyi Zavod and Kondrovo. The fighting was particularly fierce in the Detchino area, along the 133rd Rifle Division's sector, where the enemy's strong points often changed hands. In Taurovo (½km south of Detchino) the division had to engage in stubborn street fighting. Only in midday of January 9 did the division's units break the German-Fascist troops' resistance and occupied Avdot'ino, Detchino, Bukrino, and Kurdyukovka. In the succeeding days the division's attack developed to the west according to a new army plan. By this time the 173rd Rifle Division, overcoming the enemy's resistance, had captured the line Lisenki-Bogrovo-Bykovo (all points 2-4 km northeast of Torbeevo) and was attacking Durovka.

During this period no less heavy fighting had unfolded along the 238th Rifle Division's sector, particularly with the enemy units defending the area of Torbeevo and Nizhnie Gorki (two km west of Torbeevo), which he had turned into a strong fortified junction. According to data from army headquarters, up to 1,500-2,000 infantry, with artillery and mortars, had been concentrated in the Torbeevo area. The enemy, in retaining this area, was evidently trying to eliminate the threat of a flank envelopment of Polotnyanyi Zavod from the southeast by our units. It was only by the morning of January 11, by enveloping Torbeevo from the north, was the 238th Rifle Division able to overcome the enemy's resistance here and force him to retreat.

In the succeeding period the 49th Army developed its offensive on Kondrovo and Polotnyanyi Zavod, carrying out the *front's* January 9 directive on destroying the enemy's Medyn'-Kondrovo-Yukhnov group together with the 43rd and 50th armies and the 1st Guards Cavalry Corps.

From the point of view of a *front* operation, the chief operation result of the 49th Army's operations under study is the fact that the Germans' resistance was broken along the sector

Nedel'noe-Bashmakovka and the Maloyaroslavets-Detchino-Kaluga railroad. Our units were reaching the area of Kondrovo and Polotnyanyi Zavod, from which it would be possible to cut the Warsaw highway.

Operational-tactical conclusions on the 49th Army's offensive

As a result of the 49th Army's offensive from December 19 to January 9 three enemy defensive centers were liquidated: in the area of Vysokinichi, in the Nedel'noe and Bashmakovka area and along the Maloyaroslavets-Kaluga railroad (along the Detchino-Torbeevo sector). The army's forces covered from 50 to 60 km, which averaged 2 ½ to 3 km per day. One should take into account the wooded terrain and the poor condition of the roads as a result of the snowfall, and the stubborn resistance by the enemy, who employed fortified points and mine obstacles.

During the 49th Army's offensive after December 20 the question of operational cooperation with the 50th Army in wrapping up and developing its fight for Kaluga became a pressing one. This operational cooperation, as we mentioned earlier, was realized by the 49th Army command ordering its left-flank divisions to launch a deep blow in the general direction of Detchino.

One should mention those instances of frontal attacks against the enemy strong points, which led to a loss of time and cost a lot of casualties. The army command, on the basis of repeated instructions by the *front's* military council, noted this shortcoming in its orders, demanding that frontal attacks be avoided and that the troops envelop and bypass the enemy's fortifications. The capture by the army's units, employing this method, of Vysokinichi, Torbeevo, and other strong points, once more confirmed the expediency and effectiveness of these tactical methods.

Among the serious shortcomings, one must note an incident of the 49th Army headquarters losing contact with some of its formations (for example, with the 173rd Rifle Division during December 27-28, while it was fighting in the area of Bol'shie Luga, Pnevo-Rakhmanovo, and Asorgino),which deprived the army of the possibility of uninterruptedly controlling them.

The activities of ski units as mobile detachments for bypassing the German-Fascist troops' strong points and striking their rear, communications and headquarters, acquired great significance.

These detachments had the greatest effect when the troops underwent special group and individual training and were supported by automatic riflemen, anti-tank rifles, and heavy machine guns mounted on skis. The experience of attaching sappers with explosives and light mortars to the ski troops justified itself. Such detachments can be entrusted with missions involving a turning maneuver against the flanks of an enemy occupying a defensive line and for carrying out deep reconnaissance. They could also be used for destroying the enemy's reserves and rear, and his fuel depots, for holding certain tactically important sectors, points and lines until the arrival of our forces. The ski detachments acquired somewhat more importance in the succeeding period.

The operations of the tank troops (just as in the other armies of the *front's* left wing) transpired in direct cooperation with the rifle formations by means of subordinating the tank units to the combined-arms commanders. This was due to the small number of tanks and the wintry conditions. Alongside this, the inclusion of small tank units in the mobile groups for enveloping the enemy and storming into his rear is instructive. In this sense, the actions of one of the 133rd Rifle Division's regiments with the 23rd Tank Brigade in the Iskanskoe area (seven km north of Tarusa) on December 17, and that of a rifle battalion from the same division with 11 tanks near Vysokinichi while crossing the Protva River on December 18, is revealing.

The development and end of the 50th Army's battle for Kaluga and its arrival at the Yukhnov axis (December 26 1941-January 5 1942. The second Half of the Kaluga Operation)

Combat activities on the 50th Army's front before the capture of Kaluga

Combat events on the front of Gen. Boldin's 50th Army following December 25 unfolded in the following manner:

The forces of Gen. Popov's mobile group continued stubborn street fighting in Kaluga, in the southern, central, and southeastern parts of the city. The Germans, as before, were holding on to the northern and western parts of the city, defending behind barricades and repeatedly launching counterattacks supported by artillery and tanks. In the daytime fighting on December 25 our troops seized six guns and two tanks. The mobile group's fighting was of the same intensity during December 26. The fighting was particularly fierce in the northeastern part of the city and in the area of the train station, which the enemy sought to retain.

On the morning of December 26 the right-flank 340th Rifle Division attacked from the line Boldasovka-Mar'ino (four km south of Boldasovka) in the direction of Kaluga. The enemy's Kaluga group (units of the 31st and 131st infantry divisions, and others), occupying the wooded area and the inhabited points east of Kaluga, was putting up stubborn resistance. During the fighting along the 340th Rifle Division's front, two groups emerged: a left-flank regiment, cooperating with the 290th Rifle Division's right-flank units, by the close of December 27 had captured Zhdamirovo (one km east of Turynino) and was attacking toward Turynino. The other two regiments, overcoming the Germans' resistance, by the morning of December 29 had reached the line Stopkino station-Voskresenskoe-height 216.1 (three km southeast of Voskresenskoe), bypassing Kaluga from the northeast.

The *front* command, taking into account the extended fighting for Kaluga, demanded in a directive to the 50th Army on December 27 that it speed up the mopping up of the city, in order that it be able, in cooperation with the 49th Army, of developing the offensive in the direction of Tikhonova Pustyn' and Polotnyanyi Zavod, with the mission of capturing them no later than December 29.

In accordance with the *front's* instructions, the army command accelerated the movement of its left-flank divisions, assigning them the mission of deeply enveloping Kaluga from the west. By this time the army's center divisions were enveloping the city from the southeast and southwest. The 209th Rifle Division was fighting its way toward Turynino, cooperating with the 340th Rifle Division's left-flank regiment. Turynino had been transformed by the enemy into a major strong point, the capture of which by a frontal attack presented some difficulties. Thus the division commander, on the instructions of the army commander, left behind a single regiment for the fight for Turynino, in cooperation with a regiment of the 340th Rifle Division. The other two regiments were concentrating in the woods south of Malaya Sloboda, with the task of bypassing Turynino from the northeast and together with the 340th Rifle Division's main forces, to attack Kaluga from the north.

The 258th Rifle Division, tasked with attacking Kaluga from the southwest, on the morning of December 26 was fighting in the area of Annenka, Zhelybino, and Romodanovo. The enemy stubbornly sought to hold these sites. The Germans, supported by tanks and artillery, repeatedly counterattacked. The fighting in the area of the above-named points continued up to December 29. By the morning of December 29 the 258th Rifle Division had concentrated its main forces in the area of Kvan' and Verkhovaya (one km southwest of Kvan') for a blow at Kaluga from the southwest; part of the division's forces was fighting for Zhelybino and the sanatorium one km west of Kaluga. On the morning of December 30 the direct fighting for Kaluga flared up with renewed strength and entered its decisive phase. During the night of December 29-30 the mobile group's units decisively attacked and by the dawn of December 30 they had cleaned the Germans out of the northwestern and northern parts of the city and the approaches to the bridge over the Oka River from the north. Following fierce fighting, by 1000 on December 30 the German-Fascist forces had been thrown out of Kaluga and began to fall back to the northwest and west. Over 7,000 enemy men and officers had been destroyed and considerable equipment captured during the fighting for Kaluga. The army's right-flank and center forces continued their offensive, pursuing the retreating Germans.

Without a doubt, the offensive by the army's left-flank divisions influenced the favorable outcome of the fighting for Kaluga, which unfolded in the following fashion: the 413th Rifle Division, the left flank of which was being securely covered by the actions of the 1st Guards Cavalry Corps, was attacking toward the northwest following the capture of Likhvin and by December 26 was located along the line Vorob'evka-Pokrovskoe and to the south. The division advanced from this line the same day and by December 30 had reached the line Kromeno-Rassudovo, from which it was developing its blow to the north.

The 217th Rifle Division, which at first was operating to the right of the 413th Rifle Division, along the front Zhelekhovo-Sel'kovo-Sinyatino (along which it was located on December 26) and attacking toward Babynino, on December 30 reached the Maloyaroslavets-Sukhinichi railroad along the Vysokoe-Babynino sector and aimed the blow of its main forces in the direction of Uteshevo. The 1st Guards Cavalry Corps, having occupied Kozel'sk on December 28 with two divisions, pushed forward two other divisions (1st Guards and 57th cavalry divisions) to the northwest and by the end of December 28 they had occupied the area of Il'ino, Kalinteevo, and Mezentsevo, in this manner cutting off the escape route of the enemy's Kaluga group to the southwest.

The blow by the 49th Army's left-flank divisions in the direction of Detchino and Torbeevo had an indirect influence on the outcome of the fighting for Kaluga. The 49th Army's hanging over Kaluga from the north correspondingly was depriving the Germans' Kaluga group of support from the area of Detchino and Torbeevo and was creating the threat of its being enveloped from the north.

Thus during the decisive period of the Kaluga operation, the fighting along the 50th Army's front was basically conducted along two sectors: the northern and southwestern, which were operationally subordinated to a single goal—the defeat of the enemy and his non-stop pursuit.

Of particular interest in the fighting along the northern sector are the following: the 290th Rifle Division's flank maneuver toward Malaya Sloboda for a joint attack on Kaluga from the north with the 340th Rifle Division; the mobile group's fighting in the city and the high morale and combat condition of the rank and file of its units, despite the exceptionally difficult conditions and, finally, the blow by the 258th Rifle Division from the southwest as one of the component parts of the plan for taking Kaluga. Along the southwestern sector the maneuver by the 217th and 413th rifle divisions to the northwest for the purpose of cutting the enemy's retreat route to the southwest is instructive. This maneuver had a positive influence on the outcome of the fighting for Kaluga. No less instructive is the arrival of two of the 1st Guards Cavalry Corps divisions in the area of Il'ino, Mezentsevo, and Kalinteevo, which also facilitated the favorable outcome of the fighting for Kaluga. In this regard, it should also be added that the offensive by the 50th Army's units unfolded in unfavorable meteorological conditions: the snowfall (December 26-27), and the frost sometimes reaching -30 Celsius (for example, December 30).

The development of the 50th Army's offensive following the capture of Kaluga to its arrival along the Yukhnov Axis

Upon capturing Kaluga, the 50th Army's units developed their offensive to the west and northwest.

According to a *front* directive of December 30, Gen. Boldin's army had the task attacking to the northwest, get into the rear of the enemy's Kondrovo group and then develop the blow in the direction of Myatlevo. No less than a single rifle division should be directed against Medyn'. The army's remaining forces were ordered to continue pursuing the enemy's defeated Kaluga group, operating toward Yukhnov.

In elaborating on the *front* directive, the 50th Army command assigned its forces the following tasks:

The right-flank 290th and 258th rifle divisions[1] and the 32nd Tank Brigade, along with attached units, were to attack along the front Pyatkovskaya-Karavai (18 km northwest of Kaluga).

Upon the two divisions reaching the appointed line, the 290th Rifle Division was to be thrown forward in the direction of Polotnyanyi Zavod, with the mission of getting in the rear and flank of the enemy operating there. The 340th Rifle Division, which had heretofore been located on the 50th Army's extreme right flank, turned over its sector to the 290th Rifle Division and was being transferred to the army's left flank for operations along the Yukhnov axis.

On the 50th Army's left flank the 154th Rifle Division, which had previously formed part of Gen. Popov's mobile group, was pulled out of Kaluga.

During the January 1-6 time period the 50th Army's fight-flank forces, in carrying out their orders, waged stubborn fighting with the German-Fascist units for the station at Tikhonova Pustyn'. The army's left flank (217th and 413th rifle divisions) continued to pursue the Germans in the direction of Uteshevo.

During January 6 the 50th Army's units, having encountered the enemy's powerful defense, were fighting along the following front: the 290th and 258th rifle divisions—the woods east of Argunovo-(excluding) Pochinka (four km south of Argunovo)-Domozhirovo-(excluding) Gorenskoe-(excluding) Krutitsy-(excluding) Annenka. The 413th Rifle Division, having taken Zheleztsovo, was attacking toward Osen'evo and Nedetovo. In these areas the division was being pressed by the enemy from the north, where units of the German 137th and 52nd infantry divisions were operating.

The 217th Rifle Division, defending with one regiment along the line Troskino-Yeremino, was covering the army's shock group (340th and 154th rifle divisions, and the 112th Tank Division), which had received orders to attack Yukhnov. The 340th Rifle Division, which had been transferred from the army's right flank, was fighting for Ugarovka and Kudinovo. By this time the 154th Rifle and 112th Tank divisions, encountering the enemy's powerful resistance, were attempting to capture Shchelkanovo and Zubovo.

The German command, which attached great importance to the area of Polotnyanyi Zavod, Kondrovo, and the Medyn'-Myatlevo-Yukhnov area, had organized a powerful defense along these axes. According to *front* intelligence, by January 7 1942 units of the enemy's 131st Infantry Division were operating and putting up stubborn resistance along the sector Argunovo-Bol'shaya Kamenka (three km southeast of the Tikhonova Pustyn' station)-Krutitsy, while units of his Thirty-First Infantry Division were defending in the area of Annenka, Pletnevka, and Dvortsy. According to the same data, the area of Kozhukhovo (two km west of Osen'evo), Nedetovo, Golovino (three km north of Troskino), and Vshivka were being held by the 137th Infantry Division, while the 36th Motorized Division and other units were defending along the sector Kudinovo-Zubovo and then to the southwest.

1 On January 6 1942 the latter was renamed the 12th Guards Rifle Division.

The *front* command's January 1 directive drew the 50th Army commander's attention to the necessity of personally organizing the battle along the axes of the main blow and conducting reconnaissance with the formation commanders along the main axis. Taking into account the great significance of the artillery's cooperating with the infantry, particularly during the offensive, the *front* command that the commanders of the rifle battalions and supporting artillery battalions be stationed in the same command post; besides this, the removal of command posts from the front line during the offensive was regulated: no more than 10-12 km for an army headquarters, and 3-4 for division and brigade headquarters.

The wintry conditions and the necessity of pursuing the enemy as rapidly as possible required the subordination of all ski units directly to the army commander, for the purpose of more effectively "employing them in the capacity of mobile groups tasked with developing breakthroughs and blows against the enemy's flanks and rear, as well as for night raids on his rear and headquarters…" (from *front* order no. 0138, issued in the first days of January 1942).

In the period following January 6, the 50th Army's forces, in carrying out their assigned tasks, waged stubborn battles with the German-Fascist forces along the Yukhnov axis.

Overall conclusions on the Kaluga Operation

With the arrival of the 50th and 10th armies and the 1st Guards Cavalry Corps at the Oka River along the sector Kaluga-Likhvin-Belev (the operations of the 10th Army and 1st Guards Cavalry Corps are fully described in the section on the Belev-Kozel'sk operation) and the capture of this line, the German-Fascist troops were deprived of an important line, which they had attempted to stubbornly maintain. Thus the Hitlerite army was doomed to a further withdrawal.

The 50th Army's Kaluga operation lasted about 19 days and unfolded along a front defined from the north by the line of the Oka River (until the arrival of the mobile group to the southern approaches to Kaluga), and from the south by the line Krapivna-Odoevo-Likhvin, and then to the northwest toward Uteshevo, and having an overall depth of 90-130 km and an offensive front of 40-50 km in width.

The average pace of the 50th Army's advance (given the enemy's stubborn defense along a number of sectors and the poor roads due to winter conditions) amounted to about six km per day. However, this pace varied along various sectors of the army's front. For example, Gen. Popov's mobile group averaged about 23 km per day during the first three and a half days until it reached Kaluga, having successfully accomplished its task. Such a rate of advance must be recognized as high, not only for the left-wing armies, but for the *front* as a whole.

In examining the 50th Army's Kaluga operation, it is necessary to note the following:

1 This operation was note preceded by a special preparatory period. It grew directly out of the Tula offensive operation and unfolded to the west and northwest. Nor did the offensive end with the arrival of the 50th Army's forces to the northwest of Kaluga, but instead developed further, with the task of carrying out the subsequent *front* operation.
2 The creation of an operational mobile group, which played a decisive role in the capture of Kaluga fully justified itself. The organization of this group according to the situation was in complete accordance with the time and place, and surprise was achieved by the suddenness of its transfer toward Kaluga. Only Kaluga's previously-prepared powerful defense hindered the mobile group in taking the city on the march. The experience of creating such groups is instructive, while the maneuver character of its operations speaks to the high combat resilience of its soldiers and commanders and may serve as an example worthy of imitation.
3 During the operation a large role, from the point of view of coordination, was played by the 1st Guards Cavalry Corps maneuver to take Odoevo, while the quick arrival of its 1st Guards and

57th cavalry divisions at the Kaluga-Sukhinichi road supported the 50th Army's further offensive to the northwest. The blow by the 49th Army's left-flank divisions, directed by the army commander toward Detchino and Torbeevo, and depriving the enemy's Kaluga group of support from this direction, rendered an indirect operational influence and assistance.

4 During the fighting for Kaluga the method of bypassing and outflanking the enemy's strong points, thus depriving him of the possibility of maintaining them, was widely employed. This method sprang from the *front* commander's instructions and was one of the more efficacious methods in the battle with the enemy's defensive tactics.

5 The army's attached tank formations (divisions and brigades) could not play an independent role due to their small numbers of tanks; they were chiefly used in direct cooperation with the infantry (for example, the 112th Tank Division and the 154th Rifle Division).

6 With the onset of winter, the problem of the combat employment of ski units as mobile detachments, tasked with the development of the breakthrough, the blow against the enemy's flanks, unit boundaries, and headquarters, became important. The character of employing ski detachments among Gen. Boldin's forces was basically the same as in the 49th Army.

7 Concerning questions of troop control, it is necessary to once again note the instructions issued by *front* headquarters and military council, which categorically demanded that the commanders at the army, division, and brigade headquarters be close to the troops and their direct control of the combined-arms battle of their units and formations.

Combat along the front of the 1st Guard Cavalry Corps and the 10th Army from December 25 1941 to January 5 1942 (the second half of the Belev-Kozel'sk Operation)

The course of the fighting for Belev and Kozel'sk

The offensive by the 1st Guards Cavalry Corps group of forces following their arrival at the western bank of the Oka River unfolded in the following manner:

According to a *front* directive, the right-flank 1st Guards and 57th cavalry divisions were to operate in the direction of Yukhnov, with the mission of getting into the rear of the Germans' Yukhnov-Kondrovo group, and by December 28 had reached the area of Il'ino, Kalinteevo, and Mezentsevo, where they concentrated. The 41st Cavalry Division was carrying out a night march from the Kamenka area (12 km northeast of Kozel'sk), with the mission of concentrating by the morning of December 29 in the area Khvalovo-Vislovo-Spas, from where it was to operate together with the 1st Guards and 57th cavalry divisions along the Yukhnov axis.

The left-flank 75th and 2nd Guards cavalry divisions, having passed through the wooded area to the east of Kozel'sk, had engaged the German-Fascist units defending the town along the line of the Zhizdra River. Both cavalry divisions were tasked with capturing Kozel'sk by the close of December 27. Following the capture of Kozel'sk, the 2nd Guards and 75th cavalry divisions were to operate along the same axis as the cavalry corps' right-flank divisions. The corps' rate of advance increased significantly after it reached the western bank of the Oka River.

The headquarters of the 1st Guards Cavalry Corps was moving from Likhvin (where it was located on December 28) to Matyukovo (seven km southeast of Babynino station). The 9th Tank Brigade, which was attached to the cavalry corps, having been delayed by snow drifts, remained in Odoevo.

The 322nd and 328th rifle divisions, which had been attached to the cavalry corps, according to data from 10th Army headquarters, were located near Belev during the latter part of December 27: the 322nd Rifle Division was attacking the city's eastern approaches, and the 328th Rifle Division was moving north of Belev, with part of its forces fighting the Germans covering the northern approaches to the city.

The *front* command, taking into account the 1st Cavalry Corps' forward location, and the fact that both rifle divisions were engaged in the fighting for Belev, in a December 29 directive resubordinated the 322nd and 328th rifle divisions to the commander of the 10th Army, as their further location as part of the cavalry corps would have restricted the latter's operations and made the problem of control more difficult. During this period there were frequent instances of a communications breakdown between the 10th Army headquarters and the 1st Guards Cavalry Corps, to which fact the *front* headquarters and the General Staff's operational directorate alluded to the 10th Army headquarters on a number of occasions.

The 330th Rifle Division's left-flank units, which were operating along the paved road running from Belev north, parallel to the Oka River along its western bank, took part in the fighting for Belev.

Intelligence data from the headquarters of the 330th Rifle Division during this period determined the presence in Belev of units of the enemy's 167th and 112th infantry divisions, along with heavy artillery and tanks.

By order of the *front* command, the control of combat operations for the capture of Belev was entrusted to the commander of the 10th Army, Gen. Golikov, who left for the Belev area with an operational group from army headquarters. By December 28 a command post had been deployed in Zhivotovo.

During the latter half of December 28 the army's 239th and 324th rifle divisions advanced in fighting to the line Kudrino-Davydovo and continued to attack to the west. The 330th Rifle Division was fighting enemy units covering Belev from the north in the Besedino-Beregovaya area; the latter place changed hands twice. By this time the 323rd Rifle Division's forward units were passing through Snykhovo, moving to the west. The 325th and 326th rifle divisions were still in the army's second echelon in the Boloto-Gorodnya-Kalinovka area.

During the course of December 27 the 2nd Guards and 75th cavalry divisions were fighting for Kozel'sk, but were not able to capture it. The Germans' 296th and 216th infantry divisions defending the town were putting up stubborn resistance. The Fascist aviation, in group and individual raids on our cavalry, made its advance more difficult. Our troops suffered significant losses. The 9th Tank Brigade, located in the Odoevo area, could not render support to the cavalry units.

Only on the morning of December 28 did the 2nd Guards and 75th cavalry divisions, having outflanked Kozel'sk from the northwest and the south, and having pinned down the enemy from the east, break into the town and, following a brief street battle, drive out the German-Fascist units. A large amount of equipment was captured in Kozel'sk.

During the latter part of December 28 the 2nd Guards and 75th cavalry divisions, with all their forces, pursued the retreating units of the 216th and 296th infantry divisions to the west and northwest.

By December 29 units of the 10th Army, in carrying out their orders for attacking in the direction of Kozel'sk, Sukhinichi and further west, reached the following areas: the 239th and 324th rifle divisions—the Kozel'sk area, where they linked up with units from the 1st Guards Cavalry Corps. The 323rd Rifle Division, moving into the same area, by the morning of December 29 was located in Kireevskoe (along the railroad 15-16 km southeast of Kozel'sk). The 328th Rifle Division, bypassing the enemy's strong points north of Belev, was moving along the route Pashkovo-Karacheevo (both locales 6-10 km east of Kireevskoe), with the mission of getting into the flank and rear of the enemy's Belev group from the area Ishutino station-Maslovo. The 326th Rifle Division was moving along the route Moshchena-Skryl'evo-Slagovishchi and on December 30 was to reach the area Lavrovskoe-Tolstoe (ten km southwest of Kozel'sk). The 325th Rifle Division at dawn on December 29 left the area Gorodnya-Kalinovka area, where it was located in the army's second echelon, with the task of reaching the Kozel'sk area. The 322nd and 330th rifle divisions continued fighting for Belev, attacking along the following axes: the 330th Rifle Division—from the north from the line Maslovo-Redova-Beregovaya, and the 322nd Rifle Division—from the east. Enveloping the enemy along several axes, both divisions were squeezing him, forcing him to withdraw to Belev with heavy casualties.

The dogged fighting for the town continued under great pressure all of December 30. The 328th Rifle Division, part of whose forces was outflanking Belev from the north and northwest with the 330th Rifle Division, took part in the fighting. By 1300 on December 31 the battle was decided in our favor and the 10th Army's forces took the town, capturing large amounts of equipment. The defeated enemy began to withdraw to the west and southwest.

During the second half of December 31 the 322nd Rifle Division continued to sweep Belev of the remaining small groups of Germans, and the 328th and 330th rifle divisions were directed to the west and northwest to further the offensive.

The development of the offensive by the 10th Army and 1st Guards Cavalry Corps following the capture of Kozel'sk and Belev

Following the capture of Kozel'sk, the 2nd Guards and 75th cavalry divisions, pursuing the retreating enemy, by the close of December 29 had reached the front: 75th Cavalry Division—Berdy-Pronino, and the 2nd Guards Cavalry Division—Plyuskovo-Kashcheva.

During the night of December 29-30 both cavalry divisions reached the area Privalovo-Ryazantsevo-(excluding) Meshchovsk (which was occupied by the enemy), where they concentrated. According to order no. 132, issued by Gen. Belov on December 29, the 2nd Guards and 75th cavalry divisions, with the onset of darkness on December 30, left the indicated area and headed along the route Beklemishchevo-Foshnya-Mochalovo, in order to occupy their jumping-off position in the area Mochalovo-Gorokhovka-Sulikhovo for an attack in the direction of Shukleva and Mar'ina. The divisions were to cut off the enemy's route of retreat from Yukhnov to the southwest.

By the morning of December 31 the 1st Guards, 57th and 41st cavalry divisions had reached the front Poroslitsy-Kurbatovo-Zubovo-Tarasova. They had the mission of capturing Yukhnov and further developing the blow toward Vyaz'ma, directing part of their forces toward Medyn', for the purpose of cutting off the enemy's retreat route from there.

Combat operations by Gen. Belov's group of forces after December 31 unfolded as follows: the 41st Cavalry Division, located along the group's right flank, with the task of breaking through along the Yukhnov axis, was fighting during January 1-4 along the front Solopikhono-Zubovo. By this time the 57th and 1st Guards cavalry divisions, having received the same assignment as the 41st Cavalry Division, was overcoming the line Zhiteevka-Sukholom-Zheremeslo (two km west of Sukholom)-Kurkino by fighting. The left-flank 75th and 2nd Guards cavalry divisions were attacking in the direction of Davydovo in order to reach the area west of Yukhnov. By January 4 both divisions had been halted by the enemy along the front Tibeki-Davydovo-Foshnya-Petushki (two km southeast of Foshnya), where firing had broken out.

On January 6 up to three regiments of German infantry, supported by tanks and aviation, counterattacked along the front Ozero-Sulikhovo-Zhivul'ki and forced units of the group's left flank to fall back to the line Davydovo-Foshnya-Beklemishchevo. A fierce fight broke out along this line. Units of the 41st, 57th and 1st Guards cavalry divisions were engaged in heavy fighting along their former front. The cavalry group's forces experienced a shortage of ammunition. In connection with this, Gen. Belov on January 7 decided to go over to the defensive. From January 8 Gen. Belov's cavalry group was turned toward Mosal'sk and was carrying out a new *front* assignment.

The forces of the 10th Army's right flank, after reaching the Kozel'sk area, were located as follows: by January 1 the 239th Rifle Division was making a fighting approach to the line Khoten'-Klesovo, trying to bypass Sukhinichi from the north. On December 29 the 324th Rifle Division reached the front Muzalevka station-Mekhovoe, with the task of attacking toward Sukhinichi from the southeast. On January 2 the 326th Rifle Division reached in fighting the line Muzalevka-Berezovka-Slobodka, operating in a westerly direction. On December 30 the 323rd Rifle Division was in the area of Volkonskoe, getting reading to attack to the west, bypassing Sukhinichi from the south. The 325th Rifle Division was concentrated in Kozel'sk. By January 1 the 328th and 330th rifle divisions were being pulled back to the Kozel'sk area as part of the army's main group. The 322nd Rifle Division was left behind in Belev as a garrison, with the task of securing the army's left flank.

During January 1-5 the 10th Army's right-flank units were attacking toward Mishchovsk and Serpeisk, while in the center (324th and 239th rifle divisions) were fighting for Sukhinichi. An attempt to take Sukhinichi by a frontal attack ended unsuccessfully. The army command decided, without halting the offensive, to block Sukhinichi. During this period the remaining divisions were completing their movement from the areas of Belev and Kozel'sk to the Lyudinovo-Kirov axis.

From this time begins a new stage in the left-wing armies' combat operations, during the course of which they fought to reach the Warsaw highway and the Vyaz'ma-Bryansk lateral railroad.

Operational-tactical conclusions on the Belev-Kozel'sk Operation

The overall goal of the Belev-Kozel'sk operation by the 10th Army and 1st Guards Cavalry Corps was the non-stop pursuit of the defeated enemy, so as to prevent him from consolidating along intermediate lines and, along with this, by capturing the Kozel'sk and Sukhinichi dirt road and railroad junctions, to reach as quickly as possible the Vyaz'ma-Bryansk lateral railroad and to cut the Warsaw highway at Yukhnov, thus depriving the German-Fascist troops of this very important artery.

Despite a number of difficulties, which our forces had to overcome, the missions assigned to the 1st Guards Cavalry Corps and the 10th Army by the *front* command, were basically fulfilled.

From December 20 to January 5, or 17 days, the 10th Army and the cavalry corps covered about 130-140 km, having begun their march-maneuver from the line of the Plava River. This amounted to about eight km a day on the average. Under conditions of winter, the enemy's stubborn defense, and the unsatisfactory condition of our rear, such an offensive pace should be seen as sufficiently high.

The 10th Army's rate of advance could have been higher if the neighboring 61st Army (Bryansk Front) on the left had not lagged behind and left the 10th Army's left flank open. This circumstance facilitated the enemy's creation of the Belev bridgehead and his stubborn defense of this locale. At the same moment when the 10th Army's left-flank divisions were fighting for Belev, by January 29 units of the 61st Army were only reaching a line south of Belev.

During December 20-31 the 1st Guards Cavalry Corps' right-flank divisions (1st Guards and 57th cavalry divisions) covered about 150 km, or about 13-15 km per day, while these divisions' rate of advance from the line of the Oka River in the area Il'ino-Kalinteevo-Mezentsevo averaged up to 20 km per day. Such an offensive pace by a cavalry corps in winter conditions, while being cut off from the right-flank divisions and rear, should be seen as good.

One of the characteristic features of the employment of cavalry in the given operation, as well as in the previous Tula operation, was the reinforcement of the cavalry with rifle divisions, with the latter subordinated to the commander of the cavalry corps. Here the experience of the Civil War was repeated to a certain degree, when the 1st Cavalry Army was also reinforced with rifle divisions (for example, in the Voronezh-Kastornoe operation of 1919). Such measures were not accidental, but each time were dictated by the conditions of the concrete situation, which justified themselves in the course of combat operations. In such circumstance the infantry reinforced the cavalry, while the latter turned into infantry up to a certain moment. In these conditions the horse served as a means of rapid maneuver in the cavalry units' approach to the objective of their attack. The number of rifle divisions attached to the cavalry corps varied, and changed depending on the situation.

Given the necessity of rapidly pushing the cavalry forward (as was the case, for example, following the cavalry's arrival at the Oka River's western bank), the rifle divisions were temporarily removed from the command of the cavalry commanders. The *front* command was pursuing the same goal in attaching tank units to the 1st Guard Cavalry Corps. Our cavalry, being reinforced with rifle and tank units, could conduct out large combat operations along the enemy's flanks and in his rear. There were a particularly large amount of such examples in the succeeding operations.

The cavalry units broadly employed night activities. All movements, and in some cases the fighting for inhabited locales, were carried out under the cover of darkness. These spared our cavalry enemy air attacks and enabled it, by unexpectedly and rapidly appearing in front of the enemy, inflict serious defeats on him. All the preparatory measures for the march and battle were carried out in daylight. Under those conditions, when the march and battle with the enemy had to be carried out in the daytime, problems of air defense became important. It is necessary, however, to note that in the cavalry units' comparatively rapid movements our air defense often failed to cope with its assignments, while its weapons were limited as well. For example, during the movement of Gen. Belov's cavalry group to the Yukhnov area, its units were subjected to the enemy's heavy air activity during daytime marches and halts.

One of the serious shortcomings, committed both by the 10th Army headquarters, as well as that of the 1st Guards Cavalry Corps during the conduct of the operation in question, were a number of cases of a loss of communications by the army and corps headquarters with their subordinate units, as well as between each other; this relates to army headquarters communications with *front* headquarters. Sometimes *front* headquarters had no information from the army headquarters on the conditions of its forces. At the same time the army headquarters did not know the true situation of its subordinate units at the front. Such a situation arose, for example, during the night of December 28-29, and during the daylight hours of December 29-30. To a significant degree this shortcoming in troop control is explained by the absence in the 1st Guards Cavalry Corps and 10th Army of a sufficient amount of communications equipment. From a report by Gen. Belov to *front* commander Gen. Zhukov, it is obvious that he disposed of only one 5-AK radio set on a sledge. The remaining radio sets had either fallen behind, or had been damaged by enemy air attacks. Snowstorms and the heavy snowfall made communications by air difficult. The German air force's increasing activity also told. A similar situation held in the 10th Army, whose divisions during the operation's latter period had to fight along a broad front.

One of the chief kinds of troop control was the interaction of the commanders with each other and the movement of the command posts directly up to the front line.

***

After January 5 1942 the *front's* left-wing armies, without halting their offensive, began a new period of combat operations. This started for the 49th Army on January 9, when its forces were ordered to take the Germans' defensive line Kondrovo-Polotnyanyi Zavod and defeat (in coordination with the 43rd and 50th armies) the enemy's Kondrovo-Myatlevo-Yukhnov group. The 50th Army, completing the regrouping of its main forces to its left flank, was attacking Yukhnov, for the purpose of capturing it and subsequently developing the blow to the northwest. The 1st Guards Cavalry Corps was aiming at Vyaz'ma, while the 10th Army received an additional assignment—to speed up its arrival to the Vyaz'ma-Bryansk lateral railroad and capture the towns of Kirov, Lyudinovo, Zhizdra, and others.

Under the banner of carrying out their assignments, the armies of the Western Front's left wing conducted their subsequent offensive operations in January 1942.

6

The overall situation on the Western Front in the middle of January. The breakthrough of the German defense along the Volokolamsk-Gzhatsk axis and the pursuit of the enemy to the Gzhatsk defensive line

The overall situation on the Western Front in the middle of January 1942

By the middle of January the overall situation on the Western Front was developing favorably for the Red Army, despite significant losses and the exhaustion of the troops as a result of the continuous and protracted fighting in conditions of a harsh winter and the enemy's stubborn resistance.

On January 14 the Western Front's military council, in directives no. K-41, K-42, and K-43, assigned its latest objectives to the *front's* right wing, center, and left wing for carrying out its plan.

The right wing's (1st, 20th, and 16th armies) immediate mission was: in conjunction with the Kalinin Front's armies, to encircle and capture the Lotoshino and Gzhatsk-Vyaz'ma enemy group. On the right, the Kalinin Front's armies were to launch their main blow in the general direction of Alferovo, Sychevka, and Vyaz'ma. The center armies (5th and 33rd) were ordered to encircle and destroy the Mozhaisk-Gzhatsk group and reach the line Gzhatsk-(excluding) Vyaz'ma. Finally, the *front's* left wing was instructed to:

1 The Kondrovo-Yukhnov enemy group, stubbornly resisting, is striving to hold the Warsaw highway and cover the Gzhatsk, Vyaz'ma and Roslavl' axes.
2. The immediate mission of the Western Front's left-wing armies is to complete the defeat of the enemy's Kondrovo-Yukhnov group and then, with a blow toward Vyaz'ma, to encircle and capture the enemy's Gzhatsk-Vyaz'ma group in conjunction with the armies of the Kalinin Front and the Western Front's center armies.

It was thus planned to carry out the encirclement and defeat of the main forces of the Germans' central group of forces by concentric blows by two *fronts*, aiming these blows in the general direction of Vyaz'ma from the north, northeast, east, and southeast.

By this time along the Western Front's right wing a turning point in the fighting had been reached. As a result of forgoing attacks against the Germans' fortified zone along a wide front by three armies and the subsequent adoption of another method of operations—a blow along a narrow front by concentrating men and suppression means from the right-wing armies along a single sector—the 20th Army successfully carried out a breakthrough along the Volokolamsk-Gzhatsk axis, which opened the prospect of operationally employing the breakthrough by the 20th Army in conjunction with the 1st Shock and 16th armies.

In the first half of January our offensive developed in the center. In the beginning the Red Army's units achieved the greatest results to the west of the line Borovsk-Maloyaroslavets, where during 15 days in January they advanced 30-50 km in a straight line, having penetrated between the Mozhaisk and Kondrovo-Yukhnov enemy groups. The offensive was still developing slowly to the north of the Borovsk-Maloyaroslavets area; on January 14 Dorokhovo was taken along the Mozhaisk axis. Events developed more rapidly along the Mozhaisk axis in the second half of January, when as a result of the advance by our units to the north and south of Mozhaisk, favorable conditions for us were created and the Germans, under pressure from the 5th and 33rd armies, began to fall back here to the west. On January 20 Mozhaisk was taken.

Our forces advanced most slowly in the direction of Kaluga and Yukhnov, near the junction of the Western Front's center and left wing. A large German group (the remains of 7-9 divisions) was stubbornly defending in the Myatlevo-Polotnyanyi Zavod-Yukhnov triangle, covering the Warsaw highway and the Kaluga-Vyaz'ma railroad. Despite the danger of being outflanked along both flanks by our forces in the center and on the left wing (43rd, 49th, and 50th armies, and the 1st Guards Cavalry Corps), and the gradual tightening of the encirclement ring during the succeeding fighting, the Germans' Yukhnov group stubbornly held on to the occupied area. The fighting here continued throughout January.

On the *front's* left wing the Red Army forces (as was just mentioned) were engaged in persistent fighting along the Kaluga-Yukhnov axis with the Germans' Myatlevo-Kondrovo-Yukhnov group and their offensive here was developing slowly. To the south our units in the first half of January were advancing along the Mosal'sk, Kirov, and Kyudinovo axes and by January 15 were already located 100-130 km from the line of the Oka River, having reached the Vyaz'ma-Bryansk lateral railroad. It was along the line reached in the first half of January that our offensive here essentially ended.

The second half of January includes the fighting against the Germans' Yukhnov group and the gradual tightening of its encirclement ring, the fighting by Belov's group for the Warsaw highway, and also the Germans' concentric offensive from Zhizdra toward Sukhinichi and their subsequent relief of the encircled garrison in Sukhinichi. On the *front's* left flank the 61st Army (transferred on January 13 from the Bryansk Front) had penetrated deeply into the rear of the Germans' Bolkhov group, having encircled it on three sides.

During the first half of January the troops of the Kalinin Front were launching their main blow in the general direction of Sychevka and Vyaz'ma, trying to cut the Gzhatsk-Smolensk railroad and highway to the west of Vyaz'ma, in order to deprive the enemy of his main communications, and together with the Western Front's forces, to surround and destroy the Germans' powerful Mozhaisk-Gzhatsk-Vyaz'ma group.

On January 15 the Kalinin Front took Selizharovo; along the left wing there was stubborn fighting with the Germans' Rzhev-Sychevka group, which was defending stubbornly while being half-surrounded.

In the second half of January the Kalinin Front developed its successful offensive to the south-west and west, having deeply penetrated the enemy front. On January 22 the Kalinin Front was reinforced with the Northwestern Front's two left-flank armies (3rd and 4th armies).

At the end of January the Kalinin Front, attacking from the area of Toropets, were fighting along the approaches to Velizh. Another group of forces was engaged in stubborn fighting in the Belyi area. A cavalry corps, sent to the south, cut the Vyaz'ma-Smolensk highway west of Vyaz'ma.

In the area of Rzhev, Zubtsov, and Sychevka stubborn fighting continued against the German group, which was stubbornly holding this area and which from time to time went over to active operations. Thus having launched a counterblow from the Rzhev area to the west, the Germans advanced here along a narrow front and cut the communications of those Kalinin Front units which were operating in the zone between Sychevka and Belyi south of the Rzhev-Nelidovo railroad. Fighting during the final days of January was waged to restore these communications.

The Bryansk Front's right wing, having turned over the 61st Army to the Western Front, occupied its previous position throughout the second half of January. Here local battles were occurring; the troops were fortifying their positions and were conducting reconnaissance. There were no large operationally-significant events along this axis in January.

The breakthrough of the Germans' defensive line along the Lama River on January 10-15 1942

In connection with the failure of preceding operations on the 1st, 20th, and 16th armies' fronts in breaking through the enemy's defense, the *front* commander, in carrying out the *Stavka's* instructions for the subsequent defeat of the Germans, issued its new decision in directive no. 0141/op.

> To the commanders of the 1st, 20th, and 16th armies. A copy for the chief of the General Staff. No. 0141/op, 01.06.42, at 0130, a 1:100,000 map.
>
> 1 In light of the fact that the 16th Army has not carried out its task of breaking through the enemy defense, the mission of breaking through is entrusted to the 20th Army.
> For this purpose the 20th Army is to be reinforced with the following units:
> a) from the 1st Army—29th and 55th rifle brigades, and the 528th Artillery Regiment, to be concentrated by January 8 in the areas of Shchekino, Pushkari, and Kalistovo;
> b) from the 16th Army—the 2nd Guards Cavalry Corps with ski battalions, 20th Cavalry Division, 22nd Tank Brigade, the 471st, 523rd, 138th, and 537th artillery regiments, two rocket-artillery battalions, and the 40th and 49th rifle brigades.
> The enumerated units are to be concentrated by January 8 in the following areas:
> The 2nd Guards Cavalry Corps, 20th Cavalry Division, and the 22nd Tank Brigade—Chentsy-Yadrovo-Rozhdestevno;
> 40th and 49th rifle brigades—Muromtsevo-Zhdanovo;
> 471st Artillery Regiment—Muromtsevo;
> 523rd Artillery Regiment—Bol'shoe Nikol'skoe;
> 138th Artillery Regiment—Zhdanovo;
> 537th Artillery Regiment—Krasikovo;
> a rocket-artillery battalion—Yadrovo.
>
> 2 During January 6-8 the commander of the 20th Army is to prepare a blow along the front Mikhailovka-Anan'ino-Posadinki to complete the destruction of the enemy's defensive zone, followed by the capture of Shakhovskaya.
> The attack is to begin on the morning of January 9.
> The first day's task is to reach the front Bol'shoe Isakovo-Kur'yanovo-Chubarovo;
> the second day's task is for the mobile group (2nd Guards Cavalry Corps, 22nd Tank Brigade, 20th Cavalry Division, five ski battalions) to seize Shakhovskaya, followed by an advance to Gzhatsk.
>
> 3 All regroupings are to be carried out rapidly and in secret.
> The command element of the formations and units transferred from the 1st and 16th armies is to be sent to Vozmishche by 0900 on January 7, in order to receive orders and

instructions from the 20th Army commander concerning reconnaissance and the occupation of jumping-off positions.

4 Report on fulfillment. The 20th Army commander is to present his operational plan by 2400 on January 6 1942.
Zhukov, Khokhlov, Sokolovskii.

Thus the *front* command entrusted the 20th Army with the responsible mission of carrying out the breakthrough of the Germans' defense along a sector of the *front's* right flank. Naturally, in connection with this, the 20th Army was to take the leading role in the forthcoming operation as the entire right wing's shock group; the neighboring 1st and 16th armies were to subsequently facilitate the success of the wing's shock group.

The 20th Army commander, in order no. 01 of January 7, offered the following description of the situation on his sector at the time:

1 Defending along the army's front are the following:
   a) Units of the 6th Panzer Division, without equipment, and the remains of the 106th Infantry Division along the line Sidel'nitsy-Timonino;
   b) Units of the 35th Infantry Division along the line Aksenovo-Posadinki-Ludina Gora-Terent'evo;
   c) Units of the 5th Panzer Division, without equipment, along the line Pagubino-Ryukhovskoe-Spas-Ryukhovskoe-Konyashino.

2. To the right are the 1st Army's 71st and 56th rifle brigades along the line Suvorovo-Putyatino-Vladychino.
The boundary line with the 1st Army is (excluding) Nikita-(excluding) Il'inskoe-Shakhovskaya-(excluding) Zubtsov.
To the left the 16th Army's 354th Rifle Division is defending along the line of the woods one km east of Chertanovo-the woods one km east of Kuz'minskoe.
The boundary line with the 16th Army is Sosnino-Chernevo-(excluding) Aleksandrino station.

With this order, in accordance with the directive received from the *front* commander, the 20th Army commander laid out the task for the formations for the breakthrough of the enemy's defensive zone along the line of the Lama River. According to his calculations, the concentration of the arriving units should be completed within the next two-three days, after which the army could begin the offensive.

The army commander's decision on the breakthrough and the army's tasks were formulated in the following manner:

> On January 9 the 20th Army is to break through the enemy's defensive zone along the sector Zakhar'ino-Timonino-Aksenovo-Posadinki and to destroy the opposing enemy forces and by the end of the day is to reach the line Bol'shoe Isakovo-Kur'yanovo-Chubarovo; upon reaching this line, the army is to commit a breakthrough development group into the breach on the morning of January 10 in the direction of Shakhovskaya.

Such a direction of the blows corresponded to the army's objective and would put our forces into the Shakhovskaya area, which was an important road junction for the development of subsequent operations to the west.

Simultaneous with this, the neighboring 1st Army on the right had the mission of taking the Lotoshino area, which in its turn corresponded with the overall goal of carrying out a serious breakthrough along one of the front's main axes.

The army's forces were assigned the following local tasks:

4 Maj. Gen. Remizov's groups (17th Rifle and 145th Tank brigades), in conjunction with Maj. Gen. Katukov's group, is to destroy the enemy in the Zakhar'ino area and then to hold the area Mikhailovka-Zakhar'ino, thus securing the offensive by the army's main forces against blows from the north.
The boundary line on the left is Mikhailovka-(excluding) Bol'shoe Goloperovo.

5 Maj. Gen. Katukov's group (1st Guards Tank Brigade, 1st Guards and 49th rifle brigades, 517th and 528th artillery regiments, 7th and 35th independent guards mortar battalions) is to destroy the enemy in the area Bol'shoe Goloperovo-Maloe Ivantsevo Goloperovo-Kaleevo and by the end of the day reach the line Maloe Ivantsevo Isakovo-(excluding) Afanasovo.
The boundary line on the left is Timkovo-(excluding) Timonino-(excluding) Afanasovo-Starikovo.

6 The 352nd Rifle Division, with the 537th Artillery Regiment and the 2nd Independent Guards Mortar Battalion, in conjunction with Katukov's group and the 64th Rifle Brigade, is to destroy the enemy in the Timonino area and by the end of the day reach the area Afanasovo-Kur'yanovo.

7 Maj. Gen. Korol' group (331st Rifle Division, 40th Rifle Brigade, 31st Tank Brigade, 138th and 523rd artillery regiments, and the 15th Independent Guards Mortar Battalion) is to destroy the enemy in the area Zubovo-137-km station and by the end of the day reach the area Kur'yanovo-Vysokovo.
The boundary line to the left is excluding Zhdanovo-Ludina Gora-Fedtsevo-Vishenki.

8 The 35th Rifle Brigade, upon destroying the enemy in the area of Ludina Gora, is to attack toward Terent'evo and Timoshevo, while using part of its forces to cover against an enemy attack from Pagubino.
The boundary line from the left is Krasikovo-(excluding) Ryukhovskoe-Safatovo-Rozhdestveno.

9 The 28th Rifle Brigade, upon destroying the enemy in the Ryukhovskoe area, is to attack toward Dubosekovo, employing part of its forces to cover against Spas-Ryukhovskoe.

It was intended that along these units' breakthrough front a breakthrough development group, consisting of a three-division cavalry corps, reinforced by a tank brigade and five ski battalions, would be committed with the task of developing the success in the direction of Shakhovskaya.

In the order this group was given the following assignment:

> The breakthrough development group (2nd Guards Cavalry Corps, 20th Cavalry Division, 22nd Tank Brigade, and five ski battalions), led by the commander of the 2nd Guards Cavalry Corps Maj. Gen. Pliev, is to concentrate on the night of January 9-10 in the area Mikhailovka-Timonino-Aksenovo, and on the morning of January 10 is to enter the breach along the sector Maloe Ivantsevo Isakovo-Bolvasovo and, attacking in the direction of Bukholovo station and bypassing Kur'yanovo and Chukholovo from the south, by the end of the day capture Shakhovskaya, with an eye toward continuing the attack toward Gzhatsk.

A reserve of two rifle brigades was concentrated for supporting the units of the first echelon and breakthrough development groups, which was given the following tasks:

11 The reserve: a) the 64th Rifle Brigade is to attack behind the 352nd Rifle Division and by a blow from the south is to facilitate the capture of Timonino. It is then to attack in the direction of Zubovo, aiding Maj. Gen. Korol' group in destroying the enemy in the Zubovo area, and then attacking behind the right-flank part of Maj. Gen. Korol' group;

b) the 55th Rifle Brigade is to enter Volokolamsk and prepare to repel possible enemy counterattacks from the direction of Ivanovskoe, Vladychino, and Volokolamsk station.

Aside from the artillery attached directly to the army's units, a long-range artillery group (ADD) was formed, consisting of two RGK artillery regiments and a single mortar battalion. The group's tasks included:

22 The ADD artillery—544th Long-Range Artillery Regiment, 471st Artillery Regiment, and the 17th Independent Guard Mortar Battalion—is to support the offensive by Maj. Gen. Katukov's group with the 352nd Rifle Division, and Maj. Gen. Korol' group. The beginning of the artillery preparation is to begin by special order, with duration of one hour. 2.5 combat loads are to be expended on January 9.

The army aviation (601st Bomber Regiment) was ordered to bomb on January 9 the enemy's reserves and rear organs in the area Bolvasovo-Chubarovo-Fedtsevo.

The beginning of the attack was designated by a special order.

As early as January 7 new units were beginning to arrive to the army (from January 6 the 55th Rifle Brigade began to concentrate in the Zhdanovo area, and the 2nd Guards Cavalry Corps in the area Chentsy-Yadrovo-Rozhdestveno).

There were no significant changes along the army's front on January 7. Remizov's group was defending in Mikhailovka, the 352nd Rifle Division—to the east of Timonino. Katukov's group was putting itself in order and making ready for the offensive. The 331st Rifle Division was fighting for Posadinki.

At the moment the order was issued the situation along the army's front was as follows.

During the night of January 7-8 the army's units carried out combat and reconnaissance activities along the entire front.

The Germans, putting up stubborn resistance, were holding the line Sidel'nitsy-Zakhar'ino-Timonino-Posadinki-Ludina Gora-Kryukovo-Pagubino-Ryukhovskoe-Spas-Ryukhovskoe. Behind the front line they were hurriedly building defensive structures. The enemy's reserves, up to an infantry regiment in strength, were located in Zubovo, Safatovo, Dubosekovo, and Klishino. Besides this, according to our aviation, reserves and enemy concentrations of an unknown number had been observed in the areas of Shakhovskaya and Sereda.

On January 8 the forces of the 1st, 20th, and 16th armies continued their combat and reconnaissance activities along their former lines.

At night the arriving units continued concentrating in their designated areas.

By January 9 the units' concentration was completed. (The army's organizational composition is shown in supplement 2).

If at the beginning of January the army's quantitative and qualitative composition testified to the fact that it could not independently, without corresponding reinforcement, conduct large-scale operations, then as early as January 9 its forces rendered it entirely capable of organizing a decisive operation.

The army's reinforcement is evident from the following table, which characterizes the change in the 20th Army's numbers during the preparatory period for the breakthrough.

By the time indicated that army occupied a front 20 km in length.

It was planned to make the breakthrough along an 8-km sector (Zakhar'ino-Timonino-Aksenovo-Posadinki).

For this purpose the following units were deployed and concentrated:

a) Remizov's group (17th Rifle and 145th Tank brigades);
b) Katukov's group (1st Guards Rifle Brigade, 1st Guards Tank Brigade, 49th Rifle Brigade, 528th and 517th artillery regiments, and the 35th and 17th independent guards mortar battalions);
c) the 352nd Rifle Division, with the 537th Artillery Regiment and the 2nd Independent Guards Mortar Battalion;
d) Maj. Gen. Korol' group (331st Rifle Division, 40th Rifle and 31st Tank brigades, the 138th and 523rd artillery regiments, and the 15th Independent Guards Mortar Battalion);
e) the breakthrough development group (2nd Guards Cavalry Corps, 20th Cavalry Division, 22nd Tank Brigade, and five ski battalions);
f) a reserve (64th and 55th rifle brigades);
g) long-range artillery (544th Long-Range Howitzer Regiment, 471st Artillery Regiment, and the 17th Independent Guard Mortar Battalion).

This group of forces ensured the following operational density along the breakthrough front: one rifle division per 1.5 km of front, 37 guns per km of front; 39 mortars per km of front, and 12.5 tanks per km of front (based upon an overall concentration of two rifle divisions, six rifle brigades, five ski battalions, three cavalry divisions, four tank brigades, seven RGK artillery regiments, and five guards mortar battalions along the breakthrough front).

Given this operational density, the correlation of forces along the direction of the main blow was as follows.

Along the holding group's sector the density was one rifle brigade for six km of front, two guns and seven mortars per kilometer of front.

These figures give only an overall impression of the correlation of forces, as data for the enemy is based upon a calculation of the German units along the breakthrough front being at 65% of their authorized strength (two regiments of the 6th Panzer Division acting as infantry, and a regiment from the 35th Infantry Division, whose main forces were opposite the army's holding group—28th and 35th rifle brigades). In all, this yields one infantry division, reinforced by an artillery regiment.

Besides this, it is necessary to take into account the fact that by this time the quantitative strength of both sides had been significantly weakened in the preceding fighting, which means that by a battalion one should understand an organizational entity numbering, on the average, some 100-150 bayonets. The enemy was in approximately the same shape. However, it is beyond a doubt that by January 10 the advantage in forces was in favor of the 20th Army. Thus the success of the planned breakthrough was supported by real combat power.

Table V/6.1 20th Army indices, January 1-10 1942

Date and month	Rifle divisions	Rifle brigades	Ski battalions	Cavalry divisions	Guns	Mortars	Tanks
January 1	2	4	–	–	229	295	50
January 10	2	8	5	3	395	450	100
Increase	–	4	5	3	166	155	50
Correlation	01:01	01:02	00:05	00:03	01:01.8	01:01.5	01:02

Table V/6.2 Correlation of 20th Army and German forces, January 1942

Men & matériel	20th Army		Germans		Correlation per km of front	
	Overall	per km of front	Overall	per km of front	Germans	20th Army
Battalions	29	3.5	9	1.1	1	3.2
Guns	300	37	90	11	1	3.4
Tanks	100	12.5	48	6	1	2
Mortars	312	39	90	11	1	3.5

On January 9 the army's forces occupied their jumping-off positions for the offensive. However, it did not take place that day, because the preparatory work had not yet been completed.

In his January 8 report the 20th Army commander reported to the *front's* military council:

1 The army's units today have been fighting fiercely along their former lines.

2 The 2nd Guards Cavalry Corps, 1st Guards, 40th and 49th rifle brigades have completed their concentration in their designated areas.
The reinforcements for the rifle brigades have fully arrived at their disembarking stations, but less than half of them have been transferred directly to their units because of a lack of sufficient vehicles for this purpose (150 vehicles are being used for this).
The rifle brigades' battalions, without reinforcements, consist of 20-50 soldiers and do not represent a real strength.

3 The army's artillery regiments, with the exception of the 523rd Artillery Regiment, have occupied their positions, although they have only ¼ to ¾ of a combat load.
Troop artillery has even less ordnance.
Only in the evening did the units send out transport to collect the ordnance at Nakhabino station, to which point the ammunition had only been delivered.

The army commander, on the basis of this information, sought to postpone the start of the offensive.

In accordance with this, the start of the offensive was moved by the *front* command to January 10. The army commander set the time for the beginning of the attack at 1030, with a half-hour artillery preparation.

During the night of January 9-10 our units carried out increased reconnaissance along the entire front and brought up ammunition to the jumping-off position.

By this time the 1st Army to the right was also ready for the offensive for the purpose of assisting the 20th Army.

The 1st Army commander's plan, in short, came down to the following: the 56th, 71st, and 46th rifle brigades, 4th and 7th ski battalions, the 701st Artillery Regiment, and the 5th Independent Guards Mortar Battalion were designated to attack on the army's left flank. These forces were to attack along the line Vladychino-(excluding) Mikhailovka, with the immediate objective of capturing Spas-Pomazkino, and then L'vov.

The 16th Army, in connection with the transfer of the majority of its units to the 20th Army (2nd Guards Cavalry Corps with ski battalions, the 20th Cavalry Division and 22nd Tank Brigade, the 40th and 49th rifle brigades, the 471st, 523rd, 138th, and 537th artillery regiments, and the 2nd and 17th guards mortar battalions) was defending along its previous front.

The general offensive by our troops began on January 10.

At 0800 the 20th Army's artillery opened fire along the sector held by the 35th and 28th rifle brigades, and at 0900 the artillery preparation began along the breakthrough front.

At 1030, following the artillery preparation, the troops of the 20th and 1st armies attacked along the entire front, accompanied by artillery fire.

The Germans, unable to withstand the simultaneous blow by our troops, began to fall back in separate groups to the west in the first hours of the fighting. The forward edge of the enemy's defense was crushed fairly comparatively quickly. However, this cost us significant efforts, because the enemy gave up his occupied inhabited points only after repeated and persistent attacks by our units.

Thus, for example, Remizov's group, following three attacks with the support of tanks from the 145th Tank Brigade, by 1600 together with the 1st Guards Rifle Brigade had occupied Zakhar'ino, where in stubborn street fighting it destroyed more than two companies of enemy infantry (400 corpses were found), which were putting up resistance from the village's homes and cellars. The enemy's small retreating groups blew up the bridge over the Yatvenka River in order to make the advance by our units more difficult. On the whole, there were up to two battalions (presumably from the 6th Panzer Division) with three tanks in Zakhar'ino. A regimental headquarters was destroyed in taking Zakhar'ino; among the killed were a lieutenant colonel and two other officers. Thus during the second half of the day the Germans' defense along this sector was factually broken.

By 1200 Katukov's group, bypassing Bol'shoe Goloperovo from the north, was approaching the woods near point 186.5, attacking in conjunction with the 1st Guards Rifle Brigade. The latter, together with Remizov's group, also took part in the fighting for Zakhar'ino.

The 49th Rifle Brigade was stubbornly fighting, together with the 352nd Rifle Division, for Timonino, following the capture of which by 1330 it was continuing the offensive toward Kaleevo and Bol'shoe Goloperovo. In Timonino the brigade's units uncovered up to 100 corpses and took ten prisoners.

A tank regiment from the 1st Guards Tank Brigade was supporting the attack by the 1st Guards Rifle Brigade with two T-34 tanks, while supporting the attack by the 49th Rifle Brigade with a single KV tank and four T-34s. While attacking in the Timonino area two tanks burned (the KV and a T-34), while another T-34 was damaged.

The 352nd Rifle Division, upon taking Timonino (where up to a battalion of enemy infantry was destroyed), continued attacking toward Afanasovo (along a front defended by up to two enemy battalions). In the fighting for Timonino the division's units captured three anti-aircraft guns and four mortars, and destroyed an ammunition dump. The enemy left up to 250 corpses on the battlefield.

By 1400 the 64th Rifle Brigade had reached the eastern outskirts of the woods south of Timonino and, leaving behind a part of its forces to rid the woods of enemy troops defending there, continued the attack toward Zubovo.

The 331st Rifle Division, in conjunction with the 64th Rifle Brigade, from 1400 was waging an unsuccessful fight with the enemy's organized defense in the woods east of Aksenovo, having encountered here his powerful fire resistance. Up to two enemy battalions were stubbornly defending against the division along the Anan'ino-Posadinki axis.

The 40th Rifle Brigade was unsuccessfully attacking toward Posadinki.

On the army's left flank the situation remained unchanged along the line Ludina Gora-Spas-Ryukhovksoe. By 1300 the 35th and 28th rifle brigades were fighting along their former lines. Their attacks, in connection with the enemy's stubborn defense of his lines, were not successful. As before, up to a regiment of infantry was defending against the 35th Rifle Regiment, and up to two battalions against the 28th Rifle Regiment.

The 2nd Guards Cavalry Corps did not take part in the fighting, remaining in its previous location. At 1300 the corps sent out forward detachments to the Ivanovskoe-Timkovo area. By 1300 on January 11 these detachments had concentrated in the Timkovo area.

The army's successfully developing offensive was not supported by army aviation on January 10, due to the poor meteorological conditions. Nor did the enemy's air force show any activity on that day. The army commander's reserves were not committed into the battle.

There was a deep snow cover (as was the case on all other sectors of the front) in the army's area; the operations by light and medium tanks on the breakthrough sector were made more difficult and, in places, impossible, and thus the tank groups' offensive on this day was not sufficiently developed. The infantry's actions also took place in difficult conditions (deep snow and a powerful snowstorm throughout the day).

Aside from this, the Germans, having abandoned a number of first-line fortifications along their left flank, fell back a comparatively short distance and by the end of January 10 had once again organized a defense, but now in the depth of the defensive zone.

As a result of all this, the first day's breakthrough was not successfully developed and the army's forces were limited to a small advance of 2-3 km to the west.

Combat control during the offensive's first day was carried out comparatively well. Communications were maintained by radio and telephone with Remizov's group and periodically with the 352nd Rifle Division. Aside from this, such means as the telegraph and communications officers were employed. Communications was maintained with the 1st Army to the right by telephone and radio and with the 16th Army to the left by communications officers in aircraft, and by radio.

Thanks to the 20th Army's operations, the offensive by units of the 1st Army from January 10 unfolded quite successfully. For example, the 56th Rifle Brigade, attacking that day toward Spas-Pomazkino, reached the woods one km west of Vladychino and continued to make a fighting advance, while the 2nd Guards Rifle Brigade attacked Sidel'nitsy and was met by the enemy's heavy defensive fire on the eastern outskirts. Despite this, at 1400 on January 11 the brigade, together with the 46th Rifle Brigade, captured the village of Sidel'nitsy.

On the night of January 10-11 the 20th Army's units were carrying out a partial regrouping, while continuing to attack along the right flank in the direction of Bol'shoe Goloperovo and Zubovo.

The Germans, through their concentrated fire from the surviving strong points and counterattacks, sought to contain the advance by the army's forces, although their attempts did not yield positive results.

At 0945 on January 11 German infantry, up to a battalion in strength, counterattacked out of Spas-Pomazkino toward Zakhar'ino, but were beaten back by artillery fire and a counterattack by our infantry and tanks from units of Remizov's group. At 1030 the Germans repeated their attack with fresh forces of up to 300-400 men, but were met with fire from our artillery and mortars and a significant part of this group was caught in the open, as a result of which the enemy, having left a large number of corpses on the battlefield, fell back to the west and southwest. At 1330 three enemy tanks and a group of infantry managed to break into Bol'shoe Goloperovo, where they remained until the end of the day. The day passed in mutual counterattacks and there were no major changes in the situation at the front.

During the night of January 11-12 the troops of the *front's* right wing persistently continued the offensive and as early as 0300, despite the enemy's powerful fire resistance and engineering obstacles, units of Katukov's and Remizov's groups reached the line of the eastern outskirts of Il'inskoe-western outskirts of Bol'shoe Goloperovo.

Throughout January 12 the Germans stubbornly hung on to every inhabited point.

By 1300 forward units of Katukov's group had reached the area of Afanasovo, where they entered the fighting with the Germans.

By this this time the 2nd Guards Cavalry Corps began to concentrate in the area Bol'shoe Goloperovo-Zakhar'ino-Mikhailovka.

On the shock group's left flank continued, involving the 64th Rifle and 31st Tank brigades, together with the 331st Rifle Division, for Aksenovo, where the Germans continued to stubbornly hold their line. Our units suffered significant losses on this sector.

Thus on the third day of fighting the units of the army's right flank had penetrated up to five km into the depth of the enemy's defense, that is, the troops had factually overcome the Germans' first defensive zone, having failed to encounter here the expected enemy resistance, due to his small numbers.

As concerns the 1st Army, it continued to attack, successfully carrying out its assignment. Its task was facilitated by the fact that the Kalinin Front's left-flank units were also successfully advancing to the west.

As early as the night of January 11-12 the 1st Army's 47th Rifle Brigade had taken Alfer'evo, while the 56th, 2nd Guards and 44th rifle brigades were fighting for Gusevo and Spas-Pomazkino, which they captured on January 12.

In connection with the successful operations by the shock group's center, the commander of the 20th Army decided on January 13 to commit the mobile group into the breach.

On the morning of January 13 the 2nd Guards Cavalry Corps moved into the breach to develop the success in the direction of Shakhovskaya, in order to carry out the *front* commander's directive to destroy the enemy group in this area.

The corps, inflicting casualties on the enemy, at 1600 on January 13 crossed the line Chukholovo-Vysokovo, attacking along two roads in the general direction of Stepankovo and Shakhovskaya.

On this day the remaining troops continued to expand and deepen the breakthrough, occupying the following front:

Remizov's group captured Il'inskoe and was attacking toward Bol'shoe Isakovo;
Katukov's group was fighting for Nazar'evo;
The 352nd Rifle Division was moving from Bolvasovo to Vysokovo, behind the mobile group's forward detachments;
By 1200 the 64th Rifle Brigade had occupied Zubovo and was attacking Fedtsevo and Chubarovo;
The 331st Rifle Division captured Aksenovo and was attacking Kozino.

The 20th Army commander, in connection with the cavalry corps' entering the breach, ordered the army's units to attack behind the 2nd Guards Cavalry Corps, with the task of reaching the line Shakhovskaya-Vishenki-Dyatlovo.

The Germans tried to organize, with the remains of their defeated 23rd and 106th infantry and 6th Panzer divisions, together with two or three infantry battalions brought up from the reserve, a new defensive line along the Kolpyana River and then to Vysokovo and Beli, so as to prevent the further advance of the army's units to the west. However, there efforts here did not meet with success.

On this day the Germans tried to halt the 1st Army's offensive along the line Gusevo-Novinki, although the attempt did not yield positive results and the army's forces continued to slowly but surely press units of the enemy's 23rd Infantry Division to the north and west, widening the breach along the juncture with the 20th Army.

Having overcome the line of dugouts in the Gusevo area and repelled the enemy's counterattack from this village, as early as 0400 on January 14 the army's units were waging fierce street battles in Gusevo and Novinki.

The Germans' resistance along this line had reached its limit. Intensive artillery and mortar fire and counterattacks along some sectors to restore the situation were all employed by the enemy in order to delay as long as possible the Red Army's advance and secure the withdrawal of their main forces in the direction of Gzhatsk.

At midday, when Gusevo had already been taken, up to 200 enemy troops counterattacked the 56th Rifle Brigade from the area of height 151.9, but the counterattack was not successful and the enemy, having suffered heavy losses, fell back to his jumping-off position.

At the same time the 46th Rifle Brigade had beaten off two German counterattacks of up to 300 men in strength from L'vov and Revino, supported by five tanks, of which two were knocked out by the brigade's artillery.

On January 14 units of the 2nd Guards Cavalry Corps were halted by a German force of up to two battalions along the line Chukholovo-Vysokovo, but supported by the 47th Air Division, Katukov's group, and the 352nd Rifle Division and its attached artillery, by the middle of the day they had destroyed the enemy in these areas and continued to move west. By the end of the day the 3rd and 4th guards cavalry divisions were fighting to the west of this line against the remains of the enemy forces, which were falling back on Gzhatsk.

In accordance with the *front* commander's new directive, which demanded that the axis of the cavalry corps' advance be changed from Shakhovskaya to Sereda and Gzhatsk (for the purpose of encircling the enemy's Mozhaisk group, which had begun to withdraw), the troops began to develop the breakthrough to the southwest. Units of the 2nd Cavalry Corps were attacking Andreevskaya, and the 1st Guards Rifle Battalion was attacking Zdenezh'e.

The shock group's advance on January 15 was insignificant: Remizov's and Katukov's groups were fighting east of the line Rozhdestveno-Sizenevo; ther 49th Rifle Brigade captured Burtsevo; the cavalry corps captured the line Andreevskaya-Novikovo.

During January 14-15 the left wing enjoyed significant success: Gen. Korol' group captured Ludina Gora (which had been fought over for two weeks), Ryukhovskoe, and Spas-Ryukhovskoe, Safatovo, and Dubosekovo. One must assume that the Germans, following the clear indications of a breakthrough along the Shakhovskaya axis, considered it necessary to abandon these points as being in danger of a flank blow from the north. This was facilitated by the circumstance that the offensive by the army's left flank from January 10 did not end. The presupposed German withdrawal along this sector was being further confirmed by the fact that the left wing, despite its comparatively weak composition, advanced 6-8 km on January 14-15.

By this time the 20th Army's front along its right wing was protruding sharply to the west, and then sharply to the east and ran in the direction of Safatovo-Spas-Ryukhovskoe. In the present case the shock group's favorable situation offered the prospect of inflicting a blow on the enemy in the direction of Gzhatsk.

Before the end of January 15 the breakthrough by the shock group developed at a comparatively slow pace. The distance from Timonino to Andreevskaya is 16 km. It required the 20th Army's shock group five days to overcome this distance. As a result, the daily group's daily rate of advance was 3.2 km (for the forward divisions). Taking into account that the active force in the army's shock group for developing the breakthrough was the mobile group (the cavalry corps with attached units), this rate of advance must be seen as low. To be sure, on January 13-14 the cavalry had to wage stubborn fighting along the line Kolpyana River-Vysokovo, although this situation did not exclude the possibility of a more rapid advance in the necessary direction, although at the price of some losses.

The necessity of a rapid advance was understood by all the units' rank and file, and particularly the cavalry corps, but the density of the inhabited points and the deep snow cover prevented us from bypassing the Germans' strong points, as a result of which it was necessary to fight for each village and terrain feature. This caused a delay in the offensive. Attempts to infiltrate between the fortified points led to large losses (particularly among the horses) and failed to yield positive results.

If the cavalry operated successfully in the summer and fall, thanks to its ability to move off the roads, in conditions of a snow-heavy winter its successes on certain sectors were comparatively limited.

The pace of the army's advance subsequently increased a bit, but nevertheless reached up to 5-8 km per day along some axes.

On the 1st Army's front to the right the offensive unfolded more slowly during these days.

On the night of January 14-15 the army only conducted reconnaissance along its front. Its units, following the daytime fighting on January 14, were putting themselves in order and preparing to resume the offensive on the morning of January 15. The Germans were not active during the night, limiting themselves to infrequent harassing artillery and mortar fire against the army's units.

At 0400 on January 15 the army's right-flank units attacked in order to pin down the enemy's left flank and thus prevent him from carrying out a regrouping in the direction of his right flank, which had been weakened in the recent fighting. The Germans on the left flank nevertheless undertook two unsuccessful counterattacks against the 46th Rifle Brigade along the line of the woods to the east of L'vov. As a result of an enemy counterattack from the northwestern outskirts of Novinki the 2nd Guards Rifle Brigade and a battalion from the 50th Rifle Brigade were pushed back to the southwestern edge of the woods south of the village, where they were putting themselves in order and preparing to attack.

As a result of the daytime fighting, the 1st Army's right-flank forces, which were attacking Maleevo, Uzorovo and Ivanovskoe and trying to cut the Brenevo-Gavrilovo road, were not successful as a result of the enemy's strong resistance and by the end of the day continued to fight fiercely on the approaches to these inhabited points.

The 16th Army on the left, in connection with the arrival of the 20th Army's units along the line Ryukhovskoe-Spas-Ryukhovskoe, from January 15 was able to advance to the west. This circumstance was undoubtedly facilitated by the beginning of the German withdrawal before the army.

The Germans, having been hit by the 20th Army in the north, evidently did not risk continuing the defensive fighting against the 20th Army with its available forces, knowing from the experience of preceding battles how good the army was.

As a result of the offensive by the 1st, 20th, and 16th armies during January 10-15 and the breakthrough by the 20th Army, the Western Front's entire right wing had the opportunity to develop the offensive further, pursuing the retreating units of the enemy's Third and Fourth panzer groups and his infantry divisions.

At this time the situation on the Kalinin Front's left wing remained pretty much unchanged. The left-flank 30th Army was attacking in conjunction with the 1st Shock Army in the general direction of Pogoreloe Gorodishche.

The pursuit of the Germans to the Gzhatsk defensive line, January 15-25

On January 16 the 20th Army's forces continued to develop the success in the direction of Sereda and Gzhatsk. Our units, not having encountered the Germans' stubborn resistance, by 1900 had reached the line Rozhdestveno-Starikovo-Burtsevo-Andreevskaya-Novikovo.

On the left wing the 28th and 35th rifle brigades, continuing to pursue the enemy, by 1800 had reached the line Novlyanskoe-Shchekotovo.

The Germans, retreating in the direction of Sereda and Gzhatsk, and trying to delay our advance, were employing mine obstacles.

Simultaneously, the neighboring armies were also successfully advancing. The 1st Army opened its attack along the entire front at 1000. The Germans, having pulled back their worn-out main forces to the west during the night of January 15-16, put up weak resistance with covering units along the line Maleevo (seven km northeast of Lotoshino)-Brenevo-Telegino-Yaropolets-Yelizavetino-Vasil'evskoe. By 1600 the 1st Army's forces had taken this line and, pursuing the enemy's small retreating groups, continued to advance to the west.

The 62nd Rifle Brigade, having taken Maleevo, reached the area of Lotoshino, which by 1730 had been taken by the 41st Rifle Brigade.

On that day the 56th Rifle Brigade took Kul'pino, the 46th Rifle Brigade—Polezhaevo, the 2nd Guards Rifle Brigade—Yelinarkhovo, and the 50th Rifle Brigade reached Aksakovo.

Thus on January 16 the army advanced 12-15 km, having encountered the enemy's weak resistance.

At 2400 on January 15 the Germans' withdrawal before the 16th Army was noted and the latter's units began immediately to pursue. As early as the morning of January 16 our forces occupied the villages of Chertanovo and Konyashino and were fighting for Kolyshkino and Ovinishche (354th Rifle Division). However, the 16th Army's remaining units had no success this day.

On January 17 the 20th Army was pursuing the Germans along all the avenues of their retreat.

By this time the following situation had arisen along the army's front:

a) Its main forces along the right flank had reached the line Shakhovskaya and to the south as far as the Ruza River (the 2nd Guards Cavalry Corps, operating against Sereda, Remizov's and Katukov's groups, the 352nd Rifle Division, 64th Rifle Brigade, as well as the 28th Rifle Brigade, which was being moved to Volokolamsk for refitting and which subsequently advanced behind the right flank in the second echelon). All the tanks, the army artillery, guards mortar battalions, as well as aviation, were supporting this group's advance.
b) The 331st Rifle Division, which disposed of an insignificant number of troops, a few of the 31st Tank Brigade's tanks (not employed, due to the deep snow) remained along the remainder of the front along the line of the Ruza River, as well as the 35th Rifle Brigade, which had up to 200 men.

Thus the 20th Army's main forces, including all its equipment, concentrating on the right flank, were attacking in the general direction of Sereda and Gzhatsk. The auxiliary (pinning) group was not actually fighting, but was moving "forward only because the enemy is withdrawing to the south without being strongly pressed by us" (from a report by the commander of the 20th Army).

The Germans, in retreating continued to put up resistance to the shock group, defending all the inhabited points and mining the roads.

Throughout January 17 the army fought with the retreating enemy along the line Shakhovskaya-Khovan'-Dubrovino-Yakshino, and further along the Ruza River, and by 1700 on January 18 its units had reached the line Zhilye Gory-Parshino-Dyatlovo-Yakshino-Bol'shoe Syt'kovo-Vasil'evskoe.

At the same time the 1st Army continued pursuing the Germans' weak covering units (platoon, company). The army got new orders at the close of January 18 from the *front* command: turn its sector over to the 20th Army and go into the *front* reserve.

At 1000 on January 18 the 1st Army's forces, having formed pursuit detachments, halted with its main forces along the line Dulepovo-Frolovskoe-Robni-Yelizarovo-Sudislovo in order to regroup in accordance with the above-named order.

On January 18 the 20th Army's right-flank forces, while continuing to attack, began to move to the northwest. The 49th, 64th and 28th rifle brigades were detached to the 1st Army's sector to relieve its units.

On January 18 the 1st Army was getting ready to regroup, while continuing the fight with the enemy with its pursuit detachments.

It was in this situation that the 1st Shock Army's combat operations as part of the Western Front essentially ended, after which (following its relief by the 20th Army's units) it was pulled into the reserve in the Klin area for refitting and reequipping.

On January 19 units of the 2nd Guards Cavalry Corps were fighting on the approaches to Sereda and, having taken that point (where the Germans abandoned a large number of killed and captured equipment), by the end of the day had reached the Merklovo area.

It was evident from the enemy' actions that his main forces facing the 20th Army were falling back on Gzhatsk. Thus the army's units should have, while pursuing the retreating Fascists, reached this point as quickly as possible, so as to cut off the chief retreat routes to the west of the enemy's Mozhaisk group, which by this time was fighting with its center forces against the 5th Army in the Mozhaisk area.

It is of interest to note a fact confirming the Germans' retreat to Gzhatsk before the 20th Army: in the village of Yakshino (five km northeast of Sereda) a Polish translator working for the Germans left us a note containing the following:

> The army corps has been defeated. The 106th, 35th and 23rd divisions are falling back on Nikol'skoe and then to Gzhatsk, with no more than 580-600 men in the divisions.

This information from an unknown patriot complete corresponded to the actual situation at the time.

Following the fighting in the Sereda area the pace of the army's units' advance increased significantly. For example, on the right wing units of the 49th Rifle Brigade on January 20 had already occupied the area of Gol'dinovka and Strelka, having thus covered 10-12 km in a day. In the center Katukov's group occupied Novye Rameshki, having advanced ten km to the southwest. The 2nd Guards Cavalry Corps advanced only slightly and by the end of January 20 had only occupied Dubronivka and Dunilovo, and was fighting for Nikol'skoe.

On January 17-18 the retreating German forces sought to delay through powerful rearguards the 16th Army's advance along the line Chernevo-Lapino-Leonidovo, but as a result of stubborn fighting the army's right-flank units captured these places and as early as January 20 were fighting for Reptino. On that day the 354th Rifle Division occupied Terekhovo, Knyazhevo, and Ignatkovo and continued attacking with its main forces in the direction of the Bolychevo state farm. The 9th Guards Rifle Division, having the villages of Soslavino, Isakovo, and Potapovo was pursuing the enemy in the direction of Myshkino.

This was the position the army was in when it received the directive from the *front's* military council, according to which the army headquarters, together with army units, was to be shifted to another direction (Sukhinichi); the army's remaining forces, along with its sector of the front, was handed over to the 5th Army.

Thus the 16th Army completed its three-week fight along this axis in its former state. It had advanced 15km along its center and 22-25km along the flanks, with an average daily rate of advance of 3-5km.

Despite the limited success achieved by the army, it played an important role in the overall system of the *front's* right-wing operations during this period as a pinning group, which prevented the enemy from employing a portion of his forces along other axes.

The departure of the 1st and 16th armies from the Western Front's right wing significantly influenced the subsequent offensive by the 20th Army, which by itself along a 40-km front was to develop the success along the Gzhatsk axis. Aside from this chief task, the army was to maintain close cooperation with the Kalinin Front, the left-flank forces of which by that time had drawn even with the 20th Army.

By January 22 the 20th Army's units had reached the line Knyazhi Gory station-Borisovka-Novo-Aleksandrovka-Kosilovo-Nikol'skoe, where they encountered comparatively stubborn resistance. These were evidently forward positions, located in front of the main resistance zone about 6-10 km to the west of this line.

By January 23 the army command (on the basis of data received from local inhabitants) was aware that the Germans in the area of Berezki, Sapegino and Ret'kov were carrying out defensive work. By this time the army's units had reached the line of the Derzha River near

Vasil'evskoe-Kuchino-Barsuki-Gravatovo, where they engaged the enemy's covering forces on the march. The covering forces failed to play their designated role and on January 24 the army's units arrived at the Germans' main defensive zone, which covered the northern and northeastern approaches to Gzhatsk.

It should be noted that as early as January 24 the Germans on some sectors of the fronts began to launch counterattacks. For example, at 1100 on January 24 Katukov's group in the Krutitsy area was counterattacked by two battalions of infantry, supported by two tanks, from the Savino area, as a result of which units of Katukov's group fell back to the western outskirts of Titovo. At about 2000 the 64th Rifle Brigade, which was being attacked by two German companies with tanks, abandoned the eastern half of Kuchino and fell back to the woods east of this locale.

This basically marked the end of the 20th Army's advance to the west. To be sure, on January 25 a few units were able to advance a little more to the west (the 2nd Guards Cavalry Corps reached the line Bol'shie Trisely-Bykovo), although these isolated successes had no significant influence on the character of the fighting.

Thus the breakthrough by the 20th Army, successfully begun near Volokolamsk, concluded with the arrival of the army's main forces by the end of January to the line indicated above. From this moment the army waged prolonged offensive battles with the Germans, who had taken up the defensive. The 6th Panzer, 106th and 35th infantry divisions continued to operate against the army. Besides this, units of the 7th and 11th panzer and 14th Motorized divisions were also observed. In withdrawing, these divisions were covered by rearguards (from a company to a battalion in strength), reinforced with 2-3 tanks and artillery.

The army's attempts to overcome the enemy defense did not lead to positive results.

On January 26 the army's chief of staff reported to the *front* chief of staff:

> The army's units have reached the enemy's intermediate line, lying along the line Vasil'evskoe-L'vovo-Krutitsy-Petushki-Palatki-Bol'shie Trisely-Bykovo.

The army headquarters at this time evidently did not have a complete picture of the defensive system it was facing and rated the main defensive line's main resistance zone as an "intermediate line." The subsequent fighting cleared up this matter.

From the moment the army arrived at the indicated line the fighting took became fierce. Both sides suffered heavy losses: during January 20-30 the 2nd Guard Cavalry Corps alone lost 340 men killed and 817 wounded. Aside from this, 338 horses were killed and 145 wounded.

By the end of January the army was in its previous organization, although its units had been greatly weakened by the fighting. Thus it is natural that with its arrival at a new defensive zone the army encountered significant difficulties, which were defined by:

a) the lack of sufficient reserves; the army's entire shock group was basically pulled into the fighting;
b) as previously noted, the lengthening of the army's front to 40 km;
c) the army's insignificant numerical and combat composition;
d) the infantry's poor supply of skis, without which the development of maneuver operations by small subunits was made more difficult;
e) the deep snow cover (reaching 75 centimeters).

All this taken together brought about a halt in the offensive. The enemy employed the pause to fortify his positions.

Operational-tactical conclusions from the experience of breaking through defensive lines in January 1942

The successfully conducted breakthrough of the Germans' defense along the line of the Lama and Ruza rivers enables us to draw the following conclusions:

1 On the whole, the German defense was built according to manuals then in use, with amendments brought about by the war itself. It is a sufficiently serious barrier for the attacker. Usually a defense, organized in conditions of limited time, lacks long-term structures, although the capture of hastily constructed wood and earthen firing points, trenches and buildings configured for defense demands no fewer efforts from the units than in breaking through a previously-prepared defense.

In organizing g the breakthrough of defensive lines it is necessary to take into account that the preparation for this must be carried out carefully, taking into account the character of the German defense. Attention must be paid to the suppression of the enemy's automatic rifle and mortar fire along the defensive lines.

2 The character of the German defense (in which the enemy proved to be sufficiently tenacious and stubborn) requires of the attacking forces the concentration of the main shock groups along a comparatively narrow front, supported by suppression means according to the appropriate calculations. Attempts to break through along a broad front without the forces commensurate to such a front do not yield positive results.

The attempt at an operational breakthrough by the 20th Army in the conditions of the Great Patriotic War is a fortunate one, because the preparation for the offensive was thought through and correctly organized, which resulted in a breakthrough that yielded great results.

The breakthrough was carried out along an 8-km front (against the army's overall 20-km front) with a sufficiently high density of means, which guaranteed not only the suppression of the enemy's defensive fire system, but the success of the army's subsequent offensive.

Attempts at breaking through a fortified zone along the entire front of the army (as was shown through the examples of the preceding offensive by the 1st, 20th and 16th armies), without concentrating large forces and suppression, means did not lead to positive results.

3 Experience has shown that in breaking through defensive lines it is advantageous to use the preparatory period for wearing down the enemy's forces and partially destroying his equipment through artillery fire and air strikes.

This method of preparing for the breakthrough was carried out in all the right wing's three armies. To be sure, it's necessary to take into account the losses suffered by our troops during this period, but the subsequent success of a decisive blow along a particular axis will justify these losses in a majority of cases. If the offensive by the 1st and 16th armies did not directly lead to a breakthrough of the enemy's defense, it nevertheless facilitated the 20th Army's final success.

It is advantageous to wage actions to wear out the enemy along a broad front in various strengths, in order to hide from him the true direction of our forces' blow. Such a method was employed by the 1st Army command, which during the course of 10-12 days successively conducted such an offensive with its flank groups.

4 The presence of a corps-sized cavalry group requires that the army commander determine the time for committing this group into the breach. This time was determined very correctly along the 20th Army's sector, although the cavalry was forced to fight at the moment it was being committed. To be sure, the latter was not conceived as an unimpeded advance by the cavalry

along the axis of the breakthrough; however, in this case it is possible that the shifting of this time to approximately January 14 would have been more expedient, as the neighboring 1st and 16th armies had by this time already achieved real results due to their offensive.

5 Reconnaissance proved to be a weak point in all the armies, as a result of which, for example, the attacking 1st Army was forced to determine that "the enemy has broken contact and begun to withdraw." And because the Germans' withdrawal was usually carried out under the cover of darkness, the effectiveness of the battle (in the sense of destroying his forces and capturing his equipment) was significantly reduced. Besides this, the same army, following two days of fighting, was putting itself in order on January 17, which gave the enemy the opportunity to elude our blows.

Thus the successful character of the armies' operations depended to a great deal on the organization of reconnaissance. The 20th Army devoted more attention to this problem, as a result of which the offensive's pace and axis (in the spirit of the *front* command's demands) was fully realized.

6 It should be noted that the success of the breakthrough of the German defense along the line of the Lama and Ruza rivers was facilitated by the circumstance the close cooperation on the flanks of the attacking armies was realized by the *front* and army commands. This factor had great significance, in the sense of securing the overall success of the Western Front's right wing.

7 The experience of organizing the rear and the breakthrough's matériel-technical support, as laid out in Chapter 11, is instructive.

7

The Mozhaisk-Vereya Operation (January 14-22 1942)

The significance of Mozhaisk as a strongpoint

The capture of Dorokhovo and the expected seizure by our troops of Ruza opened the possibility of an attack on Mozhaisk.

Among the numerous strong points, upon which the enemy sought to delay our offensive, Mozhaisk doubtlessly played an outstanding role.

It is located along a very important route leading from west to east; its significance is increased by the large number of intersecting roads here; aside from this, Mozhaisk, due to its natural conditions, may be easily fortified: it is defended from the west by the strong Borodino position, and from the east the approaches to Mozhaisk are covered by forests and gullies that are not easily transited.

Having fortified Mozhaisk, the Germans hoped to maintain their retreating front along this meridian. A large number of wooden and earth firing points half-surrounded Mozhaisk. A large amount of artillery was concentrated in the town; strong points were located along the approaches to the town.

The plan of the Western Front Command for taking Mozhaisk; measures adopted by the Army command

The 5th Army's center and left wing forces, having captured at Dorokhovo at the end of January 14, reached the line Fedotovo-Aleksino-Modenovo-Novo-Nikol'skoe.

The 33rd Army, pursuing the enemy, was approaching at that time the line Simbukhovo-Klin-Ivkovo-Blagoveshchenskoe. To its left the 43rd Army was successfully attacking; on January 14 it captured Medyn'. The 33rd Army's flanks were secured and before it arose the prospect of inflicting a blow against the enemy's Vereya group and then developing the blow: to the west—across the enemy's Vyaz'ma front, or to the northwest—outflanking the Germans' Mozhaisk group.

At first the *front* command adopted the second variant. After the 33rd Army captured Vereya, it was to be directed to Vaulino and Yel'nya, into the rear of the enemy Mozhaisk group, which was to be destroyed in conjunction with the 5th Army.

However, from January 5, when this order was given, to January 14, when the 5th Army's forces took Dorokhovo and Ruza was on the verge of falling, the situation changed: by this time Mozhaisk stood in the capacity of a forward point of the enemy's defense; his main group of forces along this axis was located in the area of Gzhatsk and Vyaz'ma. It was now necessary to direct the combined actions of two armies not toward the capture of Mozhaisk, but toward the destruction of the enemy's Gzhatsk-Vyaz'ma group.

Thus the commander of the Western Front Gen. Zhukov, in his January 14 directive, laid out the tasks for the 5th and 33rd armies.

> The enemy is attempting to delay the offensive by the 5th and 33rd armies, it states in the directive. "The immediate objective of the center armies is to encircle and destroy the enemy's Mozhaisk-Gzhatsk group.
>
> The objective: 1) the 5th Army, no later than January 16, is to capture Mozhaisk and then develop the blow toward Gzhatsk. The boundary on the left is the line Novo-Nikol'skoe-Yel'nya-Bol'shie Lomy.
>
> 2) the 33rd Army, while continuing to develop its main blow toward Vaulino and Vereya, bypassing Mozhaisk, by the close of January 15 is to complete the destruction of the Vereya group and capture Vereya. The army is then to attack toward Ragozino and Komyagino," that is toward Vyaz'ma.

In carrying out the *front* commander's instructions, the commander of the 5th Army gave his forces the following orders: "The 5th Army is to take Mozhaisk, enveloping it from the southeast and southwest. The objective for January 17 is to reach the line Il'inskii-Borodino-Artemki, with a forward detachment along the line Bezzubovo-Koloch' station-Yel'nya." In accordance with this, the divisions were directed in such a manner that the axis of the main blow was on the left flank.

The 33rd Army, at the moment it received the *front* commander's directive, was attacking Vereya. The commander of the 33rd Army left his previous orders to his divisions in place, emphasizing the actions of the army's right flank, which was to outflank Vereya from the north.

The combat correlation of men and matériel

On our side two armies—5th and 33rd participated in the Mozhaisk-Vereya operation, and on the enemy side two army corps—IX and VII.

The correlation of forces was as follows:

Soviet		German	
Rifle Divisions	13	Infantry Divisions	6
Motorized Rifle Divisions	1	Motorized Divisions	1
Rifle Brigades	1	Panzer Divisions	1

The two sides' front was 50-60 km in breadth. Given the enemy's group of forces in the areas of Mozhaisk and Vereya, it was planned to conduct the operation to a depth of 40-50 km.

Our side had a superiority in men. However, it is difficult to establish this superiority according to the data cited, insofar as the losses on both sides had been great and not subject to exact calculation. Besides this, given the situation, an exact calculation of men and equipment that took part in the Mozhaisk operation is probably not of decisive significance, because arithmetical data were not the most important factor here, but rather the troops' political-morale qualities and the commanders' ability to control their subordinate units in conditions of a harsh winter.

In December the Germans suffered a defeat along both flanks of the troops attacking toward Moscow. In January these flanks were falling back more and more under the Red Army's blows, placing those German units in the center in an unfavorable situation. These units continued to defend stubbornly and it was to a significant degree on this premise that the Fascist command hoped to hold its front. However, the center's operational situation was unstable and was now subject to blows from the flanks, and the troops' political-morale condition had fallen.

The Soviet troops' mood, as opposed to the Germans', was good. The Red Army's units were pursuing the enemy, imbued more and more with a confidence in final victory over him. This multiplied their forces and increased the command's creative initiative.

Combat activities in the Mozhaisk Operation

Continuing to pursue the enemy after Dorokhovo, the 5th Army's center and left-flank divisions—144th, 50th, 82nd, 108th, and 32nd rifle divisions—on January 16 reached the line Kostino-Krasnyi Stan-Zachat'e-Aleksandrovo-Mikhailovskoe-Bugailovo. The 5th Army, with its left-flank 32nd Rifle Division, was getting into the flank of the German group that was defending Vereya at the time. The 32nd Rifle Division, having taken Korovino and Lytkino, was supposed to blockade Borisovo, in order to prevent the enemy from aiding his Vereya group. Thus the actions of the 5th Army's left-flank units made it easier for the 33rd Army to carry out its assignment of capturing Vereya.

On January 16 the 33rd Army's main forces had reached Vereya and began fighting on the southern and southeastern outskirts of the town, trying at the same time to outflank it from the north. The enemy put up stubborn resistance, trying to pull back here those units that at the time were located along the front Tyutchevo-Kupelitsy-Klin.

At 1000 on January 16 the 222nd Rifle Division took Monakovo and began fighting for Kupelitsy. The fighting yielded no definite results until the 1st Guards Motorized Rifle Division arrived to help. With its arrival the Tyutchevo-Klin enemy group was in danger of being "bagged," and its systematic withdrawal to Vereya was disrupted. Fighting broke out in the Kupelitsy area, where the Fascist units suffered heavy losses.

However, the enemy stubbornly held his positions. Vereya did not surrender and the fighting here became fierce and prolonged. The 1st Guards Motorized Rifle Division, having broken into the town from the outskirts, had to fight for almost each house in which the Fascists were located. The enemy often counterattacked, and was beaten off by our forces with heavy losses.

The fighting which began near Vereya on January 16 lasted into the night and continued until dawn on January 17. The remains of the German units defeated near Kupelitsy arrived at Vereya during the night, as did severely battered units from Vasil'evo, Kolodezi, and Panovo. The enemy was bringing up his forces to Vereya and concentrating them, so that in case of encirclement they could break out from here to Mozhaisk.

At the same time the fighting was unfolding near Vereya the 5th Army's left flank and center continued to attack toward Mozhaisk. By the morning of January 17 the army's 50th Rifle Division had captured the village of Pervomaiskoe; the 82nd Rifle Division and the 60th Rifle Brigade were fighting for Chentsovo and Chertanovo; the 108th Rifle Division, having crushed the enemy's resistance, had occupied the edge of the woods south of Otyakovo and cut the Yamskaya-Vereya road; the 32nd Rifle Division was blocking Borisovo and moving its forward detachments to the west.

The communications between the German garrisons in Mozhaisk and Vereya were broken as a result of these actions and they were isolated from each other. Vereya was outflanked on three sides and its fate must be decided within the next few days. The 5th Army's offensive was squeezing Mozhaisk from the east and southeast and its fate was only a question of a few days.

On the night of January 16-17 the enemy began withdrawing from Ruza and on January 17 the town was already in our hands.

With the fall of Ruza the 19th Rifle Division, 20th Rifle and 43rd Tank brigades, which had been besieging it, were freed up and they joined the forces attacking Mozhaisk. But it was still difficult to capture the town as long as there remained in the rear of the 5th Army's attacking troops enemy units occupying Vereya. From this point the question of Mozhaisk was linked with the preliminary elimination of the enemy's defensive stronghold in Vereya.

On January 18 the 222nd, 113th rifle and the 1st Guards Motorized Rifle divisions were involved in heavy fighting near Vereya and in the town itself; the 33rd Army's remaining divisions were destroying the small garrisons of the strong points to the northwest of Vereya, cutting off the enemy's path of retreat along this axis.

At 0430 on January 19, following heavy fighting, Vereya was captured by our troops. The enemy's defeated units, waging rearguard actions, fell back to the west.

With the capture of Vereya the threat to the rear of the 5th Army's left-flank units attacking toward Mozhaisk lessened. On January 19 the situation of the German garrison in Mozhaisk became extremely serious. From the north the 5th Army's 19th Rifle Division was fighting for Natashino, Kuryn', Khanevo, and Shebarshino, trying to reach the line of the Moscow River in the direction of Bychkovo and Garetovo. The 144th Rifle Division was fighting to approach the line Prudnya-Pavlishchevo; the 50th Rifle Division, in conjunction with the 20th Tank Brigade, was consolidating in the area Makarovo-Teterino; the 108th Rifle Division was fighting for Yazevo. The "pincers" outflanking Mozhaisk were penetrating further to the west and were squeezing the town ever more tightly.

During the night of January 19-20 the 19th Rifle Division, following a fierce fight, took Garetovo and Khotilovo with its ski detachments; the division was pursuing the defeated enemy in the direction of Uvarovo. At the same time, the 32nd Rifle Division on the left flank, following the breakthrough of the enemy front along the sector Yazevo-Lytkino, was moving along the Moscow-Minsk highway and had occupied Bol'shie Ponferki. Mozhaisk was in danger of being completely surrounded; the Germans, seeing the impossibility of holding it, began to fall back.

Our units (82nd Rifle Division), crushing enemy resistance, burst into Mozhaisk at 1330 on January 20. By 1330 they had passed through the town and had arrived to the west of the town along the line east of the woods-northwest and west of Kukarino. The 5th Army captured a lot of equipment, including 20 guns, 76 motor vehicles, three dumps with ammunition and quartermaster stores and other isthe enemy to create another new link along the roads leading from Mozhaisk to Gzhatsk.

It was for this purpose that the pursuit of the Germans in the direction of Uvarovo was organized immediately following the capture of Mozhaisk. Their flight, particularly through the Borodino battlefield, in many ways was reminiscent of the French army's hurried withdrawal to the west, when it was forced, after the frosts had already arrived and following the battle near Maloyaroslavets (October 24, 1812), to return along the old route of the devastated Smolensk road, by which it had arrived. The retreating German troops, wrapped up in scarves, dressed in peasant knee-length coats, felt boots, hats with ear flaps, and women's fur coats taken from the local population, resembled Napoleon's detachments as they ran out of Russia. They did not manage, contrary to their habit, to destroy the monuments to the glory of Russian arms on the Borodino battlefield; they torched the Borodino museum in senseless anger. The Soviet troops followed on their heels of the retreating enemy, routing and destroying his rearguards.

The Germans' attempt to delay in Uvarovo ended unsuccessfully for them. On January 22, following stubborn fighting for the town, it was taken by the 5th Army. At this the Mozhaisk offensive operation came to an end.

Conclusions

The following highlights should be noted in the Mozhaisk-Vereya operation:

1 The operation unfolded as the totality of mutually-dependent events—the capture of Dorokhovo and Ruza, the capture of Vereya and, finally, the attack against Mozhaisk. They were all in logical connection with each other and flow from a beginning event—the capture of Dorokhovo. The success at Dorokhovo had an immediate influence on the fate of Ruza and Vereya and created the prerequisites for taking Mozhaisk.

2 Dorokhovo, Ruza, Vereya and Mozhaisk were heavily fortified, but nevertheless they could not be held for long and fell as soon as they were threatened from the flanks. From this it follows that the defense of this or that site will be stable when it is linked with the solid defense of its neighbors. The strength of modern defense is defined not only by its depth, but by its sufficient breadth, which deprives the enemy the opportunity of raking the defending area with fire.

3 The morale factor—the moral superiority of our forces over the Fascists—played an enormous role in the fate of Ruza, Vereya and Mozhaisk. It guaranteed the success of an operation conducted in difficult conditions.

4 One should note in our troops' tactics:

a) the skillful organization of the 5th and 33rd armies' offensive: as a rule, the enemy's fortified points were taken not by frontal attacks, but by outflanking and enveloping them;
b) a superiority of force was created along the decisive sectors, which enabled us to quickly achieve success; on the left flank of the 5th Army and on the right flank of the 33rd.
c) the offensive was conducted, in spite of the difficult winter conditions, at a sufficiently high pace: in six days (January 14-20) several of the units (for example, the 32nd Rifle Division) covered a distance of 50-60 km, while fighting, and without halting, continued pursuing the enemy;
d) among the operation's shortcomings, one must note the heightened caution of our units around Mozhaisk itself, which was the result of poorly organized reconnaissance; at the same time the forces outflanking Mozhaisk (50th, 108th, 32nd rifle divisions) moved forward somewhat slowly, afraid of subjecting themselves to a flank attack from Mozhaisk, there were no longer any enemy troops in the town, except for a small group of automatic riflemen covering the withdrawal of their units; our forces' lack of information gave the enemy the opportunity to avoid a more serious defeat here.

One must note the following in the activities of the German troops defending Ruza, Mozhaisk and Vareya:

a) the skillful employment of large inhabited locales as strong points; persistence in fighting along with a sensitivity to a threat arising along the flanks; the Germans would abandon their strong points, centers of resistance, and other areas when they were outflanked: persistence in fighting would disappear; the German-Fascist troops would abandon their positions and equipment when our units maneuvered sufficiently energetically against their flanks.

8

The offensive by the left-wing armies on Kondrovo, Yukhnov, Kirov, and Lyudinovo, from January 5-9—31 1942

The situation along the *Front's* left wing by January 5 1942

The situation in the operational area of the Western Front's left-wing armies by beginning of the fight for approaches to the Vyaz'ma-Bryansk lateral railroad and the Warsaw highway was particularly complex.

Having sustained a defeat in the fighting around Vysokinichi and Detchino and having lost the line of the Oka River, the German-Fascist troops, in retreating to the west under our forces' attacks, sought to linger on other previously-prepared positions. Such positions were the fortified line Kondrovo-Polotnyanyi Zavod, the defensive lines to the northwest and west of Kaluga, on the approaches to the Yukhnov bridgehead, the important railroad junction of Sukhinichi, the Mosal'sk-Meshchovsk-Kirov-Lyudinovo-Zikeevo-Zhizdra area, and other strong points and centers of resistance, which the enemy continued to strengthen by bringing up reserves from the rear. In particular, the fresh 208th Infantry Division, arrived from France, and units from the 4th Panzer Division, arrived in the Zhizdra-Zikeevo area by January 12, that is, at the time of the greatest fighting along this axis. The 211th Infantry Division was brought up to the Lyudinovo area from Smolensk, as well as other units.

It follows that the fighting of the left-wing armies along these lines was conducted under conditions of the enemy's growing resistance. On the other hand, this fighting was seriously complicated by the winter conditions in which our troops had to wage the offensive. If one takes into account the fact that the army's units were roundly exhausted by the preceding battles, then the complexity of the situation in which we had to begin the fight for the Warsaw highway and the Vyaz'ma-Bryansk lateral railroad becomes understandable.

During this period the most powerful enemy group was the Kondrovo-Yukhnov-Medyn' one, the rapid defeat of which would have opened the road to Vyaz'ma to the left-wing armies' main forces.

It was for the resolution of this objective that there were concentrated, according to *front* directive no. 269 of January 9 1942, the efforts of the 43rd, 49th and 50th armies, and the 1st Guards Cavalry Corps.

The 10th Army, securing the *front's* extreme left wing, was to attack to the west and cut the Vyaz'ma-Bryansk railroad in the Kirov-Lyudinovo area, thus depriving the enemy of maneuver along this artery.

The disposition of the enemy's forces facing the *front's* left-wing armies as of January 5 1942 is shown in the table below.[1]

Table V/8.1 Correlation of Soviet and German forces, Western Front left-wing armies, January 5 1942

Formation	Germans			Red Army			
	Combat Personnel	Guns (all types)[2]	Tanks	Army	Combat Personnel	Guns (all types)	Tanks
268th Infantry Division	4,000	up to 40	–	49th			
260th Infantry Division	3,000	35	–				
52nd Infantry Division	5,000	45	–				
137th Infantry Division	3,500	35	–				
17th Infantry Division	3,500	35	–				
Total	19,000	190	–		37,700	295	–
131st Infantry Division	4,000	40	–	50th Army and 1st Guards Cavalry Corps			
31st Infantry Division	3,000	35	–				
36th Motorized Division	3,000	40	–				
19th Panzer Division[3]	up to 1,000	up to 30	15-20				
Total[4]	11,000	145	15-20		37,500	271	34
296th Infantry Division	3,000	35	–	10th			
216th Infantry Division	6,000	50	–				
56th Infantry Division	3,000	35	–				
10th Motorized Division	2,500	40	–				
A company from the 19th Panzer Division[5]	–	15	10				
Total	14,500[6]	175	10		48,250	203	–
TOTAL ON THE LEFT WING	44,500[7]	510	about 30		123,450	769	34

Notes:

1 The data regarding our troops is cited according to the Western Front headquarters materials (delo no. 14, for 1941).

2 Division artillery guns were included in the total data: 252 guns against the 49th and 50th armies (Yukhnov axis); 96 guns against the 10th Army (Sukhinichi axis).

3 According to data from the General Staff's Intelligence Directorate (delo no. 3/1), by December the division was operating as an infantry division (73rd Infantry Regiment) in the area south of Yukhnov; the main body of tanks had been sent to Roslavl' for repair.

4 Taking into account the 230th Infantry Division, which was in reserve, the overall strength of the rank and file facing the 49th and 50th armies and the 1st Guards Cavalry Corps was 33,760 men.

5 The text should read: The number of men is not counted.

6 Not counting the 56th Infantry Division (which then operated against the 10th Army), which had been pulled into the reserve, the enemy's strength against the 10th Army by January 5 was 11,500 men.

7 48,260 men, counting the 230th Infantry Division.

The correlation in men, artillery and tanks by army, according to the data presented in the table, was as follows:

49th Army:
Men—2:1 (in our favor)
Artillery—1.55:1
Tanks—0

50th Army and 1st Guards Cavalry Corps:
Men—3.5:1 (in our favor)
Artillery—about 2:1
Tanks—2:1

10th Army:
Men—about 3.5:1 (in our favor)
Artillery—1.16:1
Tanks—1:0 (in favor of the enemy)

This calculation shows that we enjoyed along the entire left wing a superiority in men, on the average, of a little more than 2 ½ to one, and 1 ½ to one in artillery. We had a nearly twofold superiority in tanks along the Yukhnov axis, whereas the enemy was superior along the Sukhinichi axis. However, during the period under examination neither side had many tanks and they failed to play any kind of significant role.

If you take into account the Germans' transfer of the fresh 208th Infantry Division, and later of the 211th Infantry Division to the Zhizdra-Lyudinovo area by January 12, as well as the 4th Panzer Division's motorized regiments, which had been brought by this time to the Zikeevo area, then the above-mentioned superiority declines, giving us an approximately twofold superiority in men and equality in artillery.

Besides this, an offensive against an enemy already prepared for stubborn defense, under conditions when the harsh winter of 1941-42 had fully come into its own, lowered our superiority in men even more and made the fulfillment of these tasks by the *front's* left wing even more difficult.

The efforts of the 49th and 50th armies, according to the Western Front's plan, were concentrated on the defeat of the Kondrovo-Yukhnov-Medyn' enemy group. This task was to be accomplished in conjunction with the 43rd Army. The 1st Guards Cavalry Corps was to support the left wing's armies with part of its forces, while its main forces would attack toward Vyaz'ma. The main mass of the 10th Army's forces were to operate in a westerly direction, having the objective of reaching the area Kirov-Lyudinovo, for the purpose of cutting the Vyaz'ma-Bryansk railroad.

Combat operations along the Western Front's left wing after January 5 1942 unfolded in the spirit of carrying out this plan.

The 49th Army's fight for Kondrovo, Polotnyanyi Zavod and the offensive's development to the army's arrival at the Warsaw highway along the Myatlevo-Yukhnov sector

After the arrival of the units of Gen. Zakharkin's 49th Army along the line Vasisovo-Burkino-Torbeevo the army command, on the basis of *front* directive no. 269 of January 9 1942, ordered its forces (order no. 01/op of January 9 1942) to do the following:

> The 49th Army (5th Guards, 133rd, 238th, 173rd rifle divisions, 30th, 34th 19th rifle brigades), in launching its main blow in the direction of Kondrovo and Voronki (eight km southwest of Myatlevo) is to destroy the enemy's Kondrovo group in conjunction with the 43rd Army and by the close of January 12 to reach the line Barsuki-Nikola-Lenivets.

In accordance with this order, the 5th Guards Rifle Division received the task: while continuing to attack in the direction of Butyrki, by the close of January 9 arrive with its main forces in the area Yablonovka-Nekrasovo-Voraksino (all locales 12 km northeast of Kondrovo), and its forward units to Adamovskoe (five km north of Kondrovo), while conducting reconnaissance toward Kondrovo.

By the close of January 9 the 19th Rifle Brigade was to reach the line Kozhukhovo-Zazhovo (one km southeast of Kozhukhovo), and its forward units toward Kondrovo. The 133rd Rifle Division was instructed to continue attacking in the direction of Ladovo, Zapol'e and Kartsevo (all locales 5-15 km east of Kondrovo) and by the end of January 9 to concentrate its main forces in the area of the latter two locales; its forward units were to be advanced to the line Kondrovo-Tolkachevo.

By the end of January 9 the 173rd Rifle Division was to reach the area of Gribanovo (eight km southeast of Kondrovo), where it was to concentrate, with the mission of attacking Kondrovo.

The 238th Rifle Division, according to the order, was to move its main forces to the Red'kino area, while its forward units were ordered to take Polotnyanyi Zavod.

In accordance with the *front's* instructions, the army command pointed out to all unit commanders to the organization of precise coordination with their neighbors, the organization of continuous communications, and the movement of headquarters closer to the troops.

Particular attention was allotted to the organization and conduct of the offensive with the outflanking and envelopment of the enemy's fortifications, and with the broad employment of ski units as forward detachments for this purpose.

Facing the 49th Army as of January 10 were units of the 260th, 137th, 52nd, and 31st enemy infantry divisions in the front line, and the 36th Motorized Division in the second; this division's main forces were located around Yukhnov. Units of these enemy divisions were simultaneously operating against the 50th Army along the Yukhnov axis.

The Germans set themselves the task of holding the line Kondrovo-Polotnyanyi Zavod, so as to prevent our forces from reaching the Warsaw highway. For this purpose the Kondrovo-Polotnyanyi Zavod area had been previously fortified and prepared for a tenacious defense. As it turned out, the inhabited locales in this area had been transformed into strong points with dugouts and wooden-earth firing points. The spaces between these locales could be raked with fire, and the Germans erected ice walls along the main axes. It follows that the 49th Army's units faced a difficult task—without ceasing their pursuit, to capture on the march this previously-prepared position, about which the army command at that time had insufficient information. The army's task was complicated by the fact that the terrain in the offensive zone was closed off and as a result of the winter conditions lacked a sufficient number of roads.

On the morning of January 9 the 49th Army's units, while continuing their offensive, reached the following lines: the 5th Guards Rifle Division, while at first encountering the enemy's comparatively weak fire resistance, by the end of January 9 was fighting along the approaches to Nekrasovo. The fighting lasted until January 11. The German-Fascist troops in the Nekrasovo area put up strong resistance. In the first half of January 11 their stubbornness was crushed and our units captured Nekrasovo. A ski battalion was dispatched on the morning of January 11 in the direction of Adamovskoe with the task of capturing the Kondrovo-Medyn' road.

The 19th Rifle Brigade, following stubborn fighting, had captured Ivanovka (four km northwest of Detchino) by the close of January 9 and, while continuing to attack, by the morning of January 10 had reached the Pesochnaya area (ten km northwest of Detchino). From this area the brigade made a fighting advance in the direction of Murzino.

The 133rd Rifle Division, overcoming the resistance of automatic riflemen reinforced by light and heavy machine guns, as well as the enemy's small units with mortars, was fighting for the line Baranovka-Korneevka-Durovka. The division's units advanced with difficulty. It was only by the morning of January 11 that the 133rd Rifle Division, having outflanked Korneevka from the north, captured the village and reached the line Ladovo-Karamyshevo (both locales two km west of Korneevka).

The 173rd Rifle Division was attacking in the direction of Durovka. Attempts to outflank this locale from the south and north were unsuccessful, as a result of the enemy's powerful flanking fire from Korneevka and Mokrishchi. It was only toward the morning of January 11 that it managed to crush the enemy's resistance in this area and capture Durovka. The 173rd Rifle Division, having left behind a detachment to clean out the Germans from the Durovka area, continued to attack toward Karamyshevo, aiding by this maneuver the 133rd Rifle Division.

The 238th Rifle Division fought a stubborn battle for Torbeevo all of January 9. Attaching great significance to this locale, the German-Fascist units put all their efforts into holding it. The commander of the 238th Rifle Division ordered his troops to bypass Torbeevo from the north and threw a part of his forces toward Mokrishchi, in order to assist his neighbor to the right—the 173rd Rifle Division.

This maneuver was successful and on the morning of January 11 the Germans' resistance in the Torbeevo area had been crushed and the units of the 238th Rifle Division developed their offensive in the direction of Polotnyanyi Zavod. In order to envelop Polotnyanyi Zavod from the southeast, an independent ski battalion was sent forward, which was moving along the southern bank of the Sukhodrev River.

Throughout January 11 and the first half of January 12, the 49th Army's forces continued attacking along the indicated axes. The German-Fascist units' resistance continued to increase along the entire front, particularly along the line of the strong points—Makovtsy-Zhuino-Zapol'e-Gribanovo-Kashenki (all locales five km east of the line Kondrovo-Polotnyanyi Zavod).

The most stubborn fighting fell to the lot of the 5th Guards Rifle Division and the 30th and 34th rifle brigades for Makovtsy and Andreevka. Particularly fierce fighting took place in Andreevka, where the enemy fought literally for every building. The fighting for this locale lasted through January 12-13. Only by the end of January 13 were we able to crush the Germans' resistance and take Makovtsy and Andreevka, after which our units' offensive developed in the direction of Adamovskoe and Akishevo (three km northwest of Kondrovo).

The 19th Rifle Brigade, in conjunction with the 133rd Rifle Division's ski battalion, on January 13 was to have occupied the area Murzino-Zhuino-Zapol'e (two km south of Bol'shaya Bolyntova), but was thrown out of there by a strong counterattack and fell back to its jumping-off position toward Bol'shaya Bolyntova, where it consolidated. On the morning of January 14 the 19th Rifle Brigade once again attacked and as a result of the fighting restored the situation.

The 133rd Rifle Division, overcoming the Germans' resistance, advanced.

The 173rd Rifle Division, having crushed the enemy's resistance in the area Gribanovo (½ km north of Red'kino)-Red'kino, captured both locales on the morning of January 14.

The 238th Rifle Division, despite stubborn resistance by the German-Fascist units in the area of Kashenka (three km south of Red'kino) occupied that locale by the morning of January 14.

Throughout January 14 the 49th Army attacked along the entire front. The troops everywhere had to overcome the fire and engineering obstacles employed by the German-Fascist troops in their retreat. On the night of January 14-15 the army's offensive continued without a halt, despite the enemy's unrelenting resistance. Having outflanked the resistance centers of Akishevo, Makarovo, Tolkachevo, and Utkino (one km north of Polotnyanyi Zavod), the 49th Army's forward detachments reached the Adamovskoe-Polotnyanyi Zavod road by the morning of January 15.

Thus the January 9-15 fighting may be described as the struggle for the enemy's defensive positions between the Kondrovo-Polotnyanyi Zavod fortified line and the Kaluga-Maloyaroslavets railroad.

As one can see from the above, combat was conducted with extreme exertion by the attacker's forces, confronted by the defender's stubborn resistence.

The *front* command, attaching great importance to the rapid capture of the Kondrovo-Polotnyanyi Zavod area, in its directive no. 412 transferred the 12th Guards Rifle Division (the former 258th Rifle Division) to the 49th Army, having assigned it the task of accelerating the defensive and reaching this area according to schedule.

According to the *front's* instructions, the 12th Guards Rifle Division was to have simultaneously put pressure on the rear of the enemy's units operating against the 50th Army along the Yukhnov axis.

As a result, it was planned to concentrate the 12th Guards Rifle Division in the area Ozerna-Subbotino (one km north of Davydovo).

Following a partial regrouping caused by the insertion of the 12th Guards Rifle Division, the 49th Army's units on January 16 resumed their offensive operations, having directed their attacks at capturing the area of Kondrovo and Polotnyanyi Zavod.

The offensive played out as follows: the 5th Guards Rifle Division, in conjunction with the 30th and 34th rifle brigades, and in accordance with the army commander's order, were directed at Nikol'skoe, bypassing Kondrovo from the north and covering itself from the direction of Kondrovo with a single rifle regiment. In the Nikol'skoe area the 5th Guards Rifle Division encountered the enemy's stubborn resistance, supported by powerful mortar fire.

The 133rd Rifle Division, together with the 19th Rifle Brigade, was attacking Tolkachevo. The division's units came under the enemy's heavy mortar barrage from the area Tolkachevo-Staroe Utkino (four km northwest of Polotnyanyi Zavod) and, having suffered heavy losses, fell back to the sector to the east of the Polotnyanyi Zavod-Tolkachevo road, where they consolidated.

The 173rd Rifle Division, attacking Utkino for the purpose of enveloping Polotnyanyi Zavod from the north, on the morning of January 17 was counterattacked by the enemy, supported by powerful machine gun and mortar fire; the counterattack forced the division to fall back on the Polotnyanyi Zavod-Tolkachevo high road.

The 283rd Rifle Division, having left a regiment near Zhil'nevo to pin down the enemy south of Polotnyanyi Zavod, had crossed the Shanya River with its main forces by the morning of January 17 and, having bypassed Durnevo, reached the eastern approaches to Beli, where fighting broke out. The division's movement was carried out under the enemy's strong flanking fire from Durnevo and Mukovinino (four km south of Polotnyanyi Zavod).

The 12th Guards Rifle Division was fighting along the western bank of the Ugra River, attacking in the direction of Malaya Rudnya; with a portion of its forces it was simultaneously blocking Sabel'nikovo from the north and east.

The overall result of our troops' offensive against Kondrovo and Polotnyanyi Zavod by January 17 was that the troops of the army's center (133rd and 173rd rifle divisions), having suffered heavy losses, failed to advance and in places even fell back. One of the reasons behind such a failure was the method of launching frontal attacks, which was employed by our forces in assaulting fortified objectives.

The *front* headquarters, in observing the failure of the frontal attacks on Kondrovo and Polotnyanyi Zavod, on January 17 demanded that the commander of the 49th Army send no less than a rifle division to bypass Polotnyanyi Zavod from the south in the general direction of Durnevo-Sloboda-Galkino.

In accordance with the *front's* instructions, the 49th Army command was to carry out a regrouping for the more successful realization of the assignment, while the 12th Guards Rifle

Division's task remained the same—an attack against the rear of the enemy operating against the 50th Army.

The 49th Army command, in accordance with these instructions, carried out a partial regrouping on the morning of January 18, the essence of which was: the 5th Guards Rifle Division continued to attack along the previous axis. The 173rd Rifle Division was directed to bypass Polotnyanyi Zavod from the south as to develop the 238th Rifle Division's blow in the direction of Surnevo, Sloboda, and Galkino; by the close of January 19 the division was ordered to reach the area of these locales so as to cut off the enemy's path of retreat to the west. Along the line Kondrovo-Polotnyanyi Zavod the enemy was being pinned down by the 133rd Rifle Division and the 19th Rifle Brigade, the active operations of which were to secure the arrival of the 173rd Rifle Division in a new area. The 133rd Rifle Division's 564th Artillery Regiment received orders to be in readiness to render fire support to the 173rd Rifle Division in the direction of Sloboda. The 238th Rifle Division's task remained basically the same—an attack to the northwest for the purpose of cutting off the enemy's Kondrovo group's path of retreat. By the close of January 19 it was planned to move the division to the Potapovo area. Finally, by the close of the same day the 12th Guards Rifle Division was arriving in the area Ozerna-Davydovo-Subbotino for a subsequent attack on Pogorelovo.

On the morning of January 18 the 49th Army's units, following a regrouping, went over to the offensive along the entire front.

The 5th Guards Rifle Division, having encountered the enemy's stiff resistance, continued fighting along the same line. The 133rd Rifle Division, bypassing Polotnyanyi Zavod from the north, took Utkino after a fight. The 173rd Rifle Division, in conjunction with the 238th Rifle Division, was enveloping Polotnyanyi Zavod from the south. By the close of January 18 Polotnyanyi Zavod was taken through the combined efforts of the 133rd and 173rd rifle divisions. The 238th Rifle Division was fighting near Beli; the enemy was stubbornly holding on to Beli with up to 500 men and heavy machine guns, seeking to prevent our advance to the northwest and to secure the withdrawal of his units from Kondrovo and Polotnyanyi Zavod. The 12th Guards Rifle Division, developing its blow in along the indicated axis, was involved in heavy fighting for Matovo and Rudnya (three km west of Sabel'nikovo), which its captured during the day of January 19.

Throughout January 19 the 49th Army continued attacking along the entire front, developing its success along both flanks. By this time the 5th Guards Rifle Division, having captured Nikol'skoe after stubborn fighting, broke through the enemy front to the north of Kondrovo. Our breakthrough created the danger of surrounding the enemy group in the Kondrovo area, as a result of which the German-Fascist units began withdrawing from this area.

Thus the maneuver by the 5th Guards Rifle Division on the right flank, and that of the 173rd and 238th divisions on the 49th Army's left flank, along with the 133rd Rifle Division's active holding actions in the center, led to a favorable outcome of the fighting for the Kondrovo-Polotnyanyi Zavod fortified line. The German-Fascist troops, having suffered a defeat in the fighting for this line, and carrying out covering actions, fell back to a new prepared position along the line Aidarovo-Kostino-Ostrozhnoe-Bogdanovo-Potapovo.

Following January 20 the 49th Army attacked in a new formation. According to a *front* directive, the 173rd Rifle Division was transferred to the 50th Army and moved to its left flank. The 12th Guards Rifle Division was transferred to the 10th Army and moved to the Sukhinichi area for operations against enemy units attacking from the area Zhizdra-Zikeevo. After January 22 the army headquarters' command post was located in Kondrovo.

Upon the arrival of the 49th Army's remaining units along the line Aidarovo-Kostino-Ostrozhnoe-Bogdanovo-Potapovo, stubborn fighting broke out again for these locales.

The 5th Guards Rifle Division, along with the subordinated 30th and 34th rifle brigades,[1] was fighting along the line Aidarovo-Kostino-Ostrozhnoe-(excluding) Bogdanovo. The Germans were putting up particular strong resistance in Ostrozhnoe, where on January 25 our forces had to engage in street fighting. The 133rd Rifle Division on January 28 took Bogdanovo and was attacking Sloboda. The 238th Rifle Division encountered the most powerful enemy resistance in Dorokhi (one km northeast of Potapovo), the fighting for which lasted until January 28.

By January 28 the enemy's resistance along the line Aidarovo-Kostino-Ostrozhnoe-Bogdanovo-Potapovo had been broken. The 49th Army's units, by outflanking and blocking strong points, by January 31 had reached the line Rudenka-Fedyukovo-Shimaevka. The enemy's attempt to delay our offensive along the line of the Izver' River was not successful.

By this time the 43rd Army on the right was fighting the enemy along the front Tetevo-Vorsobino-Myatlevo. On January 29 the 415th Rifle Division, together with the 1st Guards Motorized Rifle Division, took Myatlevo after fighting.

After January 31 the 49th Army, in conjunction with the 50th Army, attacked to the southwest along the Warsaw highway, enveloping Yukhnov from the northeast.

Thus the 49th Army, during the course of the January 9-31 offensive, had to break through two of the enemy's fortified defensive lines.

Despite the tactical possibilities offered by the envelopment of some of the Germans' strong points, the 49th Army was operationally forced to attack the enemy's Kondrovo group with a frontal, almost headlong blow. This was one of the reasons for the comparatively slow development of combat operations.

The neighboring 50th Army, being pinned down by the Germans' stubborn defense to the northwest of Kaluga and around Yukhnov, was not able to carry out the *front's* directive for getting into the rear of the enemy's Kondrovo group. The 1st Guards Cavalry Corps was also unable to take Yukhnov from the march and with another part of its forces reach the Medyn axis in the rear of the Germans' Kondrovo group. This was due to the growing enemy resistance on the ground, his increased air activity, and the difficult conditions of a harsh winter. Poor matériel-technical supply, a shortage of communications equipment, and the exhaustion of men and horses, which were carrying out difficult marches over a prolonged period, also played a role.

The 50th Army's offensive in conjunction with the 1st Guards Cavalry Corps, on Yukhnov and the Warsaw highway

Upon the completion of the Kaluga operation the operations by the main mass of the 50th Army developed along the Yukhnov axis. The most stubborn fighting occurred along the front Kudinovo-Zubovo (southeast of Yukhnov), where the enemy's most powerful group was concentrated. Arrayed against it was the 50th Army's shock group, consisting of the 340th and 154th (minus the 437th Rifle Regiment) rifle divisions and the 112th Tank Brigade,[2] with reinforcements. Stubborn fighting also occurred on the army's right flank, to the northwest of Kaluga, where the Fascist troops, relying on a prepared defense, were delaying our offensive.

The Western Front command, in its directive no. 269 of January 9, defined the 50th Army's objective as follows:

1 By January 26 the 19th Rifle Brigade was also subordinated.

2 By a decision of the 50th Army's military council, the 112th Tank Division, owing to its small size, was redesignated the 112th Tank Brigade.

> ... To the commander of the 50th Army—defeat the Zubovo-Yukhnov group and capture Yukhnov no later than January 11 1942; then, in conjunction with Belov's group, attack with your main forces in the general direction of Slobodka (27 km northwest of Yukhnov) and Vyaz'ma. The right flank, in conjunction with the 49th Army, is to attack in the general direction of Pushkino (15 km northeast of Yukhnov), keeping in mind that the army's left flank is being secured by the movement of two rifle divisions in the area of Chiplyaevo and Zanoznaya stations (east of Spas-Demensk)...

The 50th Army commander, in accordance with the *front* directive, assigned his forces tasks, according to which the shock group would continue fight against the enemy's Zubovo-Yukhnov group; the 154th Rifle Division and the 112th Tank Brigade were to take Yukhnov, outflanking it from the southwest, and the 340th Rifle Division was ordered to cut the Warsaw highway on the night of January 9-10 in the Strekalovo area (nine km northeast of Yukhnov). The right-flank divisions were to continue attacking in the previously ordered direction. The 217th Rifle Division was assigned the task of securing the army's shock group from the north and northeast.

The 7th Guards Cavalry Division[3] was to remain in the Matovo-Vnukovo area with the task of carrying out reconnaissance to the northeast and north.

Thus the center of combat operations following January 5 shifted to the army's left flank, where its main group, composed of the 340th and 154th rifle divisions and the 112th Tank Brigade, was formed for operations along the Yukhnov axis.

The *front* command, in directing the 50th Army's forces on Yukhnov and then Vyaz'ma, assigned it the objective of deeply enveloping (in conjunction with the 1st Guards Cavalry Corps and the 43rd and 49th armies) the enemy's Medyn'-Kondrovo-Yukhnov group. With the defeat of the latter and the arrival of the left wing's forces at Vyaz'ma, the deep envelopment, in conjunction with the Kalinin Front's right wing, of the enemy's central group in the area Rzhev-Vyaz'ma-Gzhatsk would be accomplished.

By January 6 our forces' front ran along a line east of Argunovo (15 km north of Kaluga)-Domozhirovo-Krutitsy-Zheleztsovo-(excluding) Troskino-(excluding) Derminka-Yeremino-east of Kudinovo-Cheremoshnya, where it turned to the west and ran along the line (excluding) Zubovo-Davydovo. It was on this line that our troops encountered the German-Fascist troops' powerful defense.

The enemy's 131st and 31st infantry, 36th Motorized, and 19th Panzer divisions were operating along this line.

Besides this, the 50th Army would have to deal with units of the 137th and 52nd infantry divisions, the main elements of which faced the 49th Army.

By January 10 units of the 260th, 263rd and 213th (354th Infantry Regiment) infantry divisions had been identified in the 50th Army's area of operations.

During January 7-8 the 50th Army attacked along the entire front. The German-Fascist troops, having organized an all-round defense in a number of locales, were putting up stubborn resistance. It was only along certain sectors that our forces managed to move forward somewhat. On January 7 the 217th Rifle Division took Koptevo and Karmanovo after fighting. By the end of January 8 the division was counterattacked by the enemy's infantry units, supported by 18 tanks carrying automatic riflemen from the area to the west of Karmanovo. The attack was beaten off and the division securely held the occupied area.

3 The former 31st Cavalry Division, simultaneously with the 258th Rifle Division, was renamed the 7th Guards Cavalry Division.

During the course of the fighting in the days following January 8 the following operational situation developed along the front of the 50th Army and the neighboring 1st Guards Cavalry Corps: on the right flank units of the 290th and 12th Guards rifle divisions, having thrown the enemy back, by January 12 had reached the line Verteby (one km south of Pyatovskaya)-Karavai-Dvortsy.

It was here that both divisions encountered the enemy's stubborn resistance, particularly in the area Pyatovskaya station-Frolovo-Zakharovo.

According to a decision by the army commander, the 290th Rifle Division, upon turning its sector over to the 12th Guards Rifle Division, was to move to the Kaluga area on the morning of January 14, from where it was to be moved to the army's left flank for an attack in the direction of Yukhnov. The 12th Guards Rifle Division was to be subordinated to the 49th Army. Having strengthened the 49th Army's left flank, it was to bypass Polotnyanyi Zavod from the south and assist the 50th Army's offensive on Yukhnov. Along with this, it was planned to put pressure on the Germans' Kondrovo group.

At the same time, the prolonged fighting for Yukhnov and the unsuccessful attempt by the 1st Guards Cavalry Corps to take the town on the march demanded that attention be concentrated on the task of taking Yukhnov as quickly as possible. This was the essence of the regrouping of the 50th Army's main forces to the left flank. The 50th Army's remaining divisions at this time occupied the following lines:

The 413th Rifle Division, with its front turned to the west, was fighting in the Osen'evo-Zheleztsovo area against a German group trying to break through to Uteshevo. This group was also opposed by the 7th Guards Cavalry Division, which was covering the Matovo-Vnukovo sector.

The 217th Rifle Division was holding the front Troskino-Yeremino with part of its forces, while its main forces had moved into the area Koptevo-Karmanovo. In attacking toward Yukhnov, the division reached the Warsaw highway by January 11 along the Pushkino-Kotilovo area, where heavy fighting with the enemy broke out on the approaches to both locales.

The 340th Rifle Division was attacking toward Upryamovo and Kudinovo. Both locales had been heavily fortified by the enemy and fitted for all-round defense.

The 154th Rifle Division continued to fight stubbornly in the area Derevyagino-Zubovo.

The 112th Tank Brigade, operating as a rifle unit, was trying to capture Zubovo (according to a report by the army commander, by January 7 the brigade contained five T-26 and on T-34 tanks).

The Germans, in holding the approaches to Yukhnov from the south and southeast, had organized an all-round defense of the area Upryamovo-Kudinovo-Zubovo-Podpolevo, having strongly fortified the villages, which were transformed into resistance centers and strong points.

Gen. Belov's neighboring 1st Guards Cavalry Corps on the left, following a series of unsuccessful attempts to take Yukhnov from the front Zubovo-Davydovo, undertaken during the first days of January, on January 8 was turned toward Mosal'sk and was carrying out a new *front* assignment: with part of its forces it was to take Mosal'sk in conjunction with the 10th Army, after which its main forces, bypassing Mosal'sk from the north, were to attack to the northwest for a blow against Vyaz'ma.

On the night of January 8-9 the cavalry corps, in conjunction with the 10th Army's 325th Rifle Division, captured Mosal'sk. After this the 325th Rifle Division was subordinated to the commander of the 1st Guards Cavalry Corps. The 10th Army's 239th Rifle Division was subsequently transferred to Gen. Belov's group.

On January 10 the 1st Guards Cavalry Corps' units were completing their regrouping and by the close of January 11 had occupied the following areas: 325th Rifle Division—Aleksino (four km north of Mosal'sk)-Rodnya; 1st Guards Cavalry Division—Pyshkino-Koshelovo-Kolpinovo; 57th Cavalry Division—Teren'kovo-Seliverstovo; 41st Cavalry Division—Yefremovo-Burmakino; 2nd Guards Cavalry Division—Seleznovo-Poskon'-Zyuzino; 75th Cavalry Division, the corps' reserve, was located in the Mosal'sk area, and the 2nd Guards Tank Brigade[4] in the area of Kalinteevo (12 km southwest of Uteshevo).

The cavalry corps, having completed its regrouping and concentration in these areas, operated in the following days in the northwestern direction, with the assignment of cutting the Warsaw highway and developing the offensive on Vyaz'ma.

As concerns the 50th Army, having carried out a regrouping of its main forces from the right flank to the left, concentrated its main efforts along the Yukhnov axis. The envelopment of the enemy's group in the Yukhnov area could be achieved by the arrival of the group of the commander of the 1st Guards Cavalry Corps beyond the Warsaw highway to the west of Yukhnov and its subsequent movement to Vyaz'ma.

However, the subsequent combat events did not unfold in the expected direction.

On the morning of January 14 the 50th Army's units were fighting along the entire front, and combat was particularly persistent in the area Troskino-Ryndino, where an enemy group, consisting of separate units of the 52nd, 31st, 131st, and 137th infantry divisions, was trying to break through in the direction of Uteshevo, in order to link up with units of the Yukhnov group in the Zubovo area. The enemy attempt was eliminated through the joint efforts of the 413th Rifle and 7th Guards Cavalry divisions and he was forced to fall back to the west through Khlestovo to Det'kovo and then along the Ugra River. After this the 7th Guards Cavalry Division was moved to the army's left flank.

On the morning of January 14 the 217th Rifle Division was attacked by fresh enemy units of up to two infantry regiments in strength along the front Pushkino-Kotilovo and fell back behind the line Sergievskoe-Ugol'nitsa-Palatki.

The 340th and 154th rifle divisions and the 112th Tank Brigade were fighting the enemy, who was firmly holding the line Upryamovo-Kudinovo-Shchelkanovo-Zubovo-Sosino-Podpolevo.

The 290th Rifle Division, with the task of concentrating in the area Davydovo-Podolesh'e and operating along the Yukhnov axis, was on the march, approachin Uteshevo, where the army headquarters was located from January 7.

The 50th Army's combat operations along the Yukhnov axis, beginning after January 15, came down to a slow offensive against an enemy stubbornly defending along fortified lines. Just as had been the case with the Kondrovo-Polotnyanyi Zavod line, the strong points were well constructed by engineers: there were barbed wire obstacles, trenches, ice walls, with flanking fire between them. The army's offensive was also complicated by the strong snow storms and snowfalls, as a result of which there were instances of the army headquarters losing contact with its divisions.

By the close of January 18 the situation along the 50th Army's front was as follows.

The 413th Rifle Division was fighting against the slowly-withdrawing enemy along the line Vshivka-Troskino. The 413th Rifle Division was subsequently moved to the army's left flank and, in conjunction with the 290th Rifle and 7th Guards Cavalry divisions, attacked in the direction of Trufanovo from January 22 in order to bypass Yukhnov from the southwest.

During the course of the day the 217th and 340th rifle divisions and the 112th Tank Brigade three times unsuccessfully attacked the enemy defending in Upryamovo and fell back to their jumping off point.

The 154th Rifle Division, having been transferred to the front Sosino-Davydovo was fighting for Kuligi and Podpolevo. The Germans were putting up stubborn resistance.

4 The former 9th Tank Brigade was renamed the 2nd Guards Tank Brigade on January 6 1942.

The 290th Rifle Division was fighting for Lipovka (one km west of Davydovo) and Prudishchi, while the 7th Guards Cavalry Division, covering the army's left flank, was attacking Gulino (one km southwest of Prudishchi) and Lenskoe.

As a result, the 50th Army's front resembled a broken line extending more than 70 km, while the troops were scattered along various axes.

As a result of this situation the *front* commander, Gen. Zhukov, on January 19 ordered Gen. Boldin to create a fist for attacking Podpolevo (south of Yukhnov) and, having captured it, to move the group on Yukhnov. It was ordered that another group be directed from the northeast in the direction of Prechistoe and Yukhnov, in order seize in pincers the enemy group holding the area Upryamovo-Kudinovo-Zubovo-Podpolevo and capture Yukhnov.

The 50th Army's operations subsequently unfolded in the spirit of the *front* commander's instructions. By the close of January 22 the 217th Rifle Division, having blockaded Upryamovo and other locales, was fighting for Ploskoe and Trebushinki. The 340th Rifle Division, upon capturing Ostapova Sloboda (four km east of Podpolevo) was attacking Ol'khi. The 290th and 413th rifle and 7th Guards Cavalry divisions were attacking in the general direction of Trufanovo.

Despite our troops' energetic actions, the enemy's resistance continued to mount. Intelligence data confirmed that by January 22 that up to 12 infantry regiments from the Germans' 31st, 131st, 137th, 213th, and 52nd infantry, and 19th Panzer divisions were facing the 50th Army.

It was in these conditions that the 50th Army commander directed his main efforts to his left flank, where the army's main group, consisting of the 344th,[5] 290th, 413th, 173rd (transferred from the 49th Army after January 20), and 340th rifle divisions was concentrated and which had been ordered to launch a blow to bypass Yukhnov from the south and southwest.

A January 27 order by the army commander to the forces of the 50th Army laid out the following tasks:

The 217th Rifle Division and its reinforcing units, while pinning down the enemy along the flanks, were to attack in the direction of Trebushinki and Yukhnov. The 154th Rifle Division, occupying the line Ostapova Sloboda (one km northwest of Sosino)-Tibeki (one km east of Podpolevo), was directed toward Yukhnov.

The divisions constituting the army's main group were to attack as follows:

The 344th Rifle Division from the area Davydovo-Zhivul'ki in the direction of Mochalovo and Dolina.

The 290th Rifle Division from the front Chernevo (one km north of Zhivul'ki)-Gorokhovka in the direction of Labeki, followed by a subsequent blow toward Shukleevo (west of Yukhnov).

The 413th Rifle Division, having blocked with part of its forces the enemy's strong points of Gorokhovka and Sitskoe, was to reach the area Mar'ino-Voitovo-Krutoe (all locales west of Yukhnov) with its main forces.

The 173rd Rifle Division, which was fighting for Barsuki, was assigned to blockade that locale and continue attacking to the northwest, with the mission of reaching the area Spornoe-Zhornovka-Semizho on January 28. The 7th Cavalry Division, which was covering the army's left flank, was ordered on January 28 to reach the area Zhupanovo-Krasnoe-Khvoshchevka.

The 340th Rifle Division, having turned over the Ploskoe area to the 112th Tank Brigade, was being hurriedly moved to the army's left flank and was being concentrated in the area

5 This division was formed in the Syzran' area, finished outfitting in Kuibyshev Oblast' and Cheboksary in the Chuvash ASSR, and arrived in the Krasnaya Pakhra area, from where it was moved on January 16 to the 50th army by order of the *Stavka*; it finished concentrating on January 22.

Lenskoe-Putogino-Kaplino, from which it was to attack behind the 173rd Rifle Division in the direction of Barsuki.

The enemy, having received fresh reinforcements, continued counterattacking. By the end of January 27 the Germans, in up to an infantry regiment in strength, with artillery and mortars, had pushed back our units and occupied Lazino, Dyatlovka, and Karpovo (all locales 1 ½ km south of Bardeno near the Warsaw highway). Heavy fighting was taking place along the front of the 173rd Rifle Division, which had cut the Warsaw highway in the Barsuki area and which was fighting for this locale. Prisoners were taken belonging to the enemy's 19th Panzer Division, which was operating as an infantry unit. The army's remaining divisions were forced to wage no less difficult battles. As a result, by January 31 we had managed to capture Barsuki and cut the Warsaw highway in several places. On the army's right flank the offensive was not sufficiently developed. The fighting for Yukhnov continued into the subsequent period and unfolded in bitter fighting along this axis.

Along the front of Gen. Belov's cavalry group to the left the following events took place during this period: the 1st Guards Cavalry Corps on January 14 cut the Warsaw highway in the Lyudkovo-Solov'evka area, directing its cavalry divisions to the northwest. On the right the 325th Rifle Division, attached to the corps, was defending the line Aleksino-Vysokoe-Khotibino-Pyshkino, covering the corps' operations. Our cavalry's offensive took place under conditions of the enemy's powerful resistance and his aviation's systematic raids. Our aviation, as a result of the airfields' remove and the snow drifts on some of them, was not able to render sufficiently effective support to the corps.

As had been the case on the 50th Army's front, the cavalry corps' combat operations following its arrival at the Warsaw highway came down to extended and stubborn fighting against the German-Fascist forces, which lasted until January 29. By that time the units of the 1st Guards Cavalry Corps, having broken the enemy's resistance along the sector of the Warsaw highway approximately from Glagol'nya to Solov'evka, crossed it and subsequently attacked to the northwest and west.

The actions of Gen. Belov's cavalry group following its crossing of the Warsaw highway unfolded in the following manner. In carrying out its assignment to move into the area of Semlevo station and linking up with Sokolov's cavalry corps (Kalinin Front), Gen. Belov's group on January 31 reached the area Gremyachee-Glukhovo-Vyazovets-Petrishchevo, with its forward units on the line Velikopol'e-Subbotniki.

During February 1 the cavalry group moved in fighting along the indicated axis. The offensive by our cavalry unfolded in conditions of the German troops' growing resistance. Enemy aviation also became more active in this area.

On February 2 and the night of February 2-3 Gen. Belov's forces were fighting along the following lines: the 2nd Guards Cavalry Division was attacking Stogovo, while the 1st Guards Cavalry Division, having captured the villages of Pokrov and Svinenki (16 km southeast of Semlevo station), was attacking toward Podrezovo. The 75th and 57th cavalry divisions threw the enemy out of Moloshino and Staroe Kapustino (1 ½ km south of Moloshino) and was continuing to fight for Mikhalevo (one km north of Moloshino); the 41st Cavalry Division, occupying the front Nikol'skoe-Debrevo and to the west, covered the cavalry group's rear.

The fighting along this line lasted until February 4. During the night of February 4-5 the cavalry group's forces continued attacking, with the task, in conjunction with the 33rd Army, of taking Vyaz'ma. Puzikovo (eight km south of Vyaz'ma) and Stogovo were captured in a nighttime attack.

During the day the cavalry group prepared its further attack, which was set for 1800 on February 5.

During the night of February 5-6 the cavalry group, as a result of the stubborn fighting along the entire front, moved forward slightly. During the night of February 6-7 our cavalry managed to take the villages of Mikhal'ki (1 ½ km southeast of Pastikhi) and Pastikha and reach the near approaches to Vyaz'ma. The attacking units penetrated into the enemy's defense.

Fighting established that the Germans had strengthened their defense around Vyaz'ma with men and matériel. The enemy's counterattacks grew stronger. Our troops beat them off with difficulty, inflicting serious losses on the Germans. By 1300 on February 8 the cavalry group's units occupied the area Selivanovo-Pastikha-Zabnovo-Lunyaki.

The German-Fascist troops' growing resistance in the Vyaz'ma area, the increased activity of the enemy's aviation, and the difficulties of the wintertime conditions forced our command to temporarily forgo the mission of taking Vyaz'ma and to turn Belov's cavalry group in a new direction. By February 11 the corresponding regrouping had been carried out.

The forces of Gen. Belov's cavalry group subsequently operated along the Dorogobuzh direction, carrying out a new task for the *front*.

On the 50th Army's front at this time bitter fighting continued along the Yukhnov bridgehead.

As a result of the January offensive by the 50th Army and the 1st Guards Cavalry Corps we were able to essentially accomplish one task—to reach the Warsaw highway followed by the cavalry's subsequent movement on Vyaz'ma. The other task—the destruction of the Kondrovo-Myatlevo-Yukhnov enemy group and the capture of Yukhnov—remained uncompleted. The Germans managed to extract part of their forces from under the blow by the 43rd, 49th and 50th armies and the 1st Guards Cavalry Corps and thus save them from final defeat. The reasons for this are the same ones we noted in summing up the 49th Army's operations. The positive aspect of the 50th Army's and 1st Guards Cavalry Corps' actions are that in spite of the difficult offensive conditions, the enemy was ultimately thrown out of his positions and once again began to fall back to the west, losing men and matériel.

Combat operations along the 10th Army's front for the purpose of reaching the Vyaz'ma-Bryansk lateral railroad, January 5-31 1942

Following the capture of Kozel'sk and the 10th Army's arrival to the west of the town the army command, fearing an enemy attack from the southwest against its left flank, planned to delay along the new line for 2-3 days, in order to straighten out its front with the Bryansk Front's lagging 61st Army.

The *front* command, in a January 5 directive, categorically demanded the continuation of a decisive offensive so as not to enable the enemy to put himself in order and bring up reserves and consolidate his position. The army was to as quickly as possibly occupy Sukhinichi and Mosal'sk and reach the Vyaz'ma-Bryansk lateral railroad.

The 10th Army commander, in accordance with the *front* directive, laid out the following tasks that same day: the 325th Rifle Division was to capture Mosal'sk by the close of January 5; the 239th Rifle Division was to reach the Meshchovsk area, with the idea of continuing the offensive toward Serpeisk. The 324th Rifle Division, with two companies from the 239th Rifle Division and a battalion from the 323rd Rifle Division, was left to blockade Sukhinichi. The 326th Rifle Division was ordered to reach the area Bordykino-Naumovo-Shlipovo by 1200 on January 5. The 323rd Rifle Division was to reach the area Polyaki-Buda Monastyrskaya-Buda on January 5. The 322nd Rifle Division, covering the army's left flank, was to concentrate on January 5 in the area Budskie Vyselki-Lashevo-Khot'kovo-Klintsy, with the task of attacking toward Zhizdra. The 328th Rifle Division was to remain until January 5 in the army's second echelon in the Kozel'sk area, from which it would then move to the Mekhovoe area, where the 10th Army's headquarters was.

According to intelligence data, by January 10 the German 296th, 56th and 216th infantry divisions and units of the 19th Panzer and 10th Motorized divisions were facing the 10th Army.

Two infantry regiments of the 216th Infantry Division and a company from the 19th Panzer Division were defending Sukhinichi. The headquarters of the 216th Infantry Division were also in the town.

Besides this, units of other enemy divisions were defending Meshchovsk, Mosal'sk and other locales. The 213th Infantry Division's 416th Regiment and the 212th Infantry Division's 316th Regiment were in Meshchovsk and Mosal'sk.

From the orders given to the 10th Army's forces, it follows that the army command, while directing the main mass of its forces in the direction of Kirov and Lyudinovo, simultaneously sought through the capture of Meshchovsk, Serpeisk, Mosal'sk, and Zhizdra to secure its flanks. The necessity of taking the first three locales also flowed from the *front's* overall task, which demanded that the rear of the 1st Guards Cavalry Corps, aiming at Vyaz'ma, be firmly secured, as well as the indirect securing of the 50th Army's left flank, which was fighting along the Yukhnov axis.

Besides this, given the movement of the 10th Army's own main forces to the area of Kirov and Lyudinovo, leaving such centers of resistance as Sukhinichi, Meshchovsk, Mosal'sk, and Serpeisk in its rear and along the flanks could create complications. Thus it was necessary to quickly eliminate the centers of German resistance.

From this it is evident what kind of situation the 10th Army would have to fight along a front up to 100 km in breadth. Special demands were made on troop control in these conditions.

Aside from this, the winter, the poor regulation of the rear's work, the increased enemy air activity, and the exhaustion of the army's forces, further complicated the situation in which combat operations would have to be waged.

The 10th Army's offensive unfolded as follows: during January 1-5 the 239th and 324th rifle divisions fought in the Sukhinichi area and completed the encirclement of this locale.

By January 5 the 325th Rifle Division had reached the front Frolovskoe-Bedritsa and began fighting along the approaches to Meshchovsk. The enemy's 406th Infantry Regiment, which was fresh and at full strength and which had also been reinforced with tanks, artillery and mortars, was putting up stubborn resistance to our forces. Units of the 325th Rifle Division, having crushed the Germans' resistance along the front Bedritsa-Frolovskoe, reached the town, where the once again encountered the enemy's powerful counterattacks. The fighting along the approaches to the town and within it lasted about two days. On the morning of January 6 the division, as a result of a fierce street battle, occupied the town, having bypassed it with part of its forces. After this the 325th Rifle Division attacked toward Mosal'sk.

The 326th Rifle Division, overcoming the resistance of the 206th Infantry Division and other enemy units, by the morning of January 6 had reached the area Azar'evo-Bordykino-Nemerzki, from where throughout the same day it continued to attack along the Sukhinichi-Spas-Demensk (13 km northwest of Bakhmutovo) railroad, with the task of reaching by the end of January 6 the area of Dabuzha station-Sobolevka-Shibaevka and capturing these locales.

By January 5th the 239th Rifle Division removed from blockading Sukhinichi and thrown toward Meshchovsk for an attack against it from the south in conjunction with the 325th Rifle Division. Upon capturing Meshchovsk, this division was to operate in the direction of Serpeisk. However, its participation in the capture of Meshchovsk was not needed, and on January 6 it was directed from the area to the south of Meshchovsk to Serpeisk. The 324th Rifle Division continued to blockade Sukhinichi.

South of Sukhinichi, in the direction of Kirov, the 330th Rifle Division was attacking, with the task of reaching by the end of the day the area Ryaplovo-Maklaki-Khludneva. Units of the enemy's 216th Infantry Division were withdrawing before the 330th Rifle Division.

By this time the 323rd Rifle Division, having occupied Duminichi station, had reached the line Buda Monastyrskaya-Polyaki, with the task of occupying the area Sloboda-Kotovichi-Zimnitsy. In the area of Bryn'-Dubrovka (four km southwest of Duminichi) the division was battling the enemy, who disposed of a reinforced battalion in each locale. By holding Bryn' and Dubrovka the Germans, evidently sought to secure the Lyudinovo, Zhizdra, and Zikeevo axis.

The 322nd Rifle Division, covering the 10th Army's left flank, by the end of January 6 had reached the line Kolosovo-Volosovo, in readiness to move by the morning of January 7 to the area Solonovka-Zikeevo-Petrovka. However, this task proved beyond the strength of the 322nd Rifle Division and it reached the indicated area only by the close of January 11 and began with part of its forces to encircle Zikeevo, which was being defended by two enemy infantry battalions, numbering up to 1,000 men.

The 328th Rifle Division continued to remain in the army's second echelon in the area Muzalevka-Zvyagino-Yanshino.

Thus the 10th Army was attacking along four axes: toward Mosal'sk, Serpeisk, Kirov, and Lyudinovo. The army's formation took on a fanlike shape and the width of its front reached 150 km. Such a formation placed great demands on the 10th Army in the organization of control and communications with its divisions scattered along a broad front. Besides this, the 324th Rifle Division was fully engaged in blockading Sukhinichi; in order to support the division, it was necessary to hold the army's only reserve along this axis—the numerically weak 328th Rifle Division.

In the second half of January 7 the 10th Army's units were developing the offensive along the indicated axes, with the task of reaching the front Mosal'sk-Ploty-Spasskoe-Novoe Selo-Bol'shoe Zabor'e-Ignatovka by the close of January 8.

In the latter half of January 7 the 239th Rifle Division occupied Serpeisk and continued to attack to the northwest. Bitter fighting continued around Sukhinichi with the surrounded units of the 216th Infantry and 19th Panzer divisions. The garrison in Sukhinichi refused our offer to surrender, opening fire on the 10th Army's parliamentarians.

During the day of January 8 the 324th Rifle Division's units went over to the attack along one of the sectors in the Sukhinichi area and occupied several buildings along the southern and southwestern outskirts of the town, but were halted by the enemy's powerful fire from stone houses adapted for defense.

During the night of January 8-9 the 325th Rifle Division, in conjunction with the left-flank units of the 1st Guards Cavalry Corps, occupied Mosal'sk, after which it was subordinated to the commander of the cavalry corps.

The 10th Army's remaining divisions, having carried out the commander's task, by the close of January 8 had reached the line Spasskoe-Bol'shoe Zabor'e-Ignatovka and were developing the offensive in the general direction of Kirov, Lyudinovo, and Zhizdra.

By the close of January 9 the 323rd Rifle Division had occupied Lyudinovo and all day on January 10 was stubbornly fighting to the west of the town. One rifle regiment was moved toward Kirov to support the 330th Rifle Division's attack on the city. The offensive by the 10th Army's units unfolded in conditions of heavy snowfall and, in places, blizzards, which slowed down the advance.

The enemy, while putting up a fight, was falling back along the following axes: the remains of the 56th Infantry Division's 171st and 234th regiments and the 10th Motorized Infantry Division along the Sukhinichi-Spas-Demensk road; units of the 296th Infantry Division along the Sukhinichi-Kirov road. The presence of the *Grossdeutschland* SS Infantry Regiment was noted west of Lyudinovo.

The 10th Army's units, continuing the attack, reached the line Uzhat' River-Kirov-Lyudinovo after January 10 and were fighting on the approaches to Zhizdra. In the first half of January 11 the 330th Rifle Division took Kirov after fighting.

On the army's left flank, in the area Zhizdra-Zikeevo, the situation began to change after January 11. The success of the 10th Army's offensive, the center and right flank of which had taken Kirov and Lyudinovo, caused the enemy to undertake some serious countermeasures. This was also caused by the desire to extract the Sukhinichi group from encirclement.

The German command was hurriedly transferring the fresh 208th Infantry Division, which had recently arrived at the Russian front from France, with ski battalions, from Bryansk to the Zhizdra area. The fresh 211th Infantry Division, also transferred in its time from France, was brought up from Smolensk to the Lyudinovo area during the latter third of January. South of Zikeevo, along the Sukhinichi-Bryansk railroad, the 4th Panzer Division's motorized regiments, reinforced with 10-12 tanks, had concentrated. The German command gave all these units the task of launching a blow against the Western Front's left wing and free up the Vyaz'ma-Bryansk railroad.

The enemy's 208th Infantry Division was to break through to Sukhinichi and relieve the garrison with the support of the 4th Panzer Division's motorized regiments, part of whose forces were operating along the Zikeevo axis with the task of delaying the advance of the Bryansk Front's 61st Army. The latter was lagging behind as before and in this way was putting the Western Front's left wing in a difficult position.

In a directive by the *Stavka* of the Supreme High Command, the 61st Army was included in the Western Front on January 13 and was to operate along its left wing.

On January 12 the Germans' offensive against the 10th Army's left flank began, which was accompanied by intensive raids by the Fascist aviation.

The 322nd Rifle Division, having lifted the blockade of Zikeevo, fell back under enemy pressure to the north and northeast to the line Ilyushenka-Petrovka.

Our offensive continued along the 10th Army's center and right flank. The 239th Rifle Division was fighting in the area Kirsanova-Pyatnitsa-Shershnevo-Krasnyi Kholm and attacking in the direction of Chiplyaevo station (eight km northwest of Bakhmutovo). On January 16 this division was subordinated to the commander of the 1st Guards Cavalry Corps.

The 326th Rifle Division, having cut the railroad, was fighting along the line Borets-Bykovo-Degonka. The 330th Rifle Division was in the Kirov area and attacking to the north of the town along the railroad. The 323rd Rifle Division was operating in the Lyudinovo area. During the night of January 15-16 the division, having left a regiment in Lyudinovo, set out with its remaining forces in the direction of Zhizdra. The division, in conjunction with the 322nd Rifle Division, was supposed to destroy the Zikeevo-Zhizdra enemy group and take Zhizdra. The 324th Rifle Division continued to blockade Sukhinichi. The 328th Rifle Division, as before, remained in the army commander's reserve.

The fighting in the area of Zhizdra and Zikeevo continued with unrelenting intensity in the days following January 13-14. The Germans' Zhizdra-Zikeevo group continued to stubbornly try to break through in the direction of Sukhinichi. On January 18 the offensive by the enemy's units in the Lyudinovo area began, and on January 19 the German forces opened their attack along the 10th Army's right flank, launching a blow from the Bakhmutovo area in the direction of Baryatinskoe station and along the Spas-Demensk-Sukhinichi railroad.

Combat operations on the 61st Army's front, following its inclusion in the Western Front, unfolded in the following manner: the army was carrying out a regrouping until January 16, operating against the German-Fascist' forces' Bolkhov group, consisting of the 112th and 167th infantry divisions and separate units of the 56th (one regiment) and 208th infantry divisions. The significance of this regrouping was the fact that the army's right-flank divisions (91st Cavalry, 350th and 387th rifle) were changing the direction of their attack from the west and southwest to the southeast. It was first necessary, in conjunction with the army's center and right flank, to deal with the enemy's Bolkhov group, which by hanging over the *front's* extreme left wing, was depriving it of the prospect of developing the blow to the west, cramped the operations of the Bryansk Front's right-wing forces, and left the 61st Army's left wing open.

The right-flank divisions, attacking in a southeasterly direction, reached the following front during the latter half of January 20: by 2300 on January 20 the 91st Cavalry Division had taken Ivanovo and was continuing to fight to the south and southeast of the village; the 350th Rifle Division took Yagoda in fighting and was attacking to the southeast; the 387th Rifle Division, overcoming enemy resistance, reached the front Nogaya-Kireikovo, capturing both locales.

Units from the 61st Army's center and left flank were waging defensive battles: the 346th Rifle Division along the line Marovka-Veino; the 342nd Rifle Division along the line Veino-Dolbino-Fat'yanovo (south of Belev); the 356th Rifle Division along the Oka River from Budgovishche to Chergodaevo.

By January 20 the following situation had developed along the 10th Army's front: in the center the army's units continued to firmly hold the area of Kirov, while along the flanks it was coming under strong enemy pressure, while his most powerful group was attacking the army's left flank from the area of Lyudinovo, Zhizdra and Zikeevo.

Despite the 322nd Rifle Division's stubborn resistance, it was forced to fall back from the Zikeevo area under pressure from a numerically-superior enemy to the northeast and on January 20 had concentrated in the area Rechitsa-Khot'kovo-Chernyshino. The 323rd Rifle Division abandoned Lyudinovo after heavy fighting and fell back to the area Shipilovka-Usovka-Ignatovka. The 10th Army's remaining units were fighting along their previous lines.

As a result, the German-Fascist units managed to break through on the left flank and by January 22 reach the area of Duminichi, from which they were thrown out by the 328th Rifle Division's ski battalion. The Hitlerite forces, having received fresh reinforcements, retook Duminichi station on January 23 and reached the line Duminichi station-Vertnoe.

By the morning of January 26 the main forces of the Germans' Zikeevo-Zhizdra group had reached the front Barankovo (two km northwest of Khludneva)-Khludneva-Bryn'-Vertnoe, where they waged a stubborn battle against our troops. During the following days the Germans advanced further along some sectors and moved right up to Sukhinichi.

As a result of the bitter fighting, the enemy managed to extract a part of the Sukhinichi garrison from its encirclement. At the end of January the German-Fascist forces were once again thrown back to the southwest. Persistent fighting with mixed success for both sides unfolded in February 1942.

Gen. Rokossovskii's 16th Army, the headquarters of which had arrived from the Volokolamsk-Gzhatsk axis, took an active part in these battles. By 2400 on January 27 the 16th Army command had assumed control over the 10th Army's forces in the zone Shlipovo (15 km northwest of Sukhinichi)-Ivanovo-Sergeevsk station-Kocheva station, on the right; (excluding) Belev-Ktsyn' (30 km southeast of Zikeevo)-Bryansk, on the left. From January 28 the 16th Army was attacking to the southwest, fighting units of the enemy's Zikeevo-Zhizdra group. The 10th Army continued its operations along the Kirov axis.

During January 20-30 the 61st Army concentrated its efforts against the enemy's Bolkhov group. The heaviest fighting took place on the right flank. The 83rd and 91st cavalry divisions, which had been unified into a group, were attacking to the south and reached the area of Uzkoe by January 30. At that time the 350th Rifle Division, overcoming the enemy's stubborn resistance, reached Vasil'evskoe. On the morning of January 30 the 387th Rifle Division began a fierce fight for Vyazovaya and Malaya Chern'. After January 20 the 346th Rifle Division became more active and on the night of January 29-30 was fighting for Serdichi and Sigolaevo. The Germans put up stubborn resistance. By the end of January 30 and the morning of January 31 the 342nd Rifle Division was waging a fire battle along its former line. The 356th Rifle Division, following attempts to attack Khmelevaya, was defending along its former positions.

Operational-tactical conclusions on the combat operations of the left-wing armies in January 1942

The Western Front's left-wing armies, despite the difficult conditions for the offensive, coped with their assignment, having cut by January 10 the Vyaz'ma-Bryansk lateral railroad reaching the Warsaw highway by the end of January 1942.

The 49th Army's pace of advance in January, which comprised an average of a little more than two km per day (in all, during January 9-31 the army covered about 50 km) is not instructive in the present case, because during the offensive two of the enemy's fortified defensive positions had to be overcome: the Kondrovo-Polotnyanyi Zavod line, and the Aidarovo-Kostino-Ostrozhnoe-Bogdanovo-Potapovo line.

Among the shortcomings in overcoming these fortified lines one must count the as-yet existing practice of attacking the enemy's strong points and centers of resistance head on, which led to excessive losses in men and time.

What is instructive is the organization of maneuver for the capture of the Kondrovo-Polotnyanyi Zavod line during the latter part of the period of the fighting for it: the blow by the 5th Guards Rifle Division around Kondrovo from the north, as well as the bound by the 173rd and 238th rifle divisions around Polotnyanyi Zavod from the southeast, in conjunction with the holding actions by the 133rd Rifle Division from the front.

As had been the case in preceding operations, the problem of coordination with neighboring armies once again acquired significance. The *front* command paid serious attention to this problem, in aiming the 43rd, 49th and 50th armies along converging axes for the destruction of the Medyn'-Kondrovo-Yukhnov enemy group. Operational coordination with the 50th Army was achieved with the 1st Guards Cavalry Corps' turn toward Mosal'sk, with a subsequent attack to the northwest toward Vyaz'ma.

Great attention in the 50th Army's offensive should be paid to the regrouping of its divisions from the right to the left flank. During the fighting it was discovered that the enemy in the Yukhnov area had put up more resistance than had been expected. The attempt by the 1st Guards Cavalry Corps to take Yukhnov on the march was unsuccessful; the corps, having suffered heavy casualties, was forced to halt and assume the defensive. This forced the *front* command to seek a solution in another place. The corps was transferred to the Mosal'sk area, after the capture of which it was to operate to the northwest for a blow against Vyaz'ma. The favorable outcome of the fighting along the 49th Army's front for taking the Kondrovo-Polotnyanyi Zavod line made it possible to shift the 50th Army's center of effort to its left flank. As a result, the army's combat operations assumed the character of an offensive with a regrouping of forces to the flank.

The armies' tank formations, in light of their few numbers (for example, as of January 7 the 112th Tank Brigade had one T-34 and five T-26s), did not play a big role. Thus they were subordinated to the rifle divisions for joint activities. In certain cases the tank formations had to operate as rifle units. We noticed a similar practice with the enemy. This employment of tanks can doubtlessly be explained, to a certain extent, by the winter conditions.

As in previous operations, the greatest offensive pace again fell to the lot of the 10th Army. In ten days of attack up to the arrival of the 330th Rifle Division before Kirov, the army covered more than 90 km, which yields an average rate of advance of 9-10 km per day. The high offensive rate in conditions of winter, given the insufficiently precise work of the rear organs, had an effect on the troops' condition. Besides this, the necessity of carrying out tasks along various axes forced the army command to scatter its divisions along a broad front, the light of which reached 150 km. Thus it is no accident that when the army's left flank came under pressure from the enemy's fresh forces, its divisions were forced to fall back in fighting, in this way enabling the Germans to relieve the garrison at Sukhinichi.

Troop control is an extremely complex task in conditions when the army commander has several formations subordinated to him (for example, there were eight rifle divisions in the 10th Army), and which are scattered over a broad front an in constant motion. Despite the measures adopted to organize communications and the employment of communications officers, in a number of cases the army headquarters experienced difficulties, being 50 km and more removed from some of its formations. The 10th Army's military council asked the *front* command about the organization of corps formations in order to make easier the army commander's control of his subordinate forces. It would have been expedient, in such conditions, to create temporary operational formations (similar to the organization of the mobile group in the 50th Army during the Kaluga operation).

9

The Medyn'-Myatlevo Operation

The operational significance of Medyn'

Medyn' is a small town in the Smolensk oblast. During the German retreat, following their defeat around Moscow, the town acquired great operational significance. Medyn' proved to be a barrier that, as the German command thought, should have covered the withdrawal of the German-Fascist troops to the west. Medyn' covered Myatlevo, through which two streams of enemy supplies and personnel could flow simultaneously: one from Kaluga to Vyaz'ma along the railroad, and the other from Maloyaroslavets to Yukhnov along the Warsaw highway. The German command attached great significance to the retention of Medyn', which is why the approaches to the town were heavily fortified.

The character of the enemy's defensive structures in the Medyn' Area

A well-outfitted road leads from Maloyaroslavets to Medyn'. The Germans foresaw the heavy destruction of this highway among their measures for defending Medyn'; all the bridges had been blown up or mines, and narrow passages were blocked; a large number of obstacles had been erected along the parallel roads.

The Germans built a many wood-earthen firing points in the large inhabited locales to the east of Medyn', having turned these places into strong points to combat our troops.

There are large wooded areas on the road from Maloyaroslavets to Medyn'. In wintry conditions they are difficult to traverse; besides, the Germans had obstructed, mined and braided with wire the passages in these woods.

As a result of all this, Medyn' was seen by the German command as difficult of approach for the Red Army's units. It considered that it could freely maneuver its forces in its rear.

The Western Front Command's plan for capturing Medyn'

The Western Front command well understood the role of Medyn' as a barrier in the way of the complete rout of those enemy groups that, following their defeats at Kaluga and Maloyaroslavets, were retreating to the west. If Medyn' were taken, one could in Myatlevo block the path of the two streams of enemy forces; in connection with the successful operations of the Western Front's left-wing armies—49th and 50th armies, and the 1st Guards Cavalry Corps—this could result in the encirclement of the enemy in the area Medyn'-Myatlevo-Yukhnov.

Thus following the capture of Maloyaroslavets by the forces of the 43rd Army, they were directed toward the capture of Medyn'.

In the *front* commander's directive no. 269 of January 9 1942, the 43rd Army (along with the 49th and 50th armies) was given the task: "To encircle and destroy the Kondrovo-Yukhnov-Medyn' enemy group and develop the blow to the northwest."

Separately, the 43rd Army commander was instructed: to defeat the enemy in the Myatlevo-Voronki area no later than January 11 and, having completed with the 49th Army the destruction of the Kondrovo enemy group, attack in the general direction of Ugryumovo station, outflanking Gzhatsk from the west.

In accordance with these instructions, the 43rd Army command issued the following order (no. 030/op, of January 9):

1 The enemy, having been defeated in the Maloyaroslavets area, is trying to delay along the approaches to Medyn', for the purpose of securing the evacuation of his rear stores and supplies.

2 To the right, the 33rd Army's left-wing units have reached the front Naberezhnaya Sloboda-Peremeshaevo-Semichevo-Fedorino-Dylkino; to the left, the 49th Army's right-wing units are fighting along the line Motyakino-Berezovka-Detchino.

3 The 43rd Army, developing its offensive and bypassing individual resistance centers, is to be fighting for the Medyn' area by the end of January 10 and is to take Myatlevo by the end of January 11.

In the subsequent order no. 48/op of January 13 1942, the 43rd Army was tasked with reaching the area of Ugryumovo station by the close of January 15.

In the tasks given to the divisions, it was emphatically demanded that the troops not launch frontal attacks against fortified inhabited locales, but rather take them outflanking and enveloping them; in those cases when it was impossible to bypass such locales, it was suggested that they be burned down, thus smoking the Germans out into the field and frost.

The combat correlation of men and matériel. The depth of the operation

The following troops took part in the 43rd Army's operation to capture Medyn': the 5th Guards Airborne Corps, 53rd Rifle Division, the 17th Rifle Division with the 26th Tank Brigade, the 415th Rifle Division, and the 194th Rifle Division with the 18th Tank Brigade. In the quantitative sense, taking into account the preceding losses, this amounted approximately to 15,000 active rifles, 400 machine guns, about 100 mortars, 50 guns, and up to 40 tanks. This worked out to 600 rifles, 16 machine guns, four mortars, two guns, and about two tanks per km of front, given an average army front width of 25 km. Thus the forces available for an offensive operation and the breakthrough of the enemy's fortified zone were quite small. However, the enemy (units of the XX Army Corps and Chevalier's group, composed of the remains of the 29th Motorized and 10th Panzer divisions, which were covering the withdrawal of the XX Army Corps) were demoralized to a significant degree; the enemy was retreating, hanging on to the inhabited strong points and striving to win time and safely evacuate his rear organs and extract his troops by means of delaying rearguard battles.

In such conditions the decisive actions of our troops, with the enormous increase in their consciousness and desire to do whatever it took to finish off the enemy, played an exceptionally important role. Through skillful actions one could achieve more than through a simple quantitative superiority. It was not possible to gain a precise impression of the number of enemy forces, but one can conclude that his forces facing the 43rd Army at the time did not exceed the forces of that army.

The operation was planned to a depth of approximately 60 km, with the mission of overcoming this distance in the course of six days. This planned rate of advance, in conditions of a winter offensive, without roads, and the presence of a large number of obstacles and mined sectors, was high. During the night of January 9-10 and during the day of January 10 the weather was not favorable to combat operations—there was a low cloud cover, a snowfall and a blizzard; visibility was 100-150 meters, and the temperature was six to nine degrees below freezing.

The attack on Medyn'

In carrying out the commander's orders, the 43rd Army's troops began their offensive on January 10. Their jumping off point was the front of the Luzha River along the sector Troitskoe-Panovo-Il'inskoe-Podsosino-Inyakhino-Yakushevo. The 5th Airborne Corps, with the army's composite rifle regiment, occupied the area Voskresenki-Kolodezi-Ivanovskaya. The army's troops, while pursuing the enemy, reached the designated front line by January 9.

At the same time as the 43rd Army was beginning to carry out its assignment, the neighboring 33rd Army to the right was fighting in the Vereya area. Its divisions were aimed in a northwesterly direction, as a result of which a dangerous gap developed between the armies; the enemy might feel it out and counterattack both armies along their flanks. The 43rd Army was ordered to close this gap. At the very moment when the army's efforts were being directed at capturing Medyn', the commander of the 43rd Army was forced to pull out one division (the left-flank 194th) from his army's operational formation and send it in a forced march to the area Aleksandrovka-Kolodezi-Sorochino, from where it was to move to the Shanskii Zavod and begin combat operations to destroy the enemy's small groups along the Shanya River. The division's actions were to secure the right flank of the 43rd Army and the left flank of the 33rd.

While the 194th Rifle Division was carrying out its regrouping from the left flank to the right and was moving into the space between the 33rd and 43rd armies, all of the 43rd Army's formations had moved forward and on January 10 had reached the line: the 5th Airborne Corps and a composite regiment—Kochubeevka-Varvarovka; the 53rd Rifle Division—Sinyavino; the 17th Rifle Division and the 26th Tank Brigade—Sokol'niki, and; the 415th Rifle Division—Stanki. The offensive was developing as planned, despite the enemy's resistance.

The Germans fought especially stubbornly for Mansurovo, Glukhovo, Sinyavino, Sokol'niki, and Stanki, where they had outfitted secure strong points. In spite of this, the Germans were thrown out of several strong points by our forces as early as January 10.

On January 12 the army's units once again advanced. On this day the 5th Airborne Corps reached Medyn' from the northwest and began fighting on its outskirts. At 1200 on the same day the corps occupied Yeleshnya-2. The army's composite regiment, in order to ward off any unexpected developments along the army's right flank, was moved to Isakovo. The 17th Rifle Division took Aduevo and by 1200 had begun fighting on the eastern outskirts of Medyn'. The remaining divisions were advancing along their axes to the west.

The outflanking of Medyn' continued on January 13, while that same day a forward detachment of the 5th Airborne Corps cut the highway to Myatlevo two km southwest of Medyn'. The German garrison in Medyn' was surrounded.

The enemy, seeing the pointlessness of resisting, threw in equipment to Medyn' on the night of January 13-14 and in small groups extracted its forces from Medyn' in the direction of Myatlevo. Some of these groups, having encountered the airborne corps' forward detachment, were destroyed, while others managed to break through to Myatlevo. By morning the town was in our hands. The following equipment was taken in occupying Medyn': 23 guns, six tanks, 666 trucks and 15 cars, 42 machine guns, 14 automatic rifles, 40,000 rounds of ammunition, more than 3,000 shells, and much more military equipment. More than 2,000 Germans were killed in the fighting for Medyn'.

The attack on Myatlevo

In the operation conducted by the 43rd Army, Medyn' was only the first stage. The operation was pursuing the objective of Myatlevo so that, ultimately, in conjunction with the 49th and 50th armies, and the 1st Guards Cavalry Corps, they could surround and destroy the enemy's Kondrovo-Yukhnov group.

The Western Front commander, in his telegram no. K-43 of January 14, pointed out to the commander of the 43rd Army (among the other army commanders) that the enemy's Kondrovo-Yukhnov group sought to hold the Warsaw highway and cover the axis to Gzhatsk, Vyaz'ma and Roslavl'.

"The immediate task of the left-wing's armies," it was noted in the telegram, "is to complete the destruction of the enemy's Kondrovo-Yukhnov group and in a subsequent blow against Vyaz'ma encircle and capture the enemy's Mozhaisk-Gzhatsk-Vyaz'ma group in conjunction with the Kalinin Front's armies and the Western Front's center armies."

For this purpose the commander of the 43rd Army was ordered to capture Myatlevo no later than January 16 and to then develop the blow in the direction of Yukhnov and Vyaz'ma. The more successfully the army could carry out the task of taking Myatlevo, the stronger would be the pressure on the flank and rear of the enemy group which was facing at this time the 49th and 50th armies and 1st Guards Cavalry Corps in the area of the Warsaw highway. The success of the Western Front's left wing, which was carrying out the extremely responsible assignment of enveloping the enemy's Mozhaisk-Gzhatsk-Vyaz'ma group from the south and southeast, depended upon the 43rd Army's successful operations.

At this time the 49th Army was attacking Kondrovo; the 50th Army was engaged in prolonged fighting on the approaches to Yukhnov, while the 1st Guards Cavalry Corps was approaching the Warsaw highway to the north of Mosal'sk.

The commander of the 43rd Army, in carrying out the *front* commander's orders, issued his order no. 50/op of January 15, in which he laid down the following tasks:

> The 43rd Army, for the purpose of defeating the enemy's Yukhnov group, is to bypass the enemy's main centers of resistance along the Medyn'-Yukhnov highway on January 16 and through a flank attack is to support the 49th and 50th armies' units in destroying the enemy's Yukhnov group.

For this purpose it was necessary to direct the army's main forces for operations along its right flank, with the task of cutting the communications of the enemy's Kondrovo-Yukhnov group with those German forces which were located in the Vyaz'ma area at this time.

The 194th Rifle Division, which had reached the area of Shanskii Zavod and had cleaned out the Fascists who had ensconced themselves there, received orders to attack to the southwest in the direction of Yukhnov, with the goal of covering by this maneuver the operations of that army group that was attacking Myatlevo. The army's composite regiment, which was occupying the Isakovo area, received orders to capture Koshnyaki station and cut the Germans' communications along the Myatlevo-Vyaz'ma railroad. Maj. Starchak's airborne detachment, which had been thrown into the Myatlevo area as early as January 3 1942, had by this time interrupted movement along the railroad along the Myatlevo-Kondrovo sector. Communications along the Vyaz'ma-Bryansk railroad and the Vyaz'ma-Yukhnov high road had been disrupted with the same success by a detachment from the 250th Airborne Regiment, which had been dropped into the Znamenki area by the beginning of the fighting for Myatlevo.

The employment of airborne landings

Airborne detachments during the Moscow operation operated in harsh winter conditions, which to a significant extent increase our interest in their combat activities.

The landing under Maj. Starchak's command was made with 416 men in the area of Bol'shoe Fat'yanovo, four km northeast of Myatlevo and two km from the Medyn'-Myatlevo highway. The choice of such a landing site was quite bold.

The landing was carried out at night. Along the way to the front line it was subjected to heavy enemy anti-aircraft fire; the planes were forced to disperse and some of them lost their way. Thus the concentration of the landing's forces in the designated area took place from 2100 on January 3 to 0200 on January 4, during which time the landing's personnel losses reached 15%.

After concentrating the detachment set out to rid the occupied territory of the enemy. In the landing zone there were 12 German wooden-earth firing points, against which they had to wage heavy fighting over several days. By blocking some wooden-earth firing points and suppressing their fire, the landing troops gradually tightened the ring around the wooden-earth firing points and then destroyed them. The garrisons of the wooden-earth firing points were completely destroyed.

At the same time another part of the landing party was engaged in destroying the rail line and destroying enemy cargoes and those guarding them. On January 5 an airborne detachment reached the platform at Kostino and blew up a nearby bridge. On January 8 the detachment occupied Myatlevo station and burned two rail trains, the first of which contained 28 tanks.

During January 8-19 the destruction of the enemy's wooden-earth firing points and the elimination of the German-Fascist forces from occupied territory took place. The detachment attacked a German transport column, which it discovered in the woods to the west of Dorokhi, as a result of which it captured 119 carts with military equipment that was later turned over to the 49th Army.

From the first day of the landing it maintained regular communications by air. At 0300 on January 4 two TB-3 aircraft appeared over the landing area, with which the landing established contact with the aid of two red rockets.

On January 5 two MiG aircrafts flew over the landing site at strafing altitude and the parachutists let them know they were in the area. At 1300 on the same day one of our U-2s landed at the Bol'shoe Fat'yanovo airfield. Seeing the parachutists and mistaking them for Germans, the pilot, without shutting off his motor, took off and flew back home.

The airborne detachment was informed that the 34th Independent Rifle Brigade was heading to its landing area. The airborne troops headed to meet it and on January 20 linked up with the brigade in the Nikol'skoe area. By this time the airborne detachment numbered 87 men; the remainder had died in the heavy 17-day fighting with the enemy.

The task assigned to the detachment had been carried out. It disrupted the movement along the Kondrovo-Myatlevo railroad for a period of time, destroyed a number of enemy wooden-earth firing points, knocked out two important trains with military equipment, and disorganized the work of the German's immediate rear. All this enabled our forces to advance more quickly and more easily overcome the opposing German forces.

However, this achievement was accompanied by great losses that must be attributed to the insufficiently well organized landing; preliminary and careful reconnaissance of the terrain and the enemy was not carried out; the reinforcement of the airborne group was not organized; the detachment was landed prematurely and as a result it was engaged in extremely heavy fighting, while encircled, for more than half a month. Thus the mission's accomplishment was carried out at the expense of the troops' selfless struggle.

The combat work of the 250th Airborne Regiment's airborne detachment began later. The operation was conducted for the purpose of aiding the 1st Guards Cavalry Corps' successful offensive and securing the advance of the 33rd Army to the west, and to aid our troops in surrounding and destroying the enemy's Kondrovo-Yukhnov group.

It was planned to make the drop 40 km southeast of Vyaz'ma, in the area Znamenka-Zhelan'e-Lugi. At the moment the drop was made this area was located 35-40 km from our front line. The broken terrain enabled our troops to make the drop in secret. The landing area cuts the Vyaz'ma-Yukhnov high road, along which the enemy's Yukhnov group was being supplied. The Lugi-Temkino road passes through this area, and close by is the Vyaz'ma-Bryansk railroad. All of these routes could be cut by the landing party.

According to our intelligence, there were no large enemy forces in the landing area. As a result of the fighting that followed, the following German units were identified: a division headquarters, supply train, rear units, 200-300 infantry, and about 100 horsemen in Znamenka; an ammunition depot , guarded by about a company of infantry, at Godunovka station; up to a battalion of infantry at Debryanskii station; two platoons of infantry in Velikopol'e; a supply train in Ivantsovo; a formation headquarters (presumably a corps) in Podsosonki, and; 300-500 infantrymen in each of the following locales—Sidorovskoe, Sinyukova, Gubino.

The 250th Airborne Regiment and the 1st and 2nd battalions of the 201st Airborne Brigade took part in the landing operation.

The landing detachment's formation and training was conducted by the Western Front's air directorate at the Vnukovo airfield. The airborne troops were divided into two battalions: the first under Capt. Surzhik, and the second under Capt. Kalashnikov. Training for the operation was completed on January 17.

The civilian air fleet's special designation aircraft, which had 21 PS-84 planes (Douglas), were used for transporting the landing, and which by the time of takeoff, were concentrated at the Vnukovo airfield. TB-3 aircraft from the 23rd Air Division were set aside from transporting the 45mm guns.

The air crews had sufficient experience in night flying and displayed excellent training and skill in carrying out landings in poorly illuminated terrain, with snow cover. The aircraft were well adapted for transport and did not require any further outfitting. They had turret machine guns for defense.

The troops taking part in the operation were divided into two groups—parachute and landing. These groups' composition is as follows:

Cargo	Parachutists	Landing Troops
Men	452	1,200
Rifles	263	300
Machine pistols (Shpagin)	142	646
Light machine guns	28	40
Heavy machine guns	10	28
Mortars	11	–
Anti-tank rifles	6	–
45mm guns	–	2

The operation was divided into three stages:

> First stage. A parachute drop to seize and hold an airfield and the adjacent area, so as to prepare for and secure the landing.
>
> Second stage. Two and a half hours after the parachute landing an advance team lands on the captured airfield to organize the landing.
>
> Third stage. Within thirty minutes of the advance team's landing the main landing begins. The landing is carried out in groups of 2-3 aircraft, so as to avoid piling up a lot of men and equipment on the airfield.

At 0335 on January 18 the first part of the landing, consisting of 16 aircraft, took off from the Vnukovo airfield. 452 parachutists were dropped in the area Znamenka-Zhelan'e before 0900.

The second group was sent to the same area at 1320 on January 19, consisting of ten aircraft. As a result of the unfavorable weather, a portion of the aircraft returned, one lost its way, and the others successfully carried out their assignment.

In all, over two days there was delivered: a command element of 55 men, 120 NCOs, and 467 rank and file soldiers; along with them were delivered 256 rifles, 325 Degtyarev and Shpagin machine pistols, 33 light machine guns, 10 mortars, 5 anti-tank guns, 78 revolvers, two combat loads of ammunition, 7 radio stations, and 350 kilograms of explosives.

From 1730 to 1750 on January 18 four PS-84 aircraft landed on the field near Znamenka, containing a group of 65 men for preparing the landing, of which 15 were from the advance group. The aircraft landed in the dark, with a snow covering of 50-60 centimeters on a field unfamiliar to the air -result of which one of the four was unable to take off and return and which was burned by the Germans on the following day.

In the course of January 19, under Capt. Surzhik's leadership, a landing site for the landing party was being prepared on the northern outskirts of Plesneva. Aside from the landing and advance teams, up to 400 partisans and local inhabitants took part in this work. At 0937 on January 20 comrade Surzhik reported: "It's possible to land on wheels; the coordinates are 38 535; come quickly. Surzhik."

Because of the unfavorable meteorological conditions, the landing party was landed on the strip near Plesneva during the course of January 20-22. By this time the enemy's aviation, having unearthed the landing area, began to carry out attacks. The airfield was subject to bombardment and strafing by machine guns. As a result of this, we had to carry out the landings at night. In all, along with the security group and the advance team, 1,643 men were dropped and landed, and with them 564 rifles, 817 Shpagin machine pistols, 31 heavy machine guns, 73 light machine guns, 11 anti-tank rifles, 34 mortars, 2 45mm guns, and 12 walkie-talkies.

As a result of enemy air attacks, of this number we lost 27 men killed and nine wounded, as well as three aircraft.

Following the parachute drop, the troops concentrated as follows: the 1st battalion in the area Plesneva-Zhelan'e-Malyi Lokhov; the 2nd battalion in the Zamosh'e area. At 1700 on January 19 the parachutists received this radiogram from the Western Front: "Zhukov has ordered: immediately capture Bogatyri, Znamenka and Zarech'e, in order to cut off the path of retreat of the enemy's Yukhnov group. Simultaneously push a security detail forward to Reutovo to prevent the enemy's arrival from the Temkino area."

In carrying out is assignment, the parachute landing simultaneously secured the arrival of new forces from the landing group; they arrived all the way up to January 22.

At 1620 on January 20 a new *front* radiogram was received: "By the morning of January 26 the locale in quadrant 7550 (Klyuchi) should be seized and, by a blow to the enemy rear in the direction of the locale in quadrant 8154 (Lyudkovo), aid Belov's group and link up with it."

The commander of the 250th Airborne Regiment did not exactly understand the task. The following explanation was sent in reply:

> First : do not leave area 4746 (Znamenka)-5342 (Zhelan'e)-5338 (Lugi) and hold it at all costs, having occupied area 4746 (Znamenka);
>
> Second: on Janury 22 our units are to enter area 2774 (Temkino) and are ordered to link up with you;
>
> Three: Belov should be aided with part of your forces, approximately two battalions;
>
> Four: at all costs halt the movement of enemy troops along the Yukhnov (6588)-Vyaz'ma (1526) high road. Zhukov.

Having received this order, the commander of the 250th Airborne Regiment made the decision to unite the 201st Airborne Brigades' 1st and 2nd battalions under the command of Capt. Surzhik; to move them to the Klyuchi area with the task of launching a blow against the enemy from the rear, so as to support the success by Gen. Belov's group.

In carrying out this assignment, Surzhik's detachment had reached Petrishchevo by 1100 on January 22 and continued to move to the south. On January 28 he linked up with Gen. Belov's 1st Guards Cavalry Corps in the Tynovka area and was operationally subordinated to him.

The 250th Airborne Regiment continued to carry out its assignment of holding the Znamenka area and block the enemy's movement along the Yukhnov-Vyaz'ma high road. On January 30 it linked up with the 1st Guards Cavalry Corps in the Glukhovo area, and on February 4, in accordance with a radiogram from the Western Front's air directorate, it was subordinated to the commander of the 239th Rifle Division, which formed part of the corps.

At this the work of the airborne detachment was completed. In the course of 12 days the detachment carried out an extremely difficult and responsible combat task and achieved significant results.

At a time when the Germans' Kondrovo-Yukhnov-Myatlevo group was encircled by our forces, the detachment cut off and heroically held over the course of several days the very important routes by which the enemy could maneuver his men and equipment. The detachment disrupted the work of the German troops' rear and eased the advance of our cavalry and rifle units to the northwest. The landing helped our troops carry out those tasks put forth by the Medyn'-Myatlevo operation.

The 43rd Army's combat operations

At the same time the airborne landings were successfully carrying out their combat operations, the 43rd Army's mission was being carried out in the following manner:

The 194th Rifle Division, having concentrated in the area of Shanskii Zavod, attacked on January 15 to the southwest. On January 16, having overcome the enemy's insignificant resistance, one of the division's regiments occupied Iznoski, another Bekleshi, and the third Domantsevo. On January 17, while pushing back small enemy groups, one of the division's regiments arrived at Izvol'sk, another occupied Tetevo, and the third arrived at Iznoski. The 194th Rifle Division's attack continued on January 18-19.

By 1500 on January 19 one regiment had captured Pupovka, another blockaded Khvoshchi, and the third was approaching Bol'shoe Semenovskoe. As it moved the division cleared the area of the enemy, but as a safeguard against unexpected occurrences, was forced to leave behind an infantry battalion each in Kuzovo and Izvol'sk. It reached Yukhnov in a weakened state.

The 43rd Army's composite regiment, operating to the left of the 194th Rifle Division, on January 13 broke into Koshnyaki station, wiped out the Fascist bridge and station security force, and destroyed the railroad permanent way. Five days after this the regiment was heroically repelling enemy attacks from the Myatlevo area, seeking to clean out the Myatlevo-Vyaz'ma sector of the railroad that had been occupied by Soviet forces. The regiment's forces melted away more and more in the unequal struggle, but it was aided by the arrival of the 53rd Rifle Division, which had been placed in the reserve following the capture of Medyn' and up until January 16 was being refitted and reinforced with weapons in Medyn'. By January 16 the 43rd Army's mission of occupying Myatlevo had not been fulfilled. This circumstance made the fulfillment of their tasks by the 50th Army and 1st Guards Cavalry Corps more difficult and drew out the conduct of the operation for encircling and destroying the enemy's Kondrovo-Yukhnov group.

This delay played into the hands of the enemy, who, taking advantage of our units' slowness was able to slip out of the encirclement. Taking this into account, the Western Front's chief of staff, Gen. Sokolovskii, in an order of January 16, demanded that the commander of the 43rd Army carry out his assignment as quickly as possible.

"The *front* commander has ordered," he wrote, "to immediately destroy the enemy along the Shanya River, capture Myatlevo and briskly develop the blow toward Yukhnov. For this purpose the 53rd Rifle Division should be rousted and thrown in to bypass the enemy defending along the Shanya River, so as to seize Myatlevo."

That same day the commander of the 43rd Army received a telegram from the commander of the Western Front, Gen. Zhukov, in which it was stated: "If you fail to carry out exactly the order to have your army's forces in the designated areas by January 16 1942, then you are frustrating the operational plan and putting the 50th Army and Belov's group into a difficult situation."

The situation along the Shanya River by this time had developed as follows: the 5th Airborne Corps, having been halted on Jauary 15 by enemy fire near Romanovo, was not able to advance. The 17th Rifle Division, with the 26th Tank Brigade, was fighting that day for Reutovo, Kosovo and Mosharovo. The 415th Rifle Division was unsuccessfully trying to take Bogdanovo and Ivanishchevo. Thus the army's core had bogged down in front of the enemy's fortifications along the Shanya River and was not in a condition to move further. Insofar as three of the 43rd Army's formations had tied town powerful enemy forces by their attacks along this sector, it was necessary to seek the resolution of the task of taking Myatlevo not in a frontal attack, but by outflanking this locale from the flank and rear. Proceeding from this, the *front* chief of staff proposed sending the 53rd Rifle Division to outflank the enemy defending Myatlevo.

At the moment the chief of staff's order and the *front* commander's telegrams were received, the division had been drawn into the fighting and was taking part in the 43rd Army's offensive against the enemy defending along the Shanya River. No less than a day was required to pull the enemy out of the battle and organize its march toward Myatlevo. The division was able to break contact with the enemy only on January 17; on January 18 it was already on the march, carrying out its assignment. Behind it, moving along another route, were five ski battalions.

At the moment when the 53rd Rifle Division was directed to outflank Myatlevo, the situation of the army's composite regiment at Koshnyaki station had become complicated and it, as a result of this, the division was forced to turn toward Koshnyaki station in order to render assistance to the composite regiment, while at the same time eliminating the possibility that the Germans could show up in its rear during the movement to Myatlevo. Fighting broke out in the area of Koshnyaki station with enemy forces that had arrived there and which were evidently searching for a way out of the encirclement being prepared for them and were thus also throwing their forces in the direction of Myatlevo and Vyaz'ma.

In an operational orientation issued by the Western Front staff on January 19, it was noted:

> Units of the enemy's LVII, XIII and XLIII army corps are in an operational encirclement, a fact which is recognized by the Germans themselves (a radio interception of January 19 1942). The enemy will attempt to break out of the encirclement. Our objective is to prevent this.

In these conditions the army's right flank, the density and firmness of our troops deployed here, acquired great significance. This density (two rifle divisions and the army's composite regiment were scattered over a 40-km front) was not great. So as to prevent the enemy from breaking out of Myatlevo, it was necessary to increase it. For this it was necessary to remove some of the troops from the group of forces that was attacking Myatlevo from the front.

On January 18 the 5th Airborne Corps was sent to the right flank. On January 19 it linked up with the composite regiment in the area of Koshnyaki station and, together with the 53rd Rifle Division, defeated the enemy troops located here. After this the 53rd Rifle Division was sent to the area where the 194th Rifle Division was fighting, while the 5th Airborne Corps and the army's composite regiment were ordered to defend the area of Koshnyaki station in order to hinder the movement of enemy forces to the west.

On January 19 the 5th Airborne Corps and the composite regiment had to withstand a stubborn battle with an enemy group (up to a regiment and a half in size), which was attempting to break out to the west in the area Trushonki-Krasnaya Polyana-Bulatovo. The enemy group was defeated and scattered in various directions.

At the same time another enemy group was attempting to break out of its encirclement through Khvoshchi; small groups of Germans were infiltrating in a westerly direction from Semenovskoe and Domanovo. The 194th and 53rd rifle divisions were routing the enemy along these routes, while the latter unit, as it cleansed the territory of Germans, gradually advanced to the southwest, increasing with its forces the density of the front, which the 194th Rifle Division had created here.

These attempts by the enemy to break out of the encirclement along the 43rd Army's right flank bespoke of the fact that the Germans did not plan to hang on to Myatlevo for long. Their main efforts now came down to getting out of the gathering encirclement as quickly as possible. Thus our forces had to more firmly lock in the enemy forces in the Myatlevo area and prevent them from getting out to the west.

As a result of this, on January 21 the 17th Rifle Division and the 18th Tank Brigade were pulled from the Myatlevo front and transferred to the army's right flank. Only the 415th Rifle Division remained facing Myatlevo, stretching its forces from Romanovo to Ivanishchevo. In the area of Koshnyaki station the 17th Rifle Division and the 18th Tank Brigade held out in a stubborn fight against the enemy's 268th Infantry Division, which was at full strength and augmented SS units.

On January 20 the enemy's more serious attempts to break the encirclement ring in the Yukhnov area began. On that day large numbers of Fascist troops attacked the 194th Rifle Division in the Pupovka area, while simultaneously pressuring those units of the 50th Army that were located at the time to the southwest of Yukhnov. The enemy sought to hang on to the Warsaw highway and secure himself from a blow to his flank and rear by the 43rd Army.

The 194th Rifle Division, under the pressure of superior forces, was forced to abandon Pupovka and organize a defense along a new line—Prisel'e-Kunovka.

The battles, which had begun along the army's right flank, unfolded from Pupovka to Myatlevo. The enemy was trying to break through to the west through Kunovka, Morozovo, Khvoshchi, Tetevo, Bulatovo, and Vorsobino. Heavy fighting was going on in all these locales, but the enemy's superiority in forces prevented our units from carrying the fighting through to a successful conclusion. The Germans were breaking through our defense and falling back to the west in small groups.

In this situation it was once again necessary to increase the pressure on Myatlevo, capture it and develop the success along the Warsaw highway, in order to get into the retreating enemy's flank and rear. The 43rd Army's forces for this were insufficient (415th Rifle Division); it was impossible to transfer units from the right flank to the given axis.

Insofar as the 33rd Army was carrying out its main mission of capturing Vereya, the *front* command decided to remove from it the 1st Guards Motorized Rifle Division and transfer it to the 43rd Army. This was supposed to strengthen the 43rd Army around Myatlevo and, as a result of joint actions by the 1st Guards Motorized Rifle Division and the 415th Rifle Division, lead to the town's fall.

The 415th Rifle Division, attacking methodically, by January 27 had reached the approaches to Myatlevo. In the evening of the same day the 1st Guards Motorized Rifle Division arrived at Myatlevo. On the night of January 28-29, following preliminary preparation, the attack on Myatlevo began.

According to the attack plan, the 415th Rifle Division organized its combat order along the left flank of the group's operational formation, with the 1st Guards Motorized Rifle Division on the right flank and in the center. The 415th Rifle Division was to demonstrate an envelopment of Myatlevo from the southeast and an outflanking maneuver from the south; the 1st Guards

Motorized Rifle Division, taking advantage of the distraction of the enemy's forces to this axis, was to launch a quick frontal blow and break into Myatlevo.

The divisions carried out their assignments exactly and at 0400 on January 29 Myatlevo was in the hands of Soviet troops. Without delaying in the captured locale and leaving the mopping up of the remains of the Fascist troops to the 415th Rifle Division, the 1st Guards Motorized Rifle Division developed the success along the Warsaw highway, pursuing and pressing the enemy's retreating forces. In the Voronki area it ran into a large German group, which put up strong resistance. Heavy fighting broke out, which blended together with the fighting that was going on at this time along the 43rd Army's right flank. The results of these actions go beyond the bounds of the Medyn'-Myatlevo operation, which may be considered to be over following the capture of Myatlevo and which constitute the content of a new operation for the enemy's destruction in the Yukhnov area.

* * *

The Germans' Kondrovo-Yukhnov-Myatlevo group, following the capture of Myatlevo and Kondrovo by our forces and the organization by the 43rd Army's forces of a barrier from the west, and the arrival of the 50th Army's forces at Yukhnov and units of the 1st Guards Cavalry Corps to the north of the Warsaw highway, was forced to try to break out of its encirclement. Its efforts were directed toward the Warsaw highway, where, southwest of Yukhnov, there were to be "gates" for those Fascist troops that had fallen into the encirclement.

From the end of January and in February fierce fighting raged in the Yukhnov area, as a result of which the enemy units were heavily worn down; their remains broke out of the encirclement and retreated to the southwest along the Warsaw highway.

Approximately half of the German forces perished while breaking out of the encirclement.

The work of the rear in the Medyn'-Myatlevo Operation

In the 43rd Army's Medyn'-Myatlevo operation the work of the army's rear is of particular interest. The operation, as we have seen, was of a peculiar character. Having begun as an offensive operation against the enemy's fortified locale and crossroads, in its development it grew into a complex combat operation—a simultaneous offensive against this locale and the encirclement of the enemy located at a remove from the neighboring troops.

The 43rd Army's encirclement actions unfolded along a significant front of 50-60 km. The delivery of the necessities to the units (ammunition, fuel, food, and forage) was a complex and difficult matter.

We had to employ light transportation means on which cargoes could be loaded for movement off the roads in winter conditions. In this sense sledge columns, moving behind the troops, performed a great service. In those places where it was impossible for ordinary horse drawn sledges to pass, aero sleighs and ski troops were dispatched. Behind the sledges were auto columns, the advance of which demanded the clearing and improvement of the roads. The 43rd Army command paid a great deal of attention to the timely fulfillment of such works.

> 15 In view of the lack of roads in the army's operational zone," we read in army order no. 48/op of January 13, the formation commanders are to put the roads in their zones into order, based on a calculation of one per rifle division.
>
> 16 The rear chief in the army' operational zone is to secure the following:
>
> a) the rebasing of all rear establishments;
>
> b) the construction of one army road;
>
> c) the restoration of existing bridges and roads.

In another order (no. 50/op of January 15 1942) the army commander demanded that the rear chief lighten the roads of transport that had built up on them. The lightness of these transports made it easier to supply the units; their accumulation on the roads unmasked the troops' work to the enemy. During the Medyn'-Myatlevo operation the question was raised of organizing transport that could have serviced units out of contact with other forces, as well as those carrying out their work in winter conditions and in the woods.

Conclusions

1 In the Medyn'-Myatlevo operation the Western Front command's plan for encircling and destroying the enemy's Kondrovo-Yukhnov-Myatlevo group was not carried through to the end.

A large German group (units of three army corps) held together as a compact mass, occupying a significant territory and interfering with the further squeezing or breaking up into parts of their combat order. Our forces needed to make great efforts in order not only to encircle the enemy group, but to break it up into individual parts, which could be enfiladed throughout by our fire. However, there were not enough forces for this, as a result of which the fighting took on a prolonged character and did not end with the complete destruction of the encircled enemy.

The 43rd Army was entrusted with a particularly difficult task—to hold against the enemy's pressure with limited forces against his attempts to break out of the encirclement to the west.

2 In the Medyn'-Myatlevo operation airborne troops were employed in conjunction with ground forces. The airborne units greatly eased the operations by the ground forces, despite the fact that the lack of organizational coordination in planning the detachments' work reduced the results of their combat activities and led to excessive losses. The experience of the airborne landings' combat actions in the Medyn'-Myatlevo operation demands:

a) a thought-out plan for the landing;
b) the preliminary and thorough reconnaissance of the terrain and enemy;
c) the exact determination of the time and depth of the landing, so that the ground forces coordinating with the landing can reach them rapidly and develop the success achieved by the landing;
d) the careful selection of personnel for the detachments and their supply with the necessary portable and powerful combat and technical equipment; the question of feeding people in the detachments should be foreseen, as well as the fight against the cold in winter conditions.

The combat employment of airborne units in the operation under study yielded the following results:

a) in two cases the employment of air drops made matters more difficult for the enemy, and at times completely excluded his maneuver of reserves;
b) the normal work of the enemy's rear was disrupted along those sectors where airborne landings were made;
c) the offensive activities of our troops were eased;
d) the encirclement of the enemy's Kondrovo-Yukhnov-Myatlevo group was speeded up;
e) aid was rendered to the 33rd Army's offensive in the direction of Vyaz'ma.

On the whole, this yielded our forces, operating on the Western Front's left wing, a number of operational advantages.

3 From the tactical point of view, one may note the following in the actions of our forces in the Medyn'-Myatlevo operation:

a) there was an exaggerated impression of the forces and capabilities of the enemy's forces. Given insufficient intelligence, this led to somewhat slower actions to encircle Medyn' and the development of the blow against Myatlevo; there were instances of standing in place, which enabled the enemy (as, for example, in Medyn') to pull out his forces even from the encircled locales.

b) the units' desire to carry out a frontal attack, head-on, against the enemy's fortified locales, despite a categorical prohibition of this. This led to an unnecessary loss of men and matériel, and a loss of time, which enabled the enemy to get out of dangerous situations he had gotten himself into. For example, we can cite the battle by units of the 5th Airborne Corps and the 17th and 415th rifle divisions along the Shanya River, which enabled the Fascists to evacuate Myatlevo.

c) the correct arrangement of forces and the expedient activities of the 1st Guards Motorized Rifle and 415th Rifle divisions in taking Myatlevo on January 29: their combined activities were so organized so that they distracted the enemy's attention and forces from the axis of the main blow, which the 1st Guards Motorized Rifle Division quickly and decisively delivered.

4 The Medyn'-Myatlevo operation also draws attention to the toughness and bravery of our troops, who were able in the conditions of a harsh winter, through deep snow and blizzards, to pursue the enemy at night, break his resistance and, in an extremely complex situation, defeat and destroy the enemy.

5 The work of the rear organs is worthy of particular attention and study. In encirclement battles, involving the movement of units over great distances over territory without roads, this work acquires serious significance; its experience should be taken into account in organizing similar work in the future.

10

The 33rd Army's offensive on Vyaz'ma for the purpose of splitting the enemy front

The situation along the central sector by the middle of January 1942

By the middle of January 1942 the situation along the central sector of the Western Front was developing in the following manner: our forces had seized the enemy's large strong point—Dorokhovo. The 5th Army's forces, aimed at Mozhaisk, were taking up position along the flank and were threatening to get into the rear of the enemy's Vereya group. Mozhaisk and Vereya were on the verge of falling. The enemy was hurriedly withdrawing his rear services and troops from here in the direction of Gzhatsk, where he inteneded, based on Vyaz'ma, to organize a new line of resistance.

On January 13 the 43rd Army's composite regiment occupied Koshnyaki station, destroyed the German security force here, and destroyed the permanent way of the Vyaz'ma-Myatlevo railroad. The flow of enemy supplies and personnel, which had earlier moved along this route, now went along the Warsaw highway to Yukhnov. In the German command's plans, Yukhnov (based on Zanoznaya station) was supposed to play the same role as a large center of resistance as Gzhatsk. Zanoznaya and Vyaz'ma were linked by a lateral railroad, along which two enemy groups, facing the Western Front's central sector, coordinated.

The main groups of German forces facing the Western Front's center in the middle of January 1942 were concentrated along the Gzhatsk axis and in the area of Yukhnov. There were few German troops between them, and these were only covering the routes to Vyaz'ma from the east.

At this time the 50th Army was fighting along the approaches to Yukhnov, and the 1st Guards Cavalry Corps was approaching the Warsaw highway north of Mosal'sk.

In such conditions it was becoming less necessary for the 33rd Army (following the capture of Vereya) to attack toward Yel'nya and Gzhatsk and in the rear of the enemy's Gzhatsk group; it was more profitable to employ the army for a deeper blow—toward Vyaz'ma, where the 1st Guards Cavalry Corps was aiming from Mosal'sk. At this time the Kalinin Front was developing its successful offensive from the north and getting into the rear of the Gzhatsk-Vyaz'ma German group.

With the occupation of Vyaz'ma, the enemy's Gzhatsk group would be cut off from its base and the coordination between two large enemy groups based on Vyaz'ma and Zanoznaya station would be disrupted.

Insofar as the 33rd Army's Vereya operation was coming to an end, the prospect of shifting part of the army's forces from Vereya and movin them toward Vyaz'ma presented itself to the *front* command.

In his telegram no. K-49, of January 17 1942, the *front* commander put the 33rd Army commander into the picture, and demanding from him "simultaneously with the elimination of the enemy in Vereya, the army's main forces are to be moved to the Dubna-Zamytskoe area from the morning of January 19, with the subsequent task, depending on the situation, of launching a blow toward Vyaz'ma or outflanking it from the south."

The *front* commander ordered the forward units to reach the Dubna-Zamytskoe area no later than January 19, and the main forces on January 20; the advance of the ski troops in front of these units should be organized.

The 33rd Army commander's measures for organising the offensive

On January 17, the day the he received the *front* commander's directive, the 33rd Army commander issued the following order (no. 021, of January 17 1942).

1 The 33rd Army's offensive on Yel'nya has been cancelled by the *front* commander because it is late.

2 To the right the 5th Army is trying to capture Mozhaisk. The boundary line with the army is the same as before as far as Novo-Nikol'skoe, and then (excluding) Vaulino-Vyaz'ma. The 194th Rifle Division to the left of the 33rd Army, not encountering any particular resistance by the enemy, has captured the area Iznoski-Koshnyaki and is attacking toward Yukhnov.

3 A favorable situation has developed for the 33rd Army to quickly advance to the Vyaz'ma area, into the rear of the enemy's Vyaz'ma group.
Simultaneous with the elimination of the enemy in Vereya, the army's main forces are to make forced marches from the morning of January 17 and to reach the area Dubna-Zamytskoe, with the subsequent task, depending on the situation, of launching a blow on Vyaz'ma or outflanking it from the southwest.
The army's forward units are to arrive in the Dubna-Zamytskoe area no later than January 19 1942, and the main forces on January 20 1942.
I order:

a) the 93rd Rifle Division, while destroying the opposing enemy, is to immediately begin a movement to the west and by the end of January 17 is to reach the area: L'vovo-Zhikharevo-Sverdlovo; by the close of January 18 it is to reach the area: Mochal'niki-Dryablovo-Kuzova; by the close of January 19 it is to concentrate in the area Dubna-Prokopovo-Stepanchiki.
The attack zone is as follows: to the right—Novo-Aleksandrovka-Nikitskoe-(excluding) Khoroshevo-(excluding) Shugailovo-(excluding) Mochal'niki-(excluding) Ostroluch'e-(excluding) Yurovka; to the left—Gol'tyaevo-Nosonovo-(excluding) Petrovsk-Kositsk-Lutkino-(excluding) Musino-Lukovo.

b) the 338th Rifle Division, while destroying the opposing enemy, is to immediately begin a movement to the west and by the end of January 17 is to reach the area Kremenskoe-Troitskoe-Ragozino; by the end of January 18 it is to reach the area Bekleshi-Podzharovka-Fokino; by the end of January 19 it is to concentrate in the area Zamytskoe-Korkodinovo-Vorkresensk.
The attack zone is as follows: to the right—the left boundary with the 93rd Rifle Division; to the left—Asen'evskoe-(excluding) Medyn'-(excluding) Kukushkino-Zamytskoe.

c) the 222nd Rifle Division, while destroying the enemy in the Myatlevo area and along the northern outskirts of Vereya, is to begin a movement to the west and by the end of January 17 is to reach the area Kulakovo-Kurlovo-Yefimovo; by the end of January 19 it is to reach the area Masalovka-Mikhalevo-Sorokino; by the end of January 20 it is to concentrate in the area Semenovskoe-Metrenino-Kozlakovo.

The boundary to the left is (excluding) Vereya-Arkhangel'sk-Mar'ina-(excluding) Raevo-Mikhailovo-(excluding) Motovkino-(excluding) Savinki.

d) the 1st Guards Motorized Rifle Division, having destroyed the enemy and captured Vereya in conjunction with the 113th Rifle Division, is to immediately begin a movement to the west and by the end of January 17 is to reach the area Fedyushkino-Kurlovo-Kamenka; by the end of January 18 it is to reach the area Nikitskoe-L'vovo-Shimnovo; by the end of January 19 it is to concentrate in the area Mochal'niki-Terekhovo-Yesovtsy. The attack zone is as follows: to the right—the boundary with the 222nd Rifle Division; to the left—Vereya-Kurnevo-Novo-Aleksandrovka-Valyutino-Skorodinka-(excluding) Semena-(excluding) Shanskii Zavod-Mar'ino-(excluding) Ogarevo-Zamyatino-Bulgakovo.

e) the 113th Rifle Division, having destroyed the enemy and occupied Vereya in conjunction with the 1st Guards Motorized Rifle Division, is to immediately begin a movement to the west and by the end of January 17 is to reach the area Vasilevo-Popovo-Y astrebevo; by the end of January 18 it is to reach the area Kukanovka-Troitskoe-Bryukhovo; by the end of January 19 it is to reach the area Shanskii Zavod-Nikulino; by the end of January 20 it is to concentrate in the area Kuznetsovo-Voinovo-Shumovo. The attack zone is as follows: to the right—the left boundary with the 1st Guards Motorized Rifle Division; to the left—the right boundary with the 338th Rifle Division.

f) the 110th Rifle Division, while aiding the capture of Vereya by the 113th Rifle and 1st Guards Motorized Rifle divisions, is to concentrate in the Vereya area by the end of January 17 in readiness on the morning of January 18 to begin a march along the route Vereya-Kamenka-Shustikovo-Nikitskoe-Sleptsovo-Masalovka. By the close of January 18 it is to reach the area Kryukovo-Shustikovo; by the end of January 19 it is to reach the area Peredel-Rakitskoe, and; by the close of January 20 it is to concentrate in the area Masalovka-Mikhalevo-Dar'ino.

4 Use the absence of significant enemy forces along this axis, in order to advance powerful ski detachments, infantry, and individual guns on sledges and tanks.

5 The division commanders, aside from sending troop reconnaissance and security units forward, are obliged to organize the reconnaissance of the routes by sappers and chemical troops.

6 The axis of the army headquarters' movement is Borovsk-Vereya-Shanskii Zavod.

The 1st Guards Motorized Rifle Division, in the process of organizing its march, was informed of a change in its movement—it was subordinated to the commander of the 43rd Army and was to take part in the attack on Myatlevo; the remaining divisions were to carry out their assignments in accordance with the 33rd Army commander's order no. 021.

The 33rd Army's attack toward Vyaz'ma

At the time they received the order of the 33rd Army commander for the movement of part of the divisions to a new concentration area for the offensive on Vyaz'ma, the army's forces were fighting around Vereya; a certain amount of time was required to break contact with the enemy and organize a march to the designate area. The first to depart was the 93rd Rifle Division on the night of January 18-19. On January 20 the 1st Guards Motorized Rifle Division, 113th and 338th rifle divisions, following the capture of Vereya, were marching to their new concentration area (the first of these, according to the *front* commander's instructions, was being sent to strengthen the 43rd Army).

On January 22 the 33rd Army (except for the 110th Rifle Division, which remained behind in Vereya) was marching to its new area. The enemy sought to hinder the troops' movement and repeatedly bombed our columns.

On this day the 113th Rifle Division was attacked on the march in the Shanskii Zavod area by a group of enemy automatic riflemen from Shevnevo, although it beat off their attack and held on to Shanskii Zavod. The division, having left a covering force here, continued its march to the west.

On January 23 the 93rd Rifle Division had concentrated in the Iznoski area, from where the 113th Rifle Division's forward units began to move into the Temkino area; the 338th Rifle Division at this time was located in the area Volkovo-Melent'evo-Volyntsy; the remaining divisions were en route to their concentration areas.

On the night of January 23-24 the 222nd Rifle Division, on the march, ran into the enemy, who had fortified in the Ponomarikhi area. Fighting broke out, which became prolonged. Further reconnaissance established that besides Ponomarikhi, the enemy had strong points in the villages of Vozzhikhino, Shevnevo, Mochal'niki, Orekhovnya, Khimino, Chelishchevo, and Ivanovskoe, that is, along the route of the majority of the 33rd Army's divisions moving to the west. Thus the divisions, in their movements, were delayed in order to eliminate the enemy's resistance that cropped up en route.

Besides the 222nd Rifle Division, on January 23 the 110th Rifle Division was also forced to deploy a single regiment and engage in fighting in the Vozzhikhino area and was also ordered to proceed to a new area.

In these battles (and they occurred during the following days) the 33rd Army's divisions usually defeated the enemy's small units, but each such battle distracted the troops moving to the west from their assigned goal. As a result of this, the 33rd Army's formations were widely strung out on the march and, for example, we have the following situation as of January 26:

> The 222nd Rifle Division was fighting for Rodionkovo, Yesovtsy, and Voditskoe.
>
> The 110th Rifle Division (minus a regiment transferred to the 222nd Rifle Division) was fighting for Shevnevo, Azarovo, and Vodop'yanovo.
>
> The 160th Rifle Division, which had been included in the 33rd Army, attacked Nekrasovo, from which it was to then take up position on the army's left flank.
>
> The 93rd Rifle Division had reached the Gzhatsk-Yukhnov high road in the area of Ugryumovo station.
>
> The 113th Rifle Division occupied Vyazishche and Lushchikhino at 1500, bypassing the enemy in Ivanovskoe.
>
> The 338th Rifle Division occupied Voskresensk and Mamushi at 0800 and, failing to meet serious German resistance, continued to attack in the direction of Zamytskoe.

The enemy sought to delay our troops' offensive, and being unable to do this to the first-echelon divisions, strengthened his attacks on the army's second and third echelons.

On January 26 the commander of the Western Front, in his directive no K-83, explained to the 33rd Army commander that on that morning the Kalinin Front's cavalry group, reinforced with motorized infantry, had arrived 12 km west of Vyaz'ma and cut the railroad and all the German troops' withdrawal routes.

The *front* commander demanded that the 33rd Army commander "reach the area Krasnyi Kholm-Gredyakino-Podrezovo by forced march and link up with an airborne landing by the 4th Airborne Corps and the Kalinin Front's cavalry."

The same directive demanded that the commander of the 1st Guards Cavalry Corps, having broken through the enemy front, to advance to Semlevo station (west of Vyaz'ma), while the commanders of the 43rd and 50th armies were tasked with speeding up the capture of Yukhnov, after which, having left a portion of their forces to eliminate the defeated enemy, were to reach the area southwest of Vyaz'ma with their main forces.

On January 27 the 113th and 338th rifle divisions, without meeting enemy resistance, captured: 113th Rifle Division—Skotinino, and the 338th Rifle Division—Dorofeevo and Kobelevo. At this time the 222nd, 110th and 93rd rifle divisions were fighting and coming under enemy air attack in their former areas—Dubna-Trosna-Mochal'niki. The weather on that day (down to -35 Celsius), as in the following days, made the troops' activities more difficult; the necessary results were achieved with a great loss of time, which, of course, did not facilitate an improvement in the overall situation.

January 28 was approximately a repetition of the preceding day. On that day the 113th Rifle Division reached the Kuznetsovka-Morozovo area, and the 338th Rifle Division the area Fedotkovo-Buslava-Abramovo, while the 160th Rifle Division moved by forced march to the west, and the 222nd, 110th and 93rd rifle divisions remained in their previous locations—the area of Dubna-Trosna-Mochal'niki—and continued to engage in fighting with the enemy that, for the time being, failed to yield tangible results.

On January 31 the 33rd Army continued to carry out the *front* commander's assignment.

The Germans, having concentrated in the area Trosna-Mochal'niki-Khimino three-four infantry regiments from various divisions, which had been operating here earlier, sought by an attack on Iznoski to cut the Shanskii Zavod-Iznoski road and delay the advance of the army's main body to the southwest. On January 31 the enemy air became more active, subjecting the army's combat and march columns to a fierce bombardment.

By this time one of the 113th Rifle Division's regiments had reached Dashkovka, another Stukolovo, and the third Zheltovka; the 338th Rifle Division's forward regiment occupied Gorby; the 160th Rifle Division reached the area Korshuntsy-Lyadnoe. The remaining divisions, while fighting the enemy, moved slowly to the west.

During January 31 the 33rd Army had to wage a bitter defensive battle with an enemy group, which was trying to attack to the south from the area Trosna-Khimino. This did not halt the advance by the army's forward divisions toward Vyaz'ma.

On the night of February 1-2 they occupied jumping off positions for the attack on Vyaz'ma: the 113th Rifle Division—the area Dashkovka-Yastrebovo, with the direction of attack toward Boznya; the 160th Rifle Division—the woods southwest of Lyado, with the direction of attack toward Alekseevskoe; the 338th Rifle Division—the woods to the west of Vorob'evka, with the direction of attack toward Kazakovo and Yamskaya.

On February 2 stubborn fighting broke out for Vyaz'ma in the Alekseevskoe area. On February 3 the 33rd Army's units around Vyaz'ma (in the Stogovo area) came into contact and established close communications with units of the 1st Guards Cavalry Corps, which endowed the struggle for Vyaz'ma with the character of a large engagement; it goes in time beyond the boundaries of our description.

At the moment when the fighting for Vyaz'ma was unfolding, echeloned behind those divisions that were attacking Vyaz'ma were the 33rd Army's divisions advancing under combat to the west.

The enemy's important lines of retreat—the Kondrovo-Vyaz'ma and Zanoznaya-Vyaz'ma railroads and the Yukhnov-Vyaz'ma and Temkino Znamenka high roads were cut by the army's forward units and the air drop made on January 20 in the Znamenka area. The enemy's front had been split; our forces were located between his main groups—Gzhatsk and Yukhnov. The Kalinin Front was successfully developing its attack on Vyaz'ma from the north. Its cavalry corps cut the railroad and auto road west of Vyaz'ma. The Germans were in a difficult situation. Such an advance opened before us the prospect of new offensive operations against the flank and rear of the enemy's main groups on the Western Front.

However, such a deep advance by the 33rd Army into the Germans' depth along a narrow front harbored within itself the danger of an attack against our flanks. It was necessary to prevent this; in this connection, the question arose of widening the breach and preventing the enemy from carrying out attacks against our flanks.

The fight for Vyaz'ma was a new page in the 33rd Army's combat work; its development lies outside the boundaries of our description.

Conclusions

The 33rd Army's offensive to Vyaz'ma, for the purpose of splitting the enemy's front, deserves great attention for the daring of its realization and the valor of the troops.

It is necessary to note the following chief points in the offensive under study:

1 We sometimes underestimated the enemy. The *front's* demand that "the army's main forces are to be moved to the area Dubna-Zamytskoe from the morning of January 19" assumed that the Vereya-Dubna-Zamytskoe sector of the front was free of the enemy, while there were actually large German forces in the area, which disrupted the army's planned realization of its offensive maneuver.

2 The realization of the assigned task demanded of the army its strict adherence to a time regime and rapidity of movement. Taking into account the distance (about 60 km) and the conditions of the situation, the army commander designated the movement for January 17. However, there was still fighting for Vereya going on at this time, in connection with which the movement was begun only on the night of January 18-19. Because of this, it was impossible to reach the designated area according to schedule. The army commander's combat order and the division's actual movements were thus out of sync with each other.

3 The movement of the troops in accordance with the 33rd Army commander's order no. 021 unfolded in an insufficiently organized manner; the divisions' main forces kept running into the enemy, which speaks of poor intelligence during the march.

4 There was no sense of firm control by the army command in the operation's conduct: some divisions advanced far ahead and ended up near Vyaz'ma itself, while others were delayed by the enemy and only managed to advance a short way from Vereya. The army, like a needle, penetrated into the enemy's body, but this cut was not fatal for him. By January 31 the army was spread out along a front approximately 30 km in width and about 80 in depth.

5 The *front* command, having assigned the army such a responsible task as the splitting of the enemy front, was unable to reinforce it with new units from the reserve; the breakthrough sector was not widened; in view of this, the 33rd Army's flanks were always under the threat of attack by the enemy.

6 The 33rd Army sought to carry out its assignment amidst hard frosts and a deep snow cover; in such conditions the forward units of the 113th, 338th and 160th rifle divisions covered a distance of 80-90 km in 12 days in fighting. This further increases their services to the Motherland in such a responsible and honorable cause.

11

Rear area organization and supply

As a result of the successful advance of the Red Army's units during the second half of December the necessity of a new rear organization became imperative.

The condition and organization of the *Front's* rear by December 25 1941

The organization of the rear by December 25 1941 was outlined in a directive by the deputy *front* commander for rear affairs of December 22 1941. According to this directive, the *front's* rear boundary was laid down along the line: Aleksandrov-Ryazan'-Ryazhsk; the boundary line with the Kalinin Front was Reshetnikovo station-Kotlyakovo-Sychevka, and with the Southwestern Front the line Malevka-Plavsk-Belev (all locales within the Western Front).

The location of the *front's* distribution stations and main bases did not change. As before, it was believed that until the troops reached the line Pogoreloe Gorodishche-Gzhatsk-Myatlevo, the existing location of the *front's* bases would guarantee the troops' supply.

In the capacity of a maneuverable reserve for the deputy *front* commander, it was decided to create branches of the *front* field depots with small amounts of food and grain feed along the line Khimki-Pavshino-Odintsovo-Podol'sk-Serpukhov. On the *front's* left wing, where as a result of the rapid advance by our troops, the delivery conditions grew worse, and *front* field depots of fuel and ammunition were established in the Tula area.

Simultaneously, preparations were being made to transfer the *front* bases to the west of Moscow to the areas where the branch ends were located, which it was planned to do once the troops reached the line Gzhatsk-Kaluga.

The following instructions were issued concerning the organization of basing.

1st Army—up to December 24 the army base was in the Solnechnogorsk area, and from December 26 in the Klin area; the head branch of the base for road deliveries was in the area of Teryaeva Sloboda and Suvorovo.

The army's supply route led through Solnechnogorsk, Klin, Vysokovskii, Teryaeva Sloboda, and Suvorovo. The army's distribution station was at Klin station.

20th Army—it was ordered to create an army base in the Istra area and the head branches of the army field depots in the area of Lesodolgorukovo.

The army's supply route led through the Moscow-Volokolamsk road, along with that of the 16th Army. In order to receive supplies from Moscow, until the bridge at Istra could be restored, the army was allowed to use the roads: Tushino, Mar'ino, Pyatnitsa, Nudol', Novopetrovskoe, Volokolamsk. The the army's distribution station was at Istra station.

16th Army—the army was ordered to establish an army base in the Kholshcheviki area. Aside from this, the army was ordered to have supplies in the Tarkhanovo area.

The army's supply route led through the Volokolamsk road (along with the 20th Army) as far as Yadromino and then over the road: Skirmanovo-Pokrovskoe-Tarkhanovo. The army's distribution station was located at Kholshcheviki.

5th Army—the army was ordered to establish an army base in the area of Kuntsevo and Golitsyno, and head branches in the area of Dorokhovo.

The army's supply route led through the Mozhaisk highway. The army's distribution station was at Kuntsevo station.

33rd Army—the army was ordered to establish a base in the area of Vnukovo and Krekshino and head branches in the Bakasovo area.

The army's supply route was the Naro-Fominsk road. The army's distribution station was at Vnukovo station.

43rd Army—the army was ordered to establish a base in the area of Podol'sk and Domodedovo, with head branches in the Kamenka area.

The army's supply route ran through Domodedovo, Podol'sk, Kamenka, and Maloyaroslavets. The army's distribution station, shared with the 49th Army, was Podol'sk station.

49th Army—the army was ordered to establish a base in the area of Sharapova Okhota, and Serpukhov, upon its units reaching the line Maloyaroslavets-Kaluga, with supplies in the area of Chernaya Gryaz' and Nedel'noe.

The army's supply route was Serpukhov-Chernaya Gryaz'-Vysokinichi.

50th Army—the army was ordered to establish a base in the Tula area and head branches in the Aleksin area. Besides these, the army was to have spllies in the areas of Krosno and Makarovo.

The army's supply route was Tula-Aleshnya-Gryaznovo-Makarovo. The army's distribution station was Tula station.

Supply for Gen. Belov's cavalry group was entrusted to the 50th Army apparatus. In order to improve its transportation service, the *front* from its reserve gave the 50th Army 150 motor vehicles, including 50 fuel-supply trucks.

10th Army—the army was ordered to establish a base in the area of Uzlovaya and Dedilovo, with head branches at Yasnaya Polyana station and Shchekino.

The army's supply route was Shchekino-Retinovka-Krapivna-Odoevo-Belev. The army's distribution station was Shchekino station.

In conclusion, one must emphasize that this new basing was organized for the purpose of securing the further offensive by our troops. The deputy *front* commander for the rear's directive of December 22 sought to eliminate the abnormal situation which obtained during the first period of the offensive, which saw the basing of several armies on one railroad or, just the opposite, the basing of a single army on several railroads, which broke the front up into strips. Individual shortcomings were later eliminated by a *front* order and the army commands. However, even after this the basing of several armies was poor.

One cannot, for example, consider the organization of the 20th Army's rear area to be fortunate. Its army base ended up being located in the rear area of its neighbor to the left, as a result of which the army was deprived of its own supply route. The army's auxiliary automobile road ran for a significant distance along its neighbor's rear area. All of this created difficulties in delivery, although expanding the 20th Army's rear area to the left could have eliminated these shortcomings.

The directive by the deputy *front* commander for the rear was carried out late in some armies, particularly in the matter of deploying railhead base branches.

The condition and disposition of the Front's matériel means by December 25 1941

By the end of December the difficulties in supplying the troops with ammunition, fuel, and other needs had increased to a significant degree in connection with the hard frosts and snow cover.

Despite all the efforts of the workers in the rear, who had carried out the mass production of munitions in the evacuated factories, as well as the measures adopted to increase the delivery of ammunition to the bases and troops, their supplies at all levels were shrinking. Besides the difficulties with delivery, the decline in supplies was also caused by the sharp increase in their expenditure in a number of armies.

On the average the army bases contained 1-1.5 combat loads of the most popular types of munitions. The prospects for quickly increasing this amount were far from rosy. Table 1, compiled on the basis of data by the second section of the directorate of the front's artillery chief, shows the condition of the *front* bases as of December 25 1941.

Table V/11.1 Condition of Western Front bases as of December 25 1941

Type of round	On hand (in thousands)	Average daily expenditure (in thousands)	Planned delivery by the end of the month (in thousands)
50mm mortar	20	5.5	–
82mm mortar	11.5	7	–
107mm mortar	2.1	1.2	–
45mm gun	50	3.5	–
76mm regimental gun	7.8	2	2
76mm divisional gun	2.2	5.8	2.7
107mm gun	7.9	0.3	–
122mm howitzer	7.6	5.1	12

The *front* was completely lacking rounds for 152mm guns at its bases.

The table shows that with the exception of 45mm anti-tank and tank artillery rounds, and 50mm mortar rounds, the availability of ammunition was completely insufficient to ensure their unbroken supply to the troops. The actual situation was even worse, because only a part of those supplies planned by the end of the month had actually been received.

The Western Front's provision with the most important and popular types of ammunition by January 1 1942 is shown in table V/11.2.

It is clear from the table that the *front's* provision with mortar rounds of all calibers, as well as rounds for regimental and divisional artillery was insufficient. The *front* was poorly supplied with ammunition for howitzer artillery, which was particularly necessary in an offensive.

Some armies were supplied even worse with ammunition. By the end of January 1 1942 there remained not a single round for regimental artillery in the 16th Army's depots; there remained only 1,000 rounds for the divisional artillery and 400 for the 152mm howitzers. There were very few large-caliber mortar rounds.

The situation was a little bit better in the 33rd and 43rd armies. However, the latter lacked 45mm artillery rounds in its army depots, which would place it in a dangerous situation in the event of a massed tank attack by the enemy.

Until the latter half of December the *front's* provision of food and fuel was quite normal. By the end of December, because of difficulties in delivery and the sharp increase in the expenditure of fuel, its supplies, particularly auto fuel, declined.

The Western Front's supply of fuel, food, and forage as of January 1 1942, is shown in table V/11.3.

Table V/11.2 Western Front's supply of ammunition as of January 1 1942

Type	In the Front base		In the Army bases[1]		With the troops	
	in thousands	in combat loads	in thousands	in combat loads	in thousands	in combat loads
Rifle-machine gun rounds	7,660	0.13	60,000	1.1	68,910	1.05
50mm mortar	3.7	0.01	181.3	0.6	225.3	0.7
82mm mortar	0	0	49.3	0.26	114.2	0.6
107mm mortar	2.1	0.15	9.8	0.75	1.8	0.15
120mm mortar	0	0	5.8	0.58	6.2	0.6
45mm gun	603	3	187.6	0.9[2]	250	1
76mm regimental gun	16	0.25[3]	16.7	0.25	69.3	1.1
76mm divisional gun	0	0	19.7	0.25	101	1
107mm gun	8	2.3	10	3	–	–
122mm howitzer	7.6	0.25	27.2	0.9	11.7	0.32
152mm howitzer	10.7	0.5	10.8	0.5	4.8	0.25

Notes
1 Not counting the 50th Army.
2 Without data on the 50th, 49th and 20th armies. Actually, the level of supply was higher.
3 Other figures are contained in some other documents.

Table V/11.3 Western Front's supply of fuel as of January 1 1942[1]

	In Front depots		In Army depots		With the troops	
	In tons	In rations	In tons	In rations	In tons	In rations
KB-70 (cracking fuel)	136	0.5	2,207	11		
Auto fuel	578	0.2	1,521	0.75		1-2[2]
Diesel fuel	799	1.75	663	1.3		
Flour, sugar, bread	1,673	3.2	4,310	8.7	–	–
Groats, macaroni	240	2.4	325	3.25	–	–
Sugar	–	–	207.3	7	–	–
Fats	12	0.2	42.7	1.1		[3]
Meat	–	–	191	0.7	–	–
Concentrates	128[4]	–	492.5	1.5-2	–	–
Oats	2,297	–	2,107	–	–	–

Notes
1 Not including the 50th Army. The equipment is as of December 23.
2 This is a collective figure, which includes KB-70 fuel, auto fuel, and diesel fuel.
3 This is a collective figure representing all foodstuffs.
4 The first helping is the numerator and the second is the denominator.

It is clear from the table that the *front's* overall level of supply of the most important kinds of fuel—automobile fuel and diesel fuel—was insufficient. The situation was complicated by the extremely uneven distribution of fuel among the armies. The 5th Army had 1.6 refuels in its army depots and about two refuels with the troops. At the same time the neighboring 16th Army, which was carrying out highly important operational tasks in January, had only 0.4 refills in its army depots and about one refill with the troops. Almost half of all army supplies of diesel fuel (270 tons, or four refills) were with the 20th Army, at the same time the 16th Army had only 0.5 refills, that is for a day and a half of work for those vehicles running on diesel fuel. The slightest breakdowns in delivery, which were quite possible even in the best weather and good road conditions, could place the 16th Army in a critical situation.

Given the *front's* overall sufficient supply of flour and groats (given another dish of concentrated food) and sugar, the food supplies in some armies were quite limited. On January 3 the 50th Army had only one ration of flour. Many of the *front's* armies lacked sugar, fats, and meat.

In regard to the situation, the deputy commander for the rear wrote in his conclusions to a January 1 1942 report:

> It is necessary to immediately deliver to the front mortar rounds, regimental and divisional artillery rounds, automobile fuel, fats, tobacco, and sugar.

The disposition of matériel supplies available to the *front* as of January 1 1942 was more even than in the beginning of December 1941. A December 22 1941 directive by the deputy *front* commander for rear affairs noted the approach of *front* and army depots to the troops, which was particularly important in an offensive operation.

Routes, delivery means, and their condition

Within the *front's* boundaries there were six main rail routes and three secondary ones, which could be used for the operational transport and transfer of military cargoes. As for delivery by automobile transportation, there were seven good paved roads and a number of secondary ones of local significance. Besides the paved roads there were a large number of good dirt roads.

The armies in the center were better supplied with roads, with the ones on the wings comparatively worse off. The rapid advance by our units along the left wing at the end of December and the first half of January, the destruction of the railroads and roads by the enemy, as well as of the bridges on the dirt roads, placed the rear of this wing's armies in a difficult situation.

The subsequent offensive by the center and right-wing armies during the latter half of January raised the problem of rapidly restoring the railroads and the paved and dirt roads along the entire front. Without this it would be impossible to guarantee the unbroken deliver of supplies for the troops.

The wintry conditions created a number of additional difficulties. The restoration of the roads and bridges was delayed as a result of the snow drifts, which demanded the organization of snow defense and the timely removal of snow.

The *front* rear directorate carried out a great deal of work toward rapidly restoring the supply routes. In the middle of January the People's Commissariat of Transport, which was in charge of restoring the railroads, was assigned concrete tasks, with instructions as to what speed this or that railroad should be restored. Simultaneously, intensive work was being conducted on the formation of road-construction and bridge-construction battalions, as well as carpentry battalions.

The hard frosts and deep snow cover delayed the restoration of the roads, especially of the railroads. The Tula-Uzlovaya rail sector was opened for traffic on December 31, while the Uzlovaya-Volovo sector was opened only in the first half of January.

By January 10 1942 traffic was restored on the Kalinin railroad as far as Manikhino station; the Moscow-Belorussia railroad as far as Kubinka station; the Kiev railroad as far as Naro-Fominsk station; the Dzerzhinskii railroad as far as Samozvanka station, and; in the direction Gorbachevo-Belev, as far as Vezhenka station. By January 20 traffic had been restored on the Moscow-Donbas railroad along the Ozherel'e-Uzlovaya sector; the Kalinin railroad as far as Rumyantsev station; the

Western railroad as far as Tuchkovo station, and; the Moscow-Kiev railroad as far as Obninskoe station.

The slow speed of rail restoration led to the troops becoming separated from their bases and an increase in the supply route over the roads. As a result, the volume of deliveries by automobile transportation grew at the same time that its work conditions became more and more difficult. The *front's* transportation equipment did not grow in correspondence to the growth in the volume and increasing difficulty of its work.

The availability and technical condition of the *front's* transport units (translated into GAZ-AA trucks) are shown in table V/11.4 (minus automobile transport for troops, special units, and services).

Table V/11.4 Western Front's transport units, January 1 1942

Unit	By January 1, 1942			
	Auto transport		Horse-drawn transport battalions	
	Total	In operation	Working	Not ready for work
Western Front	1,749	1,448	–	–
1st Army	365	310	–	–
20th Army	300	200	–	–
16th Army	233	233[1]	–	1
5th Army	503	422	–	–
33rd Army	450	350	1	1[2]
43rd Army	774	774[3]	–	–
49th Army	186	145	1	–
50th Army	651	454	1	–
10th Army	528	528[4]	1	–
61st Army	–	–	–	–
TOTAL	5,739	4,864	4	2

Notes

1 For lack of data regarding its technical condition, the army's entire complement is counted as being in operation.

2 The battalion was being accepted by the army in its formation area.

3 For lack of data regarding its technical condition, the army's entire complement is counted as being in operation.

4 For lack of data regarding its technical condition, the army's entire complement is counted as being in operation.

It is clear from the table that the *front's* auto transport increased only by 25% for the first half of January, while at the same time the delivery distance over the paved and dirt roads increased to a significantly greater degree. Aside from this, the arrival of the hard frosts and frequent blizzards sharply lowered the effectiveness of the automobile transportation's work.

The doubling of the number of horse-drawn transport battalions did not bring about any fundamental changes. Because of the poor care of the horses along the route and their poor forage supply, the battalions would come under *front* control with an exhausted horse complement. In the first half of January there were essentially no fully capable horse-drawn transport battalions. In the second half the situation with horse-drawn transport improved; the battalions, having harnesses and sledges took up their full-time duties.

Table V/11.5 Western Front's transport units, January 15 1942

Unit	By January 1, 1942			
	Auto transport		Horse-drawn transport battalions	
	Total	In operation	Working	Not ready for work
Western Front	2,640	2,063	1	–
1st Army	409	368	1	–
20th Army	265	145	–	–
16th Army	191	163	1	–
5th Army	560	560[1]	–	1
33rd Army	325	325[2]	1	–
43rd Army	927	810	–	–
49th Army	431	367	1	–
50th Army	526	443	–	1
10th Army	872	747	1	–
61st Army	–	–	–	2
TOTAL	7,156	5,991	6	4

Notes
1 For lack of data regarding its technical condition, the army's entire complement is counted as being in operation.
2 For lack of data regarding its technical condition, the army's entire complement is counted as being in operation.

By January the *front's* transportation equipment had been significantly better distributed than in December. With the exception of the 49th Army, the *front's* left wing was relatively better supplied with auto transport than the other directions. Three quarters of the horse-drawn transportation battalions were in the left-wing armies, were they were especially needed.

An extremely difficult situation arose with supplying the *front* with special automobile transport. Within the fuel supply companies there was a 70-75% shortage of authorized fuel trucks. The *front* required more than 400 additional vehicles to fill out its medical transport. The situation in some armies was even worse: the 20th Army had 15 medical vehicles and the 5th Army all of ten, instead of the authorized number of 90.

The command and the rear area workers searched for a way out of the existing vehicle delivery situation by improving the work of the available transport and in more fully employing the railroads, as well as employing local horse-drawn transport for work at the troop and army level.

The *front* command, in its December 22 directive no. 027 to the armies' military councils, demanded the complete employment of division auto transport, freeing it from hauling cargo unnecessary at the present time. Simultaneously, the army rear chiefs were ordered "to guarantee the maintenance and servicing of the two-way auto roads" through a strictly-organized traffic control service.

Concern for road cleaning and repair in the troop rear, the organization of a traffic regulation and lighting system for them, were entrusted to the formation commanders.

A December 22 *front* command directive was particularly valuable, but its fulfillment in the first half of January was slowed down by the almost complete absence of road-exploitation units. Without them it proved impossible to establish clear-cut order along the army supply routes and to observe a movement schedule. The shortage of road-exploitation units also told negatively.

The local population readily responded to the command's appeal to help the troops in repairing roads, in organizing their defense against snow, and cleaning up obstructions and snow. However, special people, that is, road units, were needed to rationally employ the local population; but the central authorities did not send them.

During the second half of December, the *front*, having received permission from the center, independently set about forming road-exploitation and other rear units from older age groups.

The formation of road units went quite quickly.

The availability and technical condition of the *front's* road units in January 1942, and their distribution, is shown in table V/11.5.

In the first half of January there were only five road-exploitation battalions, while there were 19 in the second half; with the exception of the 5th Army, all the others now had road-exploitation regiments. This was secured by the matériel base for creating well-equipped roads and the organization of precise order along them, without which, as experience has shown, the effective employment of automobile transport is unthinkable.

The amount of road-exploitation battalions did not increase in January, but in the second half of January they became more full-bodied and were better supplied with tools and specialized equipment. Besides those shown in the table, the *front's* auto-road section numbered 14 construction battalions, which had been transferred by the *front* command from the military-field construction command.

Table V/11.6 Western Front's road-exploitation and construction units, January 1 1942

Name	By January 1				
	Road exploitation units		Road construction units		
	Regiments[1]	Battalions	Road battalions	Bridge battalions	Carpentry battalions
Western Front	2	–	1	–	1
Main Highway & Road Directorate	–	–	6	2	–
1st Army	–	–	2	–	–
20th Army	–	1	2	–	–
16th Army	–	–	2[2]	–	–
5th Army	–	1[3]	1	–	–
33rd Army	–	1[4]	–	–	–
43rd Army	1	1	–	1	–
49th Army	–	1	2	–	–
50th Army	–	1[5]	–	–	–
10th Army	–	1[6]	–	–	–
61st Army	–	–	–	–	–

Notes
(1) One of these was only then being accepted into the forces in its formation area.
(2) One of these was only then being accepted into the forces in its formation area.
(3) This unit arrived at Aprelevka station on January 5.
(4) This unit arrived at Aprelevka station on January 5.
(5) This unit arrived in the Tula area on January 5.
(6) This unit arrived in the Tula area on January 5.

Table V/11.7 Western Front's road-exploitation and construction units, January 15 1942

Name	By January 15				
	Road exploitation units		Road construction units		
	Regiments	Battalions	Road battalions	Bridge battalions	Carpentry battalions
Western Front	2	–	1	–	1
Main Highway & Road Directorate	–	–	2	1	–
1st Army	–	1	2	–	–
20th Army	–	1	2	1	–
16th Army	–	2	1	–	–
5th Army	–	–	3	–	–
33rd Army	–	2	1	1	–
43rd Army	1	1	2	1	–
49th Army	–	1	2	1	–
50th Army	1	–	–	1	–
10th Army	–	1	–	–	–
61st Army	1	–	–	1	–

* The road exploitation regiments, with the exception of one, were of the two-battalion type.

The distribution of the road-exploitation and construction units among the armies proved to be less purposeful. From the left-wing armies, which were especially in need of road-construction battalions, only the 49th Army was sufficiently supplied with them.

In summing up what has been written, it's necessary to emphasize that the condition of the *front's* matériel supply situation as of December 25 was significantly worse than by the beginning of our counteroffensive. Nonetheless, the available supplies and the proximity of Moscow with its industry, guaranteed the offensive's continuation.

The rear apparatus, as did that of the *front* and the armies', accumulated the experience of working in winter conditions and learned to work more precisely and purposefully. With the exception of the 10th Army, in the remainder of the armies the basic links of the rear apparatus by this time had been fully outfitted.

The organization of transport and supply

In the *front* command's December 22 directive to the armies' military councils, the latter were ordered to "put an end to sloppiness in the expenditure of ammunition, fuel and food, and try to achieve the strictest economy and accountability." These instructions formed the basis for the organization of supply and transport.

The deputy commander for the rear demanded the maximum use of local food and forage resources and ammunition gathered on the battlefield or captured from the enemy. It was suggested that in calculating and planning the troops' supply that they be based upon the economic expenditure of matériel. Thus the release of ammunition and fuel was chiefly carried out according to the demands of the armies and units, but no more than those limits established by the plan.

The determination of limits, particularly for ammunition and fuel for combat vehicles, is a complex and difficult matter.

The deputy artillery *front* artillery commander for supply established for January a definite coefficient for each army. Depending on the operational situation and the tasks being carried out, this coefficient was equivalent to one in some armies, 0.8 in others, and 0.6 in still others. This made calculating supply easier, but did not guarantee the purposeful and economic employment of munitions.

In breaking through a previously-prepared fortified zone, not only were more munitions required, but definite kinds of them (predominantly high-explosive howitzer rounds). On the other hand, the employment of large-caliber artillery in mobile fighting, particularly in winter conditions, as the experience of the December fighting showed, is extremely difficult. In the meantime, the reigning principle in planning the distribution of ammunition did not fully take this into account.

At the end of December the troops of the right wing and, in part, the center had reached the enemy's previously-prepared fortified line. Despite the stubborn fighting, our units, beginning on December 25, were unable to advance. The enemy lacked such serious fortifications facing the *front's* left-flank armies and the center's right-flank armies, and thus they continued to advance without particularly difficulty.

The *front's* task consisted of defeating the Mozhaisk-Vyaz'ma enemy group. To this purpose the right wing, operating in a southwesterly direction, and the left wing—in a northwesterly one, were supposed to surround and destroy the enemy forces tied down by our center.

Proceeding from the operational situation and mission outlined above, the chief of artillery supply laid out the following coefficients for January: for the 1st, 20th, 16th, and 33rd armies—1; for the 5th, 43rd, and 10th armies, and Gen. Belov's group—0.8, and; for the 49th and 50th armies—0.6.

In the plan for supplying munitions for the center and right-wing armies, which was drawn up on the basis of these instructions, it was planned to supply more rounds for large-caliber and howitzer artillery than was indicated by the established coefficient. Further changes were made in the process of carrying out the plan. The 20th Army was allotted an additional 2,100 107mm gun rounds and 2,100 120mm mortar rounds, which had previously not been planned for this army at all.

The supply of the *front's* armies with munitions and its completion is evident from the enclosed plan.

In analyzing this plan it is necessary to take into account the following amendments. During our counteroffensive a large number of domestically produced and German munitions suitable for use by our weapons park, were captured from the enemy or picked up on the battlefield.

Part of those munitions delivered directly to the troops from the People's Commissariat of Defense's depots by the Supreme High Command's auto transport was not taken into account, and therefore was not reflected in the corresponding documents. According to the data by the 20th Army's rear directorate, the armies units received 7,500 50mm mortar rounds, 3,200 107mm gun rounds, and 7,000 122mm howitzer rounds more than was indicated in the *front's* reports.

The operation's high maneuver character, the consecutive concentration of men and matériel first on one, then on another sector or axis, demanded the maneuver of reserves and supply vehicles by the units and rear organs in organizing supply. During January 1-5 1942 the composition of a combat load in the 10th Army increased by 50% for rifle-machine gun rounds and 50mm mortar rounds, several times for 120mm mortar rounds, and 70% for 152mm howitzer rounds. During this same time the composition of a combat load in the 5th Army for 82mm mortar rounds decreased by 40%. Oftentimes an army would receive new equipment that it had not previously had, or the existing equipment was out of action. In the first case it was necessary to immediately deliver ammunition for the newly arrived equipment, while in the second it was necessary to organize the removal of ammunition and its transfer to another army. All this demanded changes in the plan and increased the significance of the distribution methods in the rear organs' work.

Taking into account the character of modern war, which demands a flexible plan allowing for amendments on the go in accordance with the changing conditions and circumstances—the deputy *front* commander for the rear in January ordered the compilation of 5-day delivery plans for all kinds of supplies. This enabled us by changing the volume of cargoes delivered to this or that army, to rectify the troops' matériel supply situation, without disrupting the entire plan.

A supply plan, drawn up for a short period, would have enabled us to maneuver reserves and equipment from the depth. The experience of the war's beginning operations showed that this was insufficient. Oftentimes, as was shown above, one or another equipment type was knocked out of action in a formation or army, while the munitions for it remained at the division exchange points (DOP) or at the army depots. If timely measures are not adopted in these situations for transferring the remaining munitions to those areas where they can be used, then there arises the danger of valuable and necessary combat means lying around useless.

An analogous situation sometimes arose when capturing enemy depots with ammunition, in which, alongside German-produced munitions we found our shells and rounds previously captured by the enemy. Such an instance occurred in the 10th Army. On January 12 the army captured at Baryatinskaya station a large amount of munitions. Of these 19,200 82mm mortar rounds, 11,500 76mm rounds, and 3,600 122mm howitzer rounds were used to supply the army's units. Besides this, 960 76mm gun rounds, 920 85mm anti-aircraft gun rounds, 5,200 107mm gun rounds, and 2,700 152mm howitzer rounds could not be used by the army because of a lack of corresponding weapons. These munitions lay for almost a month at Baryatinskaya station. It was only on February 5 that the 10th Army's supply organs put in a request to the chief of the second section of the *front* artillery directorate to use these stores.

This was not the only instance of this. During the Western Front's January offensive we captured from the enemy a large number of munitions suitable for use by our equipment.

In the 20th Army captured munitions and munitions picked up off the battlefield (that could be used by our weapons) accounted for 30% of the rifle and machine gun rounds the army received by the army or which arrived with the troops, about 20% for 82mm mortar rounds, more than 50% for 107mm mortar rounds, and more than 30% for 122mm howitzer rounds. We could not allow the use of captured enemy stores to drift along like this and it was necessary to include them in the supply plan.

In the beginning the rear and supply workers could not cope with the organization of maneuvering reserves. The situation changed as they accumulated experience in working in combat conditions. In January there were instances of transferring munitions from one army (or formation) to another. In certain cases excess supplies were transferred to the army field dumps. For example, on January 1 1942 the High Command's automobile reserve transported 720 120mm mortar rounds from the 412th Mortar Battalion to one of the army's railhead depots.

Despite an entire series of shortcomings in the artillery supply apparatus's work, the attacking troops were supplied in a timely way at the decisive moments. Overcoming enormous difficulties, manifesting initiative and inventiveness, the artillery supply workers made their contribution to the defeat of the German-Fascist hordes around Moscow.

No less difficulty arose in calculating and planning the troops' supply with fuels and lubricants. In order to compile a realistic plan it was necessary to take into account and foresee a large number of extremely changeable factors.

Automobile fuel supply at the end of December was made more difficult in connection with the shortage of railroad tank cars, discharge storage facilities at the army field dumps, fuel trucks, and smaller equipment for delivery fuel to the troops over paved and dirt roads. These circumstances demanded the precise planning of supply and the economical use of the available fuel reserves.

At the end of December the *front's* and army fuel supply sections compiled a monthly plan for the units' supply with fuels and lubricants. In compiling this plan, they calculated the presence

Table V/11.8 Western Front's plan for supplying the Front with ammunition for January 1942 and its fulfillment

Weapon	Allotted to the front			Allotted to the right-wing armies			Allotted to the center armies			Allotted to the left-wing armies		
	In thousands of rounds	In combat loads	% fulfillment[1]	In thousands of rounds	In combat loads	% fullfillment	In thousands of rounds	In combat loads	% fullfillment	In thousands of rounds	In combat loads	% fullfillment
Rifle & machine gun rounds	72,500	1.12	40	23,237	2.6	11	31,000	0.95	6.5	12,311	0.25	8
50mm mortar	440.6	1.3	12	40	0.87	5	157	2	8.5	75.5	0.74	0
82mm mortar	223	1.18	64	22.2	1.5	74	45.2	1.1	31	26	0.7	61
107mm mortar	37.6	2.9	135	6.2	2.3	130	13.7	3	36	4.9	1.1	89
120mm mortar	21.2	2	about 50	0.8	0.35	75	7.2	2.7	38	0.5	0.1	60
45mm gun	68.4	0.5	–	67.8	2.4	4	164.5	2.3	15	121.1	2.9	15
76mm regimental gun	207	3	37	32.7	2.3	85	61.1	3	22	30.8	1.2	68
76mm divisional gun	256.7	3	32.5	59.5	5.2	63	40.3	1.1	70	61.8	1.8	35
107mm gun, 1910/30	4.6	1.3	128	–	–	–	4.9	3.3	4	–	–	–
122mm howitzer	56	1.7	120	5	1	50	28.5	3.1	88	8.3	0.9	25
152mm howitzer	34	1.7	190	12.1	3	108	20.2	2.4	90	7.1	1.2	110

Notes
1 Received by January 27, according to the January plan, plus materiel delivered through January 18 according to the December plan.

of their equipment at the end of the month and the average daily expenditure of fuel in the last ten days of December established for transport vehicles at 0.5 refills and for combat vehicles at 0.3 refills per day. In accordance with this, it was planned to deliver in January 15 refills for each transport and 10 refills for each combat vehicle.

Aside from the monthly plan, ten-day (15 days in some armies) supply plans, were drawn up to make corrections in light of the new situation and conditions. In some cases these plans were put together sloppily and thus did not achieve their purpose. For example, the *front* allocated the 5th Army 266 tons of diesel fuel for the second half of January, the same as for the first half. Meanwhile, the army's supply of this fuel type fell from 53 tons on January 1 1942 to 34 tons by January 10, and to 20.5 tons by January 20. As a result, while the army's actual demand for diesel fuel during the latter half of January did not exceed 125-150 tons, it still got 266 tons.

Similar miscalculations by the planning organs led to the transportation arm being overloaded with cargoes unnecessary for the moment and to the accumulation of large amounts of certain types of fuel in the troop and army rear. In the beginning of January a half of all the *front's* supplies of cracking fuel (KB-70) were in the 43rd and 20th armies. The first of these had 27 refills and the second had 24, which would satisfy the 43rd and 20th armies' KB-70 fuel requirements for two months.

Aside from the danger of storing such an amount of fuel in the immediate vicinity of the front, the dispatch of excess fuel to the armies and formations caused the idling of railroad fuel cars and fuel trucks and led to its uneconomical expenditure.

There were no major problems in January in supplying the troops with food and forage. Supply from the deep rear, in conjunction with the organized employment of local means, completely covered the troops' requirements. Scattered breakdowns in the supply of troops were caused by the insufficiently organized work of the quartermaster and rear apparatus. Part of the apparatus's workers was of the opinion that nothing could be gained from those areas which had been occupied by the Fascist marauders. Actually, this was not quite the case. Away from the main roads (where the Germans were afraid to go) there were stored, sometimes in large amounts, vegetables, forage, and other products. Even in the cities the Germans (not finding supporting among the Soviet population) were not able to full use the available reserves. In the depots in Istra a thousand tons of salt remained after the Germans left. Beside this, the 16th Army, which took the town, had a great need for salt until it was brought up from the rear.

There, where the quartermaster and rear workers showed initiative and energy in seeking out means and methods for ensuring the troops' regular supply, they succeeded. Despite the extreme difficulties in delivery and in organizing stockpiling in conditions of a rapid offensive, the command and workers of the quartermaster apparatus of the 217th Rifle Division (50th Army) were able to ensure the unbroken supply of the troops and commanders. During heavy snowfalls the auto transport bogged down, as a result of which the danger of an interruption in supply arose. The division's rear workers got out of this difficulty by mobilizing the civilian sledge and horse-drawn transport (67 carts) and in this way secured the timely delivery of the necessary products.

Among the 33rd Army's forces (with the exception of the 222nd and 338th rifle divisions, where there were instances of a breakdown in supply) the troops and commanders regularly received a hot meal twice a day. In order to achieve this, the rear workers had to overcome enormous difficulties.

It proved to be especially difficult to ensure the matériel supply of the mobile groups. In the middle of January the *front's* rear directorate reported to the center: "The transports sent to the group (Gen. Belov's group) with ammunition and fuel cannot break through; Belov's auto transport also remains in the Podkopaevo area. It is possible to supply the group with ammunition, fuel and food only by air."

The group's rear workers found another way out. They mobilized the local horse-drawn transport. In those places where not only the automobile, but authorized horse-drawn transport bogged down, the local collective farmers found field and forest roads, along which they delivered the necessary supplies to the troops.

The matériel provision of the 20th Army's breakthrough on the Lama River

The 20th Army's rear apparatus, almost completely outfitted with workers called up from the reserves, did not know the rear service art very well and was insufficiently coordinated. As a result the army's rear worked unsatisfactorily in December, deliveries were carried out in an unorganized fashion, the location of division exchange points (DOP) often did not correspond to the operational situation, and the troops sometimes did not know where they were located. As a result, the troops received even bread intermittently. In the 331st Rifle Division bread was not distributed for two days.

The *front* helped the army with its automobile transport and sent workers who taught the reservists the vagaries of rear service on the spot. This had a great significance not only for eliminating shortcomings in the army rear's ongoing work, but also in training rear workers and in putting together a rear apparatus. Upon the appointment of several experienced rear workers to the 20th Army, its rear apparatus was transformed into a completely capable organ, which could independently organized the matériel supply of the army's troops.

The 20th Army's material supply situation at the beginning of January did not vary from the average norm at the front. The army had with the troops and in the army field dumps (PAS) 1.5-2 combat loads of munitions, three refills of fuel, 6-8 rations of food (excluding fats), and 4-5 rations of forage. Beside this, the army was entrusted with a difficult and responsible operational mission. Following successive attempts to break through the enemy's fortified zone along a broad front, the command decided to concentrate a shock group along the 20th Army's sector. For this purpose, a large part of the 16th Army's forces were transferred to the group, while at the same time measures were taken to bring up their strength to the authorized level. It was ordered that the preparations for the breakthrough operation be started on January 6 and completed on the 8th.

The command and rear workers had to carry out a great deal of work. In order to carry out the operational mission, the 20th Army required a large amount of munitions, especially for howitzer and large and medium-caliber artillery, with high-explosive shells. However, it transpired that the army was poorly supplied with these. The established January limit for the release of munitions did not eliminate this shortcoming.

The munitions available in the 20th Army by January 1 1942 are shown in table V/11.9.

Table V/11.9 20th Army munition levels, January 1 1942

Type	Combat loads (in thousands)	With the troops and in army field depots (in thousands)	Quota for January (in thousands)
Rifle & machine gun rounds	4,435.50	11,701	18,677
50mm mortar	26	37.1	80.1
82mm mortar	17.9	18.6	32.2
107mm mortar	0.5	0.15	1.9
120mm mortar	0.7	1.5	1.5
45mm gun	12.2	36	79.1
76mm regimental gun	5.2	4.5	21
76mm divisional gun	10.8	15.6	39.1
122mm howitzer	1.3	3	3.9
152mm howitzer	11.1	2.15	4.7

The fierce fighting of the first days of January exhausted these munitions. By January 4 the 20th Army was supplied worse with mortar rounds (excluding 120mm rounds) and rounds for its divisional artillery than it was on December 25.

The basing conditions also developed unfavorably for the army. The army's rear area made the organization of supply more difficult. At first the army lacked its own automobile road; an additional supply route ran across a neighboring army's rear zone for a significant distance. Things were better with the army's road units. It had one road-exploitation battalion and two road-construction battalions. These units were quite sufficient to establish the necessary order on the supply routes and to ensure the roads' timely repair.

The army's transport equipment ensured the delivery of the army's daily demands. It had (expressed in GAZ-AA trucks) 1,500 automobiles, of which about 300 were in army transport. With the increase in the snow cover there arose a need for horse-drawn transport, because the auto transport's work along the country roads was becoming more and more difficult.

The army's command and rear workers had to carry out a great deal of work in a short period of time. On January 6 1942 the *front* allocated to the army 5,500 107mm mortar and 1,700 120mm mortar rounds. 16,100 artillery rounds were issued for regimental artillery, and 5,200 for divisional artillery, 7,300 rounds for 122mm howitzers, and 10,000 152mm howitzer rounds; aside from this, 5,400 mm rounds for the newly-arrived 107mm artillery, and 2,000 203mm rounds. This is more than was allocated for the 20th Army according to the January plan, but as the number of guns rose to an even greater degree the supply of ammunition remained lower than that called for by the January plan.

The issue of fuels and lubricants and food for the army also grew. Besides this, large deliveries of winter clothing and other property had to be made.

The preparation for the matériel support for breaking through the enemy's position began with the issue of rear order no. 11 of January 7 1942. It was ordered by the beginning of the breakthrough operation to: create reserves to the amount of 2.5 combat loads, to increase the reserves of fuel within the units to two refills and to one in the army field depots, have five rations within the units and two rations in mobile food detachments, to disembark the medical services, and to move the medical-evacuation equipment closer to the units; to subsequently be ready to deliver daily 0.25 combat loads.

Until January 9 the army base remained in the area of Nakhabino station, and the branch of the field fuel depot in the area of the intersection of the paved road and road to Chismeny. From January 9-15 it was proposed to have the base in the Istra area. The chief of the army's military communications was ordered to adopt measures to develop the Dolgorukovo and Volokolamsk stations, preparing them in the capacity of basing areas.

Before the start of the operation the divisional and brigade exchange points remained as before; when the units reached the line of Shakhovskaya, they were to be moved to the line Bol'shoe Isakovo-Kur'yanovo-Chubarovo.

The main supply and evacuation route was Nakhabino-Volokolamsk. For sledge and tractor delivery it was 1) Den'kovo-Shilovo-Novo-Plavskoe-Shit'kovo; 2) Chismeny-Gusenevo-Shishkino-Lyskovo-Chentsy-Gorki-Pushkari-Ivanovskoe and Mikhailovskoe.

The army's automobile-road section was ordered to organize traffic control along these routes, with a post and team of 10-15 men every kilometer for the repair and cleaning of the road.

In the area of bridges it was proposed to have a reserve of construction materials. By January 8 it was ordered to prepare bypasses for every place which could be destroyed.

The release of matériel was set for January 7. In order deliver everything necessary to the units on time, the formation commanders were ordered to force the delivery and transfer of munitions, fuel, and forage, using the entire available transportation means.

The rear apparatus did a great amount of work. Despite the mistakes made in preliminary calculations (it was planned to deliver four combat loads for the operation) for supplying the troops with munitions, the rear workers determined the amount of necessary matériel, the volume of the work at hand, and distributed it in accordance with the plan for conducting the operation according to time.

The securing of unbroken supply and the effective employment of auto transport was placed in the center of the army rear directorate's concerns. This was a completely correct decision, but in order to carry it out it was planned, as we saw earlier, to expend an enormous amount of energy.

The directorate's concern for the concentration of a reserve of construction materials and the timely creation of bypasses in the areas where bridges were is quite valuable and educational.

In reality not everything went as planned. Most of all, there was not enough transport for bringing up reinforcements and replacements, or for the delivery of everything the troops needed. The delivery of just munitions and fuel allotted to the army required 1,500 motor vehicles. The same amount was necessary for the delivery of a day's rations and bringing up the mobile food reserves to normal.

The plan for matériel support had major shortcomings. It lacked a precise definition—when and by what means, from where and to where supplies are to be sent, as well as by whom, where and how the deliveries are to be carried out. As a result, during the first days the available auto transport worked poorly and the roads were not cleared of snow in a timely manner.

The army's automobile-road section was late with the delivery of replacements allotted for the army, as well as the necessary matériel. By January 8 only half of the replacements had been delivered. The army commander reported to the *front* that by this time from 0.2 to 0.75 of a combat load was in the army's artillery regiments. In the troop artillery regiments there were even fewer munitions. "It was only in the evening that the units sent their transport to Nakhabino station to get their munitions, which had only been delivered by that time." In the conclusions to its report the army command requested that the *front* commander change the date for the army's offensive to the next day. This was done and the offensive actually began on January 10.

The rear apparatus took its mistakes into account and subsequently worked more precisely and purposefully. By the end of January 11 1942 it was clear that the army had managed to break through the enemy's defense. This raised the possibility of operational maneuver. For the purpose of securing the army's further operations, on January 11 rear order no. 012 was issued, according to which the army base was to move to the Istra area while at the same time forced work was to be carried out to restore the railroad sector as far as Volokolamsk.

The chiefs of the combat arms, services, and supply sections were ordered on January 11 to dispatch reconnaissance groups from the army field depots to Istra to determine in what area the depots should be housed, so that by the end of January 11 its representatives and worker's teams should be there in complete readiness to receive and distribute cargoes in the new area. For this purpose, it was planned to transfer reserves there from Nakhabino station by auto transport.

The railhead branches of the army field dumps—food, fuel, and munitions—were ordered to deploy in the Volokolamsk area by 0800 on January 12.

The army quartermaster, for the purposes of maintaining the mobile field bakeries and bread factories in reserve, arranged for the baking of bread in stationary bakeries in Volokolamsk and Novo-Petrovskoe. In the event of an advance, on January 19 a special reconnaissance detail was dispatched to Shakhovskaya to determine the productive capacities and condition of the former bakeries. Worker's detachments, made up of specialists, were created to repair and restore the bakeries in the army destroyed by the enemy.

During the breakthrough of the enemy's defensive zone and during the subsequent offensive, the rear apparatus widely created reserves on the ground, thanks to which the army was supplied without a break.

Despite the extremely difficult supply conditions, the army did not experience either with munitions or other matériel during the operation to break through the enemy's defense and during the subsequent offensive. This was possible because a significant part of the troops' needs, not only in vegetables, forage and food, but in munitions as well, was covered by stockpiling of local stores, gathering up supplies from the field, and through captured enemy stores.

The experience of the rear workers in making use of local resources is deserving of careful study.

The expenditure and arrival of munitions to the 20th Army for January 1942 is shown in the following table.

Table V/11.10 Expenditure and arrival of munitions to the 20th Army for January 1942

Type	Arrived in the Army (in thousands)		Expended			Combat loads available with the troops, or in army field depots by January 12
			In January	During January 10-11		
	Delivered from depots, or arrived with the troops	Seized from the enemy, or collected on the battlefield		In thousands	In combat loads	
rifle-machine gun rounds	5,593	2,850	6,361.50	230.3	0.06	2.3
50mm mortar	29	7	29	0.3	0.01	2.9
82mm mortar	24	28	23.7	2.2	0.12	0.3
107mm mortar	8.5	0.4	6.2	1.2	2.8	3
120mm mortar	4.9	0.4	8.4	0.9	1.3	5
45mm gun	37.7	3	26.8	3.7	0.3	0.8
76mm regimental gun	21.2	1.8	13.2	3	0.57	2.6
76mm divisional gun	30.2	0.8	11.8	6.7	0.67	1.1
107mm gun	4.5	5.3	7.1	2	1.5	–
122mm howitzer	5.7	3.3	6.3	1.4	0.5	1.7
152mm howitzer	15.2	–	13.1	3.4	0.4	3.5

It is clear from the table that the number of 82mm mortar rounds captured from the enemy and collected from the battlefield covered their monthly expenditure, with some to spare; that the monthly expenditure of 107mm gun rounds was covered by more than 2/3, and more than half for 122mm howitzer rounds.

Along with this, the table shows the relative weight of the expenditure of certain types of munitions during the breakthrough of the enemy's defensive position and the other days of fighting. Rifle-machine gun rounds were expended relatively less during the breakthrough of the enemy's defense than during the remaining days. A different picture emerges with the expenditure of artillery rounds, particularly divisional artillery, and 122mm gun and 122mm howitzer rounds.

The rear apparatus coped with its assignment. The army's military council rated the rear's work as satisfactory and nominated the most distinguished workers for government awards. This success was not achieved easily. In order to achieve the unbroken supply of the troops, the rear workers had to overcome enormous difficulties caused by hard frosts and frequent blizzards, which disrupted delivery and evacuation and made the organization of equipment repair extremely difficult.

All of these difficulties were overcome thanks to the close contact between. the staff's work and that of the rear directorate, as well as the rear apparatus's numerous internal links. During the operation the command assigned the rear services specific tasks and through its staff kept it informed of the operational situation and its own intentions. The top rear workers, in their turn, took advantage of any opportunity to get acquainted with the operational situation. The deputy army commander for the rear, in his report to the *front's* military council, maintained that his workers "are always aware of the operational situation."

Of even greater significance was the hands-on leadership and very strict control on the part of the army's rear directorate. "As regards all questions of the rear services," the report stated, "they established the strictest control by means of personal association with the units, formations and the section chiefs."

The *front* apparatus rendered a great deal of help in ordering the work of the 20th Army's rear. Its representatives taught the army workers by example. Upon the basis of this experience, which has a practical value, one should study how to lead one's subordinates.

The successful completion of the breakthrough of the enemy's defensive position on the Lama and Ruza rivers and the continuing advance of the left-flank armies opened broad operational possibilities for the *front*. The deputy *front* commander for the rear, in order to support the subsequent offensive, issued his new directive no. 029 on January 17.

This directory to the supply directorates ordered that the *front's* main reserves be deployed in the area of Moscow and to the west of the city. As for the rest, the rear organization remained as before, with the exception of the 10th Army, which was ordered to deploy its base in the area of Gorbachevo, and its field depot railhead branches in the area of Manaenki station and Vezhenka.

The 61st Army, which had been subordinated to the *front*, was ordered to deploy its base in the area of Arsen'evo station and the army's distribution station at Gorbachevo station. As actually transpired, the army was only managed to move its railroad mobile groups as far as Arsen'evo station, and even that was only at the end of January.

In order to economize auto transport, it was forbidden to dispatch army transport to the *front* bases. The supply directorates and sections were ordered to organize the delivery of the necessary matériel to the armies as far as the army distribution stations, and from there the delivery of supply cargoes would be carried out by railroad mobile teams. Staging posts, subordinated directly to the *front*, were organized in the areas of Aleksin and Belev for the maximum employment of railroad transport. Later a similar base was created in the area of Khanino station.

Of great interest is the rear's work for the matériel supply of the left-wing armies during the second half of January. Below we will speak primarily about the rear's work at the *front* and with the left-flank armies.

The organization of supply and delivery in the left-wing armies

The successful advance of the left-wing armies and the delay in restoring the railroads and bridges on the paved and dirt roads led to the army bases lagging behind and to an increase in delivery difficulties. In a number of armies the apparatus did not guarantee the unbroken supply of the troops.

For the purpose of putting the supply and delivery on the *front's* left wing in order, on January 18 the deputy *front* commander for the rear issued directive no. 030, according to which the *front's* auto-road section was to create *front* military-automobile road no. 2 along the route: Khanino-Peremyshl'-Babynino-Mishchovsk-Mosal'sk. 150 motor vehicles were placed at the disposal of the chief of the military-automobile road (VAD) no. 2 from the *front's* auto reserve.

For the purpose of moving the *front's* reserves close to the troops it was ordered to create a *front* staging post in Khanino, with field depot branches for artillery, fuel, food, and forage, and to be ready to distribute these supplies to the troops by the close of January 20 1942. A railhead branch for the *front* base, with the same depots, was being organized in the Meshchovsk area.

At the same time, the deputy *front* commander for the rear, Maj. Gen. for Quartermaster Services Vinogradov, ordered the chief of the organizational-planning section of the *front's* rear area directorate to dispatch his representatives to these places to control and assist the army workers in carrying out rear directive no. 030. With their assistance, it was possible to organize the delivery of 250-33 tons of supplies along the narrow-gauge railroad Tula-Khanino station.

Great difficulties were encountered in organizing deliveries along military-automobile road no. 2. The *front's* automobile-road section failed to allocate the prescribed number of motor vehicles. The technical condition of the motor vehicles allocated to the chief of the military-automobile road proved to be so low that half of them were sent for repairs. Besides this, defense from the snow and the timely cleaning of the road from snow was not organized on the auto road; nor were there traffic-control posts, refueling or repair installations.

In response from a demand by the *front* workers for the organization of defense against snow, a sector of the road was entrusted to each of the nearby settlements, leaders were appointed, with responsibility for organizing the population and for making sure they showed up for work on time along their sector. The leaders were also responsible for overseeing the work norms and quality of the work.

With the subordination of two horse-drawn transportation companies to the chief of military-automobile road no. 2, they were dispatched immediately to assist the delivery of supplies to the west from Mosal'sk, and it was planned to employ auto transport (including that belonging to Gen. Belov's group) for work on the automobile road.

However, the group's rear chief did not agree with this and sent the horse-drawn transportation companies back for work on the military-automobile road and kept his own auto transport.

The deployment of the depot branches in the base's railhead branches was late. It was only by the end of January 22 that the main depots were ready to disburse supplies to the troops. This significantly improved supply conditions. Nevertheless, the chief interest is in the creation of new links in the supply chain.

The apparatus of the staging base and that of the railhead branch of the *front* base were outfitted with workers from the directorate of the chief of the Tula *front* base. The men and transportation equipment were gathered by the transfer of the 43rd Army's worker and auto transport company. Thus by means of maneuvering the available forces, the work was guaranteed in three places.

This is not the only instance when one establishment was used to carry out work in several places, which had been operating independently.

The group of Quartermaster Lt. First Class Sergeev did a great deal of work in establishing order at the staging base at Khanino station.

The work experience by the staging base at Khanino station showed that by skillfully dispersing supplies and observing masking discipline, it is quite possible to create supply dumps in the open.

The system of delivery in the left-wing armies is of particular interest. While the gap between the troops and their bases was more or less equal and did not exceed 100 km, a system of parallel work by the army and division auto transport, delivering cargoes to the division exchange points (DOP), and rarely directly to the units, was employed. With the increase in the distance between certain armies or divisions from their bases, we began to employ a mixed delivery method. The organization of supply in the 10th Army is typical of the latter method.

In a January 6 1942 directive for the 10th Army rear, it was directed that food from the 324th, 325th, and 326th rifle divisions should be delivered by army transport from Khanino station to the divisional exchange points in full, with half for the 323rd Rifle Division, while the division should get the other half using its own auto transport. The divisions based on Shchekino station and Vezhenka (239th, 330th, 328th, and 322nd rifle divisions) would deliver all their supplies using their own auto transport, with the exception of munitions. All munitions for all the divisions would be delivered by army auto transport.

With the large gap (more than 100 km) between the troops and their bases it was more expedient to employ army transport (reinforced in certain cases from the *front's* automobile reserve) in order to create forward branches of the army base, from which the cargoes could be gathered up by divisional auto transport and delivered to the divisional exchange points. This manner of delivery frees up the army transport from searching for the divisional exchange points and also excludes the possibility of delaying the army auto transport in the units. These delays, as is known, were a common phenomenon and caused a sharp fall in the work effectiveness of the army and *front* transport.

The organization of rear control in an offensive operation

The armies' advance, particularly rapid on the *front's* left wing, where from time to time an extremely difficult operational situation arose, the shortage of communications equipment and the winter conditions made control of the rear extremely difficult. The elongation and lagging of the rear services, inevitable in an offensive, demanded from the rear workers' service the manifestation of ingeniousness, flexibility and initiative in control questions.

In order to move the rear leadership closer to the troops, in a number of armies there were created small operational groups from the rear workers, stationed at the command post. These groups were obliged to clarify the degree of the troops' supply with the necessities, their need for these or other supplies, and to transmit the collected information to the army staff's second echelon for the adoption of corresponding measures.

In this way the operational groups, imparting flexibility and mobility to the rear's work, rendered a great service to the troops. However, in certain cases, when the operational group's workers were not given specific tasks, and when their activities were not controlled, the rear directorates operational groups not only did not facilitate but, quite the opposite, interfered with the troops' timely matériel supply.

An example of this is the 49th Army's operational group, which displayed laziness and inefficiency, which led to breakdowns in supply.

The enthusiasm for allocating a large number of representatives to various places led to the dispersal of the organizational-planning section's workers. Meanwhile, according to the volume and character of this section's work, a well-put together and smoothly working collective is required, in which each man, in close cooperation with others, carries out his part of the work. Thus the creation of operational groups or the allocation of individual workers for carrying out specific assignments on site should be carried out with the necessary circumspection.

The organization of transferring the 16th Army's directorate and rear services

The experience of organizing the carrying out transfers of large combined-arms formations, directorates and rear services contains much that is of interest for the Red Army's command element. A highly-maneuverable war often makes it necessary to carry out such transfers and that side which carries them out more secretly and more quickly, while expending fewer men and matériel, gains a great advantage. Thus the lateral movement of the 16th Army's directorate and rear services from the *front's* right flank to the left, which was carried out in the second half of January, under difficult road conditions, is worthy of attention.

An order by the *front* command for transferring the 16th Army's directorate and rear services from the area of Lesodolgorukovo station and Novo-Petrovskoe to the south, to the area of

Kudrinskaya station (later to the area of Khanino and Babynino) followed on January 21 1942. The order planned to carry out the transfer of the men and part of the equipment using the army's own auto transport. All supplies, with the exception of fuel, which was transferred to the neighboring army, were to be transferred by rail. It was planned to begin the transfer on January 23.

Having received the *front's* order, the 16th Army's rear apparatus drew up a plan, in which it was laid out who was to do what and when, route to be taken, the time, the order in which columns should be formed and the time for their departure. Refueling, repair and feeding stations were prepared along the appointed routes. In order to avoid the bunching up of vehicles during delays and to ensure the uninterrupted flow of traffic, the composition of an automobile column did not exceed 20 vehicles.

However, as a result of poor control of the preparation and insufficient leadership in dispatching the columns, this plan was violated from the very beginning, as a result of which the transfer to a new area was completed with a delay of 10-12 days.

The unfolding of the work by the 16th Army's apparatus and rear units in the new area was delayed by frequent changes in the arrival area. The previously-indicated area of Kudrinskaya station was changed along the way to the area of Khanino and Babynino, and then to the area Shchekino-Odoevo-Kozel'sk.

The 16th Army's transfer to the *front's* left wing required a new organization of its rear and supply. *Front* rear directive no. 033 of January 26 laid out the necessary instructions. The 10th Army was based on the railroad branch of the *front* base in Meshchovsk. The army's rear organizations and units, together with the most basic supplies, was transferred to the area of Pletnevka and Kudrinskaya station, so that, having restored the Naro-Fominsk-Sukhinichi railroad, organize an army base there.

In order to increase the delivery equipment on military-automobile road no. 2, the deputy *front* commander ordered the 10th Army's rear chief to subordinate an auto company to the road chief; the 16th Army, lacking its own transportation equipment, had an automobile battalion and horse-drawn battalion temporarily subordinated to it. Along with this, the supply of the 16th Army's units (consisting at this time of five rifle divisions), was entrusted to the 10th Army's rear apparatus, which was still insufficiently organized.

The supply of tank units in winter conditions

With the worsening of the frosts and the increase in the snow cover the supply of the tank units became more and more difficult. Oftentimes the situation forced us to supply tanks with munitions and carry out refueling in concentration areas. There were incidents of refueling tanks at their jumping-off positions for attacks. Motor vehicles (even those with heightened cross-country capability) often were not able to break through to their tanks.

The "Comintern" and "ST-35" type tractors proved more capable in getting through. In those situations when they could not reach the tanks, munitions and fuel were towed to the tanks on sledges. Ordinary sledges were not cut out for this, but those specifically constructed for the job often fell apart or turned over, leading to a loss of extremely necessary munitions and fuels and lubricants.

A major shortcoming of the tractors and tanks used for towing matériel supplies was the loud noise produced by them, which made it difficult to mask their movement. Circumstances sometimes required the observation of the strictest secrecy when bringing up munitions and fuel to the tanks, as, for example, when they were located in an ambush and required refueling. In such situations they usually resorted to horse-drawn transport, which could get through better than any tractor and makes almost no noise. In special situations (when careful concealment was required), munitions and fuel were delivered to the tanks on small sledges, which were pushed by people.

Given the great variety of transportation equipment employed in winter conditions for the delivery of munitions and fuel to the tanks, the most successful and most often used was horse-drawn transport. On the basis of the experience accumulated by the 26th Tank Brigade in the course of a lengthy time, the deputy commander of the 43rd Army for armored troops wrote in his report: "In tank operations off the paved roads, the best means for delivering fuel and munitions is horse transport; it's noiseless and gets through anything." According to his calculations, it's necessary to have five sledges per tank battalion, which is quite sufficient to service the battalion's operations in a 20-30 km radius.

During the fighting by the 5th Tank Brigade (from December 18 to January 9), fuel and munitions were delivered exclusively by horse-sledge transport. The 20th Army's deputy commander for armor considered it necessary to attach horse-sledge transport to the tank units.

* * *

The Western Front's January offensive raised an entire series of specific tasks for the rear workers. The overall volume of supplies delivered to the troops rose and the character of these supplies changed. Thus, for example, the expenditure of fuels and lubricants rose significantly. On certain days up to one refuel of automobile fuel was expended, compared to the daily expenditure of 0.4 refuels in December. On the other hand, the expenditure of munitions declined significantly. Besides this, a large amount of captured munitions was used. These two circumstances explain the fact that if during the December offensive (December 6-22 1941) the average daily delivery of munitions to the front was 861 tons, then during the January offensive (December 22 1941-January 31 1942) it was only 389 tons.

The expenditure of munitions in combat loads during the December and January offensives is shown in table V/11.11.

Table V/11.11 Expenditure of munitions in combat loads during the December and January offensives

Type	Front expenditure		Army expenditure	
	December	January[1]	10th Army	20th Army
Rifle-machine gun rounds	0.7	0.5	0.4	1.6
50mm mortar	1.4	0.7	0.25	1.1
82mm mortar	1.7	1	0.75	1.3
107mm mortar	2.1	1.9		
120mm mortar	2	1.5	2.4[2]	11.5[2, 3]
45mm gun	1	0.6	0.35	2.2
76mm regimental gun	1.8	1	1.25	2.5
76mm divisional gun	1.7	1	1	1.2
107mm gun	6.7	6	–	5.2
122mm howitzer	3.5	2.3	1	4.5
152mm howitzer	5	2.6	1.8	4

Notes

1 This figure is calculated according to the actual expenditure for the first 20 days and, for the remaining ten days, according to the average daily expenditure for the first 20 days.

2 The expenditure of 107mm and 120mm mortar rounds is conflated for both armies.

3 The number of heavy-calibre mortars in the army increased considerably more from January 7 than is shown in the table, and the calculation of ammunition expenditure is shown by the condition of the equipment as of January 1.

To illustrate the expenditure of munitions in certain armies, armies in a variety of operational situations are shown. The 10th Army was primarily engaged in maneuver fighting and did not face the enemy's serious fortifications, while at the same time the 20th Army was breaking through the enemy's fortified positions. This explains the fact that the expenditure of munitions in the 10th Army, with a rare exception, was less than the average for the *front*, while that of the 20th Army was significantly higher.

Conclusions

In an offensive operation, as the experience of the Western Front shows, a constant readiness for maneuvering supplies, rear units, and supply routes is required. In the operation's course the command and rear chief more and more felt that necessity of creating for themselves a maneuverable reserve of all kinds of matériel and transport means. Given the absence of such reserves, they resorted to redirecting supplies or transferring men, matériel, and supplies from one army to another. Nonetheless, this was not a way out of the situation; the high mobility of modern operations demanded a mobile reserve at all levels.

The unwieldiness of the modern rear apparatus and the variety of its duties has made it necessary to echelon some rear links in the chain to a significant depth. In order to maintain communications and troops, operational groups for running the rear were created.

The offensive at the end of December and in January (which unfolded as a pursuit on the left wing) demanded significantly fewer munitions that the counteroffensive. Moreover, the main mass of munitions was expended among the armies of the center and right flank, which were forced to break through previously-constructed enemy defensive positions.

The *front's* and armies' rear apparatus worked more precisely and purposefully in January than in December. The rear and supply workers made up for the allocated but unsent equipment by widely using local resources (including captured munitions). Only by the end of January did their shortage in the armies begin to tell sharply.

In conclusion, one must emphasize that the comparatively small expenditures of matériel, particularly munitions, in the battle for Moscow, was a result of both general conditions, characteristic of the stage of the war under study, as well as specific ones that came together around Moscow at the end of 1941 and in the beginning of 1942. This should be taken into account in calculating the matériel supply of modern operations.

12

Conclusions on the January fighting

1 The operational-strategic situation of the sides along the Moscow strategic direction by January 1942 was sharply different.

The Red Army's forces, as a result of the Germans' December defeat around Moscow, particularly the defeat of their shock flank groups, was free to operate and could continue its further offensive to completely destroy the German-Fascist forces facing the Western Front. From the end of December the Western Front's armies carried out this offensive from the line of the Lama, Ruza, Nara, and Oka rivers. By this time units of the Red Army had already suffered serious losses, and their exhaustion by prolonged and unending fighting was telling on them; the harsh winter placed its retarding stamp on the troop's operations. However, the favorable operational situation that had come about, and the high political-morale condition of the Red Army's units enabled us to count on further successes by our troops in January.

2. The German-Fascist troops, routed around Moscow and having lost a large amount of men and matériel (including almost all of their tanks), were falling back to the west under the Red Army's blows. The Germans' condition was most serious along the flanks, which were subject to the greatest defeat and which were being pursued by large forces of the Red Army. The center had suffered less and the situation there at first was more stable. Along the line of the Lama, Ruza, Nara and Oka rivers the enemy had halted so as to consolidate and bring up the necessary reinforcements, and planned to remain there until spring. In the rear, in the event of the loss of this defensive line, other fortified lines and areas were hurriedly being constructed according to a system of strong points and centers of resistance along the most important sectors and axes.

Such important areas in the rear of the German forces, the loss of which would make it impossible to maintain their communications and wage a stubborn defense over a lengthy period of time were:

a) The area of Rzhev, Zubtsov, and Sychevka along the boundary of the Kalinin and Western fronts, for which a stubborn battle was waged throughout all of January and subsequently.
b) The area of Gzhatsk and Vyaz'ma, which covered the junctions of the most important rail and dirt road supply routes (from the rear to the front), as well as the lateral (along the front) ones. The country's most important auto highway of Moscow-Gzhatsk-Vyaz'ma-Smolensk-Minsk passes through this area.
c) The Medyn'-Polotnyanyi Zavod-Yukhnov triangle, which blocked the exit to the second auto highway located in the Western Front's area of operations—the strategic Moscow-Warsaw highway; it simultaneously covered the important Kaluga-Vyaz'ma axis, including the railroad and enabled us to bypass the Gzhatsk-Vyaz'ma area from the south.
d) The Sukhinichi area as a large rail junction toward Smolensk, Roslavl', Bryansk, and Kaluga, which was simultaneously the area covering in the south the communications along the front: the

lateral railroad through Sychevka, Vyaz'ma and Bryansk, and the Gzhatsk-Yukhnov-Sukhinichi-Bryansk road.

Through the stubborn defense of these areas the Germans sought to create a certain solidity to their operational front and sought to cover their main railroad and highway arteries for supply, evacuation and supply along the front. As a result their rear was to be solidly based. Without holding these areas and communications junctions, the Germans would not have had secure communications and thus could not have counted on a prolonged and stubborn defense, so as to sit it out here until the spring and keep the enemy from the line Rzhev-Vyaz'ma-Orel.

This is why during the Red Army's January offensive the above-named areas were the arena of fierce and stubborn fighting. The Red Army's main blows were directed here for the purpose of splitting the enemy front into pieces, so as to then encircle and destroy the enemy in detail. The Germans held on stubbornly to these areas, even at the risk of their encirclement by Red Army units.

3 During January Soviet troops achieved major operational results. Along the majority of the *front's* operational directions successful offensive operations were carried out. We managed to carry them out in the following sequence:

In the first half of January the offensive by our left-wing forces developed quickly south of the line Kaluga-Yukhnov. The 1st Guards Cavalry Corps cut the Warsaw highway. The 10th Army's forces reached the Vyaz'ma-Bryansk lateral road, having advanced 120 km to the west of the Oka, although this marked the end of their achievement in January. The center carried out a consecutive offensive, at first more successful in the zone to the west of the line Borovsk-Maloyaroslavets, penetrating to a depth of 30-50 km between the Mozhaisk and Myatlevo-Yukhnov enemy group. The *front's* right wing during the first ten days of January did not advance and only beginning from January 10 did the 20th Army manage (at first slowly and gradually) to break through the Germans' fortified defense and exploit the breakthrough along the Volokolamsk-Gzhatsk axis.

During the second half of January the *front's* right wing successfully developed its operational breakthrough along the Volokolamsk-Gzhatsk axis and advanced 50-60 km, reaching as far as the Gzhatsk defensive line. In the center the 5th Army was also attacking in the direction of Mozhaisk and Gzhatsk. The 33rd Army, which found itself facing the weakly defended space between the Gzhatsk and Yukhnov enemy groups, was boldly developing its offensive toward Vyaz'ma. The 1st Guards Cavalry Corps also broke through there in the last days of January. The 43rd Army, cooperating with the 49th and 50th armies, was outflanking the enemy's stubbornly defending Yukhnov group from the north at the same time the 49th and 50th armies were outflanking it from the east and south. The 10th Army, which had spread out along a broad front, was holding the Vyaz'ma-Bryansk lateral road near Kirov, and fighting against the enemy's Zhizdra group, which was launching a counterblow toward Sukhinichi. On the *front's* left flank the 61st Army, having outflanked the Germans' Bolkhov group from three sides, was waging a persistent fight against it.

As a result of all these activities, the enemy was dealt a series of local defeats and our forces advanced to new lines and liberated a large amount of Soviet territory from the German-Fascist aggressors. The German troops' operational situation worsened considerably. They suffered heavy casualties in the fighting, were exhausted, and the integrity of their operational front was disrupted. The harsh winter and the absence of warm clothing also made the Germans' situation more difficult. More than once they were on the edge of a complete rout and catastrophe.

However, the enemy continued to put up stubborn resistance against our advancing forces, using any opportunity and favorable condition to launch counterattacks and counterblows.

These are the peculiarities of the operational situation at the end of January:

a) The Kalinin Front, successfully attacking, had reached the enemy rear west of the line Rzhev-Sychevka, having thrown forward cavalry west of Vyaz'ma. Thus the Western Front, in conjunction with the Kalinin Front, was trying to surround the Germans' large Rzhev-Gzhatsk-Vyaz'ma group. To be sure, there were as yet insufficient forces in our flanking groups in order to close the encirclement ring and achieve decisive results from the penetration of our troops into the enemy's operational rear.
b) The Western Front's right-wing armies had advanced all the way to the Gzhatsk defensive line and had begun the fight to take it.
c) The center armies had inflicted a serious defeat on the enemy. Along the Vyaz'ma axis the enemy's front was split and our troops, airborne units, and partisan detachments were operating in the operational depth.
d) The left-wing armies (in conjunction with the center's 43rd Army), as a result of sustained fighting, were surrounding the Germans' Yukhnov group. Part of these forces were advancing deeply along the Roslavl' axis, cutting the Vyaz'ma-Bryansk lateral road, repelling enemy counterblows toward Sukhinichi, and fighting the half-encircled Bolkhov group along the left flank.
e) The unity and integrity of the enemy's operational front was disrupted. It was split into four parts:
   - the strongest was the Vyaz'ma group, which was under the greatest danger of encirclement by our forces; it was covered from the by the Germans' stubborn resistance along the Gzhatsk defensive line;
   - the Yukhnov group was almost surrounded, but was putting up stubborn resistance and was the connecting link between the Vyaz'ma and Zhizdra groups;
   - the Zhizdra group was becoming more active along the *front's* left flank; it was launching a counterblow in the direction of Sukhinichi in order to relieve the besieged German garrison and was being reinforced from the depth, possibly in an attempt to split the Western Front's left wing;
   - the Bolkhov group was fighting half-surrounded, covering the Orel axis, with its front stubbornly defending to the east and west.

4 The overall character of operations in January was determined by the plan of the Red Army high command for routing the enemy along the Moscow strategic direction through the forces of two *fronts*—the Kalinin and Western, as well as by the specific situation that had come about in the theater of military activities. At the same time the Western Front, attacking to the southwest, west, and northwest, was inflicting a series of defeats on the opposing German forces and was splitting them into several isolated groups, the Kalinin Front was getting into the rear of the powerful Rzhev-Gzhatsk-Vyaz'ma enemy group. A favorable situation was being created for defeating the main forces of the Germans' Army Group Center.

At this stage of the fighting the proper operational coordination of the Kalinin and Western fronts' forces for surrounding and defeating the highly important Rzhev-Gzhatsk-Vyaz'ma enemy group was acquiring particularly significance, along with questions of the *fronts'* strategic coordination. The completion of this operation and its final results relate to the subsequent months; they lie beyond the bounds of our description. Thus here we can only note at the present stage of the fighting the important role of the close coordination of the two *fronts* for the encirclement and defeat of the opposing enemy forces in January. Here, in essence were not two independent *front* operations linked only by a single strategic plan, but a single big offensive operation (involving the forces and equipment of two *fronts* and the Supreme High Command), conducted directly by the *Stavka*. The *fronts*, in the present case, were the executors not only of the strategic, but of the operational plans of the Supreme Commander-in-Chief. Only by understanding this peculiarity of the operation and having embraced from a single operational-strategic point of view the events that unfolded in January on the Kalinin and Western fronts can one properly understand and evaluate the operations of the Western Front's forces. This is important for the January period namely because in the given concentric operation there was demanded and carried out a closer operational coordination of two *fronts* than in operations that develop straightforwardly. The close connection and coordination here deal not only with the neighboring units and formations along the boundary of the Kalinin and Western fronts, but embraced the main forces of both *fronts*, striving to surround and defeat a single overall enemy group.

5 In examining the combat events along the Western Front in January it should be noted the different, as opposed to December, overall style and character of the *front* operation.

First of all, in December on the Western Front a counteroffensive was carried out, that is, an offensive in response to the enemy's offensive and directly connected to the operational defense that preceded it. The counteroffensive began with a struggle for the initiative. In January the initiative was in our hands. We conducted the subsequent development of the December offensive from the line of the Lama, Ruza, Nara, and Oka rivers and the Fascists were forced to defend.

Secondly, in December we had dealt with a more sharply defined outline of a *front* operation and its more precise and simple development. Its formation is easily explained: two leading wings moving forward, with a stable center, which gradually becomes more active. This operation's form may be simply shown graphically. The actual development of the Western Front's operations in January unfolded along a more complex and torturous path. At first glance, in examining the course of events, the unified purposefulness, the overall connection and mutual dependence of phenomena is weakened in the scale of a *front* operation. It is displayed with sufficient fullness only in a deepened examination of these events. In the mosaic of separate local operations (army or groups of armies) and battles the *front* command's initial plans are broken up and refracted in various directions. Unnoticed here are the sharply drawn operations along the wings, which was a characteristic feature of the December counteroffensive. The armies (particularly in the beginning) carried out independent tasks along their own axis, cooperating with neighbors. The Yukhnov group's stubborn resistance required the involvement of several armies. Here were directed the efforts of the 43rd, 49th, and 50th armies and the 1st Guards Cavalry Corps, as well as airborne landings, and here the *front* command exercised the coordination of several armies on the boundary between the *front's* center and left wing.

The development of the *front* operation in January was uneven and unfolded in the following sequence:

a) The rapid and deep movement of the *front's* left wing to the Vyaz'ma-Bryansk lateral road. The slow unfolding of events along the Kaluga-Yukhnov axis and the center's more rapid advance to the west of Borovsk and Maloyaroslavets around the Medyn'-Yukhnov group. A stable situation on the *front's* right wing as a result of the enemy's stubborn defense.
b) The unfolding of an operational breakthrough on the *front's* right wing and the advance of the right wing's forces (and part of the center's) in the direction of the Germans' Gzhatsk defensive line. The start of the envelopment of the Myatlevo-Yukhnov group by the adjacent flanks of the *front's* center and left wing. The situation remained unchanged on the remainder of the left wing.
c) The encirclement of the Yukhnov group and the offensive's development toward Vyaz'ma in order to split the enemy front. The gradual slowing of the offensive on both wings with a partial retreat under enemy pressure in the direction of Zhizdra and Sukhinichi.

Such a development of the *front* operation was being determined by the concrete conditions of the fighting, which had come to pass in January along the Moscow strategic direction. Such a consecutive unfolding of the *front* offensive operation has its own regularities and internal logic, which we sought to show in all of the preceding material.

The Soviet forces' January offensive achieved, as we have already demonstrated, major positive results. Along with this, one should keep in mind that such a "broken up" character of the offensive's development, with the gradual shrinking of the scope of the operations conducted, as well as the results achieved, often serve as a sign that the troops' offensive capabilities are beginning to wane and are close to their limit, and that the offensive is on the decline. If a fresh infusion of forces does not follow or a sharp change for the better in the situation, the offensive can die out and come to a halt.

As far as army operations and larger battles are concerned, they (in the confines of those overall conditions created by a single *front* operation, such as a more or less uniform enemy, similar natural conditions, etc.) were distinguished by a great variety and many of them are quite instructive. One may find here maneuver operations along a broad front (10th Army), on a narrow sector (20th Army), and other various types of tactical and operational actions. They are described in detail in the preceding chapters, where partial conclusions are made.

The same may be said in relation to the employment of the various combat arms in January. The corresponding descriptions, evaluations, and conclusions were listed above.

In the course of combat operations the Red Army, as we have seen repeatedly, sought to encircle this or that German group. These encirclements were carried out on various scales, beginning with small units or detachments (1-2 reinforced regiments) up to large operational groups (Yukhnov, Rzhev-Gzhatsk-Vyaz'ma). However, they often failed to end in the final defeat of the enemy's forces on the battlefield or the capture of the encircled enemy.

In those cases when the enemy disposed of sufficient forces and held on stoutly, he managed to sit it out for a significant period in the encircled area and then, having chosen a favorable moment or having received support from without, would break through and withdraw the greater or lesser part of his forces from the encirclement.

The January fighting offers valuable and instructive material for judgments as to the means of encirclement and completing it with the defeat of the enemy's encircled forces, as well as fighting while encircled.

The combat and operational experience received demonstrates that the enemy's encirclement on the operational or tactical scale is even now the more decisive form of battle and operation. It should always be attempted when the possibility arises. For encirclement the following is usually required: the defeat of the enemy's units on the flanks of the encircled group, accompanied by a frontal offensive; the rapid and decisive advance on the flanks by mobile formations (and sometimes by airborne landings) to reach the enemy's rear. The encirclement may become secure only when it is completed by the rifle troops. However, the fact of encirclement alone does not signify the enemy's defeat. If the enemy is stubborn and skillful, if he has sufficient men and matériel to organize an all-round defense, then the struggle with the encircled enemy (depending on the scale and conditions of the encirclement) may be drawn out.

In order to achieve rapid and decisive results it is necessary that the attacking units be able not only to encircle this or that enemy group, but that they have sufficient men and matériel for inflicting crushing blows against the encircled group, splitting the enemy's combat formation into separate and isolated pieces and gradually squeezing the encirclement ring. The January fighting showed that encircled forces can put up serious and lengthy resistance if they are deployed in a compact manner in one area favorable for defense and can maneuver their forces and can maintain coordination between their units and combat arms. In order to break the enemy's organized resistance and to disrupt the defense's unity and integrity, it is necessary to split up his combat order by concentrated blows along narrow sectors into separate pieces of such size that they can be enfiladed throughout by crossfire. In these conditions it is difficult for the defender to hold on for an extended time and each of the cut off and isolated units may be destroyed separately. An encirclement completed in this fashion may yield a decisive result: the complete rout and destruction of the enemy on the battlefield, or the capture of his encircled forces.

6 In describing the January battles, serious attention should be paid to studying the problems of organizing the rear and the matériel-technical support of the Red Army's attacking troops. It was necessary to understand how this work was organized, what kinds of difficulties arose for the rear organs at various stages of the operation, and how these difficulties were overcome. The materials cited in the section of the rear show the entire difficulty and peculiarity of the work carried out on the Western Front under conditions of a harsh and snowy winter. Of the questions connected with the offensive of this or that army (or group of armies), particularly deserving of attention is the matériel-technical support of the 20th Army on the Volokolamsk-Gzhatsk axis (an army breakthrough), as well as the organization of supply to the attacking troops of the left wing during their rapid advance and at a significant remove from their bases.

7 The amount of ammunition expended during our offensive in December and January is of particular interest. This small expenditure of ammunition is reflected in the corresponding tables. However, along with this one should take into account the overall character of combat operations, the conditions and supply opportunities which our forces were in. It should also be kept in mind that over and above those munitions issued by the supply organs and shown in the tables, our troops used a significant amount of captured ammunition. Their actual expenditure was thus greater than indicated in the supply documentation.

8 The acquired experience enables us to draw several overall conclusions about operations in winter conditions.

Winter conditions enable us to wage large operations (*front* operations and the joint operations of several *fronts*), but particularly emphasize the necessity balancing the available men and matériel with the goals being pursued by the operations.

The most suitable form in conducting a *front*-level offensive operation is the operations by several shock groups along various axes, followed by the encirclement and destruction of definite enemy operational groups.

During wintertime the troops (with the exception of ski units) have fewer opportunities for maneuver than in summer; in connection with this the planning of winter operations requires especial purposefulness.

Large-scale winter operations are essentially planned at the *front* level. The armies resolve limited operational tasks. An army usually attacks along a single axis, having a single shock group. The resolution of large operational tasks requires, as a rule, the efforts of several armies.

Operational combinations connected with the encirclement of a large enemy group, are carried out on a *front* scale.

The organization of the combined-arms battle along the main direction of the army's offensive is carried out by the army command, which, which organizing the efforts of the divisions and attached army equipment, directly organizes the fulfillment of combat assignments by the combat formations operating along the main axis. Given a large number of formations as part of the army, the divisions operating along an auxiliary axis may be unified into an operational group.

The success of winter operations depends to a great deal on the carefulness of their preparation, particularly on the precisely thought-out work of the rear down to the last detail.

9 The present description of operations along the Moscow strategic direction is basically completed on January 31 1942. To be sure, the events that unfolded here had still not reached their logical culmination by this time. The operations did not end and no operational pause ensued and combat operations continued to develop into the subsequent period. However, these are the subject of a separate examination.

Part VI

Overall conclusions on the Moscow Operation

The overall course of the Moscow Operation

The current study examines events of great political and military significance, which unfolded along the Moscow strategic direction and embraced the period of time from the middle of October 1941 to the end of January 1942, that is three and a half months of the Great Patriotic War.

Here briefly is highlighted the failure of the first (October) German offensive against Moscow, which involved them in extended fighting along the Kalinin, Moscow, and Tula axes, without achieving any decisive results.

The weakening of the intensity of combat activities from the beginning of November along the Moscow direction (for the purpose of carrying out regrouping, bringing up for and the German's preparation for a new offensive) was a necessary operational pause and also, in examining the overall course of events, represents a logical boundary that divides the end of the first offensive from the beginning of the second.

From the middle of November the Germans' second general offensive on Moscow began. These and the following events, in accordance with their overall course, may be divided into the following complete periods (stages).

1 The German-Fascist troops' second general offensive on Moscow and the defensive battle on the Western Front (November 16-December 5 1941).

As a result of this period, the German-Fascist troops on both flanks moved forward, having deeply penetrated our position, and hung over Moscow from the north and south. But in the course of the fighting the correlation of forces and the mutual situation of the sides changed. The Germans became exhausted in the stubborn fighting with the Red Army's forces; by the end of this period they no longer had the forces for a further offensive and had to go over to the defensive in an unfavorable situation, preparing to fall back under the Red Army's growing blows. The Red Army's forces wore out and exhausted the enemy, waging a stubborn and active defense along the far and near approaches to Moscow. By the end of the period the Western Front's forces, reinforced with the Supreme High Command's reserves, had halted the enemy and forced him to go over to the defensive in conditions unfavorable to him and were preparing for a decisive counteroffensive along both flanks, now having a superiority in forces over the Germans and occupying a more advantageous operational situation.

2 The Red Army's counteroffensive on the Western Front and the defeat of the German-Fascist forces around Moscow (December 6-24).

As a result of the December counteroffensive by our troops the enemy suffered a severe defeat. Both his flank shock groups were routed and were hurriedly falling back to the west. His center held off the Red Army's attacks for the time being. The Germans subsequently managed to temporarily halt our offensive along the northern wing along the fortified line of the Lama and Ruza rivers. In the south our forces quickly forced the Oka River between Kaluga and Belev and, swiftly developing their blow, were pursuing the enemy.

3 The subsequent offensive by the Western Front's troops from the line of the Lama, Ruza, Nara, and Oka rivers (December 25 1941-January 31 1942).

This period (almost equal in its length to the two preceding ones) yielded a large territorial victory to the Red Army; the enemy suffered a series of heavy local defeats; the integrity of his front was disrupted and favorable prerequisites were created for the encirclement by the troops of two fronts (Kalinin and Western) of the Germans' main forces along the Moscow strategic direction. But the events that unfolded in January (described in the work's third part) did not achieve at this time their logical culmination and continued to develop in February. For ease of examination, this period may be divided into three shorter periods of combat in accordance with how the center of events shifted on the scale of a *front* operation.

From December 25 to January 10 the troops' main advance and the chief events occurred on the *front's* left flank, where they reached the Vyaz'ma-Bryansk lateral road.

During January 10-20 we have the breakthrough of the German defense on the right wing and the development of the offensive on the Gzhatsk axis.

During January 20-31 the chief events unfolded in the center: the encirclement of the Yukhnov group and the splitting of the front in the direction of Vyaz'ma.

All of these activities were connected between themselves by the fact that they occurred within the confines of a single *front*, as well as by the sequence of development within the confines of its wing or center. Sometimes events within the confines of a wing did not end completely in the given time, but continued subsequently to this. But the center of the fighting on the *front* scale and the main events shifted in the following sequence: the left wing until January 10; the right wing during the second ten-day period in January, and; later in the center and adjacent axes.

In accordance with the division of the Moscow operation into its main stages, the present study contains and examination of these stages, as well as conclusions for each of them.

The command's work

The Moscow operation places extremely high demands on the command element and troop control.

The German-Fascist command, in drawing up a plan for seizing Moscow and defeating the Red Army, was pursuing decisive goals, which should have, according to their design; result in the rapid end of the war. This was the plan of and experienced and skillful predator, striving to quick gain and dreaming of living off someone else's goods. But the German command underestimated the Red Army's powers of resistance and cruelly miscalculated.

Having suffered a defeat around Moscow, the German command renounced active operations and sought to hold out along a series of defensive lines. In this fighting the Germans displayed great doggedness in defense. However, the Red Army's far-reaching offensive operations, which unfolded during the course of the winter, placed the enemy troops in a difficult situation. General von Bock's entire central group of armies was more than once on the edge of a complete catastrophe.

In the December 6-January 15 time period, that is a month and ten days of the Red Army's offensive operations, the German army lost on the Soviet-German front 300,000 men and officers in killed alone.

During this period the Soviet troops captured 4,801 guns, 3,071 mortars, up to 8,000 machine guns, more than 90,000 rifles, 2,766 tanks, and 33,640 motor vehicles. More than 1,000 enemy planes were destroyed.

This data clearly shows what a serious defeat the German-Fascist army suffered around Moscow and along the other sectors of the Soviet-German front.

The rout of the Germans at Moscow was accomplished according to the plan of the Supreme Commander-in-Chief, comrade Stalin, and under his personal control. We closely examined the preparation and realization of comrade Stalin's design for defeating the Germans. This was a wise plan. It took into account the experience of our country's great past and reflected an unshakable faith in its great future. Its roots were deep in the life of the people.

The Supreme Command of the Red Army manifested great operational-strategic prudence and foresight in organizing the repulse of the Germans at Moscow. The necessary amount of troops was allocated to the Western Front for an active defense, which relied on a system of fortified lines. In the immediate rear was organized the Moscow Defense Zone, which with its troops and fortifications was a sort of covering army for Moscow and simultaneously a source of additional reserves of all types for the *front*. In the country's depth new reserve armies were being created, which were concentrated in a timely manner, by order of the *Stavka*, along both sides of Moscow, behind the Western Front's flanks.

During the course of the fighting on the approaches to Moscow the Red Army's Supreme High Command displayed a great deal of firmness, courage, and skill. Despite the extremely difficult and tense situation at the front, the main reserves were saved until the decisive moment for active operations and were deployed in those areas were the fate of the battle was being decided and where they were most needed. During the moment of supreme crisis during the battle of Moscow the Supreme Command's reserves were committed into the battle and guaranteed the Red Army's success. The Red Army Supreme Commander-in-Chief's iron will crushed all obstacles on the path to victory.

Along with this, the Red Army command manifested at the necessary times a great deal of flexibility, soberly evaluating the developing situation, and adopted decisions that were the most advantageous in the given situation. We have seen how the scope of our counteroffensive grew consecutively, while taking into account the development of events: from the rout of the German's flank groups by the Western Front's wings to the encirclement of the remaining forces of the German's central group of armies by the forces of our two *fronts* and the *Stavka*. The Red Army command, having seized the initiative in the beginning of December, firmly held it in its hands throughout the entire winter offensive.

The design and plan of comrade Stalin, the Supreme Commander-in-Chief, found talented organizers and executors amongst the command of the Western and Kalinin fronts. To him belongs the lion's share of the credit for defense of Moscow and the defeat of the German-Fascist hordes on its approaches.

It's especially necessary to single out the leadership of the commander of the Western Front, army general comrade Zhukov, who in the very difficult conditions of defense and retreat, followed by a subsequent counteroffensive, displayed examples of bold and striking decisions, firmness and resourcefulness in choosing the means and methods of operations, as well as skill in organizing the repulse of the enemy in the most difficult conditions, and to prepare his subsequent defeat.

The work of the Western Front's command is an example worthy of profound study. We referred to this more than once in our examination.

The role of the army commanders in the dynamic and rapidly developing events was also extremely responsible. It was on the basis of their bold and well-grounded decisions, their energy and organizational capabilities that so much of the course and outcome of the fighting depended. The army commanders' work in controlling their forces embraced operational and tactical situations. It was subjected to examination and evaluation by us throughout the entire work.

We saw how in the difficult days of defense and retreat under the pressure of the enemy's superior forces, the 16th Army commander, Gen. Rokossovskii, and the commander of the 5th Army Gen. Govorov (along with the other armies), tenaciously and skillfully defended each line and blocking the enemy's path to Moscow. Under their cover deep reserves were concentrating and occupying previously-indicated areas in the overall operational formation. The 50th Army, under the command of Gen. Boldin, wrote amazing pages in the history of war with its repulse of enemy attacks around Tula.

We also noted the extremely important significance of our going over to a counteroffensive played by the operations of the 30th and 1st Shock armies, under the command of generals Lelyushenko and Kuznetsov, as well as the 20th Army, and in the south—Gen. Golikov's 10th Army and Gen. Belov's 1st Guards Cavalry Corps.

They, together with the commanders of the central armies, who successfully carried out their missions, deserve great credit in the cause of Moscow's defense and in the defeat of the German-Fascist aggressors.

On the character of operations

A study of the operations by both sides along the Moscow strategic direction for the three and a half months clearly shows the great scope that can be attained in modern operations by large numbers of troops, pursuing very important and decisive goals in conditions of maneuver warfare, along broad fronts, and given relatively small operational densities.

The army and *front* operations along the Moscow strategic direction during the period under study had their characteristic features and peculiarities, one which we will dwell later. However, alongside the army and *front* operations, we have also seen at certain times operations by groups of armies (within the bounds of a *front* operation), while the entirety of the struggle along the Moscow strategic direction, doubtlessly, extended beyond the bounds of the *front* operation and outgrew them.

The Moscow direction was an extremely important one; here the most important goals were pursued. Thus the struggle took on such acute character and such a scope, which could not be contained within the confines of even such a broad *front*, which had such a large number of forces as the Western Front.

Actions on the Moscow direction, on the whole, were a large strategic-scale operation (a strategic operation), for the realization of which the men and matériel of two-three *fronts* and the High Command, controlled by the Supreme Commander-in-Chief comrade Stalin, were drawn in during the course of the fighting. At certain periods the Supreme High Command's reserves and equipment played a decisive role in this large operation.

The achieved level of technical development is also conducive to the broadening of the boundaries of modern operations. Aviation, motor-mechanized formations, modern communications equipment, and others, have broadened the bounds of operations and increased the possibilities of controlling them. They increased the pace of the operations' development, made it possible to quickly overcome great distances, and to achieve decisive operational and strategic results in limited periods of time (given the presence of favorable conditions).

Alongside this a characteristic feature of modern operations is the continuity of combat activities over a prolonged period. One operation immediately grew into another and the boundaries between them were being erased; the presence of operational pauses between local operations was a comparatively rare phenomenon. On the main axes we often observed an unbroken series of consecutive operations and battles.

In the Moscow operation the *Stavka* had to not only coordinate on a strategic scale the efforts of two *fronts*, which were directed toward the achievement of a single goal, but in certain periods directly conduct this large operation, trying to achieve (when this was necessary) the close operational coordination between the *fronts* to resolve the overall task. This close operational coordination (in accordance with the concrete development of events) was required not only for the adjoining troops formations along the *front* boundaries, but sometimes embraced the main forces of the two *fronts* (for example, during the second half of January).

The Western Front's activities offer valuable material for conclusions as to the front operation. They have often been put forward by us in the previous exposition. However, it is necessary to keep in mind that the Western Front (in accordance with the importance of the Moscow strategic direction) was not **atypical** front in the Great Patriotic War. It was distinct from the neighboring *fronts* by its size and large numbers of troops. The capital of the Soviet Union—Moscow, was in its immediate rear. This put a stamp on the scale and character of the Western Front's operations. In relation to the neighboring *fronts* (Kalinin and Bryansk), it should be noted: first, their lesser organizational stability (as organizational-strategic unions of several armies), they were created or had their existence terminated in accordance with the development of the situation; secondly, a certain breaking up into smaller pieces of the *fronts* and *front* operations and the narrowing of these operations' goals and tasks.

According to the experience of the Western Front, the characteristic features of the ***front* operation** are:

1 A *front* operation pursues a major strategic goal; its achievement exerts an immediate influence on the course of the campaign and war. The modern *front* operation in its development resolves strategic and operational tasks.
2 The *front* operation unfolds along an important strategic direction, combining an entire cluster of mutually-connected operational directions, along which armies or groups of armies operate.
3 The *front* operation units the actions of several armies, operational mobile groups, *front* aviation, and airborne landings, assigning them local objectives and laying out goals leading to the achievement of the operation's overall goal.
4 The great mutability of operational forms and the content of operational forms, depending on its plan and the specific conditions of the situation. The uneven development of the operation along different axes, the growth of one form into another, and the prospect of the operation's actual unfolding, is different from that which was foreseen by the initial plan.

Operational forms may change at each stage of the operation, and sometimes even during a single stage. This was mentioned in the examination of the December counteroffensive.

The *front's* operational formation included two wings and a center (consisting of field armies), mobile groups, *front* aviation, and *front* reserves. The length of the winding front line was quite inconstant (from 250 to 700 km). All the *front's* armies were deployed, as a rule, in a single echelon. The *front* reserves (divisions) were located at a remove of 15-30 km from the front line. The *front's* operational formation in the majority of cases was characterized by its linear character and an insufficient amount of reserves. However, it should be noted that the intensity of the fighting demanded from the *front* command the unbroken supply of its armies engaged in heavy fighting, while the necessary depth of the troops' operational echelonment and the presence of large reserves were acquired at the expense of the Moscow Defense Zone and the *Stavka* reserves, which were stationed within the confines of the Western Front and which disposed of large forces.

Army operations were usually a component part of one of the stages of a *front* operation. Their goals and tasks were determined in accordance with the idea of the *front* operation. An army's size and composition depended on the place and role of the given army in the *front's* operation (the main or auxiliary axis), and on the character of the task being pursued; its composition sometimes changed significantly during the fighting, when the army received a more important task.

The form of an army operation was determined by the goals assigned to it, and it depended upon the enemy's forces and situation, on the number of men and matériel in the army itself, and the character of the terrain. For the most part, a blow was launched from a single general sector and along one axis. An operational encirclement required the participation of several armies.

The army's operational formation usually was as follows:

> In the offensive the divisions were in a single echelon (sometimes in two), with the army reserves at a 12-15 km remove;
>
> On the defensive the divisions were, for the most part, in a single echelon; the second-echelon divisions (when we had them) were located 8-15 km from the front line; the army reserves (a regiment or division) were at a 12-15 km remove.

The army operations' general character depends (along with other considerations) also on the army's organizational composition. An army of a given organization (the actual composition of various armies on the Western Front has been repeatedly cited in the corresponding chapters) was an operational-tactical combination of forces. The army operation on the Western Front became smaller: its goals became narrower; its goals and objectives became smaller. The role of each army operation and its independence became smaller in the overall *front* operation.

Alongside of this the role of tactical elements in the armies' activities rose sharply. The battle was by no means always conducted within the confines of the division. Upon the abolition of the corps organization, the army commander was the organizer of the combined-arms battle along the main axis. This extremely important function could by no means be removed from his authority. An insufficient understanding of this problem by some armies at first resulted in the crisis of the combined-arms battle along the main axis. In a number of cases the operational task being carried out (for example, the encirclement of an enemy group) could not be immediately concluded and realized at the tactical level: the defeat and destruction of the encircled group (Klin, Sukhinichi, the Yukhnov groups, etc.) on the battlefield, or its capture.

Thus the operational element in the army was reduced, while the tactical one grew. The Western Front's experience shows that despite the broad fronts and a relatively small operational density, the modern army comparatively rarely resolves an independent task along a separate operational axis. This happens more often on the defensive than in an offensive. Usually two or three armies jointly resolve a single overall operational task.

According to the Western Front's experience, an army on the defensive is capable of waging battle with an attacking enemy within the confines of the tactical zone, using for this purpose its first-echelon divisions and the army reserve. If the attacker's forces did not exceed by too much the defender's, then the army in a number of cases had the opportunity to halt him on this or that line (the defense along the Nara River in the Aleksin area, etc.). However, if the enemy attacked with an operational shock group (particularly if he had managed to break through to the operational depth with mobile formations), then the army usually lacked insufficient means to destroy this group on its own. The *front* command's energetic assistance was required, with air, tank and cavalry formations, rifle divisions, equipment, and munitions (the defense by the 16th, 30th, and 50th armies in November and the beginning of November). The decisive role in counterblows in the operational depth belonged to the *front* reserves.

The peculiarities of the operations that the armies had to conduct also consisted in the fact that these were local operations of a consecutive type, lacking a definite boundary in time and growing from one into another. Some army operations were conducted in one group to the entire depth. These armies often lacked a second echelon.

A peculiarity in the operations of the 16th and 10th armies was expressed, by the way, in the fact that the width of their operational zone changed sharply. Thus, the 16th Army in the middle of November occupied a front of about 70 km, with part of its forces in the second echelon. In retreating under the Germans' pressure to the near approaches to Moscow, its front gradually shrank to 30 km, and was even smaller when it went over to the counteroffensive. This enabled the 16th Army to achieve a good operational troop density by the end of the defensive period and abetted its subsequent assumption of the counteroffensive.

In the 10th Army the offensive front varied significantly. This army entered the Tula operation in December, operating along a 100-km front. By the end of the operation the 10th Army's front was no more than 30-35 km in width. The army also operated along this front width during the first stage of the Belev-Kozel'sk operation. In this case (as the actual course of events showed) the armies could have a strong second echelon, consisting of 2-3 rifle divisions, which as combat progressed were moved to the army's first echelon along those axes where it was necessary to strengthen or develop the offensive. Following the 10th Army's arrival to the west of the Oka River, the width of its front sharply increased and reached 150 km. In this case the army's second echelon was almost absent, if one does not consider a single understrength division.

In the armies that had to carry out operations along a broad front and had to have a large number of directly subordinated formations (for example, the 10th and 50th armies each had eight rifle divisions, not counting other units and formations), there existed the major problem of troop control, particularly when communications were often disrupted. In such instances it evidently would have been expedient to unite the divisions operating along an auxiliary axis into an operational group, in order to lighten the load at the army level for dealing with the main axis.

In the process of the successful development of military operations, while pursuing the retreating enemy, and in organizing a breakthrough along a narrow front, we observed army operations of a more developed type. But as soon as the enemy's strength and activity would increase, his resistance would grow, and it would become difficult for a single army to resolve independent operational tasks. Then there would appear sharply defined operations by groups of armies within the confines of the ongoing *front* operation (for example, of the *front's* right and left wings in December; the operations of the central armies for encircling the Kondrovo-Yukhnov group in January, and others).

The *front* also directly controlled these operations by groups of armies. But the necessity of coordinating several neighboring armies arose often; the coordination itself had to have a tighter operational-tactical character. The situation often required the unification of several armies and the control of their actions. At the same time, the *front* was bulky (10-11 armies); the front instance was quite overloaded. Given the great length of the front line, the control of the *front* could not be direct everywhere and had to be carried out from the depth. Operations by groups of armies (even when conducted successfully) were not completely satisfactory for a variety of reasons, including, possibly, as a result of the insufficiently coordinated work of those armies resolving a single overall operational task.

On the conduct of operations

The protracted and stubborn fighting in the Moscow area, conducted in a cold and snowy winter, was a harsh school for our troops. An enormous exertion of moral and physical efforts was required in order to first, withstand the German's destructions armored wedges and hold Moscow, and then to smash the enemy's stubborn resistance, inflict a defeat on him and drive him to the west. In this titanic struggle our forces were tempered and acquired valuable experience and learned how to defeat the Germans.

Limited by the boundaries of an operational study, we were able only in brief strokes to show the epic picture of the Soviet people's struggle and to very briefly characterize the heroism, bravery, and self abnegation of some individuals and entire units, which were manifested in the fighting around Moscow in these great days. Entire volumes will be written about them and, undoubtedly the far and near approaches to Moscow will become those sacred places, which millions of Soviet people will visit with reverence, in order to honor the memory of the heroes of the great battle for Moscow. Their glorious deeds will live in the people's memory forever.

However, we have another task. We must show here what the experience of the fighting in the Moscow area gave of tactical value, in what way our theory and practice of waging battle were enriched as a result of the Red Army's victories operations in the Moscow operation.

The experience of the Red Army's combat operations (as well as that of other *fronts*) found its expression in those *Stavka* directives issued in the winter of 1941-42. These were directives on the fundamentals of conducting the battle and employing the combat arms. The organization of the artillery offensive, the basic principles of employing tank units and formations, the use of aviation and engineering troops, which are now part and parcel of the Red Army, reflect to a significant degree the victorious Moscow operation's combat experience.

From this point of view, the Western Front's guiding directives and orders, summarizing by the summer of 1942 the experience of conducting offensive and defensive battles against the Germans, deserve particular attention.

As concerns the Red Army's conduct of the offensive battle, it was pointed out that the Germans, operating along an extended front, were not in a condition to create a continuous and dense defense everywhere. The Germans' defense, as a rule, was built around outposts in the form of strong points, connected as centers of resistance (company and battalion). Their base is usually inhabited points, groves and other convenient local landmarks, carefully adapted to defense. A great deal of attention is given to organizing a fire system primarily using the infantry's fire weapons.

Such a defensive formation, given the presence of a series of favorable factors, allows for breaking through the front and makes it possible to infiltrate between the strong points and launch a blow against the defender's flank and rear. The capture of a strong point disrupts the usual defensive system and gives our forces access to the depth of the defensive zone.

For counterattacks, the Germans usually collect reserves from the depth and from neighboring sectors. The counterattacks are most often carried out by battalions supported by tanks, striving to launch flank blows against the attacking troops. Powerful mortar and artillery fire is employed. The Germans do not spare the ammunition, although the fire is usually not aimed and is area fire.

The success of our offensive operations was achieved on the condition of careful reconnaissance of the enemy, the correct preparation of the troops for battle, the precise organization and coordination of the troops, the skillful and firm direction and the good matériel-technical supply of the battle. Artillery, mortars and the fire from guards mortar battalions have an enormous significance in preparing for and conducting the offensive; however, it is impossible to carry out a breakthrough of the defense without organizing the attacking infantry's fire. One should take into account the fact that the enemy (as soon as our success becomes evident) throws in his air power against the attacking troops, and thus it is necessary to have a well-organized PVO system.

Tanks are usually employed along the main axis. The tank attack must be sudden and massive. Aviation and artillery prepare and accompany the tank attack throughout its entire depth.

The rifle regiments' first combat echelons continue the forward advance without lingering on the forward edge of the defense. Capturing the strong points that are still holding out is the second echelons' task. In the case of our successful offensive, the enemy seeks to quickly organize counterattacks. Thus consolidating the successes achieved and putting the captured points into a condition for defense has decisive significance. Having disrupted the enemy's counterattacking ranks with fire, our infantry and tanks (with the active support of artillery, mortars, and machine guns), themselves launch a headlong attack.

When our troops conduct a defensive battle, it is necessary to take into account that the Germans, in preparing for an offensive, systematically study our defense down to the last detail. In an offensive organized by the Germans, we see the employment of massed air, tanks, artillery, and mortars along the sector of the main blow. Along with this, by breaking through our lines and infiltrating groups of automatic riflemen into the depths of our defense, the Germans try to create the appearance of the rapid encirclement of our defense, seize rear arteries, sow panic in the rear, and disrupt control and supply. Combat practice testifies to the smooth coordination of the enemy's air with his attacking ground forces.

From this it follows that the defense should be organized as follows, so as to:

1 to impede the enemy's reconnaissance of or defense; for this purpose, disguise, vigilance, and military secrecy must be observed; to deceive the enemy by organizing a false forward line;
2 in constructing the defense it's necessary to study the terrain well and correctly use it; the approaches to the position from the enemy's side must be carefully observed and enfiladed;
3 the defense should be anti-artillery, anti-tank, anti-aircraft, and anti-personnel; in accordance with these requirements, measures should be carried out to most fully and expediently employ masking, firepower, and local lines. Each strong point and battalion area should be outfitted as anti-tank areas.

The fundamentals of waging the defensive battle:

1 Aviation and long-range artillery must strike the enemy's attacking units on the far approaches. Upon the enemy's reaching the edge of the security zone he is engaged by specially weapons from temporary firing positions. Upon the enemy's reaching the jumping off point for the offensive, our artillery, aviation, and mortars launch powerful blows against concentrations of infantry and tanks.
2 Upon the start of the enemy's attack, the artillery, mortars, and part of the heavy machine guns lay down fire against the attacking infantry's columns.

   With the enemy's approach to the line of attack all our firepower powerfully opens up. When the enemy's tanks join in the attack our artillery shifts its fire to the tanks. The anti-tank defense's task is to beat off the attack by the enemy's tanks and to prevent them from breaking through the forward edge of the defense.

   The task of all the strong points' and artillery's fire weapons (not engaged in battling the tanks) is to cut off the enemy infantry from his tanks, force it to the ground, defeat it, and prevent it from attacking the forward edge of the defensive position. All the fire means from neighboring sectors not under attack are to join in repelling the attack.
3 Should the enemy pierce our defensive depth, the regimental and division commanders are obliged, while continuing to defend the strong points, to halt the enemy's advance with massed fire and organize a counterattack with second-echelon forces, supported by tanks.

   Groups of automatic riflemen, which have infiltrated beyond the forward zone, are to be destroyed by flanking fire from the neighboring strong points, as well as from those strong points situated in the depth, as well as by local counterattacks by nearby companies and battalions.

   In attacking and defending under harsh winter conditions, of great significance are the troops' toughness and their training for operating at night, in hard frosts, in a snowstorm, on skis, etc. The troops must be carefully trained beforehand for these kinds of combat activities.

The experience of organizing the rear and matériel supply

During the course of the battle for Moscow the rear and supply organs carried out an enormous amount of work.

During the defensive period—in a situation involving the massive evacuation of the population, industrial equipment, and supplies, in conditions involving the sudden change of supply lines and the enemy air's systematic attack of our rear organs and supply routes—the rear apparatus, on the whole, coped with its tasks and guaranteed the troops' unbroken supply and prepared the matériel basis for our decisive counteroffensive.

With the beginning of the counteroffensive, new and various tasks arose for the rear and supply workers: to organize the restoration of supply routes, secure the delivery of significantly-increased amounts of supplies along lengthening dirt roads; to change its work methods in accordance with the new situation. The rear did not completely resolve these tasks. At the end of January the troops' level of matériel supply fell considerably and breakdowns in the delivery of supplies to the units occurred more often.

The work experience of organizing the rear and the matériel supply of the troops in the Moscow operation has great significance. The battle for Moscow unfolded along a broad front. Along with this, the main forces were grouped along the decisive axes and the density of the troops' operational deployment was uneven. Modern armies' great maneuver possibilities enabled the sides to change their troop dispositions and shift the center of their efforts from one axis to another. The rear had to take these conditions into account and adapt itself to them.

The timely complete matériel supply of the troops in such conditions (as the experience of the rear area's work in the Moscow operation shows) reauires:

1 The establishment of a firm limit in the expenditure of matériel by operational stages and axes, determined not by a quick calculation or prewar norms, but based upon the realistic needs of the troops in a given operation.
2 The creation of supply and evacuation routes with the established traffic control and repair-restoration services; the presence of the necessary transport at the commander's disposal and a reserve of basic matériel needs.
3 The close and continuous communication between the rear commanders and the staffs, for the purpose of fully and in a timely manner keeping the rear informed of the operational situation and the command's intentions.

Of no less significance, as experience has shown, is the rear's secure and swiftly operating system of communications with both the troops and between the different rear organs, which guarantees the control of the matériel supply situation, the expenditure of supplies, and the organization of the maneuver of matériel.

The disruption of rules established by experience and poor communications led to breakdowns in supplying units, and to the irrational expenditure and even loss of valuable and very necessary supplies.

In mobile defense, given the enemy's superiority in motor-mechanized units, the rear organization (the placing of personnel, the grouping of supplies, and work methods) must guarantee unbroken supply even in cases in which the troops' communications with their rear units are disrupted and to simultaneously exclude mass losses of matériel. The creation of a small mobile reserve and the stationing of small depots along the road junctions answer this demand, as well as the organization of operational rear groups and their disposition and in communications centers.

Distribution methods predominated in the rear's administration during the defensive period. However, given the absence of a plan they turned into emergency methods, which sometimes led to a breakdown in supply and the mass loss of supplies. The planning of deliveries along railroads, paved, and dirt roads is the core of in planning the rear's work overall. Difficulties in the rear's work and breakdowns in supply at the end of December and in January were brought about, to a significant degree, by the incomplete employment of existing transportation means, as well as their insufficient expansion during the period of our troops' rapid advance (particularly on the left flank).

The precise and, at the same time, flexible planning of the rear's work and matériel supply while breaking through the enemy's previously-fortified position during the offensive is very important. Without a careful and well thought out deployment of forces, the positioning of supplies and the distribution of the entire volume of work in time and space, a lack of coordination in the work of the numerous rear sections, the non-focused use of matériel, and breakdowns in troop supply are inevitable.

The organization of the rear and matériel supply for ten army formations proved to be bulky and complex. For the purpose of lightening the load for the *front* apparatus, the matériel supply of the shock (reserve) armies, operationally subordinated to the *front*, was for a time entrusted to the central directorates. During the first stage, while the enemy was enveloping the Western Front's armies in a semi-ring, the rear chief's directorate and the supply directorates coped with their tasks. As a result of the defeat of the enemy's enveloping wings and the beginning of our advance, the front expanded greatly, the delivery tasks became more complicated, and communications with the left-flank armies was often disrupted.

For the purpose of improving the matériel supply for the left-wing armies, a railhead branch of the *front* base was created and an operational group for rear administration was also organized. These measures improved the left-flank armies' supply somewhat; however, the difficulties connected with an overly large number of formations being supplied and the increasingly lengthy front line, were not fully eliminated. The creation of a special apparatus for supplying the left-flank group of armies would have been more expedient.

On the whole, the command and rear apparatus in the Moscow operation received rich and extremely valuable practice in rear organization and the matériel supply of the troops in various kinds of combat and operational activities. The experience of the rear's work in the Moscow operation is very instructive.

* * *

The shift from defense and retreat to a decisive counteroffensive on a broad operational-strategic scale and the defeat of the enemy's attacking forces is one of the most difficult and complex operations, and which place extremely high demands on the moral strength and bravery of the troops, and on the quality of the commanders and their control of the troops. Such operations reach the heights of military art. Military history knows few operations like the one at Moscow.

Here there came together as one the brilliant foresight and wise leadership of the Supreme Commander-in-Chief comrade Stalin, the great patriotism of the Soviet people, and the valor and skill of the Red Army, which became insuperable for the enemy.

The Moscow operation is an extremely varied and dynamic phenomenon. Almost all kinds of operational and tactical actions found their application here. Maneuver battles and engagements on the offensive and the defensive, the breakthrough of the front and encirclement, the operations of mobile formations and airborne drops, and the rapid change of operational and tactical forms—fill out the period under consideration. The Moscow operation, to a great extent, enriches our conception of the modern battle and operation. It warns us against a routine and schematic approach to military affairs.

It is necessary to profoundly and seriously study the Moscow operation. The way of the further development of the Red Army's military art lies through the most rapid and complete mastering of the experience of the Great Patriotic War. One of the most outstanding and stirring pages in its history belongs to the Moscow operation.

Annex A

The combat order of the enemy facing the Western Front as of January 5, 15, and 25 1942

Operational direction	Infantry divisions		Motorized divisions		Panzer divisions		Total divisions and frontage
	Front line	Reserve	Front line	Reserve	Front line	Reserve	
THE ENEMY ORDER OF BATTLE FACING THE WESTERN FRONT, JANUARY 5 1942							
Volokolamsk-Gzhatsk							
Against 1st Army	23rd	–	14th	–	7th, 2nd	–	4 divisions– about 30 km
Against 20th Army	35th	106th	–	–	6th, 5th	–	4 divisions– 20 km
Against 16th Army	SS Infantry, 252nd	85th	–	–	11th	10th	5 divisions—25 km
Mozhaisk							
Against 5th Army	78th, 87th, 267th, 197th, 7th	107th, 63rd, 255th	3rd	–	–	20th	10 divisions—50 km
Medyn'							
Against 33rd Army	292nd, 258th, 183rd, 15th	–	–	–	–	–	4 divisions—50 km
Against 43rd Army	98th, 34th, 263rd	–	–	–	–	–	3 divisions—15 km
Yukhnov							
Against 49th Army	268th, 260th, 137th, 17th	230th	–	–	–	–	5 divisions—30 km
Against 50th Army	131st, 31st, 52nd	–	36th	–	19th	–	5 divisions–about 150 km
							10 divisions—about 180 km
Sukhinichi							
Against 10th Army	296th, 216th	–	10th	–	–	–	3 divisions—about 100 km
TOTAL	25	6	4	–	6	2	43 divisions—about 470 km
THE ENEMY ORDER OF BATTLE FACING THE WESTERN FRONT, JANUARY 15 1942							
Volokolamsk-Gzhatsk							
Against 1st Army	23rd	–	14th	–	7th, 2nd	–	4 divisions—30 km
Against 20th Army	35th	106th	–	–	5th, 11th	6th	5 divisions—20 km
Against 16th Army	SS Infantry, 252nd	85th	–	–	–	10th	4 divisions—25 km
Mozhaisk							
Against 5th Army	78th, 87th, 197th, 7th	63rd, 107th	3rd	–	–	–	7 divisions—45 km
Against 33rd Army	258th, 183rd, 267th, 15th, 98th	292nd	–	–	20th	–	7 divisions–about 100 km
Yukhnov							
Against 43rd Army	34th, 263rd, 17th, 260th, 268th	213th	–	–	–	–	6 divisions—30 km

Operational direction	Infantry divisions		Motorized divisions		Panzer divisions		Total divisions and frontage
	Front line	Reserve	Front line	Reserve	Front line	Reserve	
Spas-Demensk							
Against 49th Army	52nd, 131st, 31st	–	–	–	–	–	3 divisions—15 km
Against 50th Army	164th, 137th, composite units	230th	–	–	–	–	2-3 divisions and composite units–about 130 km
Roslavl’							
Against 10th Army	296th, 56th, 211th, 216th	–	29th	–	19th	4th	6-7 divisions—100 km
Bryansk							
Against 61st Army	208th, 167th, 112th	–	–	10th	–	–	4 divisions and independent units—90 km
TOTAL	29-30 divisions and composite units	7	2-3	1	6	3	48-50 divisions and composite units—about 550-585 km
THE ENEMY ORDER OF BATTLE FACING THE WESTERN FRONT, JANUARY 25 1942							
Novoduginskaya							
Against 20th Army	106th, 23rd	35th	14th	–	7th, 6th	2nd, 5th	9 divisions—35 km
Gzhatsk							
Against 5th Army	252nd, 87th, 255th, 197th, 7th	78th, 63rd, 107th, 85th	–	3rd	–	10th	11 divisions—50 km
Yukhnov-Vyaz’ma							
Against 33rd Army	267th, 183rd, 292nd, 258th	15th	–	–	–	–	5 divisions—50 km
Against 43rd Army	52nd, 98th, 34th, 263rd, special units	–	–	–	–	–	4 divisions and special units—about 75 km
Against 49th Army	17th, 260th	–	–	–	–	–	2 divisions—15 km
Against 50th Army	268th, 31st, 131st, 137th	230th	–	–	–	20th	6 divisions—60 km
Spas-Demensk and Sukhinichi							
Against 10th Army	213th, 164th, 216th, 208th, composite units	–	–	10th	19th	–	6 divisions and composite units—215 km
Bryansk							
Against 61st Army	296th, 112th, 56th	167th, 211th	25th	–	–	4th	6 divisions—115 km
TOTAL	28 divisions, composite, and special units	8 (211th Infantry Division?)	2	2	4	5	49 divisions, composite and special units—600-615 km

Annex B

The 20th Army's combat composition as of January 10 1942

Rifle and cavalry formations	Tank	Artillery
331st and 352nd rifle divisions, 1st Guards,[1] 17th, 28th, 35th, 40th,[3]49th, 55th, and 64th rifle brigades, 108th, 109th, 110th, 112th, and 113th ski battalions, 2nd Guards Cavalry Corps, (3rd and 4th guards and 20th cavalry divisions)	1st Guards[2], 17th, 22nd, 24th, 31st, and 145th[4] tank brigades	517th Artillery Regiment (High Command Reserve), 544th Long-Range Howitzer Regiment, 138th, 471st, 523rd, 528th, and 537th artillery regiments (High CommandReserve), 55th and 53rd armored trains, 2nd, 7th, 15th, 17th, and 35th independent guards mortar battalions
Engineering	**Communications**	**Rear Units**
85th Bridge Construction Battalion, 226th Engineering Battalion, 127 and 129th sapper battalions, and the 352nd Engineering-Construction Battalion	104th Communications Regiment, and the 713th Cable-Laying Battalion	796th Auto Battalion
TOTAL: 2 rifle divisions, 8 rifle brigades, 5 ski battalions, 3 cavalry divisions, 395 guns, 450 mortars, 100 tanks, 6 tank brigades, 7 artillery regiments (High Command Reserve), 1 anti-tank artillery regiment, 5 independent guards mortar battalions, 2 armored trains, 5 engineering battalions, 1 communications regiment, 1 independent cable-laying battalion, and 1 auto battalion.		

1 Remizov's group.
2 Kautkov's group.
3 Kautkov's group.
4 Remizov's group.

Index

INDEX OF PEOPLE

INDEX OF PLACES

INDEX OF GERMAN MILITARY UNITS

INDEX OF SOVIET MILITARY UNITS

INDEX OF MISCELLANEOUS TERMS